The End of the Old Regime in Europe,
1768–1776

FRANCO VENTURI

The End
of the Old Regime
in Europe,
1768–1776

The First Crisis

Translated by
R. Burr Litchfield

PRINCETON UNIVERSITY PRESS

Princeton, New Jersey

Published by Princeton University Press, 41 William Street,
Princeton, New Jersey 08540
In the United Kingdom: Princeton University Press, Guildford, Surrey

This translation has been made possible (in part) by *The Davide and Irene Sala Award of the Wheatland Foundation*

This book has been composed in Linotron Baskerville

Clothbound editions of Princeton University Press books
are printed on acid-free paper, and binding materials are
chosen for strength and durability. Paperbacks, although satisfactory
for personal collections, are not usually suitable for library rebinding

Printed in the United States of America by Princeton University Press,
Princeton, New Jersey

Library of Congress Cataloging-in-Publication Data
Venturi, Franco.
[Settecento riformatore. English]
The first crisis / Franco Venturi ; translated by R. Burr Litchfield.
p.   cm.
Translation of: Settecento riformatore.
Includes index.
Contents: v. 1. The end of the old regime in Europe, 1768–1776.
ISBN 0-691-05564-5 (v. 1)
1. Italy—History—18th century. 2. Europe—History—18th century. I. Title.
DG545.V4513 1989
940.2′53—dc19   88-39914
CIP

Contents

Translator's Note

FRANCO VENTURI, FOR MANY YEARS PROFESSOR OF MODERN HISTORY
at the University of Turin and editor of the *Rivista Storica Italiana*, has
long been recognized as one of the most wideranging and brilliant of
recent Italian historians. His works extend from Russian history to the
Italian and European Enlightenment of the eighteenth century, for
which he is well known among scholars and on which he is acclaimed as
the greatest living authority. In Russian history his *Il populismo russo* has
been published in English as *Roots of Revolution* (London: Weidenfeld
and Nicolson, 1960 and Chicago: University of Chicago Press, 1983), as
has the collection of essays entitled *Studies in Free Russia* (Chicago: University of Chicago Press, 1983).

Venturi's work on the Enlightenment is relatively unknown to English readers. Only two short works, his Trevelyan lectures at Cambridge
in 1969 (*Utopia e riforma nell'illuminismo* [Turin: Einaudi, 1970], translated as *Utopia and Reform in the Enlightenment* [Cambridge: Cambridge
University Press, 1971]) and a collection of essays entitled *Italy and the
Enlightenment: Studies in a Cosmopolitan Century* (London: Longman,
1972), have appeared in English. Venturi's work on the eighteenth century has appeared in many short studies and articles, beginning with his
early work on Diderot and the *Encyclopédie*, but chiefly in a series of massive volumes with the general title *Settecento riformatore* (The eighteenth
century of reforms). This volume, and the one that will follow it consti-
tute volumes 3 and 4 of this work. They have been chosen for presentation to English readers at this time under the general title *The End of
the Old Regime in Europe. Settecento riformatore* is a wideranging work. The
first volume (*Da Muratori a Beccaria* [Turin: Einaudi, 1969]) traces the
cultural history of Italy from the 1730s to the work of the Milanese reformers of *Il Caffè* in the 1760s. The second volume (*La chiesa e la repubblica dentro i loro limiti, 1758–1774* [Turin: Einaudi, 1976]) is devoted to
problems of the Enlightenment and the Catholic Church, focusing on
the Italian and European debate that accompanied the successive crises
of suppression of the Jesuit order. Volumes 3 and 4 of *Settecento Riformatore* (*La prima crisi dell'Antico Regime, 1768–1776* [Turin: Einaudi,
1979] and *La caduta dell'Antico Regime, 1776–1789. 1: I grandi stati
dell'Occidente; 2: Il patriottismo repubblicano e gli imperi dell'Est* [Turin: Einaudi, 1984]) are a distinct part of the series. Here Venturi has focused
on two problems of particular interest to cultural history: the develop-

vii

ment of Italian and European public opinion through late-eighteenth-
century journalism, and the cosmopolitanism of the Enlightenment,
seen here in the reflection of interactions between politics and opinion
in Europe in general through the "prism" of Italian awareness and publishing in the two decades before the French Revolution. His treatment
is thus European, or rather Western, in scope and Italian in focus. This
approach is somewhat similar to Venturi's work on the historiography
of modern Italy ("L'Italia fuori d'Italia" [Italy outside of Italy], in *Storia
d'Italia*, vol. 3 [Turin: Einaudi, 1973]), where he discusses the ways in
which non-Italians have seen the history of Italy. Volumes 3 and 4 of
Settecento riformatore thus present a vast tapestry of European opinion in
the last two decades of the old regime, as viewed from the standpoint of
Italy. Volume 5, in the course of publication, returns to themes with
which the series began, that is, the practical achievements of reform in
Italy from the 1760s to the 1790s. A full bibliography of Venturi's works
can be found in *L'età dei lumi: Studi storici sull settecento Europeo in onore di
Franco Venturi*. 2 vols. (Naples: Jovene, 1985).

   This translation is an updated and slightly augmented version of the
Italian original, with a new preface by the author incorporating themes
from the earlier volumes of the series. Translation has required some
care in presenting the linguistic range of works cited by Venturi in the
text. To avoid confusion for readers and excessively long footnotes, titles of published works that Venturi cites in the original languages have
been left in the original languages, except for foreign titles that he
translated into Italian. I have translated these into English. To preserve
the flavor of the original, I have left poetic citations in the original languages, and have provided translations in the footnotes. I thank Professor Venturi for his lively interest in this project and for reading a draft
of the translation to ensure that it reflected his intended meaning accu-
rately and in detail. I also thank Dalia Lipkin for her careful copy edit-
ing of the final manuscript.

R.B.L.
Providence, Rhode Island, 1988.

Preface

THE FIRST LINKS IN THE LONG CHAIN OF REFORMS AND REVOLUTIONS, projects and delusions, rebellions and repressions that led in the eighteenth century to the collapse of the old regime, are to be sought not in the great capitals of the West, in Paris and London, or in the heartland of Europe, in Vienna and Berlin, but on the margins of the continent, in unexpected and peripheral places, on the islands and peninsulas of the Mediterranean, among lords and peasants in Poland and Bohemia, and in Denmark and Sweden to the north. There emerged the passions and hopes, and the revolts and protests of the sixties and seventies, which proved in the end to be incompatible with the political and social realities inherited from traditions of the past. The end of the old regime presented itself at first as a peripheral event in the Europe of the Enlightenment. The first crisis appeared in diverse and contradictory forms, which contemporaries perceived as a series of distinct and detached episodes rather than as a unified movement. Nowhere did it lead to an overthrow of the basic foundations of society or the state or to the creation of durable new institutions. But it did not pass without leaving a profound mark. It revealed deep discontents, bursting aspirations, hopes that were incompatible with the traditional order, and an unexpected will to fight in vindication of past and present oppression. Corsicans and Montenegrins, Greeks of the Peloponnesus and of the islands, the Cossacks of Pugačev, and Russian and Bohemian peasants were momentarily the protagonists of rebellions that astonished and frightened contemporaries, who were anxious themselves, like historians of today, to understand the origins and significance of these underground movements breaking out on the margins of European society.

When confronted with such strangely diverse phenomena the most sensitive men of the sixties and seventies did not close their eyes. Rousseau intervened in the Corsican revolution, and then in that of Poland. In Italy, Tuscans like Del Turco, Venetians like Caminer, and Neapolitans like Pagano attempted to interpret the movement that led the Greeks to struggle against Ottoman oppression. The Pugačev revolt seemed mysterious and disquieting in the eyes of European intellectuals. How could one not take it into account when judging Catherine II's effort at enlightened despotism, as well as her effort to give an appearance of civilized value to Russia's grandiose expansion toward the south and the east? Voltaire and Diderot, in their responses to these

difficult questions, opened a debate that continued through the concluding decades of the old regime. Even more intriguing was the European discussion of the Polish crisis, at the time of its first partition in
1772. Republican liberty and monarchal power, reorganization of the
army and the privileges of nobles, the profound weakness of the old
regime and a renewed will to survive, tightened a knot around Poland
in which all Europeans could find elements of their own situation, made
all the more sad, on the banks of the Vistula, by the agony of an ever
deepening peril of death. Of the great states of the old regime, Poland
was the first to succumb.

It seemed for a moment, around the year 1770, that something similar might happen in the Ottoman Empire. Soon it would be the turn of
England and that of its colonies. Holland then entered an irreversible
crisis. Before the end of the eighties France had crossed the threshold
of that phase of its history which we call revolution but which many
contemporaries understood as anarchy—that is, a malady, of its political
and social body, similar to the one that had struck Poland during the
first crisis of the old regime. Developments in the Scandinavian states
between the sixties and the seventies intersected with those of Poland.
The fear of a partition effected by Russia was one of the most important
reasons driving the young king Gustavus III to his "revolution" in the
summer of 1772. Shortly before, nearby Denmark had provided an example of an attempt at internal transformation based on increased freedom of the press, a reform of education, and, last but not least, a more
intense preoccupation with the fate of the peasant class. The catastrophe that ended this intense reform effort, that is, the execution of the
minister Johann Friedrich Struensee on 28 April 1772, attracted the attention of all Europe. This was a dramatic episode, painted in the vivid
colors of a polemic against morality and traditional religion, which demonstrated once again how difficult the path of enlightened reform in
Europe was during these years.

To contain within a single perspective such diverse events as those of
the first crisis of the old regime naturally requires the selection of a
point of view from which to observe them. It should be close enough to
discern the most significant details of events, engaged, so as to react with
intensity, but sufficiently detached from the policies of the great powers
to permit the formation of an independent image of the new reality that
was emerging. It should also permit sufficient involvement in the conflicts of ideals and politics of the time so as not to risk falling into indifference. Among the many possible viewpoints, I have chosen—or perhaps it is more proper to say that the research on the eighteenth century
in which I have been engaged for decades has chosen for me—Italy of
the Enlightenment, between the sixties and the eighties. I could cer-

tainly have followed what is generally considered to be the main road of eighteenth-century studies—France in these decades. I would then have been able to observe from Paris the echoes and reverberations of world events. But the resulting picture would have been seriously distorted. The Corsican revolution had its own logic and justification, quite distant from, and indeed opposed to, the politics and propaganda of Louis xv. The Mediterranean expedition of Catherine ii and the Greek uprising of 1770, like all the events that followed it, from the Peloponnesus to Egypt, were consciously inspired by an effort of Russian and English policy to oppose and dislodge the traditional domination of France in the Levant. The partitioning of Poland, and the Cossack and peasant uprisings of the seventies, demonstrated that the French monarchy was no longer in a position to effectively oppose changes in Eastern Europe. The Swedish "revolution" of 1772 was a political and ideological victory for France, but a fragile and uncertain one, as the events of the following years soon demonstrated.

In the sixties and seventies Paris remained at the center of the debates that accompanied the first crisis of the old regime throughout Europe. But when we observe the discussion more closely, it is difficult not to be struck by its contrasts and uncertainties, whereas in Paris itself the conviction that the "party of *philosophes*" increasingly needed to find a new road and new direction deepened. The truths achieved in the fifties were not sufficient to understand or dominate these new developments on the margins of the European world. The *Encyclopédie* was completed in 1765. The publication of Boulanger's posthumous works, with their new and original interpretations of the origins of Oriental despotism, as well as the series of works written or inspired by Baron d'Holbach, culminating in the *Système de la nature* in 1770, responded in different ways to the growing need for new and more active truths. The physiocratic movement produced new tools for understanding the developments in France and Europe, even if the application of this new science often divided people of the Enlightenment. The position they took with regard to the Polish drama was a typical example. Admiration and respect for the British model, with heated discussions and contrasts among intellectuals, led to an increasingly complex vision of the fundamental problems of authority and political liberty. On France itself, in the last years of Louis xv and until his death in 1774, settled an atmosphere of failing confidence, almost of desperation. Men like Diderot, Helvétius, and Deleyre received the fall of the *Parlements* as proof that the nation was profoundly corrupt and decadent. Before the eyes of the creator of the *Encyclopédie* appeared the image of Medea, who "returned her father to youth by cutting him into pieces and having him boiled up." Could only a revolution lead France out of the blind path into which the monarchy had drawn it? "My fatherland is now under the yoke of despotism. . . . This fallen nation is the scorn of Europe. No salutary crisis will restore its liberty; it will die of consumption," concluded, for his part, Helvétius.

Leaving the philosophes thus caught in a seizure of discouragement, should one cross the English Channel to seek in England the best observation post for understanding the Europe of the sixties and seventies? The ebullient political life of London in the age of Wilkes invites us, as it invited so many men of the eighteenth century, to look at the world through English eyes. The journals were of extraordinary vivacity (there was an abyss of difference between the *London Chronicle* and the *Gazette de France*), the parliamentary debates were impassioned, and England's foreign policy was active and enterprising. The end of the Corsican revolt was widely felt as a national defeat and a demonstration of the failing initiative of government. The Russian expedition into the Mediterranean was a British undertaking as much as the initiative of Catherine II. The most energetic and farsighted works in defense of Poland were born and developed in London, where, even in this case, there was a profound distance between writers and administrators. But beyond the English Channel a growing sense of impotence in government dominated the beginning of the seventies. There grew, without any apparent remedy, a distance, and then a break, between the mother country and the American colonies, which soon dominated political and military affairs. Observing the first crisis of the old regime from the viewpoint of London would be a useful and fertile historical experience, but one that would lead one to concentrate on internal problems, on the changing relationships among England, Scotland, and Ireland, on the constitutional questions that were becoming more and more acute, and on the first efforts at parliamentary reform, rather than on the symptoms of revolts and transformations that were appearing on the margins of the European world. The United Kingdom was a world unto itself, rich and energetic, which contemporaries often felt to be isolated and enclosed, almost as if it were an exception to the past and future of the continent. This isolation began to be broken precisely in the sixties by the great Scottish historians of the age of Robertson, the authors of works that were fundamental to European society and did not focus only on the past of the British Isles. Translations and comments showed the interest with which this new point of view was welcomed everywhere. But, at the moment of the old regime's first crisis, we are still at the beginning of a movement that developed more rapidly in the following years.

Italy, on the other hand, was a land open to winds from the west and east, from the south and north. It did not have a stable structure, divided as it was into a collection (or, better, museum) of monarchies and republics (including that singular elective theocratic monarchy, the Papal States). It was open to the political and cultural influence of the Empire, of Spain, and of France. No coherent political will held it together. It was furrowed instead by a thousand vile and tenacious urban and territorial rivalries. What united it, even in its extraordinary fragmentation, was its history, as Antonio Muratori, the man who more than anyone else of his generation had studied the political, social, historical, and geographical reality of Italy in the first half of the eighteenth century, knew very well. When he finished his *Annali*—of a thousand seven hundred and fifty years of history—Italy had embarked on a period of peace and reforms, which lasted from 1748 until the nineties of the eighteenth century and the unleashing of the wars of the French Revolution. This was the longest period it had ever gone without armed conflict in its territory. For nearly fifty years Italians could reflect on their past and on the situation in which they found themselves. They could look at the world to seek out suggestions and advice and observe and criticize themselves and others. The springtime of the Enlightenment in Italy came in the sixties, when Cesare Beccaria wrote *Dei delitti e delle pene* and Pietro Verri created *Il Caffè*, the most lively of the numerous periodicals beginning to multiply at that time in various parts of the peninsula. In these years the *Corriere letterario* of Venice gave way to the *Europa letteraria* and *Giornale d'Italia*, gazettes that showed from their beginnings to what extent academic tradition was left behind, and that one had entered the broader fields of the cosmopolitanism and patriotism of the Enlightenment. In Naples the reforming will of Antonio Genovesi came to maturity in this period. In all parts of the peninsula a new awareness, refracted by the most diverse realities, produced unexpected and varied perspectives. Naples, Rome, and Florence reacted in their own ways to the calamities that struck Italy in the sixties: famine and hunger struck the lands of the south and center, claiming innumerable victims and unleashing infinite miseries. Despite the efforts of the minister Tanucci, backed by Genovesi, a thicket of privileges blocked and made impossible all efforts to free the grain trade in Naples—the only remedy, according to an increasingly numerous group of economists and politicians, to the organic ills of Italian agriculture. In Rome, the efforts of the papal government to reform production and trade in grain were particularly weak. In Florence the presence of a young and active grand duke, Peter Leopold, supported and encouraged by an elite group of ministers and economists, made it possible to create the bases of one of the most successful experiments of liberalization and modernization in Europe at that time.

The participation of Italy in the major conflict that affected all Catholic countries in the sixties was naturally active and often central and decisive. The rapid expansion of the polemic against the Jesuits, the unexpected and violent intervention of the government of Portugal, the action of the French Parlements, and the decisive blow the king of Spain administered to the Society of Jesus led, after other developments, to the suppression of this body by the Roman pontiff himself in 1773. Like the first crisis of the old regime, this religious conflict did not draw its roots from the polemics of the Enlightenment, nor did it find its origins in lands that were the most developed or open to modern thought and politics. With great surprise contemporaries saw the anticlerical storm appear in superstitious Portugal, find support in Spain, famous for its Inquisition, and then develop through the meanders of Roman politics, before finding its conclusive outcome in the policy of Clement xiv. The different parts of Italy, touched by winds that blew from Portugal, Spain, and France, rediscovered their own local traditions. In Venice and Naples the images of Sarpi and Giannone reappeared. And when, under French influence, the duchy of Parma seemed to want to deny its old, typically Guelf traditions, around the year 1770, and welcome more open jurisdictional and enlightened ideas, the compromise made two centuries earlier by the Counter Reformation seemed in peril and close to collapse. Even if history and tradition won out here in the end and the young ardent minister Du Tillot was obliged to flee, the consequences were serious for papal authority, which was not only obliged to bend to the suppression of the Society of Jesus, as the Bourbon courts wanted, but also to take notice of a new party born in Italy, in which anticlericalism and polemics against the Roman Church joined ideas inspired by the *Encyclopédie* and the physiocrats. In 1767 this party found its passwords in elements from both religion and politics. The thirty-year-old Carlantonio Pilati demanded a "reform of Italy" in a thick pamphlet of the same title, which he had printed in Chur in the Grisons; it was undoubtedly one of the most lively and energetic works of the eighteenth century.

The debate about the Corsican revolution was drier and harder, but not less revealing of the new and more profound relationships crystallizing in the Italy and Europe of the Enlightenment during the sixties. Just as Montenegro and the 1770 Greek revolt revealed the hidden and obscure forces that menaced the age-old dominion of Venice in the Adriatic, thus also, in the Tyrrhenian Sea, the old dominion of Genova was brought into question by a series of recurrent revolts and attacks from the patriots of this island, which were never completely suppressed. Beginning in the twenties, two generations passed before the revolt found a leader in the person of Pasquale Paoli and matured in him with its own "justification"—an exposition of the motives that animated the insurgents in their bitter struggle against the mercantile and banking aristocracy of the republic of Genova. It was a struggle of poor against rich, of mountaineers against city dwellers, of proud enclosed islanders against a city that had been for centuries a center and symbol of seafaring cosmopolitanism, a bitter and continually renewed battle that attracted the attention of Rousseau and Boswell, of Tuscan writers in the age of Peter Leopold, of Dutch patriots and the young Goethe, of the Verri brothers in Milan and Rome, of the "Knights of Corsica" in the cities of New England, of Catherine II, and of Joseph II. Corsica thus became for a time the unexpected and impassioned symbol of a revolt that remained mysterious in its motivations and whose origin and nature it was difficult to know, but that still expressed the growing contrast between virtue and corruption, between liberty and military and government coercion, that deepened in the Enlightenment in general during the sixties and the seventies. "Fatherland and Liberty," the war cry of the Corsicans, could not help but impress even the French officials Louis XV sent to occupy the island after having bought it from the republic of Genova. And among these French were men like Dumouriez, Mirabeau, and Pommereul. In England, and above all Scotland in the wake of Boswell, there was a response to the authenticity of Corsica and an increasing enthusiasm for the nascent political liberty that emerged from the military resistance with which the islanders struck daily at Genova and France. John Symonds, the Cambridge historian and professor who gave so much to aid the Corsican revolution and who wrote the most vivid work among the many published in the British Isles at that time, judged the regime of Pasquale Paoli the second freest in the world after England.

In Italy, many young men associated the springtime of the Enlightenment with the experience of Corsica. In Turin, Francesco Dalmazzo Vasco, a noble from Mondovì and a student of economics and law who was connected with the Milanese group *Il Caffè*, threw himself into a plot to try to insert ideas he had drawn from a comparison between Montesquieu and Rousseau into the Corsican drama. He ended up paying with long years in prison and isolation for his animated effort. The events in Corsica aroused strong interest in Lombardy, for example, in Giuseppe Parini, director of the *Gazzetta di Milano* in the final years of the Corsican revolution. Tuscany was the chief center in Italy of the philo-Corsican movement. In Florence and Livorno the significant political and historical works of Raimondo Cocchi and Luca Magnanima came to light, and in these places circulated the broad network of partisans and collaborators of Paoli. These Tuscans received with greatest bitterness the reproaches Paoli addressed to them in one of his last letters written before his defeat and exile. He called them whitened sepulchers. They were favorable to him, his sympathizers, but they had not, like him, thrown themselves into the open struggle. His call had remained unheard. To the pain of defeat was thus joined the bitterness of regret and an acute sense of solitude and isolation. Southern Italy had been Paoli's homeland. He had lived there as a boy, the son of an exiled father, as a student at the University of Naples, and as an official in the garrison of Sicily, before taking command of his partisans on the island. He was a member of the multicolored cosmopolitan military elite that operated in the Bourbon monarchy in the south, but he found a fatherland in Corsica. Antonio Genovesi, who had been one of his professors, called him the Epaminondas of his generation. The theme of exile and a fatherland to reconquer remained at the root of his destiny in England under George III, where he remained at length, and in France under the national assembly, before which he gave a memorable speech, in his rebellion against the Jacobins, in his effort to create an Anglo-Corsican state, and finally during his long sunset in London, in the age of Napoleon.

The Corsican revolution, and its multiple refractions in the political discussions of Europe and Italy, is the natural point of departure for anyone attempting to penetrate beyond diplomatic and military contingencies and into the true character of the rebellions of the sixties. Certainly politics had a great importance for Pasquale Paoli's island, and the absence of any active or coherent English policy in the Mediterranean even more so. Undoubtedly the revolt of the Peloponnesus was instigated, and at least in part organized, by Catherine II and the Admiral Aleksej Orlov. Certainly the Russian intervention in Montenegro created an unexpected wrinkle in the movement led by Stephen the Little. But the closer we observe these incidents the more we become aware that what counted most, and what left the deepest traces, was the new patriotism arising everywhere, in Corsica and in Montenegro, as well as in Greece. From the guerrilla fighters' hard and difficult new experience came the roots and development of a new hope for liberty and equality. Beyond the defeats and massacres shone the vision of a rough and violent equality on Europe's horizon, in which some contemporaries saw, or hoped to see, a gleam of democracy.

We are in the age of Ossian. In 1763 the Italian version of the "ancient Celtic poem recently discovered and translated by James Macpherson" appeared in Padova. The extraordinary diffusion, everywhere in Europe, of these songs has been studied minutely from the point of view of literary history. They now have to be reread in relation to the obscure conflicts of the sixties and to the emerging patriotism of the age of the Enlightenment. We can do this through Cesarotti's version, which I have just cited. The Italian translator and commentator showed that he had understood the social and political character of Ossian's message: an archaic world in which the state did not exist, where elders and lords dominated and were responsible for the destiny of communities. In these we can recognize the "conspicuous," the "principals," the "heads" who dominated the Corsican and Greek revolts. Their power, as one of them, Antonio Psaros, explained to Catherine II, consisted in arming "the greatest number of relatives and friends." "An eternal vengeance" marked their relations. The conflicts among the chief families were relentless. These were societies of clans, in the Highlands of Scotland, as among the Maineotes and Corsicans. There were certainly strong differences among different regions and situations, but common to all of them was the vision of a world without any law other than that of tradition, and of a free society, poor and independent. The term *clan*, which Cesarotti knew well ("a union of different families descended from one stock, corresponding to the term *gens* in Latin"), was the chief symbol of these rudimentary states. This was not quite the primitive and savage image evoked by Rousseau in his second *Discourse*, but it can be recognized in the rebellions of the sixties. In Corsica and in Greece, as historians such as Francis Pomponi and Apostolos Vacalopoulos have demonstrated, the "principals" had emerged through a slow but effective development of economic and social life in these lands during the seventeenth century. In the eighteenth century, as their rebellions erupted, their patriotism took on varied and diverse forms. Scotland shows how important contact with more developed and wealthy societies was in this process. In Macpherson's *Dissertation*, which accompanied the edition of Ossian's poems, it was noted that "the genius of the Highlanders has shown a considerable change since the period when communications were opened with the rest of the island." "The introduction of trade and manufactures has destroyed that indolence in which they were formerly occupied." "Many have now begun to leave their mountains," "interest in genealogy has much diminished. . . . The men have become less attached to their leaders." The great hospitality they offered to foreigners who visited them was one of the most palpable signs remaining of the customs of former times. Long and bitter was the road, to use the expression of the Greek patriot Ademanzio Koraís, that led peoples to become nations.

In northern Europe, a revealing historical discovery was connected, between the fifties and sixties of the eighteenth century, with the diffusion of Ossian and the news of revolts coming from the Mediterranean. Paul-Henri Mallet, a young professor in Geneva inspired by Montesquieu and guided by a love for the primitive world, had published in Copenhagen in 1755 his *Introduction à l'histoire du Danemarc*. In the *Edda*, the sagas of the world of ancient Germanic stock, he had found the doc-

uments that permitted him to trace the origins of modern political and
social liberty. In the "numerous revolutions" in which Scandinavians
had been protagonists he sought, and found, that "restless spirit, indomitable, ready to arouse itself even at the mention of subjugation and
constraint," that "ferocious courage born of a wild errant life," in which
was nourished the "spirit of independence and equality" of modern Europe. Their ingenious system of local autonomous assemblies and "états
généraux" constituted a true model of free government. We find these
ideas taken up and reelaborated by Scottish thinkers, and, in Italy, they
were familiar to Cesarotti, the Paduan commentator on Ossian.

The idea of Stephen the Little to call himself Peter III, and thus to
take up the name of the Russian emperor who fell victim to the *coup
d'état* of his wife, Catherine II, seemed even more enigmatic in the sixties. Thus, a type of organization of popular protest touched the Adriatic—preoccupying not only the government of St. Petersburg, but also
Venice—which had shown itself repeatedly in the Russian world of the
past, where "pretenders" and "usurpers" had multiplied for centuries.
It found its most significant and violent expression at the beginning of
the seventies in the figure of the Cossack Pugačev. His was the mystical
image of a sovereign who appears to ensure and guarantee liberty to
the people, eliminating the oppression of the state and the exploitation
of the nobility. The "usurper" not only proclaimed himself czar, but was
also the reincarnation and personification of an epoch that predated the
appearance of absolutism. These were obscure forms, difficult to understand, and they were concealed as much as possible by Catherine II. Voltaire and the Venetian journalists were amazed by them, but, if one
looks closely, they also reflected the crisis of the state of the old regime
in an unexpected way. Between the Cossacks of the Jaik, where the revolt of Pugačev began, and the dispute of Louis XV with the French
Parlements, there was an enormous difference. Nevertheless, the mechanism that unleashed the conflict was similar: a defense of traditional
privileges imperiled by the centralizing will of the state. From this struggle, in the name of Peter III, sprang the first sparks of the Pugačev revolt. And how could one not see a connection between what happened
in Russia and the unleashing of the Polish "confederations"? Many contemporaries talked of this in their search for common causes of the
crises of the sixties and seventies. Was not even in Montenegro a central
fact of developments in the years of Stephen the Little the passage, if
only on a tiny scale, from a society of clans toward a state, however un-
intentionally modern? The form of this mutation in Montenegro was
borrowed from Russia, but the social and political reality was similar to
that of the Peloponnesus at the time of the 1770 revolt.

Curiosity, doubts, and discoveries were present in all contemporary debates about the first crises of the old regime, and they found their center particularly in the periodicals of these years. In those modest and gray pages, not easy to find now—not even in the most imposing libraries—, in those sheets, which sometimes do not even have a title, and where space was so dear that the editor often did not even start a new paragraph when passing from one country to another, rests the evidence of the growing Italian interest in what was happening throughout the peninsula, as well as beyond the Alps and the seas. Indication of the origin of the news, which was presented and published without comment, is lacking, although we can hear the echoes of Dutch, French, and Swiss gazettes. Thus, a whole European journalistic world is reflected in these pages, filtered through the local controls of Tuscany, Venice, and Naples. We can discern here clearly the curiosity that pushed readers to seek to know what was happening in the world. Cosmopolitanism celebrated a triumph in these journals. Each reader was a citizen of the world, each piece of news was a surprise, an adventure. One can easily imagine such journals in the hands of a Candide. Their function was to excite curiosity rather than to satisfy it. And when we come to the end of a year, the index the publisher provided was even more chaotic than the text, at least to our own eyes, habituated to see news in newspapers subtitled, explained, interpreted, and summarized. Instead, eighteenth-century journals were in the realm of events, and precisely for this reason they are such useful and precious documents for following curiosities that appear and die, and for tracing reflections of the world as it appeared in centers like Venice, Florence, and Naples. To be sure, these were not daily newspapers. They generally came out twice a week. The staff of journalists was small and gathered around a single table, as is shown in the engraving the *Notizie del mondo* presented to readers in 1769. Perhaps a dozen workers composed and printed the newspapers. In 1780 the number of copies that the Florentine journal I have just cited printed reached 1,700, while the other gazette of the same city, the *Gazzetta universale*, reached 2,500 copies. A small but active world clustered around these little enterprises: providers of capital, bookstores, distributors, and, especially editors. Until quite recently, this was a forgotten world. Now, thanks to the studies of Maria Augusta Timpanaro Morelli on Tuscany, of Marino Berengo on Venice, and of Giuseppe Ricuperati and Marco Cuaz on other regions of Italy, we know better at least some of the editors, who often did not have easy relationships among themselves. They were disliked by the ecclesiastical authorities. We can indicate one here, Filippo Mazzei, the Tuscan who became the friend and collaborator of Thomas Jefferson. The most recent scholar to be concerned with him, Edoardo Tortarolo, has given us excellent information about his Tuscan roots, as well as of the cosmopolitan undertakings of his long and active career.

The gazettes were unevenly distributed throughout Italian territory. They were rare in the kingdom of Sardinia; only in Nice, in 1773, was a true and proper sheet of news published. In Turin one must wait until 1780, and even then the publication was of brief duration, lasting only one year. In Austrian Lombardy there was the ancient seventeenth-century *Gazzetta di Milano*, which continued its hardly luxurious life until 1782. True development, of other titles, came mostly in the eighties and nineties, not only in the capital but also in provincial cities, particularly Cremona. But one should note for the extent of its diffusion and its ideas in Lombardy, the *Nuove di diverse corti e paesi*, which was published at Lugano. For the whole period studied in the pages that follow this was one of the most important and significant biweeklies in the Italian language. In the Venetian republic facile and bland was often the *Nuovo postiglione*, which continued to be published through the second half of the century. In 1766 the first daily of Venice appeared, the *Giornale veneto*, but it was only a sheet of local news, and this was followed by the *Novellista veneto*, which was published daily in 1775–1776. The gazettes then multiplied and reveal even in their mastheads the readers' curiosity about what was happening more widely in the world: hence the *Lettere istoriche, curiose e interessanti sopra gli affari correnti d'Africa e d'America*, which appeared in 1775. Three years later the bookseller Antonio Graziosi, the leading publisher in Venice at that time, launched a gazette that presented itself as a continuation of the Florentine *Notizie del mondo* but preserved only the title, and, independent of its model, it soon became one of the most important Italian publications. Genova and Lucca were not cities with gazettes, whereas the *Gazzetta di Parma*, restored by Du Tillot, permits us to follow closely the conflicts developing around that city in the sixties and seventies. The duchy of Modena became a center of exceptional vigor in everything related to political publication but expressed itself more in the form of journals than of gazettes. Tuscany was undoubtedly, besides Venice, the chief center of Italian journalism. By following the complex fortune of the newspapers published there from the sixties onward, one can follow closely, day by day, the lively relationship between the development of journalism and the reform policies of Peter Leopold as they grew and diversified. A glance at the Papal States makes us again aware of the extent to which this place differed profoundly from the others. But if the *Diario ordinario* of Rome, which continued throughout the century, was of unimpressive poverty, the provincial journals, that of Pesaro, for example, are not lacking in interest and merit deeper study than they have thus far received. It is enough to think of Bologna to see how the ceremonial and political squalor of Rome contrasted with the quite different life of the Legations. In the kingdom of Naples there was much variation according to circumstance. Often the productions were single sheets, but these also reveal the growing curiosity that prompted booksellers and journalists to seek to establish more frequent relations with the periodicals of central and northern Italy.

Naturally, besides the gazettes, I have taken into consideration the numerous erudite, historical, technical, and scientific periodicals that were published throughout Italy, as well as political journals, which on the model of Linguet's *Annales* and then Brissot de Warville's *Correspondance politique* became diffused, especially in Tuscany. I have taken up the translations of foreign works, which became more and more numerous and were designed to satisfy the curiosity of those who were not able to read Montesquieu, Voltaire, and d'Alembert in the original French. There were many facets of the "Italian prism" (this fine term was suggested by the American historian Marion S. Miller), and they are all useful, indeed indispensable, for anyone wanting to look at Europe from the point of view of Italy. I have not omitted, on Ranke's advice, even diplomatic dispatches. They have generally been read up to now to discover the petty secrets of small eighteenth-century Italian courts, but when observed from another point of view, they reveal the fears and hopes aroused by daily happenings in the world. But the gazettes were replacing the dispatches. Often the ambassador, instead of telling anew what he had read in print, folded up the newspaper in his dispatch and sent it to his minister. This, as well, was a typical example of the formation, throughout Europe, of general public opinion, born and developed through the multiplication and diffusion of gazettes, which were gaining the upper hand over diplomatic tradition.

We will follow the formation and development of this public opinion in Italy and Europe through the first crisis of the old regime. The movements of Corsica, of Greece, of Russian Cossacks, and of Bohemian peasants were ended and defeated; the brief moment of the reforms of Turgot, the "*guerre des farines*," and the smarting disappointments that followed the renewed hopes of the Enlightenment in France rapidly opened and closed. Not one blow of this last effort to undo the knot of the old regime in France peacefully was lost on readers of Italian publications. Public opinion was surprisingly informed as well when there began to arrive, along with the news from France, the first echoes of the long and obstinate struggle of the American colonies. An epoch closed and another opened. The second and decisive crisis of the old regime began with the revolts and skirmishes in New England. In 1776 attention was fixed on this distant land, and the second volume of this work will take up from that point.

This book is an updated and, I hope, corrected, version of the volume entitled *La prima crisi dell'Antico Regime* contained in my *Settecento Riformatore*. It was dedicated to my students at Turin in the year 1977–1978 and to those in Chicago in the fall semester of 1978. To this gratitude and thanks I must add more now, to all those who have helped me continue to work on this extraordinary turn of European history. I am particularly grateful to my friend and colleague R. Burr Litchfield, who so generously took on the task of making my work known to readers of the English language.

Abbreviations

A   Archivio
AMAE   Archives du Ministère des affaires étrangères (Paris)
AS   Archivio di Stato
B   Biblioteca
BN   Biblioteca nazionale
PRO   Public Record Office (London)
TREVISO   B. Comunale di Treviso

The following works are indicated in abbreviated form:

DBI   *Dizionario biografico degli italiani*, Enciclopedia Italiana, Rome
DBL   *Dansk biografisk leksikon*, Copenhagen
DBN   *Dictionary of National Biography*, London

Riformatori   Illuministi italiani, vol. 46 of the collection *La letteratura italiana: Storia e testi*. Milan and Naples: Ricciardi, 1958–65. Vol. 3: *Riformatori lombardi, piemontesi e toscane*, ed. Franco Venturi. Vol. 5: *Riformatori napoletani*, ed. Franco Venturi. Vol. 7: *Riformatori delle antiche repubbliche, dei ducati, dello Stato pontificio e delle isole*, ed. Giuseppe Giarrizzo, Gianfranco Torcellan, and Franco Venturi.

Italian journals listed in the *Bibliografia storica nazionale* and non-Italian journals listed in the *International Bibliography of Historical Sciences* are abbreviated as follows:

Arch. stor. lombardo   Archivio storico lombardo. Giornale della società storica lombarda. Milan.
Eng. Hist. R.   English Historical Review.
Rass. arch. stato   Rassegna degli archivi di stato. Rome.
R. stor. ital.   Rivista storica italiana. Turin and Naples.
Sirio   Sbornik Imperatorskogo russkogo istoričeskogo obščestva (Miscellany of the Imperial Russian Historical Society).

The End of the Old Regime in Europe,
1768–1776

———————

I

⁓⊛⁓

Despotism, Reform, and Revolutions between Muscovy and the Near East

IN SEPTEMBER 1768 THE EVER MORE PRESSING INTERVENTION OF Catherine II in Poland unleashed war between Russia and the Ottoman Empire, a war destined to last until 1774. At first it seemed as though the conflict would unfold once again in places that had seen so many battles in the preceding decades, on the Danube and on the northern coast of the Black Sea. In fact, decisive encounters did develop there, but this war, from the beginning, showed a tendency to expand geographically and to have deepening political consequences. Soon the whole Black Sea was involved, from the Caucasus to the Dardanelles. To the astonishment of all, the Mediterranean, from Gibraltar to Syria, was repeatedly crossed by Russian naval expeditions, shaken by sea and land battles, and troubled by a swarm of plots and rebellions in the Ionian Islands, the Morea, the Aegean, and the lands of Egypt. Unexpectedly the Italian states, especially Venice, Tuscany, and Naples, came to find themselves at the center of these events, aroused by Russia's decision to combat the Turks not only in the north, but also by launching a series of diversions in the south.

On 17 July 1769 Empress Catherine II reviewed the naval squadron of about fifteen units that was to embark the following day under the command of Admiral Grigorij Andreevič Spiridov. Soon the Russians' situation became difficult. The ships were old, badly equipped, badly maintained, and tempests were not lacking. Less than one-third of the little ships were effective when the squadron came in sight of the English coast. Only assistance of every kind offered by Great Britain, from repairs to the recruitment of officers, permitted the Russian squadron to reach the Mediterranean, after a voyage of about six months. A sec-

3

ond squadron, entrusted to the Scottish captain John Elphinston, soon
followed. It embarked on 20 October 1769 and entered the Mediterranean in May of the following year. Three more expeditions followed,
commanded by the Dane J. N. Arff, the Russian V. Ja. Čičagov, and the
Scot Samuel Greig (become for the occasion Samojl Karlovič Greich).
There were five squadrons in all, composed of twenty ships, five frigates, and numerous auxiliary pieces, to which were added eleven frigates bought in the Mediterranean and one ship and ten other frigates
conquered from the enemy. More than 12,000 men participated in the
five expeditions, and of these 4,516 did not return. The cost was close
to six million rubles. It was, in sum, "one of the most spectacular historical events of the eighteenth century."[1] Despite all its errors and defects,
it impressed contemporaries deeply. Many concluded that, "considering
the lack of experience, and the obstacles, actual and artificial, which they
had to face, the Russians carried through the movement of their ships
to the Mediterranean with admirable tenacity and courage."[2]

As audacious as the expedition itself was the diplomatic and political
preparation that preceded and accompanied it. Russia knew how to
profit from the rivalry and hostility between France and England, and
between the Bourbon courts and the powers of the north. It succeeded
in avoiding open French intervention and knew how to act on its own,
even when Great Britain made clear that it did not want to risk war to
support Catherine II. It thus played on the weakness and indecision of
the major powers, insinuating itself with seeming disinterest into the
Near East, where the influence of British trade was in decline and where
France was not willing to risk much to maintain its customary position.
In the search for support and contacts in the Mediterranean, where the
Russians were penetrating for the first time, the empress relied above
all on her military and naval forces; nevertheless she did not entirely

---

[1] Evgenij Viktorovič Tarle, *Česmenskij boj i pervaja russkaja ekspedicija v Archipelag (1769–
1774)* (The battle of Chesmé and the first Russian expedition into the Archipelago [1769–
74]), now in id., *Sočinenija* (Works), vol. 10 (Moscow: Akademija nauk SSSR, 1959), pp. 9ff.
(this is a study rich in military information, of nationalist inspiration, but entirely blind to
the ideological and more properly political significance of these events); Matthew Smith
Anderson, "Great Britain and the Russian fleet, 1769–1770," *Slavonic and East European
Review* 31, no. 76 (December 1952): 148ff.; and id., "Great Britain and the Russo-Turkish
War of 1768–1774," *Eng. Hist. R.* 69, no. 270 (January 1954): 39ff. See also the catalogue
compiled by Anthony Cross for the exposition at the University of East Anglia, in Nor-
wich, England, on the occasion of the conference on Anglo-Russian relations in the eighteenth century in July 1977. On pp. 21ff. documents and portraits are described regarding the British and Russian navies. For an insertion of the Russian expedition in the events
of the first Turkish war, see Isabel De Madariaga, *Russia in the Age of Catherine the Great*
(London: Weidenfeld and Nicolson, 1981), pp. 208ff.

[2] Anderson, "Great Britain and the Russian fleet," pp. 148, 154.

abandon the idea of supporting and making use of ferments of revolt in Corsica, the Balkans, Greece, Egypt, wherever the old equilibrium and old forms of domination could be put in doubt or in peril. She also knew how to make use of the sympathy and admiration that her program of enlightened reform had aroused even in the lands of the Mediterranean. Revolts and reforms thus intersected in her scheme in an unexpected way, arousing doubt and perplexity, but also surprising agreement and enthusiasm.

The Italian politics of Catherine II began to enter an active phase with the nomination of Marchese Pano Maruzzi as Russian representative in Venice "i pri drugich italianskich oblastjach" (and to the other provinces of Italy) in the spring of 1768, that is, before the outbreak of the war with Turkey.[3] The empress thus resumed an effort begun by Peter the Great. In 1711 Venice had been the site of the second consulate opened by Russia, after Amsterdam, followed by Hamburg, Paris, Antwerp, Vienna, and so on. Its consul had been Demetrio Bozis, a Greek educated in Venice, and its diplomatic representative had been Matteo Caretta, accredited to "the most serene republic of Venice and the other Italian states" in the hope of enticing them into war against the infidels and obtaining "at least some assistance in the form of galleys and mariners."[4] There had been no results from this or from other similar efforts in Genova and Livorno. Only a few pieces of marble from Carrara arrived in St. Petersburg, brought by English ships.[5]

A half-century later, in 1768, Russian foreign policy was still dominated by its struggle with the Ottoman Empire, but the situation was significantly changed. It had become more difficult to persuade Venice to fight the Turks. If Catherine II could not give up the idea of having the most serene republic on her side, it would have to be done in a hidden way, with Venice aiding the Russians without too much being made known. Why did Venice continue to collaborate with infidels fighting against Christian peoples in revolt against the Sublime Porte? The re-

[3] The act signed by N. Panin and A. Golicyn on 10 March 1768 and the instructions of the same day are in Sirio, vol. 87 (1893), pp. 43ff. This affirmed that "the republic of Venice had for a long time shown a desire to establish direct contact with the Russian Empire," but that nothing concrete had occurred when a minister to negotiate a commercial treaty was sent. The Venetian ambassador in Vienna had initiated a formal demand. The commerce was to operate not only across the Baltic, but also in the Black Sea. The Russian reply was affirmative, but nothing concrete had resulted. Maruzzi was accredited not only to Venice, "but also to the other Italian commercial cities."

[4] V. A. Uljanickij, "Istoričeskij očerk russkich konsul'stv za granicej" (Historical study of Russian consulates abroad), in *Sbornik moskovskago glavnago archiva Ministerstva inostrannych del* (Publications of the central archives of the ministry of foreign affairs) (1893), pt. 5, p. lxix, instruction of 6 July 1711.

[5] Ibid., p. 35.

public "could stop making those scrupulous arrangements with the Turks and leave these people to arrange as they might with the people of Montenegro," explained, not without irony, the empress' minister of foreign affairs, Panin, writing to Maruzzi on 26 November 1768.[6] Why not, for example, create "on the frontiers of Dalmatia, near the border of the Montenegrins, little stores of munitions and provisions that could be seized and used against the Turks"? The prudence that inspired Venice could not have made it forget its past struggle with the Ottoman Porte. To be sure, it was not a question of taking the initiative, "but we believe her too prudent to neglect the occasion, if she finds it, of repairing losses she can never forget." Panin, however, could certainly not have been unaware of how many obstacles Maruzzi would have to overcome to obtain such a result. "We know well that patience is needed with a government as circumspect as that of the Venetians."[7]

Even the other "provinces" of Italy appeared to be solidly anchored in the status quo.[8] Genova offered money. Panin responded that "the finances of Her Majesty are such as to need no help," but he left the door open for the future.[9] And, in fact, two years had hardly passed when Catherine requested and obtained significant financial support from Genova.[10] Politically, the situation was less easy. The republic of Genova rotated in the orbit of France, as the recent ceding of Corsica to Louis xv had demonstrated. But the Russians still hoped that because of "the free form of its government" Genova would in the end support the Russian fleet.[11] The kingdom of Sardinia would certainly have been a useful ally in Italy. Its "essential interests" and its "delicate position between the Bourbons and Austria" would naturally have moved it to favor Catherine ii. It did not want to break with the Turks, but it would still probably have closed an eye if the Russians remained in its territory for only a brief period, or so Panin thought.[12] Turin, otherwise, was startled and surprised by the unusual diplomatic accreditation of Maruzzi "for all of Italy." If this person expected to represent Catherine ii to Carlo Emanuele iii, he should present himself in Piedmont. The Sardinian minister of foreign affairs "would be charmed to see him in Turin." The empress was struck with this problem. "Mr. de Panin should inform me at length about this," she wrote in the margin of a

---

[6] Sirio, vol. 87, pp. 217ff.

[7] Ibid., p. 506, letter of Panin to Maruzzi, 18 October 1769.

[8] For a general treatment, see Giuseppe Berti, *Russia e Stati italiani nel Risorgimento* (Turin: Einaudi, 1957).

[9] Sirio, vol. 87, p. 327, 31 January 1769.

[10] Giuseppe Felloni, *Gli investimenti finanziari genovesi in Europa tra il Seicento e la restaurazione* (Milan: Giuffré, 1971), pp. 459, 575.

[11] Sirio, vol. 1, p. 129, instructions of Catherine ii to Rear Admiral Arff, 5 June 1770.

[12] Ibid., p. 8, reply of Catherine ii to Aleksej Orlov, 20 January 1769.

dispatch from Maruzzi.[13] As for the kingdom of Naples, there was little hope, given the ties that bound it to Versailles. "It dances with its minister to the sound of the French flute, and this flute is not in harmony with the voice of Russia," Catherine II wrote to Aleksej Orlov on 6 May 1769.[14] The political realities of Italy seemed, in the eyes of the empress, both complicated and immobile.

Thus Catherine took the only paths that seemed to open before her. First she supported the only force that had risen in revolt against the equilibrium of Italy and against France: the Corsica of Pasquale Paoli. She tried to profit from the spontaneous revolts that were beginning to ignite in the Slavic world of the Balkans, especially among the people of Montenegro, with their hope that the neutrality of Venice was wavering. She hoped to make use of the Order of the Knights of Malta in her struggle against the Turks. Above all, she created a net of agents and listening posts in Italy and thus set in motion a type of diplomacy quite different from the traditional one.

"One of the more important affairs currently developing in your quarter," wrote Panin to Maruzzi on 11 October 1768, "is that of Corsica." "It justly attracts the gaze and attention of all the courts." He thus requested "sure and well-considered information on everything regarding that little republic." He urged him to establish a secret correspondence with the Corsicans, who, that very day, had begun their war with France. "If your contacts are wide and sure enough to have direct communication with Paoli, I beg you to neglect nothing, provided always that you do not compromise the court in any way. We would be very glad to have positive knowledge of the resources of this defender of Corsican liberty against the court of Versailles, his hopes, and the prospects of his affairs."[15] At the same time Panin began to sound out the British ambassador Lord Cathcart to see if it was the intention of England to assist Corsica. He was assured that England intended to cooperate with its ally fully in this matter as well. If assistance to Paoli could not be arranged "under the protection of the British flag," the empress "would furnish an appointment of arms, cannons, and ammunitions for seven thousand men of which H. M. might do the honours." Panin had to admit his information was drying up. "No friend or correspondent of Paoli who might give some information and advice that might be worth considering" could be found in St. Petersburg.[16] But these diffi-

---

[13] Ibid., vol. 87, p. 265, dispatch from Venice, 6–17 December 1768.

[14] Ibid., vol. 1, p. 17, letter of Catherine II to Orlov, 6 May 1769.

[15] Ibid., vol. 87, pp. 165ff., May 1769. See Franco Venturi, "Pasquale Paoli e la rivoluzione di Corsica," *R. stor. ital.*, fasc. 1 (March 1974): 5ff., and id., *Settecento riformatore*, vol. 5, ch. 1.

[16] Sirio, vol. 12, p. 389, Cathcart to Weymouth, 12–23 October 1768.

culties did not discourage Catherine II. She confirmed personally to
Lord Cathcart that "while Paoli continued to deserve as well as he does,
and that there are people of spirit and honesty in the world, he never
can want friends."[17] During the winter of 1768–1769, when Paoli appeared to be capable of resisting the troops of Louis XV, the interest of
the empress of Russia grew still more. She asked the British ambassador
for Boswell's famous book describing his voyage in Corsica and had
translated into French the pages about General Paoli, "which she told
me had given her great pleasure in perusal,"[18] Lord Cathcart reported
on 17 May 1769. She added that she was ready to aid the resistance of
the Corsicans with ten thousand guns and cannon, but this project was
made difficult by the war with the Turks. Her "good intentions towards
Paoli" were always firm. She wanted to establish a direct relationship
with the Corsican general to ask him of what he had particular need. By
way of Maruzzi, Paoli responded that the empress was free to choose
the aid she might want to give, and he declared he was willing to put at
the disposition of the Russian fleet, if it had arrived in the Mediterranean, all the bases he controlled. "Even if we have no ports for now, we
control at least some places of disembarkment" (pereput'e).[19] On 20 May
Maruzzi had orders to intensify his relations with Paoli and inform him
"that the Empress had long watched with admiration the courageous
efforts of that intrepid republican to extricate his nation from the yoke
imposed by injustice and ambition, and that she sincerely hoped a cause
so good as his would be crowned with success." She would have liked to
offer more assistance "to the maintenance of Corsican liberty," if she
were free of the "problems of her own war." To the "brave defender"
of the island, the empress meanwhile offered "a gift from the products
of her states: linen, hemp, leather, and grain," which Paoli would be able
to "convert into means to aid his resistance." Some English ships were
to carry Catherine's homage. In this way as well the empress hoped to
"confound the ambition, plots, and excessive intrigue of the oppressor
of Corsican liberty." In exchange, Paoli would facilitate as much as possible "operations we might undertake in the Mediterranean" and grant
"free entry into all ports" to Russian ships, which would be able to supply themselves, by payment, with whatever they needed.[20]

[17] Ibid., p. 408, Cathcart to Weymouth, 28 November–9 December 1768.

[18] Ibid., vol. 12, p. 431, dispatch of Cathcart to Rochford. Boswell's book was "translated in Livorno in 1769 from English into German and now into Russian," one reads in
the version that appeared from the Cadet printing house in 1773. See *Svodnyj katalog russkoj knigi . . . XVIII veka (1725–1800)* (General catalogue of Russian books in the eighteenth century [1725–1800]) (Moscow: Biblioteca V. I. Lenin, 1962), vol. 1, p. 124 n. 713.

[19] Sirio, vol. 1, p. 20, 6 May 1769, letter of Catherine II to Orlov.

[20] Ibid., vol. 87, pp. 436ff., Panin to Maruzzi, 20 May 1769.

Another aspect of the situation that attracted the attention of the Russians was the presence on the island of colonies of Greeks, who might be used in some way in the incipient struggle against the Turks. One should ask Paoli where these were located and have him indicate "their disposition in the present circumstances of the country." They thought "one of these colonies was in Ajaccio," but they did not know its importance, whether "the port was able to receive large ships, and whether it was actually occupied by the French as were Calvi and Bonifacio." The old maps were useless, one should know exactly which cities were in the hands of the French and which were held by "nationals."[21] When these words were written, Paoli had already been defeated in Pontenuovo. But his hope for aid from Catherine II was still present when, six months later, Muscovite ships appeared in the Mediterranean. Those Corsicans who still resisted said they were convinced that the "Russian fleet was to give them aid."[22] In the autumn of 1769 Bertellet, the French representative in Florence, after having spoken of Russian plans in Greece, informed his government that "the Corsicans refuged in Tuscany had, from Paoli's recent letters, orders to be ready to go to Corsica at the first news, imagining that their chief would embark on this squadron which was destined to descend on the island and attempt to chase out the troops of the king."[23] The same news was taken up a bit later: "The refugees, intoxicated with hope, say loudly that Paoli will embark on the Russian squadron."[24] From Versailles came the following reply on 16 January 1770: "Nothing could be more false and absurd than the rumors that are spread of the coming arrival of Pascal Paoli on the island and his presumed embarcation on the Russian squadron."[25] For many months gazettes and diplomatic circles continued to attribute the exile of Paoli to his intention of putting his sword to the service of Catherine II.[26]

---

[21] Ibid., pp. 445ff., Panin to Maruzzi, 3 June 1769. Sabatier de Cabre, the French ambassador at St. Petersburg, was aware of the empress' efforts. "I have always suspected," he wrote to Choiseul on 13 October 1769, "that the brothers of Count Orlov are waiting for a favorable moment to give help in the form of money to Paoli, who has had some part of the enthusiasm of Catherine. She has often given her approbation and has indicated rather openly her great desire to attract him to her service" (ibid., vol. 143 [1913], p. 43).

[22] Turin, AS, *Materie politiche estere in genere*, mazzo 55, 1770, handwritten sheet of information, Rome, 13 January 1770.

[23] AMAE, *Toscane*, 132, F. 146, Livorno, 29 September 1769.

[24] Ibid., F. 150, 6 October 1769. See as well F. 208, 29 December 1769.

[25] Ibid., *Toscane*, 133, F. 14, 16 January 1770.

[26] Incisa di Camerana, the representative of the king of Sardinia in Venice, after having followed the long pilgrimage of the exiled Paoli to Mantova and Verona, and after having awaited him, like so many others, in Venice, announced on 19 August 1769 that

This was a missed contact, therefore, between Russia and Corsica (which nonetheless contributed, as we have seen, to coloring the Mediterranean image of Catherine II with republican hopes and thoughts of liberty). Another difficult contact, apparently impossible but nonetheless bearing fruit, was between the empress and Montenegro. In these mountains there developed at the end of the sixties a kind of prologue to the Russian intervention in the Mediterranean, the Balkans, and Greece, a prologue that seemed to be made on purpose to surprise and to arouse the curiosity of contemporaries.[27]

The Russian intervention did not at first have an official form. Instead, the popular myth of a usurper who pretends to be a restored sovereign brought echoes of an old Muscovite tradition to the shores of the Adriatic. Stephen the Little, who appeared in Montenegro in about 1766, although not openly declaring himself to be Peter III, the suppressed husband of Catherine II, took on the manners of the czar and permitted himself to be called by his name. He was by no means of Russian origin but, as far as one can tell, came from Dalmatia or Montenegro. The name he assumed was essential in making him a rough but an effective leader of a new type, one determined to contain and repress the struggle of local clans and to put in motion a process of unification for his little nation through a series of assemblies of reconciliation, directing all of its energies against external enemies, and thus against the Turks. In this work, Stephen the Little was both supported and entrapped by the clergy. His new power cut into the traditional political authority of the Petrović, the metropolitan of Montenegro. Nonetheless, religion was one of the essential bases of his politics. The spring that seems to have moved Montenegrins was, in the words of the Venetian administrator of Cattaro on 20 October 1767, "the spirit of novelty and enthusiasm that easily agitates a superstitious people."[28] They had allowed themselves to be persuaded by "an ignorant foreign vagabond" who had taken on "the air of being a legislator and sovereign," succeeding "in moving the will of the people," Antonio Renier, the provisor of

he had taken the road toward Vienna instead, setting out for St. Petersburg "to enter an honorable employment in the military service of the empress of Russia." Turin, AS, *Lettere ministri, Venezia*, 40, 19 August 1769. The *Notizie del Mondo*, no. 78, 30 September 1769, p. 641 (The Hague, 12 September), wrote: "The empress of Russia here offered General Paoli a shining place with her troops, and Paoli not wanting to accept it, she nonetheless offered him in Petersburg a palace, servants, a stable, and a large pension."

[27] Details of Russian-Yugoslav relations in the second half of the eighteenth century are in Ariadna Pavlovna Bažova, *Russko-jugoslavskie otnošenija vo vtoroj polovine XVIII v* (Moscow: Nauka, 1982). On Stephen the Little see pp. 87ff.

[28] Šim Ljubič, "Spomenici o Sčepanu Malome" (Memoirs of Stephen the Little), *Glasnik srpskog učenok Društva* 3 (1870): 17.

Dalmatia, explained at about the same time. "Fanaticism was ever seen to be increasing in the multitudes."[29] His message was "of peace, harmony, and moderation."[30] He was able to direct the assemblies he convoked with great ability. He was effective in the struggle against vendettas and factions.[31] Reading these Venetian reports and other documents about Stephen the Little, and following the vicissitudes of his fortunes, the curious situation of Montenegro becomes clear. It is difficult not to compare his work with that of Paoli, who also had to confront the fundamental problems of a society still organized in clans.

Both strange and effective was the way of presenting himself of this leader who came up from obscurity and succeeded rapidly in collecting around himself a large part of the Montenegrin warriors. Arriving in Cetinje in January 1768, he proclaimed himself emperor of Russia before the people, "declaring, however, not to want to be called emperor in the future, but rather Stephen, and not assuming in his official acts any other title besides that of *Stephen, little with the little, good with the good, wicked with the wicked.*"[32] Writing from Maina to the Venetian administrator on 5 October 1767, he signed himself "the littlest Stephen in the world, until the Lord lets him grow."[33] Soon after having arrived in Cetinje "he went, with the leaders of the people, to the monastery of Stanjevici, where he cast out all the monks and took into custody the *vladika* Savva, taking a hundred sheep from him."[34] Thus neutralizing the two chief centers of ecclesiastical power (the vladika Savva was legally also the political head of Montenegro), he began to exercise a severe and rigorous justice, intervening in private vendettas and quarrels.[35] The war against the Turks and the Venetians, in the summer of the same

[29] Ibid., pp. 20, 24.

[30] Ibid., p. 33.

[31] Michael Boro Petrovich, "Catherine II and a False Peter III in Montenegro," *American Slavic and East European Review* 14, no. 2 (April 1955): 169ff. See Philip Longworth, "The Pretender Phenomenon in Eighteenth-Century Russia," *Past and Present*, no. 66 (February 1975): 61ff., who excludes the "fascinating figure of Stepan Malyj" because he operated outside of the confines of Russia.

[32] Demetrio Milaković, *Storia del Montenero* (Ragusa: Carlo Pretner, 1877), p. 117.

[33] The document is reproduced photographically in the *Istorija Crne Gore* (History of Montenegro), vol. 3: *Od početka XVI do kraja XVIII vijeka* (From the beginning of the sixteenth century to the end of the eighteenth), part 1, ed. Gregor Stanojević and Milan Vasić (Titograd: Redakcija za Istoriju Crne Gore, 1975), p. 378. The *Gazzetta di Parma* called him the "famous little Stephen," no. 3, 16 January 1770 (from Constantinople, 20 November 1769).

[34] Milaković, *Storia del Montenegro*, p. 117.

[35] Ibid., p. 118. Among other things he "shot and then hanged a certain Šujo Radanović, from lower Cetinje, who had killed his own brother in a quarrel." As recently noted, "this was the first person in the history of Montenegro to be shot because of a homicide" (*Istorija Crne Gore*, p. 392).

year, 1768, came to occupy all the energies of the Montenegrins and of Stephen the Little. Slightly more than 10,000 men fought against more than 50,000 opponents. Venice made the situation of Montenegro more difficult by prohibiting the export of materials of war and "garrisoned with troops the entire border of the Bocche di Cattaro, from Herzegovina to as far as Turkish Albania."[36] But good fortune or, as everyone thought, the hand of God favored the Orthodox. After a courageous partisan war (in vain the Turks called the Montenegrins "mouse brains" and invited them to come out of the bush to fight in the plain), when it seemed as though they might run out of munitions, a fortunate turn permitted them to gain control of a large store of gunpowder. October 28 was their day of victory, and on November 1 an enemy camp was blown up when struck by lightning. Even the Venetians were obliged to withdraw.[37] But they did not fail to avenge themselves against communities of Montenegrins under the rule of the republic since 1718. Two partisans of Stephen the Little were condemned to death, and "others were made outlaws and their houses were burned." The historian Milaković adds that during his time, a century ago, "one could still see in the heights of Maina the walls of burned houses where Stephen had his residence."[38] In all these encounters and conflicts Stephen played only a minor part. His power was political rather than military, and his mythical relationship with Russia was an important element.

Precisely for this reason Catherine II decided to intervene in Montenegro, compelled as she was by the desire to root out the shade of Peter III even there and to include this center of anti-Turkish resistance in her plan of war against the Sublime Porte. She explained in every way possible to the "nobles and esteemed lords of the Serbian lands of Macedonia and Skanderia, Montenegro and the Littoral," that Peter III was indeed dead. She organized a kind of military mission to Cetinje headed by Prince Jurii Volodimirović Dolgorukij, who was furnished with a manifesto in which it was remembered "the zeal with which the Greek Orthodox and Slavs had defended, and would continue to defend, their faith and ancient liberty, their hereditary patrimony." "Reflecting on their anguish heroically suffered, our philanthropic heart breaks, fervent as it is, and full for the true faith." Thus she promised her "true protection" and encouraged them to fight if they wanted "not only to guarantee the remains of your ancient and precious liberty, but to extend it to that high level appropriate to the ancient conquerors and rulers of the better part of the world then known, from whom you de-

---

[36] Milaković, *Storia di Montenegro*, p. 120.

[37] François Lenormant, *Turcs et Monténégrins* (Paris: Didier, 1866), pp. 194ff.

[38] Milaković, *Storia del Montenero*, p. 122.

rive your ancestry." "The outcome is now in your hands and depends entirely on yourselves." If they were "united in heart and forces" they would be able to extend their conquests and victories "as far as Constantinople itself, capital of the ancient Greek empire and glorious for the holy relics that now cry to heaven for a day of vengeance!"[39] This is a typical example of the great distance separating the programs of Catherine II from the reality of a place like Montenegro, which was intent on giving life, in unexpected ways, to its first unity and political organization.

Dolgorukij, after having hidden for some time in Italy under the name of a merchant, departed from Ancona and disembarked at the end of July in Spizza, "a tribal place in the district of Antivari, near the confines of Montenegro," as Milaković explains. He tried in vain to avoid the attention of the Venetian authorities, but he succeeded in getting through the mountains and reaching Cetinje, where he was received by a great assembly of local leaders. He did his best to try to keep them united against the Turks, a task made more difficult by the fact that he was also expected to eliminate the only recognized political authority of the place—Stephen the Little. Stephen at first hid in the mountains, holding that the men of Dolgorukij were false Russians, "Latins"; but he realized that he would be able to maintain his power only if he confronted the envoys of Catherine II in person. He presented himself, was disarmed, interrogated, chained, and confined to a convent. But it did not take Dolgorukij long to understand that he would have no possibility of taking the place of the false Peter III, either in dominating internal feuds or combatting external enemies. The Turks had begun the siege of Montenegro. The Venetians hindered any contact of the Russian mission with Count Orlov, then in Pisa. The Montenegrins showed even more clearly their desire not to be used in any way, not to be disarmed or disturbed in their houses by foreign troops, as well as their anticipation of preserving all their ancient liberty. They asked that their elected representatives reside permanently in Cetinje in order to participate in its government.[40] The atmosphere became more and more difficult for Dolgorukij. The rumor circulated that the Venetians intended to poison the Russians. The Turks hoped to blow up the munitions of the expedition. Dolgorukij, on 12 October, decided to leave Montenegro, taking with him the Serbian patriarch of Peć, who

---

[39] Ibid., pp. 124ff. The manifesto is dated 29 January 1769.

[40] *Žurnalnaja zapiska po proisšestvijam vo vremja ekspedicij ego sijatel'stva knjazia Jur'ja Volodimiroviča Dolgorukova . . . Černuju Goru* (Journal of events in the period of the expedition of His Excellency Prince I. V. Dolgorukov to Montenegro), ed. Petr Bartenev, in *Russkij Archiv*, vol. 1 (1886) (3 August 1769), pp. 405–6.

had become too compromised with him. He declared to Stephen the Little that the crime of proclaiming himself Peter III merited death, but that he would pardon him and make him a Russian official. He put him again at the head of his "capricious people," with written orders, consigning to him a Russian uniform, arms, and the money he had brought with him.[41] "Stephen resumed his power over the Montenegrins and began to rule even better than before, provided as he was with means, however small." He gave himself over to building roads, worked, and was gravely wounded by the untimely explosion of a mine. "When they went to get him on a stretcher to take him to the convent of Vrčele, they said he was quietly singing."[42] He created an embryonic judicial body, selecting "ten among the leaders of the place." Five commissioners with a monk at their head organized an elementary census. He acted as a king and "considered himself a successor of the last Serbian despots."[43] He was not lacking in admirers, even among Venetians.[44] But the means at his disposal were extremely limited. The armed party making up his guard consisted of ten to fifteen persons. "His activity," concluded Grigor Stanojević, "led necessarily to despotism, which was essential in order to check the anarchy of the tribes."[45] But in the second phase of his rule he did not proceed much farther along this path. War against external enemies and the struggle against internal vendettas went hand in hand even for him; when the external tension lessened, the internal part of his policy became less active. To be sure, as the same Yugoslav historian has noted in another work, Stephen the Little did not succeed in creating "any administrative apparatus that could be inherited and utilized after his disappearance from the scene. After the death of Šćepan Mali it was necessary to begin everything anew and return to the old political practices of Montenegro."[46] Despite these limits, what M. B. Petrovich has written remains true: Stephen the Little demonstrated that he was "one of the best rulers of Montenegro up to that time."[47] Perhaps the instigators of his death were Turks, or perhaps they were

[41] Ibid. (13 October 1769), pp. 427–28.

[42] Milaković, *Storia del Montenegro*, p. 131.

[43] *Istorija Crne Gore*, p. 391. The paragraph following it is dedicated to the "significance of Stephen the Little in the history of Montenegro," pp. 390ff.

[44] "His discourse is always of peace, concord and equity, he is affable in manner, his answers are prompt and wise, his mind is always clear, and he does not lack good ideas for governing a province." Report cited by Milaković, *Storia del Montenegro*, p. 134.

[45] *Istorija Crne Gore*, p. 393.

[46] Grigor Stanojević, *Crna Gora pred stvaranje države, 1773–1796* (Montenegro before the formation of the state) (Belgrade: Istorijski institut u Beogradu, 1962), p. 134 (with a summary in French).

[47] Petrovich, "Catherine II and a False Peter III," p. 193.

Venetians. What is certain is that a Greek from the Morea was hired, became the servant of Stephen the Little, and cut his throat, from ear to ear, on 22 September 1773.

If this experience demonstrated quickly how difficult it was for the Russians to utilize the conflicts of Montenegro, the obstacles to their attempt to draw Malta into the orbit of Catherine II proved to be greater still.

The effort of Russia to establish new relations with the Order of Malta began in a classic manner, in 1769, with the mission of Marchese Giorgio Cavalcabò, who was supposed to persuade the knights to resume their struggle against the Turks.[48] But the envoy of Catherine II encountered strong French influence, and he soon had to be content with the fact that there was not much else to do except persuade a member of the order, such as the Piedmontese Count Masino, to join the Russian fleet.[49] Reawakening the spirit of struggle against the infidels was quite impossible. Speaking of the Knights of Malta, Catherine II concluded, "The order has fallen from its vows, our intentions could not have been better."[50] Even here the Russian effort was accompanied by popular movements and disorder. In 1774 the Russian representative was accused of having set off a commotion on 9 September of that year, when the peasants fell in with the knights. Three were condemned to death, others to prison. After this, as Cavalcabò writes, "a knight no longer dared leave the city, and a peasant feared to spend the night there."[51] The French held that everything was caused by the Russians' intrigues, and Count Masino, who had just returned from Russia, had

[48] The *Notizie del mondo*, no. 39, 15 May 1770, p. 308 (St. Petersburg, 3 April), reports the credentials of Cavalcabò. The answer of the Grand Master is in no. 40, 19 March 1770, p. 315 (St. Petersburg, 10 April), where there is also the "Lettera dell'ammiraglio Spiritoff a S.A. Eminentissima il Gran-Maestro di Malta, scritta da Maone il dí 26 dicembre 1769 e tradotta dal segretario Sergio Barbiukow, interprete di S.E."

[49] A. A. Aljab'ev, "Snošenija Rossii s Mal'tijskim Ordenom, čast' 1 (do 1789)" (Relations between Russia and the Order of Malta, part 1 [before 1789]), *Sbornik moskovskago glavnago archiva Ministerstva inostrannych del*, fasc. 5 (1893): 173ff. Count Masino "had been educated in Turin, was a good engineer and a good mathematician" (ibid., p. 194). On 24 September 1770 he returned to the Russian fleet. We find him in Livorno in Russian service and in close contact with Aleksej Orlov at the end of 1770, from a dispatch of the consul of the king of Sardinia, Rivarola, who hastened to assure Turin that Cavaliere Masino preserved "the greatest attachment to the king, our sovereign." He was enthusiastic about the Russians who in the Levant had "made miracles." The "idea of Muscovy," he said, "was to chase the Turks out of Europe completely, distributing their provinces to other sovereigns, except for those that will be united to the empire, and no one wants the islands." Turin, AS, *Materie politiche estere in genere*, mazzo 55, 1770, Livorno, 12 December 1770.

[50] Aljab'ev, *Snošenjia Rossii*, p. 202.

[51] Ibid., p. 204.

to offer himself as the champion of the empress, declaring that he would fight a duel with anyone who offended Russia. Two years later Cavalcabò was in Rome, where he died soon after.[52] On Malta disorder had become endemic. Ange Goudar, the "political historian of the century," as he was called in the *Novelle Letterarie*, counted six uprisings on the island in the last fifteen years and tried to come to a general conclusion about the deeper causes of the disquiet that dominated the declining century.[53] Even Malta, he said, was at the crossroads of the ever increasing conflicts between church and state throughout Europe, which grew along with economic discontent. As for Russia, diplomatic relations remained interrupted until 1783, when Antonio Psaros was sent to Malta, a Greek who, as we shall see, was one of the most active Russian collaborators in the years when the fleet of Orlov sailed in the Mediterranean.

Corsica, Montenegro, and Malta were still only elements, staying points in the grand plan, the "hazardous project" that was revealed to Europe between the summer and autumn of 1769, awakening everywhere curiosity, incredulity, and surprise: that is, the penetration of Russian politics into the Levant and the revolt of Greece against Ottoman domination.[1]

In Italy commercial expeditions preceded military ones. An undated *Mémoire sur l'utilité d'une correspondance directe entre la Russie et l'Italie* had explained how it would have been possible to make more than a million rubles' profit by establishing direct relations between St. Petersburg and Italy. It took up with "reciprocal utility" the proposal of English, Dutch, and German merchants who served as intermediaries between the two lands.[2] Another memoir, in Russian, from about the same period, had

[52] See *Carteggio di Pietro e di Alessandro Verri*, vol. 2, ed. F. Novati and E. Greppi (Milan: Cogliati, 1911), p. 206 n. 1.

[53] *Novelle letterarie*, no. 5, col. 79ff., and Ange Goudar, *Reflexions sur la dernière émeute de Malthe, suivie des Remarques politiques sur celles qui ont troublé les différents états de l'Europe à la fin de ce siècle* (Amsterdam [actually Florence: G. B. Stecchi and A. G. Pagani], 1776).

[1] The definition is by the Duc de Choiseul, in a letter to Honoré-Auguste Sabatier de Cabres, the ambassador in St. Petersburg. He called the expedition into the Mediterranean "a Russian swagger," although still admitting that it made "some noise in all the southern courts of Europe." Sirio, vol. 143, p. 29, 19 September 1769. It seems that the first news of the mysterious Russian preparations was published in the gazette of Utrecht, no. 60, 28 July 1769, with the following comment: "The public exhausts itself with guesses about the destination of the fleet; however, time will unveil the mystery." Cited, with some comment by French diplomats, in *Correspondance secrète du comte de Broglie avec Louis XV*, published by Didier Ozanam and Michel Antoine (Paris: C. Klincksieck, 1961), vol. 2 (1767–74), p. 192 n. 2.

[2] I. S. Šarkova, "Russkie i ital'janskie zapiski ob ustanovlenii prjamych torgovych svja-

sustained the usefulness, even for Russian manufacturing, of contacts with Italy, suggesting the possibility of trade even across the Sea of Azov.[3] In 1764 a Russian company for commerce was founded in the Mediterranean, and it was to focus chiefly on Italian ports.[4] Two years later, in 1766, the first Russian ship reached Tuscany. "The Muscovites, who were in Livorno with the remainder of the cargo carried by the ship of the Muscovy Company, sold all and left in the middle of November for St. Petersburg," wrote the consul of the king of Sardinia on December 3, adding that one did not know "whether they will return next June; appearances are against it."[5] As the Livornese would soon be able to tell, the Russian presence in their port in the following years was quite different. Still, the first commercial undertakings were of no small importance; they furnished the first financial basis for the politics of Catherine II in Italy and in the Balkans.

The empress did not limit her attention to mercantile and military problems. She also had a lively interest in the intellectual life of Italy, although she knew it mostly through the medium of Paris. The note she wrote to Elagin, who was to some extent her minister of culture, asking him for information about Beccaria, like her repeated insistent efforts, even through Maruzzi, to have the Milanese philosopher brought to her, were closely tied to her foreign policy plans. *Dei delitti e delle pene* seemed to her still another motive for a polemic with France, where this work, she had been told, had been prohibited because it was "lacking in respect to legislation," "a new crime" that permitted the empress to pretend to be a paladin of liberty.[6]

As is well known, Beccaria did not go to St. Petersburg. Catherine

zej meždu Rossiej i Italiej v poslednej trei XVIII v. (po materialam archiva Voroncovych)" (Russian and Italian declarations on the establishment of direct commercial ties between Russia and Italy in the last third of the eighteenth century [from documents in the archives of Voroncov]), in *Vspomogatel'nye istoričeskie discipliny*, vol. 7 (Leningrad: Akademia nauk SSSR, Otdelenie istorii, 1976), pp. 302ff.

[3] Ibid.

[4] "Extrait de l'état et des conditions de la Compagnie de commerce de Russie qui négocie avec la Méditerranée," Turin, AS, *Materie politiche estere in genere*, mazzo 51, 1764. The shares were three hundred rubles each. The document gives the name of the principal shareholders: "Ivan Volodimerov [member of the great family of Muscovite merchants descended from Tichon Volodimerov, supplier of Peter the Great], 100; Michaela Gribanov, 10; Monsieur le conseiller actuel Teplov [Grigorij Nikolaevič Teplov], 20, and others."

[5] Turin, AS, *Materie politiche estere in genere*, mazzo 52, 1766, information from Livorno, 5 December 1766.

[6] Cesare Beccaria, *Dei delitti e delle pene*, con una raccolta di lettere e documenti relativi alla nascita dell'opera e alla sua fortuna nell'Europa del Settecento, ed. Franco Venturi (Turin: Einaudi, 1965), p. 630.

was the one who presented to the world, and even to Italians, his program of reform. Her *Nakaz*, the Instruction to the commission convoked in 1767 at the Kremlin for the reform of the law codes of Russia, was supposed to be a kind of synthesis of European political thought, where elements taken from Beccaria had a central place.[7] With this work in his hands, Aleksej Orlov, the commander in chief of the Russian expedition in the Mediterranean, would soon present himself in Tuscany. One of the two editions of the *Nakaz* that appeared there (edited by Giovanni Del Turco), which had a clearly official character, was dedicated to him. On this Pisan edition was based the Greek version of the Instruction, almost a programmatic manifestation of the ideas the empress expected to apply in lands she promised to liberate from the Ottoman yoke.[8] In the dedication to Orlov one read that "the elements of the new legislation" "put forth with such nobility," "with immense wisdom and sacred philanthropy" by Catherine II, constituted "a necessary as well as a useful guide to the virtue and happiness of the human race," and thus had been translated into many languages so as to become "common to all the people of Europe." Greece had particular need of a work of this kind, deprived as it was of books and "cruelly oppressed." Reading it, "my compatriots will have its fruits in the field of virtue, and assistance in their unhappy condition." They will receive "from divine providence, through the empress, a philosophical and philanthropic legislation." The great hope of the wise Plato to see Greece "at the height of human felicity" would finally be satisfied. The "warm invocation of God by a poor people," their "tears" shed night and day, will have been heard. Greece will be "governed also by the laws of the philosophical empress." Orlov was to be the instrument of this "glory of the Russian race," of "paternal love," and of "other virtues" that had made him famous "in all the lands of Europe."[9]

The initiative the empress took in this period to open public debate on the condition of peasants in her empire also had a large effect.[10] In

---

[7] See Erich Donnert, *Politische Ideologie der russischen Gesellschaft zu Begin der Regierungszeit Katharinas II* (Berlin: Akademie-Verlag, 1976), pp. 29ff., and the rich bibliography.

[8] The frontispiece of this work, which appeared in Venice "from Nicola Gliki di Giannina" in 1770, declared that the text was "translated from the Italian language" and was dedicated by the printer "to the illustrious lord Count A. d'Orlov." A copy is in Venice in the Biblioteca Marciana with the call number 75.C.139. On the publisher see Georg Veloudis, *Das griechische Druck- und Verlagshaus "Glikis" in Venedig (1670–1854)* (Wiesbaden: Otto Harrasowitz, n.d.).

[9] I thank Professor Maria Sandra Bosco in the Istituto di glottologia of the Faculty of Letters of the University of Turin for having translated the dedication to Count Orlov from the Greek edition of the *Nakaz*.

[10] Donnert, *Politische Ideologie*, pp. 133ff.

1767 through the Free Economic Society of St. Petersburg, Catherine II asked enlightened Europe "whether it was more advantageous and useful to the public good for peasants to possess their own lands or only mobile goods." The responses were numerous and animated, even from Italy, where debate about the small holdings of peasants was active in these years. Thus both Francesco Dalmazzo Vasco and his brother Giambattista responded to the inquiry, and the second brother's essay, published with the title *La felicità pubblica considerata nei coltivatori di terre proprie*, was one of the works of greatest importance in Italy in the eighteenth century. It was soon translated into French and published in Lausanne by Giovanni Vignoli, who had procured in Zurich one of the three Italian versions of Catherine II's Instruction.[11] The little volume was something more than an homage to Catherine's intentions of reform. It attempted to push her in the direction of a more profound transformation of Russia, an exhortation to keep faith with her own policy, to take seriously the reformist propaganda that the empress had made into an instrument of foreign policy. Dedicated to the princes of Württemberg, exemplary enlightened lords of those years, this little book reminded the empress, through the mouth of Beardé de l'Abbaye, the winner of the competiton of the Free Economic Society of St. Petersburg, that her true historical task was to "carry forward greater prodigies than her predecessor [Peter the Great] by giving soul, light, and life to numerous persons of serfs, who have a half-existence, and by making men out of thousands of automatons." Nor should the empress fear disorder or catastrophe in her approaching work of transformation. "That happy change will not make the state experience any shock. Liberty, always preceded by the desire to be free, gives serfs the disposition to promise and carry out everything. Half-savage and barbarian peoples will become active, vigilant, zealous, and industrious when they are civilized."[12] On the other hand, through the mouth of Giambattista Vasco, the empress was exhorted to take a greater step along the road in which she found herself. The question of "whether it is advantageous to the state that peasants own land" should be changed to another, more rad-

---

[11] *La félicité publique considérée dans les paysans cultivateurs de leurs propres terres*, traduit de l'italien par Mr. Vignoli, précédé de la *Dissertation qu'a remporté le prix de la Société libre et économique de St. Pétersbourg en l'année 1768* (Lausanne: François Grasset, 1770). See Franco Venturi, "Giambattista Vasco in Lombardia," *Atti dell'Accademia delle scienze di Torino* 91 (1956–57): 19–98. The disquisition of his brother is included in Francesco Dalmazzo Vasco, *Opere*, ed. Silvia Rota Ghibaudi (Turin: Fondazione Einaudi, 1966), pp. 199ff.

[12] *La félicité publique*, p. 52. On the Württemberg see Mario Mirri, "La cultura svizzera, Rousseau e Beccaria. Variazioni settecentesche sul tema della virtù," in *Atti del Convegno internazionale su Cesare Beccaria: Memorie dell'Accademia delle scienze di Torino, Classe di scienze morali, storiche e filologiche*, 4th ser., no. 9 (1966), pp. 133ff.

ical, one: "whether it is advantageous to the state that any besides peasants own land," that is, whether nonpeasant landholding should be considered legitimate. In the same vein, and thus accentuating the polemic
against the oppression exercised by the rich and powerful, the work of
Vasco was interpreted by Isidoro Bianchi, who reviewed the Italian edition in the Florentine *Novelle letterarie*, and by Alberto Fortis, who wrote
about it in the Venetian *Europa letteraria*.[13] Bianchi wholeheartedly seconded Vasco's proposal, "to promote the division of land among the
largest possible number of owners, place obstacles to the concentration
of land under the dominion of one owner, and oblige men to cultivate
their own lands themselves."[14] Fortis wrote that, even if Vasco's plan
were never realized, the author should be given the merit for having
"transported his readers into the space of a new world."[15] In general,
the Italian echo of Catherine's inquiry was favorable to peasant property, although this judgment had different shadings. Even the conservative *Notizie letterarie*, in discussing the essay of Beardé de l'Abbaye,
praised it precisely because it supported "maxims tending to reform the
abuse practiced in many parts of the north of holding peasants in miserable slavery." This, indeed, was the intention of the "Russian sovereign." But it hastened to add that a program of this kind was more
adapted to Russia than to other lands. "The judgment of the author,
who proposes to give ownership of some portion of the land as a reward
to the diligence of peasants, is applicable to Muscovy, a vast and in large
part an uncultivated empire, but it is not equally suited to other states
where the same circumstances do not occur, and where there are not
the same motives and causes."[16] Because Tuscan peasants were paid laborers or tenants, property should be given as a reward only to Muscovites. The discussion extended through the following years as well. In
the gazette of Mantova of 1773, for example, we find eulogies to the
"beneficent attention" that Catherine II paid "to the important class of
people in the countryside." "In most of the provinces of this empire, and
the nearby kingdoms, they have shelter only in such low huts that one
cannot stand up in them, buried in the earth, covered with mud, with
only a miserable bed for the father of the family, and everyone else
spread out over tables; thus men, women, children, animals, and everything else are mixed up together." The work of peasants was very hard.
"Her Majesty, however, moved by the aspect of such a deplorable state
of affairs, has ordered that this part of her subjects be procured larger

[13] Venturi, *Giambattista Vasco*, pp. 36ff.
[14] *Novelle letterarie*, November 1769, col. 8.
[15] *Europa letteraria*, 1 August 1769, p. 86.
[16] *Notizie letterarie*, no. 25, 18 August 1770, cols. 399ff.

and healthier dwellings where it would be possible at least to enjoy a tranquil rest and console oneself that one was, although the most unfortunate part of humanity, still the most useful."[17]

One finds these discussions and hopes in the principal publication appearing in Italy on the occasion of the naval expedition of Catherine II, the *Storia della guerra presente tra la Russia e la Porta ottomana*, published, as we will see, at Venice during the course of the events starting in 1770. After recounting how the king of Denmark had wanted to free the serfs in his country, "so that by removing them from slavery, agriculture might flourish in the lands of his dominions," the work continued as follows: "The freedom of peasants was also understood by Catherine II, empress of Russia, to be a principal means of enriching her vast dominion and of returning those men, perhaps the most productive of all, to a state appropriate to humanity: slavery belonged to beasts and not to human nature."[18] "But the execution of this generous and praiseworthy project was still a delicate task." The bonds that united serfs to their masters were particularly rigid in Russia. "The powerful and the rich, besides the products of their lands, extract the larger part of their revenues from the individuals who cultivate it, and these, almost like beasts, are chained in the most harsh slavery, so that their masters can even take their lives." They had to pay "an annual tax to their lords" and were sold along with the land, but also sometimes individually, "being passed like sheep from one master to another." They were even rented out for periods of time, "almost in the way one rents out steers or horses."[19] "The women peasants in particular are sold and resold more than the men."[20] Against such brutality the sovereign had promoted the famous competition of the Free Economic Society and called together the Commission for Legislative Reform. "All Europe admired the method of a sovereign, who, one might say, set out to change the whole character of civil society in her empire." Thus, by "reducing the new law code to a social contract that no one could disobey, in a sense she shook off that sovereignty, which in Russia sometimes arrived at the point of despotism" and, "amid the jubilation of the Russians," published the Instruction and called together an assembly to carry out reforms.[21] Russia was a European nation, and corresponding with its character, the "wise and lasting legislation" that Catherine II was preparing

---

[17] *Mantova*, no. 34, 20 August 1773 (St. Petersburg, 13 July).

[18] *Storia della guerra presente tra la Russia e la Porta ottomana*, edizione adornata di carte geografiche, ritratti, piante di fortezze, ecc. (Venice: Antonio Graziosi, 1770), vol. 3, p. 60.

[19] Ibid., p. 61.

[20] Ibid., p. 62.

[21] Ibid., pp. 66ff.

would be effective "because [it was] drawn up and decreed with the consent of her subjects, whose genius was consulted."[22] The author of the
Storia seemed to be convinced that the new legislation had been approved and sanctioned. He thought of the *Nakaz* as if it were the law
code of the Russian Empire.

[22] Ibid., p. 71.

II

❦

The Greek Revolt

RAPIDLY AFTER 1767 THE THREADS OF DISCUSSION IN ITALY THAT the political initiatives of the empress had created crossed and interlaced with the weft of a more or less clandestine organization intended to prepare the Greek uprising against Turkey. The conspiracy evolved at Venice, Trieste, and Livorno. The propaganda was sent out from these places. Even the command of the enterprise was based there.

The plots that preceded the expedition of 1770 are, naturally, anything but easy to follow.[1] The most detailed narrative is still the very effective one put together by the eighteenth-century French historian Claude-Carloman de Rulhière in book 11 of his *Histoire de l'anarchie de Pologne*, published posthumously in 1807. The text is based on accurate research in the sources and on the numerous memoirs of participants in the events, and it has the great merit of preserving intact the sense of surprise and discovery of an unknown world that many contemporary witnesses revealed.[2] To use Rulhière's work fully one needs to return to the sources he used himself, which were preserved by his descendants and were used, if not always in the best way, by Alice Chevalier in a work

---

[1] The most recent study, rich in information but with some errors, is by Ariadna Camariano-Cioran, "La guerre russo-turque de 1768–1774 et les Grecs," *Revue des études sudest européens* 3, nos. 3–4 (1965): 513ff. On pp. 317ff. is the section "Préparation de la révolte." For the background of these events in the modern history of Greece, see Nikiforos P. Diamandouros, "Bibliographical Essay," in *Hellenism and the First Greek War of Liberation (1821–1830): Continuity and Change*, ed. John A. Petropulos (Salonika: Institute for Balkan Studies, 1976), pp. 191ff. Franco Venturi, *La rivolta greca del 1770 e il patriottismo dell'età dei lumi*, with an introduction by Otto Kresten (Rome: Unione internazionale degli istituti di archeologia, storia, e storia dell' arte, 1986).

[2] See the recent republication of Claude-Carloman de Rulhière's *La "sainte insurrection" des Grecs pendant la guerre russo-turque (1768–1774) (L'action politique et militaire de Adamopoulos, Benakis, Maruzzi, Mavromicalis, Papasoglis, Psaros, Tamaras)*. An extract from the *Histoire de l'anarchie de Pologne*, annotated by G. Papasogli (Rome: Pontificia universitas gregoriana, 1968).

published just before World War II.[3] From these it appears that book
11, about the Greeks, was written in 1781, partly on the evidence of
reports by Abbé Bertrand, the French consul at Trieste and later at Naples, a specialist in questions relating to Italy, and even more on a memoir by Antonio Psaros, a Thessaly merchant, whom we have already encountered as Russian consul on Malta in the eighties. He sent Rulhière
a narrative written in Italian, entitled "Relation of Occurrences in the
Expedition of Muscovites in the Morea and the Archipelago," which
would be interesting to know in a more complete form.[4] A recent book
in Greek has taken up the threads of these events and has sought to find
a social explanation in them, without, however, shedding much new
light on the preparations of the Russians.[5]

The first, and most important, element in the net of pro-Russian
feelings in Greece was Giorgio Papasoglis, whom Rulhière calls Papaz-
Ogli and whose name is variously reported by others. "He is alternately
called Grégori Papapoulo, Papadopuolo, and Papas-Oglou, the latter
being the most popular," T. Blancard writes.[6] As a merchant from
Macedonia, he had been in contact with Orlov for some time and on his
advice had traveled for three years in the lands of Greece to inform
himself of the inhabitants' state of mind. The mission was financed by
profits from the commercial enterprises Catherine had organized in Italy. The sums received were supposed to be used by Papasoglis "to buy
presents in Italy for the chief churches of Greece, which Papas-Ogli was
to make on his own initiative in the name of the empress."[7] As Consul
Bertrand recalled, Papasoglis "came to Trieste, where he encountered
Greeks from the chief families of the Morea, and placed himself in accord with them, letting them know the aim of his voyage." "At the same
time he had printed in Venice a book he had written in Greek on Russian tactics, and on the composition and maneuvers of their troops."[8]
The work appeared in Venice in 1765.[9] Giorgio Papasoglis went on to

[3] Alice Chevalier, *Claude-Carloman de Rulhière, premier historien de la Pologne. Sa vie et
son oeuvre historique d'après des documents inédits* (Paris: Domat-Montchrétien, 1939).

[4] Ibid., 347ff.

[5] Tasos A. Gritsopoulos, "Ta orlophika. E en Peloponneso epanastasis tou 1770 kai ta
epakoloutha aftes" (The war of Orlov. The revolution of 1770 in the Peloponnesus and
its consequences), in *Mnemosine* (Athens, 1967).

[6] T. Blancard, *Les Mavroyéni* (Paris: E. Léroux, 1909), vol. 1, p. 59.

[7] Claude-Carloman de Rulhière, *Histoire de l'anarchie de Pologne et du démembrement de
cette république* (Paris: H. Nicolle et Desenne, 1807), vol. 2, p. 335. See Gritsopoulos, *Ta
orlophika*, pp. 41ff. See Doriana Dell'Agata Popova, "Due donazioni di Caterina II alle
chiese greche di Livorno e di Porto Mahon," in *Miscellanea Agostino Pertusi*, vol. III: *Rivista
di Studi Bizantini e Slavi*, year 3 (1983), pp. 343ff.

[8] Chevalier, *De Rulhière*, p. 351.

[9] A copy of this *Didaskalia*, signed by Giorgio Papasoglis, "an artillery official in Rus-

the Morea, "where he spoke to all the leaders of the Maineotes," and then he returned to Italy to report on the results of his findings.[10]

Only an indirect echo of his report has come down to us, like that of other Greeks sent to Russia in these years. To be sure, the Morea appears with utopian hues in the words of these men. The Maineotes, descendants and successors of the Spartans, or as Rulhière would have it of Messenians, had apparently preserved their liberty through the centuries. They declared they were ready to sacrifice themselves for their Hellenic brothers. In the Peloponnesus, every village, every little town, with names often evoking illustrious places of antiquity, offered men and goods to the common land. Harsh indeed was the "slavery of the Greeks" under Turkish domination, but even this oppression did not seem to be without "a shadowy image of their ancient liberty."[11] In the Morea, after so many centuries of foreign domination, "almost all wealth was in the hands of Greeks, and the number of those able to bear arms was more than one hundred thousand. They alone cultivate the land . . . , they alone are occupied with useful trades. This enslaved folk, debased and degenerate, could today be regarded as the most spirited of barbarians."[12] The situation in Greece was no longer the same as when the Venetians had been obliged to abandon their last dominions in the Morea. The rule of St. Mark had been so harsh that the Greeks seemed to favor the Turks' return. Then their mode of life had changed. "A long period of peace, and that softening of manners that always follows a time of security, had brought more sweetness into their social relations." A desire for independence had reappeared in that fa-

---

sian service," is dedicated to Gregory Orlov, brother of Aleksej and a favorite of the empress, and is in the British Library in London with the call number 868.C.4. On Demetrio Teodosio, editor of the *Didaskalia*, "printer privileged by the Serenissimo Dominio for Greek print," who came under suspicion by the state inquisitors, but in reality, we are assured, "had St. Mark truly at heart," see G. S. Ploumides, *To benetikon typographeion tou Demetriou kai tou Panou Theodosiou (1755–1824)* (The Venetian publishers Demetrio and Pano Teodosio [1755–1824]) (Athens, 1969), with a summary in Italian, p. 122 n. 27. The *Giornale d'Italia* reviewed this work in vol. 2, no. 1 (6 July 1765): 4ff.: "We do not know if this work written in vulgar Greek is good or bad, not understanding the language. We are, however, informed that it contains information on the art, method, and discipline current in the Russian army and those of other European powers, details on the duties of officers from the lowest to the highest marshal, how an army from eighty to a hundred thousand men should operate, its divisions and subdivisions, the infantry, cavalry, artillery, or corps of engineers; and some rules and observations on naval armament and firepower, and that it ends with some moral injunctions on the life and duties of officers and soldiers. Too many things for such a small book."

[10] Chevalier, *De Rulhière*, p. 351, and De Rulhière, *Histoire de l'anarchie de Pologne*, p. 355.

[11] De Rulhière, *Histoire de l'anarchie de Pologne*, p. 357.

[12] Ibid., pp. 359–60.

mous land. Astute and powerful leaders were taken with it. In the Morea the most important was Panajotis Benakis, who through a thousand schemes had ended up favorable to the Russians. "He was a rich old man, with a fine figure and a venerable appearance—always notable advantages, and even more so among barbarian peoples. He has added to these gifts of nature a supple and cunning wit."[13] Everywhere in the society of Greeks of the Morea, one could see a strange mixture of democratic forms and aristocratic traditions.

From that mixture of ancient Messenians, of Spartans, of the most distinguished families of Greece, and those who reigned in Constantinople and in Trabzon, was formed the little nation known today with the name of Maineotes. They were divided into several tribes still free in the mountains, courageous to the point of ferociousness, proud of what the blood of so many imperial houses had mixed into the blood of their citizens, and still more proud after so many centuries, and despite their extreme ignorance, to be taken for descendants of Spartans. . . . Their impenetrable crags give them courage against the largest armies, the austerity of their life gives a great virility, and the liberty they enjoy in a poor and barren countryside inspires a mistrust for the riches acquired by other Greeks in slavery. The habit of peril has given even their women a tough audacity and has made them, if not deserving of this fame, at least deserving to boast of it. A vague tradition has kept alive a memory of undying independence.

Their customs also reflected ancient traditions, which were finally flowering anew. "Even today the bloody and torn clothes of sons killed in combat are brought to their mothers. Friends gather to sing hymns of consolation and triumph around these sad vestments."[14]

   Again it is difficult not to think of Corsica. More study is needed of the parallel development of these Mediterranean societies emerging from the crisis of the seventeenth century in order to observe more closely the effects whatever limited economic progress had on the formation of the power of the "principals," the "heads," of the new political elites, and also on the roots of their movements for independence and national renewal.[15] It should not surprise us to learn that Paul Rancurel,

   [13] Ibid., pp. 361ff.
   [14] Ibid., pp. 369ff.
   [15] On Corsica see Francis Pomponi, *Essai sur les notables ruraux en Corse au XVIIe siècle* (Aix-en-Provence: Faculté des Lettres, 1972), id., *Histoire de la Corse*, and F. Venturi, *Settecento riformatore*, vol. 5 (Paris: Hachette, 1979), pp. 3ff. On Greece see Apostolos E. Vacalopoulos, *The Greek Nation, 1453–1699* (New Brunswick, N.J.: Rutgers University Press, 1976). Suggestive parallels between Corsica and Greece are in Tommaseo Nicolò, *Storia civile nella letteratura* (Rome, Turin, and Florence: E. Loescher, 1972), pp. 409ff. See on pp. 433ff. the parallel between Paoli and Capodistria. "Cephalonia is the Ionian island most similar to Corsica," one reads on p. 439. For a recent history of the Maineotes see Kyprianos D. Kasses, *Syntome historia tes Manes apo ten proistoria mechri semera* (A brief history of Maina from prehistory to the present) (Athens, 1977).

a contemporary and an admirer of Rousseau, went from Corsica to Greece in his search for authentic democracy, hoping to find it first in the island of Pasquale Paoli, and then among the Maineotes who were preparing themselves for an insurrection.[16]

Besides this utopian element, there was a reflection of prophetic themes from the sixteenth century.[17] Toward the end of 1769, Agnelli, the editor of the gazette of Lugano, the *Nuove di diverse corti e paesi*, looked up the article "Mahomet" in Bayle's dictionary and found reference to a 1570 book, according to which Muscovites and Venetians were destined to be instruments in the future destruction of the Ottoman Empire. There were persons in Paris, the article continued, "who seriously say a defeat by Russians of the Ottoman fleet, the present state of the Turks, and the unrest of the Montenegrins are signs of the realization of this prophecy, which is to come in the next campaign." This was "a great revolution" already foreseen in a manuscript of Paolo Sarpi. And the Turks were quite fearful of it. "Leo, the philosopher emperor of Constantinople," had foreseen the end of Ishmael at the hands of a "blond race." "This emperor mentioned a column in Constantinople with the inscription, which the Greek patriarch explained in this way, 'That the Venetians and Muscovites would take the city of Constantinople and after various differences elect together a Christian emperor.' " "This is the reason," the gazette concluded, "that the Turks are all sworn enemies of the Russians, because they are almost all blond."[18] We find this vision elsewhere. Rulhière thought "the old prophecy of the Russians destroying the Ottoman Empire" had "become a popular belief."[19] The image of a "blond man" reappears often among Greeks in revolt during the following decades.[20]

[16] See *Correspondance complète de J. J. Rousseau*, ed. R. A. Leigh (Banbury: The Voltaire Foundation, 1975), vol. 24, p. 355, where a letter by Giovanni Bianchi to Isidoro Bianchi from Rimini, dated 30 March 1769, is cited. "That philosophe [Paul Rancurel] . . . will be in Venice and then in Albania to see if there might be there the democratic republic he seeks, and not finding it he will go on to the Morea to see if it is still among the Maineotes, who are the remains of the ancient Spartans." He was also advised to seek "that republic" in the Grisons, "without searching the barbarian lands from Albania to the Morea." See also his relations with Pasquale Paoli and Jean Jacques Rousseau.

[17] See Carlo Dionisotti, "Le guerre d'Oriente nella letteratura veneziana del Cinquecento," in *Lettere italiane*, vol. 16, pp. 233ff., and Paolo Preto, *Venezia e i turchi* (Florence: Sansoni, 1975), pp. 67ff.

[18] *Nuove di diverse corti e paesi*, no. 50, 11 December 1769 (Paris, 27 November). Note GG in the article "Mahomet" in Bayle's *Dictionnaire historique et critique* contains an extraordinary collection of prophecies about the end of the Ottoman Empire. Blonds are among those most often credited with this enterprise, and they are generally identified with Muscovites, although sometimes with Swedes or Hungarians.

[19] De Rulhière, *Histoire de l'anarchie de Pologne*, pp. 383–84.

[20] See the numerous examples cited in Camariano-Cioran, "La guerre russo-turque," p. 517 n. 10.

Giacomo Casanova also spoke of the prophecies that accompanied the Russo-Turkish war in his *Confutazione* of Amelot de la Houssaye. "I have found," he said, "in a manuscript by Fra Paolo Sarpi, a prophecy of the Turks that their empire will be put to an end by the sword of Christians. When they mention this eventuality in their prayers they howl like beasts." Casanova also reported the prophecy of the end of the Ottomans coming through the work of a "blond race." But these old stories were reduced to triviality by his pen. "The empress, from what I saw, and close by, is dark; and she is not Russian, she is German. An old man worthy of belief assured me that she appears to be dark, but she is blond. Another person of great credit told me that up to age eleven she was blond, and that an illness made her turn suddenly dark. But whatever it is, she seems to me dark. I know also that she has wit enough to appear what she is not when the good of the state requires it."[21]

Far from such musings and fantasies was the harsh reality Giorgio Papasoglis explored during his long and frequent pilgrimages across the lands of Greece. But even his own travels were soon shrouded in legend. It has been recently supposed that he might have been Agi Murad, who traveled across the Morea dressed in the "costume of an iman," and of whom there are ample traces in the pages of a later French traveler, A. L. Castellan.[22] Certainly he was the chief person responsible for the secret organization built up in Greece. He encountered many obstacles. The brothers M. and G. Mikalis, who were important among the Maineotes, explained that these people were invincible in defense, but weak in offense, because of the continual internal struggles among their different families. They would not be able to take much initiative. In general, they were surprised to see Papasoglis present himself without any credentials from Catherine II. He had more success with Panajotis Benakis, another leader, who assured the participation of many of his followers and received the promise of a large body to be sent from Russia in exchange. Many followed the example of Benakis. The clergy were particularly active. The bishops of Corinth and Patras, the former bishop of Patras, and many others took up the thread of the plot. Numerous notables of Sparta "and several among the rich" gave their support.[23]

[21] Giacomo Casanova, *Confutazione della storia del governo veneto d'Amelot de la Houssaye* (Amsterdam [actually Venice], 1769), p. 1, pp. 377ff. n.

[22] See De Rulhière, *La "sainte insurrection" des Grecs*, p. 23 n. 31, and Antoine-Laurent Castellan, *Lettres sur la Morée et les îles de Cérigo. Hydra et Zante* (Paris, 1808), pp. 59ff. n. 1. See also Camariano-Cioran, "La guerre russo-turque," p. 520.

[23] See Panteles M. Kontoyiannes, *Oi Ellenes kata ton proton epi Aikaterines B' rossotourkikon polemon, 1768–1774* (The Greeks at the time of the first Russo-Turkish war, 1768–1774) (Athens, 1903), pp. 70ff. A French translation of these pages is in De Rulhière, *La*

Antonio Psaros, another important organizer of the insurrection of 1770, was firm in his own convictions but realistic in his evaluation of the conditions of his own country. He was the one who explained during a visit to St. Petersburg "that the Greeks had the best intentions in the world," but that they would not be in a position to maintain their promises "unless the Russians send a considerable force to support them." One should not harbor illusions: "Greeks of today, raised from their childhood to fear the Turks, will never be able to stand up to them." His resolution nonetheless made a good impression. The empress wanted to see him. At court "he was called a true Greek, a Greek of the good old days."[24] The vision of antiquity thus, even in this case, intruded between the reality of the Morea and those who expected to intervene there, as later happened for one generation of philo-Hellenes after another. In vain Psaros tried to explain how things stood for Fedor Orlov, an intelligent man, but with "an imagination inflamed from reading ancient history and mythological tales." The age of Miltiades and Leonidas had now passed, he said.[25] He insisted that the Macedonians were not the same as those of antiquity. They came from Epirus. The republic of Venice and the kingdom of Naples used them as soldiers and called them Macedonians "to make them seem more respectable, more conspicuous. . . . This name is better sounding; it is a matter of vanity."[26] As for the Maineotes, the basic element in their society was the influence of their leaders. "Power belongs to those who can arm the largest number of friends and relations." Among families there often reigned "unending vendettas." To persuade oneself of this it was enough to observe Maineote families who had emigrated to Corsica, who were in a perpetual struggle among themselves.[27]

More optimistic instead, or so it seems, was another important explorer and Russian agent in Greece, Vasilij Stepanovic Tomara, "a gentleman of the Ukraine," then in his twenties (he was born in 1747), who had studied at the Accademia dei Nobili in Turin before leaving for a long voyage to Italy, Corfu, the Epirus, "and to many other possessions of the Turks where the Greek religion is widespread." He had collected many useful notes "on the situation of these provinces, the forces the Porte maintains there, and the population, character, and in-

"sainte insurrection" des Grecs, pp. 36ff. n. 32ff. The principal work on the Morea in the eighteenth century is by Michael B. Sakellarios, *E Peloponnesos kata ten deuteran tourkokratian, 1715–1821* (The Peloponnesus under the second Turkish domination, 1715–1821) (Athens: Verlag der "Bizantinisch-neugriechischen Jahrbücher," 1939).

[24] Chevalier, *De Rulhière*, p. 352.
[25] Ibid., p. 353.
[26] Ibid., p. 355.
[27] Ibid., p. 356.

clinations of the Greeks."[28] He ended up persuading himself that "the ferment" in Greece was intense. "According to him it was necessary to give the Greeks only arms and munitions, and this would be easy through different Italian ports where during certain seasons of the year everything is allowed to enter and leave without dues or inspection." The Turks would soon be slaughtered. "One hundred and fifty thousand francs given to the right hands would be sufficient to secure a great and sudden revolution."[29]

It seems that Angelos Adamopulo was also quite active. Aleksej Orlov sent him a letter at Pisa at the end of 1769, whose authenticity it is difficult to determine, but which seems to reflect well the state of mind of those days of anxious preparation: "I hope you have safely arrived in Trieste with the 5,000 zecchini. Remain there as short a time as possible and try to embark as soon as you can. See that our friend Benachi makes his preparations well, and you will be assured that a larger sum will soon follow. The friends of M. [probably Mauro Mikalis] can count on the fleet's setting sail toward the end of April, if it is not overtaken by some accident. Farewell, be prudent, and remind yourself that all your services will be rewarded."[30]

It seemed for a moment that even Giuseppe Gorani would be induced to become an instrument in the politics of Catherine II in Greece. He had just finished writing *Il vero dispotismo*, and in the summer of 1769 he was in Geneva seeing to its publication. Voltaire, whom he had gone to venerate in Ferney, discovered that Gorani's sister had married "the last legitimate heir of the emperors of Constantinople and Trabzon, Count Alexis Comnène." Why not make use of this illustrious name to raise Greeks against the Turks?[31] There was even an effort to put this plan into action. Gorani returned to Italy, making the voyage with a Russian officer charged with "arranging with other officers the means to make enormous provision for land and sea forces the empress was to send into the Archipelago against the Turks." But, once in Italy, the dreams of Voltaire and Gorani vanished without a trace.[32]

---

[28] Sirio, vol. 143 (1913), pp. 43ff., dispatch from St. Petersburg by Sabatier de Cabre to Choiseul dated 13 October 1769. Tomara later had a career in the foreign affairs and senate of Russia and died in 1819; see Tatiana Bakounine, *Répertoire biographique des francs-maçons russes (XVIIIe et XIXe siècle)* (Paris: Institut des études slaves, 1967), p. 544.

[29] De Rulhière, *Histoire de l'anarchie de Pologne*, pp. 384–85.

[30] Reported by Joseph Von Hammer, *Geschichte des Osmanische Reiches* (Pest: C. A. Hartleben), vol. 8, p. 355 n.

[31] Giuseppe Gorani, *Dal despotismo illuminato alla rivoluzione (1767–1791), Memorie*, vol. 3. ed. Alessandro Casati (Milan: Mondadori, 1942), p. 148.

[32] Ibid., pp. 150–51. On Don Claudio Antonio Comneno, see ibid., pp. 125ff., 383, 392ff.

For a while, a large part of the Russian armament around Greece was controlled from Venice through Marchese Pano Maruzzi's operation. Unlike other agents of Catherine II, he did not have to disguise himself in the clothes of a merchant, a traveler, or an archaeologist. He was, as we have seen, officially accredited to the republic of St. Mark. He shared his hopes with his compatriots, if not always their illusions. The Maroutsis family, originally from Epirus, had established itself in Venice, where trade had given them considerable wealth.[33] He represented well that active world of entrepreneurs in Greek trade, which the agents of Catherine were exploring, and he put himself rapidly into motion when the Muscovite fleet reached the Mediterranean.[34]

It soon became clear, however, that the direction of the Greek affair as a whole, as well as the preparations for the coming naval expedition, would have to be consigned to more energetic hands. The initiators of the undertaking, the two Orlov brothers, Aleksej and Fedor, transferred from St. Petersburg to Italy "at the end of 1768, at the first hint of war," Rulhière writes.[1] They were the brothers of Gregory, the great favorite of the empress and had at their backs the coup d'état of 1762 and the elimination of Peter III. Before them was a world to conquer and glory

[33] See Camariano-Cioran, "La guerre russo-turque," p. 521. See as well Turin, AS, *Lettere ministri, Venezia*, 40, dispatch by Incisa di Camerana, 28 October 1769. "Greek of origin and religion, born a subject of this republic, made a knight in Muscovy." G. Casanova also speaks of him in his *Confutazione* of Amelot de la Houssaye: "A year after my departure [1766] there arrived in St. Petersburg a Venetian who had success. But one should know that this Venetian was Greek and rich. There was a grand welcome for him in St. Petersburg in all the houses where he presented himself because the sovereign, whenever he appeared at court, took care to distinguish him from the crowd and did him the honor of always addressing some word to him. Love, despite his riches, abused him, but he departed covered with honors, decorated with the order of the Knights of St. Anne, and with the title of general agent of Her Imperial Majesty not only in Venice, but from what I was told, in all Italy." Casanova, *Confutazione*, p. 1, pp. 43ff. n. He came from a family that distinguished itself by founding an important Greek school at Janina. See. G. P. Henderson, *The Revival of Greek Thought, 1620–1830* (Albany: State University of New York Press, 1970), p. 43.

[34] See Nicolas G. Svoronos, *Le commerce de Salonique au XVIIIe siècle* (Paris: PUF, 1956), with an ample treatment of commerce with Italy also: Livorno, pp. 166ff.; Venice, pp. 169ff.; and so on. Interesting as well is the article by Basile Sfyroeras, "Les Mavroyéni et la vie économique de la mer Egée," in the acts of the conference *L'époque phanariote*, 21–25 October 1970 (Salonika: Institute for Balkan Studies, 1974), pp. 327ff., as well as the essay by George B. Leon, "The Greek Merchant Marine (1453–1850)," in *The Greek Merchant Marine*, ed. Stelios A. Papadopulos (National Bank of Greece, 1972), pp. 13ff., with a long bibliography. See particularly the section "Commercial Expansion and the Emergence of the Greek Merchant Marine," pp. 25ff.

[1] De Rulhière, *Histoire de l'anarchie de Pologne*, p. 386.

to win. They had no scruples. They were ready to use the same violence and energy in the Mediterranean that they had shown in gaining power in St. Petersburg. The face of Aleksej, marked by a horrible scar, showed who this man was whose followers called the "slashed." Fedor, "the youngest of the Orlovs, the most intellectual of the five brothers," was the only one to have profited from the "elevation of his family" to "acquire a little education." He had "a more effeminate beauty than Alexis, but a truer courage."[2]

The snares of a world they hardly knew awaited the Orlov brothers. Catherine, as we have seen, had explained to them the diplomatic situation in Italy. But in the Balkans they had to entrust themselves to the uncertain light provided by their agents, explorers, and local leaders. Papasoglis immediately proposed holding a conference in Venice "of deputies of Greeks from the Morea and the islands," so that the Orlovs "could see for themselves the truth of what he had promised."[3] This was done. The prospects seemed to be encouraging. But the activity of the Orlovs made the Venetian republic more and more diffident and fearful. The two brothers declared that they had come, motivated "by an aim of honest curiosity," expecting "after a stay of a few weeks to pass on to Tuscany and then make a tour of Italy," as Incisa di Camerana, the diplomatic agent of the king of Sardinia, announced to Turin. But "their long stay, their frequent meetings with Greek nationals, and their sending and receiving couriers from their court" evidently led one to believe that they were the center of Russian activity in the Mediterranean.[4]

The threat to Venice was not only the unwelcome one of being involved yet again in the rivalries and quarrels of the three great empires along her borders—the Turkish, Russian, and Austrian empires. The peril was also closer. Venice was certainly aware of the fact that its own subjects of Greek religion and nationality were the originators of the plot now in the hands of the Orlov brothers. The matter had been put directly to the brothers by Catherine II in May 1769. "Greeks of our rite, Venetian subjects," had sent a letter from Trieste to Prince Dmitrij Michajlović Golicyn, the Russian ambassador in Vienna, with the signatures "of more than ten persons, who say they are ready to attack Turkish vessels and subjects with their ships."[5]

Venice was all the more embarrassed by such threats to its tranquillity and the integrity of its dominions, because it was at the decisive mo-

[2] Ibid., p. 387.
[3] Chevalier, De Rulhière, p. 351.
[4] Turin, AS, Lettere ministri, Venezia, mazzo 40, 18 March 1769.
[5] Sirio, vol. 1, p. 19, letter by Catherine II to A. Orlov, 6 May 1769.

ment of a struggle that Venice, with other Italian states, was carrying on with the Roman Curia. In March the Senate disallowed the papal bull *In coena Domini*. There was discussion and deliberation about holidays, convents, and mortmain.[6] With reluctance the different parties detached themselves from these problems to fix their eyes on the new reality growing around them. Still, in May 1769 the representative of the king of Sardinia was convinced that Venice could hope to avoid being menaced by Russian policy. The Russian fleet would come, he said, "to assist General Paoli and his party in Corsica against the French, to counteract the moves made by France to involve the Turks in the war in Poland, and to make raids against Ottomans on the Greek islands."[7] This diversion, in other words, was not aimed at the Adriatic. Still, it was easy to answer, How could Venice not be involved in a conflict involving the Ottoman Empire? Even on this point the Serene Republic was in a state of crisis. The patricians were preoccupied with the difficult choice of a new agent in Constantinople. Should it be Paolo Renier or Alvise Vallaresso?[8] Even here, internal politics and the balance among the great families prevailed over international concerns. There was also Vienna to be taken into account. In June there began talk about Austrian demands that the Republic reinforce its naval squadron and prepare to defend itself. Kaunitz intended "to rouse Venice from the decadence of its military affairs" and prepare it for an eventual alliance against the Ottomans, with the end, among others, of securing the commerce of Trieste with Venetian arms.[9] Venice responded in the negative. In the autumn the Senate reviewed the cost of the small force that could be counted on. On land, theoretically, there were 18,000 men, when in reality there were 7,000. "The result of old corruption," said the agent of the king of Sardinia. It would be necessary to reorganize the navy, bringing the number of warships and frigates to ten. In the spring the command was entrusted to Angelo Emo, "a subject of distinct merit and well-known and acclaimed capacity."[10] In reality Venice became still more rigid in its "exact neutrality." It did not want to offend the Russians or to be lacking in its treaties with the Turks. As for the Greeks, how could one forget the importance of merchants of that nation in the economic life of the Republic? "Subjects or neighbors," these merchants "have a central place in the best and most lucrative part of

---

[6] Franco Venturi, *Settecento riformatore*, vol. 2: *La chiesa e la repubblica dentro i loro limiti, 1758–1774* (Turin: Einaudi, 1976), pp. 101ff.

[7] Turin, AS, *Lettere ministri, Venezia*, mazzo 40, 20 May 1769.

[8] Ibid.

[9] Ibid., 14 June 1769.

[10] Ibid., 7 October 1769.

the commerce of this place with the Levant."[11] Pano Maruzzi was their spokesman as much as he was the spokesman of Catherine II. On the other hand, "many Ottoman nationals or subjects, Bosnians and Albanians, who traffic here in the trade of wax, wool, and tobacco," would be opposed to "any kind of favor or partiality for Muscovy, or even private interest that Venetian nobles might show in the course of the war."[12] The mercantile traditions of Venice made it difficult to choose or decide. Meanwhile the coals of war in the Balkans reignited. The gazette of Lugano did not doubt that the Montenegrins would finally declare they were on the side of Russia, "as soon as the Russian fleet arrives in these waters, in which case the Porte will be obliged to carry out a diversion, and Dalmatia could become a theater of war."[13] The delicate fabric of Venetian policy seemed more and more menaced. And just then, between September and October, came the news that the fleet of Catherine II had weighed anchor in Kronstadt and had reached Denmark.[14]

To welcome the fleet, the Orlovs had for some months been preparing a base of action in Tuscany. Already on 20 May 1769, the minister Rosenberg was informed of the possibility that "certain Orlov brothers, Muscovites, who have left Venice and transferred themselves to Pisa," might have the intention "of buying vessels in Livorno to supply arms to Greeks in Albania and Dalmatia against the Turks." He even feared that "they will try to send artists to Muscovy, as it is assumed they have done from Venice."[15] The presence in Pisa, a few days later, of the Greek commander Panajotti Alessiano with the Orlov brothers also confirmed "the feared suspicion of armament under the Russian flag."[16] In the summer the Russian colony, including the Dalmatians who had joined it, reached fourteen persons with twenty-four servants.[17] "Lieutenant Schowalow" was "at Bagni with six servants and a prince—whose name I cannot spell—who is the bodyguard of the empress of Russia": Dolgorukij, one reads in another report.[18] In August there was a big

[11] Ibid., 23 September 1769.

[12] Ibid., 28 October 1769.

[13] *Supplimento delle Nuove di diverse corti e paesi*, no. 42, 16 October 1769 (from Dalmatia, 3 September).

[14] Turin, AS, *Lettere ministri, Venezia*, mazzo 40, 23 September 1769, and *Nuove di diverse corti e paesi*, no. 41, 9 October 1769 (Copenhagen, 15 September). Spiridov and Elphinston, one reads, were at the head of a great naval squadron, with "many pieces of artillery," "landing troops numbering 10,000 men," "transport vessels," "fire ships and armed galleys"; "thus there is no doubt that their destination is the Mediterranean."

[15] Livorno, AS, Governo, *Lettere civili al governatore di Livorno*, filza 7, 20 maggio 1769.

[16] Ibid., 28 May 1769.

[17] Ibid., filza 8, 31 July 1769, letter by Andrea Fortuna, captain of the Bargello of Pisa, who gives details of the names and places of habitation.

[18] Ibid., 31 July 1769.

business of buying ships in Genova and Portoferraio, "for the Levant." Guesses about their intentions multiplied. "Some say they might be pirates." But this seemed improbable because of "their bearing, their style of life, their clean clothing."[19] Objections were raised in July, even by Horace Mann, the English representative, to their intention of buying the English vessel *Rachel*, which "appeared most recently in Livorno after its voyage from Corsica, where Mr. Clemente de Paoli and other Corsicans embarked."[20] But in September it was clear that "England was in accord with the Russians," and that the Russians were in Italy not as privateers, but to prepare for the fleet of Catherine II, "expected certainly in the Mediterranean."[21]

The thread of the plot for the Greek uprising was pulled tighter in Tuscany in the last months of 1769. The *Storia della guerra presente* assures us that

there came to ratify the treaty (stipulated at St. Petersburg) not only various Maineotes, but also other Greeks from the Romelia, and it was decided to conquer the Morea. At this point Giorgio Papasoli from the Romelia, along with Angeli Adamopulo and Giovanni Palatino, left Tuscany for the peninsula, where they confirmed the treaty with the leaders at Maina and Calamata. . . . The people were assured that the Russians would land in these places with a large number of warships and transports, and that they would put ashore many troops to support the nationals . . . well trained in regular service. At this meeting there were solemn oaths, and the archbishop [of Malvasia], as well as the aforementioned leaders, signed to serve the undertaking with fidelity and zeal.[1]

The Orlovs intensified their recruitment of Slavs and Greeks, without paying much attention to whether they were Turkish or Venetian subjects.[2] At the end of January a manifesto in the name of Catherine II was published; it was addressed to "all Orthodox peoples groaning under the Ottoman yoke." These were called "deserving of prompt assistance for being so renowned" in antiquity and religion.[3] The Moslems

---

[19] Ibid., 14 August 1769.

[20] Livorno, AS, *Governo, Copialettera della segreteria civile*, 31 July 1769, the governor of Livorno to minister Rosenberg.

[21] Ibid., 18 September 1769.

[1] *Storia della guerra presente*, vol. 6, pp. 111ff.

[2] Camillo Manfroni, "Documenti veneziati sulle campagne dei russi nel Mediterraneo 1770–1771," in *Atti dell'Istituto veneto di scienze, lettere ed arti, 1912–1913*, vol. 72, 8th ser., vol. 15, p. 2, p. 1157.

[3] The manifesto was dated 19 January 1769, old style, that is, 30 January 1770. A copy is attached to a dispatch by Horace Mann from Florence on 7 April 1770. PRO SP 98/75. The English resident in Tuscany explained that "the inclosed manifest has been privately printed here, which is to be dispersed among the Greeks of the Morea and the neighbouring provinces which they inhabit." With numerous variants, this proclamation to the

were "attempting to drown Moldavia, Walachia, Bulgaria, Bosnia, Herzegovina, Macedonia, and the other states, in an abyss of misery," threatening "unspeakable calamities, most oppressive contributions, harsh conditions, never-ending injustices, extreme misery, and cruel slaughter, without the liberty of building churches or professing freely the Catholic religion." Earlier "great Peter, our uncle of immortal fame, most glorious emperor, and the most worthy empress Anna, daughter of John, our aunt of venerated memory," had worked for the liberation of the oppressed without success. Now Catherine, as her policy in Poland also demonstrated, "intended to liberate the Orthodox from the barbarians." "Such a war will be one of eternal glory and praise . . . , it will reestablish, indeed resurrect, entire peoples and vindicate ancient dignity, decorum, and splendor." "We hold close to the glory of our famous ancestors, who left Russia to found kingdoms, filling the world with glorious feats of arms, and thus were rightly Slavs, that is, glorious." Catherine II would provide them with "every comfort and advantage through the great deeds against the common enemy . . . which they would be certain to see in the present war."

In the winter of 1769–1770 Tuscany rapidly became the ideal base for the effort to carry out this program. Russian relations with Tuscan merchants, especially in Livorno, had continued to improve. Bertellet said that when "the Muscovite squadron" arrived, Tuscany would give it every welcome, because of the "great profit this state would gain by furnishing the provisions it needs."[4] The gazette of Leiden even attributed the high price of meat in Rome, at least in part, to "the extraordinary quantity of provisions the Russians have made in Tuscany for their squadron."[5] At the beginning of the new year, the Russians were viewed in Livorno as being particularly welcome and festive hosts. "Messieurs the Generals Orlow and Schuvalow, and Monsieur Prince Dolgorouky himself, who was for a time in charge of the Montenegrins, to whom he delivered arms, munitions of war, and money, had come here [to Livorno] from Pisa the fourth of this month [January], and returned the ninth where they and the officers of their party were entertained handsomely by the governor and the English consul, with whom they have close ties."[6]

"Illirian nation of Orthodox confession" is reproduced in the *Storia della guerra presente*, vol. 5, pp. 143ff.

[4] AMAE, *Toscane*, 132, 3 November 1769.

[5] *Nouvelles extraordinaires de divers endroits*, year 39, 15 May 1770 (Civitavecchia, 20 April).

[6] AMAE, *Toscane*, 133, 12 January 1770. Ivan Ivanovič Šuvalov, a great figure in the period of Empress Elizabeth, went abroad on the accession of Catherine II. She nonethe-

The Russian fleet left Port Mahon at the beginning of February, heading east. In Livorno, Orlov awaited a "favorable wind" to join it and take command.[1] Soon the news came that Russian ships had been seen near the Ionian Islands, showing themselves in the Adriatic, whereas others continued on course toward the Morea. As the *Gazzetta di Milano* reported on 21 March, in a communication from Livorno of the fourteenth of that month, "the Russian fleet is becoming more and more formidable and holds all Europe in apprehension."[2] It was a fear born not only of the disruption the fleet of Catherine II brought to the balance of diplomacy and commerce, but also, as immediately appeared, of provoked desertions and raised revolts. "We hear from the Levant that on the islands of the Venetian republic there have been uprisings of Greeks, which cause much disturbance to that government," it was reported from Florence.[3] The empire of the Turks was affected as much as that of the Venetians. In a communication from Naples the *Gazzetta di Milano* reported that "the uprising of Montenegrins and people of Georgia is like an epidemic spreading to every corner of those provinces, which keeps the Divan in high anxiety."[4] Even the empire of Maria Theresa was concerned. "The court of Vienna," wrote an informant of the government of Turin from Rome, "is disturbed about the Russians, because there are five hundred thousand Greeks in that state." The Orthodox became agitated, "above all now since they see the progress of the Russians, who call them brothers."[5]

Kaunitz, although not concealing the danger, was still convinced that a firm and resolute policy would succeed in dominating the situation. The important thing was to be sure that the weakest and most menaced state, Venice, did not give in to the Muscovites' threats and boasts. On the sea, Austria would have to give way to the English and the Russians. But on land it intended to remain the strongest. As Gradenigo, the Venetian ambassador in Vienna, revealed, Kaunitz spoke about this clearly on 28 April 1770. Austria was ready to "make war whenever the Russians want to *casser les vitres*." Venice should not permit itself illusions. The empire of Catherine II was weaker than it appeared to be. "The Russians cannot sustain the present war for long, since they already feel the consequences. They have had to raise new taxes, they have coined rubles that are almost entirely false," besides having to tri-

---

less made use of him in cultural and diplomatic missions, above all in Italy. See the entry in the *Russkij biografičeskij slovar'*, Šebanov-Šjutc, 1911, pp. 476ff.

[1] *Notizie del mondo*, no. 26, 31 March 1770 (Livorno, 28 March), p. 205.
[2] *La gazzetta di Milano*, no. 12, 21 March 1770 (Livorno, 15 March).
[3] *Notizie del mondo*, no. 26, 31 March 1770 (Livorno, 28 March), p. 205.
[4] *La gazzetta di Milano*, no. 9, 28 February 1770 (Naples, 13 February).
[5] Turin, AS, *Materie politiche estere in genere*, mazzo 55, 1770, Rome, 24 Febuary 1770.

ple recruitment.[6] These were lessons in realism that found ears well disposed to hear them. As Erizzo, the Venetian ambassador in Rome, explained to the representative of the king of Sardinia, Rivera—who passed it on to Turin on 13 January 1770—the rumor that "the Venetians could now think of joining the Muscovites to reconquer the Morea" did not have "the slightest foundation." "The republic is not in a state," he said, "to put together the necessary land or naval forces."[7]

But how was it possible to remain neutral before the rebellions, tumults, and desertions provoked by the Russians? Even foreign courts were aware of the difficulty Venice found itself in. "It is natural that the republic should think very seriously about the seditious activities of Greek subjects partial to Muscovy," wrote the foreign minister of Carlo Emmanuele III.[8] "All the Greek nation seems determin'd on a general insurrection and revolt," wrote the British representative in Venice. The Greeks showed they were openly "attach'd to the Muscovites by inclination and the most sanguine hopes." "The same fanaticism reigns among the Venetian subjects in the adjacent islands."[9]

The first "Muscovite warship, of Dutch origin, called the *Orka*, arrived unexpectedly in this port," Corfu, and it was sufficient to put "into a fever the Greek nationals of this coast."[10] Sailors and captains of ships went over to the service of Catherine II. Among the first was a certain "Palicucchia, a native Venetian subject from Castelnovo, and currently a licensed captain commanding a large tartan owned by some of the merchants of this place [Venice], with about twenty pieces of cannon and eighty men. Leaving Zante, he sent the representative there the license and flag of St. Mark, and raising that of Muscovy, went to join the aforementioned Russian boat, the two sailing together in those waters." The gesture was repeated often and spread to "Dalmatians and Slavs trading in this sea." The "movements of the Montenegrins" became more and more menacing.[11] News of vessels "that have taken the Rus-

[6] The passages in Gradenigo's dispatch were taken from an article by Roberto Cessi, "Confidenze d'un ministro russo a Venezia nel 1770," in *Atti dell'Istituto veneto di scienze, lettere ed arti*, vol. 74 (1914–15), p. 2, pp. 1592ff. This is the most important treatment of these developments. One should still keep in mind that it is strongly influenced by the interventionist atmosphere of the days when it was written (the proofs were consigned on 29 June 1915).

[7] Turin, AS, *Lettere ministri, Roma*, mazzo 262, 13 January 1770.

[8] Turin, AS, *Lettere ministri, Venezia*, 1770, mazzo 40, 31 March 1770.

[9] PRO SP 99/75, F. 15, 1 April 1770.

[10] Turin, AS, *Lettere ministri, Venezia*, 1770, mazzo 40, dispatches by Incisa di Camerana dated 24 February and 10 March 1770.

[11] Ibid., 10 March 1770. On Captain Palicucchia see also Manfroni, "Documenti veneziani," pp. 1156–57. On his death in battle, see *Supplemento alla Gazzetta di Parma*, no. 51, 17 December 1771 (Venice, 8 December).

sian flag" spread rapidly.[12] The violence of such mutinies was a cause for concern to the Russian commanders, who at least officially had to appear to respect Venetian neutrality. Horace Mann, the British representative in Tuscany, noted the "great concern" of Russians confronted with the "indiscreet zeal of the Greeks who inhabit the island subject to the Republick of Venice." Catherine II, at least in appearance, intended to live "in good harmony" with the Republic of St. Mark.[13]

The situation came to a head when the squadron commanded by Fedor Orlov appeared in the Gulf of Coron. On 28 January 1770 it entered the port of Vittulo and made its first contact with bands of Greeks in revolt. On the Ionian Islands everything was put into action immediately. "The Greeks of the islands of Corfu and Cephalonia, even the Jesuits established there, favor the undertaking of the Russians."[14] The echoes of these events traveled a long way. In Rome, as an informant of the government of Turin wrote, it was said that "on Cephalonia and Zante the Greek population has taken arms as threatening rebels, and they shout long live the empress of Russia. In the first of these places soldiers sent to control them have been shot. . . . The Russian ships continue to show themselves and to strengthen the ferment."[15] The uprising was particlularly violent on Cephalonia, where the brothers Spiridone and Giovanni Metaxà placed themselves at the head of one hundred or more men and went over to the mainland to take an active part in the insurrection on the Morea.[16] On Corfu, as on Cephalonia, the uprising took on the aspect of a revolt of minor villages against the provincial capital.[17] "The inhabitants of Theace, a small place not far from Corfu, gave a lively and clamorous expression of their common joy on hearing the rumor of the arrival of the Russian fleet," wrote the representative of the king of Sardinia in Venice.[18] From

[12] *Notizie del mondo*, no. 40, 19 May 1770 (information from Corfu dated 10, 28, and 30 April).

[13] PRO SP 98/75, 7 April 1770.

[14] *Mercure historique et politique*, May 1770, p. 320. The news seems to be derived from the *Supplément aux Nouvelles extraordinaires de divers endroits* (gazette of Leiden), no. 36, 4 May 1770.

[15] Turin, AS, *Materie politiche estere in genere*, mazzo 55, 1770, Rome, 24 March 1770. There is also a trickle of news about mutinies, recruitments for the Russian fleet, rebellions, and so on.

[16] Marino e Nicolò Pignatorre, *Memorie storiche e critiche dell'isola di Cefalonia dai tempi eroici alla caduta della Repubblica veneta* (Corfu: G. Nacamulli, 1887), vol. 1, p. 185. Incisa di Camerana sent notice to Turin of this "tumult in a corner of the island of Cephalonia, which qualifies for the term *sedition*." Turin, AS, *Lettere ministri, Venezia*, 1770, mazzo 40, 24 March 1770.

[17] Manfroni, "Documenti veneziani," p. 1157.

[18] Turin, AS, *Lettere ministri, Venezia*, 1770, mazzo 40, 24 March 1770.

Zante a large number of inhabitants went over to the Morea. People even imagined that among them was "a colonel and party of Venetian troops." Everywhere the insurgents resorted to the "most barbarous disorders, pillaging wherever they go, and killing any who resist."[19]

In the eyes of the Venetian authorities this picture was more than disquieting. Here is what Andrea Donà, the general provisor of the sea, wrote from Corfu on 23 February 1769 v.s. (that is, 1770): "To the enthusiasm aroused in subjects of this province, following passage of the Russian ship, have been attributed tiresome occurrences on the island in recent days, which are still developing." On Zante, the night of 28 January, there had been a sea raid on a Turkish village. On Ithaka the "syndics and leaders" begged for the means to "restrain a kind of fanaticism that had arisen recently in the majority of the inhabitants, who are going about armed and devising pernicious plans against the Ottoman mainland. They have imposed subjection and terror on the general inhabitants of the island." On Cephalonia the situation was even worse. "With the passage in these waters of the Russian ship a large group of armed people from the most agitated villages came to the fortress." This "village tumult" "continued to the point of gunshots in the outskirts," but it was "resisted by the inhabitants." The "most perilous innovations" inflame the minds of the islanders, a letter to Donà from Zuanni Pizzamano, the provisor of Cephalonia, reported on 11 February. "The uniformity of religion, the renown of the presumed conquests, the ascetic insinuations of the priests, ambition, indigence, the quantity of idlers, bandits, and criminals are the physical and moral causes" of the disorders. "With the appearance of the Muscovite *Urca* in these seas a crowd of about 1,000 evildoers from the most seditious villages assembled in the locality of the fortress. . . . The first to arm their houses were the merchants . . the fear spread to the lower classes raising a defensive fear in them; as a result there are guards throughout the city and incessant alarms. . . . Cephalonia had the appearance of a sea swept by a violent storm."[20] Thus a "spirit of faction" had arisen that nothing could stop. Spiro Metaxà, "in an odious affront to public authority, abuses that influence his family has always had here." "The worst is that this fanaticism arouses the inhabitants to the point that they abandon their wives and children, the better part of their attention, and makes them think it right to do anything they want. I don't see anything that can be done effectively to stop the natural evils of a ferment that is called a war of religion."[21] The "spirit of piracy" was mixed with the desire to serve the

[19] PRO SP 99/75, dispatch by Robert Richie, 11 May 1770.

[20] Venice, AS, *Provveditori da Terra e da Mar*, filza 1018, dispatch 130 (I owe this documentation and the rest taken from this filza to Marino Berengo).

[21] Ibid., dispatch from Corfu 132, 6 March 1770.

Russians. "They give the name religious crusade to what is in fact no more than a lust for loot."[22] On 12 March a proclamation prohibited any form of emigration whose purpose was "to take service with the chief warring parties."[23] But the "rising of villains," and their passage to the Morea, did not stop; instead, it increased.[24]

It seemed for a moment that Greece was about to liberate itself from the Turks.[25] There was talk of a Greek and Russian army of 50,000 "select troops" that was "growing every day among people coming in crowds from all of Romelia, from upper and lower Epirus, and from the nearby islands," "so many followers, aroused by revenge, religion, and nationality, that however fertile the fields of the Morea and Achaea there will not be grain enough to feed them."[26] Exciting news kept coming in, even though it raised the prospect of massacres and horrors. "This war will be the most atrocious ever seen, because the Turks will slaughter any Greeks they capture, and no quarter will be given by Greeks or Muscovites to Turks or Jews."[27]

The Florentine *Notizie del mondo* viewed the insurrection not only with interest, but also with a certain good feeling, symptomatic of Tuscan policy in general toward the Russian Empire in the Mediterranean. The 21 April issue announced that "fourteen thousand Lacedaemonians have revolted in the strongholds of the Morea and have incited all the Greeks there." "The Russian fleet has arrived in the Morea, where, with the help of the Maineotes, or rather Spartans and other Greeks living in that kingdom, who have come like ants with arms in hand to join and support the troops favorable to the Russians, a large army has been raised. This has conquered the strongholds of Modon, Mistra (ancient Sparta), Gastouni, Patras, and other cities." "The Muscovites who have joined the Greek people are resolved not to leave any place subject to the Turks, but to reduce them all by force of arms."[1] In the following issue, dated 24 April, there was a detailed chronicle of the "general up-

[22] Ibid., dispatch from Corfu, 12 April 1770.
[23] Ibid., addendum to dispatch from Corfu 134, 13 March 1770.
[24] Ibid., dispatch 135, 18 March 1770; 145, 28 April 1770; and in many successive documents.
[25] For a description of these events, see Andrej Nikolaevič Petrov, *Vojna Rossii s Turciej i pol'skimi Konfederatami* (The war of Russia against Turkey and the Polish confederates) (St. Petersburg: E. Vejmar, 1866), vol. 3, pp. 360ff.
[26] Turin, AS, *Materie politiche estere in genere*, mazzo 55, 1770, information from the Levant, from Corfu, 10 April 1770.
[27] Ibid. There is an interesting echo of these events in the *Gazzetta di Parma*, no. 6, 6 February 1770 (Constantinople, 4 December 1769), and in the subsequent issues.
[1] *Notizie del Mondo*, no. 32, 21 April 1770, pp. 256ff. (Naples, 10 April, Corfu, 13 March).

rising among Greeks, allied with the Russians by inclination, religion, and flattering hopes and anticipations." Readers were even prepared for a landing at Montenegro, "as seems likely." In Constantinople reigned "great confusion."[2] The tone was still optimistic in April and May. "The discipline of the Russian ships and troops is said to be admirable and in good order, and all are content." "The Muscovites, along with the Mai-neotes, have conquered all of the Morea and are about to conquer Nauplia and Corinth." The movement seemed to be growing more and more. "There has been an uprising of 10,000 Cephalonians who want to give their land to the Russians but have not succeeded. However, six thousand of these and four thousand from Zante, with many nobles, raising the flag of Muscovy with beating drums, have passed into the Morea and taken Gastouni and Lipirgi. Many from Prevesa, Vonitza, Santa Maura, Ithaka, and Missolonghi have gone with the Muscovites into the Morea and taken all the Turkish fortresses."[3]

But soon news of a strong Ottoman counteroffensive began to arrive. "In the city of Thessalonica the Turks and Jews have united and have cut to pieces all the Greeks of that city in revenge for what was done to the Turks in the Morea, keeping only the women and children for a worse fate."[4] Not long after, news from the Levant became anything but favorable to Orlov and his men. The *Notizie del mondo* still persisted in its optimistic tone, which one might suspect was inspired by the Russians. "Count Orlov," we read in number 50 dated 23 June, "who had already taken Modon and Coron, has even made himself master of Corinth. . . . There is nothing to fear from the sea, thus soon the rest of the kingdom will be in the hands of the Muscovites. Count Orlov is very content with the fervor of Greek cooperation in their liberation." Writing his "first report" to Catherine II, he told her that he had no "need to trouble himself with animating this nation or arousing its interests to its own advantage." "I have needed instead to restrain the great impulsive fervor to pull down crescents all at once, and raise crosses and Russian eagles." Orlov had only praise for the "spirit" and "ease" with which Greeks submitted to "military discipline," thus putting themselves in a position to "secure their ancient glory."[5]

Finally, even the *Notizie del mondo* had to give in to the facts and take note of the failure of the Greek uprising. They published a long and interesting article, a "detailed account of what has happened in the Morea since the campaign began," with ample detailed reports of the pil-

[2] Ibid., no. 33, 24 April 1770, p. 259 (Venice, 17 April).
[3] Ibid., no. 40, 19 May 1770, p. 328 (Corfu, 10 and 28 April).
[4] Ibid. (Corfu, 28 April).
[5] Ibid., no. 50, 23 June 1770, p. 416 (Naples, 12 June).

laging and massacres that followed in that unfortunate undertaking. The candid tone corresponded, certainly, to the truth, but it was also a ploy in defense of Russian policy, since it laid at least part of the responsibility for the defeat on the insurgents. Thus, for example, Patras was sacked by men from the Ionian Islands, who, in turn, perished under the blows of the Dulcignian pirates. The "same barbarity" was displayed "in other strongholds nearby." "Mistra was also sacked by Greeks of the mountains, and the rich spoils were taken off to the inaccessible crags where they live." "The butchery" in Tripolitza was "horrible." The Russians were unable to protect all the people seeking their aid.[6] In July the *Notizie del mondo* had to admit that there had been a total defeat. "A body of Albanian Turks, commanded by a sanjak, of twenty thousand men, entered the Morea and in a short time crushed the Russo-Greeks. . . . General Orlov was wounded and Dolgorukij killed. The Greeks and Russians were obliged to make a hasty retreat to their ships."[7] A torrent of refugees tried to get back to the Ionian Islands. "The Venetian islands of Cephalonia, Zante, and Corfu are packed with more than twenty thousand who have fled from the Morea and the nearby islands of the Archipelago and who will probably never return to their cities." From Venice it was reported that these exiles hoped to "live in greater peace under the kind and moderate laws of our government."[8]

A more detailed account of these events, even more hostile to the Greeks, was provided in the *Storia della guerra presente*, which appeared at Venice in the same year, 1770—one of the most interesting of the contemporary histories that replaced in the Republic of St. Mark, at least in part, the more lively journalism of Tuscany and other parts of Italy. "A large part of the information" came, we read on page 147 of the fourth volume, from "Doctor Pietro Romanelli, a Greek, doctor of the pasha of the Morea, who was a spectator of all the events in the peninsula [the Morea]."

The *Storia* avoids any mention of facts directly related to Venice. The insubordination and rebellions on the Ionian Islands are glossed over in silence or are carefully veiled. The movements of the Russians are followed with interest and admiration, whereas the Greeks are considered to have been too undisciplined to have succeeded in their undertaking. From the beginning of the campaign, Fedor Orlov did not succeed in coming to an accord with them. The Maineotes had attacked without his consent. The Russian commander "thought they were incapable of sub-

---

[6] Ibid., no. 53, 3 July 1770. p. 436 (Venice, 27 June).
[7] Ibid., no. 56, 14 July 1770, pp. 462ff. (Venice, 6 July).
[8] Ibid., no. 60, 28 July 1770, p. 493 (Venice, 21 July).

ordination and discipline, and irresolute."[1] Other Greeks, it is true, were
more deserving of praise: the bishops were generous in their support,
the sailors and merchants were active and capable. A lieutenant immediately distinguished himself; he "served at the same time as an inter-
preter" and was called Andromachi, from the island of Tine, "aged
about thirty-five years," and "previously a trader carrying wine with
small boats to different places."[2] But the land war had proved to be particularly difficult and risky. Before Mistra, "the ancient Sparta," the Russians were the ones who had secured victory and then had turned to
defend Turkish prisoners from the pillage and "most inhuman barbarity" of the Maineotes.[3] After the unfortunate siege of Coron, "glutted
with booty, the Maineotes stayed in their mountains and showed no disposition for further operations. They would not have followed in pursuit had it not been for the hope of further spoils. The plan was to
march on Tripolitza."[4] The assault of this city, with "forty Russian soldiers at the head of a few thousand Maineotes," also brought to light the
particular horror of the war.[5] Before the battle the Turks took three
Greeks from the prisons of the city and cut their throats. "They painted
the heads of their horses and even the hands of their troops with their
blood."[6] "When the combat was ended and the insurgents defeated,
some inhabitants of Tripolitza were found among the dead. The Turks
and Albanians returned to the city, accused all the others of being rebels
. . . and all Greeks, of whatever sex or condition, were indiscriminately
slaughtered, their bodies burned and their houses pillaged."[7] The fate
of Patras, "a city with a Greek archbishop, adorned with several fine
mosques and four synagogues, and with many merchants of silk, coral,
honey, and cheese, was not that different."[8] The massacre the Albanians
carried out on Good Friday was horrible. "Those who did not perish in
the flames or by the sword were bound with chains and sold as slaves
for the small price of a few piasters, particularly the women and children, who were saved, but only for slavery."[9]

At first the prospects of the Greek campaign had seemed favorable
to the arms of the Christians, thanks to the military prowess demonstrated by Fedor and Aleksej Orlov. Navarino was conquered by Dol-

---

[1] *Storia della guerra presente*, vol. 6, p. 115.
[2] Ibid., pp. 115ff.
[3] Ibid., pp. 117ff.
[4] Ibid., p. 122.
[5] Ibid.
[6] Ibid., p. 123.
[7] Ibid.
[8] Ibid., p. 125.
[9] Ibid., p. 126.

gorukij "and by Brigadier Annibal, an Arab moor and a great soldier and officer, with the help of a few hundred Maineote Greeks and some from the islands of the Archipelago."[10] Other strongholds, among them the castle of Arcadia, also fell into the hands of the Russians (even here there were some scenes of cruelty on the part of the Maineotes which the Muscovite officers thought were the "excesses of barbarians").[11] As Pierre-Charles Levesque, a French historian of Russia, wrote some years later, the Russians had seized control "of ancient Sparta, celebrated for its ferocious courage, as well as of soft Arcadia."[12] A solemn religious ceremony in the mosque of Navarino, reconsecrated as an Orthodox church, was supposed to celebrate these successes and create that unity of action and spirit between Russians and Greeks which military discipline had tried so hard to produce. On 29 May, "the divine service ended, Count Orlov had the intentions of the empress his sovereign read to all," a manifesto addressed "to all Christian Greek Orthodox who find themselves under the rule of the Turks." It spoke of persecutions, of the "sadness of heart" of all Christians; it recalled that "Russians of the same Orthodox faith," since the time of Peter and Anna, had thought of "raising and liberating . . . the whole Greek nation." Now Catherine II, moved by an "ardent zeal for the holy faith, would complete this holy undertaking." While the Turks had lost 600,000 men, the Russians had liberated Moldavia and Walachia and were moving toward Bulgaria.[13] To the two fleets already sent to the Mediterranean would be added a third "to free the Greek nation from the slavery of the insufferable tyranny and inhuman cruelty of the Turks." It was hoped "shortly to drive out the tyrant and proceed to Constantinople." Orlov asked the Greeks to "work together with our armies, with longing,

[10] Ibid., pp. 129ff. We have already encountered Jurij Volodimirovič Dolgorukij in the account of his expedition to Montenegro. Ivan Abramovič Gannibal was the son of the "Arab of Peter the Great," as he was called later by Puškin, who was his great-nephew; the mother of the poet was the daughter of Osip, brother of Ivan, and another son of Abram. An entry is dedicated to Ivan Abramovič in the *Russkij biografičeskij slovar', Gaag-Gerbel'*, 1914, pp. 217–18. The poet remembers him in his *Memoirs of Carskoe selo*, where he mentions "the hero of the Archipelago, the Hannibal of Navarino," and also in *My Genealogy*, where he remembers the participation of this ancestor in the battle of Chesmé. See Puškin, *Polnoe sobranie sočinenij* (Complete works) (Moscow: Akademija nauk SSSR), vol. 3, pp. 190, 263.

[11] *Storia della guerra presente*, vol. 6, p. 132.

[12] I cite the Italian translation: *Storia della Russia* (Venice: Domenico Costantini, 1784), vol. 6, p. 20.

[13] *Storia della guerra presente*, vol. 6, p. 142. The Venetian chronicler confronted with the figure of 600,000 men felt he had to note the following: "This proclamation was translated faithfully from Greek."

zeal, and vigilance for the faith, the fatherland, liberty, and their own happiness."[14]

With every passing day, however, it became more difficult to establish the necessary discipline and coordination between Russians and Greeks. If anything, this was because of the small number of Russian troops in the Morea. Even the assault on Modon was made more difficult by the untimely effort of the bishop and a few Greeks to incite an insurrection inside the city—an attempt followed, as elsewhere, by terrible massacres.[15] To counter obstinate Turkish resistance, "the assailants were reinforced every day by Greeks who had come up from Romelia and the nearby islands, as well as by many Maineotes, but with the aim more of enriching themselves in the pillage than of exposing themselves to danger."[16] The Turkish counterattack was energetic. "They took the Muscovites between two lines of fire, despite the courage and discipline of which they gave shining examples." In the end they had to give in. Dolgorukij was wounded, and Fedor Orlov slightly hurt.[17]

From this point on the destiny of Greece was sealed. The Albanian offensive crushed all resistance. "It is impossible to give an adequate picture of the horror that appeared before Navarino." There were too many people to load on the ships. Many fled to the mountains, while the few who had money "thought it was their good fortune to leave the country by paying enormous sums to barbarous captains ready to profit from the misery of others." The Morea was "reduced to extreme desolation. The harvest from its fertile lands was already lost, the land trampled under, and the peasants slaughtered . . . more than twenty thousand inhabitants left, made exiles in neighboring lands, besides those killed by the sword, fire, or deprivation."[18]

These events were painted, as one sees, in all their tragedy, despite the effort to conceal everything relating to the Republic of St. Mark and its subjects. It is enough to open the *Mercurio storico e politico*, published by the bookseller Luigi Pavini in Venice at that time, to see another aspect of the cautious and veiled censorship that accompanied the nonetheless notable informative effort of Venetian publicists. It is enough to note that the *Mercurio* translated the most important political journal in

[14] Ibid., pp. 139ff. A copy of this proclamation of 21 April–2 May 1770 is in Turin, AS, *Materie politiche estere in genere*, mazzo 55, 1770.

[15] *Storia della guerra presente*, pp. 147ff.

[16] Ibid., p. 148.

[17] Ibid., p. 150.

[18] Ibid., pp. 151ff. It has been recently held that 40,000 were killed, enslaved, or had to flee from the Peloponnesus after the insurrection of 1770. See Hélène Antoniadis-Bibicou, "Villages désertés en Grèce. Un bilan provisoire," in *Villages désertés et histoire économique, XIe–XVIIIe siècles* (Paris: SEVPEN, 1965), pp. 343ff.

Europe at that time, the *Mercure historique et politique*, printed in Holland and republished at Lausanne, in order to see the breadth of interest it attempted to satisfy. But a comparison between the original and the Italian version reveals a series of revisions and deletions of some significance. In a series of communications from Otranto, in the Venetian edition, news arrived of the Russian landing in the Morea and the manifesto of the empress of Russia committing herself "to liberate Greeks from the Turks and restore Greek rule in its ancient force and splendor."[19] There was a narrative of events, but no mention of happenings on the Ionian Islands. The cruelty and acts of banditry accompanying the insurrection were emphasized.[20] After the defeat it was reported that "the Greeks abandoned their country in great numbers to save themselves from extermination, and more than 15,000 took refuge on the nearby islands."[21] One month later, when the tragedy was over, there was word of the part subjects of the Republic of St. Mark played. From Zante, Corfu, and Cephalonia, it was said, had come down warriors and pillagers, who were soon checked by the counterattack of Turks and Dulcignians.[22] Only the Maineotes succeeded in defending their lands. The Albanians "tried to penetrate even into the region of Maina, but they were always repulsed." Elsewhere in the Morea "extreme desolation" reigned.[23]

This tragic end soon prompted, even in Venice, more and more insistent questions about the real intentions of the Russians and their good faith. But the doubts seemed to clear suddenly with the arrival of news of the amazing battle of Chesmé. The squadron of Orlov, on 7 July, not far from Chios and Smyrna, attacked and completely defeated the Ottoman fleet. The news appeared in *Notizie del mondo* on 21 August and 4 September.[24] From Venice dispatches by the representative of the king of Sardinia were still full of reports of massacres of "fugitives from the Morea" and other disasters "of unfortunate Greeks," when one reads that letters by Angelo Emo, at sea near Corfu, had reached the Senate with news of a Russian victory in the Levant. It was talked about everywhere in Venice. "Mad partisan feelings for one side or the other" gave

[19] *Mercurio storico e politico*, vol. 678, March 1770, p. 12 (Otranto).

[20] Ibid., vol. 629, April 1770, p. 14 (Otranto).

[21] Ibid., vol. 631, June 1770, p. 17 (Otranto).

[22] Ibid., vol. 632, July 1770, p. 23 (Otranto).

[23] Ibid., vol. 635, October 1770, pp. 21ff. (Otranto).

[24] *Notizie del mondo*, no. 67, 21 August 1770, p. 552 (Malta, 20 July), and no. 71, 4 September 1770 (Livorno, 31 August). (They are talking about the "bay of Seime [Chesmé], between the island of Scio [Chios] and that part of the continent of Asia once called Ionia.")

rise to interpretations and comments that were difficult to disentangle.[25] On the first of September Incisa di Camerana assured Turin that the "naval victory" of the Russians was certain. "An English ship that had arrived in Livorno gave the details."[26] "The Russians have exceeded every anticipation." The "maritime expedition," at first thought to be a "chimerical project," had ended by "increasing the prestige of Muscovy." Whereas in July Maruzzi had tried in vain to obtain "from these merchants a million ducats in loan" and had seen the senate refuse to support him, "now many merchants of the German nation here have pledged a million florins."[27] It was widely hoped that the Russian fleet would be able to enter the Dardanelles. "We are about to tie the knot."[28] It seemed as though the pressure of Orlov's fleet would decide the outcome of the war.

In reality Orlov had not tried to attack the heart of the Ottoman Empire. He was strong enough to create a "Russian Levant," as it began to be called, but not strong enough to attack the mainland.[1] The Greeks of the Morea had paid dearly for the initial Russian illusion of being able to gain control, with support from the inhabitants, of whole territories of the Sublime Porte. The expedition into the Mediterranean was a diversion, despite its extraordinary successes, and it was destined to remain so, without transforming itself into the main force of an attack on Constantinople.[2]

If this was true militarily—which the following years only confirmed—from a political point of view Catherine II's initiative had a profound impact. Despite its delusions, 1770 was the initial date of the national rising of Greece.[3] For the Ionian Islands this was even more evident: from here began the complex movement of detachment from Venice that channeled the islands into the course of the Greek national movement. The continuity between the events of 1770 and those at the

---

[25] Turin, AS, *Lettere ministri, Venezia*, 40, 11 and 18 August 1770.

[26] Ibid., 1 September 1770.

[27] Ibid., 21 July and 8 September 1770.

[28] Ibid., 15 September 1770.

[1] *Gazzetta universale*, no. 31, 16 April 1774, p. 244. A subtitle of this Florentine gazette read *Russian Levant*.

[2] See Tasos A. Gritsopoulos, "Oi Rosoi eis to Aigaion kata to 1770" (The Russians in the Aegean in 1770), in *Athena* 71 (1970): 85ff.

[3] The declaration of the son of Benakis, the most important Maineote leader, at the beginning of the new century, was characteristic of the delusions: "I would not destroy my country again, as my father did," cited, among other testimonies, Ariadna Camariano-Cioran in "Les îles ioniennes de 1795 à 1807," *Acts of the Third Panionian Congress, 23–29 September 1965* (Athens, 1967), vol. 1, p. 111.

end of the century was even greater on Cephalonia, Zante, and Corfu than it was in the Morea.[4]

The difficulty the Venetian authorities had in suppressing unrest on the Ionian Islands demonstrated this. The first measures, taken in March when the Russian ships first appeared, were intended chiefly to maintain the prestige of the Republic. Work in the Arsenal was speeded up; new soldiers and sailors were recruited. But it soon became clear that measures were needed not only to preserve an equilibrium among Venice, the Empire, Turkey, and Russia, but also to control Venice's own subjects on the Ionian Islands.[5] In May Admiral Emo left for Corfu with three frigates. Two other ships were readied, one of which was entrusted to "the newly elected General Querini."[6] In the Senate "an old zealous senator" proposed creating an "extraordinary commission for military affairs, as was done three or four years ago for matters regarding the Church," thus taking up again the idea of a commission similar to the one elected *ad pias causas*.[7] It was proposed to mobilize 16,000 men "truly at arms," who would substitute for the 18,000 who theoretically constituted the military force of the republic. The money saved by pensioning off two thousand men could serve to increase "the pay of officers." This would be "an incentive to noble subjects of the mainland to join the forces of Venice rather than to go into foreign service." Carrying out the plan would cost 1,300,000 ducats.[8] But before the project was undertaken a dispute began about the appointment of a commander in chief. There was a long discussion about Schulenburg, who had been in the army of Hanover and was supported by England. Andrea Tron was the most in favor of his appointment and read the letter of recommendation of the king of England in the Senate making a "long florid speech" in praise of the candidate, underlining "the political con-

---

[4] On developments on the Greek islands between the eighteenth and nineteenth centuries, see Gino Damerini, *Le isole jonie nel sistema adriatico dal dominio veneziano a Buonaparte* (Milan: Ipsi, 1943); Norman E. Saul, *Russia and the Mediterranean, 1797–1807* (Chicago: University of Chicago Press, 1970); Augusta Michajlovna Stanislavskaja, *Rossija i Grecija v konce XVIII—načale XIX veka. Politika Rossii v Ioničeskoj respublike, 1798–1807* (Russia and Greece between the end of the eighteenth century and the beginning of the nineteenth. Russian politics in the Ionian republic, 1798–1807) (Moscow: Nauka, 1976); Grigorij L'Vovič Arš, *I. Kapodistrija i grečeskoe nacional' no-osvoboditel'noe dviženie, 1809–1822* (The Capodistrians and the movement for Greek liberation, 1809–1822) (Moscow: Nauka, 1976).

[5] Turin, AS, *Lettere ministri, Venezia*, 40, 17 March, 21 April, 5 May 1770.

[6] Ibid., 12 May 1770.

[7] See Venturi, *Settecento riformatore*, vol. 2, p. 136. The deputation was established on 12 April 1766. Robert Richie, the British representative, also spoke of an "extraordinary military deputation" in his dispatch dated 13 June 1770. PRO SP 99/75, p. 29.

[8] Turin, AS, *Lettere ministri, Venezia*, 40, 21 July 1770.

sideration the republic should have for the court of London." But this
selection seemed a threat to the independence of Venice, and he received only 50 votes, with 121 against.[9] It became urgent to make a decision. The situation was becoming more and more chaotic. Conflicts,
emigration, piracy, tumults, and reprisals grew on the Ionian Islands.
One episode gives an idea of the situation. "Two ships of Dulcignian
pirates arrived at Zante," we read in a sheet of news, "unloading the
bishop of Romelia, who was to be sold as a prize, after which there was
a riot with many dead and wounded on both sides. But the Zanteans,
on the advice of Lord Emo, who was in the port, took the bishop; the
Dulcignians left; and all returned to quiet."[10]

There was particular concern about reprisals the Turks would undoubtedly make for the hospitality Venice had finally given on its islands
to Greeks who were fleeing the massacres of the Albanians. The Senate
seemed to be ceding to the demands of the pasha of the Morea. "The
unhappy Greeks" would have to be sent back. But what would happen
if they refused to leave? Venice played for time; it requested guarantees
for the reception the exiles would receive. It explained that there were
many, 30,000. If they were done away with, the Turks would risk finding themselves rulers of "a land denuded of inhabitants."[11] The exiles,
as was to be expected, declared that they were "resolved to risk worse
conditions, even death, rather than return to the Morea . . . , since they
were certain that despite the most solemn promises and assurances they
would be butchered on their arrival." They felt the support of other
inhabitants of the islands grow around them. "Greek nationals who are
[Venetian] subjects, naturally, would not look with indifferent eyes on
the sacrifice of these unfortunates, with whom they have a common origin, tongue, religion, interests, and perhaps the same views and chimerical hopes." But their staying on the Venetian islands raised problems. The territory of Zante is "small and unfruitful, so that its products
are not sufficient to maintain its ordinary population of nearly 24,000,"
making it necessary "to bring in stores of grain every year from the
nearby Morea." The situation on Cephalonia was somewhat better,
where "vast, largely uncultivated lands" could be colonized.[12]

In conclusion, after a long delay, the order was given to return the
Greek refugees, accompanied by "a secret order to suspend the effect
[of the decree]." It was thus hoped that the Turks "would be content

---

[9] Ibid., 11 August 1770.
[10] Turin, AS, *Materie politiche in genere*, mazzo 55, 1770, Venice, 10 November.
[11] Turin, AS, *Lettere ministri, Venezia*, 40, 4 and 11 August 1770.
[12] Ibid., 18 August 1770.

with fine words spoken lavishly."[13] In reality the Sublime Porte was much too preoccupied with the new direction of the war to act against Venice. There was even a kind of tacit agreement between the Republic of St. Mark and the Russians, at least regarding their Greek rebels policy. Colonel Dadich, a Venetian envoy, was sent to Orlov. He listened to the taunts of the commander against the "imbecility of the Greeks" and their "cowardice" and received a promise of punishment for the Russian captain who had first induced the subjects of St. Mark to desert and another promise not to admit more rebels and pirates into his ranks.[14] Naturally, the Russians did not raise a finger to help the Venetians reestablish their own authority on the Ionian Islands. The Republic would have to act alone. General Pier Antonio Querini went to Cephalonia "with the intention of returning the sullen and uncooperative inhabitants of that island to duty."[15] The task was not easy. The expedition of Metaxà into the Morea had unleashed a whole series of quarrels and vendettas. When General Querini tried to arrest Count Spiridone Metaxà, he "was so gallantly defended by his people that the soldiers were obliged to withdraw."[16] Problems with the Sdrin family arose as well. "The inhabitants of Pirgos, Racli, Coronus, Scala, and Catoleo, tired of the harsh yoke under which they languished, and induced by the immunity they hoped to obtain, having seen other recent examples, arose and sacked the rich houses of the Sdrin for two whole days, giving to the flames what they could not carry off."[17] Appeals to the capital, and Querini's intervention, had no effect. In the winter of 1770–1771 "the island was in a state of terrible anarchy, with no restraint by a legitimate authority. Evildoers went about with open pride, and wayfarers could escape only by fleeing."[18] To this disorder was added that of the local chieftans. "The Metaxà brothers set up a kind of tribunal in Cocolata, allowing no one to pass without paying tribute or homage."[19] There was a violent repression leading to arrests and shootings among the different parties, who became bandits and even pirates. It is not surprising

[13] Ibid., 3 November 1770.

[14] Manfroni, "Documenti veneziani," pp. 1162ff. See Venice, AS, *Provveditori da Terra e da Mar*, filza 1018, ins. 157, 18 June 1770. Orlov spoke of the Greeks "as qualified for no other occupation than the odious exercise of pillage" and assured Dadich that he had "harshly repulsed the noted Metaxà brothers" and others "when they presented themselves to offer their services, saying that the fleet needed men of honor and not pirates."

[15] Turin, AS, *Materie politiche estere in genere*, mazzo 55, 1770, sheet from Venice, 29 September 1770.

[16] M. and N. Pignatorre, *Memorie storiche e critiche*, vol. 1, p. 185.

[17] Ibid., p. 186.

[18] Ibid., p. 187.

[19] Ibid., p. 188.

that the nineteenth-century chronicler of Cephalonia, after having told
the story of the island from the time of the ancestors of Ulysses onward,
when he reached 1770 wrote, "then began our civil discord," and when
he reached 1772 he added, "the civil discord increased."[20] Even here the
arrival of Orlov's fleet marked a profound change.

In the autumn of 1771 famine aggravated the situation on the islands. On Corfu, "the great lack of provisions that afflicts this island,
and the disorders of every kind that consequently follow day by day,"
soon obliged the Republic to intervene urgently by sending grain "to
those hungry people, before the problem grows worse and there are
greater troubles."[21]

On Zante the most significant example of the general local unrest
involved Count Demetrio Mocenigo. He had been educated in Venice,
in the same Mocenigo family of whom one was then provisor of St.
Mark and would soon be doge. Demetrio came from a lateral branch of
this great family. He was Orthodox. Family ties and education could
have made him a member of the patriciate in which his father had circulated and he himself was educated. But Demetrio did not want to ab-
jure his faith, "not through superstition," as his friend Semen Romanovič Voroncov wrote, "but because he thought it unworthy to leave the
faith of his fathers. He left to God the choice of prayers most pleasing
to himself."[22] Thus, instead of going into the service of Hanover, as his
grandfather had done, or into that of the Empire, as other Venetian
patricians did, he looked toward Russia. It would not have displeased
him to be appointed to Maruzzi's place. But since he was not that lucky,
there was nothing left for him to do but to return to Zante. He never
imagined that a Muscovite fleet might arrive in his port, but when this
happened he gave body and soul to save the shipwrecked, to furnish sea
charts, and to warn everyone against the perils they might face in a sea
unknown to them and in the midst of an uncertain and mysterious political situation. He, among others, persuaded the Russians that they
had the legal right, and military duty, to enter the Adriatic and attack
the Dulcignian pirates before these took the opportunity of joining the
Tunisians. In other words, he became a zealous Russian agent, although
he thought the title "colonel" Orlov gave him was inappropriate, since
he continued to aspire to a diplomatic post. Thanks to his friends in

[20] Ibid., p. 322.

[21] Turin, AS, *Lettere ministri, Venezia*, 41, 9 November 1771.

[22] "Pis'mo grafa S. R. Voroncova k P. V. Zavadovskomu. O grafe Močenige" (1777) (A
letter by Count S. R. Voroncov to P. V. Zavadoskij. On Count Mocenigo), in *Archiv knjazja
Voroncova* (Voroncov Archive), vol. 16: *Bumagi Semena Romonaviča Voroncova* (Papers of
Count Semen Romanovič Voroncov) (Moscow: P. Lebedev, 1880), p. 153.

Venice he was able to give the Russian command copies of reports of the Venetian agent in Constantinople, as well as information about "what happened in the Venetian Senate." As Admiral Spiridov wrote, he "was our savior, our faithful guardian. Our security rested on his intuition. It is impossible to reward the excellence of his services."[23] He was also the protector of Greek refugees on Zante. He aided them in every way possible and made plans to make them colonists in the Russia of Catherine II.

Demetrio Mocenigo thus became a thorn in the side of Venetian domination.[24] They did not dare do anything to him for fear of Russian reprisals. They tried to intimidate him. Finally the authorities decided to take steps against all partisans of Catherine II, among whom was "a certain Count Mocenigo, a man—they say—of imprudence and irregular conduct," Incisa di Camerana wrote to Turin.[25] A little later the *Notizie del mondo* announced the arrest of a "disturber of public quiet on the island of Zante."[26] It was "a very secret affair."[27] "Fearing a rising of the populace to protect him," four hundred soldiers were sent to Zante. He himself, from a balcony, persuaded his followers not to free him with force. In prison, if we are to believe what his friend Voroncov tells us, he was saved from the poison that Venice "not rarely" employs through the able action of Admiral Spiridov, who hastened as a reprisal to imprison some merchants of the Republic. In fact, the Senate did not want to displease the Russians. At the moment of the arrest they made known in St. Petersburg that they were willing to release Count Mocenigo and were sure "this affair would end to mutual satisfaction." Finally he was consigned into the hands of a Russian admiral in Paros.[28] Exiled and deprived of all his property, Count Mocenigo became ever more involved with the Russians. In August 1776 word spread in Italy that he had been approinted "general consul for the seas of Tuscany to reside in this city" (Livorno).[29] In October the *Nuove di diverse corti e paesi* announced the following in a communication from Pisa of 27 September: "The other evening about eight o'clock arrived here, after a thirty-

[23] Ibid., p. 158.

[24] The earliest information about him is in Venice, AS, *Provveditori da Terra e da Mar*, filza 1018, no. 133, 11 March 1770.

[25] Turin, AS, *Lettere ministri, Venezia*, mazzo 43, 20 November 1773.

[26] *Notizie del mondo*, no. 97, 4 December 1773, p. 791 (Venice, 27 November).

[27] Turin, AS, *Lettere ministri, Venezia*, mazzo 44, 8 January 1774.

[28] Ibid., 12 March and 16 April 1774. See *Notizie del mondo*, no. 1, 1 January 1774, p. 6 (Venice, 25 December 1773 and 18 January 1774). On the consignment see no. 11, 5 February 1774, p. 86 (Venice, 29 January), and *Gazzetta universale*, no. 17, 26 February 1774, p. 132 (Ancona, 16 February).

[29] *Notizie del mondo*, no. 70, 31 August 1776, p. 538 (Livorno, 28 August).

three-day journey from St. Petersburg, Signor Conte Demetrio Mocenigo, as general commissioner of the Russian fleet in all the ports of Italy and as credited minister of Her Majesty the Empress of Russia to all Italian powers."[30] In 1783 he was made the Russian chargé d'affaires in Tuscany, where he remained for ten years.[31] His tomb is in the church of San Giorgio dei Greci, in Venice, in front of the iconostasis. As is well known, his son Giorgio would have an important role in developments on the Ionian Islands in the period of the French Revolution.

As the experience of Cephalonia, Corfu, and Zante shows, Venice was obliged to make a serious effort to contain popular unrest and the discontent of nobles on the islands. The diplomatic and military apparatus of the Republic was put under a severe strain, and it had difficulty finding ways and means to try to contain the social, religious, and national pressures that tested the coherence of its Adriatic dominions. From this arose conflicts within the patriciate itself, cases of corruption and perhaps even betrayal, as is shown by the general provisor Pier Antonio Querini, who was active on the Ionian Islands in these years. In the spring of 1773 he was arrested and charged for "serious crimes, and as they say, peculation, for having sold to Russian vessels powder, arms, war materials, and other things of this kind."[32] This was a serious matter that led to his arrest and sentence "to ten years in the fortress of the Lido."[33] This, like other cases, and the policy of the Senate in general in this crisis, merits closer study. Materials are not lacking in the archive of the Frari.[34] But we will limit ourselves to following the echoes of developments in the Adriatic and Levant in Venetian public opinion.

From the first there was a strong demand for information. The curiosity of Venetians was aroused, and many worked to try to satisfy it. The Savioni press and the bookseller Graziosi published a series of large handsome maps, taken from French models and replete with annotations, brief geographical dictionaries, and political and historical comments.[35] Antonio Graziosi, who had been one of the most active book-

---

[30] *Nuove di diverse corti e paesi*, no. 41, 7 October 1776, p. 328 (Pisa, 27 September 1776).

[31] Friedrich Winter, *Repertorium der diplomatischen Vertreter aller Länder*, vol. 3: *1764–1815* (Graz and Köln: H. Böhlaus, 1966), p. 365.

[32] The news in Turin was given by Incisa di Camerana on 13 March 1773, Turin, AS, *Lettere ministri, Venezia*, mazzo 43.

[33] Ibid., 24 April, 8 May, 12 June 1773; and mazzo 44, 8 January 1774.

[34] See Venice, AS, *Consiglio dei dieci, Registri criminal*, 190, F. 1, 15 March 1773, for the dismissal and arrest of Querini following "many evils and great disorders that have afflicted the islands of the Levant, with total subversion of public law and all discipline, and the considerable wasting and damage of the public purse that occurred." (I owe this reference to Marino Berengo.)

[35] *Descrizione istorico-politico-geografica delle provincie, mari e fiumi principali compresi nella*

sellers in the anticlerical debates of the immediately preceding years and had published some of the most lively works against the Jesuits and against mortmain, soon took the initiative of publishing a narrative of contemporary events, the *Storia della guerra presente*, which I have cited at length. Its handsome cover was engraved with a portrait of Catherine II. In the back of volume 8, after page 137, was the publisher's current catalogue, which advertised, along with the three pieces of historical geography already mentioned, a "portrait in large quarto of Catherine Alexinova . . . crowned empress of all Russia on 3 October 1762," along with portraits of the king of Poland and of Peter III. "Signor Baratti," it added, "and his assistants executed these novelties, and many others, of which there will be advance notice when they are closer to publication," that is, portraits of the "Prince of Gallitzin, of Mustafà III, of the grand vizier," a map of the Morea, a "plan or description" of Constantinople and the "fortresses of Oczakow, Bender, and Ibrailow."[36] The little volumes of the *Storia* came out rapidly. Thus, distant Russia came closer to Venetian readers. The first volume attempted to provide a detailed account of the recent history of that country. The parts concerning laws and religion were taken directly from Voltaire. The policy of Peter III was described in minute detail. The death of this emperor was referred to without much concealment. The scenes of drunkenness and disorder in the capital were noted, "its being customary in St. Petersburg on such occasions to permit the people to carry out pillage of this kind so they do not pay attention to what is happening."[37] The second volume gave the reader an idea of the proportions the war assumed. "It is calculated that Europe contains 150,154 square miles, of which 57,600 belong to Russia, besides the vast lands in its possession in Asia."[38] One-third of Europe was Russian. There Catherine was in action. Besides the attempt

---

carta prima geografica del teatro terrestre della guerra presente tralla Russia, la Polonia e la Porta Ottomana (Venice: Stamperia Savioni, 1770) (there is a description of the Ukraine, Bessarabia, Kuban, and so on). A second volume, published by the same bookseller on the same date, was dedicated to Poland, with some twenty interesting pages on the history of that country. The third volume was entitled *Descrizione storico-geografica dell'Arcipelago, suoi litorali, isole, provincie adiacenti e stati ottomani in quelle parti compresi nella terza carta geografica del teatro della guerra presente tralla Russia e la Porta Ottomana* (Venice: Graziosi, 1770), with a reference to a map of "Greece, a famous part of Europe subjected to the Turks." Another volume followed: *Descrizione del regno o sia penisola della Morea compreso nella quarta carta geografica del teatro della guerra presente tralla Russia e la Porta Ottomana e lo stato delle forze ottomane tanto terrestri che marittime, col dettaglio di ogni ordine di esse, delle rispettive insegne, de' vari corpi sì di cavalleria che di fanteria* (Venice: Graziosi, 1770) (there was, among others, a detailed explanation of the Timariot fiefs).

[36] On Antonio Baratti and his workshop see the notice of Alfredo Petrucci in *DBI*, vol. 6, pp. 2–3.

[37] *Storia della guerra presente*, vol. 1, p. 85.

[38] Ibid., vol. 2, p. 11 n.

to bring up-to-date the problem of serfdom among the peasants, which I have already discussed, there was talk of foreign colonists, of efforts to establish new relations with foreign countries and to develop schools and academies. In the volumes that followed, the development of the war naturally took up more space, but Russia's work of internal transformation was never forgotten.

Who was the author of this *Storia*? Speaking of the reforms of Catherine II to improve the condition of peasants, and the essay that won a prize at the competition sponsored by the Free Economic Society of St. Petersburg, it was recorded that this essay existed in "a careful summary in the Venetian journal *Europa letteraria*, the volume for March 1770, along with another essay published at Brescia with the title "Della felicità pubblica" in the volumes for September and November 1769."[39] Both were important reviews of works by Beardé de l'Abbaye and Giambattista Vasco written by Alberto Fortis. This and other evidence lead us to believe that the *Storia* emerged, in fact, as is traditionally thought, from the Venetian group of writers and publishers headed by Domenico Caminer, in which Elisabetta Caminer, the daughter of Caminer, and Caminer's friend Alberto Fortis, played an important part.

The *Storia* was a great success. In early 1771 there was a Neapolitan edition. On the first of February Vargas Maciucca permitted a reprinting, which appeared in eleven volumes.[40] Even the maps, portraits, and historical illustrations were taken from the Venetian edition. In 1771 a German edition published in thirty-six parts by Johann Cristoff Schmidlin began to appear.[41] At Venice itself, between 1770 and 1773, there was a Greek translation, edited by the bookseller Teodosio, in six volumes.[42] In 1776, also at Venice, a second edition of the Italian text appeared.[43]

[39] Ibid., vol. 4, p. 43 n.

[40] *Storia della guerra presente tra la Russia, la Polonia e la Porta Ottomana colle particolarità della morte della imperatrice Elisabetta, detronizzazione di Pietro III, accessione a quel trono di Caterina II, morte di Augusto III, elezione di Stanislao Poniatowski ed origine e proseguimento della guerra, arricchita di aneddoti, note, autentici documenti ed articoli del S. de Voltaire ed adornata di ritratti e carte geografiche per intelligenza delle operazioni dell'armata* (Naples: Vincenzo Flauto, a opera di Giacomo Antonio Vinaccia, 1771). From what I have seen, this is a complete and faithful reedition.

[41] *Geschichte des gegenwärtigen Krieges zwischen Russland, Polen und der Ottomanischen Pforte* (Frankfurt and Leipzig, 1771–74). It is necessary to correct Basil von Bilbassoff's view in *Katharina II. Kaiserin von Russland im Urtheile der Weltliteratur* (Berlin: Johannes Räde, 1897), vol. 1, p. 168, that the Venetian text was a translation from German.

[42] It is cited in the bibliography of Sakellarios, *E Peloponnesos*, p. 19, and in Ploumides, *To benetikon tipographeion tou Demetriou kai tou Panou Theodosiou*, p. 123 n. 54.

[43] *Storia della ultima guerra tra la Russia e la Porta Ottomana* (Venice, 1776). (The engraved frontispiece shows that this is a second edition made by the same Graziosi.)

On a more modest level the events were narrated with a great abundance of detail and documents by the *Storia dell'anno*, which had been published in Venice for thirty years and which tried to give a complete picture of world events taken from gazettes from every corner of Europe.[1] At the end of the narrative for 1769 the *Storia* had also expressed great surprise at the appearance of the Russian fleet in the Mediterranean. "The great distance of the place, the difficulty of sailing so far, the boldness of the enterprise, and the great cost its execution necessarily entailed resulted in a disbelief not only by common people, but also by some cabinets, which considered it an imaginary or a fabulous event."[2] But it was necessary to believe the facts. The volume for the following year was full of the undertakings of Orlov and his fleet. Documents involving relations with Malta were reproduced at length. There was an echo of the "thousand guesses and predictions" that even in Italy accompanied the Russian fleet before its arrival in the Morea.[3] The encounter with "deputies of Mistra and with the Maineotes" opened a surprising and tragic prospect, which the Venetian chronicler narrated with much diffidence toward the Greek insurgents, and a knowing silence toward the participation of the Ionian Islands that does not surprise us. "A mass of a disordered and rapacious populace, composed partly of the Greeks of the realm and partly of others from neighboring regions, believed it was able to drive out the Turks," illusions that soon turned to tragedy.[4] But at the end of the year the Morea had receded into the distance, and the Venetian chronicler turned instead to recount in detail the particulars of the great victory of Chesmé. The Greek insurrection had become an incident in a huge war, which the *Storia dell'anno* continued to follow with great attention in later volumes.

In 1771 a curious little work clearly favorable to the policy of Catherine II called *Il cittadino politico e imparziale d'Amsterdam. Lettera di un olandese a un suo corrispondente di Marsiglia dopo l'arrivo della flotta russa nel Mediterraneo* was published at Venice, with the imaginary place of Cosmopolis.[5] It was the Italian version of a work that followed Russian propaganda so closely that it led one to suspect it was published in St. Petersburg. Other circumstances, such as the Russian terms contained in

---

[1] See G. Ricuperati, "Giornali e società nell'Italia dell' 'Ancien régime' (1668–1789)," in *La stampa italiana dal 500 all' 800*, ed. Valerio Castronovo and Nicola Tranfaglia (Bari: Laterza, 1976), p. 240.

[2] *Storia dell'anno 1769* (Venice: Francesco Pitteri, 1770), p. 271.

[3] *Storia dell'anno 1770* (Venice: Francesco Pitteri, 1771), p. 43.

[4] Ibid., p. 45.

[5] See Von Bilbassoff, *Katharina II*, vol. 1. p. 182 n. 200. Notice of this work, said to be thirty-nine pages long, is given in the *Notizie letterarie* of Florence, no. 10, 18 April 1772, col. 258.

it, and the great rarity of the work in the West, seem to confirm
Bil'basov's hypothesis.[6] Since I have not been able to put my hands on
the *Cittadino politico*, I am obliged to cite it in French, making use of the
only copy I have been able to find, in an American library. The foreign
policy of Catherine II, her stand with regard to the French merchant
marine, and her interpretation of international law were heatedly defended. Even more interesting was the effort to give Russia a grandiose
image, rich and heroic all at once. The products of the empire were
enumerated with great satisfaction. "Russia produces an infinity of
products that are objects of commerce. Was there need of wood for car-
pentry, planks of oak, masts for ships? Its forests provide enough to
furnish all the timber yards of Europe."[7] Iron, precious metals, hemp,
cordage, tar, wool, leather—these were a fine basis for the economic expansion Russia saw coming in the not too distant future.

Russia's men were no less vigorous. Aristotle had been right: the
winds of the north "produce vigorous men." And he had been proven
right by "Lord Bacon, that English Aristotle."[8] It was enough to see the
Russian fleet to be persuaded of this fact. The frugality of the sailors
was extraordinary. In general, "disdaining riches," the Russians "make
better cheer with a sea biscuit called *suchari*, *quas* [kvas], a kind of small
beer, and a clove of garlic than a foreign sailor eating his portion." The
expedition of Orlov into the Mediterranean, like the battles on the Black
Sea, was proof of the qualities of the commanders as well as of the sailors. "Look at General Orlov, that great man. . . Admiral Spiritoff, the
dauntless image of a Morosini, the worthy Admiral Gregg, animated by
love of his new country; look at the soldiers who are used to prefer glory
to booty."[9] At the head of Russia stood Catherine II, "that first legislator
of her people whom the ancient Greeks, according to the Solomon of
the North [Federick II], would have placed between Lycurgus and So-
lon." "Yes, that princess, it can be admitted with impartiality, knows perfectly the genius and disposition of a civilized nation which, convinced
of the wisdom of her plans and won over by the mildness of her government, has shed its old errors and recognizes joyously that its sovereign
undertakes nothing that does not further its happiness."[10]

---

[6] See Von Bilbassoff, *Katharina II*, vol. 1, p. 145, p. 160. It was entitled *Le bourgeois
politique et impartial d'Amsterdam. Lettre d'un Hollandais à son correspondant de Marseille sur
l'arrivée da la flotte russe dans la Méditerranée* (Amsterdam, 1771). We cannot exclude the
possibility that this work of Russian propaganda, as well as its reedition, was the work of
an Italian press.

[7] *Le bourgeois politique*, pp. 29ff.

[8] Ibid., pp. 40ff.

[9] Ibid., pp. 57ff. This is an allusion to Francesco Morosini (1619–1694), called "Il Pe-
loponnesaico," the defender of Candia and conqueror of the Morea.

[10] Ibid., pp. 62ff.

Another text Graziosi circulated in 1772 is interesting: *Osservazioni sopra le passate campagne militari della presente guerra trà russi e ottomani, sopra il militare dei turchi e la maniera di combatterli*. It was dedicated to "His Excellency Count Alexis d'Orlov, to the hero who has filled all the world with his name," and it contained a vivid and interesting discussion of the tactics and strategies necessary to arrive at victory over the Mohammedans.[11] It was a partial translation of a work published at Breslau one year earlier.[12] This came from the lively pen of General Charles-Emmanuel de Warnery, who was born at Morges, not far from Lausanne. The author had first been in the army of the king of Sardinia (his baptismal name was a clear sign of his family's orientation toward Piedmont), and he then passed in 1737 into the service of Austria, migrating to Russia, and in 1742 to Prussia. For Prussia he fought in the Seven Years' War. Passing on to Poland, and sensing a new conflict approaching with the Ottoman Porte, he put down his plans and projects in 1767, consigning them into the hands of Prince Adam Czartoryski. A first edition of his work was circulated without his consent. He published the second edition himself, in 1771, with the bookseller Korn of Breslau. It was an openly pro-Russian work. He knew the language and admired the tenacity, courage, and intelligence of the Russians, while he was profoundly convinced of the serious military weakness of the Turks. He hoped that not only Russia but also Austria would attack them. He was thus full of advice and warnings, taking much pride in noting from time to time that many of his ideas had been accepted by Catherine II's generals. General de Warnery was not lacking in flare and imagination, and this helped him to understand and appreciate men like Aleksej Orlov. He dedicated an important part of his book to the Russian expedition in the Mediterranean, which many had thought a mere chimera when it was being planned.[13] But he never doubted "that the Russians would be as brave on the sea as on land; this is in the nature of a people that scorns death. One sees the English fight equally well in both elements."[14] Everywhere "Russian soldiers have no equals. . . . always in good spirits,

---

[11] See Von Bilbassoff, *Katharina II*, vol. 1, p. 175 n. 188.

[12] *Remarques sur le militaire des Turcs et des Russes; sur la façon la plus convenable de combattre les premiers, sur la marine des deux empires belligérants, sur les peuples qui ont joint leurs armes à celles de la Russie, tels que les Géorgiens, Colchidois, Mainottes, Monténégrins Albanois, chretiens Grecs etc. etc., avec diverses observations sur les grandes actions qui se sont passées dans la dernière guerre de Hongrie et dans la présente en Moldavie, comme aussi sur l'expédition de la flotte russe en Grèce et sur celle du comte Tottleben, avec des plans, par ms. de Warnery, major-général* (Breslau: Théophile Korn, 1771). The *Gazzetta di Parma*, no. 39, 24 September, and no. 40, 1 October 1771, dated Breslau, 25 August, furnished an ample and accurate summary of this work.

[13] Ibid., p. 165.

[14] Ibid., p. 152.

even in great misery, they sing their heroes and their victories; they have singers who can compose a couplet as quickly as a French grenadier." This was a good soil in which to grow a new spirit: "At present they are full of patriotism."[15] All of Russia had been transforming itself in recent years, since the Seven Years' War. "I have known the Russians for only thirty years: at present I find them quite changed, and to their advantage. The freedom Peter III gave to gentlemen, which Catherine II confirmed, has undoubtedly contributed much to this happy change: a slave can only think like a slave."[16] The experience of officers and soldiers in Germany had had a great influence on them. "The lower officers and soldiers who believed before that outside of Russia there was no bread, no health, no happiness, and that they alone were men, have seen a lot in other lands."[17] The religious policy of the emperors also had a good effect. "Tolerance undoubtedly has done the most to banish superstition from Russians, who before were carried away with it."[18]

The Russians had thus placed themselves in a position not only to defeat their enemies militarily, but also to gather around themselves politically myriad peoples who would help them defeat the Ottoman Empire. The situation was particularly favorable. Even the Corsairs of Barbary, "I mean the cities of Algiers, Tunis, and Tripoli," who constituted the most important maritime force of the Porte, had "almost entirely shaken off its yoke and are regarded more as allies than as subjects." They would not even arm a frigate against the Russians. "Their force is so diminished that they are feared only by small merchant vessels."[19] Certainly there was no dearth of pirates in the Mediterranean: it was enough to think of those of Dulcigno, and it was surprising that they were permitted to operate "under the eyes of Italy."[20] Meanwhile, the great weakness of the Turkish empire potentially activated any who could still hope to make themselves free and independent, peoples of the east like the Georgians and Kalmucks, and of the west, the "Walachians and Moldavians," who spoke "a corrupt Italian"[21] and, he expected, one day would be united, and the Maineotes.[22] The last were like "the Waldensians of Piedmont, they are mountain men." They lived "where the ancient Lacedaemonians had been, although they are not

[15] Ibid., p. 127.
[16] Ibid., p. 126.
[17] Ibid., p. 124.
[18] Ibid., p. 134.
[19] Ibid., p. 113.
[20] Ibid., p. 116.
[21] Ibid., p. 67.
[22] Ibid., p. 158 (Georgians), p. 145 (Kalmucks, descendants, he said, of the Huns), p. 67 (Walachians and Moldavians).

descendants. . . . a different lot of Greeks has taken refuge there." Their way of life resembled that of the Cossacks. They could furnish from twelve to fifteen thousand armed men, "but I think that outside of their mountains one would not get much help from them, like the Waldensians I spoke about, who fight well in their own territory, but in the plane are good for nothing."[23] Besides the Maineotes, the Russians could count on the "Albanians or Christian Arnautes, whom I would compare to Savoyards" because many are scattered through the cities of the Ottoman Empire in search of employment. "There are more than forty thousand in Constantinople, where they are bakers, carpenters, masons, porters, water carriers, and so on. They are a very courageous people." The kingdom of Naples had known how to make use of them, having recruited "a regiment that is surely not the least of its army."[24] Another group seemed to be missing from the roll call: the inhabitants of Crete. "The Cretans live in a land of mountains, in a corner of that island, where they have preserved a kind of independence, like the Maineotes, but up to the present they have been very quiet." As for the Greeks of the Archipelago, they could furnish the Russians with stores and pilots, vessels and seamen, but they were "too degenerate to expect much service from them."[25] Russia should decide what it truly wanted to get out of its penetration into the Levant. Should it take control of an island with strategic and commercial importance? "Would not an island important in these prosperous parts be worth as much as the Falklands or Corsica?" But what does one do with Greece? If one wanted to make republics out of it, as in antiquity, they would not last long. "These are no longer the same Greeks; they want to be governed in the manner of the Turks. A high-placed person among them has assured me that they are incapable of governing themselves; they are base, cunning, and have an excessive ambition to dominate their equals."[26] It would be better to make up regiments of Albanians and Illirians, whose officers "at least speak Italian or Slavic." It would be easier to take advantage of the situation in the east than in the west. General Tottleben in the Caucasus had operated well with a population of a quite different military value from that of the Greeks, "among whom a large part do not know how to load a gun."[27] In the final analysis the problem was political. Russia would have to make a special effort if it wanted to continue to intervene in the Mediterranean. A poorly thought out policy would be counter-

[23] Ibid., pp. 161ff.
[24] Ibid., pp. 162ff.
[25] Ibid., p. 165.
[26] Ibid., p. 168.
[27] Ibid., p. 170.

productive. "The Russians must manage these peoples, who are devoted
to them, most carefully, and never attempt to incite them without being
able to give them assistance. The Walachians and Moreïtes are more
unhappy than if the Russians had never appeared among them, and in
the end the Greeks might be victims as well, especially if no power close
to them takes up their cause, because the Russians are not in a situation
to give them sufficient support."[28]

In Venice a book that best explains the character of Russian involvement in the world of the Slavs was also published at this time. Demetrio
Teodosio, the editor of many Greek works, put out in 1772 two ponder-
ous volumes containing the life of Peter the Great.[29] It was written "in
the Slavic language," that is, in a language departing from Old Slavonic
that tried to be closer to Russian and Serbian. The author was Zacharija
Orfelin, who, some years before, in 1768, had tried to bring to life in
Venice the first journal ever published for southern Slavs, the *Slavenso-
serbskij magazin*. He published in it a biography of Feofan Prokopovič,
the right arm of Peter the Great in his reform of relationships between
church and state, attempting even here to remain loyal to Orthodox traditions and to a culture that was beginning to open to a dawn of enlightenment. Orfelin was a man of many capacities and trades, a writer and
an administrator, an engraver and a scientist. He was a kind of Griselini
who had come out of the Slavic world, much less cultivated and modern,
much more limited by ecclesiastical and national traditions; still, he had
taken the same road as the Venetian publicist. The example of Russia
was fundamental to him. He dedicated his biography of Peter the Great
to Catherine II. Among the engravings with which he adorned the biography was a medal showing the empress enthroned "for the salvation
of the faith and the fatherland." From the "*Storia della guerra presente*"
he took the image of the "Dialogo del turco e del russo sui Dardanelli,"
perhaps the best graphic representation of the impression the naval expedition of Orlov had made in Venice. Orfelin signed the engraving
with his own name and surname, adding the epithet "member of the
Imperial and Royal Academies of Arts and Letters of Vienna." His text
was open to ideas circulating both in Venice and in Russia. He provided
ample information on the state, culture, and customs of the Russians,
offering a large bibliography, in which recent works by Miller, Lomonosov, Emin, and Ščerbatov were included, along with classics by Pufen-

---

[28] Ibid., pp. 263ff.

[29] Zacharija Stepanovič Orfelin, *Istorija o žitii i slavnych delach velikago gosudarja impera-
tora Petra Velikago* (History of the life and glorious undertakings of the grand imperor
Peter the Great) (Venice: Dimitrij Theodosij, 1772). A copy of another, unillustrated, edition is in Venice, at the Biblioteca Marciana and has the call number 171.D.63.

dorf, Catiforo, and Voltaire. His was a voice from the Mediterranean in the general debate about Peter the Great then developing in Russia.[30]

There were also echoes and discussions in the Venetian journals of these years. Thus, the June 1771 edition of Caminer's *Europa letteraria* mentioned the French edition of the *Nakaz* that Rey had published at Amsterdam. Finally the Russians were free: "Their fathers had known only violence, terror, and servile obedience; but now they would be moved to obedience by the sweet impulse of filial tenderness; the first were serfs, the second subjects; their fathers had been forced to carry out the orders of an imperious lord, whereas the sons freely adopt the laws of a just sovereign."[31] A little farther on this journal mentioned the book by John Cook, *Voyages and travels through the Russian Empire, Tartary, and part of the Kingdom of Persia*, which appeared in Edinburgh in 1770, as well as the famous Voyage by the Abbé Chappe, against which Catherine II launched her *Antidote*. The review was optimistic: "It is necessary to admit that the Russian nation is far from being ignorant and groaning under the yoke of despotism."[32] In the same issue it said "there was nothing more marvelous or at the same time more rapid than the changes that have occurred in Russia. Posterity would hardly believe this had witnesses whose authenticity cannot be challenged not reported it."[33] The August 1771 issue was devoted entirely to Russia. "It was good to see, when the rapid advance of Russian arms demonstrated to Europe how much their nation was advancing in military affairs, that we were also informed of their progress in literature."[34]

The discovery and apology for the Russia of Catherine II found their points of arrival in the conjunction of the work of two men: the French writer Ange Goudar, a guest of the Republic of St. Mark; and Francesco Griselini, one of the most active Venetian writers of the age of the Enlightenment. The first published in 1772, with a dedication to Gregorij Orlov, considerations about Russia to which he added a eulogy to Catherine II.[35] Like the greater part of the work of this adventurous econo-

---

[30] See Arturo Cronia, *Storia della letteratura serbo croata* (n.p.: Nuova Accademia, n.d); Jovan Skerlić, *Srpska kniževnost u XVIII veku* (Serbian literature in the eighteenth century), in Id., *Sobrana dela* (Collected works), ed. Midchat Belić (Belgrad: Prosveta, 1966), vol. 2 (with a bibliography at the end of the work, on p. 225), and id., *Istorija nova srpske kniževnosti* (History of modern Serbian literature), ibid., vol. 3, 1977, pp. 71ff. The publishing house Prosveta published in 1970 a two-volume translation of this work "in contemporary" Serbian, with a comment by Radmila Michailović and Milorad Pavić.

[31] *L'Europa letteraria*, June 1771, pp. 30ff.

[32] Ibid., July 1771, pp. 71ff, and August 1771, p. 35.

[33] Ibid., p. 102.

[34] Ibid., August 1771, p. 72.

[35] Ange Goudar, *Considérations sur les causes de l'ancienne foiblesse de l'empire de Russie et de sa nouvelle puissance. Avec un Discours oratoire contenant l'éloge de Catherine II, aujourd'hui*

mist and writer of projects, this one is by no means without interest. The work of Peter the Great was in his eyes, as in those of Voltaire, a true and proper revolution, even a new creation, which had drawn Russia out of a long, millennial void of political existence. This land was too large and too poor, with too small a population, to arise little by little out of barbarism. Only a complete reform could give it life. Up to that time Russia had been in a state of nature. "Muscovy was bereft of institutions, of laws, of regulations; the government was without a constitution; the empire without a system; the state without police; the prince without principles; the subjects without education."[36] There was neither justice nor culture. The czars had the vices and cruelties of all tyrants, without either effectiveness or political energy. Despotism itself was an anomaly in Russia. Implanted in a cold country—which was thus naturally inclined toward liberty—despotism had become stronger than in the empires of Asia—which instead were naturally inclined toward slavery. From this arose an "excess of tyranny." In general, as the example of Denmark demonstrated, "when a nation naturally free becomes enslaved, it is very much enslaved."[37] "In Asia, where despotism is natural, it has bounds: if there are no laws, manners and customs give it limits." In Russia such limits did not exist. The Boyars did not have a representative function. "Religion, which ordinarily is a check on despotism, drove this one on."[38] Absence of liberty gave a vacuous and casual quality to the entire history of Russia. But there was an opportunity, a possibility through the reforms attempted by Peter, reforms that would have been impossible to carry out in a country like Turkey. The czars, in their continual effort to maintain their power, in their cruelty itself, had demonstrated that "violent government is not natural to Rus-

régnante (Amsterdam: Au dépens de l'auteur, 1772). The central part of this work was also circulated with a different cover (see the following note). Both editions appear to have been Italian, perhaps Milanese. On Goudar, see Lew S. Gordon, *Studien zur plebejisch-demokratischen Tradition in der französischen Aufklärung* (Berlin: Rütten und Loening, 1972), and the bibliography by Goudar edited by Francis L. Mars in the review *Casanova Gleanings* 9 (1966): 1ff. An interesting piece of information was transmitted on 11 January 1772 to Turin by a Venetian informant: "It has been revealed that Sig. Goudard has had secret conferences with persons of the government, both of a political and of an economic nature, and he plans to give the republic plans on these subjects since he is soon to depart for Moscow." Turin, AS, *Materie politiche estere in genere*, mazzo 56, 1772. For the relationship between A. Goudar and A. Tron, see Giovanni Tabacco, *Andrea Tron (1712–1785) e la crisi dell'aristocrazia senatoria a Venezia* (Trieste: Facoltà di lettere, Istituto di storia medievale e moderna, 1957), pp. 20 n. 4, 21 n. 1, 166–67.

   [36] Ange Goudar, *Considérations sur les causes de la foiblesse et de la puissance de l'empire des Russie* (Amsterdam, 1772), pp. 21–22.

   [37] Ibid., pp. 46–47.

   [38] Ibid., p. 49.

sians."[39] It was even true, after the revolution, after the death of Peter, that women had been able to govern Russia. The parallel with England was illuminating. "The two governments of Europe most different in their maxims and principles, since one passes for being very free and the other for being very much enslaved, have both been governed by women from time to time, without that having weakened the two empires."[40] Russia was taking the same road as the governments of European states. The transformation was made possible especially by the inclusion of Russia economically, culturally, and militarily in the European world, from which it had long been excluded. Peter had been right, whatever Rousseau might have said in the *Contrat social*, to oblige Russia to follow the example of Europe, to draw from it ideas and institutions, to open the gates of his empire, traveling and allowing others to travel. He had been right to make himself a workman among workmen, a sailor among sailors, a soldier among the soldiers of Europe. He had been justly harsh in carrying out his plan. How could one have waited, according to Rousseau's design, for the situation to mature? "The Muscovites were degenerating through time: a nation will not of itself take to reform out of corruption. Should one have waited for the end of the world to police Russia?"[41] It was not true that Peter, with his reforms, had spoiled and corrupted the customs of Russians. Intervening in a debate that was then spreading in the West and that found expression even in St. Petersburg in the pages of Prince Ščerbatov, Goudar made light of such scruples and fears. It was enough to think of the history of France to understand the motives that pushed Peter into action. Was it thus necessary to blame Francis I and Henry IV for having "enervated the political power of that monarchy by trying to reform it"?[42] If one looked at Russia the conclusion was clear. "What was needed was a general plan for reform. Passing remedies would only have palliated the evil without curing it. . . . He threw down the old edifice of government and showed all the pieces, which he then returned to their places."[43]

To this justification of Peter's revolution was added, in Goudar's book, a eulogy to Catherine. In the first part he voluntarily averted his eyes from the "present state of Russia, which gives an example to the universe" to concentrate instead on the bases of the history of that

[39] Ibid., p. 51.
[40] Ibid., pp. 52–53.
[41] Ibid., p. 171.
[42] Ibid., p. 181.
[43] Ibid., p. 94.

land.[44] Instead he wanted to observe the work of Catherine in all its fullness. In page after page he described and extolled her ideas and undertakings.

The *Discours oratoire*, "which had recently appeared in the French language" "with the consent of the author," was translated and published by Griselini.[45] The edition was dedicated to "His Excellency Signor Marchese Maruzzi, Councilor of State of Her Majesty the Empress of all Russia, her chargé d'affaires to all the powers of Italy, and Knight of the Order of St. Anne." The translator added a *Nota* intended to give a complete idea of what the Russian fleet had done in the Archipelago from the "beginning of the expedition to the battle of Chesmé," and to publish "the plans of the maritime fortresses attacked and taken by the same."[46] Two years had passed since the attack on the Morea: Russian and Greek events could be narrated with a more objective and detached tone. Venice continued to be kept out of every dispute. Attention was paid to the Russian agreements with the Maineotes. The declaration with which the Russians had promised to restore that people "to their ancient liberty and free them from the Ottoman yoke" was not forgotten. Here again the responsibility for failure was placed on the Greeks. "The bad faith, the vileness, the greed for spoil, and the indiscipline of the Maineotes themselves made it impossible to proceed with the felicity that was expected."[47] The Russians instead, even in the most difficult situations, remained "intrepid . . . and sold their lives dearly."[48] Their maneuvers were related with more grace and completeness, leading up to the "memorable day of Chesmé, in consequence of which the Russians, with the destruction of the Turkish fleet, gained control of the sea and were in a position to give laws to the islands of the Archipelago, to block the passage of the Dardanelles, and to withhold stores from Constantinople and control its shipping for the remainder of a war that will be memorable in all time."[49]

[44] Ibid., p. 3.

[45] *Elogio di Catterina II imperadrice delle Russie, scritto da celebre autore francese in occasione dei gloriosi trionfi riportati dalle armi di questa sovrana nella presente guerra* (Venice: Giammaria Bassaglia, 1773). The permission of the Riformatori of Padova was given on 16 October 1772 and was signed by Angelo Contarini and Alvise Vallaresso. See Gianfranco Torcellan, "Francesco Griselini," in *Riformatori*, vol. 7, pp. 91ff., now in id., *Settecento veneto ed altri saggi storici* (Turin: Giappichelli, 1969), pp. 235ff. Griselini's rendition is generally faithful. It is curious to note that on p. 30 (see p. xliv of the French text) he skips the following phrase: "Indigence is good for nothing besides making men unhappy, and the unhappy ruin the state. Hunger and thirst have always been the worst economies."

[46] *Elogio di Catterina II*, frontispiece.

[47] Ibid., p. 55.

[48] Ibid., p. 56.

[49] Ibid., pp. 62ff.

The *Elogio di Catterina seconda* has to be read in the light of these significant events. The admiration of the author for the internal policy of the empress was unbounded. She understood that the art of government was "a most complex science" founded on all modern culture and knowledge.[50] With the disappearance of Peter III, Catherine II had carried out that "revolution of Russia" which ensured the peace of Europe.[51] She then concentrated on improving and reforming the country. "Oh Russia, become my fatherland . . . receive the oath that I make to you to do nothing unworthy of the glory of Peter the Great."[52] For this reason she had facilitated the entry of foreign colonists and fought against the excessive wealth of the clergy.[53] Having seen that the laws of Russia were reduced to a "formless monument," she decided to remake them. "But our heroine did not want to act in this reform as an absolute ruler or give new strength to the old despotism."[54] The empress had known that "direction of general opinion" was the "only remaining means to change the genius of a nation."[55] She was inspired in this by Montesquieu and had based her *Nakaz* on him. The highest aim of this "patriotic queen" was to "unite the empire of St. Petersburg with that of the provinces," thus bringing together heterogeneous and divided peoples.[56] The basic instruments were to be "agriculture, commerce, industry, and finance."[57] She struggled, therefore, against all kinds of privilege and private interests and carried out a policy that was "splendid without ostentation, magnificent without profusion, generous without prodigality."[58] She would not be one, like other sovereigns, to raise with "the goods of the poor" any "houses of pleasure." "She does not force nature, or change the order of the seasons, but makes it a duty to breathe the same air as her subjects."[59] Even when she had to take recourse to arms, the empress directed her armies against Turkey, "a monstrous government," which "it should be the policy of Europe to annihilate, whereas the current policy maintains it."[60] The organizing capacity of Catherine II was not to be doubted. "It was well known that

[50] Ibid., p. 6.
[51] Ibid., p. 8.
[52] Ibid., pp. 16–17.
[53] Ibid., pp. 18–19.
[54] Ibid., p. 20.
[55] Ibid., p. 41.
[56] Ibid., p. 25.
[57] Ibid., p. 27.
[58] Ibid., p. 30.
[59] Ibid., p. 32.
[60] Ibid., p. 37.

Russia had ships, but Europe did not know it had a fleet."[61] "Oh you famous Strait of Gibraltar, that joining so many seas have brought about the ruin of so many peoples, you who gave us luxury unknown to our forefathers, and thus did as much evil to our customs as heresy once did to religion. Imagine how you were awakened from your stupor perceiving between your banks a fleet of which you had never seen a parallel, a unique happening, occurring only once in the world!"[62] "A great man" was that Orlov who knew how to realize the plans of the empress.[63] Not one word of this eulogy was for the Greeks. Catherine was the model of an enlightened sovereign. Her victories, her successes, should become incitements, even in states of the West, to proceed along the road to reforms. The memory of rebellions was now put aside.

Giacomo Casanova took a similar position when he undertook a continuation of his *Istoria delle turbolenze della Polonia*, of which the first three volumes appeared in Gorizia in 1774, a continuation that never saw the light of day and has only recently been published.[64] After having described at length the events of the war in 1769, Casanova reevoked the moment of stupor many felt when it seemed as though the Turkish empire was going to collapse under the blows of Catherine II, and that she would soon "make a reality of the title empress of all the Greeks in the east." "The plan was undoubtedly worthy of the high mind of that great lady and was the best that could be conceived by the imagination of a grand monarch," even if it involved, as many thought, "insuperable difficulties."[65] Not least of which, as soon appeared, was the irremediable indiscipline and rioting of the peoples the Russians expected to support in their revolt against the Turks. The Maineotes, whom others idolized, were considered by Casanova "an iniquitous race." Old rancors were reborn. Venice had lost Crete and the Morea because of the "betrayal of the Greeks, who in other places may be humane and good, but are criminal and ill natured in those places." The valor of the descendants of the ancient Lacedaemonians really consisted "in making slaves of Turks and Christians alike." "They are perfidious, as much with the first who are their rulers, as with the second whom they abhor all the more if they are Roman Catholics." How could one trust such people? "If the Russians had been well informed, they would never have entrusted themselves to the assistance of those barbarous slaves, as are all those of their rite under Ottoman rule. They are always inclined to libertinage, pil-

---

[61] Ibid., p. 38.

[62] Ibid., pp. 39ff.

[63] Ibid., p. 49.

[64] Giampiero Bozzolato, *Casanova: Uno storico alla ventura. Istoria delle turbolenze della Polonia* (Padova: Marsilio, 1976), pp. 141ff.; and Giacomo Casanova, *Istoria delle turbolenze della Polonia*, ed. Giacinto Spagnoletti (Naples: Guida, 1974), pp. 482ff. I cite the latter.

[65] Casanova, *Istoria delle turbolenze*, pp. 533ff.

lage, and larceny, as a reward for their wickedness, which reduces them to the same condition as the Jews."[66] Thus, archaic Venetian conservatism focused on what Casanova thought was Russia's blind gesture in attempting to resurrect Greece. How had they thought to provoke a "general revolution" and "total subversion" in the Morea? What had happened in Venetian territory was particularly instructive. Casanova recalled the example of Count Metaxà and other "rich lords of the island of Zante," who presented themselves in the Morea as defenders of the Greeks, only to reveal that they were incapable not only of military discipline, but also of the most elementary honesty. "That expedition, which did not last two months and cost the Russians many millions and much blood, procured them the great advantage of being undeceived, but it was surprising that Count Orlov needed such a cruel experience to persuade him." For three centuries the Greeks had been "subjected to the Turks, who have always kept the scimitar raised over their heads." They had never succeeded in liberating themselves. "It seems that God wants them to remain in that state of dependence." "The thousand lessons history presents to those who read them" should have persuaded the Russians not to trust "that miserable folk."[67]

This was a skeptical and mistaken vision that no longer corresponded to reality. The very interest with which Venetians had listened to the news of events in the Morea demonstrated it. The Greeks themselves in the years when they followed the arrival of Orlov in their lands were seeking and finding a new relationship with Russia. In St. Petersburg a symbol was soon erected to remind passers by of this. In the image of Catherine II's will to continue and renew Peter's policy, in the famous monument Falconet sculpted for the square in front of the Senate, there stood and still stands, although it is now enclosed, something connected with the events in the Greek islands during the Greco-Turkish war. The statue by Diderot's friend is famous. But its base, the mass of raw material on which the artful flight of the emperor rests, is justly famous too.[68] It was brought there, with great difficulty, by a technician from Cephalonia, born in its capital Argostoli, who received a degree at the University of Padua and, after emigrating to Russia, took the name Lascaris, from the illustrious Byzantine family, although in reality he

---

[66] Ibid., p. 594.

[67] Ibid., p. 603.

[68] The gazette of Mantova wrote on 26 February 1773 that "the pedestal, which is usually an extraneous thing, which indicates nothing and should indicate nothing, here is united with the principal figure. It joins the action expressed by the sculptor and becomes a necessary part." *Mantova*, no. 9, 26 February 1773 (St. Petersburg, 19 January). This idea was taken up by and paraphrased in the *Notizie del mondo*, no. 19, 6 March 1773, p. 148 (St. Petersburg, 28 January).

was called Marino Carburi.[69] In 1777 he published a beautifully illustrated book in Paris to tell how that rock came to be in Russia, where it
is not found at all, and how he succeeded in bringing it by land and sea
to the capital of Catherine II.[70] In the "Avertissement" of his book he
explained how "an impetuous passion in his youth, a hundred times
worse in Mediterranean climates," had driven him "to commit an act of
violence." Voluntary exile was "the most cruel punishment, undoubtedly, for one who had the good fortune to be born a subject of a wise
and enlightened republic."[71] The Melissino family, from Cephalonia, received him in Russia. Pietro Melissino was the remaker of the Russian
artillery; Giovanni, his brother, was rector of the University of Moscow;
both were tightly knit into the intellectual life of Russia in the second
half of the eighteenth century and into the masonic movement developing there.[72] Arriving at the center of Russian life, Marino Carburi
could thus observe with lively interest "the great and rapid means that
absolutism used to create a nation and found an empire."[73] He was
happy to be able to offer his own technical abilities to this land in the

[69] He was one of the three Carburi brothers, Giovanni Battista, Marco, and Marino,
who, each in his own way, represented an interesting aspect of the contacts between the
culture of the Ionian Islands and Italy. Giovanni Battista Carburi was a professor of medicine in Turin from 1751 to 1764 and traveled widely in Europe. A friend of Trudaine,
he was with him in Genova, in Tuscany, and in Rome in 1770 (see Turin, AS, *Lettere ministri, Roma*, mazzo 262, Rivera to Raiberti, 7 April 1770). Marco Carburi was an expert
on metals, a professor at Padova, and the furnisher of excellent cannons to the Venetian
navy in its last battles against the Barbary pirates. See Antimo Masarachi, *Vite degli uomini
illustri dell'isola di Cefalonia*. Italian translation from Greek by N. Tommaseo (Venice: Gio.
Cecchini, 1843), pp. 51ff., 143ff., 155ff.; M. and N. Pignatorre, *Memorie storiche e critiche
dell'isola di Cefalonia*, vol. 2, p. 197 (where there are references to Giovanni Battista Carburi, who was welcomed in England by Robertson and Hume), pp. 199ff., 207ff., 212
(with letters by Angelo Emo on the "marine mortars" of Marco Carburi, "the best in Europe"), and *DBI*, vol. 19, pp. 725ff.

[70] *Monument élevé à la gloire de Pierre-le-Grand, ou relation des travaux et des moyens mécha-
niques qui ont été employés pour transporter à Pétersbourg un rocher de trois millions pesant, destiné
à servir de base à la statue équestre de cet empereur, avec un examen physique et chimique du même
rocher par le conte Marin Carburi de Ceffalonie, ci-devant lieutenant-colonel au service de S. M.
l'impératrice de toutes les Russies, lieutenant de police et censeur, ayant la direction du corps noble
des cadets de terre de Saint Pétersbourg* (Paris: Nyon et Soupe, 1777).

[71] Ibid., p. 2.

[72] See Masarachi, *Vite degli uomini illustri dell'isola di Cefalonia*, pp. 433ff., where there
is mention of "a society of persons of importance called the 'Filadelfica,'" that was occupied "with science and studies." In reality the Masonic role of Pietro Melissino was of the
first order, as venerable, until 1782, of the "Discretion" lodge and as creator of a "Melissino rite," influenced by the Grand Orient of Paris. See Georg V. Vernadskij, "Russkoe
masonstvo v carstvovanie Ekateriny II" (Freemasonry in Russia in the reign of Catherine
II), in *Ogni* (The fires) (Petrograd, 1917), index, and particularly p. 228, and Bakounine,
Répertoire biographique des francs-maçons russes, p. 331.

[73] Carburi, *Monument élevé à la gloire de Pierre-le-Grand*, p. 4.

process of transformation. "Mechanics" opened "to talent the broadest career." "This is related directly to the needs of man and it increases his faculties all the more through achievement of new discoveries." Mechanics permitted him to praise Peter, the "generous reformer of Russia."[74] His work done, he decided to return to his own land, "to the perfect tranquillity that the wisdom of the first republic of the world has always ensured." On Cephalonia, "once warlike and unhappy and now peaceful and fortunate," he continued to work for reform and to meditate on the cosmopolitan events of contemporary politics. Under the peaceful government of Venice his thoughts turned to Catherine, who made "flower in the land of Hyperboreans the laws of Rome and the arts of Athens."[75] He had rejoined his brothers Marco and Giambattista, who were famous scientists.[76] He became the improver and colonizer of his native island, importing seeds, methods of cultivation, and exotic plants that until then were unknown in the island, such as indigo and cotton. He looked to the model of the American colonies, then in the midst of their struggle for independence. On Cephalonia a new passion, a new interest, animated the minds of cultivated people. Even there, as in every corner of Europe, arose an agrarian society to keep together and spur the new good will. "What pleasure, sirs," wrote the secretary of this association in a fine report about the exotic plants imported by Carburi, "to see stirred by our winds, or shaded by our trees, sustained by our earth, surrounded by our grass, these rich daughters of Hindustan, of the Canaries, of Brazil, of the Antilles!"[77] Marino Carburi had indeed thrown himself into transforming the landscape and economy of the island. To cultivate the new plants, he brought in a few hundred laborers from the Peloponnesus. He could not avoid coming into conflict with the other proprietors of the island, who were more traditional than he in matters of civic custom, commons rights, and agricultural improvement. In the period when the Russian ships showed themselves before the Ionian Islands, the Venetian peace that Marino Carburi had come to seek in his fatherland was broken, and conflicts among families glowed like coals beneath the ashes. His efforts at reform ended in tragedy. He was murdered by his Greek laborers, and there continued to be

[74] Ibid., pp. 32, 6.

[75] Ibid., p. 4.

[76] On the role of Marco Carburi in the Venetian Masonic world, see Carlo Francovich, *Storia della massoneria in Italia dalle origini alla rivoluzione francese* (Florence: La Nuova Italia, 1974), index.

[77] "Storia della pubblica Academia agraria ed economica di Cefalonia compilata dal D. Gio. Francesco Zulatti, segretario della medesima letta nella pubblica sessione tenuta il di 23 maggio 1796 s.v.," in M. and N. Pignatorre, *Memorie storiche e critiche dell'isola di Cefalonia*, vol. 2, p. 172.

suspicion and gossip about the part his rivals, the noble landowners of the island, might have played in his assassination. "The barbarous inhabitants of the land of Lycurgus and Leonidas cut down this fine citizen who had come to enrich us with the fruits of his long study and kindle in us the fire of his noble enthusiasm to bring here the rarest products of the two Indies."[78]

For Marino Carburi, as for Demetrio Mocenigo and many other fugitives and exiles, seamen and merchants, the Russian expedition into the Mediterranean marked a decisive moment in their lives. The ancient and wise republic that, even for them, remained for so long the model toward which they naturally turned their eyes was rudely confronted, in different ways, by distant realities: the national hopes of the Greeks and problems of reform in the immense Russia of Catherine II. As the example of Marino Carburi shows, once these men were taken up in the swirl of new aspirations and changes, their views rapidly enlarged to encompass new ideas and problems, from Freemasonry to the new agricultural methods of the United States of America.

Eugenio Voulgaris, another and a more famous son of the Ionian Islands, became an important spokesman for the new relationships that were being established between the Greek world and the world of Catherine II. Born on Corfu in 1716, he grew up intellectually in the shadow of Antonios Katephoros (Catiforo), the learned author of a biography of Peter the Great published in Italian and Greek at Venice in 1736 and 1737. Through this mentor he became linked to the Byzantine tradition, although he was at the same time open to the thought of the West and perhaps already to the philosophy of Locke, which was to have some influence over him. He became a deacon in 1738, choosing the name Eleutherios, and began his career as a teacher, which carried him to the school of the Maruzzi in Janina, to the monastery of Althos, and to the Academy of the Patriarch in Constantinople. He was always a difficult professor who demanded much of himself and others in his effort to hasten forward along the road of culture. He made enemies and had quarrels, but he succeeded nonetheless, despite all, in introducing into Greece the new physics and mathematics, as well as Antonio

---

[78] Ibid. The *Notizie del mondo*, no. 59, 23 July 1782, p. 472 (Trieste, 9 July), published the news of Carburi's assassination "by the Greeks he employed on the peninsula in the cultivation of sugar and indigo, the success of which had seemed secured." Seven were the "stab wounds of his wife . . . who nonetheless survived." The assassins were arrested "with all the stolen jewels and gold." A Frenchman whom Count Carburi had brought there from Martinique to run his plantations so as not to neglect anything necessary to the cultivation of these articles, which he wanted to make indigenous to his country, was also murdered.

Genovesi's *Elementi di metafisica*. In 1759 he was obliged to leave Mount Althos. In 1762 he left Greece and did not return before the end of his long life in 1806. In 1766 he published his *Logica* in Leipzig. His other philosophical works appeared much later, at the end of the century and the beginning of the next, and were all published abroad, at Venice, Moscow, and Vienna. This was also a symptom of the obstacles that presented themselves everywhere in Greece to the penetration of new ideas. For him as well the Russo-Turkish War was the moment of his greatest political involvement. He began in 1768 by translating into Greek and publishing in Leipzig the *Essai historique et critique sur les dissensions des églises de Pologne*, Voltaire's most important pamphlet in defense of the policy of religious toleration of Catherine II. He added numerous long notes intended to support and further discuss, although with moderation, the idea of "anexithreskeia," that is, religious toleration (it may be that he was even the one to give the Greek language this word). He kept the views of an ecclesiastic: toleration could be only political, not religious. But his effort to relate his ideas to Voltaire is still striking. He remained very close to the policy of Catherine II, was appointed librarian in St. Petersburg in 1772, was made archbishop of the Ukraine, then returned to the capital in 1779, and finally retired to a monastery, where he died. He always tried to emphasize the classical character of his Greek, refusing to write in any language besides the traditional one, and he devoted himself among other things to a Hellenic translation of Virgil, which was published in sumptuous volumes at St. Petersburg and naturally was dedicated to the empress. Meanwhile his works were slowly diffused through the world of emigrés and in lands dominated by the Turks and contributed much to what has been called the "reeducation" of Greeks between the end of the eighteenth century and the beginning of the nineteenth.[1]

---

[1] Henderson, *The Revival of Greek Thought*, p. 1. This work as a whole is particularly useful and illuminating on Voulgaris and his times. For a general view of Greek culture in the eighteenth century, see C. Th. Demaras, *La Grèce au temps des lumières* (Geneva: Droz, 1969). The most recent work on this period is by Paschalis M. Kitromilides, *Iosippos Moisiodes: Hoi syntetagmenes tes balkanikes skepses tor 18 aiona* (Iosippos Moisiodes: The coordinator of Balkan thought in the eighteenth century) (Athens: Cultural Foundation of the National Bank of Greece, 1985). This has material of interest also on the relations with Italy of eighteenth-century Greeks. By the same author see also "War and Political Consciousness: Theoretical Implications of Eighteenth Century Greek Historiography," in Gunther E. Rothenbey, Béla K. Király, and Peter F. Sugar, eds., *East Central European Society and War in the Pre-revolutionary Eighteenth Century* (New York: Columbia University Press, 1982), pp. 351ff. I have taken up some problems suggested by these works in an essay entitled *La rivolta Greca del 1770 e il patriottismo dell' età dei lumi*, published in 1986 by the Unione internazionale degli Istituti di Archeologia, Storia, e Storia dell'Arte in Roma. See also Roxane D. Argyropoulos, "Patriotisme et sentiment national en Grèce au temps des lumières," in *Folia Neohellenica* (Amsterdam, 1984), vol. 6, pp. 7ff.

III

⊛

Russians in the Tuscany of Peter Leopold

THE EXPERIENCE OF MUSCOVITES IN THE TUSCANY OF PETER LEOPOLD was different, and perhaps freer and more varied. The Russians were awkward guests in the port of Livorno, where for year after year, from 1769, there were ships from Kronstadt continually going back and forth from the Levant.[1] The Russian sailors presented a variety of problems to the urban authorities, from religious (sacraments taken to the sick in the hospitals) to disciplinary ones (thefts, and so on).[2] But on the whole the documents give an impression of notable tolerance on the part of Tuscans and of organization on the part of the Russians. The Russians did not display excessive luxury, even if Orlov could not help attracting attention by going about "with two lackeys, two aides, and two eunuchs taken from a seraglio, their costumes trimmed with gold."[3] His request "to blow up one of the vessels of his squadron" must have seemed strange and disturbing. He invited the grand duke himself to enjoy the spectacle, but the grand duke did not accept.[4] Aside from these pictur-

---

[1] A printed bulletin listing the ships in port and the exchange rates was published in 1770 and in the years that followed. Many of these bulletins are found in AMAE, *Toscane*, 133, 1770, for example at fol. 226.

[2] Livorno, AS, *Governo, Lettere civili al governatore di Livorno*, filza 11, fol. 43, 28 January 1771, and filza 14, fol. 262, 21 May 1771.

[3] Torino, AS, *Materie politiche estere in genere*, mazzo 56, 1771, Livorno, 2 January 1771.

[4] Livorno, AS, *Governo, Lettere civili al governatore di Livorno*, filza 123, 25 March 1772. It was Orlov's own idea. He said that "since painters did not show the fire of the Turkish fleet in the port of Chesmé well in their pictures, he wanted to burn and blow up one of his ships, which had been condemned by the shipwrights, so that the painters could get a better idea and show it better on their canvas." He said he would even "wait for the return of His Royal Highness from the Maremma so he could be present." Firenze, AS, *Segreteria di Stato*, 26 March 1772, no. 2. One can find a reproduction of an engraving from a painting by Richard Paton of the battle of Chesmé in the volume *Russia in the Second Half of the XVIII Century*, in *Očerki istorii SSSR* (Essays on the history of the USSR), ed. N. M. Družinin

esque elements, the important fact is that the Russians established many solid ties with Tuscan culture and journalism.

The adventurous life of Giovanni del Turco is perhaps the most significant example. Contrary to what his name implies, he did not belong to the patrician family of the Rosselli del Turco. He was born in Florence on 28 December 1739. His father, Ranieri Valentino, was the anatomical dissector at the hospital of Santa Maria Nuova in Florence and at the University of Pisa.[5] Pisa gave him his education, and he followed the precepts of De Soria, a well-known professor at the University of Pisa, who opened before him the study of mathematics and the humanities.[6] We find him in 1762 among the correspondents of G. Fontana, attentive to what was published and said by Paolo Frisi, Count Radicati, Marchese Lomellini, and to news from abroad about Jean Jacques Rousseau, who was then a refugee in Neuchâtel under the protection of Frederick II. He was already employed "from morning to night" putting in order the "library of the institution," that is, the University of Pisa, of which he had become assistant librarian in 1762.[7] His soul was full of gratitude for "the incomparable Dr. De Soria, to whom I can assure you," he wrote to G. Fontana, "I owe everything."[8] "For his *own* study and his *own* pleasure" he had put together an exposition of the system of Newton, which was later published in 1765.[9] Together with De Soria he planned a journal, the *Atti letterari*, which was supposed to be published, with his book, by Coltellini in Livorno, and he hoped to obtain the collaboration of Beccaria and Frisi.[10] But publication of the *Atti* was always put off, and finally he was obliged to give up the enterprise.[11]

et al. (Moscow: Historical Institution of the Academy of Sciences of the USSR, 1956), p. 355. On R. Paton (1717–1791), a marine painter, see *DNB*, vol. 44, p. 37. The painting was in the castle of Gatčina.

[5] Firenze, Archivio dell'opera di Santa Maria del Fiore di Firenze, *Battesimo, maschi, 1738–1739*, Oratorio di San Giovanni. On his father, see Firenze, AS, *Reggenza*, 637, ins. 41, and *Reggenza*, 1006.

[6] On the ideas of De Soria see Antonio Rotondò, "Il pensiero politico di Giovanni Gualberto De Soria," in *L'Età dei lumi: studi storici sul Settecento europeo in onore di Franco Venturi* (Naples: Jovine, 1985), vol. 2, pp. 987ff.

[7] Firenze, BN, Ms. Palat. 1197, letters to G. Fontana, vol. 81, Pisa, 5 March 1762. See also other letters by G. Del Turco, from Pisa, 16 April and 13 August 1762.

[8] Ibid.; see also the letters dated 16 April and 13 August 1762. There is no information on the administrative career of Del Turco in the manuscript of Bartolomeo Polloni, *Istoria del I. e R. Università di Pisa*, 1833, Pisa, B. Universitaria, Ms. 517, p. iii. But see in Florence, AS, *Segreteria di Stato*, 1768, 24 December, no. 4.

[9] *Illustrazione di Giovanni Del Turco, sottobibliotecario dell'Università di Pisa, ai principî mattematici di filosofia naturale d'Isacco Newton* (Livorno: M. Coltellini, 1765), preface.

[10] A. Lay, *Un editore illuminista: Giuseppe Aubert nel carteggio con Beccaria e Verri* (Turin: Accademia delle scienze, 1975). Aubert to Beccaria, Livorno, 28 June 1765, p. 60.

[11] Ibid., p. 71, Aubert to Beccaria, Livorno, 8 February 1766.

He encountered further obstacles in Florence, where he spent some time.[12] He had started to translate and comment on the *Iliad*, which he interpreted in the light of literary and political ideas from beyond the Alps and beyond the English Channel, but not, as we shall see, without an independence of judgment. He published the first book in 1767, accompanied by an ample *Esame de' poemi d'Omero e della presente traduzione*, a substantial work, which it was possible to obtain for two paoli separately from the translation: "And to receive it address yourself to the author."[13] His ambition was to do in Italy what Pope had done in England. "He has made Homer almost as familiar in Great Britain as Tasso is in Italy."[14] He thought the interpretation of La Motte, which "sits beside Homer like a church of Borromino beside the portico of the Pantheon," was outdated.[15] One should let oneself be taken by the sense of nature at the heart of the Homeric poem and not be intimidated by the great distance of time, the "diversity of customs," separating the modern world from that of the *Iliad*. "In the same way one can read with pleasure Ariosto, and other poets of romances, whose style is now almost as distant from us as that of Homer."[16] One should read this last poet "with the same kind of veneration one experiences in hearing about the customs and modes of life and behavior of the great men of our old republics."[17] To be sure, Greece was barbarous in the age of Homer, "close to its beginnings."[18] But the modern world has taught us to understand people distant both in time and in space. The Greeks, after the age of the Titans, had the kind of life "some wild populations of Africa and America have in our own time."[19] Their history was like the recent history of non-European continents. Pelloutier, De Guignes, and Banier had helped us understand those "most ancient revolutions."[20] Del Turco was convinced that the "events narrated" in the *Iliad* "could be dated about the year 1184 before our era."[21] With this historical method and chronology he set out to reconstruct the development of the "governments of Greece," with the "warriors of their first settlements . . . elected

---

[12] Ibid.

[13] *Dell'Iliade di Omero trasportata in ottava rima da Giovanni del Turco*, vol. 1 (Florence: Gio. Battista Stecchi e Giuseppe Pagani, 1767).

[14] Ibid., "Discorso preliminare. Esame de' poemi d'Omero e della presente traduzione," p. 3.

[15] Ibid., p. 4.

[16] Ibid., p. 6.

[17] Ibid., p. 7.

[18] Ibid., p. 10.

[19] Ibid., p. 23.

[20] Ibid., p. 24.

[21] Ibid., p. 48.

as leaders," kings who "had at the same time the functions of judges and rulers," while "the function of making laws resided in the people."[22] Tensions among these different powers resulted in the formation of republics. The rich enlisted and armed the poor, "almost in the way noblemen in feudal governments armed their dependents."[23] Even religion changed. "I cannot believe the gods in Homer were allegories." The political life of the gods was the same as that of men. Finally, "the light of reason" had come "to undermine the delights of fantasy."[24] Arts and letters developed from "Egyptian models," becoming "more advanced than in Mexico or Peru when the Europeans invaded those realms." "It is clear that Greek architecture in the time of the republics was improved Egyptian architecture. . . . As for science, I believe all can be reduced to the understanding of certain facts of nature . . . astronomy, medicine . . . the way our peasants still know it."[25] As for poetry, the Greeks, like other peoples, demonstrated that this was age-old. "The Celts had the poems of Ossian without knowing how to read, and the Peruvians and peoples of the Orient had excellent pieces of poetry while still barbarians."[26] The "character" of these nations was not unlike that of "savage populations": "ardent, sincere, grateful for good done and resentful of injuries, ferocious, vindictive, as extreme in friendship as in hate." "Such were the Germans of Tacitus, the Celts of Ossian, and the Mexicans of the time of Hernando Cortez."[27] In fact, this phase ended with writing. One should "consider a strange fact: the great and original poets . . . were always from nearly barbarous nations where the sciences and most of the arts that are the comfort and ornament of cultured peoples were almost entirely unknown." It was enough to think of Italy to persuade oneself of this fact. "The Florentines began to change the customs of the ancient peoples beyond the Alps precisely at the time of Dante—since I do not doubt putting our Dante among the original poets, as much for his invention as his style, which, although sometimes incorrect, no one has ever exceeded in its vividness of pictures and its force and brevity of expression, which makes his images express more than words." But if the example of Dante confirmed the relationship between poetry and "nearly barbarous" nations, the example of Milton might contradict it. Certainly his "invention is original and his poetry sublime," although not without "exaggeration." The "reason for this sin-

[22] Ibid., pp. 48–49.
[23] Ibid., p. 51.
[24] Ibid., p. 54.
[25] Ibid., pp. 55–56.
[26] Ibid., p. 57.
[27] Ibid., p. 59.

gularity" seemed to him to be "particularly" in the "manners and social circumstances" in which he, like other sublime poets, operated. "Men of mediocre intellectual capacities have to compensate for their poor spirit with the delights of fantasy, which are easier to come by. Thus among men who live heroic lives, and among barbarians, storytellers and poets are highly honored. They exercise a necessary trade. . . . Among culti- vated peoples, craftsmen of pleasures and pastimes are despised if those who exercise them fail to rise above lazy mediocrity."[28] Mediocrity is tol- erable only "in necessary and useful arts," but not in poetry, he con- cluded.[29]

Politically, Homer seemed to him important in the period of forma- tion of the Greek republics. "Perhaps he wanted to incite the Greeks of his age to glorious deeds by making flattering depictions of past triumphs."[30] Thus he had a role not dissimilar to that of the "Provençal troubadors," who, "by depicting knightly manners in their romances," set "the taste of invention for five centuries."[31] Legislators of ancient Greece understood that publication of the Homeric poems was "a means to marvelously further" their political aims.[32] To provide a visual demonstration of his interpretation, Del Turco designed an engraving, with a varied and complex Homeric iconography done painstakingly by himself, and placed it at the beginning of the book as a kind of votive temple in honor of the poet.[33]

He could not have had much success with his version of the first book of the *Iliad*. Still, he also published the second, with a dedication to Firmian, governor of Lombardy, appealing to the "glory of the Ital- ian name," to the "interests of the common fatherland," and showing that he was ready to transfer his hopes to "one of the greatest and most beautiful parts of Italy," that is, "Austrian Lombardy," where the arts and sciences were "favored and encouraged" by "the wealth and splen- dor of the cities" and the "security of citizens." There the university was "enriched with new men and new regulations," and the senate was "wor- thily filled."[34] But even this call got no reply. He continued to publish

[28] Ibid., pp. 72–73.
[29] Ibid., p. 74.
[30] Ibid., p. 5.
[31] Ibid., p. 75.
[32] Ibid., p. 5.
[33] The engraving carries the following inscription: "L'autore inv. Gregorj scol." The full explanation of the "Monumenti omerici" is on pp. 75ff.
[34] *Dell'Illiade d'Omero trasportata in ottava rima canto secondo* (Florence: Stecchi e Pagani, 1768). The dedication to Firmian is reprinted in the *Novelle letterarie*, no. 38, 16 September 1768, col. 593.

his *Rassegna delle navi, ovvero la Beozia*, but abandoned his study of Homer.

Nonetheless the history of archaic Greece and the medieval world were themes that continued to fascinate him. In June 1768 he had read the manuscript *Storia d'Italia* by Alessandro Verri and discussed it with Agostino Paradisi, one of the chief experts on Italy at that time. He was convinced that there was still much to find out "about the origins of government in the Italian republics that arose out of the weaknesses of feudal rule under the emperors." Despite what was already written about it in Tuscany, this was an "open field." He urged Verri to go into the problem more deeply. "Your serious, judicious, and philosophical way of thinking, revealed to me in the few conversations I have had with you, is such that I can imagine how the subject would be treated by you, and I have no doubt that you have something to contribute to the glory of the nation." "On this subject the best thing I have seen is the study by President Neri of the origins of the Italian nobility, although the subject is not developed much by him."[35]

Del Turco's unhappiness grew. The example of men like Cesare Beccaria was before his eyes. His desire for action became greater the more miserable and useless the fate he was condemned to as a librarian seemed to him. A common friend, Cosimo Mari, writing to Beccaria at the end of 1768, depicted the state of mind of "our Abate Del Turco," who "also rejoices in the public recognition your sovereign has bestowed on your merits [Beccaria had been appointed professor of political economy], and sends through me his respectful compliments. This poor young man has been made most unhappy by the neglect of the governors of this university and has not heard with indifference this year of the election of four professors through an intrigue that entirely ignored many others of merit." He was scandalized to see how many resorted to such plots and the "other abuses that arise through ministerial pride." He was among the rejected, as Cosimo Mari explained, "for many years as librarian he has done backbreaking work incompatible with his talents, with recompense of only one hundred scudi a year." He was so "disgusted with this neglect" that he would willingly "seek his fortune under other skies." "Do you think he might hope to obtain some chair in that university? He is known by Count Firmian and others. I beg you

---

[35] Modena, B. Estense, *Carte Paradisi*, busta 4, no. 32 346, Pisa, 20 June 1768. On the report of Neri, see Franco Venturi, *Settecento riformatore*, vol. 1: *Da Muratori a Beccaria* (Turin: Einaudi, 1969), pp. 325ff., the review article by Cesare Mozzarelli, "Stato, patriziato, e organizzazione della società nell'Italia moderna," *Annali dell'Istituto storico italo-germanico in Trento* 2 (1976): 471ff., and especially Furio Diaz, *Il Granducato di Toscana: I Medici* (Turin: UTET, 1976), pp. 369ff.

to let me know if you could further his hopes. The special friendship I have for him does not allow me to be inactive, and I ardently seek some means for consoling him."[36]

In the spring of 1769 Del Turco found unexpected support for his will to action, as well as for his thoughts about reform, poetry, civilization, and the Hellenic and barbarian worlds, among the Russians who came to Pisa to prepare the great naval expedition of the following year. Precisely when he became acquainted with their leader, Count Aleksej Orlov, we do not know. Surely, as we shall see, their relationship soon became very cordial. His Muscovite adventure had begun.

With great rapidity he translated for publication in Pisa Catherine II's *Nakaz*.[37] As the title showed, it was a kind of official edition, promoted by Orlov himself. What text did he use in the translation? The work said "translated from the original." The Instruction, which Catherine II wrote in French, appeared initially at Moscow in 1767, in German and in Russian.[38] It was then translated into English the following year and was finally published in the official edition in St. Petersburg in 1769 with the title *Instruction de Sa Majesté impériale Catherine II pour la Commission chargée de dresser le projet d'un nouveau code de loix*. Del Turco based his version on this later edition, and not on one of the two that had already appeared in French the same year at Yverdon and Lausanne.[39]

His was one of the three Italian versions of the *Nakaz* that appeared in 1769, a reminder, if needed, of the extraordinary interest the politics

[36] Milano, B. Ambrosiana, *Carte Beccaria*, b. 232, no. 115, Cosimo Mari to Beccaria, Pisa, 12 December 1768.

[37] *Istruzione di Sua Maestà Cesarea Caterina II imperatrice delle Russie alla Deputazione sopra il piano di un nuovo codice di leggi, insieme col Regolamento per la medesima Deputazione, trasportata dall'originale e dall'editore dedicata a Sua Eccellenza il sig. Co. Alessio d'Orloff, tenente generale, aiutante di campo generale di S.M.I., tenente colonnello del reggimento delle guardie di Preobragensky e tenente del corpo delle guardie dei cavalieri, cavaliere degli ordini di S. Andrea e di S. Alessandro Neusky ecc. ecc.* (Pisa: Agostino Pizzorno, 1769).

[38] Antonij Florovskj, "Die erste deutsche Übersetzung der Instruktion der Kaiserin Katharina II," *Zeitschrift für osteuropäische Geschichte*, 2 (1912): 1ff.

[39] On the composition of the *Nakaz*, see Nikolaj D. Čečulin, *Nakaz imperatricy Ekateriny II, dannyj Kommissii o sočinenii proekta novago uloženija* (The instruction of the empress Catherine II to the commission to carry out the project of new legislation) (St. Petersburg: Akademija nauk, 1907). On the different editions, see Von Bilbassoff, *Katharina II*, vol. 1, pp. 80, 83, 106, 125. The eight editions of the *Nakaz* that appeared in Russia during the eighteenth century are listed and described in *Svodnyj katalog russkoj knigi . . . XVIII veka*, vol. 1, pp. 333ff. For the versions appearing in different parts of Europe, see William E. Butler, "The Nakaz of Catherine the Great," *American Book Collector* 16, no. 5 (January 1966): 19ff. For a general orientation see I. De Madariaga, *Russia in the Age of Catherine the Great*, pp. 151ff.

and problems of Russia aroused in Italy.[40] The first translation, by Giovanni Vignoli and published at Zurich, contained the first twenty chapters taken from the German edition published at Moscow in 1767. Then, before the end of the year, came the edition of Giovanni Del Turco, and another in 16[mo] from the French text printed in Lausanne, that was published in Florence in the Stamperia Bonducciana.[41] These are works "that much attract the attention of the public," Giuseppe Pelli, in Florence, wrote in his diary in November 1769. Even he hastened to read these "instructions," persuading himself that they were "conceived and written with justice, imagined with wisdom, displayed with dignity." If the empress brought herself to complete her program she would be forgiven for "the means with which she had ascended and secured her throne." To be sure, all was not perfect in the *Nakaz*. "I see some spots . . . and defects in the order of things. Nevertheless, the basis of the doctrine is excellent." The Russian sovereign gave other sovereigns, and the grand-duke of Tuscany himself, the valuable example of a complete reordering of laws, "consistent with modern principles established by a few great sages for the benefit of humanity," and removing "confusion, error, barbarism." And it was good for her to have published an instruction "so that the crowd of deputies involved in the plan of codification would act energetically." But how was one to balance this reforming zeal, Pelli ended by asking, with the "current wars"? Would they not "disturb such a noble effort"?[42]

---

[40] Von Bilbassoff, *Katharina II*, vol. 1, p. 126.

[41] *Istruzione emanata da Caterina seconda imperatrice e legislatrice di tutta la Russia stante la Commissione stabilita da questa sovrana per la reduzione* [sic] *di un nuovo codice di leggi tal quale è stata impressa in Russia, in Alemagna e in Francia. Tradotta nuovamente dal francese in lingua toscana* (Florence: Stamperia Bonducciana, 1769). The interesting "Prefazione degli editori" (Editor's preface) has a comparison between the work of Peter, who "disciplined the Russian slaves to make them victors in battle," and the work of Catherine in a country like Russia who tended "to weaken despotism and make just authority respected." It expressed a happy surprise to see a country like Russia, where the people were treated still "a short time ago with greatest disrespect and the harshest oppression," and to put itself first in the way of reform and use of absolute power in a new sense. This was translated from the preface of the Lausanne edition, published in the same year, 1769, by François Grasset. The derivation explains the typographical anomaly on p. 11 of the "Prefazione." At the end one reads 'Avan =,' not followed by any text on the next page, which is entirely blank. The translator had begun to turn into Italian a text in which Grasset apologized to readers for the delay with which his book had appeared, a delay caused by the illness of the engraver of the portrait of the empress (which does not appear in the Florentine edition). This apology seemed absurd to the Italian editor, who left the next page without text. On the bookseller Andrea Bonducci, the publisher also of Beccaria, see *Edizione nazionale delle opere di Cesare Beccaria*, ed. L. Firpo (Milan: Mediobanca, 1984), vol. 1, pp. 404ff.

[42] Giuseppe Pelli, *Efemeridi*, Florence, BN, MS. N.A. 10501[1], vol. 25, F. 23, November 1769. On the contact of Pelli with Del Turco, see *Lettere a Giuseppe Pelli Bencivenni, 1747–*

The aim of the dedication to Orlov, which Del Turco put at the beginning of his version of the *Nakaz*, was to respond to such preoccupations and to praise the work of Catherine. The empress had wanted and knew how to found a society in which "the common good" coincided with that of "private individuals." "Wisdom understood the interests that move men to action; humanity felt the ills that individuals in society can be subjected to, and from which they seek relief; unusual generosity had sacrificed to common security rather than to the idol of power." Under the laws of Catherine it would not be possible "for a sad pretext of public security to offend private security."

A man who cannot be conclusively proven guilty of an act against public security can never be deprived of life, goods, or liberty; and, if nothing is proved against his honor, he cannot lose the right all honest men have to be believed. Thus society will never lack men who can be useful in some way, and the equity of the laws will mitigate extremes of rigor taken against public and dangerous enemies. Such extremes will be made impossible by making the civic virtues and talents that are useful to society into secure and certain means for satisfying the desires that nature and civic usage infuse in men. Such has been the fortunate situation of Russia since the happy accession of the glorious reigning empress.

As a reminder of the inspiration behind the *Nakaz* Del Turco even cited the ability and humanity shown by the "many Russians traveling in Italy" whom he had met in Pisa "from so many and such distant provinces of the Empire. The contentment and jubilation that the name of their empress arouses in them are undeniable proofs of public happiness."[43]

The year of the great events, 1770, the uprising in the Peloponnesus and the Russian victory of Chesmé over the Turkish fleet, passed for Del Turco apparently as usual, between the library in Pisa and his search for new employment (in April, according to what Pelli tells us, he seemed about to accept a post as tutor to one of the daughters of Lapo Niccolini, who had died).[44] He returned to his literary studies and published a small work on the Italian theater.[45] In the century of Trissino and Rucellai a "too servile imitation of Greek masters" had been a grave obstacle to the perfection of drama. "The respect we owe to venerable antiquity and the gratitude we justly owe to the first inventors of things

1808, ed. M. A. Timpanaro Morelli (Rome: Archivi di Stato, 1976), index. I am glad to thank Maria Augusta Timpanaro, who carried out in the Florentine Archives and sent to me much of the research I used in these pages.

[43] *Istruzione di Sua Maestà Cesarea Caterina II*, dedication to Orlov, pp. ivff.

[44] Pelli, *Efemeridi*, vol. 25, F. 173, 18 April 1770.

[45] *Ragguaglio succinto della storia e dello stato del teatro tragico italiano, del signore abate Giovanni Del Turco* (Florence: Gio. Battista Stecchi and Anton-Giuseppe Pagani, 1770).

should not be obstacles to admitting what in them might be lacking."[46] In this century the "extravagances of the seventeenth century" have multiplied, and music and drama have been too closely united, thus reducing the "theaters of Italy . . . to meeting places, where [only] from time to time there is some passable air."[47] Positive, nonetheless, were the works of Apostolo Zeno, Metastasio, Maffei, Gravina, and even Conti (Conti "lacked only poetry").[48] Their work was a guarantee that in the future the wisest and best spirits of Italy might know how to renew "the divine art of enlightening, and tuning to their talent the taste of a rational and delicate audience."[49]

In December 1770 the Russian fleet returned from the Levant. "On the eighth, Doctor Del Turco, a very learned young man, librarian of the University of Pisa, went to pay his respects to Count Orlov," the consul of the king of Sardinia in Livorno wrote. "The count opened his arms and embraced him for having his company during his quarantine."[50] This made an impression: the governor of Livorno referred it to Florence and Grand-Duke Peter Leopold responded by telling the Russian admiral that he was "glad this had happened, since, with the company of the said Doctor, his stay in quarantine would be less trying."[51] Certainly his ties with Russians and with Orlov became still closer.[52] On 1 June 1771 Del Turco asked, and received, a leave of absence from his post as librarian, "having been given the opportunity to make a few months' journey in the Levant."[53] The duke evidently accepted his transformation into a kind of secretary of Aleksej Orlov.

He now entered into contact with the numerous Greek captains tied to the policy of Catherine II. An indirect, but a significant, source even attributes to him the most important political document to come out of the group which wanted the war to continue and the struggle to liberate Greece to resume. This was the "Voti dei greci all'Europa cristiana,"

---

[46] Ibid., p. vii.

[47] Ibid., p. xvii.

[48] Ibid., p. xxviii.

[49] Ibid.

[50] Turin, AS, *Materie politiche estere in genere*, mazzo 55, 1770, Livorno, 12 December 1770.

[51] Livorno, AS, Governo, *Lettere civili al governatore di Livorno*, filza 10, 15 December 1770.

[52] See Pisa, B. Universitaria, MS. 165, *Corrispondenza di Slop*, no. 39, Del Turco to Borisov with the request that this Russian commander permit Slop, "the astronomer of Pisa," to visit the Russian ships in the port of Livorno; and Florence, BN, *Autografi Gonnelli*, 39, no. 2, Del Turco to Giuseppe Benvenuto de' Venuti, Pisa, 19 August 1771, where he speaks of Orlov, "who is trying to liberate Greece from the yoke of barbarians and reestablish there that liberty that nourishes the arts and sciences."

[53] Florence, AS, *Segreteria di Stato*, 1771, 1 June, no. 1.

which was published in numbers 54 and 55 of the Florentine gazette *Notizie del mondo* on 6 and 9 July 1771 and had wide echoes in Italy, Germany, St. Petersburg, and the lands of Romania.[54]

In 1772 Del Turco was absent from Pisa.[55] He had got as far as St. Petersburg. The echoes of his impressions circulated in Florence. Pelli refers to them in his *Efemeridi* as follows: "We have a Dr. Del Turco, son of one of our surgeons, a youth of many talents, and librarian of the University of Pisa, who has accompanied one of the Arlow [*sic*] brothers to St. Petersburg and written many curious things about that land to Dr. Raimondo Cocchi, leading us to believe that that city is becoming beautiful, that Catherine is a woman who thinks of everything at once. . . . Commerce with the Russians, and travel to Moscow, is now as open as with other more cultivated lands, something that would make our ancestors marvel if they could see the present world."[56] In July Del Turco asked for an "extension of his leave, having found an opportunity to go from St. Petersburg to Walachia."[57]

In 1773 he was in the Levant, with the Russian command, and received vivid and interesting impressions that he recounted in a long letter, which he finished writing on 2 June 1773 in his "retreat at Colossilo, in the valley of Drimalia on the island of Naxos." There he found himself "in a very good state . . . on the Chesmé, with Count Alexis."[58] Ear-

---

[54] The scholar Ariadna Camariano, in her essay "Voltaire şi Giovanni del Turco traduşi in limba română pe la 1772" (Bucharest: Extras din volumul omagial C. Giurescu, 1944), pp. 175ff., cites an eighteenth-century Greek manuscript where Demetrio Razis, the copyist of the *Voti*, said they "were composed by a Florentine philo-Hellene with the first name Giovanni and the last name Delturcos when he was in the east with the Russians in the war against the Turks" and adds that the Hellenic version was the work of Eugenio Voulgaris. This completely contradicts the testimony of Antonio Gicca in 1777, one of the most ardent and capable officials in Russian service, of Albanian origin, who said he was the author of the *Voti*, a tract, he added, that was "printed in the Italian language and has been said in Italy to be an important work." There are no reasons to doubt his testimony, which Gicca made when he was considered as an adviser to the Russian embassy in Naples. See chapter 4. But the possibility of a collaboration with Del Turco should not be excluded. The attribution to Voulgaris of the translation into Greek of a text like that of the *Voti* is improbable, since it was probably written in this language. In the essay I have cited A. Camariano indicates another Romanian version of the *Voti*, put together in May 1772 with the works of Voltaire supporting the policy of Catherine II in the Levant. The manuscript with this version is in the Bucharest Accademia rumena, MS. 499. I thank my colleague Ariadna Camariano for kindly having sent me her article.

[55] For the problems this posed for the administration of the library, see Florence, AS, *Segreteria di Stato*, 1772, 7 July, No. 4, letter of Antonio Marmorai, 9 January 1772.

[56] Pelli, *Efemeridi*, vol. 29, pp. 39–40, 25 April 1772.

[57] Florence, AS, *Segreteria di Stato*, 1772, 7 July, no. 4. The extension was given "until the academic year 1773."

[58] Florence, BN, MS. 2, 197, no. 12, "copia di lettera mandata dal dr. Giovanni Del Turco ad un suo amico in Toscana." Antoine de Zuchmantel, the French ambassador in

lier he had described the situation of Constantinople in a letter that I have not succeeded in finding. He discussed a problem of particular interest to the Russians: a military attack on the capital of the Ottoman Empire. In this second letter he gave a vivid description of Smyrna, which he had visited earlier. It seemed to him a return to the Homeric world that had fascinated him when he was translating the *Iliad*. The antique visions evoked in his commentary seemed to come to life again in the reality he had before his eyes. "There is no Greek village so poor that it cannot claim to be the place where the washerwoman mother of Homer gave birth to him on this branch of the Melete: such is still the fame of that great man after three thousand years." On Chios he did not fail to remember the ancient custom of "some grammarian reciting Homer to his students, just as in Florence there had been readings of Dante for centuries, which have now changed into readings in the Tuscan tongue." He sensed that the reality around him was deeply rooted in antiquity and in the history of these lands. "The present state of Smyrna resembles Constantinople only in what is bad about it, that is, narrow streets and decaying houses keeping the light from one another. . . . Only the houses of the Franks [Europeans] are good looking, and with better materials they would be beautiful . . . if the same designs were carried out in stone or marble. The side of Smyrna occupied by the Franks would be a marvelous sight quite similar to what I imagine the most beautiful ancient cities are, or of Palmyra, as the English have laid it out."[59] He went into the surrounding countryside, observed Ottoman society, and concluded that its landholding and military organization was "quite similar to the feudal one in the time of Charlemagne." No "Asian softness!" "Great and small alike are given over to vigorous exercise. . . . Thus personal bravery and vigilance are common, like the courage created by continuous civil war." But still there was little discipline. "Their disorder when fighting in a body is such that all their bravura serves for nothing in a battle with Europeans."

It must not have been easy to return to the Pisan library after these eastern adventures.[60] The scientist and traveler J. Bernoulli described this "first librarian" in 1777 as a "very courteous and agreeable man, who has made journeys to Russia and other distant lands." Evidently Del

Florence, wrote to Versailles at the end of 1773 of the connections of "the said Turco, of the Tuscan nation, with Mocenigo, the leader of the Russian faction on the island of Cephalonia." Paris, AMAE, *Venise*, 234, F. 337, 4 December 1773.

[59] He alluded to Robert Wood, *Les ruines de Palmyre, autrement dite Tedmor au désert* (London: A. Millar, 1753).

[60] Cesare Malanima, a professor of Oriental languages, had substituted for him. Florence, AS, *Segreteria di Stato*, 1775, 28 September, no. 79, Cesare Malanima to the grand duke, 22 August 1775.

Turco had spoken to him about his foreign travels, as well as about his version of the *Iliad*.[61] But his professional efficiency was not very great. The grand duke himself thought it would be better to "recommend him for a lectureship."[62]

At the beginning of 1776 "that pathetic Abate Del Turco," as Marco Lastri called him when writing to Giulio Perini, left for Venice "without saying a word to me, as he has done with all the others, so that he is thought to have escaped from Florence for some secret motive."[63] When he returned, he fought with Angelo Fabroni, the provisor of the university, with "some insolent words." Fabroni hoped for a time that he would return "to the right path" but concluded: "The man is not ill intentioned, but extravagant, and if the library were abandoned to him it would soon become unusable."[64] At the end of 1777 Del Turco's father died, and he obtained a leave of two weeks.[65] Then he returned to his life in Pisa, to his quarrels with Angelo Fabroni, and to a life he thought was limited and vile.[66] We catch a glimpse of him again when in contact with Vittorio Alfieri, who enjoyed his company, as well as Lampredi and a few other Pisans.[67] And he continued to be in contact with "his friend Captain Panaiotti," one of the most active Greek seamen in Catherine II's service.[68]

His unsettled nature finally got him into a difficult situation in the Spain of Charles III. In October 1784 he "left from Livorno suddenly, without telling anyone where he was going." This also surprised and concerned the authorities because in the spring of that year he had somehow been involved in a series of intrigues, about the Levant and French policy on Crete, which he had reported in detailed notes to the

[61] Johannes Bernoulli, *Zusätze zu den neuesten Reisenbeschreibungen von Italien* (Leipzig: Caspar Fritsch, 1777), vol. 1, p. 320.

[62] Pietro Leopoldo di Asburgo Lorena, *Relazioni sul governo della Toscana*, vol. 2: *Stato fiorentino e pisano* (Florence: Leo S. Olschki, 1775), p. 321. And in fact, in 1775 Del Turco was appointed instructor of history and geography to the Carovana, that is, the Knights of St. Stephen. But this did not deprive him of his place in the library.

[63] Florence, AS, *Acquisti e doni*, cart. 94, ins. 120, Florence, 24 January 1776.

[64] Florence, AS, *Reggenza*, 1301, no. 44, Pisa, 17 February 1777. Here one finds a detailed and interesting official report on the situation of the library in Pisa, signed by A. Fabroni, with the same date. A thick memorial by Del Turco on the functioning of his library, summaries of regulations, and so on, are in ibid., *Reggenza*, 1052, ins. 13.

[65] Ibid., *Reggenza*, 1301, no. 66. Valentino Del Turco was buried in Ognisanti on 11 December 1777. Florence, AS, *Camere di Commercio*, reg. 188, col. 133.

[66] Ibid., *Segreteria di Stato*, 1781, prot. 45, no. 8.

[67] Vittorio Alfieri, *Epistolario*, ed. Lanfranco Caretti, vol. 1 (1767–1788) (Asti: Casa Alfieri, 1963), p. 65; letter to Enrico Gavard from Rome, 28 December 1782. There is a copy of *Virginia* with corrections by Del Turco at Asti (ibid., p. 141).

[68] Firenze, AS, *Segreteria di Stato*, 1781, prot. 45, no. 7. See the index for more on Panajotti Alessiano.

grand-duke.[69] For a while no more was heard of him. Finally, as he himself recounted to Peter Leopold, in October 1783 he had met in Livorno "the Tripolitan Turk Acmèt Coggia, named ambassador of the pasha of Tripoli in Morocco." Together they had decided to organize a complicated traffic in grain, taking advantage of the diplomatic privileges of the Tripolitan. With this prospect Del Turco had become creditor to this man for a considerable quantity of merchandise. But the ambassador had disappeared.

Departing on an English ship in an attempt to follow him to Algiers, Tangiers, and Cadiz, Del Turco did not give up the idea of "returning next November" to resume his "duties in the service of His Royal Highness of Tuscany."[70] But his adventure had hardly begun. His contact with Acmèt Coggia proved to be more interesting than "he could ever have imagined."[71] The effort to get his money back led him to Spain, where he hoped to find a court capable of defending his interests. Thus he became involved with a colony of Italians residing in Malaga and in Madrid—Vincenzo Salucci, from Livorno, Antonio Avanzini, from Genova, and Luigi Timoni, born in Constantinople—as well as the Spanish Marquis of Manca, who had made "voyages in Russia and Turkey,"[72] and was "sent with a commission to the court of St. Petersburg, and then as minister plenipotentiary to Denmark."[73] Perhaps for business reasons (these people were all involved in law cases), perhaps, from what one can guess from Del Turco's writings, for political reasons, this group of mariners, merchants, professors, and diplomats became embroiled with the minister, Count Floridablanca. Some of the most ferocious satires against him were attributed to them. The Marquis of Manca belonged to a family "called De Litala [i.e., Of Italy]," which had fought for the Empire in the War of Spanish Succession and of which one branch had emigrated to Sardinia. Old rancors and new troubles led the whole group to prison, including Del Turco. He was not even spared torture, which he described minutely in the report of his misfortunes to Peter Leopold. His imprisonment was long and hard. The authorities did

[69] Florence, AS, *Segreteria di Gabinetto*, 155, with much curious information about the Levant.

[70] Ibid., *Memoria per S.A.R.*, undated.

[71] Ibid., Dar el Beida, 1 May 1786.

[72] Ibid., "Memoria del dottor Giovanni Del Turco sopra il suo arresto, detenzione in carcere e condanna in Madrid." Florence, 10 August 1791.

[73] In this period of his life Del Turco refers to a letter by a member of the well-known Belgian family Neny to Giuseppe Antonio Slop in which they say they received him with great pleasure in Madrid. "His instructive and amusing conversation was my good cheer and consolation during an illness I had." Pisa, B. Universitaria, MS. 168, *Corrispondenza di Slop*, vol. 4, Tournay, 22 May 1788.

everything to prevent any contact of the prisoners with the imperial ambassador. In vain Del Turco energetically denied the accusations made against him, always trying to defend his rights as a Tuscan subject. He remained a prisoner for "twenty-three months, in secret, without any accusation, or any criminal condemnation, at the simple caprice of the Secretary of State and Decrees, Count Floridablanca."[74]

His conclusion, when he was finally freed in 1791, was clear and short. In Spain what ruled was not "that law that sleeps uselessly in famous voluminous codices, on which Spanish jurisprudence in imitation of Roman jurisprudence prides itself, but instead the arbitrary procedure of the ministers of justice." "Consequently it is no wonder that authors who have tried to introduce principles of eternal justice, illuminated by the irresistible light of reason, into the practice and tribunals of Europe, are not allowed in Spain. The treatise *De' delitti e delle pene*, which was translated into Castilian under the direction of the celebrated Campomanes, governor of the Supreme Council of Castile, has been prohibited with great rigor for some time, and an equal proscription has been extended in recent days to the work, honored by all Europe, of Filangieri."[75]

Who knows if he ever thought he would have experienced a similar disappointment if he had turned his gaze toward the Russia of Catherine II, which he had praised and supported with so much enthusiasm twenty years before? There, in 1791, Aleksandr Radiščev was imprisoned, condemned to death, and sent to Siberia for his *Voyage from St. Petersburg to Moscow*. What we know for certain is that, even in the service of the grand-duke, Del Turco always wanted to underline his independence and determination. His obstinate character ended up, he said, by "becoming a proverb": in Spain he was "nicknamed the 'Protestant.' "[76]

When he returned to Pisa, he recounted "various curious and interesting things" about the land where he had been in prison, "and particularly about its letters and sciences." Despite his misfortune, he was impressed by the intellectual life of Spain. "He said the physical sciences were cultivated there as much as anywhere else, as well as pleasurable literature." He insisted on the example of Camponanes and on the diffusion of Beccaria's ideas. "History, theology, and jurisprudence are cultivated infinitely more than in any other land of Europe, so that our

---

[74] On the adventures of Del Turco in Spain see F. Venturi, *Settecento Riformatore*, vol. 4: *La Caduta dell'Antico Regime (1776–1789)*, part 1, "I Grandi Stati dell'Occidente," pp. 320ff.

[75] "Memoria del dottor Giovanni Del Turco sopra il suo arresto."

[76] Ibid.

wisest jurists and theologians cannot measure up to the theologians and jurists of Spain." He was very impressed by their theater, "as much ancient as modern," adding that many "original comedies and tragedies come to light almost daily in that kingdom." He thus approved of the defense of Spanish culture by such men as Lampillas and Andrés. He made his listeners reflect on their error in not paying attention to Spanish literary works, "while we are enthusiastic to the extent of obsequious pedantry about works of others that came from beyond the Alps," Domenico Anguillesi concluded after conversing with Del Turco.[77]

He had returned to Pisa. The "room situated in the observatory connected to the library," where he had lived earlier, was now occupied "in service" of the library, and they gave him another room.[78] He intended to resume work, but soon in Madrid the authorities declared they were ready to reopen his trial, and he asked for a new leave "to support his case." Respectfully, but energetically, he tried to obtain the support of Grand Duke Ferdinando III.[79] In February 1794 he was in the Spanish capital for the "case he and his other associates have brought against Count Floridablanca." He even thought, while awaiting the conclusion of his trial, of taking "a trip to Morocco, because of the suggestion of a subject of his acquaintance in that land . . . , who, through a privileged place near the person of the present sultan, has obtained an invitation for him to go there, and a general assurance of privileges in commerce, particularly in the grain trade."[80]

In the summer of 1794 Giovanni Del Turco's brother, Pietro, a doctor of sacred theology and chaplain of the court of Peter Leopold and after, said that he was still in Morocco and asked for assistance in collecting his stipend (in Pisa Cesare Malanima continued to substitute for him at the university).[81] In the end he probably settled in Africa. In 1799, the Order of St. Stephen requested, due to Del Turco's long absence, that the "quarter in the Orivolo Palace be assigned to someone else." The "history master of the Carovana" had occupied it long ago, and it served "from time to time as the summer lodgings of someone from Livorno."[82] In April 1800 the authorities noted the irregular "service of the nominal lector, who since 1775 has hardly been here contin-

---

[77] *L'Epistolario, ossia scelta di lettere inedite*, year 2, Venice, 1796, 39, 5 October 1796, pp. 310ff. C. Domenico Anguillesi to de Coureil, Pisa, 8 July 1791.

[78] Florence, AS, *Segreteria di Stato*, 1792, prot. 1, no. 54.

[79] Ibid., 1792, prot. 34, no. 26, with a detailed and an interesting letter from Florence of 21 August 1792.

[80] Ibid., *Reggenza*, 1040, fasc. for 1794, no. 1, Madrid, 17 February 1794.

[81] Ibid., *Segreteria di Stato*, 1794, prot. 25, no. 6. The response is dated 4 July.

[82] Ibid., *Segreteria di Stato*, 1799, prot. 4, no. 9, 20 August.

uously for two years together."[83] The regime changed in Tuscany, but the problem of Del Turco's absence continued. The provisional government was preoccupied with it in 1801.[84] Finally, in October of that year, Cesare Malanima received a raise of forty scudi for his work in the library of Pisa.[85] By then Del Turco was dead, but we do not know exactly the time of his death or the place. His life probably ended in Morocco at the dawn of the new century.

We have followed to the end the career of a man, who in these years was undoubtedly the most sensitive and intelligent link between the Russian world and Tuscan culture. But it is time to return to Livorno in the months when it served as Catherine II's base of action in the Mediterranean. From Livorno, Marco Coltellini, that noted writer and printer with whom Del Turco had planned to organize his "Atti letterari," left for St. Petersburg. "Under the sign of truth," he had been, from 1762, the editor of Algarotti, of the *Gazzettiere americano*, and of Pietro Verri. At the beginning of 1764, he gave over his bookshop to Giuseppe Aubert.[1] He became at first court poet in Vienna, succeeding Metastasio, and then went on to Russia. In Italy he had written a number of dramas, which had philosophical undertones. In Russia, in April 1768, for "the anniversary of the birth of Her Imperial Majesty Catherine II," his musical drama *Ifigenia in Tauride* was recited, and it was published in St. Petersburg the same year in the original Italian, in French, and in Russian.[2] Other performances followed in the next ten years, with music by Salieri, Galuppi, and Paisiello.[3] The thought of ornamenting the new political and military glory of Catherine II with Italian verse and music was certainly not unexpected, and there were other sonnets and songs praising the empress.[4]

[83] Ibid., 1800, prot. 35, no. 17, 11 April.
[84] Ibid., 1801, prot. 40, no. 30, 13 and 27 June.
[85] Ibid., 1801, prot. 85, no. 4, 22 October.

[1] Lay, *Un editore illuminista*, index. On Coltellini see Edizione nazionale delle opere di Cesare Beccaria, vol. 1, pp. 389ff.

[2] Von Bilbassoff, *Katharina II*, vol. 1, p. 105 n. 112.

[3] See the list of the Russian version of these dramas in *Svodnyj katalog russkoj knigi . . . XVIII veka*, vol. 2 (Moscow, 1964), pp. 55 nn. 3048–55.

[4] See, for example, Michelangelo Giannetti, *Alla sacra imperiale maestà di Caterina II* (Lucca, 1770); and Paolina Suardo Grismondi, *A Caterina II imperatrice di tutte le Russie* (Parma: Giambattista Bodoni, [1774]). We read from the latter: "Un'altra Roma io veggio / risorta in Pietroburgo, un'altra Atene / . . . / Mi si affaccia al pensiero l'altera imago / del tuo grand'avo, che a destriero ardente / il dorso preme e che dal volto spira / e prudenza e valor." ("I see another Rome / arisen in St. Petersburg, another Athens / . . . / The thought and high image comes to me / of your great ancestor on a bright charger / his back raised and from his face breathing / prudence and valor.")

Even the active propaganda put out by Voltaire in favor of Catherine II had some influence in Tuscany. In Florence, Giuseppe Pelli, at the end of 1770, read with great curiosity a work that was presented as "the French translation of a German poem by M. Plokof, Councilor of Holstein, on the present Muscovite war." In reality it was Voltaire's work, an appeal to princes and Christian republics to support Russia in its war with the Turks.[5] "We will perhaps not find again such a good chance to push the plunderers of the world back into their ancient bog," the philosopher had written, to urge on a war that had nothing to do with a crusade but instead anticipated the partitioning of the Ottoman Empire.[6] The lion of St. Mark seemed ready to put itself in motion. "The land of Themistocles and Miltiades shakes its chains in seeing the distant flight of the eagle of Catherine, but still it cannot break them. What? Is there in Europe only a small neglected folk, a handful of Montenegrins, an anthill, that dares follow the path this triumphant eagle shows us high up in its imperial flight?" It was an aggrieved appeal, which ended on a tone of ironic skepticism, almost of delusion. "Thus speaks ... a citizen in love with great things. He detests the Turks, the enemies of all arts; he deplores the fate of Greece; he grieves for Poland, which tears its entrails with its own hands rather than uniting behind the wisest and most enlightened of kings. He sings in German verse; but the Greeks know nothing of it, and the Polish confederates do not listen."[7] Giuseppe Pelli thought of translating it. "I wanted it to be done in Italian, but the difficulty of succeeding made me give up." The echo of Voltaire, even in Tuscany, remained in its French text, which must have circulated widely, although it is not always easy to follow its traces.

More original was the effort to make Russian literature known to those who had been impressed by Orlov's naval undertakings. In 1771 a work entitled *Essai sur la littérature russe contenant une liste de gens de lettres russes qui se sont distingués depuis le règne de Pierre le Grand* was published at Livorno. The identity of the author has been much discussed. But the translator is certain: Dominick von Blackford, a journalist active in making known political and literary novelties on both sides of the Alps. In contact with Domenico Caminer in Venice, and with Pelli in Florence, he succeeded in circulating the first literary history of Russia

---

[5] Pelli, *Efemeridi*, vol. 26, p. 184, 1 December 1770. The "Traduction du poème de Jean Plokof, conseiller de Holstein sur les affaires présentes," was already in circulation in June. It is published in *Oeuvres complètes de Voltaire*, ed. L. Moland (Paris: Garnier, 1879), vol. 28, pp. 365ff.

[6] "Traduction du poème," pp. 366–67.

[7] Ibid., p. 368.

to appear in Italy.[8] It had notable success. The Florentine *Novelle lette-rarie* wrote, "in this little book is a succinct account of forty-two writers, for the most part still living, who have brought to light something of their own or made translations from French." The picture of the past was a good indication of the future. "On this basis Muscovy in a short time will not bow to other nations, if it profits from so much encourage-ment from Catherine." It expressed the hope that the author might bring out, as he promised, a history of the Russian theater as well. "Everything about this glorious empire currently interests the curious public."[9]

But the *Notizie letterarie*, also published in Florence, was more skep-tical. The list of forty-two writers listed in the *Essai* did not arouse the enthusiasm of the editors of this periodical. "Truly up to now the sci-ences do not seem to have taken much root in that vast empire; it may be that the indefatigable vigilance of that empress will contribute much to make them flower in the future; in fact, she seems to regard writers with much distinction."[10] But the welcome in Venice and in other Italian centers was very good. *L'Europa letteraria* wrote the following in August: "It was good to know, at the same time that the rapid progress in Rus-sian arms demonstrated to Europe how much their nation had ad-vanced in military affairs, that we should also be informed of its prog-ress in literature."[11] In Rome the *Efemeridi letterarie* reviewed the *Essai*, remarking, "The Russian name, which is now on the lips of all Europe, begins to make itself known with distinction in letters."[12] Noting the names of Feofan Prokopovič, Tredjakovskij, Lomonosov, Sumarokov, and so on, the Milanese *Gazzetta letteraria* continued: "Muscovy, as all know, up to the time of the celebrated czar Peter, lived in rough barba-

[8] Pavel N. Berkov, "Dominik Blekford i russkaja literatura," *Naučnyj bjulleten' lenin-gradskogo Universiteta* (Scientific bulletin of the University of Leningrad), no. 8 (1946); F. Venturi, "Qui est le traducteur de l'Essai sur la littérature russe?" *Revue des études slaves*, vol. 38, 196: *Mélanges Pierre Pascal*, pp. 217ff.; and B. F. Martynov, "Opyt istoričeskogo slovarja o rossijskich pisateljach N. I. Novikova" (For a historical dictionary of Russian writers by N. I. Novikov), in *Russkaja literatura* (Russian literature), 1966, fasc. 3, pp. 184ff. On the relationship with Domenico Caminer, see *L'Europa letteraria*, August 1771, pp. 72ff., and with Pelli, *Lettere a Giuseppe Pelli Bencivenni*, index. Blackford wrote to his cor-respondent from Pisa in May and June 1771 (nos. 3799 and 3840), when he was in that city to edit the *Essai*, then he returned, through Parma, to Zweibrücken, a noted center of publicists (no. 3158). The following year we find him in Prague (no. 4098), in Nuremberg (no. 4188), and in Erlangen (no. 4236). In November 1773 he returned to Zweibrücken (no. 4571). This is a typical itinerary of this cosmopolitan journalist.

[9] *Novelle letterarie*, vol. 2, 1771, col. 316.

[10] *Notizie letterarie*, no. 42, 19 October 1771, col. 659.

[11] *L'Europa letteraria*, August 1771, pp. 72ff.

[12] *Le Efemeridi letterarie*, 1772, p. 364.

rism, and its peoples considered themselves the most uncultivated and savage of Europe. Peter was the first to introduce arts and sciences among them. . . . Russian literature is rapidly growing and has acquired much fame among the cultivated nations of Europe."[13]

The diffusion and discussion of Russian matters in Tuscany passed above all through the periodical press. The tone was not only attentive, but also generally well disposed toward the policy of Catherine II. The French representative in Florence complained continually of this. During the struggle in the Morea the presentation of facts in the columns of the *Notizie del mondo* appeared to Du Trouillet "all in favor of the Russians."[14] Information arrived slowly and in a contradictory way, and there were many uncertainties, as we have seen, even in this gazette. But the general direction of the Tuscan press is not in doubt. It is to be seen on the day when news came of the victory at Chesmé. A special sheet was published—*Narration of the last two battles between the Ottoman and Russian fleets that occurred on 18 and 31 July 1770*—where one read: "With what interest the public has always received news of encounters in the Morea between the Muscovite and Ottoman fleets, even when they could not be sure they were genuine."[15] Now there was finally news as certain as it was pleasing.

For all the years of the war the *Notizie del mondo* accompanied its military bulletins with a series of reports on Russia's internal life. This was not always pleasant news. Instead, as we will see, this period ended for Florentine journals, like those throughout Italy, with the echoes of Pugačev's terrible revolt. But before that, in the autumn of 1771, an epidemic in Moscow had been accompanied by serious disturbances. These were not concealed by the press, but their reactionary origins were emphasized, as was Catherine II's generous policy to control them. Dated 18 October 1771 the Florentine paper announced from St. Petersburg that in "Moscow disorder has entirely ceased, and the epidemic of malignant fevers is notably diminished. None of the mutineers was even punished, although it has been recognized that the instigation of clerics, and a misunderstood devotion, led to the murder of the archbishop and the uprising."[16]

[13] *Gazzetta letteraria*, 3 February 1773, p. 33.

[14] AMAE, *Toscane*, 132, 27 April 1770, F. 67.

[15] A copy of this four-page sheet is in ibid., *Toscane*, 133, F. 164.

[16] *Notizie del mondo*, no. 95, 26 November 1771, p. 732 (St. Petersburg, 18 October). In no. 93, 18 November 1771, p. 715 (St. Petersburg, 11 October), there was a first summary description of this "revolution." In no. 97, on 3 December, p. 751 (Livorno, 29 November), there was "a true account of the uprising," and it was concluded that "the people of Moscow have given a demonstration as displeasing for us as it is miserable for humanity in

With this support the repeated news of celebrations for Russian successes in the Mediterranean and on the Danube resounded all the more. A great ball was organized for the victory of Chesmé, with Argonauts, Christian slaves, Peter I, Minerva, Jason, and the genius of Russia.[17] In the autumn of 1772 another festivity saw the empress take an enemy standard and carry it to the grave of Peter, "the creator of our fleet and founder of this vast empire. Whereas before this hero was hardly known in Europe, now he equals the greatest powers and even arouses their jealousy."[18]

In the winter of 1772–1773 a large part of Europe was struck with serious famine. Tuscans were particularly attentive to the reaction of the government and public opinion in Russia to this scourge. The *Notizie del mondo* spoke at length of the inquiries undertaken by the Economic Society, referring to the principal theses published in its journal and underlining the fact that "the deputation" of this society "was the one in the recent famine to courageously oppose the Senate in urging Her Imperial Majesty to permit free export of grain, with which many provinces of Russia are well furnished, without success." Free export was finally granted through Arkhangel'sk. Around this port, "for a great distance nothing grows at all, but still this city saved Germany and Holland." "Free export has made the fortune of many Russian provinces, where grain was abundant and could be shipped through the port."[19] An unexpected news report from Hamburg shortly before confirmed the image of Catherine and her liberal policy of 1772–1773 as the salvation of Europe. "A work published here is singular for several reasons," read the *Notizie del mondo* of 16 February 1773. "This is a letter written by the Printers' Society of this city to the Order of Freemasons and the Economic and Literary Society." The first was urged to "rebuild the temple of Solomon, understood in the idea of personal enlightenment," the other to turn attention toward philosophy based on experience. The author ended the letter with a fervent wish to see erected a statue of Catherine II, the autocrat of all Russia, for which it furnished the following inscription:

general. The people are the people everywhere." "The further news we have from that city is that the people are most repentant of what they have done and seem to look with horror at what enthusiasm made them do."

[17] Ibid., no. 93, 20 November 1770, p. 756 (St. Petersburg, 12 October). The description fills two pages of the journal.

[18] Ibid., no. 84, 24 October 1772, p. 697 (St. Petersburg, 15 September).

[19] Ibid., no. 16, 23 February 1773, p. 123 (St. Petersburg, 16 January 1773). On the problems of the Economic Society, see Michael Confino, *Domaines et seigneurs en Russie vers la fin du XVIIIe siècle* (Paris: Institut des études slaves), 1963.

Caterinae
Piae, Augustae, Felici
Ob Lusitanos, Hispanos, Italos, Brittanos,
Germanos, Gallos, Suecos, Danos a Fame
Europam bis Asiam semel a Bello

Utramque a Peste
Sarmatos, Graecos, ipsumque Commercium
a Servitute ipsoque Metu Servitutis
Heroice defensos

L. N. Q. P. C.
Fautores Commercii.[20]

One year later the Florentine gazette concluded the following: "The commerce of this empire has changed remarkably during the reign of the august Catherine II. The grain trade was made free from Arkhangel'sk at all times for foreign export, and in years of good harvest it was freed in all ports of the empire. The crown has entirely withdrawn from trade in rutabagas, potassium, and leather, in favor of individuals. . . . All monopolies and exclusive privileges for factories and mills for refining sugar have been suppressed, and all are permitted to erect factories of their own to produce raw materials of raw and dyed silk, cotton, wool, and thread, on the condition that the work is to be of better quality than what was done in the country before." "The Free Economic Society contributed to obtaining these new regulations."[21]

Thus, in the famine of 1772–1773, the export of grain from Russia began to weigh into the European situation, and it was destined to increase very rapidly, as is known, in the following decades. Under the standard of free trade, and through the work of intellectuals and Freemasons, came the first symptoms of an economic phenomenon of great importance: the development of Russian foreign commerce. The end of the war and the victory made the importance of this fact even clearer. While the problems leading to the American Revolution made trade in the Atlantic more precarious, Russia saw the way to the Mediterranean open in front of it. "This opens the way of Russia to Italy and the Levant," wrote the *Nuove di diverse corti e paesi*. "The best hopes of this power

---

[20] "Merchants dedicate this to the pious, august, and prosperous Catherine for heroically defending the Portuguese, Spaniards, Italians, British, Germans, French, Swedes, and Danes from famine; [for defending] Europe and Asia from war; and plague; [and for defending] the Poles, Greeks, and their commerce itself from slavery and fear of slavery." *Notizie del mondo*, no. 14, 16 February 1773, p. 109 (Hamburg, 27 January 1773). On Hamburg intellectual circles in these years, see *Gelehrte in Hamburg im 18. und 19. Jahrhundert*, ed. Hans Dieter Loose (Hamburg: Hans Christians Verlag, 1976).

[21] Ibid., no. 15, 19 February 1774, p. 114 (St. Petersburg, 10 January). See *Gazzetta Universale*, no. 28, 5 April 1774, p. 224.

are founded on the outlet of the Black Sea." "There two great rivers, the Dnieper and the Don, carry all the products of the Russian Empire."[22] Far away were hopes for the liberation of Greece. At the beginning of 1775 a Russian consul came to Coron in the Morea, the first port where the fleet of Orlov landed in 1770, "to establish an office for the commerce of his nation." Experience, though, was not lost. "This office will be put in a state of defense against the possible actions of thieves, of whom there is a large number in this province, and against those of the pasha, who is often more dangerous than the thieves themselves."[23] In a few years southern Russia would be open not only to Italian trade, but also to Italian emigration. The gazette of Leiden already spoke of this in 1783, giving notice of "Italian colonists going to Kherson, a newly constructed Russian city on the Black Sea."[24]

Information even multiplied, in the last period of the Russo-Turkish war, about the agrarian policy of Catherine II, which was an object of increasing interest for Tuscans. We read in the *Notizie del Mondo* at the end of 1773 that the Free Economic Society continued to receive assistance and support from the empress.[25] In the summer of 1774 the same gazette referred to the effects reformist ideas would inevitably have on the condition of Russian peasants. "The empress has had an ordinance published to aid the peasants. It is said in the preamble 'that arts and commerce cannot survive in this land if agriculture is neglected; agriculture cannot progress where peasants do not own anything themselves, since no one would interest himself with passion in something that does not belong to him and could be taken away at any moment.' "[26]

And this greater liberty did not refer only to peasants and merchants. In the 6 September 1774 issue of the *Notizie del mondo* there appeared the remarkable news that "Her Majesty the empress of all of Russia has thought proper to permit freedom of the press in the city of Oberpahien in Estonia, where there is a fine press not subject to any

[22] *Nuove di diverse corti e paesi*, no. 4, 27 January 1777 (The Hague, 8 January). The *Notizie del mondo*, no. 67, 23 August 1777, p. 534, gave news of the first Russian ship to reach Taganrog from northern Europe passing through Constantinople. The same journal, no. 80, 5 October 1776, p. 614 (St. Petersburg, 6 August), had examined at length the commercial propects of the traffic across the Black Sea.

[23] *Nuove di diverse corti e paesi*, 19 February 1776, p. 59 (Coron in the Morea, 1 December 1775).

[24] *Nouvelles extraordinaires de divers endroits*, no. 50, 24 June 1783 (Livorno, 4 June).

[25] *Notizie del mondo*, no. 101, 18 December 1773, p. 818 (St. Petersburg, 4 November). "They have already published important memoirs, which have been well received by Her Majesty the Empress, who deigned to write a letter to that society in which she approves and praises their proposed plan and provides funds for the enlargement of an economics library."

[26] Ibid., no. 70, 30 August 1774, p. 555 (St. Petersburg, 22 July).

censorship."[27] This information was part of a regular campaign to persuade readers that Catherine was favorable to freedom of the press. When the prince was "wicked," despotism was "jealous." But "in the hands of Catherine sovereign power is only the laws." "The sad consequences" that might result from "the vague category of crimes of *lese majesty*" were well known. The empress of Russia knew that words "were not crimes, but only indications of crimes." "Her Imperial Majesty does not want a rigid and scrupulous examination of books that might contain something against the government," convinced as she was that "such investigations weaken the spirit, which remains inactive when constrained and submitted to certain bounds. . . . This new policy replaces the ignorance that suppresses talent and extinguishes the will to write." These considerations were all the more significant because at this time the Pugačev revolt had hardly ended. Certainly, it was right to condemn him to death. But "if a seditious book had been written for the expressed purpose of rousing the people and had an effect, he would have merited a less serious punishment, because his crime would have been less serious. Some evil-minded individuals use words spoken by chance, and equivocal phrases, to accuse people of high treason. Thus the hands of justice are stained with the blood of innocents, as has happened in this empire and in other places as well."[28]

For Tuscan readers interested in what was happening in the empire of Catherine II, the central problem at the beginning of the seventies still seemed the growth and transformation of Russia, a historical prodigy on which many continued to focus their attention. Announcing the birth of a Muscovite journal, of which two issues had appeared in 1773 with a series of documents on the Russian past, the *Novelle letterarie* expressed the hope that "the continuation of this journal will be translated into a common European language," and added: "Who would predict that the Medicean heroes who recovered the sciences of Greece would see them established three centuries later on the Gulf of Finland?"[29] Even the Tuscan edition of the *Vita* of Marshal Münnich written by the celebrated German geographer and polygraph A. F. Büsching, which C. G. Iagemann translated "to illustrate the modern history of the Russian Empire," responded to the general interest in knowing more detail about the recent past.[30] The translation was official and was dedicated

---

[27] Ibid., no. 72, 6 September 1774, p. 572 (Revel, 10 August).

[28] Ibid., No. 54, 5 July 1774, p. 427 (St. Petersburg, 27 May).

[29] *Novelle letterarie*, 1773, col. 463.

[30] *Vita del conte Burcardo Cristofano di Münnich general feld-maresciallo delle truppe russe, scritta da Antonio Federico Büsching, consigliere del Concistoro supremo del re di Prussia e direttore del Collegio illustre di Berlino*, tradotta dall'abate Cristiano Giuseppe Iagemann, confessore della Corte reale di Toscana, che può servire per illustrare la storia moderna dell'impero

to A. Orlov. The "motive" was "the desire to make known to Italians events and undertakings of the valorous and powerful Russian nation against the Turks and Tartars under the command of Field Marshal Count Münnich." "The intrepid valor of Russians in battle, and their singular patience in withstanding fatigue, their sober existence when rations run short, and finally their ability to undertake any kind of hard task and carry it out perfectly" were emphasized.[31] With even more warmth, and in the name of the "illustrious Tuscan nation," the author exhorted "Count Alexis Orlov" to complete the "great work" he had undertaken, adding, "that end most suited to the true utility of the human race."[32] The political picture presented in this work is truly worth considering.[33] The career of a German technician like Münnich had been difficult in the period from the last years of Peter the Great to the beginning of the reign of Catherine II. There were internal struggles among generals and courtiers, intrigues and betrayals, unexpected arrests, and sentences to be drawn and quartered and finally commuted to long exile in Siberia. But what extraordinary satisfactions! To be able to transform the whole water system connecting Lake Ladoga and the sea by way of the Neva. To be put at the head of an army that, through a thousand difficulties, would sack the capital of the Tartars in the Crimea and seize Očakow, the principal Turkish fortress on the shores of the Black Sea. Unheard-of sufferings were experienced in these undertakings (and Büsching did not try to hide the cruelty, violence, and terrible wrath of Münnich). Such efforts had little political outcome, without decisive victories or substantial annexations. But something emerged: an army and a country. "In the Russian army there are no

delle Russie (Florence: Gaetano Cambiagi, 1773). The dedication is dated 20 December 1772. On the author of this version, see Maria Teresa dal Monte, *Christian Joseph Jagemann. Un italianista del Settecento in Germania* (Imola: Quaderno dell'Istituto di filologia germanica dell'Università di Bologna, Galeati, 1970).

[31] Büsching, *Vita*, pp. 3ff.

[32] Ibid., pp. 5ff.

[33] The Venetian *Storia della guerra presente* had already understood the exemplary value of Münnich's career and published in an appendix to volume 4 a *Compendio della vita del celebre maresciallo Münnich*. It even remembered his project to take up the policy of Peter the Great for the liberation of the Orthodox under the Turkish yoke. See Francis Ley, *Le maréchal de Münnich et la Russie au XVIIIe siècle* (Paris: Plon, 1959), pp. 118, 244, where it is noted that the projects of Münnich were known in Europe thanks to what Algarotti had written in his *Saggio di lettere sopra la Russia*. In the second edition, which appeared in Paris, from Briasson, in 1765, one read on page 131 that "the great design of the Russian genius" consisted in "conquering the Crimea, the chief granary of Constantinople" and, "if fortune does not turn her face, who knows? It might be possible to divest the Turks of Europe and of the seat of the Greek empire, since they look to the czar as their leader and turn their souls to him, inviting him, calling him, and asking to enlist under his banner."

desertions."[34] This was a passing observation, but no eighteenth-century reader would have failed to make a comparison with the armies of other countries, always in a state of flux with desertions, pardons, returns, and new desertions of soldiers. Büsching explained the reason for this difference. The Russians had as enemies peoples with different religions and customs. The problem of frontiers was fundamental in the military and political life of Russia. Religious prejudices dominated the army of the czar. "Almost three quarters of the year Russians have to abstain from eating fat, and the superstition of the people is so great that if the synod did not give a dispensation while the army is on campaign, few would serve in it, and the others would more readily die than contaminate themselves with eating meat." The resistance of the troops was exceptional. "Common soldiers are used to sleeping on the ground without using straw, or any other cover or tent." To be sure, even they got sick.[35] "It was usual for one-third of the troops to die of disease." But still they went on fighting, even in the most unfavorable conditions. This phenomenon was only partly explained by the severity of the circumstances. The extraordinary mobility of those whom Iagemann called the "Cossacks of the Don," the reputed willingness of commanders and soldiers to correct mistakes, to put behind them sorrows and losses of the previous day and return to action, had resulted in a series of victories, partial but significant. And their commander in chief was equally constant. When Peter III ascended the throne, Münnich, then an eighty-year-old man, returned from Siberia after twenty years of exile. He still had faith in the deep hidden force of Russia. "God has given to Your Imperial Majesty," he said to the czar, "an empire of which the confines have not even been measured and a people whose numbers have never been counted, who for many reasons merits preference over all the other nations of Europe." He was persuaded of this by, among other things, "the great work for the canal of Ladoga," and on campaign "in the deserts when water and provisions were lacking." "Where else would one find a people who would dare cross the whole of Europe without food, or the widest rivers without bridges? Who would eat the flesh of horses, drink their blood, or dine on wild apples and other such things, as Cossacks of the Don and Kalmucks do? They live without houses in huts, they neither sow nor reap grain, they do not make hay, are not used to eating bread, and nonetheless are the most fastidious soldiers, observing every detail of military discipline, and so vigilant that they cannot be surprised in the field or on the march."[36] The fact that Büsch-

---

[34] Büsching, *Vita*, p. 147.
[35] Ibid., p. 148.
[36] Ibid., pp. 269ff.

ing put only a thin veil over the incapacity of St. Petersburg to make use of such human capital and did not hide the internal dissent that had paralyzed the government of Russia made the reader think of the future and of the possibilities that Russia might offer if a ruler appeared who was capable of carrying out what Münnich had proposed to Peter III. More and more, Catherine II appeared to be the answer to the historical problems of Russia.

These were distant visions, arousing hopes that made even more acute the problems evoked and left in suspension by the intervention of the Russian fleet: the fate of Greece. Expectations remained alive in Tuscany. Although, as we have seen, the Venetian press was anything but favorable to the Greek movement, the Tuscan press, along with that of Naples, was openly philo-Hellenic. The reason is clear. The Republic of St. Mark was threatened directly in the Ionian Islands and in its commercial relations. In Florence, Pisa, and Livorno new horizons were opening toward the Levant. The presence of the Russian fleet made the problems of the Greek mainland and the Archipelago seem closer and more vivid.

The *Notizie del mondo* in 1771 reflected not only the aspirations of numerous active captains from the Archipelago, but perhaps those of some of the Russian officers as well. The columns of the Florentine journal published the most important philo-Hellenic appeal not only of Italy, but of all of Europe, which was destined to echo well beyond Tuscany. In number 54 (6 July 1771) one read "from the Archipelago, 25 May": "The following *Voti* were collected from the Greek nation of this place, which we present to the public translated into Italian." And in two installments the journal published these "Voti all'Europa Cristina": "The happy times of ancient Greece," the free governments that flourished there, "when our progenitors governed their free homelands," "the upright administration of justice," "the dexterity at arms," "the knowledge of science and the fine and useful arts, and above all the universal exercise of every public and private virtue" constituted the distant shining base on which lay the broken wreck of the Greek peoples, now forced to live under the Ottoman yoke "without laws to protect them; the vile instruments of their rulers." Nonetheless the land and the people were not changed. "The same religious persecution that separates Turks from all other peoples had the singular effect of keeping their ancient lineage pure among the Greeks." It was thus not surprising that in the 318 years since the fall of Constantinople, Greeks had not been able "to accustom themselves to servitude" and had tried continually "to break their fetters, either to regain their liberty, or at least to live in peace under the moderate government of some Christian prince." It was no wonder, given the situation in which they found themselves, that "the arts and sciences were little known" among them. This was the natural consequence of a "barbarous government under which knowledge is useless or dangerous." "It is surprising instead, in such a calamitous situation, that so many Greeks find themselves scattered in so many European universities to do their studies." The arts and commerce of the Greeks support the Turks. "And if any find it strange that among a people kept in slavery for three centuries there should not be some who are infected with the vices of servitude, we ask them to remember that any active virtue is a crime for men living in such conditions." When "sincerity and courage, through a badly constituted government, make men unhappy," nothing remains but to invoke the work of "a wise legislator" capable of changing the situation. "In the practice of virtue and in the public good that will result, all citizens will recover their private happiness." "The courageous virtues"—"and among these particularly that generosity with which men, setting aside all private advantage," sacrifice everything "to support religion and the good of their fatherland: . . . possessions, kin, their dear children, and their own lives"—were not spent or even "extinguished in the hearts" of Greeks, as they had demonstrated every time "Christian princes" took the initiative of fighting against the Ottomans. "The Venetians should acknowledge all the blood shed in the conquest of the Morea," as well as in the "long and costly siege of Candia." From the sixteenth century to its last encounters in 1737, "the glorious house of Austria" had the Greeks at its side. But there was no time now for memories and regrets. The important thing was for everyone to be aware of the condition in which the Greeks found themselves. "It is not to glorify ourselves that we recall what we were, what we are, and what we might be, but rather not to be abandoned by our Christian brothers in the fatal situation that has overcome us." They no longer had even a choice between "apostasy and slavery." Now they had to choose between "apostasy and destruction," with "all the horrible tortures these barbarians employ in human slaughter." In the past they had looked to Venice and Vienna; now they were tied to "the unconquered heroine who rules over Russia, and who with wise measures and a humane and prudent legislation establishes the eternal happiness of so many peoples among her subjects." "The rapidity and greatness of her victories, and the abasement of the tyrant over us, made us think the moment of our liberation had come." Thus they would "be able to live with their own laws, and Greece, through its well-employed liberty, would in a few years be restored to its ancient splendor." In contrast, the example of the Morea showed what would happen if the Turks returned to be rulers of those lands. The massacres in Smyrna after the battle of Chesmé and other similar episodes confirmed what the Greeks had to expect. "Our total extermination is the least ill that could afflict us. But we fear still more for the weak who will not be able to resist their nefarious pressure, and abandoning Christ, will prefer their present lives to their eternal salvation." There could be no illusions: no pact or intervention would contain the "military license" of the Turks. They now saw in the Greeks "a domestic enemy that must absolutely be crushed." "The Turks have discovered that between us and the Russians communication is greater and better ordered than with any other Christian nation." Only through a massacre would the Turks be able to avoid being "trapped in a peril as great as they have judged themselves to have risked in this war."[1] Would the "principle of European equlibrium" permit such massacres or push into apostasy millions of Christians? One should not forget that "fierce janissaries among our brothers were once Christians, like the Albanian Turks and the Bosnians, whose valor is much praised." The Turks had used Christians to improve their military situation. Were not the engineers and technicians who fortified the Dardanelles Christians? Had not the French (who are not named but are clearly implied) reached the point of obstructing the Russians, and thus stopping "the arm that seemed guided by providence" from obtaining the liberation of Greece? Was this where "raison d'état" had led? One should not forget that there could be no true peace between Christians and Turks. These were always moved only by the "immutable principle of destroying or converting, or at least reducing to slavery." "For our part, poor Greeks," we read in conclusion, "we only ask the Christians whether they want, in opposing our liberation, to sacrifice millions of innocents to certain and rapid extermination and thus put themselves in peril of suffering a similar fate. In sum, the only grace we ask of our Christian brothers is their simple consent to not let us perish. These are the wishes humbly sent to you, at the moment before our end, by the unhappy nation of Greeks."[2]

The author of these *Voti* was Antonio Gicca, an official from Epirus in the service of Russia, whom we will find again at the center of the group of philo-Hellenes in Naples and who was close to Giovanni Del Turco in 1773 during his stay at the "port of Chesmé."[3] His appeal was

---

[1] "Voti dei greci all'Europa cristiana," *Notizie del mondo*, no. 54, 6 July 1771, pp. 426ff.

[2] Ibid., no. 55, 9 July 1771, pp. 436ff. The complete Greek text of the *Voti*, printed on a broadside, is reproduced in Filippos I. Ilios, "Prosthikes stin Elleniki bibliographia" (Additions to the bibliography of Greece), in *Diogenis* (Athens, 1973), pp. 290ff. The text is attributed to Del Turco and the Greek version to Eugenios Voulgaris. This is an error demonstrated by the documents on Gicca (see below) and from what one reads in the *Notizie del mondo*.

[3] "Copia di lettera mandata dal dr. Giovanni Del Turco." "In this port on the *Chesmé*

not directed to Europeans alone. It carried as well an exhortation to the empress and to Russians to carry forward their action against the Turks in favor of Greece. Certainly it had echoes in Russia, where one version was published on 8 August 1771, in number 65 of the *Sanktpeterburgskija vedomosti* (News of St. Petersburg). In the same summer the *Voti* were translated into French and appeared in the *Courrier du Bas-Rhin*, a gazette published in Cleves, in Prussian territory, and one of the most influential political journals of the time.[4] Aleksandr Radiščev, a Russian student sent by Catherine II with a group of young men to the University of Leipzig, was struck by the text. He must have heard talk, in 1768, three years before, of the empress' great Mediterranean projects from the mouth of Aleksej Orlov himself, who had passed through Leipzig in his first voyage from Russia to Italy and had passionately discussed the philosophy of Helvétius with these Russian students in Germany. Now Radiščev took stock of the consequences and difficulties of this policy. The Russians were victorious in the Levant, but the Greeks were still under the Turks. Clearly interested, Radiščev took to translating the text of Gicca but did not complete his version (in October he returned home). The fragment remained among the papers of the man destined to become the first *intelligent* revolutionary of his country and was published only much later after his death.[5]

The relationships among Russians, Greeks, and Tuscans continued to develop in the last years of the war. Perhaps the most interesting episode, which deserves to be studied more closely, was the attempt to create a school for Greek exiles in Pisa, and precisely for those who had taken refuge from the Peloponnesus on the Ionian Islands after the retreat of 1770. The *Notizie del mondo* dated 23 October 1773 reported that

where I find myself with Count Alessio I have received your welcome [letter] of 27 December, including [the one] to Signor Antonio Gicca, who is on the same ship."

[4] *Courrier du Bas-Rhin*, no. 58, 20 July 1771, p. 463, "Cleves, 20 July. We have received from the Archipelago, by way of Italy, a piece that circumstances make very curious and very important." The text was published in its entirety in ensuing issues. On the editor of this journal, Jean Manzon, a Piedmontese, see Franco Venturi, "L'Italia fuori d'Italia," in *Storia d'Italia*, vol. 3: *Dal primo Settecento all'unità* (Turin: Einaudi, 1973), p. 1047. Further on him see the dispatch from Warsaw from the nuncio Durini, on 27 April 1771: "That journalist, up to now entirely sold to the Russian party, now begins to sing his cursed recantation, even if he still cannot resist some foolish flattery of the empress." Agostino Theiner, *Vetera monumenta Poloniae et Lituaniae gentiumque finitimarum historia illustrata* (Rome: Typis Vaticanis, 1864), vol. 4, pt. 2: *1697–1775*, p. 390. In reality, Manzon was always closely associated with the policy of Federick II.

[5] Aleksandr N. Radiščev, *Polnoe sobranie sočinenij* (Complete works) (Moscow and Leningrad: Akademija nauk SSSR, 1941), vol. 3, pp. 255ff. See A. N. Radiščev, *Viaggio da Pietroburgo a Mosca*, ed. Gigliola Venturi and Franco Venturi (Bari: De Donato, 1972), pp. 18ff.

a ship laden with grain had arrived in Livorno and had stopped in Zante
to take on "thirty-two young Greeks from different families in the Morea
who had taken refuge on that island, with some women in their service
. . . to pass on to the city of Pisa and the college founded there by His
Excellency the Russian general Count Alexis Orlov, on orders from his
sovereign, to better study the sciences." On the same day a French vessel
left Zante "with a similar number of youths for the same purpose."[6]

As one sees from this episode, an important development occurred
after 1770. Although earlier the principal object of the Russians seems
to have been continental Greece and the Ionian Islands, after that date
a large part of their attention turned to the Archipelago, the Levant,
and that multicolored world of merchants and seamen about whom the
Florentine gazettes gave frequent news. This world with its officers, its
encounters with ships from other lands, and its various undertakings,
came to symbolize Greece in the eyes of many observers, even among
Tuscans.

The merchants and the seamen of the islands ultimately became the
allies of the Russians, more so than the warriors and mountain men of
Sparta. In the Morea the rebellion was crushed. At the center of the new
movement was the Archipelago, with its commerce and antiquities.[1] Antonios Psaros, who as we have seen was an active participant in the 1770
insurrection, can be considered a typical representative of these island
men. He certainly was not beaten by the disaster in the Morea, nor was
he among those who tended to attribute the responsibility for that de-

---

[6] *Notizie del mondo*, no. 85, 23 October 1773, p. 696 (Livorno, 20 October). See no. 93,
20 November 1773, p. 760 (Livorno, 17 November): "The quarantine of the Russian warship called the *Gregory*, which has arrived here recently from Paros, is ended. Her crew
and the thirty-six Greek youths have been sent on to Pisa to the new college founded by
the empress of Russia." This nucleus of a school had a brief life. After the war the idea
was taken up again, but in St. Petersburg and no longer in Pisa. In the *Notizie del mondo*,
no. 84, 21 October 1777, we read of the "new corps of cadets composed of foreigners
professing the Greek religion . . . organized by the special wish of Count Alexis Orlov,
who in the period of the late war had founded a similar seminary in the city of Pisa in
Tuscany." The students were drawn "from Italy, Poland, the Ukraine, European Tartary,
the Crimea." "Besides Russian, German, French, Italian, Turkish, and modern Greek,
they are instructed in the principles of religion and learn arithmetic, algebra, geometry,
history, geography, drawing, dancing, and so on."

[1] On the economic development of the Archipelago, which was furthered by the
Russo-Turkish war at the beginning of the seventies, see Leon's lucid pages in "The Greek
Merchant Marine," pp. 31ff. A view of all these problems is in the ample and interesting
essay by Traian Stoianovich, "Pour un modèle du commerce du Lévant: Économie con-
currentielle et économie de bazar 1500–1800," in *Bulletin de l'Association internationale
d'études du sud-est européen* 12 (1974): fasc. 2, pp. 61ff.

feat to Russia. "Losing a thousand persons," he said ten or so years later, "signified nothing. Even if half the Greeks perished, the other half would learn to find the courage and glory to defeat the Turkish yoke. Peter I sacrificed hundreds of thousands of Russians in raising and enlightening his country. Don't think you can rise up from slavery without grief." Pushed on by this will, and most faithful to Russia, he maintained close ties with Greeks still under the Ottomans and turned over in his mind projects for action he thought would be useful to the policy of Catherine II. At the beginning of 1784 he was on his way to Malta, where, as we have seen, he was appointed the Russian representative, but he declared he was ready to return quickly to the continent if necessary.[2] Psaros ended his life in 1811, at Taganrog, on lands the Russian government had given him.[3]

In Livorno a *Breve descrizione dell'Archipelago* written by Henry Leopold Pasch van Krienen was published. Van Krienen was of Dutch origin and had been an official in the fleet of Catherine II. The local history of the islands occupied by the Russians and archaeological information were mixed in this work. The author excused himself for writing in a language not his own: he wanted in this way to give homage to Italy, "which has been, after Greece, the mother and master of the sciences."[4] What struck him most in his voyages was the contrast between the glorious past and the miserable present: "The peoples who today inhabit the islands are quite different from the ancient Greeks. Among the ancients the masters of all sciences and arts were venerated; but the moderns are pitied for their general ignorance. This is not surprising, because they have lost their sense of ancient greatness; with downcast spirits they struggle against indigence and misery and must necessarily see a great contrast with their ancient customs."[5] "The wrongs the people are subjected to for various reasons" under the rule of the Turks were infinite.[6] Melos still had 50,000 inhabitants at the time of the Venetians, now there were about 500.[7] Nor was the situation of the other islands any better. Rude neglect reigned everywhere, with few exceptions. On Naxos, for example, besides a few traces left by ancient noble

[2] Letter by S. R. Voroncov to A. A. Bezborodko, Venice, 20–31 January 1784, in *Archiv knjazja Voroncova* (Voroncov Archive) (Moscow: P. Lebedev, 1880), vol. 13, pp. 174ff.

[3] Aljab'ev, *Snošenija Rossii*, p. 205.

[4] *Breve descrizione dell'Arcipelago e particolarmente delle diciotto isole sottomesse l'anno 1771 al dominio russo, del conte Pasch di Krienen con un ragguaglio esatto di tutte le antichità da esso scoperte ed acquistate e specialmente del sepolcro d'Omero e d'altri celebri personaggi* (Livorno: Tommaso Masi, 1773), "Prefazione," p. iv.

[5] Ibid., p. 6.

[6] Ibid., p. 7.

[7] Ibid., p. 11.

families, such as the Sanudo and Crespo, there were only inhabitants who were mistrustful, "vicious, and inclined to evil; so dogged in hate and envy are they that they persist to the death in their quarrels; they don't even speak to each other but carry out mutual attacks in illicit ways. The women are even more perverse than the men, excessively proud, obstinate, and petulant, intruding in each other's affairs with insolent affronts and combining the extravagant and indecent mode of their dress with that of their manners."[8] The men emigrate from Mykonos and become servants and artisans or try to make a living by "playing the guitar and singing" so as not to return to their "initial misery"; thus women are in the majority on the island.[9] On Tenos, where emigrants return and "buy pieces of land to become the gentlemen of the island," they still have "an exterior of ostentatious officiousness, . . . malicious, proud, violent, and brutal."[10] On Paros, the headquarters of the Russian naval forces in the Archipelago, one saw "total ruin" amid many relics of the past.[11] Still, the land was excellent and, if well cultivated, could "produce enough to support four garrisons similar to the present Russian one."[12] Through military intervention in the Archipelago, and behind a growing interest in archaeology, was revealed a harsh and difficult human reality. The Russians, through the work of Pasch van Krienen, intervened to their own advantage. As an official declaration dated 6 August 1771 stated, he had also visited these places to "enlist young Greeks of the islands for regular service of Her Imperial Majesty."[13] In the book he published two years later in Livorno this tangle of problems was expressed to Italian readers in a lifeless way but with a great deal of facts and dates.

Thanks to the tireless traveler and chronicler Giovanni Mariti, another aspect of the Russian intervention in the Levant became widely known in Florence, one involving Egypt, Syria, and the revolt and war of Ali Bey in 1771 and the years immediately following. All the Italian gazettes reported with interest the events of this first and ill-fated attempt to extricate Egypt from the power of the Ottoman Porte, with the more or less secret intervention of the Russians. But the most detailed accounts came from Florence. On 3 October 1772 the *Notizie del mondo* published an announcement that Allegrini and Pisoni were offering to sell an *Istoria della guerra accesa nella Soria l'anno 1771 dall'armi di Aly-Bey*

---

[8] Ibid., pp. 69ff.
[9] Ibid., pp. 82ff.
[10] Ibid., p. 90.
[11] Ibid., p. 119.
[12] Ibid., p. 121.
[13] Ibid., p. 143.

dell'Egitto.[14] The book was interesting, not only because of the breadth of information, but also because it exposed the reader to the central political problem of these years, exploring the dialogue of reform, revolt, and despotism in an unlikely corner of the world. The volume was to a certain extent a collective work, the result of Giovanni Mariti's experience in the east, as well as that of Antonio Mondaini, "our Tuscan," and of Stefano Saraf, "a great merchant" from Edessa, who, after a long stay in the west and east, had found a more secure peace in Italy, "driven in 1769 to take shelter in beautiful Tuscany under the happy auspices of Peter Leopold, its august sovereign."[15] Turning the pages one almost seems to come upon an animated discussion in one of Livorno's warehouses, among merchants commenting on the most recent news and remembering the years they had spent in Cyprus, Acre, and Egypt. The variability of political events, the continual change of scene, even the capricious fortunes of individuals (Ali Bey, it was said, had been a Georgian Christian, then a Moslem slave, then regent of Egypt, and his adventures were not yet finished), came, they were convinced, from a vice rooted in the political system of those countries. "Asiatic despotic government, bad as it is, and the Mohammedan religion professed there are at the origin of all this. These produce the many apprehensions of these people, always uncertain as to the possession of their goods, their dignity, and life itself. . . . There one sees slaves and servants easily raised from low places to the most prominent ones, whereas those born to greatness or meriting it fall as easily to extreme misery from the highest point of their greatness."[16] The frequent revolutions lack all perspective; they look not forward, but backward, or rather they seem to be only a fugitive moment in a process that is always the same. Revolts take on an aspect of the defense of sovereigns, rebellions are colored with a zeal for authority. Certainly Ali Bey succeeded in providing a greater sense of stability and security. "The rich found themselves somewhat more content, since their houses were more secure; they were

---

[14] *Notizie del mondo*, 3 October 1772, p. 654. The complete title was *Istoria della guerra accesa nella Soria l'anno 1771 dalle armi di Aly-Bey dell'Egitto e continovazione del successo a detto Aly-Bey fino a quest'anno 1772*, con aggiunte e note di Giovanni Mariti accademico apatista (Forence: Allegrini e Pisoni, 1772). Pt. 2 followed: *Proseguita fino alla morte di Ali-Bey dell'Egitto*, da Giovanni Mariti fiorentino (Florence: Gaetano Cambiagi, 1774). On the Egypt of this time see Peter Malcolm Holt, "The Pattern of Egyptian Political History from 1517 to 1798," in *Political and Social Change in Modern Egypt*, ed. P. M. Holt (London: Oxford University Press, 1968), pp. 79ff. On "Alì Bey, usually entitled 'the great,' but known in his own time by the nick-names of 'Balut kápan,' 'the cloudcatcher' or 'Jinn,' the demon," see ibid., pp. 8off.

[15] Mariti, *Istoria della guerra accesa nella Soria*, pp. 5ff.

[16] Ibid., pp. 239–40.

not pillaged in his time, nor were they subjected to the insolence of the people."[17] Cairo's "low people," by nature turbulent and unruly, had made their discontent heard, but that was because of the "famine that afflicted Egypt in 1770 and 1771."[18] After the death of Ali Bey they would soon turn again to the past, more content than before "because their insolence is tolerated and because they get their bread more cheaply."[19] But one should not blame the people alone for the continual disorder. The "cruel and tyrannical" government succeeded in "arousing a spirit of rebellion and innovation in the hearts of subjects." "And from this the desire to change lords and pass under another rule originated."[20] The situation was the same throughout the Ottoman Empire. "The pashas, governors, judges, and ministers, all estranged from their proper duties, pursue luxury and money; all ways open to them are used to gain more; their appetites have no bounds, . . . the people do not know to whom to appeal; everywhere there is injustice and tyranny; they suffer and are patient out of fear and find no remedy other than imagining relief from so much suffering."[21] When hostilities with Russia began, "one saw clearly how far the subjects' aversion to their chiefs had gone. One began to hear nothing but revolts and infidelities; it seemed that the time for vengeance had come, factions were everywhere and authority was despised."[22] Ali Bey had been able to profit from this in his meteoric rise to power. The Russians intervened without a precise program and without specific knowledge of the situation. For them Egypt was even more of a diversion than their landing in the Morea had been. Ali Bey had done what he could to obtain their help, and to this end he sent to St. Petersburg "a capable subject in his trust," as well as "his advice to Vice Admiral Count Spiridow on the island of Paros." "From the latter was immediately sent" a squadron of about twenty ships, some commanded by Greeks, such as Antonio Psaros and Panajotti Alessiano, who "toward the end of May arrived in the sea of Egypt."[23] Russia, "always anxious to procure its own interests," hastened to send engineers to Jaffa, "who began to improve the disposition of the camp, raise breastworks for the installation of batteries, and form the

[17] Ibid., p. 260.
[18] Ibid. See André Raymond, "Quartiers et mouvements populaires au Caire aux xviiie siècle," in *Political and Social Change in Modern Egypt*, pp. 104ff., which calls attention, on p. 114, to the resumption of endemic popular movements in Cairo after 1770, and especially after 1780, due to the rising cost of living.
[19] Ibid., pp. 252, 260.
[20] Ibid., pt. 2, p. 40.
[21] Ibid., pp. 41–42.
[22] Ibid., p. 42.
[23] Ibid., pp. 43, 46.

necessary plan to start a regular siege."[24] On 6 October Panajotti Alessiano opened fire on Turkish ships before Damietta and sank them. Continuing to Jaffa on 18 November, his squadron became "the terror of those seas."[25] But the Greco-Russian intervention did not save Ali Bey. His attempt to take Jerusalem failed. Everywhere the famine became worse. On 28 April 1773 he was defeated, and on 7 May, after receiving care and honor from his victors, he died. The last episode of the Russian intervention in the Mediterranean had ended. The 27 August issue of the *Notizie del mondo* published the text of the treaty of Küçük Kaynarca, which put an end to the Russo-Turkish war.[26]

In Tuscany, and especially in Livorno, there was concern in the immediate postwar period. What would happen with "the end of Russian money"? How long would it take "to resume the Levant trade"?[27] Otherwise Orlov's ships did not seem to be in any haste to leave the beaches; nor had the surprises they had aroused in recent years come to an end. Rivarola, the consul of the king of Sardinia, wrote the following on 26 February 1775: "On a frigate brought for the purpose a lady who has been much talked of was sent away; she is thought to be a sister of the king of Poland. But Count Orlov says she is a Russian lady of great distinction, whom he knew before, who has come here in misery. She was recommended to him for assistance on her return journey, to ensure that she would be served with distinction."[28] These were sweet lies to hide the abduction of Princess Tarakanova, feared by Catherine II as a possible rival to the throne. She was imprisoned as soon as she arrived and later died of consumption in her cell in the fortress of Peter and Paul. The shadow of usurpers, from Stephen the Little to Tarakanova, was present from the beginning to the end of the Muscovite expedition in the Mediterranean.

In Livorno on 7 July 1775 the Russian ships, three frigates, that remained in port celebrated "the anniversary of the day in 1770 when the Russian fleet won its victory over the Turks" with "a royal salvo of artillery."[29] A few days later, on 26 July, dropped anchor "in this port the Russian war frigate *Saint Paul terror of infidels*, coming from the Archipelago and commanded by Captain Panaiotti Alexiano."[30] The great

[24] Ibid., pp. 102ff.

[25] Ibid., p. 125.

[26] *Notizie del mondo*, no. 69, 27 August 1773, p. 551 (Bologna, 24 August).

[27] Turin, AS, *Materie politiche estere in genere*, mazzo 58, 1774, Livorno, 14 August 1774, letter by the Sardinian consul Rivarola.

[28] Ibid., mazzo 59, 1775, Livorno, 26 February 1775.

[29] *Notizie del mondo*, no. 55, 11 July 1775, p. 438 (Livorno, 7 July).

[30] Ibid., no. 61, 29 July 1775. See no. 99, 10 December 1774, p. 790 (Livorno, 7 December): "One hears . . . that General Orlov in the name of his sovereign has decorated

Russian adventure was becoming a distant memory. Greeks who had become an important part of the military and civil service of Catherine II remained. They were not numerous, but they were active and enterprising, and they made their weight felt in the course of Russian life in the period of Potemkin and beyond.[31]

with the honorable military order of St. George Captain Alexander Alexiano, brother of Captain Panaiotti Alexiano, having first conferred on him the rank of captain of infantry in recompense for his many brave undertakings faithfully executed for Her Russian Majesty during the recent war with the Porte." Thus, in no. 1, 3 January 1775, p. 4 (Livorno, 30 December 1774), we read: "On Wednesday the Muscovite warship *St. Paul* set sail from this port, commanded by Captain Cav. Panajotti Alexiano, headed for Paros, together with another transport ship." And still again in no. 7, 24 January 1775, p. 55 (Livorno, 20 January), we read that the British governor of Minorca and his wife lodged, when they had arrived in Livorno, "in the house of Sig. Cav. Panajotti Alexiano and served with the carriage of Sig. Cav. Dick, British general consul in the seas of Tuscany, who entertained them."

[31] See V. A. Karidis, "The Formation of Greek Communities in Southern Russia, 1774–1821," *Study Group of Eighteenth-Century Russia. Newsletter*, no. 5 (September 1978): 7ff.

IV

Echoes in Naples, Piedmont, and Lombardy:
The Image of Greece in Europe

ALONG WITH VENICE AND TUSCANY, NAPLES WAS THE PLACE IN ITALY
that reacted with the greatest intensity to the developments of 1768–
1774.[1] To be sure, it did not have a periodical press comparable with
that of Venice or Florence. The *Foglio straordinario*, which began to be
published in Naples at the beginning of 1769, lacked the *Notizie del mondo's* richness of news and comments. But from its first issue, on 6 January, this journal was full of news about Russia: conflicts in Poland, the
embarrassment of Venice, war between Russia and Turkey, money offered by the empress for the translation of "useful foreign works into
Russian," and the charge to "Counts Orlow and Schuvalow and to Signor Kosizhi" for the distribution of prizes to those who succeeded best
in this enterprise.[2] The second issue, in a communication from St. Petersburg dated 15 November, told how Catherine II had been "inocu-
lated against smallpox" and how preparations for war along the Polish
frontier were being intensified.[3] Soon there appeared news of the first
Turkish measures taken against the Greeks of the Archipelago, of Venice's insistent precautions for "some rebels" arrested in Cattaro, and of
the first encounters between Venetian Slavs and Dulcignian pirates.[4]
Thus, even Naples was prepared for the outbreak of war on 18 November 1768, which was announced with a "special sheet"—no. 7, on 14

[1] See Franco Venturi, "Neapolitanskie literaturnye otkliki na russko-tureckuju vojnu
(1768–1774)" (Neapolitan literary echoes of the Russo-Turkish war), in *XVIII vek*, vol. 10:
Pamjati P. N. Berkova (In memory of P. N. Berkov) (Leningrad: Puškinskij dom, 1975),
pp. 119ff.

[2] *Foglio straordinario*, no. 1, 6 January 1769 (Vienna, 18 December; Venice, 10 December; St. Petersburg, 5 November).

[3] Ibid., no. 2, 10 January 1769 (St. Petersburg, 15 November).

[4] Ibid., no. 4, 24 January 1769 (Venice, 31 December), and no. 6, 7 February 1869
(Venice, 14 January).

Febuary 1769. A little more than a month later "letters from Capo d'Is-
tria" assured that "Stephen the Little had again placed himself at the
head of the Montenegrin rebels and was being supported by the Russian
court to create a diversion against the Ottoman Porte's forces in Albania."[5] The long delays in transmitting news accentuated the sense of
distance surrounding these events. In Naples, even more than elsewhere, the landing in the Morea must have come as a surprise. If the
two sheets entitled *Copia di lettera* with the dateline "Malta 1770" are
Neapolitan, as they seem to be, we can get an idea of how news of the
events in the Peloponnesus arrived. The first successes of the Russians
and insurgents, we read,

encouraged all the Greeks generally, who do nothing but discuss war and think
about it, so none of them are content if they are not in an encampment or at
arms. To better ensure success, they have sworn fidelity among themselves, with
solemn promises never to abandon one another; thus bound together they go
about looting and taking places from the enemy. Not a day goes by when their
force is not enlarged by thirty or forty persons, who come to the camp from all
parts to join them. If this force stays united and lets itself be led by the Muscovite command, it will do much damage to the enemy and have a considerable
advantage."[6]

But soon there was delusion. In the second issue of the *Copia di lettera*,
one read that the "Greco-Russians, up to now victorious and superior
after some favorable encounters, had succumbed and avoid encounters
with the enemy as much as possible." The battles and retreats were narrated in four tiny pages. "The casualties of the Greco-Russians cannot
be described."[7]

The victory of Chesmé, to be sure, did not remedy the ruin of the
Greeks. But it contributed, even in Naples, to the attention given to the
undertakings of the Russians. Local particulars were not lacking: the
Albanian and Macedonian regiments, the Orthodox Church in Naples,
and the growing number of Greeks thrown off by their country coming
to take refuge in the kingdom of Ferdinando IV. This does not take into
account Russian troops themselves who, although small in number, began to circulate in the capital. Here is a typical picture from 1771: "Last
Sunday," reported the *Notizie del mondo* from Naples on 16 March, "the
Russian officers . . . went to hear divine service in the Greek church and
were accompanied by the marshal of the Albanians and many officers
from that nation, and afterward two batallions of the Albanian regi-

[5] Ibid., no. 12, 21 March 1769 (Venice, 25 February).
[6] *Copia di lettera*, Malta 1770, 30 June 1770, of which there is a copy in Turin, AS,
Materie politiche estere in genere, mazzo 55, 1770.
[7] Ibid., 2 July 1770.

ment, unarmed, drew up in file on both sides of the Russian officers, accompanying them to their lodgings."[8] Russian Easter was celebrated when "Lieutenant General Schuwalow, the Russian, and another officer who has volunteered in the army of that Crown" arrived in Naples. "Their devotion was exemplary."[9]

An anthology entitled *Componimenti poetici di vari autori in lode di Caterina II, augustissima imperatrice di tutte le Russie* was published in Naples.[10] Literary and learned Neapolitans, Greek emigrés, among whom was Gicca, the author of the *Voti*, joined in these pages to sing the praises of Russia and augur the revival of Hellas. Although filtered through ample rhetoric of all kinds, there emerged in this collection, if not a political program, at least a vision of the present and the future. As the authors explained in the dedication, or rather in a "supplication" to Fedor Orlov, "lieutenant general of the Russian army," they attributed to the "happy booming of repeated Russian victories against the Ottomans" the reawakening "on Pindus from their profound sleep" of the "slumbering Greek muses," who "beginning to pluck their long abandoned zithers" had "formed the following verses." The authors appealed to Catherine II to find in their work a witness to the "disposition of the Greek spirit." The empress was also expected to find in the verses an invitation "to accomplish great things," making herself "a new Judith to a nation that, although celebrated itself in all virtues and arts, when adorned with so many good things by Her Imperial Majesty, would not be lacking in thanks and deeds." In short, they hoped for a recovery from the defeats in the Morea.

The author of many of the verses, the "inspiration and guide," and the "censor and improver" of verses of the other collaborators, was a "field marshal and colonel" who signed himself "C.G.C. of the Arcadian academy," that is, Count Giorgio Corafà, the commander and historian of the Royal Macedonian Regiment of Naples. His career was described in the preface, "From the Printer to the Reader." He was born "in the state of the most serene republic of Venice," on Cephalonia, in a place, that is, "where the ferocious Ottoman 'breaks his own swelling waves.' " He received his "noble education" at Parma, in the famous college of the Jesuits, and learned from them "bright poetic ideas" and "solid thought." Entering Neapolitan service, he became field marshal and colonel of the Royal Macedonian Regiment, about which he published

[8] *Notizie del mondo*, no. 22, 16 March 1771, p. 174 (Naples, 5 March).

[9] Ibid., No. 32, 20 April 1771, p. 253 (Naples, 9 April).

[10] At the foot of the advertisement of the "Stampatore a chi legge" is written the following: Naples: Benjamino Rinaldi, 1771. The only copy I know of is in Naples, B. Universitaria, and has the call number R.xxxvi.8.

at Bologna in 1768 a *Dissertazione istorico-cronologica.*[11] His origins and profession made, one reads at the beginning of the *Componimenti poetici,* "flow naturally" the "zeal" with which he burned for the "common good" of all Greeks, and the enthusiasm he demonstrated for a sovereign who wanted their liberation. "And truly could a generous heart not warm to the fact of that nation, which was the master and teacher of all other nations in the arts and sciences and all good things, beginning to extricate itself from its chains? Could a Christian heart remain insensitive to the new Helen who would again unearth the cross of Christ and raise it in those lands where it worked our redemption?" Judith and Helen: the empress of Russia was arising as the "redemptress of Greece."

From the first sonnet Corafà recalled how the celebrated scholar Moreri, "historian and professor of Paris," had held that "the Muscovites were originally from Greece." Thus all the glory of Greece had come down to Russia. The duty of Catherine II to slay the "Thracian monster" was all the more evident. The Greeks would be able to obtain their liberty only through Russian intervention. They had no other hope. Appealing in the name of Greece to the "illustrious Russian nation," he concluded:

> né di sperar che il nodo sia disciolto
> per altre man che per la tua mi lice.[12]

More duties and grand hopes, which contrasted with the hard reality of the moment. "Grieving Greece" was not unaware that

> ormai ciascun de' difensori è oppresso.[13]

The weight of defeat and ruin was heavy and all the more difficult to bear in the absence of any people prepared "to fully pity" that unhappy land. Still, Greece continued to have "hopes of liberty" and, turning her gaze to Catherine II, it consoled itself.

> Ogni tristezza mi fugge lontano
> e si cambia in trionfo ogni mio danno.[14]

The need was great:

---

[11] See Emile Legrand, *Bibliographie ionienne* (Paris: E. Leroux, 1916), vol. 1, p. 124 n. 398; Masarachi, *Vite degli uomini illustri dell'isola di Cefalonia,* pp. 391ff., and M. and N. Pignatorre, *Memorie storiche,* vol. 2, pp. 227ff.

[12] *Componimenti poetici,* p. 1. "Nor do I hope that the knot be undone / by other hands than thine."

[13] Ibid., p. 2. "Now all the defenders are oppressed."

[14] Ibid., pp. 3, 5. "All sadness flees me / and all my injury turns to triumph."

> Arma il tuo zelo, Caterina, e desta
> nel cuore de' prodi tuoi l'ardir guerriero:
> In te sola la Grecia ansiosa e mesta
> di sua speme ha rivolto ogni pensiero.
> Il primo aiuto a' lidi egei s'estenda
> pria che del trace l'orgoglioso sdegno
> Sparta ed Atene a incenerir discenda.

From the Aegean Catherine II would be able to strike

> . . . quel covil indegno
> ove il fiero tiran par che contenda
> d'Eusin il passo e l'usurpato regno.[15]

In the Russian navy Greeks had found a first occasion to reassert themselves.

> Ardir c'ispiri e coll'ardir c'insegni
> sotto i vessilli suoi quanto siam forti.

Only under the Russian aegis would Greeks be able to unite.

> Ma senza te le forze sue non sente.[16]

All these hopes would collapse if Russia made peace with the Turks. Corafà begged the empress to reject such a policy and

> . . . proseguire la gloriosa guerra.[17]

Like ancient ilium, modern Constantinople would fall only if the combat did not cease.[18] Alexis Orlov had said

> Popoli dell'Egeo, è tempo ormai
> d'uscir dall'ombra ove finor giaceste.[19]

---

[15] "Arm your zeal, Catherine, and make rise / in the hearts of your men the ardor of war: / To you alone Greece, anxious and downcast / in its hopes, has turned all its thoughts. / The first help to Aegean shores extends / before Thracian proud disdain / makes Sparta and Athens descend in flames." ". . . that unworthy place / where the proud tyrant seems to control / the outlet of the Euxine and its ursurped kingdom." Ibid., p. 7, "In occasione dell'ingiusta guerra mossa dall'impero ottomano al russo, la Grecia così parla all'Imperatrice."

[16] "Ardor inspires us, and with ardor teach us / under your ships how strong we are." "But without you we will not feel your force." Ibid., p. 10, "La fiducia della greca nazione sotto i vessilli delle vittoriose arme di S.M.I."

[17] ". . . carry forward the glorious war." Ibid., p. 13, "Presagio alla città di Costantinopoli."

[18] Ibid., p. 22

[19] "People of the Aegean, now is the time / to come out of the shade in which you have languished." Ibid., p. 22.

The Greeks had followed his call and had not forgotten the deeds he had accomplished.

> Per te sorse la Grecia e il ferro strinse.[20]

To him above all the Greeks now turned.

> Entra in Bisanzio e noi sarem tua guida.[21]

Praises and hopes were also directed to all those who had fought against the Turks: Golicyn, Rumjancev, Panin, Dolgorukij.[22] The appeal extended finally to "Christian princes" and above all to the republic of Venice. The homeland of Count Corafà, "the sunny land of the Ionian Sea," became a kind of symbol of the will of the Greeks to have the Most Serene Republic at their side.

> Che il russo sia teco e ti sovvegna
> che Candia e Cipro sono in man de' cani.[23]

The second part of the collection shows the diffusion of this type of ideas in Naples. It contained "the poetic jests of Abate D.T.V." (Don Tommaso Velasti), which were also intended to praise Catherine and to dispel the danger that she might make peace with Turkey.[24] A long eulogy in Latin followed, entitled *Pacem inter Russos ac Turcas non nisi ad Plutonis senatum agitari*.[25] After the victories of the Danube and the Aegean, even after Egypt had been put in motion, how could one think of putting down arms? One should keep in mind the prophecies, well known to the Turks, according to which, as D. Niccolò Timoni, who came from Chios, wrote in an afterthought to these verses, "Muscovy will be their ruin."[26] The tasks of Catherine II became greater and greater. Anything but peace! God himself entrusted her with the duty of "uniting our two churches."[27]

The other collaborators were priests and military men, Italians and

----

[20] "For you Greece has risen and taken arms." Ibid., p. 31.

[21] "Enter Byzantium and we will be your guide." Ibid., p. 32.

[22] "Field Marshal Prince Alessandro Golitzin, who won the first battle against the Turkish army in 1769 and was then promoted to vice chancellor of the Russian Empire" (we read in a note on p. 44), was Aleksandr Michajlovič Golicyn. Pietr Aleksandrovič Rumjancev was field marshal (see p. 45). "The taker of Bender" (p. 46) was Petr Ivanovič Panin. "Lieutenant General Prince Dolgoroucki who conquered the Crimea (see p. 47) was Vasilij Michajlovič Dolgorukij.

[23] "Because Russia is with you and supports you / and Candia and Cyprus are in the hands of dogs." Ibid., p. 48.

[24] Ibid., p. 63.

[25] Ibid., pp. 66ff.

[26] Ibid., p. 67.

[27] Ibid., p. 103.

Greeks, lovers of classical culture, and admirers of the Russian empress. They were small figures whom we would hardly notice, but together they made up a small crowd: Giorgio Condili, Marchese Cinciglia, Conte Milonopulo, Giuseppe Piromallo Barone di Monte Bello, Pasquale Passari, Giuseppe Santuccio, Pasquale Siccardi, Bartolomeo Masnata, "patrician of Albenga and member of the Accademia Ereina of Palermo" (who set out to write a long *Epistola ai principi dell'Europa*, proposing a complete reorganization of the political map of the continent when the Ottoman Empire was defeated), and Father Antonio di Demetrio, a carmelite of Larissa. The name Pasquale Baffi is striking. A native of Santa Sofia d'Epiro, in Calabria, Baffi was from a Greco-Albanian family who had emigrated in the fifteenth century; he completed his first studies in the Italo-Greek college of San Benedetto Ullano to pass on, when he was barely twenty, to the chair of Greek at the University of Salerno. He was still there when he contributed to this collection a composition in Greek and Latin on the victory of Chesmé.[28] His later life sheds a different light on what might be thought the simple linguistic exercise of a young professor. In 1773 he came to Naples, to the Nunziatella, and soon became an active participant in the revival of Freemasonry, ending up in prison in 1776. He was one of the founders of the lodge of the Illuminati and an active participant in the republic of 1799. He was hanged during the reaction, on 11 November of that year.[29]

Among these men we find Antonio Gicca, the author of the *Voti*, with a first sonnet entitled "For the Recent Happy Successes of Russian Arms in Walachia, Moldavia, and on the Danube," which was published both in Italian and in "vulgar Greek," and a second entitled "To the Glorious Muscovite Troops." He had vivid hopes of rebirth.

> Cada il Trace e Bisanzio: alfin risorga
> dalle ceneri fredde il greco impero.[30]

His relations with Corafà went well beyond this collection of verses. A fellow officer, a propagandist, and a diplomat, Gicca was charged with a mission to the commander of the Royal Macedonian at Palermo. The *Nuove di diverse corti e paesi* mentioned him and took the opportunity to present Count Giorgio Corafà to their readers, "from the Greek nation, and one of the most illustrious, powerful, and rich families of the island

---

[28] Ibid., p. 115.

[29] See the notice by C. Francovich and A. Petrucci in *DBI*, vol. 5, pp. 175ff. There is information about an ode he wrote for Catherine II, preserved in Florence, B. Marcelliana, B.I., 18.CC.285, ff. 2ff. See Uberto Caldora, "Pasquale Baffi," in id., *Fra patriotti e briganti* (Bari: Adriatica, 1974), pp. 113ff.

[30] "Thrace and Byzantium fall: then arise / imperial Greece from the cold ashes." *Componimenti poetici*, p. 111; here his name is Antonio Gica.

of Cephalonia," known not only "for his military and political talents," but also "for his literary productions, among which there is to admire a judicious and erudite work on Mount Vesuvius."[31]

At the end of the war it was possible for Gicca to enter, with some difficulty, the complex Russo-Greco-Italian world that the conflict was bringing into being. Here is how his life is narrated in a ukaz of the Russian college of foreign affairs on 4 May 1777, when his appointment as councilor of the Russian embassy in Naples was proposed, an appointment approved by the empress on 21 May.

Count Antonio Gicca was born into a noble family of Albania; his father, Strati Gicca, is in Neapolitan service with the title lieutenant general and colonel of the Royal Macedonian Regiment, made up of Albanians, and he enjoys a particular fame in Naples, which he won during the last wars in Italy, especially at the battle of Velletri. The Albanians of Greek denomination asked him, when he left their province for Naples, to leave them one of his sons for instruction. Count Antonio was chosen. The fact that he came from a family that has always been important in Albania and had an education appropriate to a noble has been the base of the influence he has always enjoyed in all matters with his people, and for this he was particularly invited by Count A. G. Orlov-Česmenskij, in the beginning, to take part in the expedition to the Levant. Count Gicca was influential in this matter among his countrymen and led them to swear loyalty to the empress, a bond he held firm through continuous contact with his land in that time of mobilization against the Turks. To further these people's collaboration with us, he was sent to Count A. G. Orlov as a plenipotentiary delegate of the Albanian nation. Count A. G. Orlov decorated him with the rank of captain and sent him back to his country to recruit Albanians for our service, which he did successfully then and later, when the Albanian legion was formed by Kammer-Junker Domašnev. His demonstrated zeal and ability with Greek and Italian troops adapted him for employment as a secretary to these last. Among his other writings, one published in Italian entitled *Voti dei greci all'Europa cristina* is affirmed in Italy to be an excellent work. At the end of the war, at a time when he was absent, Count Aleksej Gregorevič conferred on him the rank of major and entrusted him with questions relating to the taking of neutral ships, in collaboration with General Hannibal, with whom he came here [to St. Petersburg], who highly praises the zeal and talent of Count Gicca. Count Aleksej Gregorevič attests to the same. Now Gicca is in a difficult situation because at the time of the insurrection that he supported against the Turks in Albania, he was obliged to promise his people not only what they could have, but still more. This savage people, not taking into account the impossibility of enriching the whole nation, have sworn undying enmity against him, divided all his lands among themselves, and deprived him of all his possessions. The resources of his father in Naples provided him a wherewithal, and now all his

---

[31] *Nuove di diverse corti e paesi*, no. 34, 22 August 1774, p. 272 (Livorno, 15 August).

desires are concentrated on the hope of being employed in that place, in the embassy, with the title councilor and a corresponding stipend.[32]

And he was accepted. At the beginning of 1778 the *Notizie del mondo* annouced the arrival in Naples, from St. Petersburg, of "Count Gicca, Councilor of the Embassy of the Imperial Court of Russia," preceded by "Count Rosomowsky [Razumovskij], designated minister of that court to our Royal Sovereign."[33]

We have seen Gicca in contact with Sergej Gerašimovic Domašnev, and we should stop for a moment to meet this official of Catherine II, because he was one of the most important links in the relationship among Russians, Greeks, and Italians of these years, in Tuscany as much as in Naples. He was perhaps the first Russian to mention Dante, in 1762, when he was still nineteen years old.[34] Some years later he became a representative of the nobility in the commission on legislative reforms convoked in the Kremlin. It is possible that he may have had an important part in the publication of the *Essai sur la littérature russe* in Livorno.[35] In Naples he was in contact with Mario Pagano and Abate Galiani. Returning home after the war, he was elected director of the Academy of Sciences and held this post between 1775 and 1783. At the time of his appointment, the *Notizie del mondo* recorded his literary and military activities in Italy.[36] He was, as one sees, a versatile and capable man, even if somewhat controversial.[37]

Many of these figures, literary and military men, reappear in another collection of verses, of a more officious and obsequious nature, published in 1773 and dedicated to Aleksej Orlov.[38]

[32] The Russian original is in Sirio, vol. 154 (1914), pp. 410–11.

[33] *Notizie del mondo*, no. 12, 10 February 1778, p. 96 (Naples, 3 February).

[34] Michail P. Alekseev, "Pervoe znakomstvo Dante v Rossii" (The first knowledge of Dante in Russia), in *Ot klassicizma k romantizmu* (From classicism to romanticism), ed. M. P. Alekseev (Leningrad: Puškinskij dom, 1970), p. 3. See p. 201 n. 21 for a bibliography on him.

[35] Grégoire Lozinskij, "La preimière histoire de la littérature russe: Histoire d'un plagiat," *Revue des études slaves* 16 (1936): 5ff.

[36] *Notizie del mondo*, no. 14, 17 February 1776, p. 108 (St. Petersburg, 9 January). "This young man has not only shown his taste and talent for literature with various works, but has also distinguished himself in sea and land service. At the time of Count Alessio Orlow's expedition to the Levant, he was at the head of the department of political affairs and commander of the Greek and Albanian legions that served in the fleet of his nation." Later this journal mentioned his part in a version of a Shamanic text. No. 16, 24 February 1776, p. 122 (St. Petersburg, 12 January).

[37] V. P. Semennikov, "Materialy dlja istorii russkoj literatury" (Materials for the history of Russian literature), extract from *Russkij bibliofil*, 1914, nos. 5–8, also published separately in St. Petersburg, 1915, index.

[38] *Componimenti poetici di vari autori in lode di S.E. il signor conte Alessio Orlow, plenipoten-*

> Bella Grecia respira e asciuga il pianto
> è teco Orlow tua speme e tuo conforto,

wrote Giorgio Corafà.[39] The Russian commander seemed to be fully conscious of the innate perils of negotiating with the Turks.

> Lusinghiero è il maneggio e il fin malvaggio.[40]

Orlov was right not to want to give in to a truce. On 9 November 1772 he ordered an attack and destroyed the fleet of the Dulcignian pirates in the Gulf of Patras. It was time to take up again the battle interrupted in 1770.

> E la Grecia avrebbe spezzata la catena spietata
> che tuttavia l'opprime s'ella,
> come si bene cominciò, costante e forte
> avesse potuto secondar la sorte.

Russia remained the only hope. Marchese Cinciglia wrote a sonnet celebrating the extraordinary history of that country.

> Per virtú, per valor, per senno ed arte
> sopra il piú illustri regni alzai la fronte.
> D'un popolo d'eroi son viva fonte
> son Nettuno nel mar e in guerra Marte.

Russia was a guarantee that

> la greca libertà dall'ire e l'onte
> vendicata sarà in ogni parte.[41]

Antonio Gicca sent his wishes to Orlov on the occasion of "his departure from Livorno for the third campaign in the Levant":

> Or che dubbia bensí, ma non gradita
> fama di pace a nostre orecchie arriva
> io sento ben che in voce alta e giuliva
> te la vittoria a nuove palme invita.

---

ziario e comandante supremo delle arme russe in Levante (n. p., n. d). There is a copy in Naples at the Biblioteca della Società napolitana di storia Patria, with the call number III. B 15/6. The illustrations, and above all the medal commemorating Chesmé, are typical of the military arrogance and neoclassical vision of these men.

[39] "Lovely Greece breathe and wipe your tears / Orlov is with you, your hope and comfort." Ibid., p. 5.

[40] "The process is deceptive, and the end evil." Ibid., p. 6.

[41] "And Greece would have broken the merciless chain / that still oppresses her if she, / as seemed at first, constant and strong, / had been able to follow her fate." "Through virtue, valor, good sense, and art / I raised my face over the most renowned kingdoms / I am the living spring of heroes: / in the sea Neptune, and Mars in war." "Greek liberty from anger and shame / will everywhere be vindicated." Ibid., p. 17.

And he exhorted him again:

> . . . l'egra gente argiva
> libera rendi dal superbo scita.[42]

A call renewed even by the "Arcadian shepherd" Giacinto di Crescenzio:

> Corona la grand'opra. Al fin la vita
> togli a quest'idra che 'l nostr' orbe infetta.

In an *Epilogo encomiastico* one read finally:

> Ergi dalle fatali tue ruine,
> Grecia, la fronte e mira Orlow invitto
>
> . . . .
>
> Pallade alfin gli cingerà le chiome
> e si vedran festose a lui d'intorno
> del bizantino mar le rive dome.[43]

The vision of the Hellenic past, and classical rhetoric, thus became a kind of mask, or a veil, drawn before the hard reality of Russian intervention in the Mediterranean. The Russians had been capable of stirring into action the peoples of Montenegro and the Peloponnesus, of the Ionian Islands and the Archipelago, but not of giving the Turkish empire a sufficient blow for these awakened aspirations for liberty to transform themselves into new political realities. Nor were the new aspirations able to crystallize themselves into precise formulas, remaining to the end a confused amalgam of Orthodox religious traditions, humanistic memories, and barely initiated discoveries of nationality among peoples under the rule of the crescent. What emerged from the years of battles and discussions was thus not new nations, and not even a new diplomatic balance able to last beyond the time when Orlov made his voyages between St. Petersburg and the Levant. What emerged in reality was a group of hardy men, of the most diverse origins, who had in common a willingness to profit from the Russian intervention so as to assert their own personalities and to make rapid and brilliant careers by insinuating themselves into the military and bureaucratic apparatus of Catherine II and by making the most contact possible with the governments of Italy, and above all with Venice, Tuscany, and Naples. Only

---

[42] "Now that doubtful, but not welcome / news of peace arrives in our ears; / I hear clearly in a high and joyful voice / Victory offering you new palms." ". . . make the sad people of Argos / free from the proud Scythian." Ibid., p. 18.

[43] "Crown the great work. Finally take the life / of that Hydra that infects our sphere." "Raise your face from your ruins, / Greece, and see undefeated Orlov / . . . / Pallas will crown his hair / and festive about him will be seen / the conquered shores of the Byzantine sea." Ibid., p. 35.

briefly were these men able to influence groups among the Epirotes, Albanians, and Maineotes. But even in defeat they remained firm, persistent in their attempt to persuade Orlov and Catherine II, and to work with sword and pen to keep the Greek question alive. With Gicca, Corafà, Mocenigo, and so many others began that Greco-Russian symbiosis that had an ever growing importance in the late eighteenth century and at the beginning of the nineteenth. They took the first uncertain steps that later led Capodistria, born on Corfu and minister of foreign affairs of Alexander I, to become the first president of the Greek republic.

They generally came from places where nobility was an aspiration rather than a reality. Venice, like Genova, and for even more important reasons the Turkish empire, did not permit the formation of true local aristocracies. The leaders emerging in these lands, Cephalonians or Corsicans, thought of the Venetian or Genoese patricians who came to govern them as rivals, not only in political life, but also in economic life, and thus accused them of corruption and of governing only to enrich themselves at their expense. Even the administration of justice in the colonies of the archaic Italian republics was sharply criticized: they were too bland and indulgent, incapable of combatting vendettas and assassins, even though they tended to make use of judicial fines for fiscal purposes, thus further harming an impoverished population.

As in Corsica, the "principals" above all desired honor and power. But to assert themselves they had to find a new relationship with their own people and push them into a struggle against the oppressors. Thus they accepted with gratitude the title of count that the Russians granted in profusion and clutched at the administrative roles Orlov and Catherine II finally gave them. At the same time they considered themselves to be natural leaders, representatives of their people and of Greece as a whole. Russian policy acted intelligently toward them, accustomed as it was to having to deal with different populations—Tartars, Georgians, Circasians, and so on.

However, this was not only a design for a new colonial policy. Russia was too influenced itself by the ideals that moved these men not to react profoundly to the response its expansion in the Black Sea and the Mediterranean aroused. Constantinople was a mirage for the Russians as much as it was for the Greeks. The city of Odessa would derive not only its name, but also its vocation, from Odysseus. And the particularly close ties with Italy remained an essential element in the lives of this group of men, and through them, in Russian life under Catherine II. Italy, thanks to them, carried out its task as an intermediary between west and east.

In Naples, and still more in Livorno, there were signs of a similar Italo-Greco-Russian symbiosis. The presence of the Royal Macedonian

Regiment, traditional ties with the Balkan world, and the presence of large urban populations who had come from the other shore of the Adriatic contributed to this. If we are to believe the Venetian resident, the men of the regiment were deserters who had committed assassinations on Corfu. The officers responded energetically, held an assembly, and finally prepared a long printed memoir, a clear reflection and curious testimony of their thought. Among them we find the "arcadian shepherd" Giacinto di Crescenzo, and "Gicca, lieutenant colonel of the Royal Macedonian Regiment." At their head was Captain Nestore Andruzzi and Adjutant Major Andrea Gini.[1] How could Venice, who "with the form of her free government has always been an ark and a temple for refugees of all the world, presume to demand this extradition?"[2] The fate threatening the men who were charged was clear from the example of others who had been given over before "to a Venetian commander sent to Brindisi with two warships by the general of Corfu." Now, he said, these were probably "hanging on a gibbet or were already buried."[3] In Venice the fact that the armies of the world were full of deserters was not taken into account. In the Neapolitan army soldiers came from France, Piedmont, Germany, and Prussia. When the emperor Joseph II came to Naples in 1769 he did not ask for the soldiers who had abandoned his armies. All armies had an international character, as the Irish, Walloon, and Italian regiments in the service in Spain also demonstrated. Was the Venetian resident thus trying to "reform the world"?[4] If they wanted, they could take it up with the Russians. Why not charge Captian Giovanni Palicuccia, who "at the first news of the arrival of the Russian fleet in the Archipelago hauled down the flag of St. Mark and raised the flag of Russia, saluting it with twenty-two cannon shots? Then he took sail . . . and went straight to the Russians, by whom he was welcomed along with his ship and decorated with an order of knighthood." Examples could be multiplied. In the exhibit of these officers there was a list of examples of Venetian subjects who had gone over to the "Russians who fought to liberate Greece." "Giovanni Valsammacci, Panajotti Alessiano, Pietro Aloysopolo, Risso, and Esparò."[5] But the Venetian claims were useless, not only with Russia, but also with Naples. Did the Republic of St. Mark not remember the rights that kings

---

[1] *Ossequiosa rappresentanza rassegnata a piedi del regal trono di S.M. in nome del reggimento Real Macedone e in ubbidienza del real comando sul punto delle reclute macedoni ingiustamente riclamate dal residente veneto.* Naples, 24 November 1772. There is a copy in Turin, AS, *Materie politiche estere in genere*, mazzo 57, 1773.

[2] Ibid., p. 5.

[3] Ibid., p. 7.

[4] Ibid., p. 12.

[5] Ibid., p. 13.

of Naples claimed in the Levant *ab antiquo*, from the time of Robert Guiscard? And did they not know how many inhabitants of the kingdom came from the east? "In one hundred and fifty towns and hamlets live two hundred thousand or more persons originally from our land."[6]

The young Francesco Mario Pagano was in contact with this world of Greeks and Russians. He was in his twenties when the war broke out, and he learned to understand and express their feelings and hopes better than anyone else in Naples. He had made the acquaintance of Panajotti Alessiano, a man of "truly Attic character and Platonic morality," and had become the friend of Antonio Gicca, Epirote, "and a 'centurion' in the Russian army."[7] What could be more dear to him—he wrote dedicating to them his *Oration to Count Orlov*—than the friendship of a Greek, who excelled not only in Attic letters, but also in those of Latium and Italy, dear to Tuscan muses, as if he were born in Italy ("How similar are the Greek and Italian characters!"). Following the example of Xenophon, Gicca had known how to join "literature with weapons, and Greek strength with the most profound love of homeland." When he had the good fortune to meet him, Pagano was well informed about the undertakings of the Russians, whose fame had spread everywhere. But it was Gicca who gave him "a true higher opinion of Russian heroes." "For in his intimate conversation," he recalled, "he constantly called forth the great names of Alexis, John, and Sergius" (that is, Aleksej Orlov, Ivan Vasil'evič Milovskij, his secretary, and Sergej Domašnev).[8] Love of his country and the liberty of "all of Greece" were always on his lips. He held a deeply rooted conviction that the Russians would liberate his land from servitude. He infused this faith in Pagano, leading him to write at one stroke, in six days, this "tumultuous oration." If Orlov, among his many other duties in Europe, Asia, and Africa, had time to take a look at it, he would know that it was not the result of flattery and be persuaded that "my character, nourished by Latin freedom and Greek education, flees from adulation and base commerce in the liberal arts." A great admirer of Greece, from his adolescence on, he had hoped from the onset of the war that the defeat of the Turks would bring the Russians great honor and strength by restoring the Greeks "freed from slavery to their ancient glory."[9] He had wanted to do something more than write in honor of the liberators. But meanwhile he gave

---

[6] Ibid., p. 16.

[7] *Francisci Marii Pagani Oratio ad comitem Alexium Orlow, virum immortalem, victrici moschorum classi in expeditione in Mediterraneum mare summo cum imperio praefectum* (n. d., n. p.), p. iii. There is a copy in Naples, BN, Collezione basilicatese, cart. XLI/5.

[8] Ibid., p. iv.

[9] Ibid., pp. vff.

Gicca, "mega Ellados fos," great light of Hellas, his warmest wishes for
a promotion through the ranks of the military hierarchy and to reach
his own land and see it "free from the barbarians."[10]

At the base of the *Orazione* was a grandiose vision of human affairs,
which, like the seasons of the year, change the fate of peoples, letters,
and laws. Thus the peoples of the east, "bereft of the light of culture,
entombed in the shadows of the most foul Turkish empire," languished
with torpor and misery in the present age. What remained of the Cal-
deans, the Indians, the Egyptians, "once brightest in wisdom"? And
what could one say of Greece, "the eye of the world," now "through
unworthy fate oppressed by Thracian fury"? With so much desolation
he compared the image of Russia, the "fearless tribe of the Muscovites,"
always militarily vigorous, until recently "fierce . . . under their harsh
sky," and now so cultivated and "polished" as to raise admiration and
envy even among peoples long civilized. Generally centuries were required to pass "from barbarity to refinement." But the maturation of
the Russians had been most rapid. "The unconquerable race of Muscovites, suddenly, in a few years, developed a glory of humanity."[11] The
credit for this went to Peter and those, like Catherine and her ministers,
who had known how to continue his work. In men like Orlov the empress had found worthy instruments for an enormous task, that of attacking and defeating the "most powerful, most ancient, empire" of the
Turks, into whose hands had fallen "the most precious part of Europe,
nearly all of Africa, and the nobler races of Asia."[12] Orlov had been
capable of this in the battle of Chesmé, reevoked by Pagano in page
after page of violent contrasts and colors. The sublime valor Orlov
showed the humanity with which he acted toward the defeated enemy,
and demonstrated along with the laws and Catherine II's "Instruction,"
the superiority Russia reached in war and in peace.[13] The Greeks could
profit from such success. In years past Orlov had shown that he too
knew how to act for their benefit. He had tolerated "patiently, and in
good humor," their flightiness and defects, "partly born from century-
old barbarism, when self-recognition had been cut short by unjust tyrants." With admirable ability, imitating the wisdom of ancient legislators, he had used the Greeks "to induce them to good actions." From
these defects he had drawn out remarkable virtues, becoming a new incarnation of the old myth of a wise shepherd of peoples. "You were like
a God among them." He had even instituted choral festivals, with the

[10] Ibid., p. vi.
[11] Ibid., p. viii.
[12] Ibid., p. x.
[13] Ibid., p. xv.

participation of the most noble Greek women, to show the difference between Turkish domination and that of Catherine II, and how "barbarous tyranny differs from a state founded on justice."[14] His task was anything but easy. "The obstacles were not easy to overcome." It was difficult to deal with peoples "long subjected to servitude," whose spirits are oppressed by fear, and give them hope of liberty. They always had before their eyes "the cross, the sword, the pitchfork, and every type of torment," as well as the angry faces of the Turks, their tyrants. "You have removed all this with your advice, eloquence, and authority." Men "broken by servitude and idleness," ignorant of the arts of war, "you lead on to freedom," preparing the best of them for the struggle with incredible rapidity.[15] The Greeks should thus finally rejoice. Aleksej Orlov was no longer among them, but he was still their best patron with the great Catherine. He was the one who had founded the college in Pisa, "where Greeks from all parts were educated in the liberal arts and sciences." In the past Greeks brought culture to the west. It was right that there should now be an exchange of this benefit. Italy would accomplish this, where in past centuries wise men hunted out and persecuted by the Turks had taken refuge. In Tuscany, Greeks and Russians, joined by the knot of religion, would tighten "the bonds of polite society, literature, and genius."[16] From a political and military point of view, Orlov's work in the Mediterranean was irreversible. The fact that he had dominated the coasts of Greece and of Asia for some years, "from the Hellespont to the mouth of the Nile," had borne fruit. Orlov had shown that the immense empire of the Turks "is like an overgrown body whose limbs are so far separated from their common center that they are weakened by the distance and cannot be reached by life's strength." Striking at the heart of the Turkish empire, Orlov had shown how little was known of its different parts, and how great was the peril of dissolution that hung over it. If you had done no other, "your way of waging war, Alexis, would make your name immortal."[17]

At the end of his *Oration*, Pagano left his hero alone before Hellas, immersed in thought of what Greece had been in the past, and what it was becoming. He imagined and reevoked his thoughts when confronted by its famous cities. In Athens (where in fact Orlov had never been), he thought of Pericles, Alcibiades, and Themistocles. "Have you equaled their glory and courage in repulsing the barbarians?" Had he been struck by the magnificent monuments of this beautiful and wise

[14] Ibid., pp. xxivff.
[15] Ibid., p. xxviii.
[16] Ibid., pp. xxviff.
[17] Ibid., pp. xxxff.

city, "most blessed" in the distant past? Had he seen how it was now hardly believable that Athens had been there? "What thoughts arose in you when you saw Sparta," the city with that virtue and discipline in war, "whose austerity your Muscovites have imitated?" And Thebes, the land of Epaminondas? "What did you think?" Only one thought could come from so much past glory and so much present horror and squalor: carry out the task, uproot the barbarians. The heroes of Hellas called him with a great voice. "What are you waiting for? Liberate Greece, their splendid prey, from the hands of barbaric bandits!" A new age would open. When Greece raised its head again, a new Homer and a new Virgil would not be lacking. In St. Petersburg would be celebrated the triumph of Catherine and of Petr Rumjancev. "You will be saluted as a new Africanus and Asiaticus." Nor would be forgotten "Panin [Count Nicolaj Panin], who is as Athena to the present Juno [Catherine II]." This would be a great triumph, worthy of the great Russian empire, of liberation from servitude and barbarism in Greece and all the east.[18]

This was a burst of neoclassical rhetoric—a youthful enthusiasm still bathed with discovery and dreams born of school benches—but also the revelation of a different and far-away world, a deep echo of the problems bubbling up in the Mediterranean at the end of the Russo-Turkish war.[19] There were traces of them in the letter that Domasnev, director of the Academy of Sciences at St. Petersburg, wrote to him between 15 and 26 May 1777. Pagano hastened to publish it in the appendix of his drama *Gli esuli tebani*. The *Foglietto di notizie domestiche* in Naples gave notice of this further contact with Russia, reevoked Pagano's *Oratio*, and said the letter of the Russian literary and military man was "worthy of attention" also "for the elegance of the Italian language," in which it was written. "The academicians of the Crusca would not find anything to correct in the selection of words and style of this Muscovite writer. Signor Pagano was addressed in kind and most honorable terms, and the letter was accompanied by two medals coined on the occasion of the hundredth anniversary of that academy. . . . The honor of Sig. Pagano resounds with greater luster in our own country, something that should interest any upstanding man."[20]

---

[18] Ibid., pp. xxxvff.

[19] On Pagano's culture and ideas between the sixties and the seventies, see *Riformatori*, vol. 5, pp. 785ff. The publication of the *Oratio* can probably be dated to 1772 or 1773, when the Pisan college for Greeks was being founded, when Aleksej Orlov was often in St. Petersburg, and when the possibilities of a Russian reconquest of Greece were still open. Pagano speaks of Gicca, who was leaving Naples at that time, and probably alludes to the period when the 1773 naval campaign was beginning. The question remains open why Domašnev, as we will see, delayed to thank Pagano until 1777.

[20] *Foglietto di notizie domestiche*, no. 4, 30 January 1778.

Other literary ties were also formed between St. Petersburg and Naples in these years. The war with Turkey had hardly begun when the jurist Domenico Diodati had the idea of dedicating a volume that he had just finished to Catherine II. He was convinced he had made a great discovery, that in Galilee at the time of Christ Hebrew and Aramaic were not spoken, but Greek was. Thus Jesus and his followers spoke the language of Hellas in their youth. It seemed to him that this was just what the empress and Russia needed. It was a kind of erudite antiquarian translation of the Mediterranean policy of Catherine II. Through Metastasio, who volunteered to send it, as well as Golicyn, the Russian ambassador in Vienna, Diodati's book arrived in St. Petersburg. A long silence followed, because "the war between Ottomans and Russians was then at its most turbulent point."[21] Finally the empress sent to Naples "two magnificent signs of her benevolent gratitude," that is, two gold medals with her own image.[22] "Not content with that, a few months later she sent him a copy of her Instruction for a new law code of the empire, printed handsomely and tastefully in St. Petersburg in four languages, that is, Russian, Latin, German, and French."[23] In Italy she had made a similar offering only to Beccaria.[24] Gregorij Vasil'evič Kozickij, the editor of this edition of the Nakaz and secretary of Catherine II, later wrote to Diodati, this learned Neapolitan who had made even Jesus speak Greek.[25] But he thought it necessary to limit his Hellenic enthusiasm. "The religion of the Russian empire, certainly, is the Greek rite," he explained, "but we Russians do not use in church any language besides that of our fatherland, and all the books for divine service have been translated into it. This was done at the time when the Christian religion was brought to us from Greece, and the custom has never been ques-

[21] Luigi Diodati, Memorie della vita di Domenico Diodati (Naples: Giuseppe Maria Porcelli, 1815), p. 13. The book is entitled Dominici Diodati I.C. neapolitani De Christo graece loquente exercitatio, quae ostenditur graecam sive hellenisticam linguam tam judaeis omnibus, tum ipsi adeo Christo Domino et apostolis nativam ac vernaculam fuisse (Naples: Josephus Raymundus, 1767). The copy in Paris, B. Nationale, with the call number X 7207, is dedicated to the famous Greek scholar Ansse de Villoison: "Doctissimo atque eruditissimo viro Joan. Baptista Gasparo d'Ansse de Villoison Dominicus Diodatus in obsequi signum d.d.". The dedication to Catherine underlined the merits of the empress in the field of culture and education but did not forget her "bellicas expeditiones" on land and sea.

[22] Ibid., pp. 18ff.

[23] Ibid., pp. 20ff, 29ff.

[24] Beccaria's copy, bound with Russian markings, is in Milan, B. Ambrosiana, with the call number Becc. B. 196. An old hand has made a list of the passages common to the Instruction and to Dei delitti e delle pene, cited in the Haarlem edition of 1766.

[25] Diodati, Memorie della vita di Domenico Diodati, p. 29. See Semennikov, Materialy, pp. 45ff., and Pavel N. Berkov, Istorija russkoj žurnalistiki XVIII veka (History of Russian journalism in the eighteenth century) (Moscow: Akademija nauk SSSR, 1954), index.

tioned."[26] To Kozickij, Diodati did well to send "the treatise of Carlantonio Broggia *Sui tributi, sulle monete e sulla sanità* and Bartolomeo Intieri's book, *Sulla stufa,* invented by him, *per la conservazione de' grani,* so that they could be translated into Russian for use in that empire." "The empress," concluded the biographer brother of Diodati, "liked to know the progress of science in foreign lands, and Diodati on that occasion succeeded in furthering the honor of his countrymen."[27]

Hellenic enthusiasm, solidarity with Greek exiles, neo-classical visions, discovery of the Russian world—these were all elements that appeared in Neapolitan culture at the beginning of the seventies. But they were limited not only by the venturesome and precarious character of Orlov's expedition, but also, one should not forget, by the aim of the government of Tanucci, the minister of Ferdinando IV, not to let itself stray in any way beyond a policy of caution, prudence, and neutrality. The elderly minister became more and more entrenched in his old convictions and hostile to grand commerce and great merchants involved in international adventures. For some time he had been convinced that Naples would not gain any advantage from the development of commerce in the Levant.[28] He had little sympathy for Russia, and he was often in conflict with Venice. Then war had unexpectedly arrived in the Mediterranean, making difficult the balance he expected to maintain between the Bourbons and the English, and between large and small powers. He was even worried about too curious Russians, like Michele Wetockinickoff (Vetošnikov), who had "shown himself in a boat scanning the crater [of Vesuvius], sketching the port, fortifications, and so on," and who did not fail to be arrested, although he was soon set free.[29]

Galiani expressed better than others this Parthenopean reserve and diffidence. His point of view was influenced by the opinions of his French friends: not by Voltaire, but by those, like Suard, who were

[26] *Notizie del mondo,* no. 3, 9 January 1770, p. 21 (Naples, 30 December). The letter was dated "St. Petersburg, 1768 A.D., 13 February, according to the old calendar we still use." In the same issue of the Florentine gazette is reproduced Diodati's dedication to Catherine II.

[27] Diodati, *Memorie della vita di Domenico Diodati,* p. 29.

[28] Francesco Barbagallo, "Discussioni e progetti sul commercio tra Napoli e Costantinopoli nel '700," *R. stor. ital.,* year 82, fasc. 2 (June 1971): 264ff.

[29] *Notizie del mondo,* no. 87, 31 October 1772, p. 718 (Naples, 20 October). The same issue of the gazette published the dispatch on Tanucci of 17 October 1772 announcing with pleasure that the suspicion had been dismissed and the Russian released, apparently after the intervention of Catherine II. This was Michael Nikolaevič Vetošnikov, a student in the academy of art in St. Petersburg, who lived for some time in Rome and Naples and died in 1791. See Petr Michailovič Majkov, *Ivan Ivanovič Beckoj. Opyt ego biografii* (St. Petersburg: Obscestvermaja pol'za, 1904), p. 207.

closer to the official policy of Louis xv.[30] To Suard he explained, in fact,
that in Naples the gazettes were worth little or nothing, and that to inform oneself it was necessary to refer to the "gazette of Florence" (the
Notizie del mondo), "which is very interesting." Even Galiani was taken in
1770 by the sense of surprise that spread everywhere when Muscovites
were seen entering the Mediterranean and stirring Greeks in the Morea. "What an adventure! We will be neighbors to the Russians, and
from Otranto to St. Petersburg there will be no more than a step and a
little bit of sea: *Dux foemina facti*! A woman has done this! It is too good
to be true."[31] But Galiani was dominated above all by the thought of the
useless risks Naples would take if it intervened among Russians, Greeks,
and Turks. Writing to I. I. Šuvalov on 1 October 1771, he did not abstain from giving advice to Russia and to Catherine II. If it had been up
to him, he would have left only a few ships in the Archipelago, thus
limiting the cost. He would have paid more attention to the threat Sweden and Denmark posed to Russia. Was Kronštadt so strong and secure
as to make it possible to keep that many ships and men in the Mediterranean? "For the rest," he concluded, "I am only a good Italian and
nothing more. In the conquest of the Crimea I see an event that is most
favorable to Italy, because I know from history that it was never so prosperous as in the time when Caffa was in the hands of the Genoese. My
advice to your sovereign is to give it back to Italians and enter into commercial relations directly with us."[32] This was a truly good example of a
realism that wanted to be Machiavellian and ended up, as not infre-
quently with Galiani, in a strange utopia flowering in a past long dead.
He would exchange these dreams later himself for more concrete projects when the opening of the Black Sea began to transform the prospect
of relations between Russia and the Mediterranean.[33] But his politics

[30] Ferdinando Galiani, *Dialogues sur le commerce des bleds*, ed. Fausto Nicolini (Milan and
Naples: Ricciardi, 1959), pp. 544, 556.

[31] Ferdinando Galiani, *Correspondance*, new ed. by Lucien Perey and Gaston Maugras
(Paris: Calman Lévy, 1881), vol. 1, p. 134, to Madame d'Epinay, Naples, 5 May 1770. See
pp. 182ff, to Suard, Naples, 30 June 1770–, pp. 95ff., to Baron d'Holbach, Naples, 7 April
1770.

[32] The letter is published, according to the Soviet custom, only in Russian (from which
it has been necessary to translate it back into Italian) in Nikolaj Golicyn, "I. I. Šuvalov i
ego inostrannye korrispondenty" (I. I. Šuvalov and his foreign correspondents), in *Lite-
raturnoe nasledstvo* (Literary heritage), vols. 29–30 (1937), p. 282.

[33] See Furio Diaz, "L'abate Galiani consigliere di commercio estero nel regno di Na-
poli," *R. stor. ital.* 80, fasc. 4 (December 1968): 854ff., and Ferdinando Galiani, *Opere*, ed.
Furio Diaz and Luciano Guerci (Milan and Naples: Ricciardi, 1975), especially pp. 770ff.
"Piano del modo come si potrebbe condurre a buon fine la negoziazione per conseguire
dalla Porta ottomana la libera navigazione del Mar nero dei bastimenti mercantili delle
Due Sicilie," of 1784. For the relationship between Galiani and Domašnev, see Domašhev's

was always, even in this camp, dominated by a deeply rooted sense of his own weakness. In his forecast for 1771 he did not exclude the possibility of a return of the Russians to Greece. He already seemed to see "an Orlov sovereign prince of the Morea," admitting this hypothesis with a kind of resigned optimism: "That will be better for us than you can imagine."[34] But he had no illusions about Catherine; he admired her precisely for the Machiavellian hard political element that inspired her policy. Voltaire seemed to be dreaming when he attributed to her generous thoughts of religious toleration. "His Catherine is a masterful woman because she is intolerant and aggressive."[35] "In politics I admit only pure Machiavellianism, unmixed, crude, green, in all its force, and with all its bitterness."[36] Galiani thus closed himself to the possibility of understanding the political debate that was developing with greater and greater intensity in Paris (the last quotation was directed against Raynal). And even in his relations with Catherine he risked more and more becoming a distant admirer, even a writer of inscriptions for the monuments of the Russian empress. He was no longer able to understand struggles and contradictions. He foresaw a further expansion of Russian power but believed that Europe would become fossilized in a type of absolutism, tempered by "slowness of procedures" and "sweetness of manners": something similar to China. "Republics will disappear in Europe: they do not march in line with monarchies; they lose ground and sink."[37] The events in Poland seemed to make him right. But in ideas, as in deep political movements, Galiani became more and more incapable of recognizing the forces that made a fossilization of the old regime, and its slow evolution toward a stability worthy of the empire of China, impossible, the forces of opposition and revolution, which Catherine in her way had contributed much to put in motion with her Russo-Turkish war.

The view of a Neapolitan publicist, Michele Torcia, was not lacking in acumen in the years when Orlov's fleet dominated the Levant. Catherine's task seemed to him difficult. If she freed the serfs "the revenues of the crown would be much diminished" and the peasants "who had become landed proprietors would perhaps grow impatient with the yoke of the government." The most positive element in the situation seemed to be the nobility, "perhaps in that century the most cultivated

letter in Naples, Società napoletana di storia patria, MS. Galiani, vol. 31, year 13, no. 24, from St. Petersburg, 3 April 1782.

[34] Galiani, *Correspondance*, vol. 1, p. 307, to d'Alembert, Naples, 24 November 1770.

[35] Ibid., p. 407, to Madame d'Epinay, Naples, 22 June 1771.

[36] Ibid., vol. 2, p. 114, to the same, Naples, 5 September 1772.

[37] Ibid., pp. 236ff., to the same, Naples, 24 July 1773.

in Europe." "There are few among them who do not have the perfect use of two or three languages. The larger part applies itself particularly to some art or science to the point of mastering it, and in general their love of culture and intellect has become almost a passion." "This nation, although the last to set itself in motion, is one of the most advanced in civilization and spiritual culture."[38]

It is not difficult to find Greco-Russian echoes beyond Venice, Tuscany, and Naples. In Piedmont diplomatic and military interests predominated. We have seen Cavalier Masino implicated in Orlov's undertaking. Count De Sylva based an important book on a similar experience.[1] The way he presented his book, with the stamp of the ecclesiastical censor, made the Principe de Ligne smile. He expressed a clearly positive judgment but had to add the following: "What troubles me, for all the effort I made to read it, is the approval of the Reverend Carmelite Father, who says it is a good book because there is nothing in it against the Catholic faith or morals."[2] Old Piedmont retained archaic forms and usages even when it opened itself to the modern world.

De Sylva had wanted to explain realistically the causes of the first Turkish defeats. For these he turned to Ottoman society itself, noting that the feudal regime of the Timariot, not unlike that of the Starostwo of Poland, brought naturally to mind "the idea of the almost extinguished old feudal government of Europe."[3] But what prevented even the Turks from reforming such inefficient structures? Fortunately for Christians they did not intend to abandon the "ridiculous prejudices"

[38] *Sbozzo politico di Europa scritto nell'inverno del 1772 e 1773 da Michele Torcia napoletano*, Regio archiviario della Suprema Real Giunta degli Abusi (Florence, 1775), pp. 75, 77. He also mentions, on p. 78, the college founded in Pisa "for the education and studies of a large number of youths, women, and men of the Greek nation to then return to their homeland and cultivate the sciences there." On this figure see Edoardo Tortorolo, "Michele Torcia: Un funzionario Tanucciano tra Magna Grecia ed Europa," in *Bernardo Tanucci e la Toscana. Tre giornate di studio. Pisa-Stia. 28–30 Settembre 1983* (Florence: Leo S. Olschki, 1986), pp. 139ff.

[1] De Sylva, *Considérations sur la guerre présente entre les Russes et les Turcs, écrites en partie au mois d'octobre et en partie au mois de décembre de l'année 1769* (Turin: Reycends, 1773). It is not certain who the real author was, but it was probably Emanuele de Sylva Taroicca, of Portuguese origin. There is some information about his family in Manno's *Patriziato subalpino*. The *Considérations* was sold together with the *Remarques sur quelques articles de l'Essai général de tactique*, by the same author and the same publisher.

[2] Cited in Max Jahns, *Geschichte der Kriegswissenschaften vornehmlich in Deutschland*, vol. 3: *Das XVIII. Jahrhundert* (Munich and Leipzig: R. Oldemburg, 1891), p. 2090. At the foot of his remarks was the permission dated 20 October 1773 by "François Marie de S. Pierre des Carmes déchaussés . . . consulteur du S. Office." For the civil authorities the permission was that of the Abate Berta and of Conte Caissotti.

[3] De Sylva, *Considérations sur la guerre présente*, p. 27.

that tied them to the past. "Even if there were some wise enlightened Moslem among them, in a state to be useful to his country, he would not dare show himself, out of fear of being the victim of jealousy and envy."[4] Even politically the Sultan was much weaker than was generally believed. "The emperor, who is believed to be so despotic, is often the slave of ignorance and superstition, of fanaticism and cabals that abuse the credulity of the people. The ulema can almost always make the Sultan tremble."[5] Without saying it too explicitly, De Sylva let one think that the Russians' superiority over the Turks consisted precisely in the capacity of the first to open themselves to the ideas of the Enlightenment. In this way advice and suggestions multiplied. This did not mean, naturally, that they were immune from tactical or strategic errors. War should be "lively and short," and all the more so because recruitment was not "so inexhaustible a resource as many imagine," and "consuming men is a matter of great consequence for an empire."[6] Russia had barely one third the population it could have. From this point of view the Turks had an advantage. Nevertheless, Russia's potential was enormous. Its infantry had become "one of the best in Europe." "That infantry is like a wall." The religious faith of the soldiers was as strong as that of their enemies. And the first had the advantage of "constancy and resolution" before the "enthusiasm" of the second.[7] "There is no soldier easier to feed than the Russian."[8] The problems were in the extraordinarily awkward organization. "The Russian army is always overloaded with baggage. It holds back what is necessary in order to have the superfluous. In vain they make regulations and give orders. These have little effect."[9] This was an acute observation, which beyond the form of the army, went to the heart of the state mechanism in Russia.

In Milan, at least through the eyes of Pietro Verri, political interests predominated: the attempt, that is, to understand how Catherine II entered the debate that was then unfolding in all of Europe between traditional and new liberties, and between absolutism and the desire for social transformation. Even in the mind of Pietro Verri the daring of the Muscovite undertaking aroused wonder and enthusiasm. But he also understood the risks of abuse of power, despotism, and the barbarism it could not help produce. The fleet of Spiridov and Elphinston was still in the English Channel when Pietro wrote the following to his

4 Ibid., p. 35.
5 Ibid., p. 36.
6 Ibid., p. 70.
7 Ibid., p. 80.
8 Ibid., p. 82.
9 Ibid., p. 85.

brother: "On one hand, I like this move: it is something grand and heroic; it takes elevation of spirit to plan such an expedition and bring it
off. From St. Petersburg to the Archipelago there is a new course, a
marvel for the Russians. On the other hand, I am sorry that a nation so
accustomed to feel the knout should come to mix itself in our affairs;
after all, the Germans, French, Spanish, Italians, English, more or less,
are a family, but the Muscovites have been civilized for too short a time;
genealogical family trees are of little use, but those of nations are quite
important."[10] He feared that the Muscovite fleet would stir up all the
problems of the Adriatic and the Aegean, bringing the Montenegrins
into the war and disturbing relations among Constantinople, Greece,
and Egypt. Provisions would be lacking, but the Ottoman capital would
not fall because it was too well defended by nature and by arms. This
was a prophecy of notable precision that, as happens sometimes in this
correspondence, arouses the suspicion that it was made *post festum*. But
the political foresight—which Pietro Verri tells us he reached with the
help of his Welsh friend Henry Lloyd—has a ring of authenticity.

But who were, and what had they come to bring, these Muscovites?
They were above all a nation in singularly rapid development. "These
Russians have truly made haste," Verri's brother Alessandro wrote from
Rome. Little time had passed since their origins and already their culture was in flower. "They already have good poets, good tragedies, have
translated many French books, and all say St. Petersburg is a Paris." But
their political life did not correspond to this development. "Despotism
is there with all its strength, and there is no law besides the caprice of
the sovereign," a contradiction that risked stopping them soon along
their way. "Without a modern government they will not get far." Excellent, still, was their military technique, as demonstrated by their artillery, which is said to be "better than any other in Europe, and thus in
the world." In fact they were making war with another despotic land,
and certainly a less cultivated one. Thus Alessandro Verri's preference
was for the Russians. "They are less cruel, less fanatical, and more cultivated." But he was still uneasy and ended up concluding that they were
"terrible, both of them." "If things go forward and one of them has a
great advantage, it could change the face of Europe."[11] He later called
Russia "a nation escaped from barbarism."[12] When they arrived in the
Mediterranean, the Russians stirred rebellions, revolutions, and attempts at liberation. In March there arrived in Rome news of the first
Venetian ships that had passed "unexpectedly into the service of Mus-

[10] *Carteggio di Pietro e di Alessandro Verri*, vol. 3, pp. 81ff., 30 September 1769.
[11] Ibid., p. 100, 7 October 1769.
[12] Ibid., p. 135, 16 December 1769.

covy."[13] The Morea was in flames. Pietro Verri, from Milan, wrote as follows: "If the Florentine gazettes tell the truth, the Spartans have united with the Russians and have already gained a foothold in many cities of the Morea."[14] Then, like the rest of Italy, the two brothers exchanged news of victories and terrible massacres. From Rome, Alessandro spoke on 18 April of rumors of a "kind of Sicilian vespers of Greeks of the islands and other places subject to the Porte," adding, "they say there has been a universal massacre."[15] To Pietro the attempt at insurrection in Greece immediately recalled the Corsican revolt, which had ended less than a year earlier with the battle of Pontenuovo. He had followed developments in Corsica to the end with great emotion, talking about them even with the Belgian Cornélius de Nény, his colleague in the Supremo Consiglio di Economia, who had had direct contact with Pasquale Paoli. Nény—Pietro recalled—had told him "that the Spartans, surrounded by Turks, have always been able to maintain themselves free in their mountains, and whenever the Turks have tried something against them they have failed; but he also said that in the last century a party of them, venturing out into the plain and surrounded by Muslims, were obliged to throw themselves onto a ship and abandon themselves to the sea, and by chance arrived in Corsica, made their homes there, and spread the first seeds of independence among those islanders."[16] Thus was born, from the conversation of two high functionaries of Maria Theresa, a kind of distant vision, a myth, that did not correspond much to immediate reality (the Greek settlements in Corsica were always viewed with hostility by Paoli and his followers), but that still expressed a deeper common element we can recognize, as we have noted, in the Corsican and Greek revolts.

Even when news came of the Russian reversals in the Morea, Pietro Verri continued to be convinced of the military effectiveness of the army of Catherine II. It was precisely the despotism of the Russian government that made the army an exceptional instrument in Europe. "An army in which no one flees, no one deserts, where there is blind obedience, where the men are robust, was made to conquer a corrupt degenerate state like that of the Turks." Poor and vile seemed, in the light of this situation, the policy of Rome, which, as he wrote jokingly to his brother, seemed to be on the side of the Turks and certainly stood for

---

[13] Ibid., p. 225, 17 March 1770.

[14] Ibid., p. 261, 25 April 1770.

[15] Ibid., p. 259, 18 April 1770.

[16] Ibid., p. 261, 25 April 1770; see also on p. 262 a note on Count Cornélius de Nény. On his activity in Corsica, see Franco Venturi, *Settecento riformatore*, vol. 5, pt. 1, p. 101 n. See also Walter W. Davis, *Joseph II: An Imperial Reformer for the Austrian Netherlands* (The Hague: Nijhoff, 1974), p. 38 n. 23.

the status quo, for a resigned preservation of the existing balance. In response, in a similar vein, Pietro wrote: "I am in this war Christian, most Christian, but you Romans, you are a little Turkish, from what I see."[17] The papacy truly did not seem able to go beyond the ancient disputes that divided the Roman and Greek churches.

For the Verri brothers, as well, the battle of Chesmé marked a turning point: the conflict at this point, even in their eyes, became less ideological and more military and diplomatic. The weariness provoked by the long war and thoughts about the huge expense weighing on Russia soon began to throw a shadow on their correspondence, especially on Alessandro's letters from Rome.[18] The fear that the liberation of Greece would remain a vain hope appeared ever more evident in Pietro's mind. The Turks, prolonging the conflict, would succeed in tiring and weakening their adversary. In October 1770 he was not yet ready to abandon his hopes: "But I still would like the fatherland of Pericles, Miltiades, Plato, and so many venerable men to change its destiny, so that the oppressor of this degraded ingenuous nation should not walk over their honored bones."[19] He did not change his position about Russian policy even when Vienna moved to limit the expansion of Catherine II.[20] But in 1772 the vigor of the Muscovite enterprise was fading, and the violence and vulgarity of men like Orlov came more and more to the center of the picture. Alessandro was struck by this when he saw the general in Rome. "He is an uncommonly tall man, with a ferocious air, strong as a Hercules, unobliging, with a deep saber scar under his left eye. I saw him at the Marchesa's when the Duke of Gloucester was there. To show his strength he took an apple between two fingers and crushed it so that half the fruit shot out across the room before the face of the duke and almost hit him. The Muscovite, not in any way seeking to slight His Royal Highness, took no more trouble than to smile in a martial way from his chair where he was sprawled with one leg crossed over the other."[21] The abduction of Princess Tarakanova naturally added a further disquieting element to the last period of the presence of Orlov in Italy.

The discussion in Italy that the consequences of the Russian penetration into the Mediterranean evoked was varied, lively, and some-

---

[17] *Carteggio di Pietro e di Alessandro Verri*, vol. 3, p. 304, 30 May 1770.
[18] Ibid., p. 428, 17 August 1770; p. 461, 12 September 1770. He received a large part of his information from Ivan Ivanovič Šuvalov.
[19] Ibid., vol. 4, p. 19, 10 October 1770.
[20] Ibid., pp. 148ff., 2 March 1771.
[21] Ibid., vol. 7, p. 152, 19 April 1775.

times profound. It brought to light for a moment a whole hidden world, from Montenegro to the Peloponnesus, from Smyrna to Egypt. Fears and hopes were aroused by the Greek revolt, and the naval and commercial developments that accompanied and followed Orlov's expedition were followed with growing interest. Then, with their departure for St. Petersburg, the fires seemed to go out. The discussions about Greece and Turkey, about Russia and the Levant, would resume only later, during the second war of Catherine II with the Ottoman Porte. By then the center of the debate was not Italy, but France, where the eighties witnessed a true flowering of neo-Hellenic enthusiasm, and a rediscovery of the Levant that took many forms. Prepared by the *Voyage littéraire de Grèce* of Pierre-Augustin Guys, which came out in Paris in 1771, fed by the researches and books of Jean-Baptiste d'Ansse de Villoison and Abbé Jean-Jacques Barthélemy, this current had, one could say, two political poles: a positive one, favorable to the rebirth of modern Greece, in Marie-Gabriel Choiseul-Gouffier, and a negative one, disparagingly hostile to the modern inhabitants of Hellas, in Cornélius de Pauw. Then the themes that we have seen passionately discussed among the agents of Catherine II, between Papasoglis and Psaros, for instance, and that appeared in Italian books and newspapers at the beginning of the seventies, returned to the stage. What was the relationship between ancient and modern Greece? Who was responsible for the degeneration of the modern descendants of Themistocles and Lycurgus? What role did the oppression brought about by Turkish conquest play? And where should the Greeks turn for help in their hope for a rebirth? This debate had something similar, and parallel, to the debate about degeneration and American slavery that Antonello Gerbi has revealed with great clarity.[1]

Naturally, the destiny of Greece touched the roots of European civilization too closely for the discussion of the eighties not to color the taste and whole political atmosphere of the period immediately preced-

---

[1] For a bibliography see Renata Lavagnini, *Villoison in Grecia. Note di viaggio (1784–1786)* (Palermo: Istituto siciliano di studi bizantini e neoellenici, 1974), p. 79 n. 250. On all these problems, see Luciano Guerci, *Libertà degli antichi e libertà dei moderni. Sparta, Atene e i "philosphes" nella Francia del '700* (Naples: Guida, 1979). On A. Gerbi, see Marcello Carmagnani, "Antonello Gerbi e il Nuovo mondo," *R. stor. Ital.*, fasc. 1, (March 1978): 165ff., and the recent revised and enlarged edition of Antonello Gerbi, *The Dispute of the New World*, tr. G. Moyle (Pittsburgh: Pittsburgh University Press). David Constantine has taken up different aspects of the Greek problem in *Early Travelers and the Hellenic Ideal* (Cambridge: Cambridge University Press, 1984), although he did not use Italian sources. Thus the insurrection of 1770 is seen through the *Gentleman's Magazine* and other London periodicals, and not through Venetian sources, which were much more attentive to developments on the Adriatic and Ionian islands.

ing the French Revolution. It is enough to open the folio volume of exquisite elegance that Choiseul-Gouffier published in 1782 under the title *Voyage pittoresque de la Grèce* to be aware of his major concern. On the frontispiece was Greece, dressed in what seemed to be a national costume and enchained, lying in the midst of her great ancestors' tombs. "This was the posterity of the Greeks."[2] It was enough to observe the Maineotes to persuade oneself: "robust, sober, invincible, free as in the time of Lycurgus." It was natural that the Russians had turned to them a decade earlier. If they had been defeated, the responsibility should lie at the feet of the agents of St. Petersburg, who, "to make themselves accepted, minimized the difficulties," and to the Russian army, which "arrived with feeble and insufficient means." "There was no accord, no concerted action, between Russians and Greeks, or among Greek chiefs. It seemed on one side and the other that everything was expected to be resolved from the first effort, and from a carefree daring." Catherine's men had acted as if it were a question of a slight of hand, not a true and proper revolution. "There were only a few conspirators, when a confederation was needed; there were only a few seditious, when what was needed were rebels." "The deaths of one hundred thousand Greeks were the punishment for such imprudence."[3]

France and the other European countries thus came, in the thought of Choiseul-Gouffier, to take the place of Catherine II, or at least to join forces with the Russian empress, in a policy of solidarity with Greece. The liberation of Hellas would not be difficult to carry out if supported "by the great powers who have a true interest in furthering the revolution." To Catherine remained the great merit of having conceived and continued to think of this possibility. She had not hesitated to call the Greeks to liberty, just as she had wanted to emancipate "the lowest class of her subjects." Now, with the support of Europe, it would be possible to create circumstances permitting the insurgents to demonstrate their discipline and their capacity to "obey their leaders and commanders." This was the indispensable premise necessary to win victory in such an "august national war."[4] This was how to achieve "a free state in the Morea."[5]

Choiseul-Gouffier returned often in the text of his work, and in the luxurious illustrations, to the exalting but wounding experience of 1770. Under the first plate one read the following: "Bellona, freeing a

[2] Marie-Gabriel-Auguste Choiseul-Gouffier, *Voyage pittoresque de la Grèce* (Paris, 1782), p. v. The preface of the work, from which these words are taken, appears to have been published in January 1783. See Léonce Pingaud, *Choiseul-Gouffier. La France en Orient sous Louis XVI* (Paris: A. Picard, 1887), p. 52.

[3] Choiseul-Gouffier, *Voyage*, p. ix.

[4] Ibid., p. xi.

[5] Ibid., p. xv.

cache of arms and followed by Russian troops, shows Greek slaves the symbol of liberty, from which they have the baseness to flee." The engraving, dated 1778, alluded to the assault on Coron. Several years had passed, but the effects of the defeat were still felt. The whole land was in misery. "All groaned under the outcome of a cruel war." Bitter were the memories of those who had acted like brigands, "who only thought of pillaging their compatriots rather than fighting for their common liberty." There could be only one explanation for their behavior: the Greeks were "degenerate, made vile by long slavery."[6] And all their hopes of liberation from the Turkish yoke were turned toward Russia, toward a state undoubtedly despotic itself. Choiseul-Gouffier asked the following question: "Would the slave of such a weak, such a decrepit, government as that of the Ottomans find support in the rigorous administration of an equally despotic state, in its infancy, one might say, with an energy the first has long since lost?"[7]

Thus, the liberation of Greece was difficult and risky, but still always possible, Choiseul-Gouffier concluded. A pure and simple illusion, C. de Pauw answered him. The "state of degeneration" into which the Greeks had fallen was such as to make any remedy impossible.[8] It was their religion, so appealing to the Russians, that was the principal cause of their decadence. It was not by chance that the Turks had left them their monasteries but had closed or created difficulties for their schools. The result was that "this people" had "returned to infancy in wanting to be theologians."[9] French writers like Guys, who held that the Greeks, once free, would return to the age of Pericles, were ignoring "the depths of darkness that surround the spirits of modern Greeks."[10] The responsibility for this situation did not belong to the Venetians or to the Turks. To persuade oneself, it was enough to observe the most independent inhabitants of the Peloponnesus, the Maineotes. Their monks in the Order of St. Basil "were bandits as dangerous as the rest of the nation."[11] "There was not the slightest appearance of liberty in a form of government where the elders on one hand and the clergy on the other oppress a nation that claims to be independent."[12]

De Pauw did not forget to mention the flight of a group of Maineotes to Corsica in 1676.[13] His polemic against the Greeks is not far

[6] Ibid., p. 3.

[7] Ibid., p. 6.

[8] Cornélius de Pauw, *Recherches philosophiques sur les Grecs* (Berlin: G. J. Decker, 1788), vol. 1, p. 100.

[9] Ibid., p. 101.

[10] Ibid., p. 103.

[11] Ibid., p. 415.

[12] Ibid., p. 419.

[13] Ibid., p. 421.

from that of many in France and England after Pasquale Paoli's defeat. Against the superstition of the clergy and the people of Corsica, France had brought, they said, an enlightened administration.[14] But even this did not seem possible for Greece, de Pauw concluded. The Muscovites were well aware of it and had soon repented "of having made ties with the most perfidious people in the world."[15]

Only at the end of the century, with the French Revolution, did the image of Greece begin to change. The Maineotes began to be observed for their dress, their mode of life, and their songs, more than for their relationship with the classical world. This romantic vision tended, if not to hide, certainly to veil the deep political and social contrasts that were revealed in the revolt of 1770. Pouqueville's *Voyage* and Fauriel's *Chants populaires* were the most significant representations of a Greece now distant from the age of Orlov and Catherine II.[1] More like the eighteenth-century view, but drained of energy and done up in a refined and sweetened neoclassicism, the last Italian fruit—or rather Venetian, judging from the surroundings in which it matured—of the interest and discussion aroused at the beginning of the seventies was Saverio Scrofani's *Viaggio in Grecia*.[2] Scrofani was in Greece in July 1794 and October of the following year. He had difficulty abandoning his mythological and sentimental visions when observing the reality of the present. "What difference does it make," he said, "if Sparta, Athens, and Corinth no longer exist? The land where they were still had buried in it the great ideas that they had generated in the past: if one knew how to excavate it the land would yield its secret, and one would see, in 1794, the Greece of Pericles and Lycurgus."[3] It was a self-induced illusion, which disappeared when Scrofani proceeded with what we might call the "folklorization" of past and present Greece. He recalled the Olympic games and compared them with spectacles that even in Italy were beginning to "be forgotten": "the *regatta* of Venice and the *cuccagna* of Naples." And he hastened to add: "antiquarians, writers, philosophers, do not grind down the teeth of my comparison." The best of the people had partici-

---

[14] Franco Venturi, "Il dibattito francese e britannico sulla rivoluzione di Corsica," *R. stor. ital.*, fasc. 4 (October 1974): 643ff., and id., *Settecento riformatore*, vol. V–1, pp. 130ff.

[15] De Pauw, *Recherches philosophiques sur les Grecs*, p. 423.

[1] François-Charles-Hugues-Laurent Pouqueville, *Voyage en Morée, à Costantinople, en Albanie et dans d'autres parties de l'Empire Ottoman pendant les années 1798, 1799, 1800 et 1801* (Paris: Gabon, 1805), and Claude-Charles Fauriel, *Chants populaires de la Grèce moderne, recueillis et publiés avec une traduction française et des notes* (Paris: F. Didot, 1824–25).

[2] Saverio Scrofani, *Viaggio in Grecia*. Edited with an introduction and philological notes by Claudio Mutini (Rome: Edizioni dell'Ateneo, 1965).

[3] Scrofani, *Viaggio*, p. 33.

pated in the contests of Hellas, like those of Italy, and had found there glory and praise. "And why are these games being forgotten? Because . . . The people, deprived of their festivals, seek fame in another direction: they have begun to agitate . . . unfortunately."[4] A knot of problems began to be brought to light by his observation, but then Scrofani hurried on. The situation of the Greeks and their right to a free and independent life appeared for an instant in his travels, but then quickly disappeared, "not to be spoken of again," as he said. The Greeks had preserved the character and even the vices of their ancestors, but, deprived of ancient Sparta and Athens, they had "exchanged sentiment for license, delicacy for pleasure, love of glory for self-interest; finally the descendants of Leonidas, of Aristides, of Epaminondas trembled before the gaze of a Turk." Still there were "five million in Europe, three million in Asia." "Their strength of character, which made them, even after so much misfortune and surrounded with barbarians, keep their own language, their own religion, their own customs, shows to the eye of a philosopher what this nation could become. Oh, if I could see it arise, reappear, show the true path. . . . I will be dead, but my wish will be fulfilled. Conquerors, make live again the honor of Athens, Sparta, Corinth, and all Greeks who blush for their state, descendants of those from whom we have inherited arts, sciences, morality, liberty: this is an undertaking worthy of you."[5] These distant visions seemed to come closer and become solid when Scrofani encountered a region in Greece with a more rapidly growing economy. On Cephalonia, he spoke at length of Homer and of the myth of Ulysses, always alive on that island, but then he passed on rapidly to note the Cephalonians' recent activities and successes. "To their natural talents they have brought a certain frankness that makes them seem inhabitants of a great capital rather than of a little island in the Ionian Sea. In recent times they have given a viceroy to Sicily (Giorgio Corafà, whom we have already encountered), a tutor to the prince of Brazil (Michele Franzi, professor in Coimbra at the time of Pombal), a great general and famous architect to Russia (Pietro Melissino and Marino Carburi, whom I have mentioned), and a peacemaker to the Porte, England, and Prussia (Spiridone Lusi, officer in the Bavarian war of succession and, in 1781, Prussian ambassador in Holland, at the time of tension with the United Provinces, Great Britain, Prussia, and then Russia in the reign of Paul I).[6] They have cultivated medicine and chemistry successfully, but navigation is their general preference. Their population barely contains 60,000 men, but they have

[4] Ibid., p. 47.

[5] Ibid., pp. 75ff.

[6] On the adventurous life of these individuals see Masarachi, *Vite degli uomini illustri dell'isola di Cefalonia.*

at sea 200 vessels and 5,000 small ships. The Adriatic, the Mediterranean, the Archipelago, and the Black Sea are filled with Cephalonian ships; they go out into the ocean, to America, and to the Indies. In the last century a Cephalonian captain was viceroy of Siam. Their capacity to emigrate cannot be separated from greed; it drives them to the point of being accused of being the best pirates. If the deeds credited to them are true, the Cephalonians, among all peoples of the Mediterranean, are perhaps the only ones capable of effective strategy. The Russians made use of them recently against the Turks."[7]

In his *Relazione su lo stato attuale . . . della Morea* Scrofani abandoned his reevocation of the past for an up-to-date, intelligent, and precise observation of the present. It was not by chance that the book was dedicated to Matteo Biffi Tolomei. The air of the Georgofili, the agrarian academy in Florence, blows through these pages. "Don't believe, my respected friend, that in Greece I pass my time by only walking and sighing among its ruins." All his attention was concentrated on the "means adopted by nature to make that soil rich and fortunate despite itself," and on the economic, technical, and political impediments making difficult and stunted the still evident revival of Greek life. The contrast with "enterprising Tuscany" was striking. Erroneous laws, barbarous customs, and oppression had made the Greeks "miserable and unfortunate."[8] The roots of this evil were many. First there was the religion of the Mohammedans. "In the middle of this century, when other religions began to decline, Mohammedanism sustained itself, and thus one sees perpetuated among the Turks inertia, poverty, and ignorance." But even here there was progress: "Disbelief, which has corrupted other religions, has spread its first light on the dogmas of Mohammed and has begun to enlighten the minds and warm the hearts of the Turks."[9] Now "the rich, the magistrates, employees in the militia and in commerce, and all those who go to the capital or travel in foreign countries no longer frequent the mosques with more than mere formality." In vain, "the mufti, the mullah, the dervish . . . denounce impiety." "Their cries hasten the revolution of the mind."[10] It must be confessed that "the

---

[7] Scrofani, *Viaggio*, pp. 20ff.

[8] *Relazione su lo stato attuale dell'agricoltura e del commercio della Morea, indirizzato al nobil uomo Matteo Biffi Tolomei gentiluomo fiorentino dall'abate Saverio Scrofani siciliano* (Florence: Gioacchino Pagani, 1798), printed without a title page and without pagination. On Matteo Biffi Tolomei see the notice by Furio Diaz in *DBI*, vol. 10, pp. 386ff. Scrofani's *Relazione* was translated into French and included in *Voyage en Grèce de Xavier Scrofani sicilien, fait en 1794 et 1795*, traduit de l'italien par J.F.C. Blanvillain, traducteur de *Paul et Virginie* (Paris and Strasbourg: Treuttel and Würtz, year 9 [1801]), vol. 3. The editor said (vol. 1, p. v) that Scrofani walked, in his work, "in the steps of Genovesi, Filangieri, Verri, and Galiani."

[9] Scrofani, *Relazione*, p. 8.

[10] Ibid., p. 9.

Greeks were more superstitious and tenacious in their belief than the Turks," even if the growing economic activity distracted them. "In fact, in lands being reclaimed and cultivated one always finds Turkish capital and Greek labor joined together."[11] Religious festivals—seventy-two a year—were a great obstacle. Despite everything, "religion totters even among them."[12] The political regime was still very oppressive. "There is not in Europe . . . an office that can be compared to that of the Pasha of the Morea. The viceroys of Sicily, Valencia, and Ireland, the Venetian general provisioners of the Levant, are shadows in their authority and profits" by comparison.[13] To religion and politics had to be added manners. The "laziness" of the Turks was remarkable. "Their hospitality seemed to result more from pride than from kindness." Nothing seemed capable "of arousing their industry."[14] Their frugality itself was an impediment to the development of the arts. "The bread one eats in the Morea is worse than in any other part of Europe, including Venice."[15] "There were no public schools, no teachers; there is no one there who cultivates the exact sciences, not to mention the principles of physics, logic, geography, poetry, and arithmetic." They were all "bored with the monotony of life."[16] They were more backward than the people the Spaniards found in America. Their whole existence seemed to confirm an obvious economic verity: "For a kingdom to flourish some luxury is required . . ., and for it to arise when depressed it is useless to expect assistance from agriculture, where commerce has not made its first profits." It was enough to look at England. "This land would not have been a strong agricultural and commercial nation if commerce had not opened the way for agriculture."[17]

Despite their difficulties, the Greeks were beginning to take this road. Certainly, they were obliged to hide their riches so as not to be robbed. Certainly, they had imitated the customs and prejudices of the Turks too much. Certainly, their way of cultivating the land was the "worst," but there was progress in specialized products such as raisins, citrus fruits, and livestock. "In the last thirty years there has been considerable progress in the Morea. The Moslem notables have tasted the profit of their capital, and the Greeks the profits of their commerce."[18] Scrofani examined different aspects of economic life of the Morea with

[11] Ibid., p. 10.
[12] Ibid., p. 11.
[13] Ibid., p. 16.
[14] Ibid., pp. 18ff.
[15] Ibid., p. 23.
[16] Ibid., p. 26.
[17] Ibid., p. 27.
[18] Ibid., p. 58.

great competence, making continual comparisons with Italy, especially with Sicily. He provided statistics and geographical information. He gave advice. In his pages the Morea became a significant example exposing reality and change in a Mediterranean land in the last decades of the eighteenth century.

He then returned to social and political problems, also making continual comparisons with the Italian peninsula. For example, he emphasized the fact that, despite appearances, the Morea "had its fiefs." "These are not hereditary"; there was no seigneurial justice. But even here the "lords extort and milk, and that is enough to vex the peasants."[19] Commerce evolved in an atmosphere of continuous conflict and contrast. "The continued war with the Barbary pirates, Neapolitans, Sicilians, Maltese, Tuscans, and Genoese, hinders commerce in the Morea."[20] On the mainland, the Albanians were a continual menace.

Still, one could not deny that there was progress. "I would rather take heart," concluded Scrofani, "in considering the secret work of time engaged in raising a great defeated nation, than grieve for the idea that it might never rise again."[21] Through this sense of hoped-for renewal, the reality of the age of Orlov now seemed put in the shade.

The century's last tribute came from Friedrich Hölderlin. At the heart of his *Hyperion* was the exultation of a Greece arising alive and perfect as in antiquity, and horror in its defeat, joy in good military action, sorrow for the dissolution of the military force, the massacre, the pillage, and the fratricidal war. We find in the German poet all the contrasts and conflicts that had accompanied the insurrection of the Morea from the beginning: the distant vision of Sparta and Lycurgus, the reality of life of the Maineotes, the uniting of all Hellenic forces, and the inexpiable internal struggles. Hölderlin's hero, Hyperion, after a long search and pilgrimage, receives from his friend Alabanda the great news: "Russia has declared war on the Porte. They come with their fleet to the Archipelago. The Greeks will be free, if they rise up, to drive the Sultan to the Euphrates. The Greeks will do their duty; the Greeks will be free. And I feel truly happy. . . . If you are what you once were, come! I am in the village of Coron, if you take the road for Mistra. I live under the hill, in the white farmhouse, on the edge of the wood."[1] Breaking with his past life, and sure to keep off forever the peril of

[19] Ibid., p. 64.

[20] Ibid., p. 75.

[21] Ibid., p. 89.

[1] Friedrich Hölderlin, *Iperione*, ed. Giovanni Angelo Alfero (Turin: UTET, 1960), p. 125.

"growing old, falling into misery, becoming a common man," Hyperion obtains the impassioned approval of his lover, Diotima, and dedicates himself entirely to the work of liberating Greece.[2] "I am at the center of the Peloponnesus," he writes a little later. "Believe that he who goes about in this land still supporting the yoke on his neck, and does not change himself into a Pelopidas, is without heart and intellect." "The people of the mountains here are burning for vengeance." Enthusiasm arouses their primitive natures. Should one fear that they are too savage? Without hesitation, it is time to put ourselves at their head.[3] Nor should one be too hesitant about the Russians, as the friend Alabanda explains. "Don't be scandalized by our allies. I know well that the good Russians want to use us like a weapon; but let them!" The important thing was that "our strong Spartans" were becoming self-conscious, coming "thus to know who they are and what they can do" and creating "their own life." To this Hyperion responds that the new life had to be worthy of antiquity. Now it was time to "take off the garments of slaves." The dawn was breaking on the "young free state of the land of Greece." At its center would be "the Pantheon of all that is beautiful."[4] "All must be redone," Hyperion writes to Diotima, "be changed from its roots. . . . Nothing, not even the smallest, most common thing is without a spirit and divinity! Love and hate and all our utterings must shun what is vulgar, and not for an instant, not even once, can we come back to the prosaic past!"[5] The army struggling against the Turks seemed to make this vision come alive and present. "The thousand bright eyes" of the combatants are a promise. "Das stolze Bild des werdenden Freistaats dämmert vor ihnen" (before them dawns the proud image of a new free state arising.) Their motto is "all for one and one for all."[6] "The twisted ways of the past" are ended.[7] "We have before us three victories in small encounters. . . . Navarino is ours, and we have before us Mistra, what remains of ancient Sparta. I have raised a banner I snatched from an Albanian horde on a ruin that lies before the city, I have thrown, for joy, my Turkish turban into the Eurotas, and now I wear a Greek helmet."[8]

But the siege dragged on. A "stormlike atmosphere" surrounds the camp. A deep threat comes to undermine the companies of warriors. "Even my own men do not please me. There is in them a dreadful pet-

---

[2] Ibid., p. 128.
[3] Ibid., pp. 136ff.
[4] Ibid., pp. 140ff.
[5] Ibid., p. 145.
[6] Ibid., p. 146.
[7] Ibid., p. 148.
[8] Ibid.

ulance."[9] Then all dissolves. "Est ist aus, Diotima! Unsre Leute haben
geplündert, gemordet, ohne Unterschied, auch unsre Brüder sind er-
schlagen, die Griechen in Misistra, die Unschuldigen, oder irren sie hül-
flos herum und ihre tote Jammermiene ruf Himmel und Erde zur
Rache gegen die Barbaren, an deren Spitze ich war" (All is finished,
Diotima! Our men have pillaged, assassinated, without distinction; even
our brothers, the Greeks of Mistra, the innocents, have been massacred,
or go without aid and with their faces undone by grief invoking heaven
and earth for vengeance against the barbarians, at whose head I
stood).[10] Before such a disaster he could only conclude that "it was a
strange plan to build my Hellas with a band of robbers" (Räuberbande).
Wounded in the effort to stop the assassination and pillage, he was
forced to witness the havoc. "Rapine sweeps through the Morea like an
epidemic, and he who does not draw his sword is hunted out, killed;
and meanwhile the madmen say they are fighting for our liberty. Another brutal band is under orders of the Sultan and does just like the
first." "The Russians who dared join our arms, forty valorous men, resisted alone and were all killed."[11]

There remained only for Hyperion to go on fighting at sea, with the
fleet, in the hope that the battle would be "a bath that would clean me
of dust."[12] And the battle came. Wounded in the battle of Chesmé,
pulled fainting but safe from the fires, when he finally learned "that the
Russians had sent up in flames the entire Turkish fleet," he cried out:
"Thus one evil cancels out the other! . . . thus tyrants rout each other"
(So rotten die Tyrannen sich selbst aus).[13]

The *Hyperion* is the reflection of Hölderlin's philosophical, moral,
and practical experience. The titanic and the search for beauty inter-
twine in this, as in other works of his. Greece is the symbol of his deepest
thought.[14] However, in filigree, there emerge, as we see, the events of
1770, from the uprising in the Morea to the battle of Chesmé, and there
are even allusions to the secret preparation for the Greek revolt (the
League of Nemesis in Trieste). The *Hyperion* is at the last point in the
discussion of a quarter-century about ancient and modern Greece, the

[9] Ibid., p. 151.
[10] Ibid.
[11] Ibid., p. 152.
[12] Ibid., p. 158.
[13] Ibid., p. 160. The texts in German are in Friedrich Hölderlin, *Sämtliche Werke und
Briefe* (Berlin and Weimar: Aufbau-Verlag, 1970), vol. 2, pp. 218, 223.
[14] From the immense literature I will cite only two Italian essays: Leonello Vincenti,
"Il motivo titanico nell'opera di F. Hölderlin," in id., *Saggi di letteratura tedesca* (Milan and
Naples: Ricciardi, 1953), pp. 82ff., and Sergio Lupi, "Destino di Hölderlin," in id., *Saggi
di letteratura tedesca* (Turin: Giappichelli), pp. 453ff.

causes and circumstances of the revolt of 1770, and the possibilities and hopes of revival. One of Hölderlin's departure points is the German translation by Heinrich August Ottokar Reichard, of the first volume of the *Voyage pittoresque de la Grèce* by Choiseul-Gouffier.[15] But his pages reveal something more, an intuition not only of the contradictions, but also of the lasting value of the attempt made in 1770 to bring the traditions and aspirations of the Greeks into the political and intellectual program of the Enlightenment.[16]

At the opposite pole from Hölderlin's work are two volumes published in 1800 ostensibly in London, but in reality in Paris, with the title *Voyage de Dimo et Nicolò Stephanopoli*. They appear to be an adventure story, but they tell of real events. The volumes read like a propaganda pamphlet, but within the many pages is a kernel of political truth: the attempt Napoleon made in the summer of 1797 to contact the Greeks of the Morea. Antoine Sérieys, the "professor of the Prytaneum" who acts as the narrator of the long tale, was not really a man adapted to guaranteeing the authenticity of the pages he put together, unscrupulous compiler and vendor of apocryphal texts as he was on other occasions. But there is in this book something that would have been difficult to invent, the artless violent expression of that hidden Mediterranean world which Catherine II discovered so many years before, from Corsica to Malta, to Montenegro, to the Peloponnesus, and which reemerged with the stronger and more penetrating blows of the French Revolution. Many of the threads we have tried to unravel in the preceding pages converge once again in this *Voyage*, before separating and losing themselves in the new century. Again the journalistic grasp of the work succeeds in giving a sensation of immediate reality.

The two protagonists of the work are Corsicans, and Maineote Corsicans, descendants of those Greek exiles who, obliged to abandon the Morea, found refuge near Ajaccio in 1673.[1] As a French chronicler said

---

[15] I thank Bernard Böschenstein, of the University of Geneva, for this and other suggestions and references. There are interesting and precise observations on the sources of Hölderlin in D. Constantine, *Early Greek Travelers and the Hellenic Ideal*, pp. 182ff.

[16] The interest of Hölderlin for revolts and rebirths of Mediterranean peoples of that period is confirmed by his reevocation of the "edel Volk . . . auf Korsika," and of Pasquale Paoli in *Emilie vor ihrem Brauttag*. Ernest Tonnelat, in *L'oeuvre poétique et la pensée religieuse de Hölderlin* (Paris: Marcel Didier, 1950), takes no notice of this historical reality. About the rapid end of the Greek insurrection, he writes: "This rapid reversal of the situation can be interpreted as a weakness in the plot" (p. 176).

[1] "We are French by adoption and sentiment, / but born Corsican of the Greek nation, / not only Greek, but your compatriots, / our ancestors were Maineotes," Dimo Stephanopoli said to the people who received him in the Morea. See his poem entitled "Viaggio

in a curious book printed at Cagliari, this colony was composed of "430 persons from the family Stephanopoli, men, women, and children, and 300 from other families, . . . peasants devoted to the cultivation of the soil who were called *popolani*."² They succeeded in transforming the land they had settled into the "garden of Corsica," but soon their life was made difficult by the hostility of the local population.³ They did not forget that they were descendants of the Comnens, emperors of Byzantium, but this was no longer something to boast of in the Year v of the Republic. Time did not pass heedlessly, even for them, and Dimo Stephanopoli studied the sciences, medicine, and botany. In Greece they were seeking both liberty and a plant that had become rare in Corsica, which they thought was a marvelous vermifuge. The presence of Bonaparte in Milan, and of Antonio Gentili, the companion in exile of Pasquale Paoli, who had become governor of the Ionian Islands on Corfu, opened for them the way to the Levant.⁴

From Livorno to Dalmatia encounters with Sanfedists, with peasants in revolt, generally Slavs, threatened the lives of Dimo and his nephew Nicolò. It was difficult to reach Greece through the world overturned by the fall of Venetian rule. The two commissioners witnessed the "planting of the liberty tree" in Argostoli, the capital of Cephalonia, on 22 August 1797. Among the inscriptions was "Love for the fatherland and hatred of privileges are the bases of democracy." "What joined the unanimous applause of the commissioners and spectators was the devotion with which the nobles threw into the flames their patents, their robes, and their wide, long, thick perukes." A "father of a family" took the platform, remembered the persecutions of the past government, and came directly to the central issue: "Forget your past interests, vile affronts, old quarrels, baseness. Arise anew, give your descendants advantages you did not receive from your forefathers, control yourself, so as to employ your actions and direct the aims of your passions to the

a Maina," in *Voyage di Dimo et Nicolò Stephanopoli en Grèce pendant les années 1797 et 1798, d'après deux missions, dont l'une du government français et l'autre du général en chef Buonaparte* (London and Paris: Guilleminet, Year VIII [1800]), vol. 2, p. 267. On the origins of the Corsican Maineotes see vol. 1, pp. 263ff.

² *Anecdotes historiques de la colonie grecque établie dans l'île de Corse en 1676,* par M.L.B.D.V. (Monsieur Le Begue de Villiers) (Cagliari, Sardinia: Imprimerie royale, 1780), p. 56. The work is dedicated to Conte de Marbeuf, "lieutenant general of the Armies of the King, commander in chief in the Island of Corsica," who had become the protector of the Corsican Greeks, with the title "Marquis de Carghese."

³ Ibid., p. 61.

⁴ See E. Rodocanachi, *Bonaparte et les îles ioniennes* (Paris: Alcan, 1899). There is an extended discussion of Dimo Stephanopoli's scientific activity in Charles Coulston Gillispie, *Science and Polity in France at the End of the Old Regime* (Princeton, N.J.: Princeton University Press, 1980), pp. 473ff.

good of the country. . . . Gently require each individual to make sacrifices to the society of which he is a member."[5]

The Committee of General Security warned the people of Cephalonia that "anyone who dares from this moment on to speak against democracy, anyone who tries to seduce the people or praises the past hated government, will be declared an enemy of the people and punished as such with all severity."[6] On Cephalonia as well the most painful memory of the past was that of justice denied. Assassins had also been absolved here for money: "Assassinations were even more frequent, and vendettas more common, than in Corsica, in the absence of any criminal tribunal." As for the nobles, they had been "petty tyrants," but it had to be remembered that some of them "fought with their talents and virtues against the stream of vices: they made it their pleasure to instruct the people and to compensate for their losses. They had prepared, or rather preceded, the revolution on Cephalonia; at the sound of their voices hatred was quieted, vendettas ceased, brotherly feelings joined hearts together."[7] The situation on the other Ionian Islands was uncertain. How could one forget "the furious vengeance" on Zante that scattered bodies on the public squares? Within three years, two thousand had died. "One said that Zante was a second Rome. It is a fact that in this capital of the world, under the reign of the popes, and particularly Pius VI, assassinations occurred in public with impunity."[8]

Dimo Stephanopoli narrated his mission to Greece, his *Viaggio a Maina*, in verse.

> Sei giorni navighiam verso Levante
> quando, di là dall'isola di Zante,
> scopriam corsari turchi pien quel mare. . . .
> Ci odiano dacché siam republicani. . . .[9]

But they succeeded in avoiding an ambush before Coron, as well as storms around Cape Matapan, and disembarked

> a piè d'un monte che domina un piano
> e dall'antica Sparta non lontano.[10]

[5] *Voyage de Dimo et Nicolò Stephanopoli*, vol. 1, pp. 79ff.

[6] Ibid., p. 86.

[7] Ibid., pp. 89ff.

[8] Ibid., p. 95.

[9] "For six days we sailed toward the east / when, beyond the island of Zante, / we found the sea full of Turkish corsairs. . . . / They hate us because we are republicans. . . ." Ibid., vol. 2, p. 256.

[10] "At the foot of a mountain that dominates a plain, / and not far from ancient Sparta." Ibid., p. 259.

Their discussions with local leaders centered on the "changes that had taken place in the political situation of Maina" in the preceding thirty years, from the time of Orlov's expedition. In the catastrophe of the 1770 insurrection the Maineotes had lost their traditional independence. They had to accept new ties of dependence on the Sultan, even if they had succeeded tenaciously in saving their autonomy. "The Maineotes agreed to accept a bey among their countrymen, chosen by the people, and a captain of each district, in charge of maintaining order and collecting the taxes they paid to the pasha of the Morea. With these conditions, it was agreed that they would remain free as in the past and able to prevent any Turkish army from entering Maina."[11] Only the inhabitants of Vitulo, from whom the Stephanopulos were descended, had refused to pay this tribute. As the Soviet scholar Augusta Stanislavskaja has noted, the structure of power was in fact changing in these years. The "principals" who had arisen after the mid-seventeenth century had perished in the repression or had seen their authority diminish. They were being replaced by captains and armed leaders, who were the heads of the military organization that stood between the population and the Turks.[12] The increasing involvement of the Morea in the Mediterranean market undoubtedly contributed to the development of these social forces. The evolution came about chiefly for internal political reasons, as the Maineote leaders explained to the Stephanopulos: "To tell the truth, during the period when we enjoyed absolute liberty, we suffered much from civil dissention." The struggles among great families divided the region. Assassins went unpunished, and the continued struggle with the Turks made economic life difficult. Finally a balance had been achieved. "The chief revenue of the Maineotes comes from the produce of their olive groves; they have agreed to sell oil to their captains at a price that permits these public officials to make a profit in the market proportionate to their needs; thus both captains and people are content."[13]

But a passion for liberty and the myth of independence remained strong in the souls of the Maineotes.

> . . . mai barbara gente
> violò i confini nostri impunemente
> . . . non ci siam punto scordati
> che siamo i discendenti dei sparziati.
>
> . . . .
>
> Senza governo e senza forza armata,

[11] Ibid., vol. 1, pp. 194, 199.
[12] Stanislavskaja, *Rossija i Grecija*, p. 261.
[13] *Voyage de Dimo et Nicolò Stephanopoli*, vol. 1, pp. 201, 203.

la nostra libertà è illimitata,
il solo tribunal dell'opinione
basta per farci star alla ragione.[14]

In vain others accused them of brigandage and piracy. "It is not for slaves to judge free men," they responded. What right did obseqnious Germans have to talk, or Italians nourished "with masses, miracles, and servile prejudices"? Or the English who measure "the weight of a people by their riches"? Only the French with their "nascent liberty" could understand them.[15] Particularly painful was their memory and judgment of the Russians. It was useless to conceal—they told the commissioners—how even in France it was held that Catherine II's men were defeated in the Morea because of the "mean spirit" of the Greek insurgents, who were supposed to have abandoned them before the enemy.[16] In response, the Maineote leader, who had the title of bey, retold all the phases of the struggle, from the surprise of the insurgents at the small number of troops landed to the lack of coordination between Russians and Greeks. Orlov's attention seemed to be fixed on the Morea, he said, "although his heart was in the Crimea."[17] In reality Orlov "appeared in the Archipelago only to carry out a diversion, to hold the Turks in check, and to weaken their army on the side of the Black Sea."[18] This was a cold calculation compared with the "great attachment" Catherine had always shown for the Greeks.[19] Even Commander Spiridov had shown a rather different understanding of them. If his had been the "chief command of the Russian army, Greece would have been delivered." Instead, Orlov, "far from expecting to save its peoples from slavery, had the different aim of disabusing them of their freedom, or rather of sacrificing them to the achievement of his ulterior goals."[20]

Russians, Turks, and Venetians had all pushed the Maineotes to the brink of ruin. The only possibility that remained for them was a long and difficult resistance, a retreat into their own traditions, their customs, their daily routine of life without abandoning the hope that a true liberator would come. Even the attention of the commissioners was di-

---

[14] ". . . barbarous people never / violated our confines with impunity / . . . we have not forgotten / that we are the descendants of Spartans. / . . . / Without government and without an armed force, / our liberty is unlimited, / the law of public opinion / is enough to keep us within reason." Ibid., vol. 2, pp. 270ff.

[15] Ibid., vol. 1, pp. 204ff.

[16] Ibid., p. 208. In the second volume as well, on p. 16, the polemic against French "scholars" continued, particularly against Choiseul-Gouffier.

[17] Ibid., p. 210.

[18] Ibid., p. 212.

[19] Ibid., p. 213 n. 1.

[20] Ibid., p. 216.

vided among a reevocation of antiquity, a search for classical monuments, exhortations to trust France, and a close observation of the social reality in which they found themselves. "While [Nicolò] Stephanopoli went out into the countryside to visit the ruins, Dimo informed himself of the customs and habits of the Maineotes; he liked to compare them with his brothers in Corsica." He wanted to "understand, so to speak, men from the moment they left their mothers' breast until the tomb."[21] Thus was born a true folkloristic and anthropological treatise on the Maineotes. It was like entering their houses after having seen them fight for survival for so long.

This was the vision that increasingly attracted the attention of the world and found its point of arrival in Claude Fauriel's famous collection of Greek popular songs. The struggle against the Turks and daily life were mixed in this work. There returned as well a sad wound, the memory of the fated 1770 insurrection, an interplay of deceptions that had sent both Russians and Greeks to their deaths. After nearly a half-century, the heroism of the combatants, the plots of Orlov, and the cautious policy of the Venetians appeared in legendary form.[22] Even the policy of Catherine II in the Mediterranean seemed to have become folklore.

But the political problems of Greece moved to the center of the picture when the Stephanopolos gave the account of their expedition to Napoleon in Paris. The report was in Italian. "Greece, citizen general, is worthy of liberty and expects it from you. . . . Byzantium awaits you; your presence is needed to carry the frontier of French and Greek liberty to the Bosporus and into the Pontus Euxinus. Carry out your great work; the Turks themselves will bless you; they already have tricolor cockades hidden in their breasts. Greeks keep lamps lit before your portrait as a sign of adoration, like a god of liberty."[23] The appeal was accompanied by a "Plan for the Morea," drawn up to give military information: "the possession of the Morea, a most fertile land," would soon make Napoleon "ruler of all Greece."[24] Even domination of the Ionian Islands was tied to this, and it depended economically and militarily on the liberation of the Peloponnesus. It was necessary to anticipate the intentions of Austria and Russia. "Now the Greeks, who are alert and desire liberty at whatever cost, will embrace the first power that presents

[21] Ibid., pp. 291ff.

[22] Fauriel, *Chants populaires de la Grèce moderne*, vol. 1, p. 114. On the Russian expedition see *Voyage de Dimo et Nicolò Stephanopoli*, vol. 1, pp. 102ff., 217ff. (where there is information about the Greeks' struggle against the Albanian invaders).

[23] *Voyage de Dimo et Nicolò Stephanopoli*, vol. 2, p. 157.

[24] Ibid., p. 167.

itself with the promise of freeing them, although they are aware that true liberty is that of the French, which you spread in Italy and the Levant. Your name and presence will do more than all the Russian and Austrian armies."[25] Or, to cite the verses with which Dimo Stephanopoli closed his *Viaggio a Maina*:

> Tutto è pronto, guerrieri e sussistenza,
> non manca piú se non la tua presenza;
> passata l'occasion, tutto è perduto;
> qualche tiran raccoglieranne il frutto.[26]

[25] Ibid., p. 189.
[26] "All is ready, warriors and provisions, / now only your presence is missing; / if the occasion passes, all is lost; / some tyrant will harvest its fruit." Ibid., p. 284.

V

The Image of Russia and the
Pugačev Rebellion

THE IMAGE OF GREECE HAS TAKEN US A LONG WAY. NOW WE MUST RETURN to the Russia of Catherine II, the first person responsible, even among Italians, for the renewed interest in the Levant. As the Turkish war neared its close, the Levant attracted more and more attention for the increasingly serious and dramatic internal problems that afflicted it. Everywhere in Italy, even in Tuscany, which showed it was the place best disposed toward the Russians, the image of military and political developments darkened after 1773. The months preceding the peace were tragic for the empire of Catherine II, which was charged with military conflicts and uncertainties. Soon there arrived, even in Italy, echoes of the terrible civil war unleashed by Pugačev, echoes that mingled with the noise of the victory that concluded the struggle with the Turks. This constituted a dramatic final act, in 1774, to the war that had started with Orlov's adventure.

In the summer of 1773 the news from St. Petersburg was disquieting: "The prohibition of speaking or writing about affairs of state has been renewed, and above all about anything regarding the government, the court, and the war," one read in the *Notizie del mondo* on 20 July. "Rash pronouncements made with little caution" had circulated. The government felt the need to "ensure public quiet and prevent disorder." It was said that, among other books, there had appeared a little work "full of free comments on the Russian constitution, the law of peoples, the law of sovereigns, and the order of succession." The author was unknown, and "the book is very hard to find."[1] In Russia, in other words, even in the capital, Catherine II's bases of power were being questioned.[2]

---

[1] *Notizie del mondo*, no. 58, 20 July 1773, p. 460 (St. Petersburg, 20 June).

[2] On the actual internal situation of these years, when the heir to the throne came of

At the beginning of the new year, the news in gazettes became still more insistent—often from Cologne and Vienna, which were clearly hostile to Russia—about discontent in the old and new capitals and the more distant provinces. On 12 Febuary 1774 the Florentine journal spoke openly of an "uprising." "The empress has left St. Petersburg secretly without its being known for what destination. It is thought that the insurgents are even being supported from Sweden." This development, together with the approaching death of the Sultan, could herald "revolutions in the affairs of Europe."[3] A few pages earlier, this journal, which was the major Italian newspaper, had brought news through a dispatch from London dated 21 January, of the Boston Tea Party, and thus, in a sense, of the beginning of the American revolution.[4] Evidently "revolutions in the affairs of Europe" were in the air at the beginning of that year. On 19 February an "Extract of a Letter from Moscow dated 23 December 1773," which passed through Cologne, reported how "for some time here the party of the court has been shifting, and how the great, kept distant for the most part from honors and dignities, have little communication among themselves. There are those who have not hidden their secret designs well, and are thus held in great suspicion by the government; consequently distrust reigns everywhere, even among individuals in the same families."[5] There was "a kind of ferment," we read a few days later, "which you can call what you like, but it creates fears for the internal quiet of this empire."[6]

On 24 February 1774 the other important Italian journal, that of Lugano, took up what the *Notizie del mondo* had explained a few days earlier, that "it is said a peasant revolt has broken out in the district of Kazan on the occasion of a levy of recruits. Some add that even the Cossacks of the Don have risen, that the commander of Orenburg was killed by the rebels, and that General Brandt, governor of Kazan, was defeated in a skirmish."[7] The *Notizie del mondo* underlined the impor-

age and married (1772 and 1773), and on the discussion, of notable ideological and political interest, which took place at that time about the value of the legacy of Peter the Great, see David L. Ransel, *The Policy of Catherinian Russia: The Panin Party* (New Haven, Conn.: Yale University Press, 1975). Also of considerable interest is John T. Alexander, *Autocratic Politics in a National Crisis: The Imperial Russian Government and Pugachev's Revolt, 1773–1775* (Bloomington: Indiana University Press, 1969). See also Isabel De Madariaga, *Russia in the Age of Catherine the Great*, pp. 239ff.

[3] *Notizie del mondo*, no. 13, 12 February 1774, p. 99 (Vienna, 31 January).

[4] Ibid., no. 13, 12 February 1774 (London, 21 January).

[5] Ibid., no. 15, 19 February 1774, p. 116 (Cologne, 4 February). See *Nuove di diverse corti e paesi*, no. 7, 14 February 1774, p. 52, "Summary of a Letter from Moscow dated 23 December," which takes this up and adds other information.

[6] *Notizie del mondo*, no. 16, 22 February 1774, p. 123 (Vienna, 10 February).

[7] *Nuove di diverse corti e paesi*, no. 4, 24 January 1774, p. 28 (from Poland, 25 December

tance of the Cossacks in the uprising. "Wherever they go they leave
signs of their fury, and the deserts that surround them . . . are used for
defense and refuge."[8] These were the first reports of the Pugačev revolt.[9] As the *Notizie del mondo* explained, the movement's center was in
the province of Kazan, "where, not counting natural Russians, there are
six or seven different nationalities, some settled and others nomadic."
Among the instigators were "a few discontented low priests" who refused "to submit themselves to the lottery of the militia." In general, the
revolt was aimed against recruitment and the head tax.[10] The gazette of
Lugano had already mentioned discontent among the lower clergy as
being at the root of the "sedition," whose location one did not yet know:
"Some say the trouble is in Moscow, others in Kazan or in the Asian
provinces."[11] The strangest rumors began to circulate. Some even said
that the people responsible for the rebellion were "a certain Jewrainoff
and Demidoff, one a manufacturer of silk cloth and the other a general
contractor of mines, who have a considerable number of workers in
their employ." The first had presented himself as Peter III returned to
life. "They say that Prince Volkonski, governor of Moscow, has been
obliged to swear fidelity to the confederation, along with many others
from the most illustrious families." It was said that they had asked "to
restore to the Senate a part of the powers taken from it, and that there
be a just balance of authority between the nation and the sovereign, or
that he no longer encroach beyond the limits once prescribed by the
estates."[12] It was not by chance that such rumors came from Poland. The

1773). In reality General Jakov Ilarionovič Brandt was governor of Kazan from 1772 on.
When the revolt became more menacing Brandt organized the defense. Kazan was not
assaulted and taken until July 1774. Then Brandt perished as well. See the notice on him
in *Russkij biografičeskij slovar', Betankur - Bjakster*, pp. 324ff.

   [8] *Notizie del mondo*, no. 15, 19 February 1774, p. 116 (Cologne, 4 February).

   [9] An interesting study of the echo of the Pugačev revolt in western Europe is by O. E.
Kornilovič, "Obščestvennoe mnenie Zapadnoj Evropy o pugačevskom bunte" (Public
opinion in western Europe on the revolt of Pugačev), *Annaly*, no. 3 (1923): 149ff. The
essay by Vladimir Vasil'evič Mavrodin does not add much, *Krest'janskaja vojna v Rossii v
1773–1774 godach. Vosstanie Pugačeva* (The peasant war in Russia in 1773–1774. The Pugačev insurrection.) (Leningrad: Izd. Leningradskogo Universiteta, 1961), pp. 261ff. Neither of these two essays focuses on Italy. For a comparison with echoes in England, see
Pearl Spiro, "The British Perception of Russian Domestic Conditions during the Pugachev
Rebellion," in *Great Britain and Russia in the Eighteenth Century: Contrasts and Comparisons*,
ed. A. G. Cross (Newton, Mass.: Oriental Research Partners, 1979), pp. 247ff. On the
character of the Pugačev movement, see Philip Longworth, "Popular Protest in England
and Russia: Some Comparisons and Suggestions," ibid., pp. 263ff.

   [10] *Notizie del mondo*, no. 16, 22 February 1774, p. 123 (Vienna, 10 February).

   [11] *Nuove di diverse corti e paesi*, no. 5, 31 January 1774, p. 37 (Warsaw, 31 December).

   [12] Ibid., no. 6, 7 February 1774, p. 43 (from Poland, 15 January). In no. 9, of 28
February, p. 70 (Danzig, 4 February), the same gazette compared the current conflicts in

Russian "revolution" was interpreted through the revolt of the Polish confederates, and a constitutional motive was attributed to a movement composed of minority peoples, lower clergy, and Cossacks, but from which rich manufacturers and provincial notables did not seem to be excluded. This gave a Polish and Western face to a reality that, as soon became apparent, had quite different characteristics.[13]

The rigid censorship made it more difficult every day to understand what was going on in Russia. The *Notizie del mondo* reported from St. Petersburg on 2 April that there was "the most profound and rigorous silence about affairs in the interior of the empire, and that it was not prudent to talk about these with people of uncertain discretion."[14] In St. Petersburg it was impossible to find out what the rebels had written. "It is impossible to have a clear and precise idea of the proclamations of Pugatschew because of the rapidity with which the government has suppressed them and also because they are written in the languages of the nomad peasant peoples, whose attention he tries to get by making them magnificent promises, or, if they do not follow him, by frightening them with the most terrible threats."[15]

In the official propaganda, the brutal and cruel aspects of the obscure rebellion were emphasized the most. Adopting the language of a proclamation of the empress on 23 December (o.s.), the *Notizie del mondo* spoke of "enormous excesses," murders "of the most barbarous kind," of officers fallen into the hands of the rebels.[16] The *Nuove di diverse corti*

Russia with those of the time of the empress Elizabeth. The family of Muscovite merchants Evreinov, beginning with Matvej Grigorevič, were the founders, in the time of Peter the Great, of trade with China and of the manufacture of silk. Akinfij Nikitič Demidov was the founder of the iron industry in the Urals, which was carried forward by his descendants. Prince Michail Nikitič Volkonskij, commander in chief of the Russian army during the Seven Years' War and deputy in 1767 in the commission for the new law code, was in 1774 the commander in chief of the garrison of Moscow.

[13] The reality of the relationship between discontent at the top of the social hierarchy and the revolt from below in the Russian developments of 1773–1774 is an open historical problem. The Pugačev revolt was certainly a response to the increasingly heavy burdens that the war against Turkey imposed on Russia, but it was also a popular reaction against modernization, against the desire for reform, enlightenment introduced from above, and the whole policy of Catherine II. In the immense literature on the uprising I cite only the excellent volume *La révolte de Pougatchëv*, ed. Pierre Pascal (Paris: Collection Archives, Juliard, 1971), and the vivid presentation by Paul Avrich, *Russian Rebels, 1600–1800* (New York: Schocken Books, 1972), pp. 179ff.

[14] *Notizie del mondo*, no. 27, 2 April 1774, p. 211 (St. Petersburg, 22 February). See also no. 29, 9 April 1774, p. 226 (St. Petersburg, 18 February).

[15] Ibid., no. 20, 8 March 1774, p. 156 (Cologne, 22 February), "Estratto di una lettera di Kiow nella Russia minore."

[16] Ibid., no. 17, 26 February 1774, p. 131 (St. Petersburg, 18 January). On 1 March,

e paesi told how Pugačev had hung "Professor Lowitz, [who was] sent from the Imperial Academy to different provinces of the empire." The same fate befell "another young man he had in his company." "A disgraceful end" had come down on "those knowledgeable men selected to improve the imperfect knowledge of the inner provinces of this vast empire through their travels."[17]

But even among readers of Italian gazettes horror did not stop the effort to penetrate more deeply the motives of the rebels. "The revolution taking place in southern Russia," said the *Nuove di diverse corti e paesi* on 21 February 1774, "has fixed the attention of the curious." It was no use trying to explain the problem with Polish or Turkish intervention.[18] It was no use trying to reduce the movement to "some bands of robbers." The revolution was "a serious affair." An adventurer making use of the name of Peter III had succeeded in putting himself at the head of 1,000,000 Cossacks and Kalmucks and "had already taken over the whole district of Orenburg." One reason for his success was that "the said Peter III exempted the people from any new levies." In the same issue a correspondent from Hamburg reported the testimony of the man who at that time was, in effect, the most knowledgeable of the region and its peoples, the traveler Peter Simon Pallas. He explained the geographical context of the outbreak of the revolt: the Jaik. The Cossacks of the region "are prowd of their liberty. . . . They do not admit foreigners to their land. . . . But they do not engage in agriculture; they are all fishermen and warriors."[19] In general, this was a "revolution formed, nurtured, and planned in deserts by nomadic peoples. . . . It is to be hoped that it will be possible to contain it and keep peace along the frontier with cultured and disciplined peoples."[20] The intentions of the insurgents were mysterious, even where their hoards were strongest. "It seems that Pugatschew has the idea, among others, of opening a way to Siberia," wrote the *Notizie del mondo*, "for a large number of unfortu-

no. 18, p. 139, the proclamation was printed as a whole. The *Nuove di diverse corti e paesi* had published it in no. 9, 28 February 1774, p. 68 (St. Petersburg, 18 January).

[17] *Nuove di diverse corti e paesi*, no. 7, 13 February 1775, p. 51 (St. Petersburg, 11 January). Georg Moritz Lowitz, originally from Nuremberg, held the chair of astronomy at the Academy of Sciences in St. Petersburg. There is information about him in the work, dedicated to his son, by N. A. Figurovskij, *Leben und Werk des Chemikers Tobias Lowitz* (Berlin: Akademie-Verlag, 1959), index.

[18] Generally, the Italian gazettes emphasized these motives, as did those beyond the Alps. See, for example, *Nuove di diverse corti e paesi*, no. 10, 7 March 1774, p. 77 (Kiev in Little Russia, 15 January), and no. 27, 4 July 1774, p. 213 (from the Turkish frontier, 1 June).

[19] Ibid., no. 8, 21 February 1774, p. 60 (from the Danube, 6 February, and Hamburg, 1 February).

[20] *Notizie del mondo*, no. 26, 29 March 1774, p. 202 (Paris, 10 March).

nates who are kept there as slaves. Some are state prisoners, some prisoners of war, but most are criminals."[21] His most active supporters were among non-Russian peoples of the empire: the "Bashkirs," a "ferocious people." Official pronouncements spoke of "other nations different in customs, religion, appearance, and apparel," forced to revolt "only for maliciousness, and because they do not understand the happiness of living under the protection of Russia."[22] The call of Pugačev elicited a large response among peasants. "He continues to publish proclamations in the name of Peter III, and in one of these he has declared peasants on crown lands free."[23] He had even sought support "in the fantasy of religion."[24] This was an aspect of the Pugačev "revolution" that interested Italian readers most. "Among other things he promises to give to some hamlets the freedom to grow beards and make the sign of the cross with two fingers, customs that Peter the Great suppressed with great difficulty."[25] In a long report from Cologne the same gazette provided curious information about this. "The rebels in the region of Orenburg have invented a stratagem one could hardly think possible. Recently their leaders have given out that, being defenders of public liberty and vindicators of oppressed people, they had taken to defend the cause of a large number of good subjects of the Russian Empire persecuted for many centuries as Raskolniks, that is, heretics . . . , they are declared enemies of despotism and look with horror on the vicious administration of those, who, under the pretext of governing the nation, do everything to weaken it with unjust exactions." Particularly active in this movement was a "dangerous and intransigent fanatic, Alessio Petrowicz Foma, who claims to be the nephew of a certain Foma, a Russian priest who was burned in Moscow in January 1715 for having preached against icons. He openly tore to pieces an icon of the Virgin in a church on St. Alexis Day and declared from the pulpit that all good Christians should shun the cult of the pretended Russian Orthodox religion."[26] "He drags behind him a portrait of the Raskolnik Foma, whose

[21] Ibid., no. 20, 8 March 1774, p. 156 (Cologne, 22 February), "Extract of a Letter from Kiev in Little Russia." The same notice on these "unfortunates who are slaves in Siberia" is in the *Nuove di diverse corti e paesi*, no. 10, 7 March 1774, p. 77 (Kiev in Little Russia, 15 January).

[22] *Notizie del mondo*, no. 25, 26 March 1774, pp. 197ff (Königsberg, 28 February).

[23] *Nuove di diverse corti e paesi*, no. 18, 2 May 1774, p. 140 (Königsberg, 13 April).

[24] Ibid., no. 13, 28 March 1774, p. 99 (Königsberg, 7 March).

[25] *Notizie del mondo*, no. 26, 29 March 1774, p. 202 (Paris, 20 March).

[26] Ivanov Foma, called Foma the Iconoclast, was a barber condemned and burned in Moscow in 1714 as an accomplice of the heretic Dimitrij Evdokimovič Tveritinov. On Tveritinov see Franco Venturi, "Feofan Prokopovič," in *Annali della Fac. di lettere e filosofia e di Magistero dell'Università di Cagliari*, vol. 21, pt. 1 (1953), extract, pp. 23ff., and James

nephew he claims to be, shows the iron with which his hand was torn off, and accuses the government of excesses committed against this unfortunate sect, which has been much persecuted up to the present reign, when persecution in matters of religion was finally prohibited." The Raskolniks still remained in the reign of Catherine, "for the most part fugitives in the deserts and forests." "It is also true that they are faithful, like Quakers, and as simple as they, but the emissaries of Foma, under the pretext of religion, have revived the old animosity of these sectarians, and every day many come to submit themselves to the pretended archbishop voluntarily." "These madmen go from village to village in the swamps and woods searching out Raskolniks dispersed there by the severity of the laws." Religious protest and protest directed against the burdens weighing on peasants were joined in their sermons.

The rebel Foma says in his proclamation, among other things, that it is unjust to force peasants to pay impositions beyond their means when they want to marry girls from different villages; that no law can make them leave their beards in the countryside . . . ; he says the Raskolniks, sentenced to severe penalties during so many reigns for having maintained true religion, should defend their desolate and oppressed fatherland with arms, and that in this case they can join in good conscience with so-called Orthodox Russians and make a common cause with them, to punish the crimes of those against whom the whole nation laments.

Certainly the mind of the reader could not help but be struck by the image of Foma, "that fanatic," his head "covered with a great hat with two pieces hanging down over his ears." "He has a long beard and wears a coat that hangs below his ankles."[27]

The defense of old autonomies, especially in the peripheral zones of the empire, peasants' aspiration for liberation, religious toleration—these were the essential elements of the Pugačev rebellion seen in Italy, although through fragmentary and distorted information passed on from Poland, Germany, and France. How could one not recognize in these deeper forces behind the Pugačev revolt the problems that Catherine II had tried to confront in her effort to give a new legal arrangement to her empire? She had done this by pushing the Free Economic Society of St. Petersburg into discussing the fate of peasants and by giving the Raskolniks some liberty. Gazettes and other works had long writ-

Cracraft, *The Church Reform of Peter the Great* (Stanford, Calif.: Stanford University Press, 1971), pp. 132ff.

[27] *Notizie del mondo*, no. 60, 26 July 1774, pp. 476ff. (Cologne, 12 July), "Extract of a Letter from Tawrow in the Duchy of Rezan of 13 June." See *Nuove di diverse corti e paesi*, no. 30, 25 July 1774, "Summary of a Letter from Tawrow in the Duchy of Rezan, 13 June."

ten of this in Italy, and they would continue to do so. But it soon became evident that there was no common language between the reforms descending from above and the Cossack and peasant revolt. Pugačev saw only two solutions, which were in reality contradictory but found a meeting point in himself: give the liberty of the Cossacks to all, and at the same time keep all united through the absolute power of a traditional czar from before the time of the reforms of Peter. He wanted to be simultaneously the free Cossack Emel'jan Pugačev, and the emperor Peter III. As for the peasants, they had no means other than a *Jacquerie*, a *bunt*, an elemental drive for justice capable of crushing everything in its path. This drive led Pugačev a long way, and it made him the leader of the greatest peasant revolt in Russian history, but it also led him to defeat and to the scaffold. He could unite Cossacks, aliens, workers of the Urals, and serfs of the Volga, but this was not enough to defeat the modernly equipped army that Catherine II marched against him.

Reform and revolution thus intersected in circumstances that ended by making it impossible for Catherine to complete her program of the seventies, and for Pugačev to win. The fundamental reason for these failures was the war, the expansionist will of the Russian government, and the internal economic and political weakness produced by the long conflict. Two worlds collided and found no outlet besides wearing out and destroying one by the action of the other.

Mysterious in its origins, obscure in its course, the "revolution" of Pugačev forced itself into general consciousness even in Italy during the spring of 1774. "This conflagration spreads through the great distances between Kazan and Tobol'sk and is worse in the south, so that it seems certain, as some reports have indicated, that many sparks of it have gone as far as the Russian Ukraine," the *Notizie del mondo* reported at the end of March.[28] "We hear from the Ukraine that the fire of revolution has already reached the region near the Don . . . ," the gazette of Lugano reported soon after.[29] At the beginning of March news arrived that the old capital was being threatened. "A troop of rebels makes sorties close to Moscow, pillaging the villages and putting all in its surroundings in confusion."[30] In June came an echo of what was being said at the fairs of Leipzig. "Greeks coming here from Russia to our fair speak of nothing else but the Cossack rebellion and have given out certain details that could fill the whole empire with fear. The conduct of the Russian merchants themselves seems to confirm their ill-omened reports. They have sold their own merchandise but will buy none of ours, for fear of being

[28] *Notizie del mondo*, no. 26, 29 March 1774, p. 202 (Paris, 10 March).
[29] *Nuove di diverse corti e paesi*, no. 14, 4 April 1774, p. 105 (Königsberg, 9 March).
[30] Ibid., no. 18, 2 May 1774, p. 140 (Königsberg, 12 April).

robbed in Russia while seeking to transport it, since the rebels are in control of part of that empire." "All are united in assuring us that Pugatschew has made great progress and that the revolution has extended as far as Moscow. The victories reported by the court of St. Petersburg make one think the problem is greater than is believed."[31] The entire Russian economy suffered from the interruption of the "Asian trade." A kind of fatal, uncontrollable determination carried Pugačev even further. "He always uses the same phrase to encourage his followers: 'There is no choice for us,' he says, 'besides winning and dividing the spoils of the enemy or dying with our arms in our hands to avoid an infamous and cruel death on the scaffold.' This inspires the rebels with such ferocious desperation that some Cossacks defended themselves for more than two days against a whole detachment."[32] The defense of Catherine's troops, as the official reports show, was for a long time unable to cope with such an attack. It was significant that the government was obliged to mobilize the nobility, explaining that it was "the shield of the fatherland, the strongest support of the throne." "The ashes of our ancestors call out to us to arm against the impostor. The voice of posterity itself reproaches us that this detestable event has come to darken the splendor of our era, during the reign of the ever glorious and immortal Catherine."[33]

Many asked themselves the secret of this "singular" man Pugačev.[34] The gazettes provided a series of biographies, one more fantastic than another. He was the empress' page, sent to Berlin "to take a course of studies." He had served in the Prussian army. He had been a "gentleman of the grand duke," "a rebellious soul" with "talent and ability."[35] But he was also talked about in more realistic terms. "He is a good soldier and well instructed in military arts . . . he has a quick eye and a more penetrating mind than many of his countrymen; he is resourceful, and when he exposes himself rashly he knows how to recover astutely, when more than courage is required." He had with him "many Montagnard Circassians . . . these are almost wild tribesmen, proud, robust men, used to the hardest tasks. They are great thieves and there is nothing they will not do to get their prey."[36] Thus, he was a good partisan and a leader of plunderers. But this was not enough to explain his suc-

---

[31] Ibid., no. 23, 6 June 1774. p. 178 (Leipzig, 15 May).

[32] Ibid., p. 181 (from Little Russia, 3 May).

[33] *Notizie del mondo*, no. 29, 9 April 1774, p. 226 (St. Petersburg, 8 Feburary), and no. 33, 23 April 1774, p. 259 (St. Petersburg, 15 March) (from which the words cited were taken). See also *Gazzetta universale*, no. 33, 23 April 1774, p. 258 (St. Petersburg, 5 March).

[34] *Notizie del mondo*, no. 26, 29 March 1774, p. 203 (The Hague, 5 March).

[35] *Nuove di diverse corti e paesi*, no. 13, 28 March 1774, p. 103 (The Hague, 8 March).

[36] *Notizie del mondo*, no. 29, 9 April 1774, p. 227 (Kamineck, 28 February).

cesses. It was necessary to penetrate the passions that might have moved him. "His fury is directed chiefly against the nobles, of whom he has slaughtered more than a thousand, among men, women, and children."[37] His pride was exceptional. When defeat put him in the hands of the government (the first detailed news of his ruin arrived in the autumn) and he was taken to Moscow "in an iron cage," his rude dignity struck many, near and far. "I am treated like a villain, because I have been an unhappy man. If I had succeeded in my plan I would not have been humiliated with having to suffer your company," he said to those around him.[38] Even on the "very high cart, all black," in which he was carried to his death, he "was nonetheless undaunted; he showed great presence of mind; he did not have the least apprehension. He had a lighted candle in his hand, and in passing prayed continually for onlookers to pardon him. . . . With indescribable frankness he helped take off his own clothes."[39]

On 18 March 1775, the *Notizie del mondo* published a long "authentic history" of the end of Pugačev. "They were supposed to cut off his limbs one after another, but by mistake the executioner cut his head off first, for which he was punished with the knout." "Three of his accomplices were hanged; another was treated in the same way as Pugatschew. After this execution the knout was administered to several other rebels; some had their noses cut off, others their ears, some were whipped, and others branded; in a word, it did not end till night." One would have thought, added the Florentine journal, that "from then on he would not be talked about, because he was no longer feared." But in reality things did not go that way. The rebellion he had led was not spent.

The news we have from the depths of the Russian Empire is not as favorable as might be desired. Several bands of Cossacks have rebelled and united with Kalmucks and partisans of Pugatschew, and they create more work for Prince Repnin's troops. This new rebellion will not be, it seems, of more consequence than the devastation inevitable in such cases. But even this is too much for a country whose population, rather than being proportional to its size, is almost entirely composed of barbarous, undisciplined tribes who are always ready to destroy themselves to protect the deserts they inhabit. This shows all the more that atrocious punishments administered to criminals are unable to prevent or retard further crimes and will be a new example to add to the comments in the famous book *Dei delitti e delle pene* by Sig. Beccaria.[40]

---

[37] Ibid., no. 80, 4 October 1774, p. 636 (St. Petersburg, 26 August).

[38] Ibid., no. 99, 10 December 1774, p. 787 (Riga, 2 November).

[39] *Nuove di diverse corti e paesi*, no. 10, 6 March 1775, p. 77, "Copy of an Authentic Letter from Moscow of 23 June."

[40] *Notizie del mondo*, no. 22, 18 March 1775, pp. 172ff. (Hamburg, 20 February). See

In the years that followed the tragedy of Pugačev, Russia seemed to reembark, although slowly and carefully, on the road of reform. The *Notizie del mondo* hailed with joy this return to an interrupted path. In February 1776 it wrote: "If Russia has been an empire slow to become civilized, it has still made rapid progress toward greatness. Peter I and his successors tried to remove from their subjects those barbarisms that made them distasteful in the eyes of other European nations." Now Catherine had returned to work. "All is foreseen in the design of this princess for an immense plan for the population and defense of her states." But economic plans were not enough. "To complete the happiness of Russia all that is missing is a form of legislation that can ensure life, honor, and property to each member. This would contribute much to making sovereign authority more respectable; it does not want to reign without equity and moderation." Catherine had not forgotten her 1766 *Nakaz*. "Despite the hindrance and clamor of war," she had continued to seek a reform of Russian law. It was indispensable to ensure justice "without any distinction among nobles, non-nobles, landowners and peasants, traders, artisans, and others." In various countries "differences of origin, condition," and the like "are often reasons that many able subjects remain useless to society; these serve as a pretext for the great to exempt themselves from the established order." Even in Catherine's empire it was necessary for all to "become useful members of the public good, from the Russian to the Laplander, from the prince to the Tartar, from the Greek Orthodox to the gentile." To carry out such a program, "in each province will be chosen, among those most instructed in the laws and customs of their region, a certain number of inhabitants from whom the tribunals will elect a certain number whom Her Imperial Highness will then designate, among those most worthy, for the administration of justice and good order."[41] According to the *Notizie del mondo*, the following were the "principal items" in the new legislation:

> 1. "Make Russia a completely European state. In the past she has used laws from Asia and Europe, which make her legislation imperfect and difficult to enforce in all the parts of the vast empire."
>
> . . . .
>
> 3. "Establish a fixed and permanent repository for legislation."
> 4. "Regulate laws on the status of subjects with regard to their situation, customs, capacity, and intelligence (and for this allow ten

Nuove di diverse corti e paesi, no. 11, 13 March 1775, p. 83 (St. Petersburg, 6 February). But the comment on Beccaria is only in the Florentine gazette.

[41] *Notizie del mondo*, no. 14, 17 February 1776, pp. 107ff. (St. Petersburg, 9 January).

years or so 'for the formation of new laws and a large number of institutions intended to improve education in all the provinces')."

5. Reduce "the number of crimes," excluding those against religion: "Religion will no longer serve as a pretext for hatred and vendettas; those who work openly to destroy religion will be judged guilty only against the same, and punished as such, because doubts, questions, and propositions are not always the result of designs harmful to religion or custom. Condemnations, however, will be only for the instruction and illumination of those who have become estranged from the general rule." "The death penalty will be rare. . . . loss of honor and liberty, a civil death, will be a prolonged death made useful to the state through the work delinquents will be condemned to."

6. Torture and any kind of violence on the part of judges will be abolished.

7. "The security of the accused who may not be guilty" will be ensured. "In this way Russia will teach other people to follow a practice founded on the light of philosophy and love for humanity; it is better to fail to punish twenty criminals than to condemn one innocent man."

8. "No one can be arrested without being condemned by a legal sentence."[42]

This hope for the restoration of the reforming will of the empress prompted the Roman writer Giovanni Cristofano Amaduzzi to say that Catherine II was doing better than Italians in this matter. He perceived the program we have just read as a reproach for "us, the reliquaries of feudal and Lombard barbarity," and he thought that "the North, in the rigidity of its climate," had earlier than Italy "felt the sweet influence of humane philosophy, and applied it to the well-being of peoples. I am not far from believing that such a code is sufficient for all nations."[43] This was a utopian moment in the long dialogue between Russia and Italy of the sixties and seventies, in which moments of drama and realism were not lacking.

---

[42] Ibid., no. 16, 24 February 1776, p. 122 (St. Petersburg, 12 January). See the same reform program in the *Nuove di diverse corti e paesi*, no. 9, 26 February 1776, p. 66 (St. Petersburg, 10 January). The *Notizie del mondo* gives the news with more breadth and comment.

[43] Milan, B. Ambrosiana, MS. T. 134 Sup., fol. 11, G. C. Amaduzzi to I. Bianchi, Rome, 30 March 1776.

VI

❦

The Peasants of Bohemia

───────────

THE RUSSO-TURKISH WAR WAS HARDLY ENDED, AND THE REVOLT OF
Pugačev crushed, when a peasant revolt broke out at the heart of Maria
Theresa's dominions, in Bohemia, in 1775. It was, so to speak, the last
echo of the movement that troubled the countryside of Eastern Europe
in the seventies. It was much less intense in its furor than the Russian
movement and had different causes and a different outcome, opening
the way to a gradual abolition of feudal dues. But the Bohemian movement still aroused hopes and fears, revolts and reactions, similar to the
ones in Russia, the Ukraine, and Poland. It did this at the center of the
Empire itself, within that state apparatus that seemed and was a model
of stability, ordered reform, and harmonious development effected
from above. The Bohemian rebellion was contained without much difficulty. But it naturally attracted throughout Europe and also in Italy, if
only for its location and the moment of its eruption, attention from all
those to wh se eyes the newspapers daily brought problems of reform
and revolutions.[1]

Strange news arrived in Italy from Bohemia in the spring of 1775.
An informant of the king of Sardinia sent from Venice, on 18 March of
that year, rumors that had arrived from Vienna: "concern is aroused at
this court by some disorders in Bohemia of Hussite heretics, because of

---

[1] For general background, see Jerome Blum, *The End of the Old Order in Rural Europe*
(Princeton, N.J.: Princeton University Press, 1978), pp. 337ff. The two principal studies
are František Teply, *Selské bouře* (Peasant revolts) (Prague: Min. zemědělství RČ, 1931),
and Josef Petráň, *Nevolnické povstání 1775* (The uprising of serfs in 1775) (Prague: Universiteta Karlova, n.d.), with a bibliography on pp. 251ff., an index of places on p. 259,
and an index of persons on p. 273. There is ample documentation in *Prameny k nevolnickému povstání v Čechách a na Moravě v roce 1775* (Sources for the history of the uprising of
serfs in Bohemia and Moravia in the year 1775), ed. Miroslav Toegel, Josef Petráň, Jin-
dřick Obršlík (Prague: Academia, 1975). Many of the texts are in German and a few are
in Latin (see, for example, on p. 128 the report on a "rebellio rusticorum," which is described in detail, or, on p. 252, the crowd of 400 peasants "baculati et panibus provisi").

which it has been necessary to send troops to control these seditious subjects."[2] In the summer, on 18 July, the same informant reported that "in Moravia and Bohemia things are not going well with the rebellious subjects." At the same time the Florentine *Notizie del mondo* gave its readers a fragmentary, but not unclear, picture of the peasant movement that disturbed the Slavic lands of the empire, in both its social and religious dimension.

After this, for week after week, the only news from Vienna was about balls, receptions, concerts, new churches, sermons, visits of princes, and announcements of new measures taken to facilitate the grain trade, production of linen,[3] and credit advanced for "new normal schools to benefit youths and children of the poor." But then came another voice from Bohemia: "The Hussites, who have grown considerably in number in that kingdom, have begun to flock together and create disorder, so that the government has had to make a rigorous use of force to put an end to the problem."[4] A few days later, on 24 March, information sent on from Zweibrücken did not conceal the extent and seriousness of developments: "They say the court and government of Vienna have been seriously occupied for some days with putting together the means to suppress the disorder of Hussites and lawless peasants in the kingdom of Bohemia. They have committed various excesses and have burned houses and villages, particularly those belonging to Prince Piccolomini, Prince Kinsky, and the prince of Paar. They have an audacious leader who directs them and provides for what they need."[5] Quieting and disquieting news followed. "They say the disturbances in Bohemia are at an end. It seems that some have been punished with death, and others arrested."[6] On 18 April the *Gazzetta universale* affirmed that the sedition had ended after the punishment of the leaders, but that the peasants "still hoped to be relieved of the harsh weight of feudal services they are required to perform."[7] The *Notizie del mondo* added other details: besides those arrested and tried there had been "several hundred dead from a volley of shots by troops on a large band of the most obstinate, who were later brought to reason by a general pardon published by the sovereign, which gave them three days to

[2] Turin, AS, *Materie politiche in genere*, mazzo 59, 1775.

[3] *Notizie del mondo*, no. 13, 14 February 1775, p. 101 (Vienna, 2 February), no. 17, 28 February 1775, p. 133 (Vienna, 16 February), and no. 20, 11 March 1775, p. 156 (Breslau, 7 February).

[4] Ibid., no. 27, 4 April 1775, p. 212 (Vienna, 23 March), and (Zweibrücken, 20 March).

[5] Ibid., no. 28, 8 April 1775, p. 219 (Zweibrücken, 24 March).

[6] Ibid., no. 30, 15 April 1775, p. 235 (Vienna, 3 April).

[7] *Gazzetta universale*, no. 31, 18 April 1775, p. 245 (Bologna, 11 April).

return to their houses, at the end of which time they were to be considered rebels and treated with the greatest severity." It was high time for "a discreet adjustment to moderate serfdom." The court of Vienna was already thinking of it. But serfdom in Bohemia was not "very arduous or vexing."[8] To encourage the government in this direction there appeared more evidence of the rebellious and hopeful mentality of the peasants. As in Russia, Sweden, and elsewhere, they committed serious violence but continued to hope that an energetic and benevolent sovereign would be able to defend them and even liberate them from their lords. "It is said that these disturbances are born of the peasants' conviction that the nobles have received a patent from their Imperial Majesties for the abolition of serfdom and the work services they are obliged to perform for the lords; and for this reason they have gone from manor to manor seeking this presumed patent and, being refused it, have resorted to violence."[9]

At the epicenter of the movement, in the "circle of Konigraz" (Königgrätz, now Hradec Králové), there was fear that the land might not be cultivated or sown. The peasants moved from place to place, drinking the beer they found and "dining at the expense of the Jews." When soldiers intervened, "the peasants threw away their clubs and began to retreat in little groups. The dragoons behind them took one hundred and fifty prisoners. . . . Another body of troops advanced toward the mutinied peasants, who retreated into the hills, taking the road for Smirzitz [now Smiřice]; thus a cordon was drawn up, forcing them to surrender, since neither the king of Pussia nor the elector of Saxony would let any of them pass their frontiers." Their violence and growing hostility to religion increasingly impressed observers. "It is not to be believed how cruel and pitiless these rebels are, and how sacrilegious and impious toward churches and the most holy things. They devastate, pillage, and kill anything they see before them." But they now hoped that one of the chief centers of agitation was under control. On 31 March Count Rais, lieutenant colonel of the Colloredo Regiment, unexpectedly surprised in session "the Great Council of Nachot [Náchod] assembled secretly by the rebels, with a printing press, to better carry out their perverse designs, and took prisoner the Obrist-Burggraff, a magistrate of Nachot called Clemens [actually Antonín] Nivell." His secretary was also arrested, as well as five councilors.

From Prague there was sad news: "Yesterday a peasant was hanged outside the Carlstor Gate, and tomorrow two more will be hanged out-

---

[8] *Notizie del mondo*, no. 31, 18 April 1775, p. 247 (Zweibrücken, 3 April).
[9] Ibid., no. 34, 29 April 1775, p. 269 (Zweibrücken, 15 April).

side New Gate."[10] The *Nuove di diverse corti e paesi* of Lugano reported equally serious news: "One hears from Prague that one of the leaders of the Bohemian rebels, whose accomplices accorded him all the honors given to monarchs, has been taken, along with twelve of his chief followers. He has devastated many villages and set fire to several castles. There is another leader above this one, who seems to be a captain of hussars, but up to now they have not been able to arrest him. Nine of the chief rebels have been hanged, and there are one hundred more in prison who are to receive the same punishment."[11]

In the summer it seemed as though the disorders would resume in Moravia. "They say the peasants have lately committed excesses in various lands."[12] But the movement was dwindling. "We understand from Vienna that eight peasants thought to be leaders of the uprising have been brought from Bohemia and imprisoned to be examined and tried. They say there were two nobles as well, one Bohemian and the other Moravian, who were masquerading as the emperor in order to stir up and incite the peasants, and that one of them is taken, but the other has escaped."[13] The initiative was now passing into the hands of the government. In Prague it was said that "the rights of the lords of Bohemia are being examined, without depriving them of their just rights, that they will lose those too close to the old feudal system."[14]

In September a fire "that caused damage worth more than 200,000 florins" in the "principal seigneury"of Count Wallenstein seemed an isolated incident. But "they do not think it is accidental, because of the discontent in that kingdom."[15] Precautions continued to be taken. "Although the peasants have resumed the work services they wanted removed, the appearance of quiet after the revolt is not to be trusted. Thus 44 battalions of infantry and 9 squadrons of cavalry are kept ready in this kingdom, and in Moravia there are 19 battalions and 9 squadrons; some peasants have been executed as examples, and fines have been imposed; but the guilty have tried to resume their pillaging, and many of them have nothing to lose." There was a rumor that an imperial proclamation had been published, which tended to make "the peasants less burdened in the future," and they would have "more time to work for themselves." "The lords will be obliged to pay for the work they do."[16]

---

[10] Ibid., no. 35, 2 May 1775, p. 277 (Prague, 2 April).
[11] *Nuove di diverse corti e paesi*, no. 22, 29 May 1775, p. 170 (from Basso Reno, 18 May).
[12] *Notizie del mondo*, no. 62, 5 August 1775, p. 492 (Zweibrücken, 25 July).
[13] Ibid., no. 64, 12 August 1775, p. 510 (Zweibrücken, 2 August).
[14] Ibid., no. 69, 29 August 1775, p. 548 (Prague, 14 August).
[15] Ibid., no. 78, 30 September 1775, p. 622 (Venice, 23 September).
[16] Ibid., no. 79, 3 October 1775, p. 630 (Prague, 4 September).

On 13 August 1775, after long delays of the imperial administration and an even longer discussion between the government and the nobles, Joseph II intervened with an edict that fixed work services legally, from a minimum of thirteen days a year to a maximum of three days a week, proportional to the taxes the peasants paid. The work day was fixed (it varied from eight to twelve hours), and the extra payments at harvest time were determined. It was a first step that led, ten years later, to the integral abolition of "robot," as the work services were called. The enforcement of this first measure was made difficult by nobles who refused to accept the will of the emperor and by peasants who continued to show their discontent.[17] The issue was so controversial that it strained relations between Maria Theresa and Joseph II. The empress was reluctant to make concessions to the peasants and was profoundly hurt by the anti-Catholic religious element among the peoples of Bohemia and Moravia and some conversions to Lutheranism. Agrarian reform and religious toleration became the objectives of her son, despite a thousand obstacles and stratagems of resistance.[18] The pressure of villagers in the years immediately after the outburst of 1775 continued to be double edged—both social and religious. "They write from Moravia," one read in the *Notizie del mondo* in June 1779, "that the recent disturbances were motivated by religion, because twenty thousand inhabitants refused to go to mass and declared themselves Lutherans, chiefly with the objective of exempting themselves from the obligation of paying tithes to the clergy. For this reason the court of Bohemia has ordered that they be treated with circumspection and has contented itself, for the moment, with sending them priests known for their ability and moderation."[19]

Later, putting in order the diary he had kept in those stormy days, Johann Ferdinand Opitz, the secretary and librarian of Prince Karl Egon Fürstenberg, concluded that the ferment of the peasants of Bohemia was a subject worthy of Count Mirabeau or of the Abbé Raynal. A history of these developments would be "instructive reading for sover-

---

[17] There are some other sporadic echoes of this situation in the *Notizie del mondo*: the decoration of General Oliver Wallis and others for their work in Bohemia as "general commissioner sent by the court to deliver sovereign orders to the peasants on the work services to do in the future," no. 7, 23 January 1776, p. 52 (Vienna, 11 January); "The trial against the forty arrested in the recent uprising in Bohemia continues, and criminial commissioners have been sent to Prague for that reason," no. 8, 27 January 1776, p. 60 (Vienna, 15 January).

[18] Franco Venturi, *Settecento riformatore*, vol. 4, pt. 2, pp. 615ff.

[19] *Notizie del mondo*, no. 51, 28 June 1777, p. 406 (Frankfurt, 6 June). On the peasant revolt and the position and responsibility of the archbishop of Prague and the Church, and the political outcome of the mission of 1777, see Eduard Winter, *Der Josefinismus und seine Geschichte* (Brünn-München-Wien: Rudolf M. Rohrer, 1943), pp. 220ff.

eigns, politicians, and philosophers."[20] After what had happened, how can one maintain that revolt was impossible in the presence of strong disciplined troops? "Ah! without thinking of Corsica, what was happening in Pennsylvania, in English America? What disasters had not the false Peter, that is, Pugatschew, wrought? The uprisings in Sicily, and particularly in Messina, like the present insurrection of peasants in Bohemia, were proof that one should always fear such evils." A *bellum servile*! "What ruin it brought to the Roman republic!" "The insurrection in Bohemia, as well, was no other than a bellum servile." With what sadness one had to admit that philanthropic sovereigns like Maria Theresa and Joseph II had to witness such disasters. Altogether, after what had happened in Bohemia, it was impossible to ignore the problems of relations between peasants and soldiers, between villages and armies. And no veil could conceal the common elements between the Mediterranean and the Russian world, and the world of Bohemia.[21]

---

[20] *Prameny k nevolnickému povstání*, document no. 2, p. 23.
[21] Ibid., document no. 549, pp. 308ff. (the text is in German).

VII

Between Monarchical Republics and Republican Monarchies: Poland

ALL OF EUROPE FOLLOWED WITH ANGUISH THE DEVELOPMENTS IN Poland in the tragic decade 1763–1772, from the death of Augustus III to the partition. This was the first state on the continent beset by a crisis that threatened to be fatal. At the same time, in about 1770, it had seemed as though the Ottoman Empire would come to ruin. Soon the turn came for the British Empire, which was broken up at the end of the seventies. Holland followed, and before the end of the eighties, France entered that phase of its history that we call revolution but that many contemporaries thought of as anarchy. Before the end of the French Revolution, Poland, despite its extraordinary effort at internal renewal, was canceled from the list of states.

Poland, in other words, was the weakest link in the long and intricate chain of states that contemporaries considered the essential elements of the European system. It did not fall into crisis between 1763 and 1772 for economic reasons. On the contrary, its agriculture and export of grain prospered and made its neighbors more and more avaricious, leading them to annex vast tracts of its territory. Neither did it fall for lack of military energy. In fact, these years saw a true explosion of belligerence in every corner of Polish territory, making it tenacious and resistant to foreign intervention. From the repeated waves of volunteers that arose in these years was born the tradition of partisan warfare, which survivors introduced into Europe as a whole in the late eighteenth and early nineteenth centuries. More than an economic or a military problem, the crisis in Poland was political. It was the first republic surviving into the age of absolutism to fall under the blows of diplomacy, the art of war, and more efficient and Machiavellian techniques of government. The tragedy presented itself as a conflict between republican liberty and monarchical absolutism. And since the Polish republic had the habit of electing a king as its leader, the contrast also became an internal struggle between the partisans of Stanislas Augustus Poniatowski and the defenders of republican law and tradition.

Precisely because of its political and constitutional character, the Polish conflict aroused passionate interest in Europe as a whole. The continent had just emerged from the Seven Years' War, in which there was no lack of heroic military episodes or famous acts of defense, and which ended with important changes of sovereignty and frontiers in America, Asia, and Europe.[1] The significance of the Polish conflict was different, because from the beginning it assumed political colors and presented itself as a struggle between republican and absolutistic ideals. The conflict was even more significant for the development of European consciousness because all states, whether monarchies or not, were in the midst of deep transformations that were influenced by the Enlightenment. The republic in Poland did not stand only for the defense of the *liberum veto*, the privileges of nobles, and that nexus of uses and customs that referred back to the Sarmatian myth. The aims of reformers were already wearing down and transforming these traditions. New constitutional plans emerged, and the first experiments that were made led to a profound transformation of the republic in the last period of its existence, between 1772 and 1794. At the same time, through a thousand difficulties and contradictions, the numbers grew of those who held it indispensable to accept the monarchical graft that Stanislaus Augustus hoped to make on the old trunk of Poland. They accepted the degree of centralization and reform that the catastrophic situation from day to day seemed to make more necessary. A progress from republic to a constitutional monarchy of the English type, a road that Poland was not fated to follow, seemed a more and more seductive possibility in the crisis of 1763–1772. Thus in Poland, as in other European states, the conflict developed not only between traditional political forms and a need for reform, between conservatives and innovators, but also among different projects for reform, and among different currents of the Enlightenment. We cannot forget that in Russia, Prussia, and Austria, the lands that held Poland in their vise, it was not traditional absolutism that was in full development, but enlightened despotism, as we have the habit of calling it—an almost paradoxical but still effective term for describing the will to reform operating in those countries. In Warsaw, as in southern Europe, Catherine presented herself with the *Nakaz* and the

[1] For Italy, see Anna Vittoria Migliorini, *Diplomazia e cultura nel Settecento. Echi italiani della guerra dei sette anni* (Pisa: ETS, 1984).

inquiry of the Free Economic Society in hand. In Poland she appeared as a defender of toleration for minority religious groups against Catholic fanaticism. Frederick II was not only a model of efficiency in military and civil reforms, he too covered his policy with a Voltairian patina. Austria was the land of Maria Theresa and Joseph II. Among the nations intervening in Poland, we cannot forget the France of Louis XV, whose policy was to be sure uncertain, contradictory, and in the end catastrophic, but that was also the center and hearth of the Enlightenment. Among diplomats and philosophes—who are less distant from one another than it might seem at first glance—the Polish problem was discussed widely in the France of Choiseul. And the first volunteers to defend a republic against the oppression of a monarchy, like that of Catherine II, came from France, the precursors of those, who a few years later, fought at the side of the insurgent American colonists.

In consequence of all this, the terms of the confrontation changed rapidly. The republicans' effort to keep faith with the old constitutional forms became no longer merely a rejection of the new political world or a defense to the death of privileges. Instead, they made an effort to go beyond traditional limits and give new vigor and force to the liberty, autonomy, and independence that they thought could not be renounced. The Poles thus found themselves at the crossroads of late-eighteenth-century political ideas. They were pulled on one side by the effort to revive their old autonomy and spirit of independence, and on the other by the need for economic and social reforms, a contrast that appeared in the most diverse and distant nations.

Yet Poland, despite the elements that tied it to Europe, did not become a model for anyone, unless it was in a negative sense. Others followed the example of England, Russia, Austria, and even Tuscany, whereas the Polish drama seemed to indicate a road that should not be taken. Poland was isolated and even betrayed by Europe. But, aside from its tragic sense of isolation, we must recognize in Poland one of the essential movements in the process that led from the age of reform to that of revolution—and the most sensitive contemporaries understood this.[2]

---

[2] The fundamental work on this period remains that of Jean Fabre, *Stanislas-Auguste Poniatowski et l'Europe des lumières* (Paris: Belles Lettres, 1952). This still has the tendency to interpret the epoch of Stanislaus Augustus more from the point of view of civilization and morality than from that of political logic. As often happens for Poland (and also for France during the French Revolution and Italy during the Risorgimento) the nineteenth century dominates the eighteenth, romanticism the Enlightenment, patriotism cosmopolitanism. Fabre's judgment of the reform movement in eighteenth-century Poland seems too narrow now, even in the eyes of the most recent Polish historians. One could say that the historical rehabilitation the French historian has carried out for the work of Stanislaus

Discussion of Poland was particularly animated and profound in France. But the Polish tragedy also invoked agonized echoes in other European countries and aroused a passionate political debate. Without this European background what was thought and written in Italy is less understandable.

The echoes in Great Britain were quite important. Stanislaus Poniatowski looked to England as a model, as did the powerful house of Czartoryski. But at the end of the sixties and the beginning of the seventies Great Britain was hardly anxious to welcome appeals from Poland. The same governments that refused to assist Pasquale Paoli were even more reluctant to commit themselves to a difficult defense of the tempestuous Polish republic. In the Mediterranean the English fleet worked with the fleet of Catherine II. If the English had wanted to oppose Russia and its Prussian and Austrian allies in the years that preceded the partition, they would have had to work with the only power that tried to act in Poland's defense, that is, France, which was generally considered the natural enemy of Great Britain. Noninterference and tacit acceptance of the fate of Poland became the only, although painful, ways of escaping the contradictions of English foreign policy.[3] But what travelers and gazettes reported about Polish internal affairs was not generally encouraging to more active participation in the affairs of this distant and little-known country. In these years, for example, John Williams tried to compare the different states of northern Europe: Holland, Denmark,

August could be extended to Voltaire, to the Encyclopedists, and to the physiocrats confronted with the problem of "Polish anarchy."

As in other fields, Stanisław Kot has opened the way for the European debate about Poland in *Rzeczpospolita Polska w literaturze politycznej Zachodu* (The Polish republic in political literature in the West) (Krakow: Nakładem krakowskiej spółki wydawniczej, 1919). For a statement of the problem, see Bogusław Leśnodorski, "Le nouvel état polonais du XVIIIe siècle: Lumières et traditions," in *Utopie et institutions. Le pragmatisme des lumières*, ed. Pierre Francastel (Paris and The Hague, 1963); Emanuel Rostworowski, "Républicanisme 'Sarmate' et les lumières," *Studies on Voltaire and the Eighteenth Century* 26 (1963): 1417; and Ryszard W. Wołoszyński, "La Pologne vue par l'Europe au XVIIIe siècle," *Acta Poloniae Historica*, fasc. 11 (1965): 22ff. There is an ample and learned anthology edited by Wacław Zawadzki, *Polska stanisławowska w oczach cudzoziemców* (Poland in the age of Stanislaus as seen by foreigners], 2 vols. (Warsaw: PIW, 1967). There are numerous insights in the essays published in honor of Bogusław Leśnodorski, *Wiek XVIII. Polska i świat* (Eighteenth century. Poland and the world) (Warsaw: PIW, 1974). There is an effort at a general historiographical discussion by Marian Henryk Serejski, *Europa a rosbiory Polski. Studium historiograficzne* (Europe and the partition of Poland. A historiographical study) (Warsaw: PIW, 1970).

[3] There is a clear exposition of these problems in David Bayne Horn, *British Public Opinion and the First Partition of Poland* (Edinburgh: Oliver and Boyd, 1945). The ample relevant discussion in the *London Chronicle* and other London gazettes in 1772 is put forth in detail on pp. 47ff.

Sweden, Russia, and Poland. He concluded that the situation in Poland was particularly unhappy. He was filled with horror by the "scene of confusion, of massacres, robberies, disorders, and devastations" that the Confederation of Bar provoked. For him there was no doubt that Catherine acted with firm steadfastness in combatting such "horrible disorders."[4] Certainly Catherine had no right to send troops into Poland to crush the liberty of that land. Yet her reforming intentions could serve as a justification: "It is generally believed that she had no other motives for taking this step than those of serving her friend Poniatowski and a desire for correcting some of the abuses that the Poles had made of their liberties." The Polish clergy, with its "obstinacy and bad conduct," only made the situation worse. Undoubtedly, at the end of the drama of Poland, at the moment of partition, the responsibility of the Empire and Prussia was greater than that of Russia. "Their supposed wisdom and policy will one day be regarded as foolishness."[5] Some day the chains they had prepared for Poland would be wrapped around their own necks. But still, the ruin of Poland could not be explained if one did not examine the internal political life of that country, as well as the political and social situation. "The government of Poland is in many respects like the ancient Celtic or Gothic forms of government, which have been corrected or altered in almost every other state of Europe." There alone still remained a "republic with the royal dignity."[6] An aristocratic and Catholic government, Poland lived under unjust and oppressive laws, which were feudal and intolerant at the same time. As a result, there was "no civilized and christian country in the known world where human beings are reduced to such a state of misery and distress."[7]

Adam Smith had much the same opinion. The modern world had passed the Polish economy by without changing it. "Poland, where the feudal system still continues to take place is at this day as beggarly a country as it was before the discovery of America."[8] Spain, Portugal, and Poland divided the little-wanted prize of being the most miserable countries of Europe.

These were strongly negative judgments, which in England, as on the continent, took root in the minds of many observers of Poland's economic and social structures. But a different picture appeared when the

---

[4] John Williams, *The rise, progress and present state of the northern governments, viz. the United Provinces, Denmark, Sweden, Russia and Poland* (London: T. Becket, 1777), vol. 2, p. 619.

[5] Ibid., p. 620.

[6] Ibid., p. 625.

[7] Ibid., pp. 642ff.

[8] Adam Smith, *An Inquiry into the Nature and Causes of the Wealth of Nations*, ed. R. H. Campbell and A. S. Skinner (Oxford: Clarendon Press, 1976), p. 256.

center of interest became the liberty of that land and its desire for independence. A writer, John Lind, tried his best to persuade the English not only that in foreign policy they should occupy themselves with what happened in Poland, but also that they should not be blind to the Poles' struggle to defend their constitutional liberties. Lind had been attached to the British embassy in Constantinople before going to Poland, where he became the director of the school for cadets and the tutor of a son of Stanislaus Poniatowski, a major general of the Polish army. He became a kind of agent of the king, an unofficial diplomat, a "private Anglo-Polish counselor," as Jeremy Bentham, his close friend in his youth, called him.[9] In November 1772 John Lind completed a large book, *Letters concerning the present state of Poland*, which was translated into German and French and was one of the most important texts of the European discussion to which the first partitition gave rise. He described vividly the tragic contest of Stanislaus, Catherine II, and Frederick II to determine which would have the right to reform the constitution of the Polish republic. There was no doubt that it needed to be reformed. Stanislaus proceeded gradually, cautiously. But he was rapidly overtaken by his rivals, for whom reform was a means and an instrument of imposing their own wills, with the result that the situation became blocked and anarchy continued.

Lind described with satisfaction the measures Poniatowski took at the moment of his ascent to the throne. Montesquieu had certainly been right when he said that "the independence of each individual is the object of the laws of Poland, and the result is the oppression of all."[10] The king thus had to fight against the resulting "oligarchical tyranny" and intervened to ensure at least the right to life of peasants downtrodden by their lords. "The old feudal system" survived in Poland, even to the extent that killing a peasant was punished merely by a fine, "and what a trifling sum of money!" "Under the present king the shocking law had

---

9 Horn, *British Public Opinion*, pp. 20ff. On the school for cadets, see Ambroise Jobert, *La Commission d'éducation nationale en Pologne (1773–1794). Son oeuvre d'instruction civique* (Paris: Les belles lettres, 1941), pp. 125, 146. On the political thought of J. Lind, see Margaret E. Avery, "Toryism in the Age of the American Revolution: John Lind and John Shebbeare," *Historical Studies* 18, no. 70 (April 1978): 24ff., where his evolution toward a more and more conservative position, akin to what happened to much of Whiggism in the age of the American Revolution, seems too much emphasized. During his eight years in Poland and in all his actions in favor of that land, J. Lind was animated by a kind of philosophical radicalism, parallel to and influenced by the ideas of Bentham. The first two volumes of the *Correspondence of Jeremy Bentham*, ed. Timothy L. S. Sprigge (London: Athlone Press, 1968), contain much precious material about him. See above all, for Poland, vol. I, p. 161 n.

10 John Lind, *Letters concerning the present state of Poland* (London: T. Payne, 1773), letter 1, p. 9 (each letter has a separate pagination). See *Esprit des loix*, book 10, ch. 5.

been abolished, and this useful body of men are reintegrated in the rights of nature." The peasants were still "attached to the glebe" and subjected to the jurisdiction of their lords, with the only exception of capital penalties.[11] The education of the "gentry" was another great preoccupation of Stanislaus. He formed a corps of cadets with the hope of taking the education of youth away from the priests. But the reforms touched a raw nerve when they approached the problem of toleration. Lind reveals that Catherine II was not moved by the "singular idea of being the first christian sovereign to employ the civil power in defence of a general toleration," but rather in her desire to attract Orthodox and Protestants and form "a strong party in the republic."[12] The opposition of Frederick II to a compromise between the king and the religious dissenters was motivated by a still lower intent (in general, John Lind was even more critical of the king of Prussia than of Catherine II): he feared that toleration in Poland might induce emigrées to abandon Prussia and return to their country.[13] But the greatest act of aggression was taken by Catherine II, in 1767, when she presumed to impose her own constitution on Poland at a single blow, thus taking control of the entire legislative authority of the country.[14] With what right? Even an absolute king, as in France or Spain, would not be able to oppose the will of subjects wanting to renounce certain ancient rights.

How could one keep the Poles from abandoning prerogatives, like the liberum veto, which threatened their very existence? What would the English say if a foreign power obliged them to reestablish their government "such as it was under the houses of Lancaster, York, Tudor or Stuart"? "Yet the empress of Russia, under pretence of reestablishing the ancient constitution of Poland, endeavoured to perpetuate abuses infinitely worse and more fatal than ever obtained at any, the most tumultuous period of the English government."[15] "Independence in the exercise of the legislative power is the first, great, unalienable prerogative of every state."[16] The confederates were right on one point: every nation had the right to change its own constitution. In Holland the stadholders were first elective and then became hereditary. Why could not Poland do the same? Liberty and independence must coincide. The abuse of power during the partition had given back this fundamental right to Poland. And neither did it concern Poland alone. "What secu-

---

[11] Ibid., pp. 28ff.
[12] Ibid., letter 2, p. 41
[13] Ibid., p. 145.
[14] Ibid., letter 3, p. 11.
[15] Ibid., p. 13.
[16] Ibid., p. 12.

rity have Denmark and Sweden, the states of Germany and Holland, the cantons of Switzerland and princes of Italy that this alliance will not be as fatal to them as to Poland? The cause of Poland is now become the cause of all Europe."[17]

Even in England this appeal was limited by the generally diffused admiration for Catherine II and the hope that her foreign policy would succeed. When the partition of Poland was announced to the House of Commons, not one voice was raised in protest. "The Parliament, after a few soft murmurs, is gone to sleep, to wake after Christmas, safely folded in Lord North's arms," Edward Gibbon wrote to a friend on 11 December 1772.[18] Lord Cathcart, who had recently returned as ambassador to St. Petersburg, took advantage of the situation and called Catherine II "the greatest character in Europe."[19] The mind of the opposition was not different. Chatham wrote to Shelburne: "Your Lordship well knows I am quite a Russ. I trust the Ottoman will pull down the House of Bourbon in his fall."[20]

Foreign policy thus seemed prevalent in English opinion, whereas in France there was a more subtle and complex mix of ideas and passions, of international relations and political thought. Voltaire opened the debate with a series of short works. The internal and foreign politics of Poland were not at the center of his interest as much as the question of religion was, the principle of religious tolerance.[1] In the autumn of 1768, when he wrote his first pamphlet, Europe as a whole was dominated by increasingly sharp conflicts between church and state. The outcomes of multiple encounters with the Roman Curia were still unresolved. Poland, Voltaire was convinced, was an excellent battleground. Here there could be an example of a rapid and profound change. The dissenters had on their side not only reason, but also long tradition. The Eastern Church could be exhibited as an example to the Western Church. "The Greek Church always submitted to the emperors up to the last Constantine; and, in the vast empire of Russia, it is entirely dependent on the supreme power." There, as in England, a division between religious and political authority was unthinkable. "That happy subordination is the only dike one can put up against theological quar-

[17] Ibid., p. 61.

[18] Cited by Horn, *British Public Opinion*, p. 10 n. 2.

[19] Ibid., p. 10.

[20] Ibid., p. 11; see *Correspondence of William Pitt Earl of Chatham* (London: John Murray, 1840), vol. 4, pp. 288ff., dated 20 October 1773.

[1] On the problems of that time, see George Tadeusz Łukowski, "The Szlachta and the Confederacy of Radom, 1764–1767/68. A Study of the Polish Nobility," in *Antemurale*, no. 21 (Rome, 1977).

rels, and the torrents of blood these quarrels set in motion."[2] As for the Protestant Poles, they could also, in a different way, be fitted into the past and the laws of their country. In the sixteenth century Sigismund Augustus had known how to show himself a "hero of tolerance."[3] Sad battles and long decades were required for the followers of the Jesuits to succeed in enclosing Poland in the horrors of intolerance again. These traditions would bear new fruits in the soil of modern liberty. It was no longer a question of going back to the example of the church in Jerusalem. "We are no longer in the time of the apostles, but instead in the time of citizens; it is a question of their rights and their natural liberty."[4] Stanislaus Poniatowski and Catherine II were in a situation to affirm and sustain these rights. Public opinion supported them. "The system of toleration has made rapid progress in the north, from the Rhine to the Arctic Sea, because reason has been heard, and it is permitted to think and read." No selfish interests were being defended, but instead a new policy, which was now growing roots even in Prussia and Denmark. As for Catherine, it would be easy for her to profit from the disorder in Poland; she would gain, at the least, useful immigrants and colonists for her empire. The new policy radiated from her. "She not only has established toleration on her own land, she also seeks the glory of effecting its rebirth in the lands of her neighbors. Her glory is unique. No ostentation in the world can provide an example like that of an army sent to a great nation to tell it to live in justice and peace."[5]

This was a perfect coincidence of principles and action. Voltaire reminded Catherine in his letters, continually, that he hoped to see it confirmed in fact. He did not doubt the good faith of Stanislaus Poniatowski, who he knew was an "enemy of disorder, zealous for the happiness and glory of his country, tolerant through humanity and principle, religious without being superstitious, a citizen on the throne, an enlightened and a spirited man."[6] His doubts about the king of Poland came from his admitted incapacity to carry it out rather than from his policy. The opposition he encountered became continually more violent, and he did not have the power necessary to dominate it. It would

---

[2] *Essai historique et critique sur les dissentions des églises de Pologne, par Joseph Bourdillon, professeur en droit public*, in Voltaire, *Oeuvres complètes*, ed. Moland (Paris: Garnier, 1879), vol. 26, p. 455.

[3] Ibid., p. 459.

[4] Ibid., p. 456.

[5] Ibid., p. 466.

[6] Ibid., p. 464. There is an excellent examination of the relationship between Voltaire and Stanislaus Poniatowski in Emanuel Rostworowski, "Voltaire et la Pologne," *Studies on Voltaire and the Eighteenth Century* 62 (1968): 110ff. There is an interesting article by Wanda Dzwigala, "Voltaire's Sources on the Polish Dissident Question," ibid. 241 (1986): 187ff.

be necessary to impose tolerance in Poland. Would Catherine, who alone could act in this sense, remain faithful to the principles Voltaire attributed to her?

Reasons to doubt this were not lacking. On the eve of the Turkish war the Russian intervention became more and more insistent. One had to close one's eyes not to see that the policy of Stanislaus Poniatowski and that of Catherine II increasingly differed. Resistance inside Poland became stronger. In the middle of 1768, there circulated in Europe a letter Voltaire had written to an English friend in which these doubts and reservations were expressed with suppressed anger. The letter is probably apocryphal, but it still reveals the line of thought that many hoped Voltaire would take. The letter seems to have been written in French, but only the English version that appeared in Great Britain in June and the Italian version that appeared in the *Gazzetta di Firenze* on 13 September 1768 are known.[7]

All over Europe, one read, discord was increasing: in Parma, in Geneva, where it had been still possible to reach an accord, and in Neuchâtel. The "domestic discussions" of Poland were particularly violent. "The citizens, under the name of confederates, destroy each other, and all for the glory of God and the honor of religion." The Russian intervention was only worsening the situation. How could one admit that "a foreign power had come with arms to force a free nation governed by its own laws to receive what it wants to impose with fixed bayonets"? "What would the English say if the king of France at the head of 100,000 men went to impose laws on England?" They would certainly respond, "after throwing enough barrels of powder in their faces: 'Sire, why are you coming to interfere in our affairs? Go back to your kingdom. You are not our legislator. Vaunt your power in your own house and leave us to enjoy our liberty.' " But the fate Catherine reserved for any who dared to pronounce such words was demonstrated by what happened to the bishop of Krakow, "confined in Schlüsselburg in the same appartment where Czar Peter III met his end." Again the image of Catherine was that of her husband's assassin, not of the liberator of Polish dissenters.

But Voltaire, in reality, continued along his path. The more tense the situation in Poland became, the more he persuaded himself that it was necessary to emphasize the polemic against the confederates,

---

[7] The Italian text was published by Joseph G. Fucilla in *Travaux sur Voltaire*, vol. 1 (1955), pp. 111ff., and the English text in *The Complete Works of Voltaire*, vol. 117: *Correspondence*, vol. 33, pp. 391ff., with the number D.15080. The Italian text is in *Gazzetta di Firenze*, no. 7, 13 September 1768, pp. 5off. It is listed with the dateline London, 23 August, and thus appears to have come from England.

against the wave of religious and political fanaticism he felt was mounting in the country. In vain Stanislaus Augustus sent him, in the spring of 1769, an envoy in the person of Salomon Reverdil—the Swiss scholar whose function we will see in the events of Denmark in these years—to explain how difficult his work as a tolerant and reforming king was. Voltaire did not let him even begin discussing the policy of Catherine II.[8] He had only one enemy, "theological Rome," along with those Poles who were ready to become its "slaves and satellites."[9] His profound horror for the absurdity of Catholicism became mixed with an increasingly clear repugnance for the political conduct of the confederates. "Do you want to be bloody assassins under the pretext of being Catholics? . . . In the name of God and nature, do not insist on being barbarians and wretches."[10] He repeated to them, wearily, the arguments he had made so many times in favor of tolerance. But why waste useless words? It was better to come to the heart of the question: "Don't you know that the Russians shoot better than you? Don't oblige your protectors to destroy you; they have come to establish tolerance in Poland, but they will punish the intolerants who receive them with gunshots."[11]

In 1775, taking up again the *Essai* he had published under the name Joseph Bourdillon, Voltaire observed the high price Poland was obliged to pay for its religious fanaticism and blind politics. Durini, the papal nuncio, had fanned the fire. The alliance between confederates and the Turks had isolated Poland more and more. As he had written in 1771 in his work entitled *Le tocsin des rois*, it was the duty of all Europe to move against the Ottoman Empire. That had not happened. The attention of reformers was more and more directed toward Russia. "It was a great prospect of a rising nation that alone everywhere opposed the pretentions of the Turks, so long victorious over Europe, and revived the virtues of Miltiades while so many other nations were declining." To Russia Poland had no other response than civil war and the attempted assassination of Stanislaus Poniatowski. "The result of so many horrors was the dismemberment of Poland." Maria Theresa, Catherine II, and Frederick II "exercised the rights they had over three Polish provinces.

----

[8] Emanuel Rostworowski, "Une négociation des agents du roi de Pologne auprès de Voltaire en 1769," *Revue d'histoire littéraire de la France*, year 69, no. 1 (January–February 1969): 39. The documents published here are of great interest and make it possible to discern the extraordinary net of intrigue and influence that surrounded Voltaire and the effort to affect his political stance.

[9] "Discours aux confédérés catholiques, de Kaminieck en Pologne par le major Kaiserling au service du roi de Prusse," in Voltaire, *Oeuvres complètes*, vol. 27, p. 77.

[10] Ibid.

[11] Ibid., p. 81.

They took them over; no one dared object. That was the outcome of Polish chaos."[12]

Still, and Voltaire knew this well, the partition did not resolve the problem of the relationship between the Enlightenment and Polish reality that had pushed him to intervene with so much insistence in the drama of the republic. The part Frederick II took was a proof of it. He sent him, on 15 February 1775, a work by John Lind in which this Anglo-Polish writer bitterly attacked the king of Prussia, as in all his other works. For Voltaire it was a kind of vendetta, or at least revenge, to vent his anger for the part Frederick II and the other monarchs who partitioned Poland had induced, or obliged, him to play. "I was trapped like a fool," he wrote, "when before the Turkish war I simply believed the empress of Russia was in accord with the king of Poland only to give justice to dissenters and establish liberty of conscience. You kings . . . you are like the gods of Homer who make use of men for their designs without the poor people's suspecting it."[13]

Destiny deflected the grand hopes Voltaire nurtured in the years before the war between Russia and Turkey. Bringing Poland into the age of natural law turned out to be a task plagued with difficulties, perhaps impossible. Prejudices and interests prevailed. But the battle he fought was the right one, the one he had shown to be the only possible one. He wanted to say this again, in his last work for the theater, *Les lois de Minos*, reinforced in his convictions as he was by the recent experience of Gustavus III, who had done in Sweden what Stanislaus Poinatowski had not been able to do in Poland. At the center of the tragedy stood the horror of religion, symbolized by a human sacrifice. The successor of Minos, Teucer, had no doubt of the need to prevent this act of sacred barbarism. But he felt he was too weak to confront the prejudices and passions of the clergy and nobles around him directly, and he sought help and assistance from his subjects and neighboring peoples. How could one find the authority needed to carry out a necessary act of civilization? The world around him was "still barbarous." How could one give a positive value to the energy fermenting within it?

> La Grèce a des héros, mais injustes, cruels,
> insolens dans le crime et tremblans aux autels.
> Ce mélange odieux m'inspire trop de haine.
> Je chéris la valeur, mais je la veux humaine.

The enemy was within the country, in its prejudices, not outside.

[12] *Essai historique et critique sur les dissensions des églises de Pologne*, p. 468.
[13] *The Complete Works of Voltaire*, vol. 125: *Correspondence*, vol. 41, p. 334, no. D.19340.

> Nos Grecs sont bien trompés: je les crois glorieux
> de cultiver les arts et d'inventer des dieux;
> cruellement séduits par leur propre imposture,
> ils ont trouvé des arts et perdu la nature.[14]

Against the laws of nature legal tradition was valueless, even if it was represented by the constitution of Minos. The constitution ordered human sacrifice. It should be done away with. Vainly an archon tries to persuade the king that the only possible policy is to give in to popular prejudices. In vain he explains

> il faut du sang au peuple . . .
> ménagez ses abus, fussent-ils insensés.
> La loi qui vous révolte est injuste peut-être,
> mais en Crète elle est sainte. . . .
> Tout pouvoir a sa borne et cède au préjugé.

To which Teucer responds:

> Quand il est trop barbare, il faut qu'on l'abolisse.[15]

In the struggle to prevent a human sacrifice, the cruel origins and barbarous horrors of Cretan law are revealed more and more. Behind Minos stands

> . . . ce monstre appelé Minotaure.[16]

But desecration makes the struggle against prejudices more difficult and bitter. The king remains alone, isolated in his will to cut the knot between religion and politics.

He hesitates, fearing a civil war, and becomes more and more unhappy.

> Faut-il perdre l'état pour mieux gouverner? . . .
> Il le faut avouer, je suis bien malheureux!
> N'ai-je donc des sujets que pour m'armer contre eux?

---

[14] "Greece has heroes, but unjust, cruel ones / insolent in crime and trembling before altars. / This odious mixture inspires in me too much hate. / I love valor, but I want it to be human." "Our Greeks are deceived: I thought them glorious / in cultivating arts and inventing the gods; / cruelly seduced by their own imposture, / they found arts and lost nature." *Les lois de Minos*, act 1, scene 1. Voltaire, *Oeuvres complètes*, vol. 7, p. 178. A contemporary Italian translation by Elisabetta Caminer Turra is included in the *Nuova raccolta di composizioni teatrali* (Venice: Pietro Savioni, 1775), vol. 3, pp. 153ff.

[15] "The people want blood . . . / control their abuses, should they be unreasonable. / The law that revolts you is unjust perhaps, / but in Crete it is holy. . . . / All power has its limits and cedes to prejudice." "When it is too barbarous, it must be abolished." Ibid., act I, scene 3; ibid., p. 188.

[16] ". . . that monster called the Minotaur." Ibid., act 2, scene 1; ibid., p. 194.

Pilote environné d'un éternel orage,
ne pourrai-je obtenir qu'un illustre naufrage?

Still, a way remains open before him: undo the archaic constitution of the country. To an archon inviting him to respect tradition and moderation, he responds:

laissez vos lois, elles me font horreur,
vous devriez rougir d'en être le protecteur.

In vain another archon invites him to exercise caution.

Proposez une loi plus humaine et plus sainte,
mais ne l'imposez pas; seigneur, point de contrainte,
vous révoltez les coeurs, il faut persuader.
La prudence et le temps pourront tout accorder.[17]

Despite all these appeals, Teucer chooses the road of action (and here the example of Gustavus III imposed itself on that of Stanislaus Augustus). He snatches the designated victim from the hands of the priests, to the cry.

Ouvrez-vous, temple horrible.

He overturns "the altar of crime" and finally proclaims that "all will change today," once "the old barbarity" is destroyed.[18]

Natural law triumphs. To gain his end he has utilized neither the moderation of Stanislaus Poniatowski nor, one should note, a foreign intervention, like that of the Russians. Voltaire does not seem to identify the people he imagines allied with the Cretans in the great work of renewal of their country with the Russia of Catherine II, and even less with the Prussia of Frederick II. They resemble rather the peoples the Russo-Turkish war had put in movement here and there throughout southern and eastern Europe. Voltaire's Sidonians seem idealized Maineotes or Montenegrins.

Ces durs Cydoniens, dans leur antres profonds,
sans autels et sans trône, errants et vagabonds
mais libres, mais vaillants, francs, généreux, fideles,

---

[17] "Must one lose the state to govern better? . . . / I must admit, I am unhappy! / Do I have subjects only to arm myself against them? / A pilot surrounded by an eternal storm, / can I only succeed in a famous shipwreck?" "Leave your laws, they fill me with horror, / you should blush at being their protector." "Propose a more humane and holy law, / but do not impose it; Lord, no constraint, / you will offend all hearts, you must use persuasion. / Prudence and time can accomplish all." Ibid., act 2, scene 2; ibid., p. 197, and act 2, scene 4; ibid., p. 203.

[18] "Open, horrible temple." Ibid., act 4, scene 3; ibid., p. 219, and act 5, scene 4, pp. 231ff.

>peut-être ont mérité d'être un jour nos modèles;
>la nature est leur règle et nous la corrompons.[19]

A new relationship establishes itself between Cretans and Sidonians, not one of conquest, but one of collaboration in a work of civilization. As one of the dignitaries says,

>Nous voulions asservir des peuples généreux
>faisons mieux: gagnons-les; c'est là régner sur eux.[20]

Voltaire, despite all, had been right. The tragedy was coming to an end; the policy of Catherine II had brought new energy to Poland and mortally wounded the sacred monster of tradition and religion. At the same time the Sweden of Gustavus III showed what a decisive will to reform could do. It was not by chance, in an appendix to his *pièce*, that Voltaire again took up his polemic against the liberum veto: "Dear and fatal right that has caused more grief than it has prevented." The Polish drama had concluded with a partition. The only possibility of salvation for Stanislaus Poniatowski lay in an energetic reform policy. "He still has a kingdom larger than France, which could be flourishing one day if it were possible to destroy anarchy there, as it has been destroyed in Sweden, and if liberty can coexist with monarchy."

In his sympathy for Stanislaus Augustus and especially in his support of Catherine II's policy, Voltaire went against the current of directives the French government attempted to follow through a thousand complications. Voltaire had on his side the Parisian philosophes, above all Diderot, who precisely in Poland's decisive years brought his own relationship with the Russian empress closer, giving her his library in exchange for a pension, as Voltaire hurried to advertise in one of his pamphlets.[21] But Louis XV's ministers could not listen to Voltaire preach about the dissolution of the Ottoman Empire without preoccupation or his exaltation of the victories of Catherine II and public condemnation of the Polish confederates, whom Choiseul, as far as he could, sought to help under the table.[22] It was not that the judgment of the French agents sent to Poland differed so much from those of the patriarch of Ferney. State policy and tradition led Louis XV to support Russia's enemies, but direct contacts with the Polish rebels were not easy to main-

---

[19] "Those hardy Sidonians, in their deep lairs, / without altars and without a throne, wandering at will / but free, but valiant, open, generous, faithful, / perhaps they have merited to be our models one day; / nature is their law and we corrupt it." Ibid., act 1, scene 1; ibid., p. 178.

[20] "We wanted to subject a generous people / let us do better: win them over; that is the way to rule them." Ibid., act 2, scene 2; ibid., p. 196.

[21] *Discours aux confédérés catholiques, de Kaminieck*, p. 82.

[22] On the policy of Choiseul, see Herbert H. Kaplan, *The First Partition of Poland* (New York: Columbia University Press, 1962), pp. 97ff.

tain, and the reactions of his agents to the fanaticism of the Poles were similar to those of the philosophes. As military men accustomed to respecting the rules of an absolutist state, they could not help but be scandalized by the lack of discipline among the troops of the confederates. Confronted with a world entirely unknown to them, they reacted with profound revulsion. "Lazy *dévots*, pious thieves," one of the agents writing to Choiseul called them. "They add an insufferable pride . . . to the basest acts. With an exterior of devotion that would make you take them for saints, they are frivolous, liars, and of worse faith than any other nation." Cruel, dirty, and robust, the first thing they said when meeting you was: "sum nobilis" (we are nobles).[23] Dumouriez, the most famous of these French, writing to the court on 15 August 1770, emphasized "the absolute ignorance of war, the bad state of the Polish troops."[24] They had no general plan and were disorganized in all their actions. Poland, "that unfortunate kingdom," had "as many particular wills as leaders in each district." Certainly the confederates represented the nation, but they were "the formal assembly of a tyrannized and unhappy people." Their "ultimate aim" was no other than the "reestablishment of religion and liberty." But their way of proceeding was such as to make them incapable of any "vigorous and useful war." "The Polish nobles are the worst kind of troops. . . . They are independent, drunkards, plotters, and pillagers." The peasants were excellent in comparison, "and one could make of them good dragoons and hussars, but it is not the nobles' policy to arm many of them." They feared above all that Catherine II and Stanislaus Poniatowski would raise the peasants against them, as had happened "in the province of Kiovia." What could one do? There was not time to "change the military constitution of Poland" in the midst of combat. It was impossible to touch the immense power of the priests, and they were also unworthy of exercising it. There was the example of the bishop of Kamienieck: "A vain man and an indecent priest, an intriguer governed easily by flatterers. . . . He has the audacity of priests, although he is a coward."[25] Plans for the general reorganization of the confederations were not lacking. But there were always insuperable obstacles, born out of the basic structure of the country itself. Massive assistance from France would only reinforce the lower nobility, which was incapable of seeing beyond its immediate advantage. The conclusion: they were "ignorant, badly brought up, pillagers, vindictive,

[23] Władysław Konopczyński, *Materiały do dziejów wojny Konfederackiej, 1768–1774* (Materials for the history of the war of the Confederation, 1768–1774) (Kraków: Polska Akademija umiejętności, 1931), pp. 25ff.

[24] Dumouriez was one of the most typical adventurers and military men involved in the revolutions of the sixties and seventies, from Corsica to America, and also in Poland and Sweden.

[25] Konopczyński, *Materiały*, pp. 53ff.

and capable of achieving the ruin of the republic instead of restoring it."[26]

There was by contrast a higher military spirit, a greater dedication to the assigned task at hand, and a more detached judgment on the part of the Polish confederates in the documents of Baron de Vioménil and his men, which were collected and published in 1808 as a companion to Rulhière's *Histoire de l'anarchie de Pologne*. These men were officers of exceptional courage (their leader, Vioménil, after Poland served with the American revolutionaries and was mortally wounded defending Louis xvi at the Tuileries on 10 August 1792). They were not led astray by the wave of discussions and polemics that flooded Poland. They tried to be technical and practical in their judgments. But even they could not help but be struck by the "fanaticism combined with intrigue," and the extraordinary mixture of courage, valor, and inefficiency surrounding them in Poland.[27] They hoped for a permanent renewal of the will to resist and counted on the increasing weariness of Russia with its greater and greater commitment to an immense conflict. But the partition put an end to all their hopes.

They discovered, as one sees, a world they had difficulty understanding and dominating. Like the Russians with the Greeks, the French also tended to deflect their blows onto those who showed they were incapable, or indisposed, to accept the norms of an absolutist state.

Nevertheless in Paris, unlike St. Petersburg, the problem of Poland was discussed with extraordinary intensity. The activity of Michał Wielhorski, the representative of the confederates in France, contributed to igniting and developing this debate, as Konopczynski, the chief historian of the events, has demonstrated. The circles of diplomats, writers, and economists were extraordinarily sensitive. From these was born one of the most important political discussions of the second half of the eighteenth century. It was a discussion, I must add quickly, of a reserved nature that, with the exception of the physiocrats, rarely spilled out beyond a nucleus of philosophes and high functionaries. Some of the principal works, such as those of Rousseau and Rulhière, came to light out of the shadow of cabinets, salons, and libraries only many years later.

The work of Rulhière, published posthmously in 1807, but which circulated widely in manuscript from in the seventies and eighties, is typical.[1] The political element predominated: the struggles of men and

[26] Ibid., p. 114, *Etat militaire de la Confédération*, 30 April 1771.

[27] *Lettres particulières du baron de Vioménil . . . sur les affaires de Pologne en 1771 et 1772* (Paris: Treuttel et Würtz, 1808), p. 93.

[1] De Rulhière, *Histoire de l'anarchie de Pologne*. On the specifically Polish aspect of his work, see Ryszard W. Wołoszyński, *Polska w opiniach francuzów XVIII w. Rulhière i jego*

circumstances, intrigues, betrayals, violence. But above this rose the desperate will of the Poles to live and act, even when everything around them was collapsing. The "unhappy republic" became the center of the drama beyond any intention or plan.[2] Increasingly its ancient constitution appeared as an element in the game of the great powers. The constitution appeared more absurd every day. The liberum veto was no other than the "mad law of unanimity."[3] Nevertheless, abolishing it might have been the removal of the first stone from an edifice that threatened to make it collapse entirely. Rulhière was similarly uncertain about the problem of religious toleration. Outside intervention supporting non-Catholic dissenters had made "the greater part of Europe favorable" to Catherine and the republic more and more unpopular. Even here the risk seemed too great for tolerance to be acceptable. In reality, the dissenters "demanded not so much tolerance, as a share in sovereignty," an enlargement and transformation of the sovereign body.[4] And with Russia's assistance they succeeded in obtaining "a new constitution."[5] That is, in a few days they accomplished the task of abolishing a whole series of privileges and corporate bodies that had taken the kings of France four centuries to do. Was it surprising that Voltaire had applauded the policy of Catherine? A closer awareness of the "national spirit" of the Poles, and above all a desire to align himself with the aims of French foreign policy, prompted Rulhière to defend the Polish nobility in its resistance to Stanislaus Augustus. But he did this without illusions: the cold, detached, diplomatic style of the French historian expressed his wish to be on the side of the confederates without becoming involved with them. He knew that the revolt against Stanislaus Augustus drew its roots from a culture and "customs one could say were formed in other centuries," that is, before the modern era.[6] He analyzed the religious character of the rebellion with great acumen as "a kind of revelation."[7] His portrait of Krasinski, the bishop of Kamieniec, emphasized this background of burning passions. He was from a house boasting its descent from one "of those Roman generals who, leaving their country when it gained a master, went searching for liberty wherever the valor of barbarians defended it against Roman arms." A great reader "of books on revolutions, conspiracies, and intrigues" in his youth, he was

---

współcześni (Poland in the opinion of eighteenth-century Frenchmen, Rulhière and his collaborators), with a summary in French (Warsaw: PWN, 1964).

[2] De Rulhière, *Histoire de l'anarchie de Pologne*, vol. 2, p. 83.

[3] Ibid., p. 249.

[4] Ibid., p. 253.

[5] Ibid., p. 255.

[6] Ibid., p. 340.

[7] Ibid., p. 427.

not fanatic in matters of religion, but in politics he was ready to use any means, including alliance with the Turks. There was no equivocation in his program: "It was liberty or death."[8] The arrest and deportation of the bishops of Kraków and Kiovia signaled a critical moment. While Catherine II seemed to put herself on the road of Pombal and Du Tillot, and Voltaire applauded, the Polish clergy reacted with greater vigor than the clergy of Portugal, Spain, or Parma and unleashed a national and religious revolt. Contemporaries were already asking what the causes for this difference were. Rulhière was convinced that it all resulted from the mistaken policy of the Russian empress. Instead of proceeding with reforms and uprooting abuses and privileges, she had made use of tolerance as a means for establishing her own domination. This was not a policy inspired by "love of humanity" and "philosophy."[9] "Catherine II filled the world with the noise of her new laws; but all her pretense and ambition reduced itself to preserving despotism in Russia and anarchy in Poland."[10]

The anarchy soon led, with the formation in February 1768 of the Confederation of Bar, to a tragic civil war. The insurgents placed their hopes in Europe and thought numerous volunteers would come to their aid. But they had deceived themselves. "It was no longer an age when Europe was filled with generous adventurers, always ready to join the armies of weak peoples defending their liberty, or when independent nobles went anywhere their courage led them to seek peril and glory."[11] The modern state, against which the confederates rebelled in Poland, had consolidated itself in Europe. Still, the confederation fought on alone. "Here was a disarmed people whose territory was occupied from one end to the other by a large enemy army that was disciplined, formidable, and continually replenished; a people betrayed by their king and by a part of their senate, a country without fortresses and even without mountains, the natural refuge of independence, but still arising on every side."[12] The confederates' problem was not insufficient foreign support, but, Rulhière was convinced, the condition of the Polish nobility. At their backs was an immense number of peasant serfs. "Slavery made the Polish peasantry useless in defending the state." Their condition was similar to that of Russian peasants, but their spirit was different. "They did not have that inert stupidity which leads the Russians to accept death, thinking they have no right even to their own lives." In

[8] Ibid., pp. 485, 519.
[9] Ibid., p. 538.
[10] Ibid., p. 553.
[11] Ibid., vol. 3, p. 51.
[12] Ibid., p. 65ff.

reality Polish peasants were more similar to the great mass of laborers covering the whole earth. "They are like that prodigious multitude of serfs who populate the land, subjected by force, bent down with sorrow and the hard necessity of their condition, habituated by their parents to patiently accept the sad fate of their birth, and capable, by a fermentation of nature itself, to open their hearts to the hope of a revolution."[13] The Russian serfs were not capable of as much, ready as they always were to die for the czar. This hatred and disdain for Russians that Rulhière derived from the Polish confederates blinded him. A few years later, in 1773, the Pugačev revolt showed that, to use his words, "the hope of a revolution" was not lacking in the serfs of the empire of Catherine II.

Rulhière's attention was directed above all—like that of Europe in general in those years—to observing the courage, daring, and venturesomeness of the confederates, as well as their exceptional capacity for resistance and renewal. But he did not forget to record how the Poles undertook an effort to relate themselves to the "best minds of Europe," thus posing the following question to the philosophes with ability and energy, a question similar to the one posed a few years earlier by Corsica: "What form of government should the Poles give to their republic after its deliverance?"[14] They posed, that is, in the most explicit way the question of the relationship between republican tradition and the necessity for reforms.

The first to respond in France was Abbé Mably, whom Rulhière himself had persuaded to think about the Polish question. On 31 August 1770 he finished his long and detailed memoir, which was read in Paris by a small and select number of people, among whom was Jean Jacques Rousseau.[15] It was a program for reform, an appeal for political action to be carried out in a risky and tragic situation. To be sure, he did not hide the difficulties; he listed and described them openly, but he did not deny the possibility of arriving at a "happy revolution."[16] The most immediate threat was foreign intervention, particularly by Russia. Only the Ottoman Empire seemed a candidate for limiting and stopping the expansion of Catherine II. The Poles should not delude themselves about the value of European equilibrium for preventing their ruin. "Should

---

[13] Ibid., p. 67.

[14] Ibid., p. 304.

[15] Published by Mably himself in 1781, this work, entitled *Du governement et des lois de Pologne*, is included in the *Collection complète des oeuvres de l'abbé de Mably* (Paris: Ch. Desbrière, L'an 3 de la République [1794–95]), vol. 8, pp. 1ff. See Gabriel Bonnot de Mably, *Scritti politici*, ed. Aldo Maffey (Turin: Utet, 1965), vol. 2, pp. 449ff.

[16] Mably, *Du gouvernement et des lois de Pologne*, in id., *Collection complète des oeuvres*, p. 231.

Poland not finally be disillusioned in seeing with what indifference Europe witnesses her misfortune?"[17] Certainly Catherine had risked much in launching her undertaking, as much financially as militarily. But Poland would be wise to accept a compromise, perhaps electing as king an Austrian archduke, seeking the support of France and Sweden, and not forgetting the Roman Curia, weak, certainly, but with an energetic man in the nuncio, Durini, who was capable of mobilizing the Polish clergy. But this foreign policy would make sense only if it were part of a profound transformation of the country. The Poles had to be ready to reform themselves all alone, with their own means and their own strength. "I would prefer you to make awkward laws and an ill-considered constitution than for you to receive better ones from your neighbors."[18] This was exactly the opposite position from the one Voltaire held. And Mably did not mean to set the history, language, and customs of Poland against those of Russia or Prussia. The problem for him was not so much national policy as the possibilities and nature of political reform carried out in a free country by free means. "Reform in a free country" was the problem the Poles had to resolve.[19]

He put aside the widely held illusion that it would be sufficient to make small adjustments in the existing constitution. Elimination of the liberum veto was not a cure-all. It was necessary to abolish the election of the kings, making them hereditary, and at the same time to take away all their effective power. The example of England showed that it was important not to leave any authority in the hands of kings. "It would be better to follow the example the Swedes have given us."[20] They had reserved for the general Diet, or the Senate, all power over "ecclesiastical, civil, and military dignities," as well as over "royal lands," even removing all financial autonomy from the king. In Poland, the Diet would become the only legislative power, reducing local assemblies, little diets, to administrative functions. The executive power would be organized in a manner somewhere between a government of rotating committees, of Venetian type, and a modern council of ministers.

But this reform should be undertaken prudently. If it were a matter "of remaking the government of a slow, docile, and timid nation, little given to agitate for liberty, it would be necessary to arouse passions and even encourage new ones." "But it is necessary to prescribe quite differently for Poland, because one does not pass from anarchy to love of law

[17] Ibid., p. 79.
[18] Ibid., p. 5.
[19] Ibid., p. 38.
[20] Ibid., p. 73.

and order in the same way that one passes from despotism to liberty."[21] Nor should one be taken in by an illusion "of a perfection that is too great."[22] It was still necessary to arouse great hopes in everyone and not make concessions. Mably seems to describe intuitively in these pages the first, idyllic and generous, moment of modern revolutions. "The time of reform shoud be, if I can so speak, a time of jubilation and indulgence. . . . Old crimes should be forgotten, grace should be prodigious so as to extinguish old resentments. . . . There should be reconciliation, all spirits must come together to establish laws that will procure the common happiness."[23]

Mably did not hide the obstacles to such a transformation. There was prejudice everywhere. The Jews, with their riches, were "the true masters of Poland."[24] The peasants, he said, addressing himself to the nobles, "will take little interest either in your prosperity or in your adversity; and if they are not stupefied by their ignorance and the weight of their servitude, they will be openly your enemies, and you will have slave rebellions, which despair sometimes makes terrible."[25] The nobility must persuade itself that it cannot be free without freeing the peasants. "Land wants to be cultivated by free hands."[26] A third estate would have to develop. The diffusion of enlightenment was also needed. The chief obstacle was that the Poles, as he had been told ("comme on me l'assure"), believed in the infallibility of the Pope. But the dissemination of good books, like those by Bossuet, Fleury, and Nicole, would be a great advantage. "This revolution needs to be prepared by a diffusion of *lumières*, which will little by little dissipate error and prejudice."[27]

Despite his great effort to interpret and give final direction to the Confederation of Bar, the Abbé Mably thus ended in the road that would be taken by his adversary and now enemy, Stanislaus Augustus. In the end enlightened reform would dominate rebellion.

Jean Jacques Rousseau proceeded in a different way. He was prompted and informed by Wielhorski, the confederates' agent; he was also aware of the work of Rulhière and of the policy of Choiseul.[28] Rous-

---

[21] Ibid., p. 19.
[22] Ibid., p. 38.
[23] Ibid., pp. 145ff.
[24] Ibid., p. 170.
[25] Ibid., pp. 231ff.
[26] Ibid., p. 232.
[27] Ibid., pp. 173, 174.
[28] The *Considérations sur le gouvernement de Pologne et sur sa réformation projectée* is in the *Oeuvres* by Rousseau, ed. B. Gagnebin and M. Raymond (Paris: Gallimard, 1964), vol. 3, pp. 951ff., with an ample introduction and numerous notes by Jean Fabre. This presentation is very critical of Mably and entirely favorable to Rousseau, thus carrying on after

seau agreed to express his ideas about Poland in October 1770. He worked intensely through the winter and finished his work in April 1771, revising it in the months that followed. Mably had a copy of it on 9 July 1771, before finishing the second part of his memoir. The fall of Choiseul, the change in French policy, and the defeat of the confederates led Rousseau not to publish his *Considérations*; the French police prohibited its publication in 1774. It did not come to light until after his death, in 1782. It had circulated as a manuscript, however, if only to a small group of people.

Strange and astonishing to the eyes of Jean Jacques seemed the spectacle of Poland. He had to ask himself how "a state so strangely put together could have survived for so long."[29] The phenomenon seemed even more surprising because all over Europe there were signs of the decadence of current political forms. "I see all the states of Europe run toward their ruin." In the midst of this decay, Poland, "that depopulated, devastated, oppressed land, open to its enemies," was releasing its energies to work toward its renewal. "It is in chains and discusses the means for conserving its liberty!" One should accept and nurture this impulse. One should appeal not to science or interest, but to the heart, to precisely those passions that Mably wanted to moderate and keep in check. One should proceed with great care so as not to risk weakening or stifling what was permitting Poland to survive and fight. Everyone criticized anarchy. But one should not forget "that it is at the breast of that anarchy, so odious to you, that patriotic souls who protect you from the yoke are formed."[30] The Poles should not choose "*quietum servitium*," but "*periculosam libertatem*," as Stanislaus Leszczyński had said.

Rousseau's aversion to civilization brought by conquest, which a few years earlier had already made him side with the Corsicans in their struggle with Louis xv, as well as his growing polemic against the philosophes, led him to a call for revolt, for originality, and for the independence of Poland.[31] He was convinced that the peril threatening the nation was terrible. The danger was not only from losing the war, from being invaded and conquered, but even more from losing one's soul, renouncing one's traditions, and losing oneself in the surrounding world. Like the Corsicans, who a few years earlier he thought were the only people in Europe still capable of liberty, the Poles were the only

two centuries the discussion between the cosmpolitan and national positions of the two philosophers. And see now Jerzy Michalski, *Rousseau i sarmacki republikanizm* (Rousseau and Sarmatic republicanism) (Warsaw: pwn, 1977).

[29] Rousseau, *Considérations*, p. 953.

[30] Ibid., p. 954.

[31] On the psychological and philosophical origins of this call, see Bronisław Baczko, Rousseau, *Solitude et communauté* (Paris and The Hague: Mouton, 1970).

ones able to defend "a national character." The other peoples of Europe all resembled each other. "There are today no longer French, Germans, Spanish, even English, despite what one says, but only Europeans." Only the Poles had preserved a "particular kind of institution" that permitted them to preserve a "national form." Their enemies were thus made all the more dangerous by presenting themselves as political, social, and economic benefactors. "Their ambition is only for luxury, and their passion only for gold."[32] And the Russians? How should one act toward these, who represented for Poland the greatest and most immediate peril? For them Rousseau developed, in a few hard and cold sentences, the final conclusions of his appeal to the Polish nation. "You will not be able to prevent them from swallowing you; make sure they cannot digest you."[33] But should the Poles, as was hoped, be victorious, and when they celebrated this event, it would not be necessary to even speak of the Russians. "It would give them too much honor. Silence, the memory of their barbarity, and the commemoration of those who resisted them will say all that is necessary; you should disdain them so as not to hate them."[34] The work of Peter the Great should serve as a negative example. In matters such as education, clothes, and laws "you should do exactly the opposite of what was done by that vaunted czar."[35] In general, one should substitute the development of forces contained in national tradition for imitation. A "noble pride" should guide the country. In this way "it will take up again, in this new age, all the vigor of a new nation."[36]

But how should one achieve such a rebirth? The task was not easy. Rousseau did not hide the contradictions in his assumptions and in his program, which was both conservative and innovative at the same time. His solutions were not intended to be compromises, but rather incentives for a deep integral change. The fact that Poland was a large state was a "basic vice" in his eyes. All great peoples were crushed "by their size."[37] A reduction of size was essential. "Perhaps your neighbors were thinking of doing you such a service."[38] Perhaps through the current war itself it would be possible to arrive at a "confederation of thirty-three little states," thus uniting "the strength of great monarchies with the liberty of small republics."[39] This was the foresight of a solution sim-

---

[32] Rousseau, *Considérations*, p. 960.

[33] Ibid., pp. 959ff.

[34] Ibid., p. 961.

[35] Ibid., p. 962.

[36] Ibid.

[37] Ibid.

[38] Ibid., p. 971.

[39] Ibid., p. 1010.

ilar to the one the United States of America later sought and achieved.
But Rousseau did not ignore the fact that in Poland the solution would
be particularly difficult because any reform risked opening a door to the
enemy. The liberation of the serfs would have been "a great and good
measure," but it was dangerous and risky at the time.[40] The central
point from which there could be no deviation was this alone: "maintain
the constitution."[41] Rousseau put himself on the road to reform, and to
improvements to the constitution, but still he declared firmly that he
wanted to maintain its fundamentals. The king should remain elective.
Poland was free because each new reign was preceded by a period in
which "the nation, restored to all its rights, and taking on new vigor,
prevents abuses and usurpations, so that legislation renews itself and
finds again its initial impulse."[42] Here the future American presidential
elections seemed to appear in the mists. It was necessary to preserve the
three essential elements of the political structure: the diet, the senate,
and the king. Rousseau held that the noblility should preserve a monopoly of political power. He even proposed adopting the *Libri di Oro*,
Golden Books, of Venice and the idea, also Venetian, of opening "the
door of nobility and honor to the bourgeoisie" through offices given to
citizens.[43] While Mably tended toward democracy, Rousseau, as one
sees, was republican; he wanted to preserve the institutions inherited
from the past. And like other republicans of those years, he too was very
much concerned about the perils threatening free governments
throughout Europe. "You have seen Denmark, you see England, you
will see Sweden."[44]

Even when he wrote about the "particular causes of anarchy," his
republican patriotism dominated his political vision. Certainly, it was
necessary to abolish the liberum veto, that "unfortunate right," because
it prevented the Polish constitution from functioning. He even proposed the death penalty for anyone who made use of this "barbarous
right."[45] But then he took the route all modern constitutions have accepted: three-quarters of the votes, not a simple majority, would be necessary to adopt particularly important dispositions. He did not want to
abolish the confederations, "the shield, the asylum, and the sanctuary of
the constitution."[46] They corresponded to Roman dictators. "Do you

[40] Ibid., p. 974.
[41] Ibid., p. 975.
[42] Ibid., p. 991.
[43] Ibid., pp. 983, 1027.
[44] Ibid., p. 992.
[45] Ibid., p. 996.
[46] Ibid., p. 999.

want to deny the republic the resource that has just saved it?"[47] "Executive power given to the confederations will always give them strength, activity, and speed at times of need, which the Diet cannot have, forced as it is to proceed more slowly and more formally and not being able to carry out a single irregular act without upsetting the constitution."[48]

These political instruments would be effective only if Poland adopted for the future an "economic system" consonant with its need for isolation, and if its foreign and military policy followed suit.[49] Here as well the parallel with Corsica was evident. In both cases there was an attempt to escape the existing political and economic system of Europe by setting aside power and riches to uphold independence and liberty. Rousseau put the Poles clearly on guard. "If you want to be only noisy, brilliant, and formidable, and to influence the other peoples of Europe," you will only need to erect a centralized and enlightened state, on the model of so many other European nations. You would thus be able to take part in the wars of the continent and even enrich yourselves. "But if by chance you would rather construct a free, peaceful, and wise nation that has neither fear nor need of anyone and is self-sufficient and happy," then you will need to close your ears to the many counsels you are offered and give life to a society quite different from that of your neighbors.[50] You will have to renounce riches to have prosperity, give the least possible importance to money and its circulation, avoid the sciences of finance and economics, assign common tasks to the labor services of all citizens, prefer taxes paid in kind, encourage the manufacture of only prime necessities, and not attend to commerce. In this way the Poles will have "neither mendicants nor millionaires." "Luxury and indigence will quietly disappear by themselves."[51]

The military system would also have to be radically different from that of other European states. Taking up and developing further the critique of standing armies typical of "commonwealthmen" among British republicans, Rousseau proposed "a good militia, a true militia."[52] The memory of Switzerland gave his proposal realistic and familiar colors. He did not disregard the intrinsic difficulties in his plan. How could one arm peasant serfs? He appealed, meanwhile, in anticipation of emancipation, to the cities. The model of western republics imposed itself on Polish reality.

[47] Ibid., p. 998.
[48] Ibid.
[49] Ibid., p. 1103.
[50] Ibid.
[51] Ibid., p. 1009.
[52] Ibid., p. 1014.

In the conclusion of his work Rousseau exhorted the confederates not to accept any compromise. Their alliance with the Turks was essential to them. After all, "the Grand Seigneur" showed in his actions "less enlightenment and finesse than integrity and good sense."[53] The important thing was not to give in to flattery and not to cede in any way to the Russians. "The Russians always look at free men as we must look at them, that is, as automatons on which only two impressions register: money and the knout."[54] It was up to the Poles to show that the Russians were wrong.

Rousseau's text is rich in perspectives and can be read from many different angles. At its base is an extrapolation on a European scale of his polemic with the "philosophes." Even the Grand Turk was better than the economists. His vision of Europe was bitterly pessimistic. Poland, after Corsica, lights up for a moment with energy and desperate struggle on an ever darkening horizon. As in his polemic with Holbach, his anguish grew as he discovered, or believed he discovered, how able, rich, powerful, and unscrupulous his enemies were, as well as the enemies of liberty. The general development of things was against him. Few and weak were those who opposed the spread of despotism, indifference, uniformity, egoism. This made him all the more enthusiastic about the patriotism of Pasquale Paoli and the Confederation of Bar. His pessimism and desperation were compensated for by the idea and conviction growing within him that all great modern states were in decline, menaced, and on the brink of ruin. In the contest between republics and monarchy, between free and servile lands, military force was still on the side of the powerful, but a mortal danger weighed even on them. For the moment, there was no other refuge of liberty than in itself, in the refusal to be oppressed and seduced. The nationalism of Rousseau—it is difficult to define otherwise some of the expressions I have cited—was born of this sense of inferiority combined with the prophecy of the enemies' approaching collapse. Survival, even for Poland, was in itself a guarantee of a reaffirmed future. This nationalism was born in the terrain of republican tradition (*libertas* is independence and liberty inseparably linked). But the tradition was colored for him by an entirely new vision of the political and social reality of Europe. In his opposition to the great states, he guessed their weak point, the inability to understand the new passion for liberty that was rising in the margins of Europe, in Corsica, Greece, and Poland. Everywhere older European states were in crisis, but nowhere was it possible to carry out necessary and indispensable political and social reforms. Denmark, Sweden, En-

[53] Ibid., p. 1038.
[54] Ibid., p. 1039.

gland, and the American colonies would demonstrate soon that his viewpoint, dramatically attuned to the limitations of enlightened despotism,
was beginning to find its response in political reality. Thus Jean Jacques
was among those who perceived with greatest sensitivity and penetration the shift in the sixties and seventies from reform to revolution.

The price he paid for this vision and intuition was great. He closed
his eyes to Russia and refused to see or hope further. In his dislike of
Voltaire he finally denied that even the empire of Catherine could be
overtaken in the great shift of the century. He did not speak about
Greece, although it was a phenomenon not that different from that of
Corsica. The fact that Orlov was involved in the events in the Morea was
enough to make it impossible for him to see the importance of this other
seed of the modern renewal. Still more, he closed his eyes to the value
of the enlightened and modernizing effort that had begun in Poland
when he wrote his *Considérations* and that became accentuated after the
first partition. In this effort Poland needed reformers, not confederates,
or rather, as soon appeared, confederates who could be converted to
reforming ideas. However, the value of Rousseau's ideas was recognized
only later. After 1781 the *Considérations* began to be seen as a prophetic
text. Jean Fabre has held that in these pages Rousseau contributed to
the preparation of Poles for the long test of total partition and for their
nineteenth-century resistance and insurrection. Modern Polish historiography tends to see the work of intellectual, political, economic, and
social transformation of the period of Stanislaus Augustus as the most
authentic cause for Polish survival after the disappearance of the ancient republic. In a sense, the eighteenth-century debate about Poland
between Rousseau and Voltaire is still alive.

Another direction, different from that indicated by Rousseau, was
taken by the physiocrats. Mirabeau saw with clarity in 1767–1768 the
peril threatening Poland, torn between reform and liberty. Even there
could be seen the "general ferment," the "appetite for economic and
political enlightenment" that affected Europe as a whole. In no other
land was it possible to see with such clarity the alternative preparing
itself. Either the government would know how to interpret these new
needs, or it, like other states of Europe, would fall "tottering." Much
depended on the position Catherine II took. Would she be capable of
abandoning her old policy of encouraging Polish anarchy to increase
her own power? Would she know how to exchange it for an open and
clear proclamation of fundamental principles, for "property, liberty, security"?[55]

[55] See Ambroise Jobert, *Magnats polonais et physiocrates français (1767–1774)* (Paris: Les
Belles Lettres, 1941), p. 21.

One of the most important followers and disciples of Mirabeau, the Abbé Baudeau, took up this theme and continued to develop it in his political activity in Poland, and later in a series of articles published between 1770 and 1772 in the *Ephémérides du citoyen*. He did not place his hopes in the empress of Russia, but instead collaborated personally and directly in the profound transformation of Polish life. In 1770 he thought the republic was in complete ruin: "No king, no senate, no ministers, no diet."[56] How had one reached such a state? A look at the history of the previous two hundred years answered the question. For some time the Muscovites had "formed a plan to dominate or destroy the two nations that serve as their barrier to Europe, Sweden and Poland."[57] Poland had collaborated in this systematic demolition. One could even say that "the Poles themselves work toward their own destruction with even more success than their enemies."[58] And whereas in Russia, after Ivan III, the "Muscovite despotism"[59] was formed step by step, in Poland, particularly after the era of Casimir III, one revolution succeeded another, which resulted in "total anarchy."[60] These interrelated and contrasting destinies found points of contact in the parallel problems the two governments had to face. Catherine II, in 1767, had followed the example suggested by Casimir III in 1336 in his project for making a new law code. The empress had been intelligent enough to publish the *Nakaz* in doing this, in which she followed the traces of Montesquieu, Beccaria, and other authors "inferior to those two." To be sure, it was "always praiseworthy to seek assistance, procedures, and advice from the most famous philosophers." But Catherine II had not always chosen well. Evidently the strong influence of German cameralists, such as Justi, displeased the Abbé Baudeau. He also did not like, in the case of both the Polish king and the Russian empress, the number of deputies admitted to the commission destined for the compilation of the new code. They seemed too numerous in both cases. It would not be possible to find that many cultivated and enlightened men. And in fact, in the assembly at the Kremlin there were deputies who "did not know how to read."[61] Under these conditions discussion became a pure formality and risked going on endlessly. Even with the central problem Catherine II raised, that of the relationship between nobles and peasants, Casimir III had committed the same error that Peter III had made

[56] "Lettres sur l'état actuel de la Pologne et sur l'origine des ses malheurs," in *Ephémérides du citoyen*, vol. 2 (1770), p. 18.
[57] Ibid.
[58] Ibid., p. 19.
[59] Ibid., p. 57.
[60] Ibid., vol. 3 (1770), p. 51.
[61] Ibid., p. 59 n.

recently in Russia. It was not good, in both cases, to begin by freeing the nobles and then asking them to liberate their serfs. "The emancipated nobles did not want their peasants to be free and would not suffer it." Hope in the generosity of nobles was as absurd as making "a code for a nation composed of arbitrary despots and slaves." Vainly Catherine had announced the competition of the Free Economic Society. The most clear and precise responses were rejected "in deference to the prejudices of the nation in truly difficult times."[62] An analysis of the past and present showed the need of undoing the central social problem of both countries. "What an absurd chimera is the idea of civilizing an empire and still leaving in serfdom all the workers of the soil."[63]

Baudeau attempted to resolve the Polish problem with great persistence, which his contemporaries unjustly thought was a spirit of intrigue. How could one effect reform without unleashing Russia's impulse to conquest and domination? How could one resolve enormous social questions without abandoning guarantees and legitimate liberties? He hoped to receive the necessary support from Bishop Massalski. He went to St. Petersburg to study the conditions of Russian peasants and sought in vain to win Catherine ii's favor. He supported the efforts of Stanislaus Augustus and hoped to draw into the party of reform at least some of the Confederates of Bar. He proposed a whole series of diplomatic plans to avoid the growing tension between Russia and France. He ended up, in the winter of 1771–1772, proposing a plan for peace, which the Abate Raimondo Niccoli, the Tuscan representative in Paris, who was in close contact with the physiocrats, was supposed to send on to Vienna.[64]

Besides Baudeau and, in competition with him, others also attempted to intervene in the debate. Thus, Le Mercier de la Rivière, who in 1772 declared the republican government "admirable," produced at the same time a thorough critique of Polish society.[65] He also said he was in favor of gradual change through necessary reforms, insisting on the necessity of proceeding not only with economic reforms, but also with change in the Polish constitution (abolition of the liberum veto, and positive mandates to the nuncios, the deputies to the Diet). He insisted above all on the emancipation of peasants and bourgeois. The Polish

[62] Ibid., p. 69 n.

[63] Cited by Jobert, *Magnats polonais*, p. 24.

[64] A large part of A. Jobert's interesting book, cited earlier, is dedicated to this incident. On Niccoli, see Mario Mirri, "Per una ricerca sui rapporti tra 'economisti' e riformatori toscani. L'abate Niccoli a Parigi," *Annali dell'Istituto Giangiacomo Feltrinelli* 2 (1959), which refers to the encounter between the Tuscan representative and I. Massalski but does not mention any attempt to mediate between Poland and Austria.

[65] Jobert, *Magnats polonais*, p. 46.

nobles, he said, must show "a firm resolution to break the chains of those to whom the laws have left only what could not be taken away from men: their form and name."[66] Education in general and in sciences in particular would contribute a great deal to transform the country. The economist Dupont also insisted on the need to free the peasants and develop schools (he was later named secretary of the commission for national education). His activity is typical of the changes occurring after the partition of 1772. Enlightenment became a fundamental premise for reforms and even, in a sense, a substitute for social transformation, so that it became increasingly difficult to turn plans into an effective reality.

These problems and hopes also echoed in Italy.[1] The debate in Italy, however, was not as intense or important as it was in England and France. There was more compassion than comprehension, more sympathy than direct participation. In the general development of the Russo-Turkish war, what most interested Italians was the Greek insurrection and the apprearance of Russia in the Levant. Poland was far away, and it was difficult to find an orientation in the intricacy of developments there. Still, the contrast between reform and republican tradition, between the culture of the Enlightenment and admiration for the Sarmatia of the north, and between foreign intervention and national independence was too important for there not to be, even in Italy, an attempt to follow intently the many political threads with which the diplomacy of Europe as a whole, and the factions in Poland, wove their Penelope's web.[2]

Let us look first at Venice. The work of petty popular chroniclers was, to be sure, not lacking. But the general curiosity could not be satisfied through pages and pages of news and comments alone. Giacomo Casanova could not avoid discussing the matter, even though it was distant from the central subject of the first part of his *Confutazione della*

---

[66] Pierre-Paul-François Le Mercier de la Rivière, "L'intérêt commun des Polonais," manuscript preserved in the BN in Paris and cited by Louis-Philippe May, *Le Mercier de la Rivière (1719–1801). Aux origines de la science économique* (Paris: CNRS, 1975), p. 91.

[1] For a general view, see Zdzisław Libera, "Rapports culturels polono-italiens à l'époque des lumières," in *Italia e Polonia tra illuminismo e romanticismo*, ed. Vittore Branca (Florence: Olschki, 1973), pp. 3ff. See also *Istituzioni, cultura e società in Italia e in Polonia (Sec. XVIII–XIX). Atti del convegno italo-polacco di studi storici (Lecce-Napoli, 10–17 Febbraio 1976)*, ed. Cosimo Damiano Fonseca (Galatina: Congedo editore, 1979).

[2] For a general orientation, see Emanuel Rostworowski, "Tentative reforms under Russia's Tutelage (1763–1788)," which is ch. 11, pp. 313ff., of the *History of Poland*, ed. Aleksander Gieysztor, Stefan Kieniewicz, Emanuel Rostworowski, Janusz Tazbir, and Henryk Wereszycki (Warsaw: PWN, 1968).

storia del governo veneto d'Amelot de la Houssaie, which was published in 1769. In his notes is a eulogy to "Zaluski, lord bishop of Kiovia, a Polish Senator . . . arrested at Warsaw in 1767 by order of the empress of Russia because he expressed the opinions of a free man, a Catholic, and a son of his country." Even the republican spirit of this prelate attracted Casanova, who called him "pious, Catholic, patriotic, zealous, a firm partisan of the general discord of the country, because it is the only source of the concord of particulars, and the mighty column supporting the ancient laws of Poland."[3] This was a country where "the desire to make innovations is the same as the desire to put everything to fire and blood," and where no one could be happy without accepting that perpetual "*discordia concors* of which Ovid writes." Casanova then narrated the circumstances that led to war between Russia and the Ottoman Empire. "Here is another marvel of this century: the Grand Turk defending the exclusive privileges of the Roman Church in Poland." As we see, anarchy and Catholicism were the first things that struck those who turned their eyes toward Poland.

Even Casanova, like so many others, and despite the interest the figure of Catherine II aroused in him, felt close emotionally to dismembered Poland. Stanislaus Augustus, this "leader of a republic," this representative of a nation "now wandering and dispersed," seemed to him pitiable. "He is a victim sacrificing himself to ambition, to the glory of being king and of raising his brothers and friends. Being made unhappy for wishing to create happiness—this was a too-austere virtue." And his abdication would resolve nothing. There was no escape from the Polish situation. "Without prejudice to the profound veneration a poor mortal owes to the dignity of a king, I cannot in the secrecy of my soul not pity his harsh destiny." He was "raised to the highest place the ambition of a citizen can aspire to," but he became "the most unfortunate of all men." "The obstinate disorder of his nation" now obliged him "to join the interests of those who are destroying it." He would never abandon the throne, if for no other reason than to "not seem a weak soul in the mind of Catherine."[4]

For these psychological reflections the *Storia della guerra presente* substituted in Poland, as it had done in Greece and the Levant, a military and political commentary that is quite interesting. The second small volume was devoted in large part to the Polish precedents of the Russo-Turkish war. The third presented "the system of Poland" or, more precisely, that country's incapacity of maintaining an internal equilibrium.

---

[3] Casanova, *Confutazione della storia del governo veneto d'Amelot de la Houssaie*, pt. 1, pp. 34–35 n., 37.

[4] Ibid., pp. 45–46 n.

The "great," exceeding "their bounds," had reduced the republic to a "frightful anarchy."[5] The nobles dominated a "people of peasant slaves, less cultivated than the animals that assist their labors."[6] The king's efforts to reform seemed fruitless. The decisive opposition of the bishops, "inspired by Clement XIII," was emphasized.[7] This problem could not help but interest Venetians who in these same years were undertaking a transformation in the relationship between church and state. Thus the *Storia* praised the policy of Catherine II in Russia and beyond its frontiers, even against the stormy Polish background. The good will of Stanislaus Augustus, "crossed in all of his plans," paled by comparison.[8] In May 1767 "civil war broke out."[9] The confederates multiplied. Developments in Poland were linked to the story of conflicts unleashed throughout Europe by the Rezzonico Pope. The fourth volume describes the facts leading gradually to general war in the style and form of a gazette. The "enthusiasms" of the Confederates of Bar are brought forth in volume 4, as well as their "sad effects."[10] In the volumes that followed events in the Mediterranean and on the Black Sea distract attention from Poland, which was seen to continue along its *via crucis*. In volume 9 accounts are totaled: the confederates appeared to have completely overturned the country. The nobles, with their disastrous policy, had destroyed their own authority. "The great have begun to be aware that the evil was too advanced." It was now too late for both themselves and Poland. "Those who were the first to establish confederations considered the state of their country in the depths of their hearts and thought the doctor was worse than the disease. The bishop of Kamieniec was one of these."[11] The capital became more insecure; in the provinces there were "the most terrible famines, which completed the desolation of the already ruined country."[12] The situation was summed up by a proclamation "on the unfortunate outcome of the confederations," a proclamation that particularly attracted the attention of the Venetian chronicler.[13] At the time of its partition Poland seemed to be a particularly dramatic element in the "general ferment of Europe in military, political, and ecclesiastical affairs."[14]

[5] *Storia della guerra presente*, vol. 3, pp. 5ff.

[6] Ibid., p. 7.

[7] Ibid., p. 31. See also p. 90: "Clement XIII encourages the Polish Catholics with various briefs."

[8] Ibid., p. 107.

[9] Ibid., p. 109.

[10] Ibid., vol. 4, p. 47.

[11] Ibid., vol. 9, p. 82.

[12] Ibid., p. 9.

[13] Ibid., vol. 10, p. 31.

[14] Ibid., p. 1.

Contemporaneous to the *Storia della guerra presente* other works reported to the Venetian interest in developments in the land of Stanislaus Augustus. The *Descrizione storico-politica-geografica del regno polacco*, which appeared in 1770, offered many critical insights. The *Storia dell'anno*, although basically oriented toward the narration of events of the war, also focused on the internal crisis of Poland. In 1771 "fatal disorders" had brought "the greatest of evils that can arise from the internal dissensions of a state." The "cruel incursions" of the confederates, infiltrated by "bandits and false confederates," had spread "terror and desolation" everywhere. The warring parties all pretended to act "for religion and liberty," but the only result was "violence, robbery, and vexations." The Russian military force had demonstrated that it was incapable of restoring order.[15] Such "horrible anarchy," as Saldern, the ambassador of Catherine II at Warsaw, reported, prepared Poland's ruin.[16] The confederates, vaunting the principles of their policy, said "they were all free sons of a free mother" since "*par super parem non habet potestatem*" (equal does not have power over equal). But despite acts of extraordinary courage and French intervention, they lost more and more the possibility of winning their difficult battle.[17] Even in the *Storia dell'anno* the Polish war seemed to crumble into a myriad indecisive military events. The year 1772 opened with a narrative of the events leading to the partition. It was clearly the most important occurrence of that year. The attempt to assassinate Stanislaus Augustus was taken to be the decisive episode. How could other states permit such a "horrible example" without "rapid punishment"?[18] The violation of the sacred person of the king and the reestablishment of legitimacy were seen as the decisive elements in the intervention of Catherine II, Frederick II, and Maria Theresa. This conservative vision, by furnishing abundant documentation for the other side, did not prevent the *Storia dell'anno* from making heard the voice of those who still nurtured the "vain hope" of outwitting the Russians and "chasing them forever from the realm."[19] There was no sympathy in these pages for "those proud malcontents," but one of their most impressive proclamations, by Pułaski, was reproduced literally. "God and fatherland," "virtue and patriotism," "liberty and religion" had moved him, he said, not to make an attempt on the life of the king, but to defeat him "in battle, joined with the cruelest of our ene-

---

[15] On the *Descrizione storico-politico-geografica del regno polacco*, see ch. 2, p. 54 n. 35. *Storia dell'anno 1771* (Venice: Francesco Pitteri, 1772), p. 66.

[16] Ibid., p. 81.

[17] Ibid., p. 83.

[18] *Storia dell'anno 1772* (Venice: Francesco Pitteri, 1773), p. 3.

[19] Ibid., p. 19.

mies."[20] The oath Puławski himself administered to his troops before the image of the Madonna of Częstochowa revealed how great was the hatred of these men for Stanislaus Augustus, "the breaker of divine and human law, the usurper of the throne of Poland, the agent of atheists and heretics, the betrayer of the fatherland, the oppressor of the nation, and the vile instrument of foreign ambition and injustice."[21] Before this unleashing of traditional and patriotic passion, the proclamations of the partitioning powers, which were also reproduced in full in the *Storia dell'anno*, seemed a return to normal politics, interweaved with reforms, economic preoccupations, and aspirations for peace and well-being. Such smiles and promises could not hide or veil "the profound sadness and agitation" the partition produced in Warsaw.[22] "This was the sad state of that unfortunate kingdom" were the last words of this long chronicle.[23]

In comparison with this still rough picture, the history of events in Poland that Giacomo Casanova began to publish two years later gives the impression of a pale and faded fresco on the walls of a Venetian villa.[24] Its pretense of lordliness and grandeur has not disappeared, but energy and originality are lacking. While seeking his fortune Casanova had lived in Warsaw and St. Petersburg. He had met personalities of the first rank in the drama he set out to narrate, but he had no important firsthand testimony to offer; he remained on the margin. His picture was colored with and continually confused by the inclusion of collateral episodes, historical background, and descriptions of persons and things. The principal personages are all handsome, dignified, magnificent, and even heroic; the events are all worthy of memory. What lacked was doubt, reflection, thought. Casanova was full of interest. He even had an up-to-date knowledge of contemporary thought. But all curiosity and vivacity were wasted away in his skeptical and weary conservatism.

From the beginning of his *Discorso preliminare* he identified the center of the story: despotism and the revolt against it. He discussed at length "the famous modern Boulanger" and his theory of the religions and

[20] Ibid., p. 21.

[21] Ibid., p. 23.

[22] Ibid., p. 60.

[23] Ibid., p. 73. An ample documentation on the partition of Poland was also collected by Alberto Fortis in *Europa letteraria* for February 1773, vol. 1, pt. 2, pp. 21ff., in his review of *Letters Concerning the Present State of Poland* by John Lind.

[24] *Istoria delle turbolenze della Polonia dalla morte di Elisabetta Petrowna fino alla pace tra la Russia e la Porta ottomana, in cui si trovano tutti gli avvenimenti cagioni della rivoluzione di quel regno* (Gorizia: Valerio de' Valeri, 1774). Two reprints of this work, with the addition of the part remaining still in manuscript, have recently appeared: Bozzolato, *Casanova*, and Casanova, *Istoria delle turbolenze della Polonia*.

theocratic origins of despotism. "Idolatry," Boulanger said, was born "of theocracy, because men became accustomed to considering God as a man; idolators then became slaves because they treated man like a god." But then he stopped, rejecting the enlightenment conclusions of the proposition. Boulanger became in his eyes a "dangerous politician," tending to cut away the roots of monarchy, as well as of despotism. The Polish example, like the Swedish one, persuaded him of the necessity of government by one person, and that the sovereign should have absolute power. Still, one should avoid abuses of this kind. He thought Boulanger's ideas were equally dangerous from the point of view of religion. "The spirit that guides Boulanger in his famous satire of despotism, where he examines, as one should, the Oriental type, is the same as that which makes him a declared enemy of all religion, against which he also speaks openly. He should be aware that he demonstrated he was opposed to the despotism of God, to prohibitions prescribed in divine law . . . , he negates revelation." Thus, pen stroke after pen stroke, the thought of Nicolas-Antoine Boulanger, one of the most interesting philosophes of the French eighteenth century, was transformed into a "satire" and a "romance," whereas Casanova turned to religious Orthodoxy.[25]

The intersection of religious and political problems still remained at the center of his attention. He tried to insert events in Poland into a conflict between Catholics and Protestants, into the anticlerical struggles of the sixties and seventies, and in general into the European religious crisis that had culminated with the suppression of the Jesuits. The policy of Catherine of favoring dissenters, or as he sometimes calls them, "nonconformists," was not interpreted as a pure and simple political ploy, but instead in its religious precedents and consequences.[26] In an ample digression he referred to the sixteenth century, describing the Protestant advance in Poland and the importance of Lelio Socino, Francesco Stancaro, and Giorgio Biandrata.[27] Precisely these past dangers induced him to justify the resistance of modern Poles against the attempt of Catherine to introduce tolerance in the kingdom. The right of intolerance seemed to him evident. "The nature of Protestantism in the end is such that if its free and public exercise is permitted in a province the Catholic religion will not remain there, or will be little by little destroyed." The Protestants make use of the idea of tolerance to undermine all religion. "This tolerance is raised by them to favor liberty of conscience, which they hold to be the most sacred among the rights of

[25] *Istoria delle turbolenze della Polonia*, vol. 1, pt. 1, pp. 8ff.

[26] Ibid., vol. 1, pt. 2, p. 21.

[27] Ibid., p. 161.

man. They do not realize that freedom of conscience, when permitted, excludes the truth of any one religion, and that it is absurd to pretend to be a good Christian when it is allowed." Even from a political point of view "diversity of religion is a most dangerous thing for any state." Louis XIV had been right to revoke the Edict of Nantes. "All claim that the evils resulting in that prosperous kingdom from this strong measure were enormous, and that the wounds are still open and cannot easily be healed, but if one wants to remove the root of continually recurrent disorders, it is best to act in that way." There was always the risk of dissenters' becoming *esprits forts*. Criticism of doctrine, free discussion, the abolition of the "magnificent ceremonies" of Catholicism, all led to shorten the step "that a Lutheran or Calvinist need make to arrive at deism."[28]

The Protestants were responsible for the difficult situation in which the kingdom of Stanislaus Augustus found itself. "These heretics, conspicuous in nobility and wealth, are scattered here and there in considerable numbers in the vastness of Poland, and they make common cause with the Orthodox, who are present in even greater numbers, together comprising the dissenters."[29] Catherine depended on them in her able, flexible, and intelligent policy, which Casanova followed in all of its turns. Against this the projects of Stanislaus Poniatowski were of little use. The projects attributed to him seemed empty dreams "remaking laws, controlling the excessive powers of individuals, abolishing slavery . . . making legislative and judicial authority reside in the king of the nation, who from that moment would become a true monarch, and thus despotic." He deprived priests of the right to interfere in affairs of state and "confined them to their dioceses to take care of their flocks."[30] Obtaining all this would require "changing the basic character of the nation."[31] His contrast between dream and reality inspired Casanova with a political portrait of Stanislaus, which was bright and effective. "Anyone who sees a king of Poland in the pomp of his royal majesty would have difficulty believing that he is not the most powerful and most absolute of all monarchs and would be astonished to know that the nobles subject to him take as a maxim to always oppose anything he wants to do or say, calling him commonly not the soul, but the mouth of the republic, like the queen bee, which is said to be without a sting, which nature has given to its subjects. He is always watched, and his great chancellor can refuse to set a seal on what he does not like. Even his first

[28] Ibid., pp. 166ff.
[29] Ibid., p. 173.
[30] Ibid., vol. 1, pt. 1, pp. 83–84.
[31] Ibid., p. 85.

chamberlain has the right to search his pockets, but he has the divine privilege of dispensing grace to his subjects at all hours of the day."[32]

Casanova followed closely the measures the king took, his efforts at reform; many of these could not help but interest his Venetian readers, particularly the dispositions regarding luxury, commerce, and agriculture in 1766, ecclesiastics in 1768, fixing the age for taking monastic vows at twenty-five for men and sixteen for women, the prohibition "for ecclesiastics to acquire noble lands by purchase," the prohibition to "dispose more than a third part of estates . . . to convents or charities." "All feast days, with a few exceptions, pending papal approval, were limited to Sundays."[33]

When Casanova came to speak of the confederates, his colorful journalistic pen strokes took precedence over any design or political reflection. The news reaching him through the gazettes was "a chaos of lies." The effort an author "would have to make to untangle them would be greater than is humanly possible."[34] All he could do was speak with detachment, coldly. But still, even through him, the reality of Poland expressed itself. The flags of the confederates were eloquent. "On one of them was depicted a wounded eagle from whose wounds came drops of blood with the motto '*vincere aut mori*' [conquer or die]. On another was a virgin and a cross with the motto '*pro religione et patria*' [for religion and country]. The confederates themselves wore crosses on their chests as did in olden days the excessively praised crusaders."[35] The terrible situation of the peasants appeared to him in equally vivid colors. "The dwelling of the Polish serf is a sad hut where his naked children, in the cold climate, live among the beasts and seem to condemn nature for not having dressed them in the same way as animals. The serf who gave them life would be glad to see his den go up in flames, since he cannot say it is his: all belongs to the lord, who can sell the plowman along with the ox; an unhappy people, among whom the cold kills many."[36] He criticized any luxury, any magnificence, among the nobles. He knew "such luxury could not help but do fatal damage in a country without industry and where the arts are unknown."[37] Still, at the end of so many contrasts, he found no more to say than this: "All tends to extremes in Poland, and it seems that even serfdom and liberty compete to destroy the realm."[38] Poland was truly a place where desires for equality and

[32] Ibid., vol. 2, pt. 1, p. 288.
[33] Ibid., vol. 1, pt. 2, pp. 103ff.; vol. 2, pt. 1, p. 31.
[34] Ibid., vol. 2, pt. 1, p. 78.
[35] Ibid., p. 39.
[36] Ibid., p. 284.
[37] Ibid., p. 283.
[38] Ibid., p. 287.

liberty were out of balance and where all social classes contributed to chaos and anarchy. This, colored by his skepticism, was the conclusion Casanova reached.

Equality is one of those truths destined to gain possession of man's reason, but not of his heart. Inequality of conditions is a necessary evil, surely, but it should be tempered at least with natural liberty and the balance of law. In Poland it is not only the people who suffer, since although palatines, castelains, bishops, and great officials are well provided for, one hundred thousand little gentlemen need to seek their bread. The nobility that seems so free and arrogant does not stop at demeaning itself by serving the rich in the most vile manner to earn a salary, in a country where trade is decreed unworthy of a gentleman, who might be a converted Jew, making as much noise in one of the local diets as an offshoot of the Jagellons.[39]

His conclusions were similar to those of Carlo Rizzardi, who, a year after Casanova, also published a *Storia della guerra*. The cause of so much tragedy was not difficult to fathom. "The Polish nation was always fond of discord and war."[40] The springs that activated the confederations were even simpler: "The leaders' only aim was to pillage the nation and make themselves rich."[41] Pułaski and his "robbers" were not seen in a better light. They had carried out "a thousand cruelties and depredations against many poor innocents." "Here is what ambition, hate, and avarice can do."[42]

As one sees, the information that reached Venice about Poland was ample, although it lacked a sense of deep firsthand awareness. The choice between the reforming impulse of Catherine II and the spirit of independence of the confederates, between the program of renewal of Stanislaus Augustus and the desire for liberty of the Polish nobles, between religious toleration and the defense of traditional religion, seemed difficult everywhere in Europe. Voltaire and Rousseau, Mably and the physiocrats debated these contradictions. In Venice there was not a decisive choice, and people often contented themselves with a distant spectacle of grand and strange events. "The unhappy destiny of that belabored republic" (the expression of Alvise Mocenigo, the ambassador of St. Mark in Paris) could not help but impress the Venetian patricians, who every day became more fearful that "such violence might easily appear in Europe." The rights of Poland had been "violated," "bit-

---

[39] Ibid., pp. 287ff.

[40] *Storia della guerra originata dalla discordia dei polacchi per la elezione d'un nuovo re, tra polacchi, russi e turchi, descritta dal principio sino alla fine da Carlo Rizzardi* (Venice: A spese dell'autore e si vende al negozio Cicerone, 1775), p. 3.

[41] Ibid., p. 39.

[42] Ibid., p. 49.

ter" was the destiny of that "unhappy and desolate nation."[43] How could one prevent a similar fate in Venice? Certainly, as the London resident Giovanni Berlendis wrote, the developments in Poland had "undermined the political system of Europe."[44] From Vienna Ambassador Bartolomeo Gradenigo sent even gloomier messages. "The unfortunate and sad events," the "dismemberment and disgrace" of Poland, seemed to him the result of "unprecedented violence. . . . One does not know to what it may lead in the future" if "the current political situation does not change" and if there is not a change of policy of "the great powers, particularly the lesser ones, and finally all of humanity." Poland must persuade itself, he concluded, that its misfortunes were the "sad result of its internal turbulence." Lack of "love of country" had "produced the massacre and ruin of both the public and the private realm, as necessarily occurs in a republic that detaches itself from its own laws and customs."[45] The ambassador at Constantinople thought this conservative lesson insufficient to confront the increasingly difficult situation appearing everywhere in Europe. The increasing size of armies and the perfecting of the "art of war" had led to the extinction of the "spirit of liberty that motivated men to great and noble actions abroad and gave them courage in internal policy to hold to a middle course between imperiousness and servility." The tradition of free republics from the past emerged weakened and gravely wounded by the Polish experience.[46]

In other parts of Italy, with some exceptions in Tuscany and Rome, participation in the affairs of Poland does not seem to have been much better. The *Gazzetta di Milano* was well furnished with news about Poland but preserved the tone of incredulity and doubt about the fate of the confederates it had adopted from the beginning, in 1770. "Strong were their plans, but they were incapable of achieving them," and they "always got the worst." "But it is unlikely that they are a mere chimera, as some put out, and thus enfold the truth in a chaos of doubts and further contradictions."[47] The violent civil war bloodying Poland was anything but a chimera. The desire to keep the spirit of reform alive, even in that

---

[43] Venezia, AS, *Senato, dispacci Francia*, filze 253 and 254, cited by Paolo Preto, "Venezia e le spartizioni della Polonia," in *Cultura e nazione in Italia e Polonia dal Rinascimento all'Illuminismo*, ed. Vittore Branca and Sante Graciotti (Florence: Olschki, 1986), p. 68 n. 26.

[44] Venezia, AS, *Senato, Dispacci Inghilterra*, filza 125, cited by Paolo Preto, "Venezia e la spartizione della polonia," p. 68.

[45] Venezia, AS, *Senato, Dispacci Germania*, filza 275, cited by Paolo Preto, "Venezia e la spartizione della Polonia," p. 70.

[46] Venezia, AS, *Senato, Dispacci Costantinopoli*, filza 215, cited by Paolo Preto, "Venezia e la spartizione della Polonia," p. 71.

[47] *La gazzetta di Milano*, no. 7, 14 February 1770 (Poznan, 12 January).

situation, was appreciated by this journal. "Among the horrors of war," one read on 21 February 1770 in a communication from Vilno, "the discord of the great, and the popular uprisings, the vigilant bishop Prince Massalski has found a way to preserve his serenity and contribute to the improvement of customs and religion." He had even offered prizes to anyone who contributed to the "resolution of the three following questions: what is the knowledge and virtue necessary for a good parish priest . . ., what education should nobles with little patrimony or fortune receive in order to make them truly useful to the country . . ., and what instruction should be given to peasants, the part of humanity most deprived in Poland?"[48] The *Gazzetta di Milano* thus paid attention to the penetration of reformist and physiocratic ideas in Poland. But the times were not favorable. In the following summer Bishop Massalski abandoned Vilno, giving up its arsenal to the confederates. The intervention of Souvorov was needed to retake it. Massalski had emigrated to Paris.[49]

Even Pietro Verri was struck by the contrast between enlightenment and revolt in Poland at the end of the seventies. When the Confederation of Bar was organized he wrote to his brother as follows: "There will be a new religious war and more human blood spilled in the eighteenth century for polemical opinion."[50] Distant news reached him through the gazette of Chur. Examples of fanaticism followed, which, he thought, could be useful in some way in Italy and serve as an argument for those writing "against the monks." But, as his words revealed, there was a big difference in tone and intensity between the Polish drama and Italian anticlericalism. He feared rather that events in Poland would lead to a general war, from which the Pope would profit "to save himself," that is, to distract from the conflicts between church and state.[51] The view of Pietro Verri, although it had less internal tension, was thus not far from that of Voltaire and of the admirers of Catherine II. More "republican" and mistrusting of Russian propaganda was his brother Alessandro, who was more conservative, and at the same time more sensitive to what sounded false in the brotherly declarations of the empress.[52] With the

[48] Ibid., no. 8, 21 February 1770 (Vilno, 20 January). The same news is in the *Notizie del mondo*, no. 13, 13 February 1770, p. 99 (Vienna, 1 February). On this competition and on Ignacy Massalski in general see Jobert, *Magnats polonais*, p. 41ff.

[49] On the departure of Massalski, see *Notizie del mondo*, no. 91, 12 November 1771, p. 699 (Warsaw, 12 October), and no. 98, 7 December 1771, p. 757 (Warsaw, 4 November), where it is reported that the bishop of Vilno "nine wagons full of furniture and other" things were confiscated.

[50] *Carteggio di Pietro e di Alessandro Verri*, vol. 1, pt. 2, p. 241 (Milan, 16 April 1768).

[51] Ibid., p. 246 (Milan, 20 April 1768).

[52] Ibid., p. 288 (Rome, 18 May 1768).

passage of years a bitter realism also took hold in the mind of Pietro. "The examples of Corsica and Poland," he wrote in 1777, "make me believe things in this world are arranged so that in such questions eloquence and the laws of nature and peoples go to one party, and victory goes to the other."[53]

In Tuscany the echoes of developments in Poland were clear and frequent. In comparison with Venice, what is most striking is the difference in style of communication and commentary on the news. Diffuse, soft, and redundant was the style of Venice; dry, often arid, but clear was that of Milan, and particularly that of Tuscany. Pietro Verri had no doubts as to which of these two political styles he preferred. "A man who is truly a man sees objects as in Chinese pictures, designated directly, dryly, and clearly; a corrupt people sees things in pastel colors with shadings."[54] In the Florentine *Notizie del mondo* he could find something to his taste. The mechanical placing of one article after another, the lack of any apparent ideological filter, the close reportage of events, and the absence of any effort to flatter the reader resulted in producing, as in the best eighteenth-century journals, a kind of distance and a lucid vision. Any reader could feel like Candide. Any notice, even the most seemingly useless, could be taken for a sign of destiny.

The first information in the *Notizie del mondo* was from Warsaw: "We are now persuaded that war is inevitable and that both powers (Russia and Turkey) are making great preparation for a war that may be the most stormy of our time."[55] In Poland "all hope is past for quieting the different confederations that have disturbed that realm for some time. They seem to become more obstinate every day." Only if Russia became completely involved in the conflict with the Ottoman Porte would it be possible to restore to Poland "the tranquillity of the republic."[56] Meanwhile, Catherine intervened ever more deeply. To the sound of trumpets she published her declaration of war against Turkey, insisting that her intention was to protect dissenters persecuted "contrary to the Polish constitution, that is, the liberty and equality of all citizens."[57] The confederates became more and more active. "The Palatinate of Krakow is menaced by new disturbances, and the number confederates of Greater Poland is now so high as to raise apprehension."[58] From Warsaw, in February, came the following news: "We are so surrounded by

53 Ibid., vol. 9, p. 85 (Milan, 17 July 1777).

54 Ibid., vol. 1, pt. 2, p. 268 (Milan, 11 May 1768).

55 *Notizie del mondo*, no. 1, 3 January 1769, p. 5 (Warsaw, 3 December 1768).

56 Ibid., no. 3, 10 January 1769, p. 19 (Warsaw, 13 December 1768).

57 Ibid., no. 7, 24 January 1769, p. 52 (St. Petersburg, 6 December 1768). The declaration of war was published in full in this and in the following issues.

58 Ibid., no. 12, 11 February 1769, p. 91 (Warsaw, 10 January).

confederates that have grown in number that the roads are no longer
secure in any direction."[59] Stanislaus Augustus resisted the demands of
Repnin, the Russian ambassador. "I have done much and who knows
perhaps more than I should, and you want, my lord prince, for me to
become the executioner of my country." The acts of resistance of the
nobles followed. Augustus Sułkowski reminded the Russians of the "critical circumstances to which they have reduced my miserable country,"[60]
declaring that he would "sacrifice for its salvation my goods and my life
to defend liberty and laws." "These are the first and chief duties I have
learned since my earliest youth."[61] "As soon as one confederation is extinguished in one part of Greater Poland, another springs up in another
part."[62]

In the south the struggle rapidly assumed a social dimension and
took on disquieting aspects. In the Ukraine, where new Orthodox colonists replaced Cossacks, the peasants had become more and more discontented, their situation tending to become like that of serfs, and they
were subjected to intense Catholic propaganda. Hatred for Jewish communities also existed. They looked to Catherine II as their liberator, all
the more so because it was said that the empress had already announced
that she was in their favor. The revolt, particularly around the city of
Humań in the spring and summer of 1768, was terrible. Thousands of
lords and merchants perished. The Polish nobles, who finally collaborated with the Russians in suppressing the uprising, blamed the disaster
as much on the policy of Stanislaus Augustus as on that of Catherine II.
Here were the results, they said, of dangling before the eyes of peasants
the hope of improvement.[63]

---

[59] Ibid., no. 23, 21 March 1769, p. 179 (Warsaw, 17 February).

[60] Ibid., no. 24, 25 March 1769, p. 186 (Warsaw, 22 February).

[61] Ibid.

[62] Ibid., no. 29, 11 April 1769, p. 225 (Warsaw, 11 March).

[63] There was an insistent echo of these events in the *Gazzetta di Firenze*, no. 11, 27
September 1768, p. 85 (Warsaw, 28 August). News was reported of a leader of "Orthodox
schismatic peasants of the Ukraine . . . [who was] impaled, his associates [were] slaughtered, and the larger part of his followers [were] condemned to irons for life." But their
"spirit of rebellion was not spent." The "Haydamacks" were distinguished in their "cruelty
against the Jews." Many cities were burned by them, suffering "the same disasters that
were suffered shortly before by the village of Humań." In no. 13, 4 October 1768, p. 100,
in a correspondence from Plosko came the announcement that "the second revolution of
the peasants of the Ukraine was not less than the first for its serious excesses. . . . what can
hardly be believed is that many gentlemen united with the rebels and shared the fruits of
their misdeeds." Rulhière describes at length the uprising of the "most execrable people,
if one can give the name people to a bunch of brigands from all nations, who have escaped
for the most part from execution," that is, from the Cossacks "who keep in Russia their
ancient name of Zaporoves, which means inhabitants of water falls, but they are called
Haydamacks by the neighboring peoples" (De Rulhière, *Histoire de l'anarchie de Pologne*,

In the spring of 1769 news of the worsening situation in the frontier region between Poland and Catherine's empire reached Florence. "The inhabitants of the Ukraine, Podolia, and other frontier provinces flee in all directions to escape the barbarism of the Tartars, who when they appear put entire regions to fire and sword and indiscriminately slaughter people of any age and sex."[64] Ten days later it became known that "the Haydamacks, risen again, had committed the most terrible devastations, but on 18 and 19 February they had been attacked and defeated by [Polish] troops in that province, and all the rebels who escaped the fury of fire and sword were taken and systematically hanged."[65] A commander, "who recently brought the welcome news of the defeat of the Haydamacks, has returned to arms after having received a fine gift of money from His Majesty."[66] But the celebration came too soon; the revolt continued. Everywhere the Haydamacks incited "Polish peasants to arise." "They have made trenches to fortify themselves and gathered

---

vol. 3, pp. 84, 91). They incited the peasant revolt. Rulhière was convinced that they had operated on the empress' orders. It had been, according to him, the Russians who conceived "the horrible plan to massacre in their houses all nobles who had signed the act of confederation." "The Zaporoves gave arms to the peasants and these took them from house to house." Thus, the nobility was "butchered." "The Jews, more hated because of their extortions, were almost all burned alive. These horrible people amused themselves by hanging on the same gibbet a gentleman, a monk, a Jew, and a dog, with the inscription 'They are all alike' " (pp. 92ff.). Rulhière had no doubt that "emissaries were sent throughout Poland to stir up the peasants" (p. 100). For an idea of the deep traces left in Poland by these events it is enough to read Joachim Lelevel's *Histoire de Pologne* (Paris: Librairie polonaise, 1844), vol. 2, pp. 246ff. The appeal to a peasant revolt finally turned back on the Russians themselves. "An electric spark went through their veins, telling them of that land invaded by their empress and arousing in them unexpected desires." And, in general, the great Polish historian was particularly interested in following all aspects of this attempt of the czars "to raise the peasants" (p. 307). Just as the name Pugačev was taken in Russia to be a symbol of nineteenth-century revolutionary movements, so among Polish emigrées, up to 1834, the group of populists of the *Lud polski* (Polish people) installed on Jersey took the name "community of Humań." Stanisław Worcell was among them and other nobles who thus used the city of this eighteenth-century Jacquerie "as a symbol of vicarious penitence for the wrongs done to the peasantry by their class," Peter Brock has written in *Polish Revolutionary Populism: A Study in Agrarian Socialist Thought from the 1830s to the 1850s* (Toronto and Buffalo: University of Toronto Press, 1977), p. 25. For the long-term development of these lands, see William H. McNeill, *Europe's Steppe Frontier: A Study of the Eastward Movement in Europe* (Chicago: University of Chicago Press, 1964). Of great interest is the essay by Jaroslaw Pelenski, "The Haidamak Insurrections and the Old Regime in Eastern Europe," in *The American and European Revolutions, 1746–1848. Sociological and Ideological Aspects*, edited with an introduction by Jaroslaw Pelenski (Iowa City: University of Iowa Press, 1980), pp. 228ff.

[64] *Notizie del mondo*, no. 26, 1 April 1769, pp. 200ff. (Warsaw, 1 March).

[65] Ibid., no. 28, 8 April 1769, pp. 217ff. (Warsaw, 8 March).

[66] Ibid., no. 33, 25 April 1769, p. 258 (Warsaw, 25 March).

together cannons taken from the Poles."[67] There followed an invasion of "Cossacks from Zaporow."[68] In June "the Cossacks of Siet and their associates the Haydamacks have again started to devastate the Ukraine and the district of Braclaw."[69]

The distant echoes were mixed with those of the increasingly bitter religions and political struggles that tore at Poland. On the will of the Catholic confederates to eradicate the Protestants, it is enough to cite the following report: "The famous Malazewski, marshal of the confederation, after having been defeated in his march near Czenstochau, arrived near Kraków, at Meseritz, the sixth of the current month with a body of four thousand men. On the way he had taken prisoner an inhabitant of Bentsch whom he had decapitated in the principal square of that place. On 8 March he marched toward the little city of Schwerin, where he made the Lutheran citizens pay him a tribute of 1,400 *écus*, and not content with this, had eight of them hanged on the column of a well, because there was not a gallows ready. He made a butcher's boy be the hangman, whom he later also had hanged. He made the magistrate swear to arrest all the Lutherans, wanting to make them all suffer the same fate on his return. He condemned to death a postillion and the son of a baker, who were Protestants. Both had ropes around their necks, but one saved himself by becoming a Catholic, and the other preferred to die for his religion."[70]

Would Poland survive such a crisis? "There was a general collapse of the state," one of the manifestos of the confederates read; everywhere "tyranny, slavery." "The pride of despotism insults and despises the nation." The rights of "national religion" were trodden underfoot. "As the arbiter of our legislation, Russia without any check has planted the foundations of a pure tyranny."[71] The war between Russians and Turks dragged on. The Russian victory at Chocim was even celebrated in Warsaw with a Te deum "in the Russian chapel . . . and the lord ambassador gave a magnificent dinner that day." The news of the defeat of their Turkish ally seemed to reduce the confederates to "ultimate despair."[72] A wind of defeat and abandonment made itself felt everywhere among the Poles. A long diatribe against Ignacy Potocki was published. "Who could have been that idiot among Christians who looked to infidels for the defense of religion?" And how could one think of confiding the safe-

---

[67] Ibid., no. 35, 2 May 1769, p. 274 (from the Polish frontier, 3 April).

[68] Ibid., no. 37, 9 May 1769, p. 291 (Warsaw, 9 April).

[69] Ibid., no. 47, 13 June 1769, p. 375 (Warsaw, 13 May).

[70] Ibid., no. 30, 15 April 1769, p. 234 (Kalisz, 13 March).

[71] Ibid., no. 64, 12 August 1769, p. 520 (Warsaw, 12 July, "Translation of the Manifesto of the Confederates of the Russian Palatinate").

[72] Ibid., no. 86, 28 October 1769, p. 703 (Warsaw, 27 September).

guard "of the laws and liberty of the state" to the "despotism of Moslems"?[73] The new grand vizier, of whom the Florentine gazette furnished a detailed biography, declared to Potocki that the sultan "did not want to hear anything more of their cursed liberty, which they claim to have lost, and that they could go to perdition with the Russians." He added that "if the Poles want to embrace the true Mohammedan religion, I would be glad to assist them."[74] The grandiose sweep of the Russian war plan for 1770 appeared ever more clearly on the horizon: the Danube, the Black Sea, the Mediterranean.[75] The initiative was effectively in the hands of Catherine II. Still, the confederates resumed their action, always standing up against "sons who have totally abandoned their country."[76] In the Florentine gazette, a detailed and uninterruped chronicle of the encounters of this endless partisan war continued. In August it reported that the confederates "were still in large numbers." The "recent deployment of Russian troops" was understood to "contain the confederates to a certain extent and to prevent them from causing as much damage as in the past."[77] In the autumn "misery was very great." "Trade has for a considerable time stopped in this kingdom, and misery increases."[78] At the end of the year the horizon was dominated by news of the Russian victory at Chesmé, of the festivities in St. Petersburg, and of the birthday of Paul, the hereditary prince. But the confederates soon returned to the offensive. It was reported from Warsaw that they were "now in a position to cut our communication with many other cities."[79] "Marshal Pulaski and his people seem determined to make the most obstinate resistance."[80] At the beginning of the new year the gazetteer cast a glance back over the just completed 1770, traced the long trajectory from Greece through the battles of Russians and Turks, remembered the "barbarity of the confederates," mentioned the revolt of Ali Bey in Egypt, and finally concluded as follows: "Italy divided into

[73] Ibid., no. 83, 17 October 1769, p. 680 (Warsaw, 12 September, "Letter from a magnate of the Russian Palatinate").

[74] Ibid., no. 88, 4 November 1769, p. 719 (Warsaw, 2 October), and no. 90, 11 November 1769, p. 736 (Warsaw, 7 October). It was said that the new vizier "had a lively talent, was enterprising, and was an unscrupulous follower of the dogmas of the Mohammedan religion. He drinks willingly of the good wines of Hungary and the most exquisite liquors and is always abundantly supplied with those from France. He likes literature, especially Italian books, of which he has a good store in his library. In his seraglio are women as beautiful as in that of the Sultan."

[75] Ibid., no. 47, 12 June 1770, p. 390 (Ploczko, 13 May).

[76] Ibid., no. 69, 28 August 1770, p. 564 (Warsaw, 1 August).

[77] Ibid., no. 66, 18 August 1770, p. 540 (Warsaw, 19 July).

[78] Ibid., no. 85, 23 October 1770, p. 695 (Warsaw, 19 September).

[79] Ibid., no. 94, 24 November 1770, p. 766 (Warsaw, 24 October).

[80] Ibid., no. 98, 8 December 1770, p. 798 (Warsaw, 5 November).

so many mild governments, which procure no other than the well-being of their respective populations, enjoyed the most enviable tranquillity."[81] The contrast with Poland could not have been greater.

Still in 1770, Luca Magnanima, an astute Tuscan writer, thinking of the fate of Corsica, which had passed the year before into the hands of Louis xv, and of Poland still fully at war, asked himself the causes of such misfortunes. The answer was clear to him. In free countries it was necessary for public authorities to intervene immediately in order to prevent the lords from "forgetting themselves and thinking the low people born to live in miserable subjection." This inequality was at the root of all evils. Not having taken the necessary remedies, Poland, "a republic that exists in our time in another hemisphere, where there are no more excellent, talented, or virtuous citizens to support it, and where everyone believes he has authority through the power of wealth, runs down into decadence. The remedies taken up to now show that there is no longer a public spirit, because they have been contrary to the interests of the nation, and the few unhappy enlightened men who may remain there serve only the purpose of foreseeing the fall."[1]

The oppression of the rich and the lack of public spirit made any reform of Poland impossible. For this reason, and for the sense of tragedy pressing down more and more, the interest this nation aroused did not diminish. Even when observed from a tranquil shore like Italy, the tempests of Eastern Europe and the Levant continued to fill the columns of the *Notizie del mondo*. Warsaw, at the beginning of 1771, was defended with trenches. "The confederates have advanced as far as Mlodzym, which is one mile from this capital."[2] With the resumption of hostilities it seemed as though Russia's enemies might be able to win. Near Kraków there was a great battle. The new ambassador, Saldern, assumed a hard line and declared that he wanted to bring the "cruel anarchy" and the abyss "of public evil to an end."[3] The confederates not only held firm, but extended their action. The "turbulence" extended even into Courland.[4] In Lithuania the hetman Michael Casimir Oginski rose up but was defeated by the Russians. His declaration dated 29 September was reported in its entirety: "I live in the most sad melancholy.

---

[81] Ibid., 1771, preface.

[1] Luca Magnanima, *Lettere italiane sopra la Corsica in rapporto allo spirito di legislazione che dovrebbe animare quel regno per renderlo felice* (Lausanne [actually Livorno]: G. Aubert, 1770); see *Riformatori*, vol. 7, pp. 816ff.

[2] *Notizie del mondo*, no. 8, 26 January 1771, p. 59 (Warsaw, 19 December 1770).

[3] Ibid., no. 57, 16 July 1771, p. 449 (Warsaw, 15 June). The declaration, of 16 May, is published in full in this issue and in the following one.

[4] Ibid., no. 77, 24 September 1771, p. 608 (Warsaw, 24 August).

... I have lost everything, money, baggage, papers, but I will never lose my constancy and courage, nor the desire to assist my oppressed country."[5]

In November the king himself was attacked. The effort of a group of confederates to abduct him made a deep impression on everyone. Disguised as peasants, the conspirators gave him a sword blow to the head. "He was made to mount on horseback ... he fell twice and was helped up, meanwhile dropping his fur coat." "The king asked his captors continually if they were ready to kill him." A fortunate encounter with a Russian picket drove off some of the conspirators. Stanislaus Augustus finally asked the one still with him to let him free. Assured of his own safety, this man "threw himself at his feet and kissed them." The two took shelter in a "wooden house," feigning to be travelers beset by robbers. The king sent a message to the commandant of the guard to fetch him back to Warsaw "amid the acclamations and tears of the people, whom the king consoled kindly and thanked, adding that this incident would serve the good of the country."[6]

This was a "base attempt," from which followed acts of beneficence by the king and pathetic scenes of emotion on the part of the people, as the Florentine gazette interpreted matters.[7] For once arid news of war and desperate political acts gave way to heartfelt effusion. Also, care was taken to note that the abductors were not from the high nobility, but "of low extraction."[8]

The "best of kings" was safe, but the destiny of the country became more and more unclear, as encounters, deportations to Siberia, and in-

---

[5] Ibid., no. 94, 23 November 1771, pp. 723–24 (Warsaw, 23 October). Long ago was the time when "Comte Ogen'ski, young, playful, foolish," had played the harp at length in the presence of Diderot in Paris in August 1760. See Denis Diderot, *Correspondance*, ed. G. Roth (Paris: Editions de Minuit, 1957), vol. 3, p. 41 (to Sophie Volland, 2 August 1761). Ogiński later became an important figure in agricultural reform in Poland, as he was in political developments during the eighties. See Fabre, *Stanislas-August Poniatowski*, index. See especially Andrzej Ciechanowiecki, *Michał Kazimierz Ogiński und sein Musenhof zu Słonim* (Köln and Graz, Böhlau, 1961).

[6] *Notizie del mondo*, no. 96, 30 Nobember 1771, pp. 740–41 (Vienna, 18 November). In the fourth issue of the *Giornale letterario* of Siena (1776), whose editor was the poet and writer Bertola, there appeared "a sublime fragment of an epic poem on the phantasm of liberty" written by the well-known Abate Francesco Zacchiroli. This was a typical example of solidarity with Stanislaus Augustus Poniatowski of an Italian literary figure (see the *Gazzetta universale*, no. 36, 4 May 1776). Republicanism was for him the "phantom of liberty." Brutus and Cassio exhorted the conspirators of the act. See Renato Pasta, "Il *Giornale letterario* di Siena (1776–1777) ed i suoi compilatori," *Rassegna storica toscana*, no. 1 (January–June, 1978): 93ff.

[7] *Notizie del mondo*, no. 99, 10 December 1771, pp. 763–64 (Warsaw, 11 November).

[8] Ibid.

terventions by foreign troops took place.[9] In Warsaw platoons of troops arrested anyone found in the cafés and inns after eight at night.[10] Pułaski, to whom the responsibility for the attempted abduction was traced, launched a final cry: "I have done all I could to distinguish my career with an unbending constancy. Neither the blood of one of my brothers shed by the enemy under my eyes, nor the cruel slavery of another, nor the sad fate of so many kin and countrymen has made me waver in my patriotism." Nor was he touched by polemics and calumnies. His gaze was always fixed on "virtue," "liberty," and "religion."[11]

But the Catholic Church itself was becoming split. Along with the increasingly sharp appeals for resistance, an important current turned to reform and helped create support for Stanislaus Augustus. The Piarist Father Konarski, the most famous scholar in Poland, wrote at that time his *Divinae providentiae specimen*, an act of accusation against those responsible for the plot against the king.[12]

Meanwhile, the preparations for the partition became clearer. In May there was talk of "a triple alliance among Austria, Russia, and Prussia," while the men of the confederation were reduced to "a bad state." They had hoped that their victorious assault on the castle of Kraków would have brought them great advantages. "They had sent to the attack on that castle their bravest officers and soldiers, but for lack of support they had to yield to the superior strength of the Russians." Twenty-four French officers were taken prisoner: The "advantage the confederates gained" in their attack not far from Warsaw was "small" by comparison.[13] The collapse of the country became imminent. "Among the many calamities that afflict us not least is the quantity of false and debased money that has been circulating in these provinces. The confederates are accused of this." But these blamed the "foreigners."[14]

"The thirty Austrian regiments that have entered this kingdom advance more and more," it was announced one week later.[15] Pułaski was

[9] Ibid., no. 9, 1 February 1772, p. 67 (Warsaw, 25 December), and no. 11, 8 February 1772, p. 84 (Danzig, 5 January).

[10] Ibid., no. 10, 4 February 1772, p. 76 (Warsaw, 1 January).

[11] Ibid., no. 11, 8 February 1772, p. 83 (Warsaw, 3 January).

[12] Ibid., no. 15, 22 February 1772, p. 117 (Warsaw, 21 January). On Konarski, see the article by Jerzy Michalski in the *Polski słownik biograficzny*, 1968, fasc. 58, pp. 471ff., with a long bibliography.

[13] Ibid., no. 44, 2 June 1772, p. 368 (Warsaw, 2 May). On these events see Jerzy Michalski, *Schyłek Konfederaciji barskiej* (The decline of the Confederation of Bar) (Wrocław: Ossolineum, 1970), with a summary in French.

[14] *Notizie del mondo*, no. 45, 6 June 1772, p. 375 (Warsaw, 9 May). On 20 June 1772, no. 49, p. 408 (Warsaw, 20 May), it was added: "There is serious thought of changing the whole monetary system of this realm."

[15] Ibid., no. 47, 13 June 1772, p. 391 (Warsaw, 12 May).

obliged to dismiss his troops and withdraw "beyond the frontier of this kingdom." The Prussians were now "only thirteen miles from this capital."[16] The occupation by the three powers did not stop; instead, it advanced inexorably. Rumors spread about what might be "the division of this kingdom."[17] The seizure of fiefs of the major houses, like that of the Lubomirski, "greatly agitated" our "great families." "Those who had been openly against the king now sought some accommodation that would be advantageous to them."[18] The end of the confederation appeared to be more evident, "which, born from the ambition of a few great families, was upheld as long as it was useful to political interest but is now abandoned to its own devices; it will be immortalized in the annals of Poland for having ruined its country."[19]

The last news of the encounters around Częstochowa were mixed with the proclamations of the great powers taking possession of the territory they occupied.[20] From day to day were displayed "the last agonies of a dying body."[21] The tenacious will of Stanislaus Augustus remained the only firm point in so much ruin. "In these critical circumstances, the king takes care to reestablish order in the kingdom as much as possible." Instead, "the authors of the disturbances of our land now gather the fruits of their intrigues, their hates, and their jealousies. . . . Now they are abandoned by the same governments on which they had founded their hopes and are in the hands of the Russians, whom they had the boldness to provoke."[22] It was not that concord reigned among the powers who were partitioning Poland; on the contrary.[23] But there was no turning back. "The confederates slowly began to return to their different lands."[24] They still had hopes for Bavaria and took as their motto *Debilitata, sed non debellata Poloniae republica* (The Polish republic is weakened but not vanquished). But the fortress of Częstochowa, "after having been their stronghold for so long, was obliged to surrender by capitulation to the Russians on 15 August, and great stores of every kind of provisions and 150 pieces of artillery were found there."[25] The "dis-

---

[16] Ibid., no. 48, 16 June 1772, pp. 399ff. (Warsaw, 16 May).

[17] Ibid., no. 52, 30 June 1772, p. 432 (Warsaw, 30 May).

[18] Ibid., no. 55, 11 July 1772, p. 455 (Warsaw, 10 June).

[19] Ibid., no. 56, 14 July 1772, p. 464 (Warsaw, 17 June).

[20] Ibid., no. 57, 18 July 1772, p. 472 (Warsaw, 17 June); no. 59, 25 July 1772, p. 486 (Warsaw, 25 June); no. 60, 28 July 1772, p. 496 (Warsaw, 27 June); no. 61, 1 August 1772, p. 504 (Warsaw, 1 July); no. 65, 15 August 1772, p. 535 (Warsaw, 16 July).

[21] Ibid., no. 56, 14 July 1772, p. 464 (Warsaw, 17 June).

[22] Ibid., no. 67, 22 August 1772, p. 551 (Warsaw, 24 July).

[23] Ibid., no. 68, 25 August 1772, p. 560 (Warsaw, 29 July).

[24] Ibid., no. 73, 12 September 1772, p. 602 (Warsaw, 12 August).

[25] Ibid., no. 74, 15 September 1772, p. 609 (Warsaw, 19 August).

memberment" continued. The "regicides," that is, those who had organized and carried out the attempt on Stanislaus Poniatowski, were arrested.[26] "The famous Lukaski," "in the chains with which he is bound, has lost nothing of his audacity and ferocity." Pułaski, it was said, had "turned toward France, consoling himself with the intention of seeking his fortune in Martinique."[27]

As if to conclude this tragic year, the *Notizie del mondo* reported the able declaration of Stanislaus Augustus and his bitter deploring of the civil war. "Legitimate power was scorned by a few, and anarchy spread to almost all provinces. All of Poland was trampled upon, impoverished, devastated, not only by its own citizens but also by foreign troops. . . . Five years of scourge and ruin have brought this kingdom low, and a rapid peace is its most urgent and indispensable need. The initiative taken by the three powers to act effectively to this end contains in itself an act full of humanity." Stanislaus Augustus nonetheless rose in protest "before the universe against any measure taken or to be taken in the dismemberment of Poland."[28]

The summer and autumn of 1772 thus changed not only the political situation, but also the state of mind of Poles, as the *Gazette de Nice* indicated in a letter from Warsaw on the first of August. "The entry of two foreign armies into our country opens before us a long train of evils; those we experience today are probably only the beginning of those that await us. We can almost regard them like lightning that announces thunder. . . . A sad prediction, which tells us of calamities we will not be able to avert." This mood favored a greater reconciliation with Stanislaus Poniatowski. "Today there is no citizen who does not recognize the advantage of living under the laws of a king of Poland. Experience has brought the people back to their senses."[29]

The fate of the "most unhappy realm" of Poland struck even Giuseppe Pelli in Florence. The partition was certainly "worthy of note," but what significance should one give to it? "Perhaps . . . it offends justice but serves humanity." And he even expressed surprise in imagining a "project that would deprive Poles forever of the misery of their senseless liberty."[30] When the partition was complete, Pelli wrote the following in his *Efemeridi*, on 8 January 1773: "the dismemberment of Poland is much discussed." His thought returned also to the other example of

[26] Ibid., no. 75, 19 September 1772, p. 617 (Warsaw, 19 September).

[27] Ibid., no. 78, 29 September 1772, p. 641 (Warsaw, 3 September). On the capture of Łukawski see no. 82, 13 October 1772, p. 673 (Warsaw, 12 September).

[28] Ibid., no. 93, 21 November 1772, p. 762 (Warsaw, 21 October). The declarations of 17 October are reported in full.

[29] *Gazette de Nice*, no. 5, 31 August 1772, p. 19 (Warsaw, 1 August).

[30] Pelli, *Efemeridi*, vol. 29, pp. 132–33 (21 July 1772).

conquest he had witnessed, Genova's ceding of Corsica. "But truly, this is a greater thing than Corsica." Nor did it to exclude the possibility that the accord would be followed by "a general war in Europe, as some believe." "But the powers who have made the partition seem well armed to sustain it." "What would a philosopher think?" he asked. "He would judge things quite differently from politicians and the powerful of the earth, leading us to dream of justice, equity, and moderation."[31]

As Count Charles François de Broglie wrote to Louis xv in February 1773, "only a revolution in that empire [Russia] could prevent the dismemberment of Poland."[32] Numerous that summer, as we have seen, were the premonitions of the Pugačev rebellion.[33] But by the time it broke out and was crushed, the partition was already complete.

While the archaic republic thus descended to its sunset, other, still more stark Polish social realities were revealed to the eyes of readers of Tuscan gazettes, which in the fall of the republic appeared in all their squalor. "In the midst of these critical circumstances" people in the countryside refused to accept "abolition of the feast days occurring during the summer months." "There is nothing of which false zeal cannot persuade a superstitious and an ignorant people." In Warsaw itself, in the "suburb called Krakow," ironmongers were obstinately "refusing to accept" the new shop regulations.[1] "In some places opposition to the suppression of feast days comes from the clergy itself, and in other places where priests are more prudent they encounter obstinate resistance from their parishioners." "The populace always acts in this way, but the situation is worse in lands where the despotism of a prince or of great families vilifies the body of the nation and the false zeal of religion provides an instrument to maintain oppression under the yoke of slavery."[2] A correspondent explained the situation of the "Polish peasant." He was ignorant of the "advantages common in other parts of civilized Europe." His dwelling place was "only one room" with "sheaves of straw" and a stove.[3] The idea began to insinuate itself that the great powers should perhaps have done something to improve everyday life in Poland. "One should hope that the revolution taking place in that realm might procure at least the advantage of a better administration of jus-

---

[31] Ibid., vol. 30, p. 118 (8 January 1773).
[32] *Correspondance secrète du comte de Broglie avec Louis XV*, vol. 2, p. 368.
[33] See chapter 5.
[1] *Notizie del mondo*, no. 67, 22 August 1772, p. 551 (Warsaw, 24 July).
[2] Ibid., no. 71, 5 September 1772, p. 586 (Warsaw, 5 August).
[3] Ibid., no. 72, 8 September 1772, p. 593 (Warsaw, 8 August).

tice."[4] In 1772 the imperial forces began constructing a "splendid road" through Lemberg.[5] In both the Lombard and Tuscan press the desire for reform was continually mentioned as a justification for the partition. Just as dissenters had been the banner of Catherine, social and administrative improvement became the program of Maria Theresa. The gazette of Mantova explained that in Poland there were only, "so to speak, two classes of men, that is, nobles and slaves." "The first seeks honor and disdains the arts and sciences, whereas the other works the land in order to nourish the luxury and idleness of its lords." "Medicine, commerce, and trades are exercised by the Jews." "The government of Austria has set out to change customs and opinions in this matter."[6] The gazette of Florence took up this theme and concluded, speaking in the name of the Poles, "We can console ourselves with being in the same condition as other peoples of Europe, but we deplore the destiny of a nation that is becoming civilized only through the force of foreigners and its own disgrace."[7] La *Gazzetta di Milano* said that "among the many abuses introduced by the despotism of the great one the maintenance by principal families of corps of troops, which often presented to the eyes of Europe great disorders and the most deplorable excesses, is quite important. The house of Potocki, in particular, had the habit of keeping a small army. The Austrian generals have told the Palatin of Kiovia . . . to dismiss all the troops in his pay, immediately and without recourse, permitting him only a few Swiss as bodyguards."[8]

In his *Saggio sulla pubblica educazione*, which was published in 1773, Giuseppe Gorani explained that the chief obstacle to "rustic education" in Poland was serfdom. "Among the many lands where I observed the sad effects" of the powers of seigneurs, "Poland was the one that presented the most lugubrious spectacle." He had seen "squalid peasants break out in sobs of happiness for crusts of black bread offered to them . . . , in that same happy season when, loaded with riches, the spacious and abundant countryside surrounds them with signs of opulence." "Born in such a fertile land, when will you have the courage to say to your tyrants, We are men with a nature equal to yours . . . ?" Fortunately, even in Poland times were changing. "A better wind already blows for you. Clemency and philosophy finally sit together on your throne." "The eminent virtues admired in Stanislaus, the beneficial institutions he planned when discord still lacerated your land, are the preludes of

4 Ibid., no. 78, 29 September 1772, p. 642 (Warsaw, 3 September).
5 Ibid., no. 88, 3 November 1772, p. 721 (Warsaw, 7 October).
6 *Mantova*, no. 19, 7 May 1773 (Leopoldstadt, 4 April).
7 *Notizie del mondo*, no. 37, 8 May 1773, p. 295 (Leopoldstadt, 31 March).
8 *La gazzetta di Milano*, no. 45, 14 November 1772 (Warsaw, 5 October).

fine hopes." "In vain the senseless politics of a few disturbers of concord opposed itself." "Perhaps peace is near. . . . The glorious triumphs of the great Catherine will end in destroying the sad monuments of the tyranny that has thus far kept you in slavery."[9]

Poland as a whole seemed to throw itself into a discussion of existing abuses and the proper means for ending them. The situation of peasants was not the only untenable one, the *Notizie del mondo* noted, but that of artisans and traders as well. How could one operate in a society where "those who want to engage in commerce are subjected to an infinity of burdens"? "Those with rights of life and death over their vassals" had "also the right of not paying." It was a question "of giving to each citizen the right to earn a living through the exercise of his own talents." The problem of the death penalty was serious. It should be removed from the hands of lords and exercised only by the king.[10] Even from an economic point of view greater liberty would certainly be beneficial for the country. "If it is true, following what the illustrious Montesquieu said, that the amount of taxes one can collect is in direct proportion to the liberty of subjects, it seems that Poland has the right to see at least reduced at this time the servitude of the most industrious part of its people." Why not give even "to free artisans the right to buy land"?[11] In some regions controlled by the Austrians it seemed that a program of this kind might be realized. At the end of 1774 the following was announced from Lemberg: "The first advantage this province has received from its separation from Poland is undoubtedly the reestablishment of order among the peasants, so that there will be a kind of space between the great and the poor, and the first will be respected and the second protected in their persons and goods." The other advantage, he added, was "the foundation of a university."[12]

Echoes arriving in Florence from various places in Poland of efforts to improve education and create new schools were continual and insistent. In December 1773 the *Notizie del mondo* reported that "many senators continue to request of the king that a university be established here with part of the property of the suppressed Jesuit order. An institution of this kind, both advantageous and necessary for our country, should, according to them, have as its object history and all the other branches of belles-lettres and be under the immediate protection of His Majesty." There would be rapid progress "through the care of such an enlight-

[9] Giuseppe Gorani, *Saggio sulla pubblica educazione* (London, 1773), in *Riformatori*, vol. 3, pp. 531–32.

[10] *Notizie del mondo*, no. 21, 14 March 1775, p. 166 (Warsaw, 11 February).

[11] Ibid., no. 23, 21 March 1775, p. 181 (Warsaw, 18 February).

[12] Ibid., no. 3, 10 January 1775, p. 20 (Leopoldstadt, 15 December).

ened monarch," in "all those sciences that create the happiness of nations." "Count Joseph Zaluski, bishop of Kiovia, has warmly recommended this project to His Majesty in a letter."[13] In June of the
following year a "plan for education" was "in circulation" that had been
presented to the commission charged with national education, a plan
attributed to Ignacy Potocki, which was minutely described.[14] The culture and society of Poland were beginning to change. Would this country furnish a model of an exemplary internal transformation? In 1776
the *Notizie del mondo* felt it could abandon itself to optimism. "Peace,
unity, and concord have reigned up to now in all our meetings. A similar patriotic spirit seems to have animated all the members of the Diet.
All this demonstrates that in the end firmness and virtue win over the
audacity of vice. . . . Our generals, who thought they were the principal
support of the nation and dared balance their power with that of our
king, are now reduced to the rank of honest and useful citizens, without
their independence giving alarm to the state." The voices of Branicki,
Rzewuski, and Oginski had echoed "highly the names and words of subversion of the laws, of slavery, and of ruin of the fatherland" in their
agitation for the phantom of republican tradition. "But such words no
longer make the same impression on the spirit of Poles, because sad
experience has made clear that these were words without sense."[15] Internal reforms were begun and pressed forward. At the end of 1776 the
Notizie del mondo assured its readers triumphantly that Poland had abolished torture, "the shame of a great part of Europe." The law, it said,
"merits imitation by peoples who believe they are more enlightened
than the Poles."[16]

But still there were doubts. Crown Marshal Francis Michael Rzewuski had remained a "fierce republican" and certainly was not the only
one to fear that Poland might end up "forgetting even the word of *liberty.*"[17] Also change came slowly and in small doses. "The only consolation of patriots is to see that the king does not give up under the weight

[13] Ibid., no. 101, 18 December 1773, p. 818 (Warsaw, 19 November). See Heinz
Lemke, *Die Brüder Załuski und ihre Beziehungen zu Gelehrten in Deutschland und Danzig* (Berlin: Akademia Verlag, 1958).

[14] *Notizie del mondo*, no. 47, 11 June 1774, p. 372 (Warsaw, 17 May). See Jobert, *La
Commission d'éducation nationale en Pologne.*

[15] *Notizie del mondo*, no. 89, 5 November 1776, p. 690 (Warsaw, 9 October).

[16] Ibid., no. 103, 24 December 1776, p. 801 (Warsaw, 23 November). The notice is
also in the *Nuove di diverse corti e paesi*, no. 52, 23 December 1776, p. 411 (Warsaw, 30
November). The law of the abolition is reported in the *Notizie del mondo*, no. 104, 28 December 1776, pp. 808ff.

[17] Ibid., no. 81, 8 October 1776, p. 624 (Warsaw, 17 September).

of affairs."[18] Confronted with facts it was necessary "to believe that the bright rays of philosophy have not entered this kingdom everywhere." In the Palatinate of Kalisz "a gentleman had nine old women burned who were accused of having bewitched the surrounding fields and caused sterility in that region." What better proof was there of the "abuse of private jurisdiction"?[19] It was necessary to wait until 1778 for the law code project, which would "perfect, clarify, and simplify the course of justice."[20] The economy of the country remained problematic. "This is a kind of crisis that shows itself in a thousand ways. The nobles limit their expense, equipages become more than simple, servants in livery, once so numerous, are reduced to a number barely necessary; the expenses of table and furniture are similarly reduced."[21]

Shade and light, delusions and hopes—these were the words that the Florentine journal used in 1775 as a provisional conclusion from the long discussion it dedicated to Poland. "There is every reason to think that this reign, which for ten years has provided so much material for the curiosity of Europe, is not yet at the end of the developments that make its history one of the most interesting of our century."[22]

A distant voice raised itself in the same year in defense of the archaic constitution of Poland, that of Luigi Antonio Caraccioli, a descendant of the Neapolitan house but for some time a cosmopolitan publicist and an author of a series of works on Pope Clement xiv.[23] His work, *La Pologne telle qu'elle a été, telle qu'elle est, telle qu'elle sera*, defended the politics of the Rzewuski, to whom he felt particularly tied and who were among the organizers of the Confederation of Bar. His position became still more explicit in a book he later published in 1782, *Vie du comte Wenczeslas Rzewuski, grand général et premier sénateur de Pologne*. Later he even defended the liberum veto and concluded that "to abandon the legislation of a people to a plurality of votes in the place of unanimity risks exposing oneself to arbitrariness, especially in a land where great lords are like so many sovereigns and have no obstacle to their wills." "A republic is in a sense destroyed when unanimity is proscribed." This should have remained the basis of "republican liberty." It was important also to erect a solid barrier against foreign ideas and customs entering Poland. "Soon people will be ashamed to appear like Sarmatians and affect the appearance of Parisians. This was a new way of acting and

---

[18] Ibid., no. 99, 12 December 1775, p. 779 (Warsaw, 15 November).
[19] Ibid., no. 100, 16 December 1775, p. 786 (Warsaw, 15 November).
[20] Ibid., no. 94, 24 November 1778, p. 753 (Warsaw, 20 October).
[21] Ibid., no. 2, 6 January 1776, p. 11 (Warsaw, 9 December).
[22] Ibid., no. 49, 20 June 1775, p. 387 (Warsaw, 24 May).
[23] See Venturi, *Settecento riformatore*, vol. 2, pp. 328ff.

thinking, a new egoism . . . detaching the republic from many of its subjects." This political and cultural conservatism did not prevent Caraccioli
from asking for the liberation of unfree peasants or from commenting
as follows: "Poland will be more at ease if it has fewer nobles and more
merchants, artisans, and workers."[24] The first of the two books echoed
in Italy. In April 1775 the *Notizie del mondo* reported that "a book in 12mo
entitled *La Pollonia tale quale è stata, è e sarà* had been published in Warsaw. The Florentine gazette judged that it was too filled with conjectures
to be truly convincing. The author explained "how the operation of the
partition had been conceived," calling it "an article to add to the great
book of small causes and great effects." In these pages one can see "exactly what is planned." "But time alone will tell if the projects succeed.
They depend on a chain of circumstances that we cannot read in the
future." "Those who want to exercise their imagination and swallow
conjectures and guesses might find pleasure in this book, especially in
its third part."[25]

Beyond Venice and Florence, Rome was the most important center
of Italian observation of events in Poland. The problem we have seen
emerge in the Republic of St. Mark and the grand duchy of Tuscany of
how the Polish tragedy insinuated itself into the incipient anticlerical
movement agitating all of Catholic Europe could not help but interest
the Roman Curia. There was, in fact, much discussion of Poland in
Rome. But there was little action, which showed the weakness and decadence of papal power between the sixties and the seventies. The reactionary policy of Clement XIII was represented in Warsaw by the nuncio
Angelo Maria Durini. The more comprehensive and indulgent policy of
Clement XIV was transmitted by his successor, Giuseppe Garampi. But
neither succeeded in effectively influencing the Polish drama, whose
deepest problems were religion and tolerance. Durini and Garampi re-

---

[24] Cited by Angelo Tamborra, "Luigi Antonio Caraccioli e la Polonia dopo la prima
spartizione," in *Italia, Venezia e Polonia*, pp. 27ff. See *Vie du comte Wenceslas Rzewuski, grand-
général et premier sénateur de Pologne* (Liège: J. J. Tutot, 1782), pp. 8, 42, 47, 67.

[25] *Notizie del mondo*, no. 32, 22 April 1775, p. 252 (Warsaw, 22 March). The book was
worth, in reality, more than what one might guess from this summary judgment. The
pages on the necessity of emancipating the peasantry are intelligent. The author felt close
to the Poles, reduced to being like poor orphans ("We are like orphans who have lost their
fathers, and our mothers are distressed as widows"). He saw the causes of the catastrophe
in the ever clearer desire of European sovereigns "to have in this world neither aristocracies nor democracies." "For a long time the liberty of Poland has irritated the other powers. An absolute monarchy does not like to hear talk of a nation that gives lessons to its
ruler. It imagines that this wounds its authority." (*La Pologne telle qu'elle a été, telle qu'elle est,
telle qu'elle sera* [Warsaw and Poitiers: Michel-Vincent Chevrier, 1775], pt. 2, pp. 71, 122,
pt. 3, p. 8.)

mained observers rather than actors. Nevertheless, their testimony is crucial.

Like Pope Rezzonico (Clement XIII), Durini was both resigned and obstinate. He knew well how inefficient the political organization of Rome was, and he did not attempt to hide the impotence of the Curia in defending even the forms of respect. He was doubtful and often pessimistic about the future of Catholicism, and not only in Poland. But he did not budge from what he took to be tradition and truth. From his dispatches appear the origins of a new type of reaction, which grew at the end of the century, in the years of the French Revolution. That Poland was undergoing a revolution Durini knew well. He reacted with a rigidity that was not blind, but severe, and that brought him to condemn, hate, and despise whoever attempted to compromise or sought a way out. This Lombard patrician was without illusions. His voice joined the many raised in Italy in defense of the Curia, and he too lamented the discomfort and disgust that awaited the defenders of Rome in these years. Even this was an aspect, if a negative one, of the decline in clerical influence taking place everywhere. Offices of state and intellectual careers brought glory and satisfaction, positions in the Church were a hardship and carried less honor and remuneration. "In this century," Durini wrote to his uncle, the archbishop of Pavia, on 17 October 1767, "service to the Holy See is the worst career one can make." When he arrived in Poland he remarked that "the task of a nuncio is now everywhere distasteful, but here it is insufferable from all points of view."[1] There were plenty of dangers. Humanistic tradition and his love for Latin verse helped him conserve a formal dignity. He published his poems, as polished as they were politically neutral, in Warsaw at the most serious point of the conflict. But privately his discomfort became greater. His dreams of revenge grew more grandiose, and his politics, directed toward a complete Russian defeat and a triumphant victory of the confederates, became more and more unreal. He tried in vain to persuade the Roman Curia of his ideas, and in order to advance them he did not hesitate to carry out a policy in Warsaw that was in clear contrast to the prudence and reserve of the Roman secretary of state.

He looked to Paris rather than to Rome and hoped for the intervention of Louis XV. In his reaction, generally, one senses something different from the numerous appeals to the Holy Faith that were heard in Italy at that time, something that brought him closer to the battle of the Sorbonne against the Encyclopedists.[2] After leaving Poland, he collabo-

---

[1] Cited by G. B. Marchesi, "Un mecenate del Settecento (Il cardinale Angelo Maria Durini)," *Archivio storico lombardo*, 4th ser., year 31, fasc. 3 (September 1904): 60.

[2] Domenico Caccamo, "Il nunzio A. M. Durini (1767–1772) e la prima spartizione

rated with Clement XIV in an attempt to find an accord with the French monarchy and became governor of Avignon when it was restored to the papacy. In 1770 he returned to Lombardy, where he spent some years in a life of luxury and patronage. He died in 1796 while he was preparing to leave with a good store of gold for Switzerland at the news of Napoleon's first victories.

Antonio Eugenio Visconti, the predecessor of Durini as nuncio in Warsaw, had warned of the perils of the Polish situation. The request for "a complete liberty of religion and for a perfect equality between dissenters and Catholics" was a move supported by Russia and Prussia, and it had also found a favorable reception within the republic. "The country lacks population and arts, and for that reason it would be good to attract dissenters to come and establish themselves in Poland. . . . The maxims that govern more cultivated people favor the dissenter cause and inspire on all sides principles of toleration." A force opposed to such aims was "the knightly order," "the small nobility," which was animated not only by a "zeal for religion," but also "by opportunism," "by a perception of self-interest, because they fear that dissenters would compete for a share in the distribution of royal charges and honors." The atmosphere was not generally favorable to the clergy. Even in Poland, I might add, reigned a state of mind similar to that elsewhere in Europe. "In general laymen feel a great animosity toward ecclesiastics . . . , the riches of the clergy, both secular and regular, are said to be immense . . . , they would like to reduce payments of tithes and taxes and to impose charges of the state on ecclesiastics." The tribunal of the nuncio was challenged, appeals to Rome were contested, and the export of money was condemned. "There is an outcry against the numerous convents and the idleness of monks thought useless to the state." All look to the "conduct of the other powers, which, especially in recent times, have administered great and palpable blows to the rights" of the Church. Stanislaus Augustus preyed on this situation. He had "talent, awareness, and above all a vivid desire to reform, if he could, in a single day, the whole country and raise it to the level of other, more cultivated nations." The "greater part of the nation" was ignorant. But "dangerous books" were published "daily."[3]

Rapidly, in the months that followed, the Russian intervention made

della Polonia," in *Italia, Venezia e Polonia*, pp. 37ff., where nonetheless the variation of policy of the Holy See during the pontificate of Clement XIII himself is not taken sufficiently into account, and then when he was succeeded by Clement XIV. See also Sante Graciotti, "Il nunzio Durini e la Polonia letteraria del tempo di Stanislao Augusto," ibid., pp. 69ff.

[3] Thenier, *Vetera monumenta Poloniae*, vol. 4, pt. 2: *1697–1775*, pp. 94ff. (Warsaw, 24 September 1766).

these problems more serious. The unity of the Catholic Church seemed in peril, as the bishops themselves asserted. In Spain and Portugal, in Naples and Venice, in Germany and Austria, disputes with the Roman Curia had never reached, according to Durini—and in this he was mistaken—"such an extremity," risking to open the road "to deism and irreligion."[4] Indifference seemed to dominate the court,[5] and against this there arose an ever more violent opposition, which refused to make concessions to the dissenters and the Russians. "The old religion and liberty" became more and more Durini's password.[6]

The dislike of the nuncio was directed against Machiavellian politicians, and all those who intended "to introduce the free exercise of all religions in this kingdom and place hands on the goods of the Church, restricting the bishops to fixed incomes, as the czarina has done in her states."[7] Durini struggled in every way to prevent the jurisdiction of the nuncio from being touched.[8] He called "execrable" a "mixed tribunal" that had been recently constituted.[9] He hoped with all his soul for the victory of the confederates, blessing their banners and their leader Pułaski for "extreme and exemplary piety."[10] His hostility to reformers of any type grew more violent, especially, as often happens, when they were men of the Church. He broke with those who, even in Poland, had received and developed the legacy of Benedict xiv and Muratori. They were abusing "the immortal name of Benedict xiv," he said at the end of 1769.[11] The man he hated the most among the reformers was Stanisław Konarski, "the principal theologian of tolerance." He found teachings inspired by him repugnant. In church schools they read "Erasmus, Woolf, and other authors of tolerance. . . . they bring in from France and England great trunks of stylish books." "If the religious raise their crests, what will laymen do?"[12] Against the "execrable abuses intro-

---

[4] Ibid., p. 202, the Polish bishops to the king, 19 December 1766.

[5] Ibid., p. 223, 9 September 1767.

[6] Ibid., p. 224, 23 September 1767.

[7] Ibid., p. 231, 14 October 1767.

[8] Ibid., p. 268, 31 January 1768.

[9] Ibid., p. 273, 5 October 1768.

[10] Ibid., p. 370, 15 September 1770. The description of Durini's journey to the confederate camp in Częstochowa is extraordinarily significant, from "the devotion of the whole people," "something never seen in Warsaw," to Pułaski kissing the hand of the nuncio and the description of this leader: "He is of few words, but of many deeds, of moderate height, quick of body, dark complexion, not more than twenty-five years old; seeing him on foot does not promise much, but on horseback he is truly an Alexander." "I was saluted by several cannon shots and by the vivat of the whole army of 4,500 men." Durini's solemn benediction followed.

[11] Ibid., p. 321, 23 December 1769.

[12] Ibid., p. 314, 7 October 1769.

duced by Father Konarski and his faction" any means seemed justified to the nuncio, from a denunciation of the Holy Office to the rebellion of the confederates.[13] The most dangerous thing in his eyes seemed to be the alliance of the king with enlightened reformers. He tried every means to break this union. He loudly affirmed that the writings of Konarski were as perilous from a political point of view as from a religious one, and that they threatened the fundamentals of both the Polish constitution and the papacy. "There reign in this man all the symptoms of an arch-heretic . . . , he writes against the liberum veto and the most solid maxims of Polish liberty."[14] And he was not alone. Father Portalupi, "the superior of the Theatines," was also "a shamefaced courtier and promoter of the Russo-schismatic system." He was, in reality, one of those who had done most to bring to Poland the Italian culture of the early eighteenth century and who was convinced that reforms could be accomplished only by supporting the policy of Stanislaus Augustus. It is enough to enter the room where the king of Poland worked, his cabinet, to see how much he prized such collaboration. Portraits of Konarski, Portalupi, and Śliwicki (the superior of the Lazarists, who was also taken by reformist ideas) were on one of the walls. Across from them were the portraits of Voltaire, Montesquieu, and Rousseau. This filled Durini with particular horror.[15] It would be hard to imagine a better symbol of the difficult, but not unfruitful, convergence that existed everywhere in Europe in those years, but the one in Poland aroused more violent reactions than elsewhere.

The results were now clearly visible. Ideas and customs were changing. "One would be much mistaken to try to base a judgment of Poles today on Poles of thirty or forty years ago, so much have they strayed from their old faith and simplicity!" The great were increasingly dominated by their political interests, reducing themselves "to the ultimate refinement of malice and cunning." Only the body of the regular clergy restrained the torrent, together with the "poor nobility." The secular clergy, with a few exceptions, thought of nothing but "getting hold of benefices, and in reaching them they have no scruple in using means most pernicious to religion." "In a word, without the regular clergy, *actum est* for Catholicism in Poland." The developments of the last years had revealed Polish reality for what it was. There was need of "a revolution in Poland to expose its indolence, and among revolutions this has most brought forth the spirit of the nation."[16] "The enormous, unheard

---

[13] Ibid., p. 315, 28 October 1769.
[14] Ibid., p. 320, 9 December 1769.
[15] Ibid., pp. 349ff., 21 April 1770.
[16] Ibid., p. 350, 21 April 1770.

1. The staff and print shop of the Florentine gazette *Notizie del mondo*, 1769.

Gazzetta

NOTIZIE
DEL MONDO
Per l'Anno
MDCCLXIX.

NOTIZIE DEL MONDO

Num. 18.

SABATO 4. Marzo 1769.

FRANCIA
PARIGI 13. Febbrajo.

Entiamo da S. Brieux, che il nuovo Decreto del Consiglio, di cui il Sig. Duca di Duras ne ha fatta fare pubblica lettura agli Stati il dì 30. del passato mese, e che rimette l'ordine della Nobiltà nel medesimo Stato in cui era per la dichiarazione dell'anno 1736. è stato inserito sul registro in margine di quello de' 30. Marzo 1768. che è considerato come se mai non fosse avvenuto.

Decreto fatto dal Parlamento del Delfinato.

LA Corte giustamente intimorita da'grandi ostacoli, che sembrano elevarsi contro la libertà del commercio de'grani, e convinta da una esperienza di 4. anni de'Reali vantaggi procurati a questa Provincia dalla Dichiarazione del 25. Maggio 1763. e dall'Editto del mese di Luglio 64. ha decretato, persistendo ne' suoi Decreti, e Deliberazioni precedenti sopra questa materia, che sia scritto al Re ad effetto di supplicarlo ad interrogare del loro voto le sue Corti avanti di accordare veruna deroga alle precedenti Leggi sì preziose pe' suoi Popoli ,, . A Grenoble 20. Dicembre 1768.

GRAN-BRETTAGNA
LONDRA 10. Febbrajo.

Il dì 3. del corrente la Camera de' Comuni dopo aver lungamente dibattuto l'affare del Sig. Wilkes pronunziarono la seguente sentenza ,, Che Giovanni Wilkes Scudiere, Membro di questa Camera, e che alla Barra della medesima si è confessato autore d'aver pubblicato quello che questa Camera ha decretato essere un libello insolente, scandaloso, e sedizioso, e che è stato giudicato reo al Tribunale del Banco del Re d'avere stampato, e pubblicato un libello sedizioso, e tre libelli impudici, ed empj, e che essendo stato condannato per Decreto del Tribunale medesimo

ГОСПОДИ БОЖЕ МОЙ! ВОНМИ МИ, И ВРАЗУМИ МЯ, ДА СОТВОРЮ СУДЪ ЛЮДЕМЪ ТВОИМЪ ПО ЗАКОНУ СВЯТОМУ ТВОЕМУ СУДИТИ ВЪ ПРАВДУ.	*Domine Deus mi! exaudi me, et da mihi intelligentiam, vt conſtituam iudicium genti tuae, quo ſecundum legem tuam ſanctam dicatur ei ius.*

НАКАЗЪ

КОММИССІИ О СОСТАВЛЕНІИ ПРОЕКТА НОВАГО УЛОЖЕНІЯ.

1.

Законъ Христіанскій научаетъ насъ взаимно дѣлаши другъ другу добро, сколько возможно.

INSTRVCTIO

Coetui ad condendam ideam noui legum Codicis conuocato, plenaque ad id donato poteſtate.

1.

Religio Chriſtiana docet nos, vt alter alteri mutuo tantum boni faciamus, quantum quidem in cuiusque noſtrum viribus ſitum eſt.

Herr mein Gott! vernimm mich, gieb mir Verstand, dein Volk zu richten, nach deinem heiligen Gesetze und nach der Wahrheit!

Seigneur mon Dieu! sois attentif à ma voix, & donne moi de l'intelligence pour juger ton peuple selon ta sainte Loi & selon la justice.

Instruction

für die zu Verfertigung des Entwurfs zu dem neuen Gesetz-Buche verordnete Commißion.

INSTRUCTION

Pour la Commission chargée de dresser le Projet d'un nouveau Code des Loix.

I.

Die Christliche Religion lehret uns, einer dem andern so viel gutes zu thun, als uns möglich ist.

I.

La Religion Chrétienne nous enseigne de nous faire les uns aux autres tout le bien que nous pouvons.

A 2

4–5. The Instruction given by Catherine II to the commission for the reform of legal codes. Edition in four languages, published by the Academy of Sciences in St. Petersburg, 1770. The reproduction is taken from the copy given by the empress to Cesare Beccaria, preserved in the Biblioteca Ambrosiana in Milan.

нѣтъ изъ нихъ ни одной, которая бы отъ прочихъ не зависѣла, и что только одно всѣхъ сихъ частей сопряженіе можетъ составить, укрѣпить и въ вѣки продлить безопасность государства, благосостояніе народа и славу Самодержца.

Подлинное подписано собственною ЕЯ ИМПЕРАТОРСКАГО ВЕЛИЧЕСТВА рукою, тако:

ЕКАТЕРИНА.

Санктпетербургъ, 1768 года, Апрѣля 8 дня.

Печатанъ при Сенатѣ.

ab reliquis; poſtremo eſt perſpicuum ſolam omnium harum partium in vnum faſcem collectionem poſſe efficere, firmam reddere, et in perpetuum prorogare ſecuritatem imperii, proſperum ſtatum populi et gloriam Imperatoris.

Autographum ſubſcriptum eſt SACRAE IMPERATORIAE MAIESTATIS *manu propria ſic :*

AECATERINA.

Petropoli anno Chriſti 1768, Aprilis die 8.

Excuſum formulis litterarum in officina Senatus.

gung dieſer Theile vermögend iſt, die
Sicherheit des Staates, die Wohl=
farth des Volkes und den Ruhm des
Souverains zu bewürken, zu befeſti=
gen und zu verewigen.

dante des autres & que la réunion
ſeule de ces parties peut opérer,
affermir & perpétuer la ſureté
de l'Etat, le bonheur des Peuples
& la Gloire du Souverain.

Das Original iſt von Ihro Kay=
ſerlichen Majeſtät eigenhändig
unterſchrieben, alſo :

Catharina.

St. Peterburg 1768. 8ten April.

Gedruckt beym Senat.

L'Original eſt ſigné de la propre main de
SA MAJESTÉ IMPÉRIALE, ainſi :

CATHERINE.

St. Pétersbourg, l'An. 1768. le 8. d'Avril.

De l'Imprimerie du Sénat.

6–7. The last page of the Instruction of Catherine II. The engraving is signed I. d. Sthelin
inv. et del. (elsewhere, more precisely, we find J. d. Stehlin or Jakov Jakovlevič Štelin). C. M.
Roth, Sculptor Acad. Sc. Petrop. Sculpsit.

въ передѣ не могъ вредить обще-
ству, и чтобъ отвратить со-
гражданъ отъ содѣланія подоб-
ныхъ преступленій. Для сего
между наказаніями надлежитъ
употреблять такія, которыя,
будучи уравнены со преступле-
ніями, впечатлѣли бы въ серд-
цахъ людскихъ начертаніе самое живое и долго пребывающее,
и въ то же самое время были
бы меньше люты надъ престу-
пниковымъ тѣломъ.

206. Кто не обемлется
ужасомъ, видя въ исторіи
столько варварскихъ и безполе-
зныхъ мученій, выисканныхъ
и въ дѣйство произведенныхъ
безъ малѣйшаго совѣсти зазора
людьми давшими себѣ имя пре-
мудрыхъ? Кто не чувствуешь
внутри содроганія чувстви-
тельнаго сердца при зрѣлищѣ
тѣхъ тысячь безщастныхъ лю-
дей, которые оными претер-
пѣли и претерпѣваютъ, мно-
гажды обвиненные во престу-
пленіяхъ сбыться трудныхъ
или немогущихъ, часто сопле-
тенныхъ отъ незнанія, а ино-
гда отъ суевѣрія? Кто можешь
говорю Я, смотрѣть на растер-

---

detrimentum, praeterea que, vt
ciues a perpetrandis similibus scele-
ribus arceantur. Ideoque e numero
poenarum tales eligendae sunt,
quae coaequatae criminibus im-
primant in animis hominum ideam
viuam ac durabilem, eodem que
ipso tempore minus, quantum fieri
potest, saeuiant in corpus facinorosi.

206. Quis est, qui non cohor-
reat, videns in historiis tot barba-
ros et inutiles cruciatus repertos
et re ipsa adhibitos sine vllo con-
scientiae ictu a viris, qui nomen
sibi sapientum indiderunt? Quis
est, cui cor intus non palpitet ad
spectaculum tot millium hominum
infortunatorum, qui cruciatus illos
perpessi sunt, hodie que patiuntur
saepe rei facti criminum, quae vix
ac no vix quidem fieri possunt,
et quae multoties intentantur ab
inscitia, non numquam a superfti-
tione? Quis, inquam, est, qui queat
oculis irretortis intueri, cum
discerpuntur magno et numeroso
cum apparatu homines ab homini-
bus, fratribus suis? Imperia et

---

bürger, ähnliche Verbrechen zu begehen,
abgehalten werden mögen. Zu dem
Ende sind solche Strafen nöthig, die
mit den Verbrechen in Verhältniß
stehen, die in die Herzen der Men-
schen einen lebhaften und lange wäh-
renden Eindruck machen, und die zu
gleicher Zeit die wenigste Grausamkeit
an dem Körper des Verbrechers aus-
üben.

206. Wer erschrickt nicht, wenn
er in den Geschichten von so viel bar-
barischen und vergeblich gebrauchten
Martern lieset, die von Leuten, die
sich Weise genannt, ohne den minde-
sten Vorwurf des Gewissens erfunden,
und ausgeübet worden? Welches
empfindliche Herz wird nicht von einem
innerlichen Schauer gerühret, bey An-
schauung so vieler tausend Unglückli-
chen, die solche Martern erlitten haben,
oder noch leiden, die oft solcher Verbrechen wegen, verurtheilet worden,
welche schwerlich oder unmöglich be-
gangen werden können, und die öfters
von der Unwissenheit, zuweilen aber
auch vom Aberglauben erdichtet worden?
Wer kann die Zerfleischung dieser Men-
schen, die mit grossen Zubereitungen,

---

toyens de commettre des crimes
semblables. Parmi les peines, on
doit employer celles qui, étant
l'impression la plus efficace &
la plus durable sur les esprits
des hommes, & en même tems
la moins cruelle sur le corps du
criminel.

206. Qui ne frissonne d'horreur en voiant dans l'Histoire tant
de tourmens barbares & inutiles,
inventés & emploiés froidement
par des hommes qui se donnoient
le nom de sages? Qui ne sent
frémir au dedans de lui la partie
la plus sensible de lui-même,
au spectacle de ces milliers de
malheureux qui les ont soufferts
& qui les souffrent, accusés de crimes souvent impossibles, souvent
fabriqués par l'ignorance & quel-
que fois par la superstition? Qui
peut, dis-je, les voir déchirer
avec appareil, par des hommes
leurs frères. Les pais & les
tems où les supplices les plus
cruels ont été mis en usage, sont

8–9. "Who is not horrified in reading the history of the many barbarous torments imposed with impunity and conceived and carried out by men who call themselves wise without experiencing the slightest feeling of conscience? What sensitive heart is not filled with an internal chill when casting a glance on the many thousands of unfortunates who have suffered, and still suffer, such torments, and are often condemned for crimes not committed, or invented through ignorance, or even at times through superstition? Who can withstand the sight of the slaughter of such men, even by their brothers, administered with such sad instruments? The times and places where the most terrible punishments were practiced were those when the most inhumane villainies were practiced." The text of Catherine II is taken literally, with some abbreviation, from the version by Morellet, *Traité des délits et des peins.* Lausanne (Paris), 1766, par. 15. "On the mildness of punishments," pp. 107ff., corresponding, with modifications, to par. 27 of the original text of Beccaria. Giovanni Del Turco, the translator of the Instruction, did not return to the Italian original, but retranslated it from French. The text above is in Russian, Latin, German, and French.

10. *Monumenti omerici.* As Giovanni Del Turco, the author of this engraving, explains, "the most singular monuments of Homer can be seen in the device facing the frontispiece of the first volume of my translation." (*Della Iliade di Omero trasportata in ottava rima tomo I*. Florence: Gio. Batista Stecchi and Giuseppe Pagani, 1767.)

11. The most important Italian translation of Catherine II's Instruction by Giovanni Del Turco.

12. Greek translation of Catherine II's Instruction, done from the Italian version of Giovanni Del Turco and published in Venice in 1770.

Geografica Dimostrazione della Propontide, dell'Elesponto,

13.   A westerner and an easterner before the Aegean, the Dardanelles, and the Black Sea, during the Russo-Turkish war of 1768–1774. Engraving by Domenico dell'Acerra, from the Neapolitan edition of the *Storia della guerra presente tra la Russia, la Polonia e la Porta Ottomana*. Naples: Vincenzo Flauto, 1771–, vol. 9.

EUROPA

MARE NIGRUM

Trojanopolis
Maximianopolis
Mesbrus
Saronea
Enos
Siragella
Traiana polis
Bergula
Tristralum
Selybria
Heraclea
Rhodosto
CONSTANTI NOPOLIS
BOSPHORVS
Scutari
Chalcedon

MARE MARMORA

Samothrace I.
Lysi machia
Gallipolis
Marmara I.
Priaxpis
Catalli
Sestos
Camp sacas
Ione
mbrus I.
Stalimene I.
Dardanella
Dardanella
Abydus
C.Dardanella
Dardanella
Thiatyra
Cyzicus
Prosias
HELLE
ILLLum Troja vetus
Loper dium
Apollunge
Tenedos I.
Alexandria Troas
nova Troja
Assus
Antandrus
ASIA
Porta ferrea
Miletopolis
Methymna
Pitana
Copcars Pergamus
Eteea
Mytilene I.

PORTVS

ARCHIPELAGVS

Bosforo, e loro adiacéze ianto nell'Europa quanto nell'Asia
Dom. dell'Acerra f.

14. Frontispiece of volume 4 of the original edition of the *Storia della guerra presente tra la Russia e la Porta Ottomana*. Venice: Antonio Graziosi, 1770.

Il Felt Maresciallo Principe di Galliczin occupa Cochtzim dopo replicate vittorie ottenute sopra i Turchi.

15. A Russian victory, 10 September 1769. "The field marshal himself crosses the river accompanied by some generals, volunteers, and others and enters the fort rendering solemn thanks to the Most High to the boom of the cannons found there; the whole army drawn up on the other bank of the river replies with a triple salute, loudly shouting, 'Long live the empress.' " (*La storia dell'anno 1769*. Venice: Francesco Pitteri, 1770, p. 265.) The feminine figures are purely imaginary. In fact, in the fortress there remained only "a few persons."

16–17. The Greek uprising and Russian assault on Coron, in the Peloponnesus. The illustrations are from the *Voyage pittoresque en Grèce* by Ambassador Choiseul-Gouffier, published in Paris in 1778. The allegory is explained by the author as follows: "Bellona, freeing a cache of arms and followed by Russian troops, shows Greek slaves the symbol of liberty, which they have the baseness to flee." Coron was attacked by troops landed by the Russians and by a corps of Maineotes in April 1770.

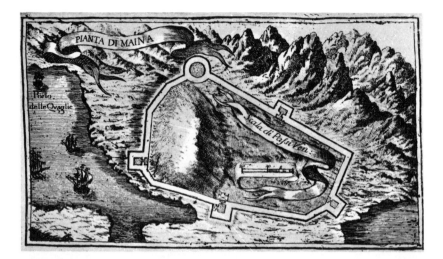

PIANTA DI MAINA

Porto delle Qvaglie

Scala di Passi Ven.

MISITRA o I. SPARTA

Navarino

Mare di Sapienza

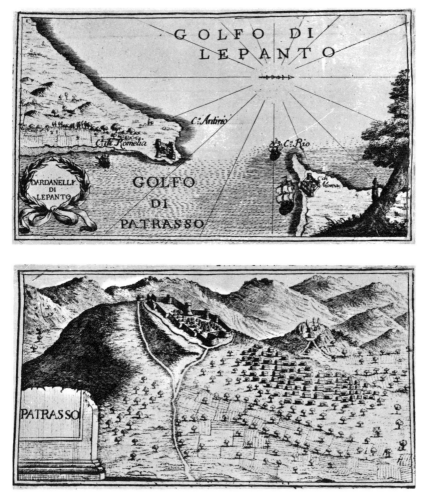

18–22.   Fortresses and battles in the Morea: Maina, Sparta, Navarino, Lepanto, and
Patras. The illustrations are from the *Elogio di Catterina seconda imperatrice delle Russie*.
Venice: Giammaria Bassaglia, 1773. A translation of the French text by Ange Goudar
was undertaken by Francesco Griselini.

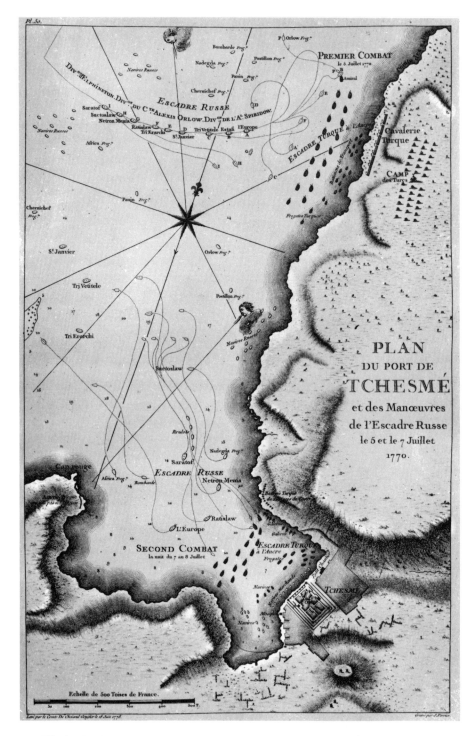

23. The battle of Chesmé, 5–7 July 1770. Drawn on 18 June 1776 by Choiseul-Gouffier.

24. Count Aleksej Grigor'evič Orlov, victor and destroyer of the Turkish fleet. The happiness and joy of Russia. Chesmé, 24 and 26 June 1770. With gratitude to the victor from the College of Admiralty. The engraving is by Giuseppe Aloja, *Componimenti poetici di vari autori in lode di sua eccellenza il signor conte Alessio Orlow.* Naples, n.d.

COMPONIMENTI POETICI

DI VARJ AUTORI IN LODE

DI CATERINA II.

AUGUSTISSIMA IMPERATRICE

DI TUTTE LE RUSSIE

PARTE PRIMA.

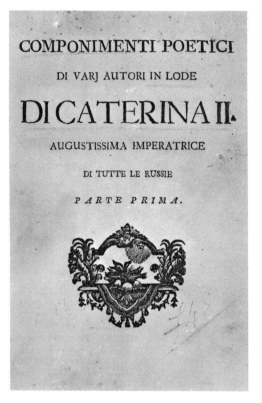

COMPONIMENTI POETICI

DI VARJ AUTORI

IN LODE

DI SUA ECCELLENZA

IL SIGNOR

CONTE ALESSIO ORLOW

PLENIPOTENZIARIO E COMANDANTE SUPREMO
DELLE ARME RUSSE IN LEVANTE
NEL 1772.

Che d'Icaro il deſtin acerbo e rio,
Se più m'inoltro, ho da temer per pena
Del ſconfigliato ardir che l'alma acceſe
            A temerarie impreſe.
Ma giacchè dee tacer l'umil mia vena,
Tu Signor non ſdegnar che il cuor divoto
T'offra ſe ſteſſo oſſequioſo in voto.

L glorioſo grido ſparſo nel
Mondo intero delle ſublimi
virtù che adornano l'Anima
grande dell'Eccellenza voſtra, e dell'E-
roiche ſue Impreſe: ſiccome deſta l'am-
mirazione e gli applauſi delle Nazioni
tutte; così di eſtraordinaria e parziale
                                          eſul-

34

Glorioſo ſcopri? Chi delle Sfere
Le diſtanze rimote
Ruppe, vinſe, e varcò? Emolo al Sole
Vince i Tempi e Natura,
Gl'Ampj Spazj del Ciel corre e miſura.
Chi vide mai nel Mondo
Coſì rara virtù? Se al Re de' Numi
Sia la gemina Prole,
O Compagno degl'Aſtri, o Figlio al Sole
Ceda Aleſſio a' vanti tuoi:
    Aleſſandro ed anche Achille,
    Se il camin de' grand'Eroi
    Già ſei giunto a ſuperar.
Ceda il Trace; e le ſcintille
    Del ſuo barbaro furore.
    Ora impari, e con dolore,
    L'empio orgoglio ad abbaſſar.

35

EPILOGO ENCOMIASTICO.

E Rgi dalle fatali tue ruine
    Grecia la fronte, e mira Orlow invitto,
Che compie a tuo favore ciò ch'hai ſcritto
De' Duci tuoi nell'opre tue divine.

L'impreſe ſue più rare e pellegrine
    Conduce a ſegno per ſentier più dritto;
E nel più duro interior conflitto
Vince gli affetti ſuoi, e gli dà fine.

Armato di valor, e d'arte adorno
    Ognun l'ammira, ognun ſtupiſce come
    Strugge le Flotte de' Nemici a ſcorno.

Pallade alfin gli cincerà le chiome,
    E ſi vedran feſtoſe a lui d'intorno
    Del Biſantino mar le rive dome.

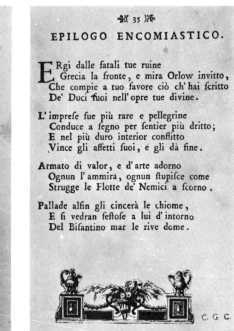

C. G. C.

27–30.   Taken from the *Componimenti poetici di vari autori in lode di sua eccellenza il signor conte Alessio Orlow*. Naples, n.d. The initials C.G.C. on the right corner indicate Conte Giorgio Corafà.

31. *"Exoriare aliquis."* The call to revolt and aid of enslaved Greece amid ancestral tombs and ruins. Taken from the *Voyage pittoresque en Grèce*, by Choiseul-Gouffier.

32. Victory or death. Thus did the Corsican Maineote Nicolò Stephanopoli describe the discovery of this bas-relief. " 'Oh heavens, what do I see!—he cried suddenly pouncing on a bit of marble—a statue of Liberty!' She held in her right hand a long pike, and in her left hand a codex topped by a crown of laurel, with the device 'Liberty or Death!' With that inscription he recognized the arms of Lacedaemon. . . . He carried away the little statue and hastened to show it to his uncle. Dimo embraced him with the joy and veneration that one would embrace a mother, and asked Démétrius to give it to him as a present to General Bonaparte; his request was granted and Dimo, returning to Paris, hastened to give it to the hero who has known so well how to propagate the cult of that goddess. General Bonaparte, receiving the statue of Liberty, said to Dimo: 'She has the appearance of a saint.' 'You do not deceive yourself'—responded the old man—'she is the first of all the saints.' " (*Voyage de Dimo et Nicolò Stephanopoli en Grèce pendant les années 1797 et 1798.* Paris: Guilleminet, 1800, vol. 1, pp. 227ff.).

ʋιμη, η θαναλος

33–34. The rock that was to serve as the base for the statue by Falconet dedicated by Catherine II to Peter I being taken along the Neva with a mechanical apparatus designed by Marino Carburi of Cephalonia. From the volume *Monument élevé à la gloire de Pierre-le-Grand*. Paris: Nyon and Stoupe, 1777.

GAZETTE DE NICE.

DU VENDREDI 4 MARS 1774.

De CONSTANTINOPLE *le 11 Janvier.*

 Uſtapha III. eſt mort aujourd'hui des ſuites d'une hydropiſie dans ſa 58me. année. Il étoit fils du Sultan Achmet III. qui fut dépoſé en 1730. né le 20 Décembre 1745 à Andrinople, il fut proclamé Grand Sultan & Empereur de la Turquie le 30 Novembre 1757; il a laiſſé un fils unique, âgé de 7 ans, qui ne lui ſuccédéra pas; le Mufti, les gens de Loi, & les Chefs de la Milice ont déja proclamé Abdulamet, frére du Grand-Seigneur. On ne croit pas que cet événement occaſionne du changement dans le ſyſtême actuel de la Porte, & dans les réſolutions du Divan. Peu de tems avant ſa mort, le Grand-Seigneur avoit reçu pluſieurs nouvelles agréables ſur l'état de ſon Empire; il avoit appris que la ſageſſe du Grand-Viſir & le courage de ſon Armée n'avoient plus laiſſé d'ennemis en deça du Danube, qu'on avoit chaſſé le dernier Détachement Ruſſe qui étoit reſté dans une Iſle de ce Fleuve, près de Siliſtrie, & que tous les poſtes ſur la droite du Fleuve, depuis Vidin juſqu'à Caraſow, ſont pourvus de nombreuſes garniſons; il avoit recueilli la ſucceſſion de Moldavangi-Ali-Pacha, ancien Grand-Viſir, ſi connu par les fautes que lui fit commettre un courage mal dirigé, & par les défaites qui en furent les ſuites; mort depuis peu d'une Apoplexie à Rodoſte; & il avoit reçu d'Egypte le tréſor du célèbre Aly-Bey qui alloit encore à trois millions de Piaſtres, tant en bijoux qu'en argent monoyé.

De la TURQUIE *le 10 Janvier.*

La nouvelle importante de la retraite des Ruſſes au-delà du Danube & de la défaite totale de leur arriére-garde par Haſſan-Pacha, près de Cſernawada, fut annoncée au peuple de Conſtantinople par l'Artillerie du Château des ſept Tours. La Cavalerie Ottomane ſe mêla dans cette Action avec l'arriére-garde du Général Unghern, qui craignant qu'elle ne profitât de ce déſordre pour paſſer le Danube avec les Ruſſes, fit couler à fond une grande partie des pontons ſur leſquels l'arriére-garde devoit traverſer ce Fleuve; cette précaution prévint ce malheur qui étoit véritablement à craindre; mais elle expoſa l'arriére-garde à un plus grand maſſacre; & l'Action fut effectivement ſi ſanglante, que les Ruſſes y laiſſerent quatre mille hommes. Haſſan-Pacha apprit au Grand-Seigneur cette nouvelle intéreſſante, & demanda qu'il lui fut permis d'inquietter à ſon tour ſes ennemis dans les quartiers qu'ils ont pris au-delà du Danube; en lui envoyant cette permiſſion, le Grand-Seigneur a ordonné au Grand-Viſir de lui fournir 15 mille hommes la plupart de Cavalerie, que le Pacha de Vidin ſoutiendra de ſon Infanterie.

De PETERSBOURG *le 20 Janvier.*

Sur les avis qui ſont arrivés de la Révolte qui a éclaté dans le Gouvernement d'Orenbourg, la Cour a fait publier ici au ſon de la Trompette & du Tambour un Manifeſte en datte du 3 Janvier, & en a envoyé des copies dans les différentes Provinces de l'Empire pour y être lues & publiées. Il eſt dit dans ce Manifeſte, dont l'Original a été ſigné de la propre main de l'Impératrice: *Que Sa Majeſté Impériale a appris avec*

35. *Gazette de Nice*, no. 18, 4 March 1774. After having recounted events in the Ottoman Empire, the gazette of Nice went on to announce from St. Petersburg, on 20 January, "the revolt that has broken out in the province of Orenburg," the insurrection of Pugačev.

36.   The execution of Pugačev. Drawing by Andrej Timofeevič Bolotov.

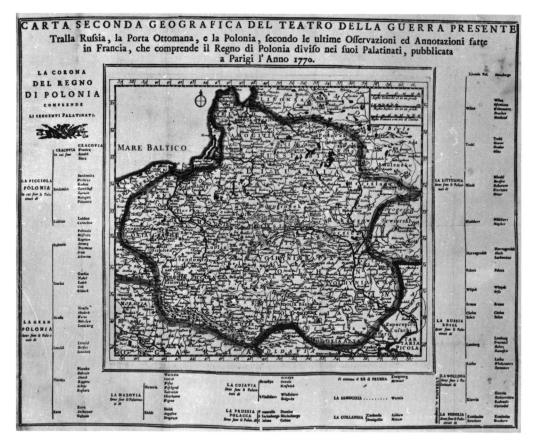

37. Poland before the partition. Venetian print.

JEAN - FREDERIC
Comte de Struensée
Premier Ministre d'Etat de sa Majesté Danoise
Décapité en 1772

38. "A pathetic history worthy of being read": Johann Friedrich Struensee.

ISIDORUS BLANCUS

O S B CONG. CAM.

Quid virtus et quid sapientia possit
utile proposuit nobis exemplar

Cornel. Höijer del.   Meno Haas sculps. Hafn. 1775.

39.   Portrait of Isidoro Bianchi, engraved in Copenhagen in 1775.

40. The Sweden of Gustavus III. Venetian print.

41. Voltaire and the peasants of Ferney. The work of Jean Huber, preserved in the Musée des Beaux Arts in Nantes, in the Cacault Collection.

NOTIZIE DEL MONDO

Num. 25. MARTEDI' 26. Marzo 1776.

FRANCIA
PARIGI 7. Marzo.

IL Re ha approvato il nuovo Piano di Lotto prefentatogli dal Conte di San Germano. Reftano in confeguenza foppreffi fino dal primo di luglio proffimo tutti i Lotti, ed anco quello della Scuola Real Militare, ed è creato in quella vece un Lotto folo col titolo di Lotto Reale, che farà quafi fimile a quello della Scuola Militare. Per evitare poi la frode, che s' introduce fempre troppo facilmente in quefte forte di ftabilimenti, e per diffipare i timori che fi potrebbero concepire, S. M. ha meffo il detto Lotto in amminiftrazione a fuo conto, e ha premeffo di non iftabilirne alcun' altro, quando non fia per rimettere in buono ftato la Compagnia dell' Indie, o per foyvenire a' bifogni del Regno in tempo di guerra. Sul prodotto di quefto Lotto farà affegnato un fondo a favore degli Alunni della Scuola Militare in compenfazione del Lotto ch' era loro accordato, e faranno egualmente indennizzati gli altri Lotti.

Il Sig. Beaucert Autore dell' Opera profcritta fopra gl' *Inconvenienti dei Diritti Feudali*, era ftato citato dal Parlamento a render conto perfonalmente del motivo, che l' aveva indotto a ftampare quell' Opera, e del principio che fi sforzava di accreditare ma il Re gli ha dato ordine di reftare a Verfaglies, dove egli è fotto la protezione di S. M., e gli ha proibito di prefentarfi al Parlamento Si afficura altresì, che ufcirà un Decreto del Configlio, che fopprimerà la Relazione del Sig. Seguier Avvocato Generale, come tendente a alterare l'autorità del Sovrano, e capace d' infpirare ai fudditi di S. M. una difubbidienza tanto più rea, in quanto che tutte le mutazioni che il Re fi propone hanno per oggetto il follievo ed il bene dei fuoi popoli, ai quali vuol render la libertà sì preziofa alla Nazione Francefe.

E' da notarfi che nel Decreto del Configlio che accennammo, fopra la foppreffione delle 5. Memorie pubblicate in ftampa a favore dei Corpi d' Arti e Meftieri, fi offerva principalmente che fe per il bene della giuftizia, e la difefa delle Parti è permeffo agli Avvocati di fare ftampare i loro Scritti, quefta permiffione non può eftenderfi fuori degli affari contenziofi, che fono o debbono effer portati nei Tribunali. Quelli che hanno firmato i detti Scritti ftampati hanno evidentemente ecceduto i limiti del loro ufizio con dare alle ftampe Opere che non hanno, e non poffono aver relazione a veruna contestazione giudiciaria In una parola tutte quefte Stampe hanno un carattere, che merita la maggior' attenzione di S. M., e la fua correzione. Il potere Legislativo appartiene a lei fola, e s' ella permette alle fue Corti di farle umiliffime Rimoftranze fopra le leggi, che ftima bene d' indirizzare alle medefime, non è mai ftato permeffo a verun Particolare di difcutere preventivamente l'oggetto, o le difpofizioni di dette leggi, o opporre per così dire un fentimento ifolato all' autorità di S. M., e di cercare di prevenire i fuoi fudditi contro Leggi emanate dalla fua faviezza, giuftizia, ed amore per i fuoi Popoli. Laonde Sua Maeftà non può troppo affrettarfi di profcrivere quefti Scritti, come contrari ai Regolamenti, e al rifpetto dovuto alla fua Sovrana autorità, e perciò proibifce a tutti i Librai, Stampatori e Mercanti di vendere, fpacciare, o in altra guifa diftribuire le dette Stampe; ordina che quelli che ne hanno degli Efemplari faranno tenuti a portarli alla Cancelleria del Configlio, proibifce a' Signori della Croix, Dareau, Saulnieer, e Leroy de Montecli, Avvocati, di ricadere in futuro fotto le pene convenienti ec.

La

43. Frontispiece by Benjamin West,
engraved by Francesco Bertolozzi, for the
Storia degli stabilimenti europei in America,
by William and Edmund Burke.

44. John Wilkes. Engraving by Hogarth.

STVPETE GENTES REPERIT VIVVM DIOGENES

BENJAMIN FRANKLIN

Ministre plenipotentiaire a la Cour de France pour la Republique des Provinces unies de l'Amerique Septentrionale.

45. In 1760, in Venice, in an engraving reproduced in volume 2 of *Settecento riformatore. La chiesa e la repubblica dentro i loro limiti*, figure 20–21, Francesco Griselini presented Paolo Sarpi as the man Diogenes was seeking. In 1780 the French artist Bligny took up this image again, substituting Benjamin Franklin. The symbols changed. A republican cap and a pike made their appearance. The American Revolution, with its thunder, had come to break the yoke. Twenty years of reforms and revolts had run their course.

of, scandal" that occurred on 24 June 1770 seemed to Durini to signal that his blackest prophecies were being realized. In was the feast of St. John. In Warsaw "all the Freemasons" had met in a building erected by them, in the midst of which stood "an altar in strange form with the following inscription: *Virtuti Sapientiae Silentio Sacrum.*" Five hundred people with carriages attended, "not to mention those on foot." There were even great ladies, and the king's cousin, Princess Lubomirska. "It was said publicly that His Majesty had donated two thousand florins to the assembly for the evening supper, and that, besides providing money for the occasion, he had even honored it incognito with his presence as a good brother." In vain Durini explained himself hoarse that there existed, against Masonry, "the famous bulls of Clement XII and Benedict XIV prohibiting such assemblies under pain of excommunication reserved for the Pope himself and enjoining bishops to implore the secular arm to prevent them."[17]

The more he shuddered to see such spectacles, in that Babylon of modern Warsaw, the more his thought turned to the surrounding regions, where in growing numbers the confederates fought, without sparing blows, for "religion and liberty." Any concession to the "Stanislaus" party—even those which the Secretary of State in Rome soon made—seemed to him errors.[18] He knew that Rome intrigued against him. But he did not intend to change. He would remain faithful to the motto of the Confederates: "*Pro fide, rege et patria*" (For faith, king and country).[19] He left Warsaw, when the order came, all the more convinced that "Catholicism and liberty go together in Poland and support each other."[20]

It fell to his successor, Garampi, to try to practice the policy of accommodation and concession that Clement XIV had initiated shortly before in Portugal and then extended to all other Catholic states. "The entire nation is disarmed and fearful," he wrote on 28 September 1772, when the earthquake the partition produced was still far from quiet. The war was over. The passion for liberty had been smothered. The three powers had taken control of the situation. And if Austria did not present a threat from the Catholic point of view, and basically Frederick II did not either, Catherine pressed on with her heavy religious proselytizing. Distant were the Voltairian programs of the outbreak of the war. The problem of tolerance was no longer in the forefront, nor was

[17] Ibid., p. 364, 27 May 1770.
[18] Ibid., p. 421, 25 December 1771.
[19] Particularly interesting in this regard is a letter by Cardinal de Bernis from Warsaw dated 30 January 1771, published by Caccamo, "Il nunzio A. M. Durini," pp. 53ff.
[20] Theiner, *Vetera monumenta*, p. 439, 11 January 1772.

there further talk of political reform; indeed, Russia became more conservative in its observance of the Polish constitution. The weight fell
most heavily on the Uniats, Catholics of Eastern rite, who were obliged
to convert to the Eastern religion. "The protection and propagation of
the schism by Russians is closely tied to their political interests; it is even
a basis of their empire."[21] In 1774 the end of the war against the Turks
and the crushing of the Pugačev revolt combined to put a seal of victory
on the foreign and internal policy of Catherine II. "Russia has never
made such a glorious or advantageous peace as this," Garampi was
forced to conclude.[22]

[21] Ibid., p. 458, 28 September 1772.
[22] Ibid., p. 594, 6 August 1774.

VIII

⁂

Between Despotism and Liberty: Denmark

——————

AMONG ENGLISH REPUBLICANS OF THE SEVENTEENTH AND EIGHTEENTH centuries, the example of Denmark was thought to be particularly significant. The abolition of the old "gothic" constitution of 1660 and its substitution with a government that was harshly absolutist impressed men like Shaftesbury and Molesworth. At that time Denmark took a road that "commonwealthmen" intended with all their strength to avoid in England, shaken as they were with profound horror by any diminution of liberty and by any religious conformity.[1] Particularly vehement was the pamphlet written by Robert Molesworth, *An account of Denmark as it was in the year 1692*, which was published in London two years later. He had no doubt that "all Europe was a manner of free country till very lately."[2] Then, instead, tyranny was canceling out one after another all free governments, in Italy, and in Europe as a whole.[3] Even in Denmark there had remained in force, until 1660, "the ancient form of government . . . which the Goths and Vandals established in most if not all parts of Europe." Up to the catastrophe of thirty years before, the estates had represented all groups in the nation, "people of all sorts." Even the peasants, "even the boors," had been able to make their voices

——————

[1] See Caroline Robbins, *The Eighteenth-Century Commonwealthmen* (Cambridge, Mass.: Harvard University Press, 1959), pp. 92ff.; and Franco Venturi, *Alberto Radicati di Passerano* (Turin: Einaudi, 1954), pp. 145ff.

[2] Robert Molesworth, *An account of Denmark as it was in the year 1692* (London, 1694), preface (not paginated).

[3] He cited as proof, on p. 42, Cardinal Guido Bentivoglio and his *Relazione delle Provincie Unite di Fiandra*, book 3, ch. 7: "Truly all kings at the beginning were chiefs and not kings, and of republics rather than kingdoms, but long habit has made people take on the usage of obedience, precisely like a plant or a human body becoming accustomed to living in a soil or a climate different from its natural one." *Opere del cardinal Bentivoglio* (Paris: Giovanni Iost, 1649), p. 49.

heard. The kings were elective and aware that their power derived "*a subditis*" (from subjects).[4] "Frequent meeting of the estates was a part of the very fundamental constitution."[5] Thus, this was an ideal model for English supporters of traditional republican monarchies. But now parliaments were suppressed everywhere, except in Poland and Great Britain. Long wars and ever pressing financial problems had broken the solidarity of the estates, depriving them of the capacity for acting together in defense of common liberties. The nobles had treated commoners and the clergy as slaves. The responsibility of the clergy in this drama was important. The nobles found themselves unable to resist when the king, in accord with the other two estates, proposed to make the crown hereditary. "To give up at once their beloved power and submit their necks to a heavy yoke was an intolerable grievance, but they saw they were no longer the masters, the commons were armed, the army and the clergy against them."[6] Thus Denmark, in four days, "from an estate little differing from an aristocracy," had passed "to as absolute a monarchy as any is at present in the world." It did not take long for the results to be felt. Taxes became more and more arbitrary and burdensome, the value of landed property diminished by three-quarters, the misery of peasants increased, justice deteriorated, and even commoners were obliged to recognize how much worse absolutism was than any kind of noble regime.[7] The entire nation rapidly became more indolent, more and more dominated by "a kind of laziness and idle despondency which puts men beyond hopes and fears, it mortifies ambitions, emulation and other troublesome, as well as active qualities which liberty and freedom beget."[8] In gloomy pages Molesworth thus described the decadence and general degeneration of the country, an example *ad deterrendum* and an exhortation to return to the way of liberty that aroused wide discussion and ended by making this work one of the classics of British republicanism.

The century of Danish absolutism, from the *lex regia* of Frederick III (1665) to the death of Frederick v (1766), was dominated by the increasing influence of the international situation in which Denmark found itself and by the increasing importance of a class of political men, administrators, and technicians who had come from abroad, especially from Germany and Sweden. Closed internally in its absolutist form, Denmark was open externally toward Europe of the early eighteenth century.[9]

[4] Molesworth, *An account*, pp. 42ff.

[5] Ibid., p. 45.

[6] Ibid., p. 61.

[7] Ibid., p. 73.

[8] Ibid., p. 75.

[9] See Ludvig Krabbe, *Histoire de Danemark des origines jusqu'à 1945* (Paris and Copenhagen: E. Munksgaard et C. Klincksieck, 1950), pp. 149ff.

The development of Russia's power carried much weight, and the policy of Peter the Great and his successors was decisive for the orientation of Danish foreign policy. The problem of Schleswig and Holstein served the diplomacy of the czars as an instrument for deeper penetration into the world of the Baltic and German states. Nor should one forget that Denmark dominated the strait across which the fleet of Kronstadt would one day pass to navigate in the open sea. Its relations with England, on the other hand, also became closer and were dominated not only by commercial considerations, but also by the presence on the British throne of a sovereign from nearby Hanover. Thus as a small country between two powers in full development—Russia and England—Denmark found itself at the center of the ebbs and flows of northern European politics. In the last years of Frederick v and the first years of Christian vii, in the sixties and seventies of the eighteenth century, when the Seven Years' War ended and the Russo-Turkish war began, the Danish situation was dominated by a weakening of French influence, by uncertainties of British policy, and by the increasingly intense initiative of Catherine ii.[10] In distancing himself from Louis xv and Choiseul, the Danish minister of foreign affairs, Johann Bernstorff—one of the most important among the numerous Germans installed at the helm of the government of Copenhagen in those years—ably sought an accord with Russia. Writing to Choiseul on 24 May 1766, he defined as precisely as possible the field of ambitions of a small country like Denmark: "We have taken stock of ourselves; we know that heaven has not given us a great deal of power or a position that permits us to influence others beyond the North; and thus we limit ourselves to that, giving all the rest of our attention to taking care of the interior arrangements of the state, the restoration of its finances, and the increase of its commerce and industry."[11] Counting on Russian support, profiting from the diplomatic errors of the English and from the growing skepticism of France, Denmark would thus remain able to block the always menacing ambitions of Sweden and concentrate on problems of internal reform.

This was a moderate and sensible program permitting Denmark to continue its maritime and commercial expansion and the active mercantilistic policy that distinguished the state in the first half of the eighteenth century. It is enough to think of the Danish penetration into the Mediterranean to realize the scope of this expansion. Contact between

[10] Michael Roberts, "Great Britain, Denmark and Russia, 1763–1770," in *Studies in Diplomatic History. Essays in Memory of David Bayne Horn*, ed. Ragnhild Hatton and M. S. Anderson (London: Archon Books, 1970), pp. 236ff.

[11] *Correspondance entre le comte Johan Hartvig E. Bernstorff et le duc de Choiseul, 1758–1766* (Copenhagen: Gyldendal, 1871), p. 240.

the two distant regions was not infrequent. Along with Swedish ships—
in all some 572 in 1762—the Danes carried fruits and vegetables from
Tunis to Livorno and Marseilles, Sicilian grain to Spain, and Moslem
pilgrims to Mecca.[12] In the summer of 1773 the *Notizie del mondo* spoke
of some 900 merchant ships in the Mediterranean sailing under the
Danish flag—and they came, I should add, mostly from Norway, which
was then part of the realm of Christian VII.[13] Their encounters with Barbary pirates became more frequent. The *Gazzetta Fiorentina* of 12 May
1770 announced from Copenhagen that "our squadron will pass into
the Mediterranean to demand satisfaction from the bey of Algiers for
having broken the peace with our kingdom and allowing corsairs to disrespect our flag."[14] It was the beginning of a long struggle, which
brought little success to the Danes (the attempt to bombard Algiers had
no result), a conflict that was naturally followed with attention by Italians.[15] After these events the thought comes immediately to mind that
the great expedition of Orlov was the most obvious and conspicuous,
but certainly not the only, northern penetration into the Mediterranean
at the beginning of the seventies.

But in Copenhagen it was clear that this was only one element, one
aspect of the economic and cultural enlargement of horizons in which
the country was involved. The exploration of little-known lands was an
important part of the program. Already Frederick V "had sent a group
of scholars to Asia to study the laws, customs, habits, religion, and politics of different states in that part of the world." The return of the only
survivor of this expedition, "Captain Niebuler" (Carsten Niebuhr, the
father of the famous historian of ancient Rome), aroused great emotion
in Denmark in 1771. "They say that among other things he has brought

[12] Claude Nordmann, *Grandeur et liberté de la Suède (1660–1792)* (Paris and Louvain:
Nauwelaerts, n.d.), pp. 268ff. nn. 104, 105.

[13] *Notizie del mondo*, no. 74, 14 September 1773, p. 602 (Copenhagen, 21 August).

[14] Ibid., no. 3, 12 May 1770, p. 301 (Copenhagen, 14 April).

[15] Ibid., no. 42, 26 May 1770, p. 340 (Copenhagen, 1 May) (the king reviews the departing fleet); no. 2, 5 January 1771, p. 12 (Copenhagen, 8 December 1770) ("His Majesty
has not only ordered that his squadron in the Mediterranean proceed against them, but
has fitted out a much larger fleet to stop the insolence of the barbarians and end their
treachery"); no. 25, 26 March 1771, p. 195 (Copenhagen, 24 February) (the failure of the
bombardment of Algiers leads to a withdrawal of the fleet). No. 62, 3 August 1771, p. 489
(Copenhagen, 8 July): "It is reported from London that peace between our court and
Algiers has been concluded through mediation by the king of Sardinia." Finally, one year
later, in no. 62, on 4 August 1772, p. 511 (Copenhagen, 11 July), the signing of a treaty
with Algiers was announced. There is an ample summary of these events in the *Storia
dell'anno 1770*, pp. 68ff. There was talk even of Struensee's intention of "sending twenty-
six Danish ships into the Mediterranean to support the Russians and English," a project
that was soon abandoned. See *Gazzetta di Parma*, no. 11, 17 March 1772 (Venice, 8 March).

a description of Arabia and a part of Yemen, with some excellently drawn maps."[16] It was "one of the most famous Oriental expeditions of the century," Arnaldo Momigliano has written in his study of its importance in the formation of Barthold Georg, the son of Carsten.[17]

These distant visions, in the Denmark of the seventies, became mixed with more immediate and compelling necessities. The bad climate seemed to oppose any will for reform and improvement: frozen seas, broken communications, scarcity, and famines were continually noted in the news from Denmark and northern Europe.[18] How was it possible to keep attention fixed on the Mediterranean, or even on Arabia? A large part was naturally concentrated on more urgent necessities: the problems of economic and social change.

In Copenhagen, among the ministers, technicians, and professors, a broad current favorable to reform emerged. These were practically all foreigners and from diverse origins, but they were united in the interest they had in their adopted country. Perhaps the most ingenious was Elie-Salomon-François Reverdil, a Swiss from Vaux, a cultivated man open to the political debates of his time. Called in 1758 to the chair of mathematics at the Academy of Copenhagen, he became the tutor of Christian VII in 1760 and then served as minister until 1767. He left a most vivid picture of Denmark in these years, to which one must turn to understand the contrasts of men and ideas spurring the country toward an attempt at rapid transformation that came suddenly to a brusque and

[16] *Notizie del mondo*, no. 103, 24 December 1771, p. 794 (Copenhagen, 26 November).

[17] Arnaldo Momigliano, "Lettere di B. G. Niebuhr sui suoi studi orientalistici," *R. stor. ital.* 72 (1960): 336ff.; and id., *Terzo contributo alla storia degli studi classici e del mondo antico* (Rome: Edizioni di storia e letteratura, 1966), pp. 197ff. See also *Notizie del mondo*, no. 95, 28 November 1772, p. 775 (Copenhagen, 4 November). ("The king has awarded a gold medal with the inscription *Pro meritis* to the councilor of state Langebeck, author of a work entitled *Scriptores rerum danicarum*. . . . Captain Nibuhz has received another. . . . The voyages of this captain and the important discoveries he has made are known by all.")

[18] *Notizie del mondo*, no. 17, 26 February 1771, p. 130 (Copenhagen, 25 January): "Navigation has been interrupted in the Sound, which causes much damage to this capital; foodstuffs and wood are much needed this season and begin to be scarce; the poor suffer much; and the rich have great difficulty providing for themselves"; no. 94, 23 November 1771, p. 723 (Copenhagen, 29 October): "The recent news from Norway is that grain is so scarce in that land that the inhabitants of the countryside have no more bread"; no. 49, 20 June 1772, p. 406 (Copenhagen, 26 May): It is "the intention of the king to provide assistance to the poor in this time of scarcity and misery"; no. 68, 25 August 1772, p. 558 (Copenhagen, 1 August): "The famine continues to desolate Norway." Only in no. 82, 11 October 1774, p. 650 (Copenhagen, 13 September), was the gazette able to publish the following: "Despite the inconstant weather the harvest has been abundant in our two kingdoms." See also *Gazette de Nice*, no. 1, 17 August 1772 (Copenhagen, 24 July): "The news one receives from Norway could not be worse; the extreme misery that desolates it drives its unhappy inhabitants to atrocious acts that make humanity tremble and nature revolt."

violent halt.[19] One can well understand, after having read the incisive pages of Reverdil, how he was worthy, when he finally returned to his homeland in 1771, of becoming the friend and correspondent of persons such as Necker and Madame de Staël, Voltaire and Meister, Bonstetten and Gorani, as well as the translator of Ferguson's *Essay on Moral Philosophy*. The members of the Hanoverian family of Bergstorf were quite different from him, but they also impress one for their breadth of culture and benevolent cosmopolitan views. The Moltke were more closely tied to the Danish world. Charles-Louis de Saint-Germain was entrusted with the reorganization of the Danish army when an attack seemed imminent by the new emperor of Russia, Peter III, in 1761, who was himself a member of the Holstein family (only his murder and the ascent to the throne of Catherine II ended this threat). The problem of recruitment was closely associated with the right of nobles to levy soldiers from their own lands: the military problem and reform of the peasantry were inseparable. Around the Count of Saint-Germain coalesced a group of young officers, also of German origin, who were persuaded of the need to proceed with reforms.

Need for economic and political renewal then led, from the fifties, to a reemergence of traditions of liberty and constitutional ideas, which had been smothered, but not eliminated, by the triumph of absolutism nearly a century earlier. Montesquieu was an inspirer of this movement, which found its most active elements among Genevans working in Copenhagen. Guided by the *Esprit des lois*, Paul-Henri Mallet, a twenty-five-year-old professor of French, discovered and made known to Europe the deep roots of the Danish past.[20] Behind the façade of a tired and narrow imitation of classicism and absolutism, he discovered a quite different reality, the world of the Germanic tribes, of the Edda, of sagas, and of an unsuspected degree of political and social freedom. His *Introduction à l'histoire de Dannemarc*, which appeared in Copenhagen in 1755, not only was at the origin of a European wave of passionate interest in the mythology and poetry of Nordic peoples, a wave comparable only to the one raised contemporaneously by Ossian, but also contributed to arousing curiosity and interest in the historical roots of modern liberty.[21] He studied the Scandinavians (whom Mallet still called Celts, fol-

---

[19] *Struensée et la cour de Copenhague, 1760–1772. Mémoires de Reverdil, conseiller d'état du roi Chrétien VII*, ed. Alexandre Roger (Paris: Ch. Meyrueis, 1858).

[20] Still of great interest is the work about him written by J.C.L. Simonde de Sismondi, *La vie et les écrits de P. H. Mallet* (Geneva: J. J. Paschoud, 1807). "He knew what importance one could ascribe to the history of the North, and that it was there that one should search for the source of our opinions, or manners, and our customs."

[21] For literary aspects, see Paul Van Tieghem, "La découverte de la mythologie et de l'ancienne poésie scandinaves," in id., *Le Préromantisme. Etudes d'histoire littéraire européene*

lowing Pelloutier) not only for their hymns and legends, but also because they had carried out "numerous revolutions" in Europe, had introduced "a form of government marked by good sense and liberty," and had exhibited "a restless spirit, indomitable, ready to rouse itself at even the words *subjugation* and *constraint*, with a ferocious courage born of a wild errant life." From them Europe derived "a spirit of independence and equality."[22] No one had ever succeeded in removing these deep roots entirely. Forms of government created by the Nordic peoples still remained in some places, and even "where it had been thought proper to abolish these forms" they were not entirely destroyed "because the habits and spirit arising from them remain in many respects." All servitude was hated; honor was given its due. Sovereignty was exercised with that "moderation" and "familiarity" and with that "respect for humanity" which "so happily [distinguishes] our sovereigns from the proud secretive tyrants of Asia."[23] Even in Denmark this modern humanity traced its origins to the government and laws "of the ancient Danes": their free election of sovereigns, their tribunals, and the simple and vigorous constitution that had ruled them in the past. In Iceland this primitive form could still be observed in all its purity. "The genius of these peoples and their natural good sense and love for liberty appear openly. The nation was left to itself and developed in a remote place separated from the rest of the world."[24] The ingenious system of local assemblies and "Estates General" constituted a true model of free government. After having minutely described the "political constitution" of the distant island, Mallet concluded by indicating how ample and deep the influence of this type of government had been on Europe as a whole. "Limitation of the authority of kings or heads of state by representative assemblies of the nation, which reserve for themselves legislative power in all important matters, was a kind of mold that for centuries shaped almost all governments of Europe." The "instinct for liberty," so deeply inscribed in the nature of the Spanish, the Gauls, the peoples of Germany, the British Isles, and the north, as well as the Thracians and Scythians, linked them indissolubly to a "form of government for which they all seem to have derived the idea from the same source." This was radically different from most of the nations of Asia, "subjected to absolute masters" and incapable of knowing anything be-

(Paris: Rieder, 1924), pp. 73ff. A review in Italian of the *Mémoire sur la mythologie et la poésie des Celtes*, published in Copenhagen in 1756, was published in De Felice in his *Estratto della letteratura europea* (1758), fasc. 1, pp. 1ff.

[22] Mallet, *Introduction à l'histoire du Dannemarc où l'on traite de la religion, des loix, des moeurs et des usages des anciens Danois* (Copenhagen, 1755), pp. 3, 5, 7.

[23] Ibid., p. 7.

[24] Ibid., p. 118.

sides "the extremities of servile indolence, or revolt and treason."[25] As Montesquieu had justly said, tyranny does no other than cut down the tree to collect the fruit, as among the savage Americans.[26]

Mallet's book, one notes, was dedicated to Frederick v, the king of Denmark. It was intended to be not only a discovery, but also a testimony that the old constitutional roots were not dead in Denmark. They had been transformed into customs and into a will to reform. But how the transformation from political to social liberty had been accomplished Mallet did not say. A book appearing a little later, also the work of a Genevan, responded to the question. In 1757 the *Lettres sur le Dannemarc* by André Roger appeared; Roger was a collaborator and relative of Reverdil (his brother had married Reverdil's sister). It was a discussion between Geneva and Copenhagen and was strongly influenced by the ideas of Montesquieu.

As the English translator of the *Lettres* later wrote, "a book about a monarchic state written by a republican of Geneva" could not help but arouse interest.[27] The Danish government was not despotic, but monarchical, according to Roger. The term "despotic" always had "something odious" about it. It poorly described "such a mild government." "It is an absolute monarchy, to be sure, but one of the most temperate governments in the world." Nor did this "mildness" derive entirely from the "personal virtues of the monarch: it was the natural fruit of the constitution."[28] How could one compare the reign of Frederick v with those Oriental despotisms that naturally aroused horror and repugnance in the "free and republican" soul of the person to whom the first of these letters was addressed, "Mr. Beaumont, advocate to the council of the republic of Geneva"? The notion of despotism should always be reserved exclusively for states dominated by the arbitrariness and caprice of their leaders. "Thus, to avoid all equivocation, and following the immortal author of *Esprit des lois*, let us apply the word *despotism* only to monstrous governments bound by fear."[29] Still, he concluded that "of all forms of government the best undoubtedly is that of an absolute monarchy in the hands of a wise and enlightened prince," capable of ruling

[25] Ibid., p. 124.

[26] Even this political conclusion in the introduction by Mallet was amply summarized in the review published in May 1775, p. 302, by the *Mercure danois*, the journal that Philibert published in Copenhagen.

[27] *The present state of Denmark in relation to its government and laws, its trade and manufactures, its revenues and forces . . . in a series of letters monthly written by monsieur Roger* (London: Th. Osborne, 1762), p. ix.

[28] André Roger, *Lettres sur Le Dannemarc.* I have used the unpaginated preface of the "new edition" (Geneva: Claude Philibert, 1767), preface, and p. 1.

[29] Ibid., pp. 2ff.

according to the laws, of applying them with moderation and sweetness, and of respecting a division of powers and the proper internal social distinctions. "The despot sees throughout his state only equal men, because they are all in an equal state of subjection. The monarch permits subordinate powers that support his throne, temper his authority, and are the canals along which power descends to its ultimate point in measured steps."[30] It is necessary to look at its codes of laws to judge a government like the Danish one, especially at its penal code. No extraordinary commissions, numerous guarantees for the accused, no torture, except for crimes of lese majesty, and even in these cases only after a death sentence, and on explicit license of the king, "who permits it so rarely that in the last twenty-five years it is hardly possible to find two persons to whom the question has been applied." With this mode of procedure monarchy was superior "in moderation" to "free governments."[31]

As he reemphasized in the second volume of the letters, the liberty of a country did not depend in the final analysis on being governed by a monarch or by a senate. It was enough to think of the past or to look around in the modern world in order to be aware of this fact. One could soon persuade oneself that "a senate could be as despotic as a Turkish emperor. The provinces of ancient Rome, and Corsica, were governed by republics with more despotism than Morocco."[32] And Hume had justly called attention in his fourth essay, "If Politics Can Be Reduced to a Science," to the bad aspects of aristocracy, when, as in Poland, the authority of nobles on their domains is unlimited. In Denmark, it was not at all true that 1660 had made "a kingdom lose its liberty, which had been free before." "It was really only the nobles who had lost liberty; the clergy and the third estate had counted for almost nothing in the assembly of estates." The nobles had profited from their liberty to acquire fiscal privileges. The "revolution" of 1660 had thus cut back a "vicious aristocracy" mounted on the "political and civil slavery in which it kept the peasants."[33] It was Frederick IV, in 1702, who had abolished peasant serfdom, while still introducing new bonds "to prevent peasants seduced by their new liberty from abandoning cultivation of the land." From the ages of nine to thirty-five they were liable for recruitment into the national militia. "This also tied peasants to cultivation of the land, but for motives that seemed more noble, and that also turned to the profit of

---

[30] Ibid., pp. 4ff.
[31] Ibid., pp. 7ff.
[32] André Roger, *Lettres sur le Dannemarc* (Geneva: Philibert, 1764), vol. 2, p. 279.
[33] Ibid., vol. 1, pp. 8ff.

the kingdom."[34] Still, it was now time to reconsider the peasants' situation and change it. Their condition could be considered "destructive to industry and population." Free possession of land would also be beneficial. "Property is a principle much more enlivening to man than continual surveillance by an inspector."[35] Nonetheless, surveillance by the state prevented proprietors from abusing their powers. Nor were peasants deprived of legal guarantees. In Norway the situation was different because there were almost no nobles. Peasants possessed land "as *fideicommis* . . . transmitted from father to sons." This was a stable situation but one that could still pose an obstacle to the development of agriculture.[36]

Thus Denmark needed reforms like any other country. But these should be carried out with the moderation and sweetness that characterized its monarchical government. There was no need for severity in a people whose "atrocious crimes are more rare than in other nations," where "violent thefts" were infrequent, even in the capital, and where the roads were secure. It is true that there had been an outbreak of fanaticism: "Some morbid men persuaded themselves . . . that the surest road to heaven was death on the scaffold." "Murders committed in cold blood" multiplied among people who sought death at the hands of justice "as a benefit." But "the length of captivity in which they were made to languish," and "the blows of the rod applied before sending them to punishment, suppressed this strange enthusiasm almost at its birth." Efficient means, for which one could substitute even better ones, to refuse "to these wretches the death they seek [are to] make them pass the remainder of their lives in labor and pain."[37] Quite praiseworthy too was the Danish principle of punishing public fraud more moderately than private theft, "a principle quite contrary to despotism."[38]

This was thus a "desirable government," which nothing seemed to menace, not even the need for change that was beginning to be felt here and there. "And why should the Danish nation fear change?"[39] The general spirit of the century, the growing importance commerce assumed, the very character of the reigning sovereign, all seemed to presage an unthreatened future. The country would continue to develop through the principles established in 1660, which ensured a proper balance between the third estate and the nobility. The peril of equality

34 Ibid., p. 57.
35 Ibid., p. 58.
36 Ibid., pp. 62ff.
37 Ibid., pp. 89ff.
38 Ibid., p. 90.
39 Ibid., p. 92.

would thus not jeopardize the land. That "extreme equality," which was incompatible with monarchy and republics, producing despotism in the first case and anarchy in the second, would be excluded.[40] Even regarding the Danish nobility the ideas of Montesquieu seemed the best and most solid.

The *Mercure danois* made a similar comparison between Danish reality and the European thought of the Enlightenment. In the year that Mallet was widely reviewed, this journal, published by the bookseller Philibert, gave prominent notice to the *Eloge de Mr. le président de Montesquieu par M. d'Alembert.*[41] Roger's *Lettres* were widely discussed, and not without reference to the polemic against Molesworth.[42] In the same issue the editor announced one of his most important works, an up-to-date reissue of the celebrated *Dictionnaire universel de commerce* by the Savary brothers.[43] The following year came the *Ami des hommes* by the Marquis de Mirabeau.[44] Books on economics were becoming more and more numerous. The geographical and historical vision of the journal enlarged, from the lands of Barbary to the *Slovo* by Strube de Piermont about the evolution of Russian law.[45] There were even echoes of Italy, as in the notices in the *Saggio sopra la filosofia degli etruschi* by Lampredi and the *Prose e poesie* by Abate Conti.[46] Often, for Italy, the *Mercure danois* let itself be guided by the indications of De Felice, whose *Excerptum*, published at Basel, was for sale in the bookshop of the Philibert brothers in Copenhagen.

The propaganda and conclusions of the Genevans, of Philibert, Mallet, Roger, and Reverdil, were widely accepted in Europe. The constitutional aspect of the Danish problem was obscured, and moderation and the spirit of reform appeared in the forefront. Voltaire, in his *Essai sur les moeurs*, recalled how the king of Denmark had been a kind of doge before 1660, while the "nobility was sovereign and the people were enslaved." "The clergy and the bourgeois preferred an absolute sovereign to a hundred nobles wanting to govern them; they made the nobles be subjects like themselves and conferred unlimited authority on the king, Frederick III." Thus, terrible were the weapons put in his hands, and he became the most absolute of sovereigns. But his successors did not abuse them. "They have known that their grandeur consists in mak-

---

[40] Ibid., p. 116.

[41] *Mercure danois*, December 1755, pp. 29ff.

[42] Ibid., July 1757, pp. 46ff.

[43] Ibid., p. 59.

[44] Ibid., January 1758, pp. 50ff.

[45] Ibid., pp. 27 ff. See Frédéric-Henri Strube de Piermont, *Lettres russiennes*, introduction and bibliography by C. Rosso (Pisa: La Goliardica, 1978).

[46] *Mercure danois*, July 1757, p. 78.

ing their people happy." Modern development and the expansion of commerce were thus obtained in a diametrically opposite way from that of Sweden: "Sweden made itself free and Denmark ceased to be so."[47]

The problem even attracted Mably's attention. Writing *De la manière d'écrire l'histoire* for the course of studies his brother Condillac was conducting for the Duke of Parma, he paused on the reasons leading the Danish monarchy to absolutism. "Oppression united the oppressed, and the estates in 1660, in destroying the authority of the senate and nobility, conferred most despotic power on the king." Apparently the king of Denmark became "a true sultan." But then why so much "moderation" in the rule of the sovereigns of this state? "It is because they were curbed by the customs of the nation, which while it became enslaved preserved some of the qualities of free peoples." Even the revolution of 1660 was not born from "fear" or from a "spirit of servitude." It had been necessary to blunt the pride of the nobles and the tyranny of the senate. The victory over the aristocracy thus veiled the servitude into which the Danish people had fallen and aroused a sense of pride. Oppressing the oppressors could seem a bizarre and even ridiculous thing. But "such strange notions, under despotism, support free and independent customs." The king himself continued to be inspired by these habits and traditions, rather than by the laws that had made him an absolute ruler of the country.[48]

But then, a little more than five years later, all these rosy assertions and forecasts were overturned. Between September 1770 and January 1772 Denmark witnessed an extraordinary period of rapid, precipitous reform, ending in a political drama that carried its first minister to the scaffold. A kind of enlightened despotism replaced the moderation and sweetness so praised by Roger. At the helm of the government stood a German doctor, Johann Friedrich Struensee, a young and enterprising "grand vizier," as Reverdil called him.[1] With the royal council, the stronghold of noble influence, eliminated, and with many of the aristocratic German families who had dominated the scene in preceding de-

---

[47] Voltaire, *Essai sur les moeurs*, ch. 188, in *Oeuvres complètes*, vol. 13 (Paris, 1878), p. 126. What Voltaire had written on Danish history was the object of a broad discussion in the *Mercure danois* at various points, beginning in July 1757, pp. 3ff.

[48] Gabriel Bonnot de Mably, "De l'étude de l'histoire, à monseigneur le prince de Parme," in id., *Collection complète des oeuvres*, vol. 3 (Paris: Ch. Desbrière, 1794–95), pp. 137ff. See Luciano Guerci, "La composizione e le vicende editoriali del Cours d'études di Condillac," in *Miscellanea Walter Maturi* (Turin: Facoltà di lettere e filosofia, Giappichelli, 1961), pp. 356ff., and id., *Condillac storico. Storia e politica nel "Cours d'études per l'instruction du prince de Parme"* (Milan and Naples: Ricciardi, 1978).

[1] Reverdil, *Struensee*, p. 178.

cades kept at a distance, he launched a series of surprising changes in the social and political life of the country.[2] There was a strong impulse to reform, and an even stronger and a more violent reaction. Struensee paid with his life for his effort to accelerate the pace of Danish development.

The experience left the capital more disquieted, the relationship between Denmark and Norway more difficult, the balance between church and civil society more bitter, the internal political debate more harsh. What were the causes and results of the extraordinary effort in the brief and intense epoch of Struensee? Did the crisis serve to further reform, or to delay it through too precipitous haste? Contemporaries, and even Italians, already asked these questions and were also struck by the singular, novelistic character of the whole affair.

On 14 January 1766 Frederick v died. Christian vii, seventeen years old, ascended the throne. His intimates, and in first place his tutor Reverdil, could not hide the fact that he was not well and progressing rapidly along the road to dementia. In his mind visions of grandeur and energy alternated with increasingly long moments of discouragement and abulia. The situation was made all the more sad, after the long reign of his father, by the hopes raised at the moment of his accession. His wife, whom he had married in September, was Caroline Mathilde, sister of the king of England, George iii. There were rapid changes in the government, where dignitaries of the preceding reign soon began to be eliminated, while the king's doctor, Johann Friedrich Struensee, gained influence. He was the son of a theologian of Halle, who was open to ideas of the French Enlightenment, a man of exceptional scientific curiosity and lucid political ambitions.[3] A voyage to France and England in the retinue of Christian vii, between May 1768 and January of the following year, set the first foundations of his power at court, a power that became total when the queen became his lover, and the king, early in 1770, fell more deeply victim to his malady. After September Struensee operated through the cabinet of the king, modeled after Frederick ii's similar organ in Prussia. Soon Berstorff was set aside, and the privy council was abolished. In the decree of 24 December, cited by the Florentine *Notizie del mondo*, it was explained that the cause of mismanage-

---

[2] See Henry Steele Commager, *Struensee and the Reform Movement in Denmark*, Ph.D. diss. (University of Chicago, June 1928); *Danmarks historie*, ed. John Danstrup and Hal Koch vol. 9: *Oplysnig og tolerance* (Enlightenment and tolerance), 1721–1784, ed. Svend Cedergreen Bech (Copenhagen: Politikens Forlag, 1965), pp. 407ff., 526ff.; and Svend Cedergreen Bech, *Struensee og haus tid* (Struensee and his times) (Copenhagen: Politikens Forlag, 1972).

[3] On his scientific activity, see Stefan Winkle, "Johann Friedrich Struensee als Arzt," in *Gelehrte in Hamburg im 18. und 19. Jahrhundert*, pp. 135ff.

ment of administration was the "multiplicity of persons of high rank participating in it." This was incompatible, it said, with a "monarchical government." The "public good" thus required the suppression of the council so as to return to the "form of government" established by "our ancestors of glorious memory," to the "constitution the nation pre- scribed for our predecessors," "without any shadow of change," as Struensee proclaimed in the name of Christian VII.[4]

This seemed to be a return to absolutism. In reality something more complex was happening, as a measure taken a little earlier demon- strated, which surprised all of Europe. In October, the Florentine ga- zette announced that the "censorship of books" was abolished in Den- mark, and that "the most ample liberty was granted to the press."[5] The news was true. With a decree dated 4 September 1770 Struensee had abolished the long series of laws and orders that regulated royal, aca- demic and ecclesiastical censorship in Denmark.[6] He had personally ex- perienced the reality of this legislation: twice he had seen a scientific journal he had produced in Altona suppressed, the authorities having considered blasphemous a part of the material he intended to publish. In vain he had appealed to Bernstorff. Now, writing to the bishops, to the rector and professors of the university, and to the religious author- ities to explain the decree, he declared he was "entirely convinced that it was perilous both for the impartial search for truth and for the dis- covery of errors of the past to prevent true patriots from writing freely in accordance with their own ideas and conscience."[7] The same Septem- ber Struensee took care to assure himself that the new liberty would be guaranteed to gazettes as well. Voltaire was exultant. Addressing him- self to Christian VII he wrote:

> Monarque vertueux, quoique né despotique
> tu rend ses droits à l'homme et tu permets qu'on pense.

In Paris, continued Voltaire, in order "to have wit" one had to go to ask permission "of the police." Throughout the whole world governments believed civil disorders were nourished, or even created, by writers. But freedom of the press was asked for with greater and greater insistence everywhere in Europe.

---

[4] *Notizie del mondo*, no. 13, 12 February 1771, p. 99 (Copenhagen, 12 January). Earlier, in January, this gazette had announced that "the king, having thought well to suppress his secret council, has dismissed those who were members of it." (Ibid., no. 4, 12 January 1771, p. 26 [Copenhagen, 11 December 1770].)

[5] Ibid., no. 83, 16 October 1770, p. 677 (Copenhagen, 18 September).

[6] Commager, *Struensee*, pp. 252ff.

[7] Ibid., p. 257.

Le Parnasse ne veut ni tyrans ni bigots
c'est une république éternelle et suprême
qui n'admet d'autre loi que la loi de Thélème
elle est plus libre encor que le vaillant Bernois,
le noble de Venise et l'esprit genevois.[8]

The new intellectual liberty that was breaking out in Europe was thus more truly free than the republican traditions of Berne, Venice, and Geneva, to which Voltaire's thought still naturally turned in search of examples and precedents. And—surprising and significant—the new liberty found its expression precisely in this land of the north, which had a tradition of and reputation for despotism.

As Reverdil tells us, there arose "a multitude of works published against the old administration." To free himself from Bernstorff and other influential figures of the past Struensee appealed to public opinion. It was difficult for the government and court to adapt itself to the new and disquieting situation produced by the abolition of censorship. "That absolute liberty of the press attached many foreign writers to the new favorite, but it did not support his aims," wrote Reverdil, who was also taken by surprise by such a radical step taken by Struensee. "Instead of attacking the former ministers, or treating boldly matters of philosophy, native writers set about criticizing the new measures taken as soon as they appeared."[9]

Since that epoch many judgments of the first results of freeing the press have been negative, the critics often calling attention to the acrimonious and libelous tone taken by writers. But even the American historian H. S. Commager, who seems to agree with the critics, has had to recognize that "many urgent reforms were discussed: land reform, abolition of service, guilds, free trade, banks, lackeyism, military affairs, the university and education and especially a Norwegian university, economic conditions in Norway and Iceland, and innumerable others. Some fundamental and startlingly modern changes in government were advanced and many of the reforms of the Struensee period anticipated."[10] The freedom of the press—precisely because the flood that responded to the measures taken by Struensee was energetic and turbulent—became the center of the political struggle. In April 1771 the

[8] "Virtuous monarch, although born despotic / you give man his rights and permit one to think." "Parnassus wants neither tyrants nor bigots / it is an eternal and supreme republic / which admits no other law than that of Thélème / it is more free than the valiant men of Berne, / the noble of Venice, and the spirit of Geneva." "Epître au roi de Danemark Christian VII sur la liberté de la presse accordée dans tout ses états," in Voltaire, *Oeuvres complètes*, vol. 10 (1877), pp. 421ff.

[9] Reverdil, *Struensée*, p. 174.

[10] Commager, *Struensee*, p. 260.

law was republished and extended. "By edict of His Majesty are abolished all taxes on books, maps, and so on, which come from foreign lands, in order to advance human knowledge and promote the greater flowering of literature. For the same motive His Majesty concedes total freedom of the press."[11]

At the same time Struensee undertook a series of measures intended to extend the area of religious tolerance. In this case it was not a question of a declaration of principles, as with the freedom of the press, but of isolated interventions on the most controversial issues. The Moravian brothers were admitted to Denmark and invited to establish themselves in Jutland. All restrictions on the Quakers were removed in October 1771. Baptisms of non-Protestants became public, "the king having promised Roman Catholics the free exercise of their religion," as the gazette of Florence announced.[12] These and other episodes made the Danish Church, which had traditionally been subservient to the state, more and more suspicious and hostile. The advance of reform continued nonetheless. The construction of a large church in the capital was suspended. The chapel of a hospital was suppressed and transformed into a department for people with venereal diseases. Laws on matrimony, divorce, illegitimacy, and infanticide became less rigid. All luxury was excluded from funerals. The dead were interred outside cities. "Those who have noble tombs in the churches will be able to erect them in the countryside and decorate them as they like."[13] At the end of 1771 Altona was declared "an absolutely free commercial city." "Liberty of conscience" was extended to "all sects, none excluded." "Any foreigners can establish themselves in that city and leave at their pleasure. . . . They may adopt whatever profession, art, or trade that pleases them most; . . . make use of their talents with full freedom, whatever their calling."[14]

All these measures made the Lutheran clergy more and more hostile to Struensee. They were already scandalized by the reputation for immorality surrounding the queen's favorite and by the advanced ideas that were attributed to him with increasing insistence. Had he not proclaimed his admiration for Voltaire openly by sending to Paris, in the name of Christian VII, a contribution for the erection of a statue to the philosophe? And was not his inspiration Helvétius, as was said?[15]

[11] *Notizie del mondo*, no. 46, 8 June 1771, p. 360 (Copenhagen, 13 April).

[12] Ibid., no. 22, 16 March 1771, p. 169 (Copenhagen, 12 February). This measure was also noted in the *Storia dell'anno 1771*, p. 113.

[13] *Notizie del mondo*, no. 46, 8 June 1771, p. 360 (Copenhagen, 8 May).

[14] Ibid., no. 8, 28 January 1772, p. 60 (Copenhagen, 28 December 1771).

[15] Commager, *Struensee*, p. 266 n. 1: the Hanseatic diplomat Meinig said that *De l'esprit* by Helvétius was Struensee's favorite book. In the work of Reverdil there is an interesting discussion of how Struensee, when alienated from the pietistic background in which he grew up, developed a skeptical attitude hostile to all religious sects. "The study of physi-

One measure in particular struck the Lutheran Church from the beginning of Struensee's rule, the limitation of religious festivals, carried out through an edict of 26 October 1770: nine were abolished and two were moved to Sunday.[16] Here two fundamental nexes of his policy were joined: the problem of liberty and that of the peasants. The freedom of peasants was as important as that of the press and civil society. The limitation on festivals was a step toward the planned transformation of village life. The greater part of reform for peasants was still to be accomplished, although for more than ten years the Danish elite had been persuaded that it would no longer be possible to tolerate the influence of noble lords over recruitment for the militia, the heavy and arbitrary work services, the system of open fields, triennial rotation, the chronic scarcity of cattle, the backwardness of agricultural implements, and in Norway, the system of the manse, which impeded any commercialization of the landholding and made economic progress difficult.

A number of academies and committees had discussed the means of escape from this labyrinth (on 31 March 1755 an edict had already stopped censorship of works on agriculture and the economy). Notable progress had been made, but not thanks to government intervention. The great proprietors themselves—the Bernstorff, the Moltke, and the monarch—had reorganized their estates, attempting to transform them into model farms. Work services and obligations for military service had been transformed into money payments. The "most hurtful communal system" was breached, and the authorities were invited to effect its abolition. In January 1770 it was abolished in Schleswig-Holstein.[17]

Men like Reverdil, who had been particularly active in this phase of preparation for agrarian reform, could hope that with the new regime the transformation would be completed on the basis of circumspect, effective, and gradual projects. But he was also the first to realize that it was difficult to create the necessary unity of intent within the elite. Projects continued, but the will to bring them to conclusion was lacking. When Struensee entered the government, in the autumn of 1770, "the

---

ology launched him into Epicureanism; uniting the experiments of Haller with the metaphysics of Helvétius he persuaded himself that our organs produce thought by themselves and that our ideas are basically no more than sensations. He concluded that our sole end should be to arrive at pleasant sensations that were not harmful to others, and that one could ignore all the perceptions and opinions of other men." Reverdil hastened to add that in judging Struensee, or others, one should not forget that "the conduct of men depends more often on their character than on their opinions, and that choice influences their fate less than circumstances" (Reverdil, *Struensee* pp. 59ff.).

[16] The edict is in *Notizie del mondo*, no. 97, 4 December 1770, p. 790 (Copenhagen, 6 November). On 28 December 1771, no. 104, p. 803 (Copenhagen, 30 November), the extension of this measure to Holstein was reported.

[17] Commager, *Struensee*, pp. 90ff.

College of agriculture was enervated and ineffective, and reform was passing from public to private hands."[18] As in other areas of activity, he soon demonstrated the need for new instruments and new men. On 19 November the College of agriculture was abolished and replaced by a general commission, in which Georg Christian Oeder became particularly active. He was a German educated at Göttingen, a doctor, botanist, and fervent partisan of reform. On 20 February 1771 came the first important result. A decree, as the gazette of Florence reported, freed "from the rule of the nobility all peasants who were not truly serfs."[19] Work services were not abolished, but the lords were no longer able to fix them at will. Instead, they had to calculate on the basis of cultivated land and the harvest—a kind of tariff imposed and controlled by the state. A maximum was also introduced, and peasants were ensured a degree of legal protection. This was not enough to resolve the problem, but the measures were nevertheless sufficient to raise the ire of more conservative nobles. The uncertain situation blocked Struensee when the general commission finally proposed to free the peasants from the heavy burdens weighing on them through recruitment for the militia. Struensee did not dare take this decisive step. Seeking some way out of the situation he put his hopes in Reverdil, requesting that he return to Denmark. "He is believed recalled to this court—we read in the *Notizie del mondo*—to carry out a project regarding improvements in agriculture, and also the freeing of peasants from serfdom, a project already prepared by the said Reverdil when he was employed here."[20] The situation in the summer of 1771 was anything but peaceful. In the variety of differences dividing lords and administrators on the royal lands from peasants, Struensee regularly took the part of the latter.[21] But when, as in Jutland, it became a matter of "a revolution on the question of the head tax," there was nothing to do but send "a detachment of troops against the insurgents" and force them to pay.[22] The situation in Norway was also disturbing, where a general commission, with an edict dated 14 January 1771, succeeded in bringing about a notable lightening of the system of the manse, opening the way to investment and improvements.[23]

[18] Ibid., p. 103.

[19] *Notizie del mondo*, no. 32, 20 April 1771, p. 249 (Copenhagen, 16 March).

[20] Ibid., no. 80, 5 October 1771, p. 619 (Copenhagen, 7 September). On the complex motives for this action, see Reverdil, *Struensee*, pp. 238ff. To be sure, as he himself says, "after the interior of the palace [the life of the court], the first object of my interest was the freeing of the peasants" (ibid., p. 270).

[21] Commager, *Struensee*, pp. 111ff.

[22] *Notizie del mondo*, no. 55, 9 July 1771, p. 434 (Copenhagen, 15 June).

[23] Commager, *Struensee*, p. 114. See Halvdan Koht, *Les luttes des paysans en Norvège du XIVe au XIXe siècle* (Paris: Payot, 1929), pp. 240ff.

The agricultural innovations undertaken by Struensee were only one aspect, although a central one, of his financial and economic policy. He, like all European reformers in the sixties and seventies, attempted to find a way to unburden the state of debts inherited from the past and to introduce greater freedom of trade. There were economies and reorganizations of the fiscal apparatus on one hand, and battles against the restraints imposed by mercantilism on the other. Simple fiscal measures would be insufficient, as he knew well, thanks partly to the technical ability of his brother Carl August. In order to balance the budget it would be necessary to transform the entire Danish economy. He began by dismantling the large, privileged companies that dominated trade with Africa, Asia, Iceland, Greenland, and so on. The example of the Mediterranean was typical: the conflict with Algiers contributed to the fiscal deficit and demonstrated the inadequacy of the traditional system of commerce. The problem was political as well: Benstorff personified mercantilism, Struensee economic liberalism. Small-scale protection of local manufacturing was abandoned, and the high customs tariffs of 1762, raised still higher in 1768, were adjusted. These were all premature efforts—Struensee was convinced—which would impoverish the country and benefit only small groups and a few individuals.[24] He found support from a few technical men, especially from Ole S. Phil, professor of political economy at the University of Copenhagen. He received support from an active group of merchants. From Norway—a nest of mariners—came pressing appeals for liberalization. For financial reasons he did not turn Copenhagen into a free port, but he rapidly dismantled internal and external trade restrictions. A provision of 3 September 1771 radically lowered tariffs on imports in all protected zones. Import of tea was freed, and the tax on rum reduced. Butter, herrings, meat, and so on, circulated more freely, as did salt from England and cattle from Sweden. The most famous of these measures was that of 26 December 1771, which established free trade in foreign grain in southern Norway. Thus ended one of the most important monopolies the Danes had reserved for themselves, which had left Norway threatened with recurrent famine. The harsh winter of 1771, and the impending peril of hunger, obliged Struensee to make a decision, and he chose the route of free trade, a decision made all the more difficult because famine, throughout his brief government, obliged him to be occupied continually with the fundamental problem of bread in the capital and provinces alike.[25]

If the agrarian reforms and economic measures Struensee took did

[24] Carl August Struensee said that "the time of large-scale manufacturing has not yet arrived in Denmark." See Commager, *Struensee*, p. 158 n. 1.

[25] Commager, *Struensee*, pp. 148ff.

not fail to attract the attention of observers, the interest he aroused by
the changes he administered to the state and judicial apparatus of Denmark was even greater. His battle against delays in the German chancery
were noted even in Italy.[26] Expectations and criteria for the qualifica-
tions of functionaries were changed.[27] Seniority would have greater importance in their careers.[28] Even more needy of reform was the judicial
apparatus. When a list of criminals in Copenhagen prisons revealed the
delays of the authorities, the names of "judges who have been lacking
in their duties were recorded."[29] On 26 April 1771 the death penalty for
thieves was abolished. "They will be publicly whipped, branded, and
condemned to forced labor for life." The wife of a condemned criminal
would be considered a widow. "Her husband, being dead to society,
should also be dead for her."[30] This reform of criminal law aroused particular interest in Tuscany. The edict of Christian VII was reproduced in
full in the Florentine gazette two months later, with an ample and interesting comment entrusted to an "Englishman who loves his country and
humanity." British law in the matter of thefts, he said, certainly needed
reform. Doctor Johnson had written justly in this matter. "The ingenious author of the *Rambler*, number 114, has some excellent reflections
on this subject. . . . To equal robbery with murder is to reduce murder
to robbery."[31] "The habit of condemning to death criminals for simple
theft was censured by Chancellor More in his *Utopia*. In a word, we are
risking taking a life that might be made useful to the public." Denmark
had given an example that others might follow. Why should "the Dane"
be "more humane than the Englishman"?[32] The abolition of torture, on
30 December 1771, also recalled a need felt elsewhere in Europe.[33]

[26] *Notizie del mondo*, no. 14, 16 February 1771, pp. 107ff. (Copenhagen, 15 January).

[27] Ibid., no. 37, 7 May 1771, p. 289 (Copenhagen, 9 April).

[28] Ibid., no. 19, 5 March 1771, p. 147 (Copenhagen, 5 February).

[29] Ibid., no. 29, 9 April 1771, p. 226 (Copenhagen, 5 March). See *Gazzetta di Parma*,
no. 15, 9 April (Copenhagen, 8 March).

[30] *Notizie del mondo*, no. 46, 8 June 1771, p. 360 (Copenhagen, 8 May).

[31] In his *Rambler*, no. 114, 20 April 1751, Samuel Johnson underlined the violent and
tyrannical character of much penal legislation. Seeing a condemned man led to the gallows, others should ask themselves: "Who knows if this man is less guilty than I?" Punishment of theft with the death sentence was an ineffective and a cruel measure. In fact,
"rapine and violence are hourly increasing" and the image of justice was becoming ever
more "sanguinary." "To equal robbery with murder is to reduce murder to robbery, to
confound in common minds the gradations of iniquity." "The frequency of capital punishments rarely hinders the commission of a crime." And Johnson concluded his article evoking the name of Thomas More.

[32] *Notizie del mondo*, no. 61, 30 July 1771, p. 481 (Copenhagen, 4 July).

[33] It was said "better that a guilty man go unpunished than that an innocent one suffer." "The instruments of torture used up to now to discover crime must be destroyed.
The confession of a suspect should be ascertained by witnesses and judicial proofs alone"

These reports and discussions were witness to the international echoes of Struensee's reforms, but for distant observers they veiled growing internal tensions in the Danish situation. As the minister proceeded on his way he continually alienated new groups and individuals. So violent were the accusations of libertinism, atheism, contempt for the traditions of the country, even expressed through pamphlets and other works, that the edict on freedom of the press, hardly a year after its promulgation, was, if not abandoned, at least qualified. On 7 October 1771 it was explained that the edict had been promulgated "with the sole end that persons zealous for the public good, and particularly the advantage of their fellow citizens, could freely make known their knowledge of the sciences." Instead, "ill-intentioned people" had intervened, printing "pernicious works worthy of condemnation." "*Libelles*" and "pasquinades," along with "other seditious writings," should be prohibited. New instructions established that "although there is no longer supervision of the press, all authors should take care that what they write is not contrary to laws and ordinances." "A publisher will not be permitted to print any work of which he does not know the author personally, for whom he must answer if he does not denounce him, so that no work can be printed without the name of the author or publisher."[34]

By the autumn of 1771 Struensee's reformist impulse was reduced to a defensive. The hatred he had aroused was embodied, in the winter, in a group of nobles and officers who found a point of unity in the pedantic and ambitious queen mother, Juliana Maria, the second wife of Federick v. The coup d'etat was carried out in the night of 16 and 17 January 1772. The order for the arrest of Struensee and Queen Caroline Mathilde was signed by the king, Christian vii, who was more and more ill and unaware. "Yesterday," wrote a correspondent from Copenhagen on 18 January 1772, "was undoubtedly one of the most memorable days of this reign."

Nor did the drama involve only the protagonists. The people of the capital intervened in the political events, giving them a significance that went beyond the intentions of the instigators of the coup d'état. An immense crowd "transported with joy . . . almost drew behind it the carriage of the king" and illuminated the whole city. Signs of loyalty to the monarchy, and of hate for the innovators, rapidly took preoccupying forms. "Damaged and assaulted by the furor of the too-zealous plebs" were "more than seventy houses of persons most suspected in this af-

(cited in Commager, *Struensee*, p. 212). A handsome print depicting penal reform is reproduced in Danstrup and Koch, eds., *Danmarks historie*, vol. 4, p. 446.

[34] *Notizie del mondo*, no. 90, 9 November 1771, p. 691 (Copenhagen, 12 October).

fair." It was necessary to announce at the sound of the trumpet that, "however content and grateful for the fidelity and love shown by all," the sovereign was greatly displeased by the disorders of the previous night and prohibited them rigorously in the future.[1] Queen Mathilde was exiled. "Count Struensee, poorly dressed, and in chains, is locked in a dark prison, where, although arousing compassion among men of feeling, the people and enemies of the disgraced minister are able to satiate their feelings of revenge through this horrible spectacle."[2]

What had happened in Denmark? In Florence, the diarist Giuseppe Pelli wondered, "truly a plot" or "a court incident"? As for the cause of the catastrophe, it seemed to him that it was "the imprudence of the queen, a rapid change in government, customs and laws in a still-barbarous nation, and the weakness of the king." His sympathy nonetheless was with the fallen minister. Even the "crimes" with which he was accused "were born more of poor judgment than of the heart." He foresaw "more victims." "Good as well," he concluded, "should be done suitably, and by all."[3]

The very detailed and exact chronicle in the Florentine gazette expressed a sense of dismay for the unexpected reversal of fortunes, and pity for the unhappy minister. There was too much disquiet and uncertainty in the situation of the court and people for the *Notizie del mondo* to accede to the official optimism. The solemn thanks to the Most High resounding in the churches of Copenhagen were not sufficient to prevent quite different voices from being heard, even from a distance. "The police court published an order by express command of the king that those who, either before or after the tumult of the seventeenth and the following days, had taken or might have in their hands property belonging to others, could return this to the court in the space of eight days to be restored to the owners without paying a fine."[4] At the same time when "the bishop of Zeeland, the faculty of theology, and all the clergy presented themselves at the palace by order of the king, His Majesty gave them hope that the change that had occurred in the court would not be displeasing to the clergy either."[5]

Struensee's trial began in an atmosphere of intense reaction. The

---

[1] Ibid., no. 12, 11 February 1772, p. 92 (Copenhagen, 18 January).

[2] Ibid., no. 14, 18 February 1772, p. 106 (Copenhagen, 15 January).

[3] Pelli, *Efemeridi*, vol. 29, p. 28, 4 April 1772.

[4] *Notizie del mondo*, no. 15, 22 February 1772, p. 115 (Copenhagen, 28 January). See no. 35, 2 May 1772, p. 294 (Copenhagen, 5 April), where it appears that the losses suffered in the sack amounted to "38,000 rixdollars." Indemnity was supplied to the extent of 6,000 rixdollars furnished by the king. "We will attempt to make up the remainder through a general collection in the churches."

[5] Ibid., no. 15, 22 February 1772, p. 115 (Copenhagen, 28 January).

scene was dominated by the theologian Balthasar Münter, "pastor of one of the two German churches of Copenhagen, a pompous and accomplished preacher who knows how to conciliate unction and vehemence," Reverdil wrote.[6] He declared the following during a solemn religious ceremony: "A few of the impious dominated us, the unjust held our temporal happiness in their hands. . . . They justified transgression and opened the way to committing it; they poisoned our manners with the corruption of their abominable example. They had no other thought than to suffocate all virtuous sentiment. . . . What terrible things had they not already done! Thanks to that providence that did not leave us in the prey of their perverse intentions" when "their bloody designs were about to show themselves in sedition and butchery."[7] Peter Frederick Suhm, "from the deputation of the tribunal of state inquisition," said no less clearly: "Enough, and for too long our religion and virtue have been cast under foot." "Then the country dissolved in tears, fear and terror reigned in every part, and the Danish name was tarnished." "Thanks to the patriots and all others whose upright and pure intentions tore the veil assunder." He begged the king to deport those who were not Danish. "Turn away from foreign languages and from traitors too lazy to learn our tongue."[8] Meanwhile there was a reorganization of the army. "The regiment of the king and that of Prince Frederick, which had been dispersed to various villages of Zeeland, have been recalled and restored to the place they occupied before."[9] "The usage has resumed of closing the city gates on Sundays and other festivals in the time when sermons are made in the churches."[10] A kind of *habeas corpus* decreed on 3 April 1771 was withdrawn, on the basis of which "everyone would enjoy in his house a full and an entire liberty and not be subjected to interference in their affairs by day or night guards of the police." Measures were taken to ensure that "order" and "good conduct" would reign in the inns and cafes. "Idlers" were not to circulate in the city.[11] As the trial of Struensee and his collaborator Brandt began, there was much preoccupation with their souls. "Preacher Münter" visited the first, whereas the second "received every day an hour's visit from minister Hee."[12] The threat of the death penalty weighed ever more heavily on them.[13] Meanwhile, disquiet among the

---

[6] Reverdil, *Struensee*, p. 427.

[7] *Notizie del mondo*, no. 17, 29 February 1772, pp. 130ff. (Copenhagen, 1 February).

[8] Ibid., no. 18, 3 March 1772, pp. 139ff. (Copenhagen, 4 February).

[9] Ibid., no. 19, 7 March 1772, p. 148 (Copenhagen, 7 February).

[10] Ibid., no. 20, 10 March 1772, p. 155 (Copenhagen, 12 February).

[11] Ibid., no. 21, 14 March 1772, pp. 162ff. (Copenhagen, 15 February).

[12] Ibid., no. 25, 28 March 1772, pp. 194ff. (Copenhagen, 29 February).

[13] Ibid., no. 27, 4 April 1772, pp. 210ff. (Copenhagen, 10 March).

populace of the capital grew. "Every day the plebes show some excess needful of correction. At night they go about in crowds shouting in the streets, breaking lampposts, windows, and doors. The disorder could lead to worse, and more will appear every day, if the tribunal of the police does not take prompt measures. To this end a rigorous edict has been published."[14] The law on liberty of the press received another blow, still without being formally revoked, with the institution of surveillance of gazettes in the capital.[15] Torture was allowed again.[16]

The trial of Struensee, Brandt, and those accused with them unfolded with tragic solemnity. "Count Brandt, supposed criminal of state," showed himself proudly indifferent. "He talks familiarly with the guards . . . this conversation and his habit of playing the flute permit him to pass the day in good humor. He plays especially when he sees Minister Hee arrive; he entertains him with some concert pieces and then asks if they are not better than all the discourse they could have together. But he still doubts he will be condemned to death and always remarks when the minister appears: 'It seems to me that my head is separating itself from my shoulders.' This idea, certainly not the most pleasant, does not make him lose the least part of his good humor."[17] The accusations directed against Struensee were colored more and more with Danish national feeling: the fallen minister had published "royal edicts in the German language." "Even military drills were being conducted in German." Only after his departure did one hear "the native tongue" in the army.[18]

Interrogators followed one after another. The threat of the scaffold arose more and more clearly, even if the rumor spread that the death sentence would be commuted "to perpetual imprisonment in the castle of Monkolm in Norway."[19] Particularly uncertain was the fate of the queen. Her brother, George III of England, intervened to protect her.[20] Thus, although she was finally confined to a castle, Struensee and Brandt had to face death. The first "implored the clemency of his sovereign," asking that the execution be shielded from the "eyes of the public."[21] On 25 April the same sentence was read for both: "his right hand will be cut off, his head severed from his shoulders, and his body cut into four pieces, which will be attached to a wheel; the head and hand

---

[14] Ibid., no. 28, 7 April 1772, p. 219 (Copenhagen, 12 March).

[15] Ibid., no. 33, 25 April 1772, p. 279 (Copenhagen, 30 March).

[16] Commager, *Struensee*, p. 297.

[17] *Notizie del mondo*, no. 31, 18 April 1772, p. 262 (Copenhagen, 18 March).

[18] Ibid., no. 32, 21 April 1772, p. 272 (Copenhagen, 24 March).

[19] Ibid., no. 33, 25 April 1772, p. 279 (Copenhagen, 30 March).

[20] Ibid., no. 37, 9 May 1772, p. 310 (Copenhagen, 12 April).

[21] Ibid., no. 39, 16 May 1772, p. 326 (Copenhagen, 18 April).

will be mounted on a stake." Struensee did not let "escape the least surprise," saying that he "had had time to prepare himself for such news." Brandt hoped to the end that his sentence would be commuted. "From then on the pastors Münter and Hee did not leave the state prisoners." On the morning of 28 April the sentence was executed. "The said gentlemen demonstrated courage and constancy on the fatal occasion. The scaffold was ringed by four ranks of soldiers and mariners, but there was not the least sign of disorder." The completed sentence was not yet published so that Struensee was only accused of "too much despotism in affairs," of having caused three million *écus'* worth of damage to the treasury, of having dismissed "a regiment of guards without reason, and of having published improper ordinances in the capital." Brandt "was condemned for crimes committed against the person of the king."[22]

At the beinning of May a thick work by Münter, entitled *Recollections of the Conversion of Count Struensee*, was published. The author intended it to serve above all to demonstrate his pastoral ability, and the great power of religion. In reality, it seems to have been interpreted more as a demonstration that the two condemned men were not, as had been said, "libertines" and "materialists," having always shown "a sensible spirit and a generous heart." "Their last wishes were to pray for the health of the king, the royal family, the people, and the state, and a moment before their death they said they pardoned with good heart the instigators of their torment and believed they had always acted with good intentions." Even the relationship between the two men was moving. Struensee "seemed to be more concerned about the disgrace of his friend than about his own."[23]

Thus the image of the condemned men changed rapidly and soon aroused no longer just astonished curiosity, but also sympathy from a growing number of people. Meanwhile, popular discontent grew. Mariners reached the point of loudly demanding to be paid monthly rather than trimonthly. The king rejected their demands but refrained from

[22] Ibid., no. 41, 23 May 1772, p. 343 (Copenhagen, 28 April). The article of the law on the basis of which condemnations were made "for having offended with words the king or the queen or having made any attempt against their life or that of their children" is published in no. 42, 26 May 1772, p. 351 (Copenhagen, 2 May). The sentence against Struensee and Brandt is reported in full in nos. 45–50 and 52, on 6, 9, 13, 16, 20, 23, 30 June 1772, pp. 374ff., 383ff., 389ff., 407ff.

[23] Ibid., no. 43, 30 May 1772, pp. 359ff. (Copenhagen, 5 May). The *Gazzetta di Parma* is also rich in details on the "striking developments in Denmark," and whole pages were dedicated to a discussion of the government after his execution. See no. 22, 2 June 1772 (Augsburg, 23 May), and no. 23, 9 June 1772 (Augsburg, 30 May).

punishing them for their audacity.[1] At the beginning of 1773 they arose again, claiming "that their officers did not respect their rights, that they received poor rations, and that agreements with them were broken." The continued agitation of mariners and the insistence with which they presented their demands made some say they had become the "Janissaries of Copenhagen." On their "fourth attempt" repression struck. Two were condemned to death, "others to the punishment of the *cat* (an instrument covered with sharp points of iron that tore the backs of its victims)." "These two, after this punishment, were condemned to forced labor for life, three others were condemned to the punishment of the cat alone."[2]

Meanwhile, political discussion resumed in a more violent manner. Many letters were published attacking Münter, who continued to pride himself on the conversion of Struensee. The latter, he said, "did not believe he was talking with a journalist when he confessed his sins." Bynch, the person responsible for this last accusation, author of a pamphlet entitled *Man of State*, was imprisoned and then freed.[3] At the beginning of the new year a "fanatic" who had "truly sought the glory of martyrdom in writing a book entitled the *Prophet*, was granted his desire" and condemned to the same sentence as Struensee. "The sentence is now under the eyes of the king, who must sign it, and he is most impatient to see it put into effect." He was called Thura, and he criticized the queen mother in particular.[4] His passionate accusation of those responsible for the trial of Struensee, the "famous victim," had the effect of "inciting the inflamed imagination of all who sought reprisal."[5] His book was "in the hands of all, despite precautions taken to suppress it."[6] The death penalty for Thura was finally suspended, and he was imprisoned in a fortress; his goods were confiscated and his works—*Teller of Truth, Response to Friends of the Country, Letter from Germany to the Hypocritical Priests of the Great Idol*—were burned by the executioner.[7] In the spring of 1773 it was necessary to state that "despite the rigorous penalties threatening printers and booksellers publishing works directed against the court, these have continued to multiply, and impru-

---

[1] Ibid., no. 54, 7 July 1772, p. 446 (Copenhagen, 13 June), and no. 56, 14 July 1772, p. 463 (Copenhagen, 19 June).

[2] Ibid., no. 12, 9 February 1773, p. 91 (Copenhagen, 9 January).

[3] Ibid., no. 73, 12 September 1772, p. 601 (Copenhagen, 18 August).

[4] Ibid., no. 12, 9 February 1773, p. 92 (Copenhagen, 9 January). The same notice is in the *Gazzetta di Milano*, no. 6, 10 February 1773 (Copenhagen, 18 January). There Thura's book was published as *Il pronostico*.

[5] *Notizie del mondo*, no. 13, 13 February 1773, p. 99 (Copenhagen, 18 January).

[6] Ibid., no. 15, 20 February 1773, p. 114 (Copenhagen, 26 January).

[7] Ibid., no. 36, 14 May 1773, p. 284 (Copenhagen, 13 April).

dent persons, like Thura, have continued to appear."[8] In Copenhagen, we read the *Gazzetta di Milano*, one continued "to talk openly of the causes of the revolution that has aroused so much uproar in this kingdom."[9]

The political situation remained tense and difficult. The news of the "revolution that has occurred in Stockholm," that is, the announcement of the coup d'état of Gustavus III in neighboring Sweden, increased the general sense of insecurity.[10] To be sure, this could be seen as a confirmation of the absolutist tendencies that seemed to be reaffirming themselves in the Scandinavian countries, a continuation of seventeenth-century tradition. Even the *Notizie del mondo* noted in November how in Copenhagen the "anniversary of the famous revolution that occurred in this kingdom in 1660, when the constitution was changed," was celebrated with particular solemnity.[11] But these historical memories were not sufficient to hide the fact that the Swedish "revolution" might prove to be a threat for Denmark, which was interested, like the Russia of Catherine II, in preserving the "liberty" in Sweden. Otherwise neighboring powers might have to fear a revival of bellicosity in the kingdom of Gustavus III. And in fact, in Copenhagen, there was an intensification of warlike preparations against Sweden and against its ally France.[12]

In reality this was a false alarm. Catherine II was too preoccupied with the war against the Turks. France preferred not to break relations. In Copenhagen the foreign threat only distracted attention from the underlying internal discontent that had played for a moment with the reforms of Struensee but now seemed to turn against the judges who had condemned them. There were other small signs of the presence of this fever. In October 1771 the sale of objects once belonging to the fallen ministers reached high prices at auction as souvenirs. "Some have put these things into cases and frames with glass to preserve the memory of those unhappy famous people."[13] In November, measures taken against "people of all ages and both sexes, and particularly against thieves who in the past anarchy committed a thousand villanies," also revived memories of the coup d'état.[14] The subsistence crisis, which con-

---

[8] Ibid., no. 32, 20 April 1773, p. 251 (Copenhagen, 30 March). On Christian Thura, see *DBL*, vol. 24, p. 87.

[9] *La Gazzetta di Milano*, no. 9, 3 March 1773 (Copenhagen, 30 January).

[10] *Notizie del mondo*, no. 74, 15 September 1772, p. 608 (Copenhagen, 24 August).

[11] Ibid., no. 91, 14 November 1772, p. 745 (Copenhagen, 20 October).

[12] Ibid., no. 78, 29 September 1772, p. 640 (Copenhagen, 1 September). In subsequent issues there was further talk of this military preoccupation. See, for example, no. 89, 7 November 1772, p. 728 (Copenhagen, 13 October).

[13] Ibid., no. 91, 14 November 1772, p. 745 (Copenhagen, 20 October).

[14] Ibid., no. 101, 19 December 1772, p. 824 (Copenhagen, 23 November).

tinued to weigh on the life of the entire country, contributed to maintain "spirits in the greatest agitation."[15]

Wearisome and difficult was, thus, the attempt at restoration, at a return, as some hoped, to the years that had preceded the advent to the throne of Christian VII.[16] The curfew in the capital, the prohibition "to all mariners and soldiers, as well as journeymen and apprentices of shops, not to appear in the streets after seven in the evening, under rigorous penalties," were insufficient. A year had passed since the arrest of Struensee, and thus since the "famous revolution." But this "had left such sad impressions that many would not be secure in their lives if care was not taken to control the plebes."[17] The day of the first anniversary did not produce disorder "among mariners, soldiers, and so on, because of the king's rigorous orders, but still in many parts of the city the people could not do less than drink to the health of Queen Caroline Mathilde, thus making known their hatred of those believed to be her principal enemies."[18]

The parallel with Great Britain in the years of Wilkes was evident: a kind of popular anarchy barely kept in check by a conservative government. Danish internal politics vacillated among the queen mother's throwing a "great sum of money to a crowd of people" from the window of her apartments, the distribution of "alms in the city to many poor people," and the harsh punishment—as we have seen—of the most riotous mariners. The last measure had "much embittered other seamen" and provoked desertions of seventy-nine men altogether. "In other seaports they are equally discontented."[19] In May of the following year came news that in Sorö there had been "uprisings of peasants," obliging "the government to send in infantry to return the insurgents to order."[20]

The fundamental problems that the Struensee years opened, from the structure of the state to peasant serfdom, thus remained without solution. But a precarious equilibrium eventually returned. In the summer of 1773 a symbol in marble was erected in the royal gardens of

---

[15] Ibid., p. 825.

[16] Ibid., no. 5, 16 January 1773, p. 34 (Copenhagen, 19 December 1772) ("It seems that they want to put things into the state they were in before the last three or four years of the reign of Frederick v"); no. 14, 16 February, p. 106 (Copenhagen, 19 January) (a reference to Adam Moltke, who "had been at the head of affairs during the reign of Frederick v"); no. 15, 20 February 1773, p. 114 (Copenhagen, 26 January) (a sense of general delusion among Danes aware "of a return to the old system").

[17] Ibid., no. 13, 13 February 1773, p. 98 (Copenhagen, 18 January). See no. 16, 23 February 1773, p. 122 (Copenhagen, 30 January) ("the people are in great agitation" against the curfew).

[18] Ibid., no. 15, 20 February 1773, p. 114 (Copenhagen, 26 January).

[19] Ibid., no. 16, 23 February 1773, p. 114 (Copenhagen, 30 January).

[20] Ibid., no. 44, 31 May 1774, p. 347 (Copenhagen, 8 May).

Rosemburg, "in a new pleasure house," to celebrate this difficult and partially achieved conservative victory, "a Sampson in the act of dismembering a lion." "This fine allegory of the recent revolution is in Italian marble, which Frederick IV sent back while traveling in that country."[21]

The nature of the political and cultural climate of Denmark in the years immediately after Struensee is recounted for us by Isidoro Bianchi, a minor figure, but one not lacking in interest for the Lombard enlightenment. He arrived in Copenhagen in July 1774 and left in May 1776. He was employed as a secretary by Prince Raffadali, the Neapolitan minister at the court of Christian VII.[1] He was an open and a curious man who observed with great attention the country in which he found himself. He was welcomed with sympathy by local erudites. The writer Charlotte Dorothea Biehl offered her services as translator for his *Meditazioni*, which had encountered obstacles in Italy (it was even said that the book could have been "written by a Voltaire and by a Rousseau"). The Danish version appeared in Copenhagen in 1774, and the year after, in the same city, there came to light a "new edition" in Italian, "reviewed, corrected, and enriched with many additions by the same author."[2] The editor dedicated the book to Christian VII. One read in the French preface of "The treatise on public and private happiness": "What object could be more proper to present to a sovereign who, on his ascent to the throne, proclaimed that he sought glory only in love of the fatherland and who has already merited the names of father and friend of his people?" Closer to the reality of the country where Isidoro Bianchi found himself were the two chapters he added to the Danish edition, of which the most important was entitled "On Sedition." When he left Sicily, where he had been a professor, echoes of the violence of 1773 were still audible. As the editor wrote, Bianchi "did not think best to publish [this chapter] in Palermo because of the critical situation of Sicily at that time." In Denmark had come the time to make his conclusions known. "Some governments are, unfortunately, organized so that from time to time they are subject to a revolution." It was the task of philosophers to discover the causes of this situation and of monarchs to

---

[21] Ibid., no. 72, 7 September 1773, p. 587 (Copenhagen, 14 August).

[1] The *Notizie del mondo* announced the first audience of the minister in no. 71 on 3 September 1774, p. 563 (Copenhagen, 8 August). On Isidoro Bianchi, see *DBI*, vol. 10, pp. 132ff.

[2] *Meditazioni su vari punti di felicità pubblica e privata. Opera del sig. abate D. Isodoro Bianchi. Nuova edizione riveduta, corretta e di moltissime aggiunte arricchita dallo stesso autore* (Copenhagen: Claude Philibert, 1775).

adopt remedies. Both one and the other had first to be aware of the instability and uncertainty in which they operated. "A lazy and libertine people is always in a state of turbulence. It takes no more than a lack of provisions, misery, or some dreamed-up grievance, to put them off balance." Nor is there ever a lack of people interested in arousing them, "the ambitious," "the dissipated." "Their quarrels with the government, with the ministry, with the provisioning authorities, their poisoned words against the prince, and their specious emphases on liberty and public good insinuate them rapidly into the hearts of the people."[3] Once in movement, they are difficult to restrain. "What a horrible tragedy is a people in revolt! How ferocious is the air of self-assurance with which an insurgent walks before monuments of justice and power! With what daring tones he addresses ministers and senators!" In an uprising the "lowest people" draw along with them "the better educated." "The interest that moves a crowd, through misunderstood public good, to fear neither law nor prince, also arouses the spirit of the upper classes, although they appear to condemn the violence and disorder of the seditious mob. Educated people have broader views and greater needs. But still, between the vulgar plebs and more noble classes there is only a slight distance. The artisan has relatives among the plebs, and also friends among them." Isidoro Bianchi had seen with his own eyes, in Palermo, the outbreak of an insurrection and the formation of a consensus of revolt among different social levels. He had become more and more convinced that a strong monarchical authority was needed. The experience of Denmark must have confirmed his conclusions: "Politicians are wrong to seek to diminish crimes of the sovereign only to increase those of the people. . . . Unfortunate is the city where base plebs, youths, and vulgar women began to cry out 'arms and justice.' "[4] Only an intelligent and firm policy of monarchs and clergy would be able to respond adequately to the needs of the times and perils of the situation. It was important not to let oneself be tempted into violence. "I myself think uprisings should be controlled more with prudence than with iron. . . . A civil war ruins a state; it does not improve it. . . . Prompt condescension and sweetness may dampen popular fury and restore the initial state of tranquillity."[5] In the long run the only true remedy was

---

[3] Ibid., pp. 158ff.

[4] Ibid., pp. 161ff. Elsewhere he returned often to the polemic against the ambitious politician, the "fanatic patriot," the "badly understood spirit of patriotism," always in contrast with the calm meditation of the philosopher or economist. His experience in Sicily led him to maintain that "factions among nobles arouse the people." But his criticism of ambition, of the ardent reformer, could also reflect his experience in Denmark in the years of Struensee.

[5] Ibid., p. 164.

diffusion of education and culture. The example of Russia seemed significant. "Everyone knows the state of Russia before the era of Peter the Great, and soon St. Petersburg will become, perhaps, the Athens of the north."[6] Thus, in Sicily, only sciences and arts would remedy the lack "of industry."[7] Sovereigns and ministers should begin by taking account of a great truth: it is "easier to govern a cultivated and enlightened nation than a stupid and an ignorant one."[8]

Isidoro Bianchi could not conceive of a spread of enlightenment detached from the economic and social problems that interested him so much in Italy, which he rediscovered in Denmark. Even here the poor cultivator, the most useful of men, was commonly the most despised.[9] The effective political level of a country could be measured by the condition of peasants. "The freedom of a nation will be greater if peasants own the land they work."[10] With a formula still echoing his discussion with Giambattista Vasco, his "learned friend," Isidoro Bianchi affirmed that "public happiness can thus be considered to be cultivation of one's own land."[11] He did not confront the problem of serfdom in Denmark directly and limited himself to praising the efforts of the agrarian society.[12] But where his preference lay, and his program, appears clearly on every page of his *Meditazioni*. In the second of the two essays added in the Copenhagen edition, entitled "Del premio dovuto ai cittadini virtuosi," he concluded the matter openly: "The peasant would be more industrious if his efforts were paid. But the unhappy cultivator, burdened with payments and taxes, finds himself condemned to work lands that are not his own and to live in hunger and misery."[13]

In a series of reports to the *Novelle letterarie* of Florence, all from 1775–1776, Isidoro Bianchi described to Italians the state of the republic of letters in Denmark.[14] He discussed the University of Copenhagen. He wrote a funeral eulogy for Jacob Langebek, "whom I have always called the Muratori of this noble part of the north."[15] He paid attention to ecclesiastical history. At the beginning of 1776 he revealed a "plan of

[6] Ibid., p. 167.
[7] Ibid., p. 173.
[8] Ibid., p. 176.
[9] Ibid., p. 189.
[10] Ibid., p. 187.
[11] Ibid., p. 189.
[12] Ibid., p. 254.
[13] Ibid., p. 257.
[14] The relationship of Isidoro Bianchi with learned Danes can be seen in the collection of letters they sent to him, which is preserved in his papers in Milan, B. Ambrosiana, T. 133 Sup.
[15] *Novelle letterarie*, no. 39, 20 September 1775, cols. 618ff. On Jacob Langebek (1710–1775), see *DBL*, vol. 13, pp. 605ff.

a work on the state of science and the fine arts in Denmark." But "the distance from our Italy, the scarcity of travelers, the difficulty of obtaining books, and the different languages," he said, "are strong impediments to our knowing one another."[16] He had become a great admirer of the Danish language, "so sweet, harmonic, expressive, and susceptible to laconic philosophy." "But there is no Dane, even among the low people, who does not understand and speak German. There is no nation in Europe with more genius and disposition than the Danes for understanding foreign languages."[17] He followed with great interest the projects for reform of the schools and university proposed by the minister Ove Guldberg, "secretary in the cabinet of His Majesty himself, a man celebrated here for his published works and for the integrity of his manners."[18] One thing that struck him most was the development of the periodical press, which was organized in part by emigré French Protestants, such as La Beaumelle, and by Germans, such as Büsching, and especially by the Swiss, such as Cramer, Reverdil, and Mallet. To Mallet, the "celebrated" author, and to Reverdil, was due the *Mercure danois*, which was worthy of "particular mention." It added to its panorama of European culture "the political news of this capital and court," and also foreign news.[19] The publisher Claude Philibert, who published his *Meditazioni*, was also Swiss. Closely related to this activity was naturally freedom of the press, granted "without any restriction" at the time of the "unhappy and famous Count Struensee." Philibert had known how to act with audacity and constancy in this situation. "He published a manifesto in which he exhorted Danes to let him know of their works of all kinds, and foreigners of all nations to send him their works through the post, reserving for himself the right to choose. In less than a month Philibert received from various places many anonymous and pseudonymous works. . . . To encourage the public to write with complete freedom Philibert resolved to proceed so that each author would be absolutely sure he would remain unknown and obtained this end by placing outside his shop a little iron box fitted into the wall with the inscription *per amica silentia noctis*. Here by night anyone, on his or her own or through an intermediary, could place manuscripts without the least danger of being discovered." The works Philibert received were often "extremely passionate." At the same time, "to maintain the decorum and reputation of his journal, he published works taken from the *Mercure de*

[16] *Novelle letterarie*, no. 2, 12 January 1776, cols. 27ff.

[17] Ibid., no. 3, 19 January 1776, col. 44. The letter is addressed to Angelo M. Bandini.

[18] Ibid., col. 48. On Ove Guldberg (1731–1808), see DBL, vol. 11, pp. 76ff.

[19] *Novelle letterarie*, no. 11, 15 March 1776, cols. 189ff., to Giovanni Cristofano Amaduzzi.

France, the *Encyclopédie* of Yverdon, the *Almanac des Muses,* the *Oeuvres* by Voltaire, the *Gazzetta letteraria di Europa,* and German works."[20] Philibert also started a literary cabinet, "consisting of a large collection of books of history, belles-lettres, poetry, romances, tragedies, comedies, and of literary and political journals of France, Holland, Germany, and England." A certain Signor Michelin, a literary man, "a famous printer . . . a friend, and a member of the Apatisti of Florence," was at his disposal to serve the public "three hours in the morning and four after dinner." These were the advantages of freedom of the press, which nonetheless, Bianchi was convinced, also had negative aspects. "Considering well the results, in any kind of government it is more pernicious than useful for a wise legislator to permit it."[21] It was enough to think of the political work of Struensee and the great number of libelles against the government appearing at that time. The example of Josias Leopold Bynch was particularly significant. He had started to put out *The Publicist,* but "in the first two issues there were such daring propositions against the government that the author, despite the freedom of the press permitted without limits, was punished with six months in prison. When he was let out he set out to publish three other issues criticizing himself, with the title *The Anti-Publicist.* Then, because he could not restrain himself from saying ill, he began another journal, with no other object than to examine with scorn the sermons and homilies of the clergy, of which he published only four issues, because the government was again aroused against him."[22] Even cultural journals, like *The Critical Spectator of Native and Foreign Literature,* exhibited "much genius and little moderation" in those years. The *New Critical Journal* edited by Baden was better. "I took myself a good way to Elsinore to have the pleasure of knowing him personally."[23] More than praiseworthy was the campaign carried out by others by means of the "important news of jurisprudence," with the aim of "ending, if possible, the prejudices of those who torture the laws to make them say whatever they want." In all six "scientific journals" were published in Copenhagen. "That demonstrates clearly the will to promote the sciences and the arts, and the number of cultivated persons who, without counting the cost, make use of this effective means of instructing themselves."[24] Isidoro Bianchi, in observing the effects of freedom of the press, thus finally

---

[20] Ibid., no. 13, 29 March 1776, cols. 218ff., to G. C. Amaduzzi.

[21] Ibid., cols. 220ff.

[22] Ibid., cols. 221ff. On Josias Leopold Bynch (1747–1779) see *DBL,* vol. 4, pp. 416–17.

[23] *Novelle letterarie,* no. 13, 29 March 1776, col. 223. On Jacob Baden (1735–1804), see *DBL,* vol. 1, pp. 608ff.

[24] *Novelle letterarie,* no. 13, 29 March 1776, col. 224.

pronounced himself openly in favor of the diffusion and increased importance of journalism. "Even the political journals have, as Your Venerated Excellency knows [that is, the Prince of Belmonte Ventimiglia, 'maggiordomo maggiore of His Sicilian Majesty'], their great utility when they are written by persons of good sense who are well instructed and know how to present things with order and precision, who follow the thread of events, reflect on certain facts, reject falsehood in time, and do not leave the public anything to desire in matters concerning politics, which have so much influence on the fate of states and on all the actions, fortunes, and lives of men." A good journalist must know "the principal languages of Europe so as to express the news he receives from foreign countries on his own." And, naturally, he must be aware "of the general interests of princes, the political economy of different nations, their land and sea forces, the names and characters of persons employed as ministers." Through the work of journalists "nations grow closer to one another, commerce expands, citizens are enlightened, and the annals of our century and the history of our lands are preserved for posterity. Our descendants will have excellent materials for knowing the history of our times, and perhaps for writing it." It was truly a shame that "in the greater part of the cities of Europe" the "public sheets" were written by "inept persons, or men who support themselves with this trade." "Even in the freest cities, and still more in monarchies, it should be the task of government to pay attention above all to the authors of national journals, since these are the depositories of new laws, the censors of manners, the recounters of civil and economic developments, the faithful custodians of public memories. . . . In our Italy, . . . in particular, one should attempt to make these interesting and useful."[25] It was true, as he wrote in dispute with the author of the *Courrier du Bas Rhin*, the Piedmontese Jean Manzon, that "commerce in gazettes is carried out with more success in free and imperial cities than in monarchies." The example of Denmark was instructive in this regard. "There is perhaps no other city in Europe where one sees as many different journals as in Copenhagen."[26] Four times a week the *Notices of Copenhagen* appeared, with news about "everything that happens daily in the city and the two kingdoms, among births, deaths, marriages, auctions, sales, litigations, trials, losses, galas, festivals, new edicts, public functions, promotions, the vessels of all nations that pass the Sound to leave or enter the Baltic, shipwrecks, names of persons leaving or entering the realm, or passing from one city to another, the plans that are made, . . . the news of other foreign countries, articles on morality, verses, precepts of economy, an-

²⁵ Ibid., no. 22, 31 May 1776, cols. 366ff., to the Prince of Belmonte Ventimiglia.
²⁶ Ibid., no. 23, 7 June 1776, cols. 379–80, to the Prince of Belmonte Ventimiglia.

nouncements of new books." Thus, anyone, "without leaving the solitude of his house," can be "instructed in the most minute things." "And
here it is truly a miracle to see that gazettes of this kind are in the hands
of the lowest plebs, and of common women, and that everyone enjoys
information about daily occurrences." Two monthly journals provided
public notices, edicts, and "pieces of history." Denmark was clearly not
a country where knowledge of laws and other regulations was reserved
for the government, as happened elsewhere. "Here even the lowest people know all about what is planned for the public good in the royal cabinet, or in the chambers of finance, and all know how they should reg-
ulate their public affairs and how they will be judged." A weekly, the
Courier of the Night, bearing "the logo of a bat with spread wings," "contains articles on morality, poetry, economics, criticism, programs, dec-
lamations, and other matters worthy of public curiosity. For the most
part students at the university submit works for this journal." There
was one journal in French, two in German, and two others in Danish.
To this one could add the numerous periodicals published in the provinces, which Isidoro Bianchi described in detail. This was "without
counting those journals that came from all the other parts of Europe.
Now this genius is unequivocal proof of the progress made here in the
sciences and arts and culture of the nation."[27]

Isidoro Bianchi dedicated a further letter to another important center of Danish intellectual life, the university. He told its medieval history
at length, followed by its development during the Reformation, but did
not examine its current situation.[28] His account of historiography was
more detailed, although it was limited to the works of the chief scholars,
Langebek and Peter Frederick Suhm, "my friend," as he hastened to
add.[29] He revealed even more about the past of Denmark in his private
letters to Amaduzzi: "I never tire of contemplating the runic monuments here. . . . Iceland is an emporium of monuments. In the Edda
there is the history of the Danish idols. Their mythology, although pa-
gan, is poetic and revealed by a thousand other memories." Thus Bianchi absorbed the ideas of Mallet, Roger, and Reverdil. Even from a political point of view his conclusions did not differ much from those of
the Genevans. "Denmark has enjoyed an enviable peace since the expulsion of the unfortunate queen. Do not believe those who talk of despotism in this kingdom. . . . Here there are clear and intelligible laws,
and the despotic sovereign himself is judged when necessary. The low-

[27] Ibid.
[28] Ibid., no. 25, 21 June 1776, cols. 410ff., and no. 26, 28 June 1776, col. 429ff., to
Carlo di Firmian.
[29] Ibid., no. 29, 19 July 1776, cols. 475ff., to Carlo di Firmian.

est of the people know the code of laws and its penalties if they are acting against the laws. . . . In sum, here people are governed more by reason than by force."[30]

A few months later, in June 1776, on his way to Italy, Isidoro Bianchi continued to send reports from northern Europe to the *Novelle letterarie*. From Hamburg he announced his intention of "meeting in person Mr. Klopstock, who is commonly called the Virgil of Germany." But he found the Academy of Commerce of no less interest, "newly founded and frequented by youths from all parts of Europe." The director, Christoph Daniel Ebeling, was then publishing the second volume of his "collection of works on commerce written by the more celebrated Italians, and has included the *Discorso sul commercio di Sicilia*" that Bianchi had published with A. Rapetti, in Palermo, "at the beginning of a new edition of the *Saggi politici sul commercio di David Hume*."[31]

At the end of 1776 he was in Milan and vividly narrated his Danish experience to Pietro Verri, who for his part transmitted it to his brother Alessandro. "The tragedy of Count Struensee and Count Brandt," was naturally at the center of the story. Isidoro Bianchi

arrived at that court when the limbs of these unfortunates were still hanging on the walls of the city. . . . Struensee was the son of a preacher and doctor. . . . The queen took a violent passion for Struensee and he the same for her. The king left things to the favorite. Struensee, covered with honors and dignities, conducted business in the intervals left to him by the love of the queen. He was a man of ingenuity who knew the principles of government and the state, with an upright heart, and great disinterest, activity, and humanity. Two defects brought about his ruin, the first even more so. It was a serious defect for him to conduct his affair with the queen, for whom the king had no interest, too openly. The second defect was to have imprudently attacked the clergy, the military orders, and the nobility, arousing all at once his most potent enemies with the project of carrying out a general reform of abuses weighing on the most unhappy part of the nation.

This political program brought Struensee to his ruin and, as one sees, was of great interest to Pietro Verri. Certainly Denmark was "a land little known in Italy," but its problems and culture could not help but be echoed in the Milan of enlightened reformers. "Bianchi says the capital is handsome. . . . The inhabitants are amiable, far from being bloodthirsty or thieving."[32]

[30] Savignano sul Rubicone, Rubiconia accademia dei filopatridi, MS. 7 A (Copenhagen, 5 December 1775).

[31] *Novelle letterarie*, no. 30, 26 July 1776, cols. 495ff. See a letter by C. D. Ebeling to I. Bianchi, undated but written in 1774, about the project of publishing his *Discorso* in Milan, B. Ambrosiana, MS. T. 133 Sup., F. 6.

[32] *Carteggio di Pietro e di Alessandro Verri* (Milan: Milesi, 1934), vol. 8, pp. 224ff., from Milan, 14 December 1776.

When he reached Germany Isidoro Bianchi thus resumed his usual literary and scholarly habits, which he tried to continue in the following years in his own country. But something remained, for himself and his readers, of his Danish experience, in which he had found, as we have seen, an extraordinary journalistic freedom and a social ferment that struck him with its deep energy.[33]

Among the many Europeans who tried to make sense of the turn of events in Denmark, the English were, because of their closeness, affinity, and interests, the most able to penetrate the logic of politics and constitutional developments. The most important contemporary work on the modern "revolutions of Denmark" was published, in fact, in London in 1774 (the work of John Andrews). It took up the discussion where Molesworth had left off: why had nothing been done to preserve liberty in 1660? This was "impardonable, absurd neglect" that had weighed down all the subsequent history of the country.[1] It was enough to think of what had happened in England, where there had also been a monarchical restoration in 1660, to understand how serious had been the surrender without conditions in Denmark and the lack of resistance of the commons and clergy. The character of the whole nation had been changed by it. "Since the abolition of the ancient constitution and the introduction of despotism in Denmark, the minds and the tempers of the natives have been gradually declining from the loftiness and generosity which accompanied the better classes and from the stoutness and courage which till then had characterised the common sort."[2] The worsening of the economic situation of the country had resulted from a similar lack of initiative and energy on the part of nobles and bourgeois.

Nevertheless, Denmark revived, and within "the course of not so many years" it had reached a relatively "flourishing state."[3] What were the reasons for such an incredible fact? The merit could be attributed to the government. "The wise management of individuals in power" had "counterbalanced the defects of an evil constitution." It was something that could happen in an absolute monarchy. But this consideration was not a justification for a political form that should continue to

---

[33] Only at the beginning of the next century, in a changed atmosphere, were his writings on Denmark collected into a volume: *Sullo stato delle scienze e belle arti in Danimarca dopo la metà del secolo XVIII. Lettere dell'ab. Isidoro Bianchi* (Cremona: Giuseppe Feraboli, 1808). One of the letters (pp. 53ff.), "on the various useful foundations and literary establishments in Denmark," was written to Gaetano Filangieri. Generally, this later correspondence did not have the interest or vivacity of the one published in the *Novelle letterarie*.

[1] John Andrews, *The history of the revolutions of Denmark, with an account of the present state of that kingdom and people* (London: J. Nourse, 1774), vol. 1, p. 312.

[2] Ibid., p. 364.

[3] Ibid., vol. 2, p. 73.

be considered bad. There were only rare cases of good administration
in absolutist states. Only "liberty, like an open high road, leads more
directly to the term proposed. . . . Despotism is, at best, but an oblique
path, subject to numberless errors and perplexities."⁴ It was enough to
observe French administration, so accurate and efficient, but yet remaining always a "tyrannical management," which was, "strictly speaking, intolerable."⁵ Whatever the circumstances, absolutism always ended
by suffocating initiative and suppressing the will of individuals: so it was
in Denmark. Even under exceptionally good sovereigns, such as Christian VI and Frederick V, with the absence of a "deeper rooted principle
of stability," of a constitution, the economic and political recovery had
been narrow and difficult. The navy had never returned to what it was
in the past, as Josiah Child had noted, "whose veracity has never been
called in question."⁶ And what had not been done in the same two decades of the late seventeenth and the early eighteenth century by two
free countries like England and Holland! "Let us not be dazzled, then,
with the pompous accounts some writers have given of the present felicity of the Danish nation."⁷ The misery, "the wretchedness" of the peasants were evident.⁸ It was precisely initiative that was lacking. The peasants worked only because they were constrained to do so. The
monarchs, for fear of "disobliging their nobility," had not dared intervene with sufficiently effective measures. When Struensee and Brandt
had then tried to cross the tacit limits, they had only prepared their own
ruin. "The late terrible catastrophes that have befallen the principal suf-
ferers of the late revolution, are by some ascribed chiefly to their having
made alterations in sundry provinces of the kingdom too advantageous
for the rural classes and too favourable to their independence to be
borne with patience by the body of the nobles."⁹ Still, the peasants had
begun to emerge from the "oppressions they endure" and Denmark
would one day follow the example of those parts of Europe "where the
importance of agriculture is well understood."¹⁰ Even here the example
of England was decisive. Already in Denmark one saw "divers estates as
judiciously and as generously administrated as in any of the British dominions."¹¹ One must have confidence in these enlightened proprietors
and in the many who, even in Denmark, informed themselves more

⁴ Ibid., pp. 74ff.
⁵ Ibid., p. 76.
⁶ Ibid., p. 94.
⁷ Ibid., p. 96.
⁸ Ibid., p. 99.
⁹ Ibid., pp. 111ff.
¹⁰ Ibid., p. 113.
¹¹ Ibid., p. 115.

widely about what was happening in England, Holland, and Flanders. This was a "patriotic enterprise" that could bring Denmark out of its traditional misery, but it found limits and obstacles in the country's form of government. Nor could Struensee's work be seen truly as a mediating effort to overcome difficulties hindering the transformation of Denmark. It was "an event of a particular nature," resulting from the "concourse of very unusual and extraordinary causes."[12] Only with difficulty could it be seen as "preparatory to any essential change in the system of the government itself." The proof of this was in the arbitrary way Struensee had treated those who opposed him.[13] To find arguments in favor of the capacity of the Danes to escape the system of absolutism, it was necessary to look at their technical capacities as mariners, the love with which peasants cultivated the little fields the lords left to them, the passion for education that pervaded all classes, the rarity of violent crimes among the Danes, which made them so different from the "lower classes in Italy, in Spain, in Portugal and in France itself."[14] Their religion was not, to be sure, as favorable to "republican principles" as the Calvinist one—and for this reason Calvinism was viewed as dangerous in Denmark. But the deference of all classes toward the Church and toward clergymen was also changing. "The insipid gravity" of the pastors was a serious obstacle, but "enlightened understanding" was making notable progress.[15] The ignorance of the clergy was such that teachers were often chosen among laymen, thus permitting a "more liberal and generous education."[16] Another source of optimism was the great moderation of the government. The sad events of the Struensee years should be considered, even from this point of view, an exception, a parenthesis. In general, it had to be admitted that what was said about the "lenity of government in that kingdom is founded on truth."[17] But how could one succeed in passing from such civility and moderation under absolutism to a policy of reform sufficient to confront the gross injustice and ugliness that still remained, overturning the "unhappy spirit of injustice and tyranny" that still pervaded state and society in Denmark, especially with regard to peasants?[18] It remained true that "few of the Danish peasants are free and independent possessors of land."[19] If this problem were resolved, "no nation in Europe could boast a better sys-

[12] Ibid., pp. 121, 124.
[13] Ibid., p. 124.
[14] Ibid., p. 203.
[15] Ibid., pp. 218ff.
[16] Ibid., p. 224.
[17] Ibid., p. 327.
[18] Ibid., p. 360.
[19] Ibid., p. 359.

tem of internal polity, and Denmark would afford the singular exemple of a people subject to absolute monarchy enjoying the most equitable laws and living under most moderate government in Christendom."[20] Perhaps, or, better in all probability, the terrible face of tyranny would reappear, revealing again "the radical deficiency" of the Danish government, that is, the lack of constitutional liberty.[21] With this alternative John Andrews closed his work, where better than elsewhere one can sense the tension between republican tradition and the eighteenth-century attempt at reform that was emerging in Denmark. The problem continued to interest John Andrews in the following years, when the American Revolution changed the bases of discussion and pushed him toward a more pronounced constitutionalism, aligned with British tradition, freedom of the press, and individual freedom.[22] About Denmark, he still held, in 1783, that it preserved "that villenage and slavery of the lower and particulary the rustic classes which is so disgraceful to mankind."[23]

But an attempt to abolish entirely the outdated system of peasant servitude in Denmark was also beginning. Whereas Russia and Poland continued to demonstrate their inability to resolve this fundamental problem, and in these countries peasants continued to be owned by their lords almost like beasts, Denmark resumed its way toward a substantial change. Andreas Peter Bernstorff, nephew of the minister of Frederick v, was put at the head of a plan for reform, and, together with Christian Reventlow, he contributed to dissolving the agrarian question without arousing a serious reaction. Between 1784 and 1788 the liberation was accomplished. At the same time there was a return to freedom of the press and to a renewed toleration. From a religious point of view, the shift from the older to the younger generation cannot be better symbolized than by comparing Balthasar Münter with his son Friedrich. They were both ecclesiastics and theologians, and both learned writers. But the father was, one remembers, the man who had converted Struensee in prison, the perfect instrument of orthodoxy, and the author of the famous book on his victory over enlightenment and libertinage, which became a classic of Protestant apologetics. It was translated into many languages, and even into Italian, in Florence in

[20] Ibid., pp. 441ff.

[21] Ibid., p. 442.

[22] John Andrews, *An essay on republican principles and on the inconveniencies of a commonwealth in a large country and nation, illustrated from ancient and modern history, and concluding with some Reflections on the present situation of Great Britain* (London: Richardson and Urquart, 1783).

[23] Ibid., p. 59.

1848.[24] His son Friedrich, on the other hand, became one of the major exponents of European Freemasonry, one of the leaders and inspirers of the Illuminati sect and, in Italy, a friend of Gaetano Filangieri, Mario Pagano, and, in general, the whole generation of the last decades of the century of Enlightenment.[25]

Even the discussions that the narrative of the conversion of Struensee aroused everywhere in Europe showed how closely political and religious problems in Denmark were linked. The government of Struensee, as a translator of Balthasar Münter's work said, represented "such a great and rapid revolution in customs, especially in the capital, that the whole world feared the unhappy outcome. There was soon a general outcry that religion was being threatened." Many were persuaded that Struensee, "impious because of libertinage, and perhaps also because of pride," had lived "without religion or morality." Nevertheless, the laws he published inspired respect and led one to think that he was "more unhappy and more to be pitied than he was guilty." In reality the clergy, the *dévots*, had overreacted, as often occurred in lands of the north, declaring "divinity outraged when they believed they themselves were offended." Only Balthasar Münter had succeeded in following the narrower path that passed "between hypocrisy and scandal."[26] To be sure, his apologetics were based on the enlightened Protestantism of the age of Lessing and on ideas and books by Jerusalem, Reimarus, Spalding, and Bonnet. He did not even shrink from discussing ideas of the most fervent writers of the French Enlightenment, such as those by Nicolas-Antoine Boulanger.

As months and years passed it became more possible to believe that the Struensee eposiode should be put between parentheses, as a curious exception to that moderation of which Denmark was so proud, and, in reality, the country showed it was capable of adopting fundamental re-

[24] G.-F. Struenzée, *Biografia religiosa. Da Baldassarre Munter pastore danese* (Florence: Le Monnier, 1848). (There is a copy in Florence in the B. Marucelliana, with the call number 7.E.X.58.) This was a version of *Le comte Jean-Frédéric Struenzée. Biographie religieuse. Traduction libre et abrégée de l'Allemand par Guillaume-Adam de Felice* (Paris: J.-J. Risler, 1838). See Balder Vermund Aage Erichsen and Alfred Krarup, *Dansk historisk bibliografi* (Copenhagen, 1917), vol. 3, p. 683, no. 13600. On the Protestant propaganda of Piero Guicciardini through the editions of Le Monnier, see Giorgio Spini, *Risorgimento e protestanti* (Naples: ESI, 1956), pp. 257ff.

[25] See *Aus den Tagebüchern Friedrichs Münters. Wander- und Lehrjahre eines dänischen Gelehrten*, ed. Øjviind Andreasen, 4 vols. (Copenhagen and Leipzig: P. Haase and Harrassowitz, 1935–).

[26] *Histoire de la conversion du comte Stuensée . . . avec la Relation de la manière dont il est parvenu à changer ses idées en matière de religion, telle qu'il l'a donnée lui-même par écrit*, publiées par le D. Munter et traduites de l'allemand (Lausanne: J. Pierre Heubach, 1773).

forms before the French Revolution at the end of the century. Mallet, the writer who had discovered the ancient roots of Danish liberty, after his *Introduction,* had given himself to writing a complete history of Denmark, reaching the third edition and the ninth volume in 1788; which was dedicated to events in the last part of the seventeenth and in the eighteenth centuries. He took up again, against Molesworth, a defense of the events of 1660. The responsibility for the rise of absolutism was again placed on the nobility, which had been incapable of understanding how low its prestige had fallen and incapable of reacting with force and intelligence. The senate and nobility thus allowed the escape of "the favorable moment to renounce the greater part of their privileges."[27] The monarch, the army, and the commons had prevailed without difficulty. There were no guarantees. But absolutism still had to be interpreted in the light of the conduct of the Danish kings during the century after the proclamation of the new royal law. This gave still further reason to "applaud the moderation, clemency, and wisdom of the kings" of the nation.[28] In vain one seeks some mention of the eighteenth-century political struggle and the Struensee incident. Mallet refused to occupy himself with internal politics and instead devoted long pages to the intricate threads of diplomacy of the kingdom, with regard to the duchies of Schleswig and Holstein. The seventies were now distant, and in his eyes enthusiasm for liberty, the constitution, and reforms was spent.

The shadow of Struensee reappeared nonetheless for a moment on the horizon of Italy before the outbreak of the French Revolution entirely changed the scene even in Denmark. Giuseppe Pelli, the writer who had recorded the Florentine echoes of what was happening in Copenhagen in 1772, received and read almost twenty years later a "history of Count Struensee and of Brandt . . . published in 1789." "This history," he noted, "is pathetic and worthy of being read."[29] The English translator of the work said it was a portrait of a politician rather than of "an enthusiastic man of feeling."[30] The means Struensee used admittedly corresponded to the "most melancholy state" in which Denmark found itself, so that his will to action could express itself only through a struggle of interests and intrigues.[31] Struensee had observed the "enor-

[27] P. H. Mallet, *Histoire de Dannemarc,* 3d ed. (Geneva and Paris: Barde, Manget et Buisson, 1788), vol. 9, p. 62.

[28] Ibid., p. 84.

[29] Pelli, *Efemeridi,* vol. 29, p. 28b. Addition before April 1772.

[30] *Authentic elucidation of the history of counts Struensee and Brandt and of the revolution in Denmark in the year 1772,* privately printed, but not published by a personage principally interested. Translated from the German by B. H. Latrobe (London: John Stockdale, 1789), p. xi.

[31] Ibid., pp. 76ff.

mous defects both in the foreign and internal state of Danish politics
with an eye of an intelligent statesman and had formed a bold plan to
thoroughly remedy both."[32] He exhibited an exceptional lucidity in his
judgment of Russia, refusing to accept the "haughty air with which the
court of Petersburg was accustomed to speak." The war with the Turks
and "the intestine commotions" of the empire of Catherine had permitted him to act without much circumspection.[33] He was less successful in
his plans regarding internal policy; circumstances pushed him to risky
and improvised action. His projects for the reform of finances and of
justice were grandiose and showed "his capacity and genious in the most
favourable light."[34] But his ambition made him adopt a mistaken policy
toward the nobility, whose privileges he wanted to remove. And in this
as in other areas "he had every advantage that a thinking and vigorous
mind could derive from an excellent theory, but he wanted that knowledge which can only be acquired by long experience and frequent disappointments."[35] Only experience would have carried him to victory.
His power was a caprice of fortune, and there could be no delay or hesitation. He had too many hopes for changing things around him.
"Struensee . . . showed, in most of his action, that he never properly
considered the power of prejudice over the human mind."[36] In one of
his reforms, that of the peasantry, he showed all of his best qualities,
demonstrating a capacity for acting gradually and wisely, and at the
same time for creating a foundation of hope for integral reform. "The
peasants throughout Denmark looked upon this event as a happy omen
of a total emancipation from slavery, and Struensee certainly intended
to complete the work he had so humanly begun, had not the opposition
of many of the lords prevented it at that time." Even here, as in his law
on the press, Struensee had operated without the guidance of immediate political prudence; it was necessary to realize that he had risked following "the false glare of the theoretical principles." He had surprised
the world by producing a law that no one imagined could be born "under the protection of despotism." Even his reform of the police, the
model to which he had attached himself, that of Paris, was little adapted
"to the taste and habits of cold and quiet citizens of Copenhagen."[37]

Thus, as an unhappy hero of the will to reform, who was required

[32] Ibid., p. 78.
[33] Ibid., pp. 80ff.
[34] Ibid., p. 88.
[35] Ibid., p. 93.
[36] Ibid., p. 94.
[37] Ibid., pp. 100ff.

to pay a price for his projects and efforts, he was overcome by the strictures of his surroundings and his own errors. The political base on which he tried to build was too narrow. He ended up being buried under a violent reaction, which he provoked. His history, as Pelli said, was "pathetic and worth reading."

IX

Between Republican Monarchies and Monarchical Republics: Sweden

IN SWEDEN, AS ELSEWHERE IN EUROPE, THE SIXTIES REVEALED A strong impetus to reform.[1] The equilibrium that the party of the Hats (nobles and philo-French) achieved painfully and with difficulty in the preceding decade did not survive the grave economic crises of the years 1763 to 1765. In the diet of 1765–1766, the longest and most tempestuous in Swedish history, which lasted twenty months, the party of the Young Caps (affiliated with the citizen class, the lower clergy, and the peasants, and in foreign policy Anglophile and more pacifistic) prevailed. An anti-inflationary and antimercantilist policy was adopted, leading many manufactures subsidized by the state to close their doors. Measures against luxury were taken. Although the liberal currents of physiocracy had some influence, full freedom of trade still did not exist. Some political reforms were quite radical. The law on freedom of the press of 2 December 1766 was the most significant. "After Great Britain, Sweden was the first country to institute this legally as a fundamental law of the kingdom."[2] On the condition that the name of the author was mentioned, the editor was exempt from all responsibility. Even criticism of the fundamental laws of the constitution was punished by only a simple fine. The ecclesiastical censorship became a mere formality. The re-

---

[1] Nordmann, *Grandeur et liberté de la Suède*, pp. 272ff. This is the major treatment by the French school of the events of the seventeenth and eighteenth centuries in Sweden. For a general view, see Ingvar Andersson, *Storia della Svezia*, ed. Silvio Furlani (Reggio Calabria: Ed. Parallelo 38, 1975). For matters regarding culture, see Corrado Rosso, "La Francia nel Nord: Le 'lumières' in Svezia nel 'Tempo della libertà' (1718–1772)," in id., *Illuminismo, felicità, dolore* (Naples: Esi, 1969), pp. 151ff.

[2] Nordmann, *Grandeur et liberté de la Suède*, p. 274. For echoes of the physiocrats see Furio Diaz, *Filosofia e politica nel Settecento francese* (Turin: Einaudi, 1962), p. 398.

sult was an increase in political debates. "A flood of anti-noble literature, in particular, poured out."[3]

But the currents of reform still did not succeed, at the end of the sixties, in dominating the reaction to liberalism, and the difficult political and social situation in general. The party of the Caps struggled more and more to keep the forces hostile to the nobility united. Nonetheless, the position of the nobles continued to be menacing. For the first time in forty years (since the fall of the absolutist regime in 1720) they were on the defensive. "The days were gone by when the Clergy or Peasants were prepared to alter their resolutions in deference to the appeals or threats or protests of the Nobility." "Cutting across the party strife of Hats and Caps there was now emerging a struggle between one Estate and the rest, a struggle of privileged against unprivileged." This was the period when the free Swedish peasant was idolized in counterpoint to the nobles. Many plans were drawn up to ensure improved rights in the countryside. A current that, with due caution, we might call democratic was felt strongly everywhere. "It seemed at least possible, in 1771 and 1772, that Sweden might be on the eve of some such revolution as was to occur in France twenty years later."[4]

That the outcome was not this but the coup d'état of Gustavus III in 1772 was due to several complex reasons. To begin with, there was the structure of the nobility itself, which, far from constituting a closed hierarchical and parasitical body, was comparatively open, mobile, and enterprising, similar to the English model. Its presence was felt in industries, especially mining, in the state administration, naturally in agriculture and the army, and also markedly in cultural life. Like the Polish nobles, the Swedish nobility was proud of the equality within its class, and of its democratic organization, as much on a local as on a national level. As in Poland, it had undertaken an energetic struggle and a resistance against absolutism. And unlike nearby and always rival Denmark, the long battle of Swedish "aristocratic constitutionalism" had ended with a victory, that is, with the inauguration in 1720 of the "age of liberty." A comparison with France is enlightening. Even there recent historians have rediscovered what Madame De Staël and De Tocqueville made clear, that the nobility at the end of the old regime was economi-

---

[3] Nordmann, *Grandeur et liberté de la Suède*, p. 275. There is ample correspondence on the freedom of the press in Sweden in the *Gazzetta estera*, published in Florence on 21 April 1767, no. 3, p. 9 (Stockholm, 1 March).

[4] Michael Roberts, "The Swedish Aristocracy in the Eighteenth Century," in id., *Essays in Swedish History* (London: Weidenfeld and Nicholson, 1967), p. 280. This is one of the most interesting essays of this excellent historian who, through the study of Sweden, has brought illuminating insights to all of modern history. See his *Age of Liberty: Sweden, 1719–1772* (Cambridge: Cambridge University Press, 1986).

cally and politically active and far from being merely a mummy from the feudal past.[5] In France also it was the nobles who created a tradition of liberal constitutionalism through opposition to Louis xiv and the long struggle of the Parlements. But in France the absolute monarchy had won; and the nobility, except for that of the robe, was no longer a true order or animated by the ideal of aristocratic equality, as it was in Sweden, Poland, Venice, and in some measure among English peers. In Sweden, in the sixties and seventies, the nobility was strong and well organized enough to resist the pressure of other orders and to impose a series of compromises on the monarchy.

If Sweden did not take the ruinous route of Poland, as many contemporaries feared and as the risky international position of the country might have indicated, this depended much on the diplomatic situation of France and England, both desirous to maintain peace, and on the Russia of Catherine ii, which was engaged with the Turks and with Pugačev. But it also depended to a significant extent on the resilience, activity, and public spirit of the orders that stood behind the nobility at the base of the Swedish constitutional regime: the clergy, citizens (especially the merchant classes), and peasants. Insistent, tenacious in their goals, capable of autonomy and great initiative, these formed the political base of the Caps and, after 1772, of the resistance to absolutism. It was precisely these groups and energies that were absent or dispersed in Poland.[6]

We must be careful not to view the political life of Sweden in this period with eyes that are too modern. The limitations of the underlying mixture of new and traditional elements in the "age of liberty" are evident. The "estates" remained "orders," enclosed in their prerogatives, customs, and habits. The Germanic world, closely affiliated with the world of Sweden, provides the best parallel. Swedish corporatism, however, was less closed than that of Germany. The tradition of autonomy originating in the Middle Ages was extraordinarily more alive in Scandinavia. As Michael Roberts has recently written, "The Middle Ages left Sweden with a pattern of grass-roots democracy which has never been erased and which provided a solid basis upon which modern democracy might build."[7] The fact that peasants had representatives and exercised their duties in the shifting political balance of the Diet is significant, and

---

[5] Guy Chaussinand Nogaret, *La noblesse au xviiᵉ siècle. De la féodalité aux lumières* (Paris: Hachette, 1976).

[6] Robert R. Palmer, *The Age of the Democratic Revolution: A Political History of Europe and America, 1760–1800* (Princeton, N.J.: Princeton University Press, 1959), vol. 1: *The Challenge*, pp. 99ff.

[7] *Times Literary Supplement*, 9 December 1977, p. 1434.

it rightly attracted the attention of contemporaries. But the cost of this traditionalism was high. The Swedish "orders" opposed not only absolutism, but also other constitutional models, such as the English one, which was the more or less secret dream of Gustavus III. Michael Roberts has considered the Swedish constitution more liberal and more refined, at least in certain respects, than the British one. The fact remains, however, that the closed corporative nature of the "orders" prevented any step toward more effective internal development and thus opened the way for the intervention of Gustavus III. The same Roberts, in splendid pages, explains what were the limits of the "time of liberty."[8] Born from the revolution of 1720, the political system continually hesitated between specific goals (control of taxation, regular parliamentary meetings, ministerial responsibility, hostility to a standing army) and the desire to establish a single fundamental constitutional law. It looked to the past, expecting to restore ancient Swedish liberties, but in reality it was constructing something profoundly new. It was inspired by Locke, by Algernon Sidney, and by republican thought, but in the end it created, not a compromise between sovereign and parliament as in England, but a form of absolutism, exercised not by the king, but by the assembly, "the absolutism of the Diet, stepping into the shoes of the royal absolutism which had been overthrown."[9] Thus what lay at the base of the constitution was not a contract, as in Great Britain, but the domination of the Diet, which was not limited by any house of lords and was reinforced by the fact that the assembly not only governed but also administered the country. At least some Swedish legists were of the opinion that the assembly was the *legibus soluta*.[10] This domination became all the more unstable and difficult given the presence of four groups or estates, whose particular interests continually threatened to override that of the Diet as a whole. Nobility and bureaucracy tended to be one. "The estate of nobility was overwhelmingly composed of officeholders." It was said in 1720 that, except for peasants, there were only a few deputies who were not in the service of the king or did not aspire to be. "And even among the peasants (who hated bureaucrats) the leaders tended to be petty local officials."[11] Salaries, prestige, and power flowed from the state, which gave the Diet even less political independence. This assembly of bureaucrats, or aspiring bureaucrats, exercised a power that, in England, had been seen only at the time of Cromwell.

---

[8] Michael Roberts, *Swedish and English Parliamentarism in the Eighteenth Century* (Belfast: Queen's University, 1973).

[9] Ibid., p. 6.

[10] Ibid., p. 10.

[11] Ibid., p. 14.

"As a legislative, the Diet was innocuous, but as an executive, it was truly formidable."[12] It failed to vote on the most needed reforms but intervened in the most minute details of the administration of the country. And its methods, when it encountered resistance, were anything but mild: the political struggle developed during the years of liberty with no holds barred. "Freedom of speech within the Estates was precarious: members who vented unpopular opinions might find themselves voted out the house. Political persecution disguised as justice was among the most odious features of the age."[13] Capital punishment was not lacking. Despite some efforts, *habeas corpus* was not adopted. A heavy atmosphere of secrecy often surrounded Swedish political life.

These problems attracted the attention, or at least the curiosity, of Vittorio Alfieri in 1770. "The form of the government of Sweden, arranged and equilibrated so as to preserve a semi-liberty, aroused in me a curiosity to know it more deeply. But unable as I was at that time to sustain any serious or continued application, I studied it only in general. Nor did I understand enough to form in my mind more than one idea: that the poverty of the four classes of voters, and the extreme corruption of the classes of nobles and citizens, produced the venal influence of the two corrupting seducers, Russia and France, and could not create either peace among the orders, or effective deliberation, or just and lasting liberty."[14] The attraction of Alfieri for the "aristocratic constitutionalism" of Sweden was spontaneous, as one sees. But his sympathy was soon checked by the picture of corruption and inefficiency that colored the view of Sweden in the eyes of the greater part of European politicians and diplomats. Gustavus III made use of this picture when he declared he was ready to reestablish authentic liberty, and a true constitution.

Certainly, there was no lack of corruption. This was a tradition as well, and a means of support for a large part of the political class. As in Poland, corruption falsified operation of the constitution and tied different ideologies to the interests of foreign diplomacy. In Sweden the defense of the constitution of 1720 became a weapon in the hands of Catherine II. The efforts to reform were utilized by France. Reading the dispatches of diplomats in half of Europe, what is most striking was the continual lament provoked by the ineffectiveness of money and the continual incapacity of foreign gold to procure the desired effects and thus truly change the course of events. The political struggle in Sweden was

[12] Ibid., p. 18.
[13] Ibid., p. 35.
[14] Vittorio Alfieri, *Vita*, ed. Giampaolo Dossena (Turin: Einaudi, 1967), pp. 97–99.

so lively and complicated that even continual, repeated, foreign dis-
bursements did not succeed in changing it in a lasting way.

An instructive way of understanding the logic of events in Sweden
of the sixties and seventies is to read the gazettes—for example, the Italian ones. Naturally, they knew little and wrote less about the secret operations and corruption that fill the dispatches of ministerial cabinets
and ambassadors. In the columns of the gazettes, and in the pages of
broadsides and pamphlets, political life resumes the aspect it had for
contemporary observers, and it stops being the continual plot of *raison
d'état* and duplicitous secret diplomacy, which many, chiefly nineteenth-
century historians, have described in detail.[15] The discovery and use of
diplomatic archives was an important step forward in the evolution of
historical interpretation. But a return to the documents that contemporaries read and commented on, to what they did and said publicly, is
indispensable for truly understanding the contrasts between liberty and
despotism, between reform and revolt that, even in Sweden, were an
essential element of the period we are studying.

Even here the Florentine *Notizie del mondo* was an important center
of contemporary journalistic attention, and its documentation on Sweden is surprisingly abundant. Alongside this journal we will assess writings of Italian witnesses to events in the north in these years.

The conflicts at the end of 1768, which centered on the threat of
resignation of King Adolphus Frederick, sounded exotic and strange to
Italian ears. This was not even a renewed threat of abdication, but a
simple refusal, a kind of public confession of his own political impotence. He could no longer command even the royal guard. In the background was a difficult economic situation. Through bitter dissension,
and not without the support peasants gave the king, a convocation of
the Diet was finally agreed on for the spring of 1769.[16] The tone of the

---

[15] A typical example for Sweden is the book, still of some value, by Auguste Geffroy,
Gustave III et la cour de France, 2 vols. (Paris: Didier, 1867). Something similar could be said
about the book by Robert Nisbet Bain, *Gustavus III and His Contemporaries, 1746–1792*, 2
vols. (London: Kegan Paul, 1894), where still there is an echo of public opinion contemporary to the events narrated.

[16] *Notizie del mondo*, no. 5, 17 January 1769, p. 34 (Stockholm, 13 December 1768):
"Yesterday the king went to the Senate, where he insisted strongly on a convocation of the
estates for a Diet, since the finances were not in a good state. . . . The king, after having
made this proposition, left the Senate, and one waits with impatience to hear what the
sentiment of that assembly will be"; no. 6, 21 January 1769, p. 43 (Stockholm, 16 December): "The senate not having given His Majesty a categorical response to his satisfaction
yesterday, he renounced the crown and scepter, which he took up again three hours
later"; and no. 7, 24 January 1769, p. 51 (Stockholm, 28 December 1768) (a long communication on the positions of various political leaders on the king's threatening to re-
sign).

correspondent of the Florentine gazette was generally quite favorable to the monarchy. "The whole people is filled with joy because the king has, for good reasons, succeeded in promoting a convocation of the estates of the realm," one read in February.[17] The transference of the Diet from Norrköping to Stockholm was emphasized. International aspects of the conflict (Norrköping could easily be threatened by an Anglo-Russian naval intervention) and elements of party rivalry (the Caps were giving in to the Hats) were not forgotten but did not appear in the foreground. In other Italian gazettes as well developments were observed from the point of view of foreign policy, as, for example, in the *Gazzetta di Milano* on 24 January 1770, when news arrived from London that a triumph of the English party at the court of Sweden, "despite the intrigues of France," was to be hoped for.[18] Generally, in Italian gazettes, the Swedish struggle appeared more as a conflict among parties and groups than among corps, orders, or constituted bodies. This was a fairly accurate interpretation. The "fundamental laws" of the country, and their different and even contradictory interpretations, were correctly portrayed. Events were observed above all as constitutional disputes. The policy of the king, the Florentine journal reported, seemed to challenge the formation of an "aristocratic state," which tended to impede the reform of "entrenched abuses."[19] Even the Venetian *Storia dell'anno 1769*, although it brought to light among causes of the Swedish crisis "the universal decline of manufactures, mining, arts, and even the well-being of citizens, and consequently the powers of the state and size of the population," underlined the "limited authority of the king," so that "the actual system of that government, from [being a] monarchy [has become] almost republican." The continual tension between the king, the Senate, and the "remainder of the nation" led to "an insidious equilibrium, which, under the appearance of quiet and harmony, is nothing other than continued arbitrary obstruction, leaving things as they are, and tending to a clear ruin of the state and of citizens."[20] Meanwhile, the debate of these themes took on a more violent tone. In February an *Advice to the People of Sweden* circulated in Stockholm, "a libelle," as reported the *Notizie del mondo*, "which treated the monarch and ministry in an unworthy manner with regard to differences with the Senate and the anticipated convocation of the Diet." "By order of the king the most thorough search is being made to discover the au-

[17] Ibid., 14 February 1769, p. 101 (Stockholm, 10 January).
[18] *La Gazzetta di Milano*, no. 4, 24 January 1770 (London, 2 January).
[19] *Notizie del mondo*, no. 62, 5 August 1769, p. 504 (Stockholm, 4 July).
[20] *Storia dell'anno 1769*, pp. 51ff.

thor."[21] In June the Florentine gazette provided a general picture of Swedish public opinion as revealed through the press. "The present Diet has given occasion to publish some tracts, whose authors have no scruple in declaring their attachment to one party or the other." A periodical, the *Aristarc*, appeared and was directed to the "Swedish people" to teach them "truth and virtue." "Liberty is the spirit animating every paragraph of this work, and it should inspire zeal in every Swedish heart." It was favorable to royal authority. "The grandeur and right of the throne are essential parts of the constitution."[22] In this, the freedom of the press was also an integral part, which, as one reads in the summer of 1769, "is maintained vigorously so that every day works on matters of great importance leave the presses."[23] Thus the resolutions of the Diet were supported in "a printed book entitled *Patriotic Thoughts*." "This attracts universal attention."[24] Against this was soon unleashed the counteroffensive of the nobility, which produced a disturbance in the "course of exchange" and elicited a printed reply from the "citizenry."[25] Libelles were put up "in public places in the city."[26] The *Free Thinker*, by Doctor Rothman, caused a scandal, and Rothman was obliged to flee the violence of the ensuing polemic.[27] In December another "seditious tract" entitled *Letter Written from Stockholm to a friend in Gottenbourg* appeared. Then it was the turn of the clergy to take offense. "The most careful search is being made to discover the identity of the author."[28] Even the Venetian *Mercurio storico e politico* provided a detailed account of these political disputes, taking notice of the work mentioned earlier, which in Venice was called the *Free Speaker*.[29]

These divisions soon involved the foreign powers. Ivan Andreevič Osterman, the Russian envoy, took issue with "a printed book entitled

[21] *Notizie del mondo*, no. 24, 25 March 1769, p. 185 (Stockholm, 21 February). See *Storia dell'anno 1769*, p. 61.

[22] *Notizie del mondo*, no. 58, 22 July 1769, p. 472 (Stockholm, 19 June). On the author of the *Aristarc*, Carl Christoffer Gjörwell, "publicist and historian, the founder of the Swedish literary and educational press," see Nordmann, *Grandeur et liberté de la Suède*, p. 309 n. 51. See *Svenska män och kvinnor* (Men and women of Sweden) (Stockholm: A. Bonniers, 1946), vol. 3, pp. 70ff.

[23] *Notizie del mondo*, no. 68, 26 August 1769, p. 551 (Stockholm, 25 July).

[24] Ibid., no. 73, 12 September 1769, p. 595 (Stockholm, 11 August).

[25] Ibid., no. 74, 16 September 1769, p. 603 (Stockholm, 19 August).

[26] Ibid., no. 76, 23 September 1769, p. 618 (Stockholm, 22 August).

[27] Ibid., no. 77, 26 September 1769, p. 631 (Stockholm, 29 August), and no. 79, 3 October 1769, p. 649 (Stockholm, 1 September). On Jacob Gabriel Rothman, see *Svenska män och kvinnor*, vol. 6, pp. 373ff.

[28] *Notizie del mondo*, no. 3, 9 January 1770, p. 17 (Stockholm, 1 December 1769). For another attack on the clergy, see no. 20, 9 March 1771, p. 154 (Stockholm, 1 February).

[29] *Mercurio storico e politico*, no. 672, September 1769, p. 92.

Letter of a Friend in the Country to His Friend in the City." "He complained about observations that could offend his nation." Thus, "freedom of the press," which "since the year 1766" had been as great in Stockholm "as it is in London," began to be at issue. "The work mentioned did not attack Russia directly, but instead some anonymous writers who exalt the victories of that power; and the author appeared to fear for his country if Russia should ever act there as it had acted in Poland."[30] These difficulties and incidents agitated Swedish political life but did not seem to interfere with the principle of freedom of the press, a fact that even the French ambassador Vergennes noted with surprise.[31]

The economic situation worsened every day. Deputies from the provinces arrived in the capital; they "represented the extreme need in which the inhabitants found themselves for lack of provisions and requested stores of grain for their subsistence. They also complained that officials of the crown took furniture and other effects from the said inhabitants for payment of taxes, so that they could no longer continue to work in the mines."[32] The scarcity of grain aroused a conflict, which continued in the years that followed, on the prospect of prohibition of distilling aquavit. Nobles would suffer because they drew "a portion of their revenue" from this industry. "It would damage citizens in the grain trade, as well as peasants, who would be deprived of a drink they like."[33] But gradually, as the crisis of provisioning became worse, this unpopular measure was imposed. With equal reluctance, but resulting from the same need, there began to be a suspension of many feast days, "although the order of peasants was strongly opposed to this."[34] Reforms became more and more necessary, but no one seemed to have the power to carry them out. The Diet did not succeed in concluding anything about feast days.[35] The situation of the finances and of state employees was quite similar. These questions were often raised but were never resolved.[36] According to the Venetian *Mercurio storico e politico* no one proposed "returning the government to its old state and annulling all that had been decreed since the year 1720 with regard to charges

[30] *Notizie del mondo*, no. 104, 29 December 1770, p. 847 (Hamburg, 4 December).

[31] Geffroy, *Gustave III*, vol. 1, pp. 141ff.

[32] *Notizie del mondo*, no. 16, 25 February 1769, p. 123 (Stockholm, 23 January).

[33] *Notizie del mondo*, no. 65, 15 August 1769, p. 528 (Stockholm, 14 July); see no. 7, 22 January 1771, p. 52 (Stockholm, 18 December 1770) ("The peasantry uselessly consume a great quantity of grain in distilling the liquor").

[34] Ibid., no. 82, 14 October 1769, p. 672 (Stockholm, 12 September).

[35] Ibid., no. 10, 3 February 1770, p. 75 (Stockholm, 30 December).

[36] Ibid., no. 92, 18 November 1769, p. 752 (Stockholm, 17 October), and no. 5 (16 January 1770), p. 35 (Stockholm, 12 December 1769).

and offices."[37] Thus, when prohibitions were imposed on the import of luxury items, such as coffee, tea, chocolate, and so on, even when adopted they remained dead letters.[38] Similar projects accumulated.[39] What was lacking was the energy to enforce them. The ominous symptoms multiplied: bankruptcies, a drop in the exchange rate, and so on.[40] It seemed increasingly necessary to "support manufacturing and commerce through cash advances" and at the same time "rigorously prohibit the introduction of forbidden products."[41] At the beginning of 1770 it was hoped that the bottom had been reached: "Money is not as scarce as it was before, and it circulates more freely."[42] "Through the wise dispositions of the Diet people will be able to return to trying to raise themselves from the misery into which they have fallen, because many have been obliged to sell what they have in order to pay their taxes."[43] But the poor summer harvest, the news of prohibitions that Russia expected to impose on its own export of grain, and awareness that export of iron was weakening—partly because England bought chiefly from Russia— soon made people again aware of the sad reality.[44]

When King Adolphus Frederick died, of indigestion, on 12 February 1771, "the scarcity of foodstuffs" was "increasing every day."[1] The atmosphere was anything but cheerful. "The regency takes every possible measure to prevent an increase in the price of necessities of life and to avoid the disapproval of the people."[2] Nevertheless, within this picture of increasing difficulties, Tuscan readers could note a positive sign, a vivid concern for the condition of the peasants. A subsidy allowing inhabitants of the countryside to buy medicine and support doctors and surgeons was made.[3] New privileges were given "to those applying

[37] *Mercurio storico e politico*, no. 673, October 1770, p. 91.

[38] Ibid., no. 9, 30 January 1770, p. 67 (Stockholm, 26 December). See no. 60, 28 July 1770, p. 492 (Stockholm, 26 June) (the prohibition of foreign wines, except those of France, the Rhine, and Portugal), and no. 101, 18 December 1770, p. 821 (Stockholm, 16 November) ("Difficulties fiscal agents encountered when they attempted to put into operation the prohibitions against luxury").

[39] Ibid., no. 14, 17 February 1770, p. 107 (Stockholm, 13 January) (fiscal easements extended to peasants and an increase of tariffs on punch, tobacco, and coffee).

[40] Ibid., no. 8, 27 January 1770, p. 58 (Stockholm, 19 December 1769). The variations in the exchange rate were in January and February.

[41] Ibid., no. 15, 20 February 1770, p. 115 (Stockholm, 19 January).

[42] Ibid., no. 23, 20 March 1770, p. 179 (Stockholm, 16 February).

[43] Ibid., no. 24, 24 March 1770, p. 187 (Stockholm, 20 February).

[44] On iron see ibid., no. 92, 17 November 1770, p. 749 (Stockholm, 18 October).

[1] Ibid., no. 14, 16 February 1771, p. 108 (Stockholm, 11 January).

[2] Ibid., no. 20, 9 March 1771, p. 154 (Stockholm, 1 February).

[3] Ibid., no. 20, 10 March 1770, p. 156 (Stockholm, 6 February).

themselves to agriculture: . . . exemption from all public burdens." Thus it was hoped that a problem leading to much preoccupation would be avoided: the emigration of many peasants to the cities. "If they do not return to their old condition, the further decline of agriculture will do much damage to our trade."[4]

On 13 February 1771, at noon, "Prince Gustavus" was "recognized by the Senate as king of Sweden, and of the Goths, Vandals, and so on." The title was solemn, but, as one sees, the Senate had the decisive vote. It seemed as though for a year everything would remain as before. There was much agitation, but it was contained within the limits of the constitution. The Diet was convoked, and as the *Notizie del mondo* reported, "it will not be different from what it was in the past." But "malcontents" were at work, and there was already talk that they intended to "change . . . the current system." Still, in general, it was thought "that their efforts will not produce any novelty."[5] The situation seemed to have stalled. For this reason the words of the young king that he wanted to "carry out the great task of removing any partiality, and of reconciling minds to the general good," resonated all the more.[6] His words had a new patriotic tone that was fully reflected in the Florentine gazette. "Born and educated in your midst, I learned from my tenderest youth to love our country, to base my greatest happiness on being Swedish, and my greatest glory on being a first citizen in the midst of a free people." In his words there was an aristocratic undertone, but he addressed himself in his vague but suggestive program to all four orders. His rule was to be austere. "I have observed that what makes a people happy is not absolute power in the hands of the prince, or luxury, or magnificence, or a treasury collected from the economy, but only love of their country and domestic peace. It depends on ourselves alone to be the most happy nation on earth."[7] These words rose above the half measures taken by the Diet, the growing disputes among the four orders, and the increasingly worrisome economic situation. They showed, above all the misery, a broad historical and political vision, which evoked the past and gave a glimpse of a better future. In the autumn of 1771 the *Notizie del mondo* reproduced in full the *Panegyric of the King of Sweden Adolphus Frederick Written by the King His Son*, which Voltaire declared to have read "with tears that welled up in tenderness and admiration." It contained a history of modern Sweden, where the brilliance of glory dissolved any conflict between absolutism and liberty, and any conflict

---

[4] Ibid., no. 72, 8 September 1770, p. 588 (Stockholm, 7 August).
[5] Ibid., no. 26, 30 March 1771, p. 202 (Stockholm, 22 February).
[6] Ibid., no. 60, 27 July 1771, p. 472 (Stockholm, 28 June).
[7] Ibid.

or rivalry between the orders and the state.[8] The grave military and political crisis that Sweden had traversed thirty years before, at the beginning of the forties, appeared, for instance, to have been resolved "by the blood of the Vasas," which showed it was above "foreign ambitions" and the "divisions of citizens."[9] Nor did Gustavus III fail to underline the work of the deceased king in economics. During his reign "agriculture was improved, the building of factories was encouraged, commerce was protected; the population grew," and "true religion" was "preserved in its purity."[10] This was a regal vision, which was received with difficulty by those who feared for constitutional liberties or expected to impose concessions on the young king.[11] Another speech by Gustavus III was censured, and it circulated on the margins of the law: "Copies circulate in manuscript and people still hope that it will be published in some small city of the kingdom."[12]

The idea guiding Gustavus III, the conviction that only through a reaffirmation of royal authority would it be possible to combat the evils imminent in the foreign and internal politics of Sweden, had its roots, as one sees, in the country's past, and it presented itself as a return beyond the age of liberty, inaugurated in 1720, to the seventeenth-century age of greatness. But this was only a historical stage set, barely concealing a modern vision that originated in France in the sixties and seventies and was produced by the hopes and fears of the age of Choiseul and Maupeou. It was also influenced by the Parisian debate on the Parlements and by the physiocratic notion of legal despotism.

This historical layering made the character of the young sovereign, which was already very complicated, still more complex and ambiguous.[13] His mother, Luisa Ulrica, a sister of Frederick II of Prussia, had an imperious mind, but she had resigned herself to the dismemberment of monarchical power by the Diet in 1720. She had a profound influence on him. His early education was entrusted to Count Carl Gustaf

---

[8] Ibid., no. 86, 26 October 1771, pp. 659ff. (Stockholm, 23 September), and the following numbers. See Voltaire, *Oeuvres complètes*, vol. 47, p. 542, letter to Gustavus III, 12 November 1771.

[9] *Notizie del mondo*, no. 87, 29 October 1771, p. 667 (Stockholm, 27 September).

[10] Ibid., no. 88, 2 November 1771, p. 675 (Stockholm, 1 October).

[11] See ibid., no. 38, 12 May 1772, p. 318 (Stockholm, 13 April).

[12] Ibid., no. 7, 25 January 1772, p. 51 (Stockholm, 24 December 1771). This speech is in no. 12, 11 February 1772, p. 93 (Stockholm, 7 January): "A general lack of specie, the poor harvest, the fear of famine, the plague and sicknesses now require unanimous attention in discussion. I would think myself fortunate if I could contribute to this meeting. I offer my person to this effect."

[13] For a recent interpretation of his personality, see Gerd Ribbing, "Reflektioner kring Gustaf III," in *Gustaf III. En konstbok från Nationalmuseum redigerad av Ulf G. Johnsson* (Stockholm: Rabén and Sjögren, 1972), pp. 9ff. (There is a summary in English on pp. 141ff.)

Tessin, a great cosmopolitan noble with a passion for the arts and letters.[14] This man, encouraged by Queen Ulrica, invented for him an education based on fables, anecdotes, images, and exchanges of letters.
When the documentation of this new pedagogy was made public in the
fifties, it was thought to be astonishing for its originality and for its willingness to break with all traditional programs for a young lord. German, English, and French versions appeared. In 1759 there was a translation into Italian,[15] a fruit of the passion this text aroused in the mind
of Vincent Bernard Tscharner, the young active center of a group of
patricians at Berne who were rediscovering Swiss patriotism and an enthusiasm for virtue and reform.[16] He dedicated "to his eminence Monsigneur Cardinal Passionei, secretary of briefs and librarian of the Vat-
ican," the "project to transplant into Italy some fruits of the genius of
the north and to establish better a literary traffic among different climates." "Happy are the nations," he added, "whose sovereigns know
how to choose as their ministers Passionei and Tessin and to thus place
between the people and the throne defenders of religion, advocates of
truth, protectors of talents, and models of virtue!"[17] This version was
made from a copy of the original text preserved in the "erudite library
of Mr. Albert Haller," and it also took the German translation into account, whereas the French translation was harshly criticized.[18] By this
unexpected route Italians were able to gain knowledge of the political
thought of the age of liberty in Sweden and to enter into contact with
the culture of the land of Linnaeus. Moral injunctions abounded, and
religious ones were not lacking. There was extraordinarily broad information about ancient history (whereas modern history was almost absent), and a disproportionate emphasis on the history of art. From such
humanistic precepts came the initial political orientation of the future
king of Sweden. He "was to reign over a free people, subject to law, but
happy in their subjection." "Through the precepts of God we are sons
of liberty." "A prince who wants to be too absolute cannot suffer that

[14] See Per Bjurström, *Carl Gustaf Tessin och konsten* (Carl Gustaf Tessin and the arts)
(Stockholm: Rabén and Sjögren, 1972). This, with its illustrations and catalogue of Tessin's collection, gives a vivid idea of the man and his epoch. His choice and taste appear
to have been most refined, but with some heavy vulgarity. Boucher and Piazzetta are the
two most significant points of reference for understanding his artistic world.

[15] *Lettere scritte al principe reale di Svezia dal conte di Tessin, ministro di stato ed ajo del
medesimo principe*, translated from Swedish at the expense of literary innovators (Berne,
1759–60).

[16] See Mirri, *La cultura svizzera*, pp. 133ff.

[17] *Lettere scritte al principe reale di Svezia*, pt. 1, vol. 1, dedication unpaginated.

[18] Ibid. *Il traduttore agli amatori di prefazioni*, unpaginated. One also reads, "Since I am
not much aware of Italian poetry, for the translation of a few verses encountered an appeal was made to the chiarissimo sig. Domenico Soresi of Milan."

word; but a prince whose chief law is the public good hears it willingly." "Such a king has the authority to bring to account those who receive pluralities of votes, who attempt to dominate him, to impede his good projects, and to make his plans, which would be good for the state, disappear." From these general statements emerges the image of a government capable of guaranteeing its subjects their liberty, along with the certainty that "the fruits of their labor would not one day become prey to someone with more power." This would be a government capable of granting "unlimited license to the import and export of all products of the country, and not have them rot in the hands of artificers or others," to store "abundant provisions against bad times," and, naturally, "to cultivate the fine arts and sciences" and improve agriculture, so that "grain and feed are always kept at a moderate and just price, but not too low."[19] Distant, but on the horizon, was the image "of the kings of China, who at the beginning of their reigns plow the earth for a whole day dressed in the clothes of a peasant."[20] Still, Tessin concluded, one must take into account the political realities beyond such happy visions, which naturally produce conflicts and unavoidable contrasts. "There is no kingdom, no republic, no province, no city into which a discordant party spirit has not put its roots." This was a necessary evil that kept people "vigilant and prudent." "Partisanship and jealousy often raise great men to action . . . and even promote virtue and glory." "Your duty, Sir, will be not to allow yourself to be slowed down for even a day by such concerns, but to provide everywhere general peace and security, to exercise an unreprehensible justice, to gain the hearts of all with humanity and sweetness, and never to ignite fires of discord which consume subjects by making them declare that they support a party. *In discordia pax civilis nullo pacto esse potest* [There is no agreement amid civil discord]."[21]

Clearly, there was no lack of contradictions in the programs Tessin had laid out. His later political experience made these even more evident. He was the leader of the Hats party and a typical example of the nobility, in manners a courtier, but also a convinced supporter of the existing constitution. "His manners were courtly, but his principles were republican," Nisbet Bain has written.[22] It did not prove possible for him to remain Gustavus III's tutor. During the reaction against the attempted monarchical restoration in 1756—the work of the queen, to whom Tessin was too bound—the Diet thought it was necessary to entrust the young Gustavus to Count Carl Frederick Scheffer, who had been Tes-

---

[19] *Lettere scritte al principe reale di Svezia*, pt. 2, vol. 1, pp. 184ff., 248ff.

[20] Ibid., pt. 2, vol. 2, p. 94.

[21] Ibid., pp. 232ff.

[22] Bain, *Gustavus III*, vol. 1, p. 18.

sin's successor in the Swedish embassy in Paris; he was an able diplomat, as well as a great Francophile and a partisan of Swedish liberties.

The young prince thus grew up in the midst of violent political struggles, and he turned to Paris as a distant and vivid beacon. The *Henriade*, of which he knew a large part by heart, and the writings of Voltaire in general had particularly influenced him. He had learned to write in French fluently and effectively.[23] What is most striking in the letters he wrote in that language was his capricious liberty, as well as his avid desire to assume styles, even linguistically, that came from afar. His prose is often an imitation, almost a mimicking, of the liberty of others, an exploration of freedom in examples that came from outside. Through all these arabesques there emerged a barely obscured desire to express himself. There is an irresistible temptation to compare Gustavus III with his uncle Frederick II of Prussia, and with his adversary Catherine II of Russia: three different styles of assimilating the French language and ideas of the Enlightenment. One would not reject the conclusion that in all three cases the Enlightenment effectively modified political behavior, even if a naked desire to dominate always returned to make itself felt. The influence of Enlightenment ideas was particularly deep in the mind and soul of the king of Sweden, so much so that they became an integral part of his personality. But political motives also rapidly prevailed. Even the ideas he had most assimilated were utilized to affirm these motives. It is enough to think of his choice of French Encyclopedists to be aware that he never forgot the difficult and risky situation he had experienced since childhood and in which he remained throughout his reign. Of course Voltaire and Grimm were chosen. He had sympathy even for Rousseau. But he had a barely hidden hostility for Holbach, Diderot, Thomas, and for anyone who in one way or another tried to be a substitute for sovereigns when carrying out reforms. Preferable, in his eyes, were men like Marmontel, who fought for the just cause of tolerance, but without the philosophic pride or "republican" emphasis that the king of Sweden could not bear.[24] He was even

[23] See Gunnar von Proschwitz, *Gustave III de Suède et la langue française. Recherches sur la correspondance du roi* (Göteborg: Akademiförlaget, 1962), with a long bibliography.

[24] Bain, *Gustavus III*, vol. 1, p. 56; Michel Launay, "J. J. Rousseau et Gustave III de Suède," *Revue de littérature comparée*, fasc. 4 (October–December 1958): 496ff., and Von Proschwitz, *Gustave III et la France*, p. 163. Part of the letter to Luisa Ulrica dated 15 February 1771 is published, in which the lack of "modesty" of the philosophes is considered a "revolting fault." Some years later Diderot wrote an imaginary interview with Gustavus III. He would have received him with honor, he said. "I would have spoken without ill-opinion and without heat, at least as long as the matter did not affect the happiness of a multitude of men, because in that case, who can answer for himself?" (Diderot, *Correspondance*, vol. 14, 1968, p. 225).

more sympathetic toward the physiocrats, especially Mirabeau, Le Mercier de la Rivière, and Turgot, from whom he derived illumination and counsel.[25]

Amid these bright Gallic colors the paler and more delicate tints of Venetian reformers were not lacking. They were carried and diffused in Stockholm by Abate Domenico Michelessi, who was not Venetian (he came from the Papal States), but he had given the Republic of St. Mark his whole soul.[1] He was born in Spinetoli, "a castle of Ascoli," on 4 August 1735. The "scarce resources" of his "honest and respected family" were soon "almost entirely squandered" by his father. Practically an autodidact, he demonstrated extraordinary linguistic ability and restlessness to seek out, in schools and churches, some way of leaving the corner of the world into which he was born.[2] At the age of twenty-six he was a master of rhetoric in Montalto, where he succeeded in making contact with the world of Venice, in meeting Marco Foscarini, and little by little in becoming friendly with the literary world that rotated around the Gozzi and the heirs and followers of Algarotti.[3]

One of his first published works was a kind of hymn to the republic on the occasion of the election of Francesco Pisani as procurator of St. Mark in 1763.[4] He exalted, "*Venetam quidem Rempublicam, lucem Italiae, religionis ac libertatis domicilium, pacis ac tranquillitatis sedem . . . optimis legibus divinitus constitutam*" (The Venetian republic, light of Italy, home of religion and liberty, the seat of peace and tranquility . . . founded divinely on excellent laws).[5] Plato himself would not have had to think up his own republic, he said, if he had known the Venetian one. Even

---

[25] Eli F. Heckscher, "Fysiokratismens ekonomiska inflytande i Sverige" (The influence of the economics of physiocracy in Sweden), in *Lychnos* (1943), fasc. 1, pp. 1ff., with a summary in English. Vieri Becagli has indicated the importance of the correspondence preserved in Stockholm between Mirabeau and Scheffer, particularly the parts regarding Tuscany, in "Il 'Salomon du Midi' e l' 'Ami des hommes.' " "Riforme leopoldine in alcune lettere del marchese di Mirabeau al conte di Scheffer," *Ricerche storiche*, year 7, no. 1 (January–June, 1977): 137ff.

[1] The only study of him is by Agne Beijer, "Abbé Domenico Michelessi någa anteckningar om honom själv och hans verksamhet i Sverige," *Samlaren*, new ser. year 1 (1920): 92ff. This does not make use of the principal source for the adventures and ideas of this writer, that is, the letters and documents that were collected with great care by Bonomo Algarotti, his correspondent and friend, now preserved in Treviso, B. Comunale, MS. 1260–63.

[2] Treviso, 1261, anonymous biographical information.

[3] Ibid., other biographical information by Pasquale Cristofori, from 19 May 1773.

[4] *Ad Franciscum Pisanum Ludovici principis filium D. Marci procuratorem oratio Dominici Michelessii* (Venice: Ex typographia Albriziana, 1763).

[5] Ibid., pp. viiiff.

the Council of Ten, "*ille quoque decemvirorum ordo summus*" (that highest order of the Ten), received his praise, which was not surprising because this magistracy shortly before had been much criticized in the *Correzione* of 1760–1761.[6] He had wanted to express these sentiments again, when, still in 1763, he pronounced the funeral panegyric of Doge Marco Foscarini, his teacher and that of others of his generation.[7] He remained in Venice as secretary to Monsignor Francesco Carafa, the nuncio to the Most Serene Republic. When this prelate was sent to represent the Pope in Cologne, Michelessi became the first member of his household to travel abroad.[8] In September 1768 he was again in Venice, dedicating himself to what became his principal work, the *Memorie intorno alla vita e agli scritti del conte Francesco Algarotti*, which Pasquali published in 1770. The dedication to Frederick the Great, the insistent praise of the Italian literary tradition, polemics against rude French translators, a defense of the character and cosmopolitan virtues of the work of Algarotti, and numerous details on his relationships with writers such as Fontenelle, Voltaire, Maupertuis, and illustrious European sovereigns and ministers made this book an elegant messenger between Venice and Italy of the sixties, and the larger world beyond the Alps. He energetically defended the legacy of Dante and Michelangelo, but his attention was turned to those who, like Algarotti, had opened themselves toward great new nations, especially to Prussia and Russia.

Almost as if to follow in their footsteps in the spring of 1770, Michelessi left for the north. At the beginning of April he was in Vienna. He took with him his manuscript *Memorie* and sent the last corrections to Bonomo Algarotti, who was to see them through the press.[9] Golicyn, the ambassador of Catherine II, told him he knew the voyage of Algarotti in Russia by memory: "He admires the author very much, although he did not know him personally." He added that he would present the *Memorie* "to the czarina" as soon as it appeared.[10] In Dresden, where Michelessi arrived next, he was overtaken by "news of the Russian fleet," that is, the expedition of Orlov. "Since the court [of Saxony] is on the side of the Turks, and the whole nation is for the confederates, it is said and believed here that there have been great atrocities, that the Russians

---

[6] Ibid., p. xix.

[7] *Laudatio in funere serenissimi principis Marci Foscareni habita coram venetis patribus a Dominico Michelessio in aede SS. Johannis et Pauli XVII Kal. Maji an. 1763* (Venice: Apud Franciscum Sansoni, 1763).

[8] Treviso, 1261, biographical information by Pasquale Cristofori.

[9] Treviso, 1260, mazzo 2, Vienna, 7 April 1770. The letters are addressed to Bonomo Algarotti unless otherwise indicated.

[10] Ibid., Venice (but he meant to write Vienna), 9 April 1770.

are already destroyed, and that the king of Poland is dethroned."[11] But
his admiration for Russia was growing. In August he was in Prussia.
"Here I am in Berlin, an immense city, magnificent; not only the most
beautiful there is outside Italy, but better than the chief Italian ones."[12]
He became acquainted with the variegated world of individuals grouped
around Frederick II—Formey, Bastiani, Catt, Sulzer, Beausobre, Bégue-
lin, Merian—and spoke of them at length in his letters to friends in Venice. He was particularly surprised by the interest many of them showed
in Italy. "The truth is that we have in Italy only a few who understand
our literature as well as they."[13] News of the Mediterranean, however,
became more scarce. "Here everyone asks me about the Russian fleet
and I know nothing."[14] He continued to think of persons to whom he
wanted his book sent: Tanucci, Du Tillot (whom he had had occasion to
describe as "an elevated and gentle genius who is making Parma a new
Athens").[15] He continued to weave his cosmopolitan web, ingratiating
himself, among others, to d'Alembert through a witty letter of introduction to Venetian men of letters when it seemed that the French mathematician was thinking of crossing the Alps to visit Italy. He wanted d'Alembert to avoid what had happened to "some German and English
scholars," who returned from Venice "without even being aware that
among that nobility were sublime Zenos and Emos, real geniuses, who
speak like the greatest philosophers in print, but who, content with
themselves, seem not to esteem the human species enough to deign to
instruct it, or are too modest to make themselves known." He added the
names of "Querini the Venetian Demosthenes, Renier the modern Aristotle, *Memmi clara propago* (the illustrious offspring of Memmius), the
eloquent politician Morosini, the solitary geometer Arnaldi, and those
pillars of our language, the Gozzi." The past and present of Venice returned impetuously before the eyes of Michelessi; but he did not forget
the world in which he had come to find himself, where he seemed to
hear "the gods speak with the mouth of Frederick."[16] The courts of Germany were opening before him: Gotha, Weimar, Brunswick. In Brunswick he had the opportunity to meet the two young sons of the king of

[11] Ibid., Dresden, 27 April 1770.

[12] Ibid., Berlin, 17 April 1770.

[13] Ibid., Berlin, 4 September 1770.

[14] Ibid., Berlin, 18 August 1770.

[15] Domenico Michelessi, *Memorie intorno alla vita ed agli scritti del conte Francesco Algarotti
ciambellano di S.M. il re di Prussia e cavaliere del merito, ecc.* (Venice: Giambattista Pasquali,
1770), p. cii.

[16] Treviso, 1261, mazzo A, to Vicentini, undated, but September 1770. See mazzo 2,
Berlin, 22 September 1770, and Brunswick, 18 December 1770: "D'Alembert was most
attentive to my letter. He has written of it to several friends to thank me."

Sweden, who were traveling toward Paris and who told him of their intention of visiting Italy as well.[17] Michelessi proposed to accompany Gustavus "privately" to Padova and Venice. The young prince struck him as cultured. "He was born to be a professor in some university." From him he discovered that the best moment to visit Sweden would be the occasion of a coming meeting of the Diet. A little more than a month later, in Dresden, he received news of the death of King Adolphus Frederick. "Thus the two princes are returning without having visited Italy." But his admiration for Gustavus was too great to relinquish meeting him again soon. "You cannot imagine this excellent not king, not prince, but private citizen. I do not know what becomes of such princes when they ascend their thrones, but I would bet that Gustavus will always be the same, and that he will welcome me in Stockholm with the same grace with which he invited me to come."

The idea of going to encounter the new king was too good for the Italian Abate to miss. Then from Stockholm he would go on to St. Petersburg. "Prince Dolgoruki, minister of Russia in Berlin, my friend, puts things up and down for me to go to Russia and this Prince Bieloseski, an intimate of Orlov, begs me to go."[18] Money, to be sure, was necessary, and Bonomo Algarotti provided it. But his pilgrimage through German territory was not yet finished. In Vienna Kaunitz welcomed him "with great kindness." "I ate with him and he said he liked me because I have an honest face." Not everyone was of the same opinion. The Venetian ambassador and a "beautiful Hungarian lady" cast doubt on this "quality," saying he had "the face of a mischievous man." In Vienna he found louder echoes of Algarotti, where his works were appearing in French.[19] Even in Italy his fame was growing. The only gray point on this luminous horizon was the Papal States. Garampi, the future nuncio to Warsaw, responded with the usual "Roman rudeness and ignorance" to his gift of the *Memorie*. "Everyone is aware that in my book there are three or four solemn truths; according to the Holy City [they are] solemn heresies or at least scandalous propositions."[20] He did not stop thinking about the world of the Church, but there grew in him daily the desire to keep away from it and to try new experiences.

"Thus I will go to Stockholm," he wrote from Vienna on 6 April.[21] The thought was no obstacle, although it crossed his mind on his way to the north that he did not know the language of the country and was not

---

[17] See Michelessi's undated letter to Prince Carlo of Sweden, Treviso, 1261.
[18] Treviso, 1260, mazzo 4, Dresden, 4 March 1771.
[19] Ibid., Vienna, 23 March 1771.
[20] Ibid., Vienna, 30 March 1771.
[21] Ibid., Vienna, 6 April 1771.

even in a position to recognize "the money, or rather the paper they give you when they change gold."[22] In June, when he reached the Swedish capital, he was immediately swept by its agitated and intense political life. "The new king is most preoccupied with the present affairs of the Diet, which is to decide the form of government, the assignment to His Majesty, and the affairs of the whole kingdom." France on one side and Russia on the other attempted to influence the nobles, the clergy, the bourgeois, and the peasants; "these four orders compose the Diet, which arranges everything, like the Great Council of Venice. The King is more or less the Doge." Two parties divide the kingdom, the nobles of the Hats and the others of the Caps. "The Holy Church, always political, gains time by amassing money from both sides." The "difficulties of a king beginning his reign," however, were considerable. Gustavus III "deigns to talk with me every day, and always with the same humanity. . . . He told me he wanted me to stay until the coronation." Even though he did not succeed in understanding a single word, he was struck by the atmosphere the king's speech created in the Diet. "I saw that whole nobility weep openly with tenderness when His Majesty spoke. I don't know what kingdom has ever witnessed a similar spectacle. Italy will never see it unless Procurator Morosini became king."[23] A French translation of the king's speech began to circulate. "Count Scheffer is the author." Michelessi translated it into Latin and sent it to Italy, not forgetting Garampi, but thinking chiefly of his Venetian friends.[24] Thus, he became rapidly a kind of spokesman for the king. He knew his program very well. "The king makes every effort to rid himself of parties and establish concord, without which the kingdom will never advance." To carry this out it was necessary to maintain contact with the most diverse groups, from the court of the queen mother to the parties that were becoming more and more active and belligerent. "Only the Abbé," it was said in Stockholm, "has the right to be everywhere."[25] He was clearly too useful to be allowed to depart, as he had intended. He was invited "with all possible flattery to spend the winter in Stockholm to see the end of the Diet." The king asked him to translate his speeches into Italian, especially the one he had given in honor of his father. [26] Ever clearer appeared in the eyes of Michelessi the difficulties within which Gustavus III was obliged to operate. Economically poor ("the palace of the king is what a gentleman in Venice would have with fifteen

[22] Ibid., Stettin, 22 May 1771.
[23] Ibid., Stockholm, 8 June 1771.
[24] Ibid., Stockholm, 2 July 1771.
[25] Ibid., Stockholm, 26 July 1771.
[26] Ibid., Stockholm, 20 August 1771.

thousand ducats of revenue"),[27] politically without power (the Diet threatened to use a stamp instead of his signature and refused to hear his deliberations),[28] a "simple executive of the resolutions of the four orders that are called estates,"[29] subordinated to the parties that alternate in power at each election and bring about a change of the laws and government at the end of each triennial,[30] and above all to the influence of France and Russia, the "adorable Gustavus" had great need for at least the support of public opinion in his own country and in Europe. For this he wanted his speeches known even in Venice, by men like Tron, Morosini, Foscari, Giustiniani, and Algarotti, about whom Michelessi had told him, and about whom he continued to speak in the diplomatic circles of Stockholm.[31]

In the spring of 1772 the conflict between the Diet and the Senate grew more acute. From being the king's spokesman, Michelessi became more and more his confidant. Gustavus III showed him the protocols of the Senate, "which no one in the world has ever seen," and had him read the speech he had given but whose circulation was prohibited. These were points of light in the dark situation of "this poor and tattered kingdom." It was time to make known the personality of the king as widely as possible, telling how he was formed and explaining what the actions of this young protagonist of Swedish history were. "The letters of the king and of Count Scheffer, his tutor, with the addition of the *personalia*—that is, the speech he had written in honor of the dead king—and the speeches thus far of His Majesty will be translated into Italian, and it would be a fine book, which with the permission of the king will be dedicated to Count Buonomo Algarotti." At the same time the speeches of Gustavus III would be translated into Latin and "dedicated to the Pope."[32] These projects grew in the following months and involved more new materials, until they became, in the following year, a book printed in Venice by Giambattista Pasquali—the richest and most revealing series of documents on the Swedish crisis that had appeared until then not only in Italy, but also in Europe.[33] The Latin version in

---

[27] Ibid., Stockholm, 16 July 1771.

[28] Ibid., Stockholm, 20 August 1771.

[29] Ibid., Stockholm, 6 September 1771.

[30] Ibid., Drottningholm, 26 August 1771.

[31] Ibid., Stockholm, 26 January 1771. Scheffer and Vergennes remembered Tron and "the procurator Morosini, who is most esteemed by Senator Scheffer and was known by him in Paris." Vergennes called himself the friend "of His Excellency Foscari and of Cavaliere Giustiniani."

[32] Ibid., Stockholm, 6 March 1771.

[33] *Carteggio del principe reale, ora re di Svezia, col conte Carlo di Scheffer, senatore del Regno, cavaliere e commendatore degli ordini del re ecc. Si aggiungono alle Orazioni di S.M., la Lettera*

manuscript is still among Michelessi's papers in Treviso.[34] Pope Ganganelli (Clement XIV) was now changing the policy of his Rezzonico predecessor (Clement XIII). It was time to try to influence even Rome.

The work was anything but light for Michelessi, who had also dedicated himself to the intensive study of Swedish, which he learned with extraordinary rapidity, in a few months, even though he was distracted by the life of the court, by the struggle with the "incredible cold" of the country, and even by the hunting of "élans," that is, elks, and especially by the writing of innumerable letters, accounts, and so on. "It is true that I work like a beast and have abandoned society almost entirely."[35] But if he did not do all this work no one could substitute for him. And with ill-concealed impatience he told his Venetian friends about the torpid intellectual atmosphere that surrounded him. In Sweden the classics were ignored. "In Upsala the professors are well paid, but they are all asleep."[36] Still, the uncertainty of the political situation seemed to stimulate him. Even communications were becoming difficult. Letters, which had to pass through Denmark, were now opened "after the revolution [against Struensee], and many letters that were favorable to that minister have been lost."[37] When in Stockholm the Caps seemed to get the upper hand, Michelessi was even more convinced of the strength of influence of Russia, which seemed truly the "arbiter of Sweden."[38] With greater obstinacy he intensified his work. It was necessary, he was convinced, to appeal more to the Swedish past, to find historical roots. It was also for this reason that he studied the language of the country, which he thought still "uncertain in its rules, and uncultivated, without a grammar or dictionaries, although rather copious."[39] At the end of March he began composing "a little work in Swedish, on the subject of Gustavus Vasa, who liberated his country from the tyranny of Christian

---

dell'abate Michelessi a mons. Visconti oggi cardinale sopra la rivoluzione, li Discorsi tenuti dal maresciallo e dagli oratori degli ordini dinanzi al re nel chiudersi la Dieta, li 9 settembre 1772. Nel fine le memorie del conte Carlo di Scheffer riguardanti l'educazione di S.A.R., alcune tradotte dagli originali francesi ed alcune dalli svezzesi (Venice: Giambattista Pasquali, 1773).

[34] Treviso, 1262, *Gustavi IIIrii Sveciae regis Orationes sveco in latinum conversae.* In a letter from Stockholm dated 13 November 1772 (Treviso, 1260, mazzo 6), Michelessi wrote that Merian had finished the printing of this work. He proposed to have an edition published in Italy but cautioned to wait for the corrections that would come from Berlin. Already in August of the same year he had written that Gustavus III had been "very pleased by the dedication to the Pope, of whom we speak often when we are together" (ibid., 11 August 1772).

[35] Treviso, 1260, Stockholm, 9 June 1772.

[36] Ibid., Stockholm, 6 March 1772.

[37] Ibid., Stockholm, 23 March 1772.

[38] Ibid., Stockholm, 7 April 1772.

[39] Ibid., Stockholm, 23 March 1772.

ii, and who from being a citizen became a king."[40] National and local elements seemed all the more important because the nobility, the party of the Hats, and the king himself appeared to have succumbed to a true idolatry of Paris and considered "anything they do in France" as "divine."[41] Gustavus iii was certainly "a truly honest king, as wise and gracious as could be, but young and in the hands of advisers who make him believe that 'there is no health outside of Paris,' a maxim more deeply engraved in his mind because his tutor, Count Scheffer, preached it to him from his earliest youth; consequently, the king does nothing but talk of Paris and Versailles." The infatuation took an aristocratic form but ended by becoming a kind of idolization of French absolutism. The king's councilors were rearranged following this model, hoping to make Gustavus iii sovereign of Sweden, "which, if I were to enter into a political discussion, I would say was only a dream," Michelessi concluded. Gustavus iii seemed too bound to one of the two parties. "All the Caps think him a Hat, and no Hat takes him for a Cap."[42] He was too partisan in his praise of senators removed by the Diet.[43] The situation the king found himself in might explain such behavior. How could one accept the painful situation of having to depend on "a crowd of villains, priests, and drunken bourgeois who attend the Diet to sponge money from Russia and France and ill-treat the princes and the king"?[44] "The fury of the people" even when it seemed somewhat "calmed" could not help make the king "agitated and taciturn."[45] The king himself emphasized the parallel between his condition and that of the doge of Venice, "a comparison that, for all his effort to evoke with philosophy and indifference the memories of what has happened and happens daily, was painful to me in my sincere attachment for this worthy prince."[46] But even in his effort to console himself, Gustavus iii still seemed pathetic. In June he declared that "since his influence could not shine in matters outside the kingdom, as he has none in the affairs of Europe, nor within the kingdom, where he is like the doge of Venice, there remains for him only to make himself loved and esteemed for acts of beneficence,"[47] like Stanislaus Augustus of Poland, we might conclude.

But the outcome in Stockholm was quite different from that in Warsaw in the summer of 1772, which witnessed the partitioning of Poland

[40] Ibid., Stockholm, 31 March 1772.
[41] Ibid., Stockholm, 3 April 1772.
[42] Ibid., Stockholm, 14 April 1772.
[43] Ibid., Stockholm, 15 May 1772.
[44] Ibid., Stockholm, 14 April 1772.
[45] Ibid., Stockholm, 22 and 28 April 1772.
[46] Ibid., Stockholm, 19 May 1772.
[47] Ibid., Stockholm, 9 June 1772.

and the Swedish revolution. Michelessi was so engrossed in his work that he was not aware that behind the appearance of dignified resignation Gustavus III was preparing a plot that would deliver the scepter of the nation into his hands. And it was precisely because of his lack of awareness of the more hidden aspects of the policy of Gustavus III that the Italian abbé in the end influenced, not events, but the coloration these assumed, contributing with his words and writings to the dilution of the aristocratic element in the actions of Gustavus III, to blunt the point of absolutism, and to create the political atmosphere that surrounded the sunset of the age of liberty.

The oration he gave in Swedish, in the presence of Gustavus III, at the academy when he was received in this assembly, pivoted around the idea of liberty. This was linguistic liberty, first of all: "Rich and sweet," poetic, like Greek and Latin, was the Swedish language when "considered in a metaphysical way," "free from the yoke of didactic construction."[48] The political roots of oratory in Sweden were not less vital. "Free lands have always produced great orators." These judgments and appreciations were tuned to support the acts of Gustavus III. "Fortunate Swedes! You also have another advantage: behold among you Demosthenes, the defender of liberty on the throne."[49] "For a year the pen of Gustavus has accustomed you to a style that bears the vigorous imprint of a free and magnanimous heart, and to the only passion worthy of a king, that is, to do as much good as possible."[50] No people other than the Venetians could understand his work. "They are republicans who praise a king when they speak of liberty. Their vote is all the more valuable because they are free to give praise or withhold it, and they are above any suspicion of adulation. Reading such speeches has kindled the imagination of my sensitive nation. Men and women illustrious of birth and genius echo your king's name on the happy shores of the Adriatic. The crown with which you have girded the temples of Gustavus is laced with Italian laurels."[51] He turned to the past, to a past of Sweden that was "more remarkable than the romances of other peoples," but he also looked ahead, to the future, and saw "the Swedish scepter in the hands of beneficence."[52] In other words, from the roots of liberty would be born policies of reform.[53] Carl Frederick Scheffer, the second tutor

---

[48] *Operette in prosa ed in verso, composte in Svezia dal signor abate Domenico Michelessi* (n.p., n.d., but Venice: Pasquali, 1773), pp. xiff.

[49] Ibid., p. xvii. On the political problem of eloquence see Jean Starobinski, "Eloquence et liberté," *Revue suisse d'histoire*, fasc. 4 (1976): 549ff.

[50] Michelessi, *Operette*, pp. xviiff.

[51] Ibid., p. xviii.

[52] Ibid., pp. xxiiff.

[53] There is a full review of this speech in the *Journal littéraire dédié au roi*, published in Berlin in November–December 1772, pp. 114ff.

of the king, minister-plenipotentiary in France, member of the council of state, and after the "revolution" author, along with Gustavus III, of the new Swedish constitution, responded to Michelessi's speech. Scheffer had been a Freemason since 1737 and was the founder and grand master of the auxiliary lodge of St. John in Stockholm. His words ably expressed enlightened hopes, memories of Italy, and the political reality of Sweden. He remembered how Italy was "the common fatherland" of the "literary societies of our days." He remembered the great Venetians—Morosini, Tron, and Algarotti—but he lingered on the modern phenomenon of the emergence of a new people "in the extreme north," who merited "more than ever to be seen with the eyes of a philosopher." He even cited Russia in the epoch of Peter the Great, which with "a sudden flight" had raised itself "from the abyss, if we can call it that, of ignorance and barbarism to the heights of greatness and glory in all manner of things." For Scheffer as well as for Voltaire, it was a question of "a remarkable turnabout, more similar to a new creation than to a reform of government."[54] For Sweden, Scheffer suggested, the problem was different, even if a new political and intellectual direction was necessary there.

Beyond academic walls these thoughts were more difficult to express. Michelessi was convinced that he should postpone publication of a poem he had in mind to write until the end of the Diet, because of the "ideas, although most just, in it concerning liberty."[55] It was not because there was censorship in Sweden—"every day libelles and satires are published, as in London"—but because "it is important not to make enemies, and about this the king himself is in agreement with me." One should do nothing to make the work of Gustavus III more difficult. The king showed him the speech he had prepared for the day of the coronation. "It would be impossible to make a more beautiful one. I am astonished," concluded Michelessi.[56] On that occasion a new official knightly order titled with the name of Vasa was instituted, "instituted by His Majesty Gustavus III to encourage agriculture, commerce, mining, and the arts."[57] The political and social significance of the gesture was clear. "Through this foundation," the king declared, according to what *La gazzetta di Milano* reported, "those who are not nobles but merit such an honor can be compensated." "I have resolved in the nomination of these knights not to pay the least attention to birth or honors, and be-

---

[54] Michelessi, *Operette*, pp. xxviiiff.

[55] It was entitled "La bontà," sang the praises of Adolphus Frederick, was dedicated to Vergennes, and was published in *Operette*, pp. xxxvff., and in the *Poesie di Domenico Michelessi* (Fermo: Agostino Paccaroni, 1786), pp. 131ff.

[56] Treviso, 1260, Stockholm, 22 May 1772.

[57] "Per l'ordine reale di Vasa," in Michelessi, *Operette*, p. xlix.

cause all my subjects are equally dear to me and I divide my love among
them without any distinction, I take pleasure on any occasion to be able
to give them signs of my benevolence."[58] The idea of an order devoted
to economic life was original and effective: in the involution of chivalric
tradition could be encased modern economic concerns. The *Notizie del
mondo* published the statutes of the "new knightly order of Vasa." The
king was to be the grand master, and no one could abolish the order.
"The king can name no knights . . . before his coronation and without
having first sworn to observe the statutes." All new members were received with the following formula: "We King of Sweden, of Goths and
of Vandals, receive you as a knight in our renowned order of Vasa: Be
worthy."[59] At the same time the king got into the habit of regularly at-
tending sessions at the Academy of Sciences and Arts when they were
devoted to "useful arts." The Tuscan gazette that published this information did not miss emphasizing that "Abate Michelessi, an Italian," was
a member of this body.[60] In Michelessi's thought and writing such royal
proposals were a hymn to human industry, to harmonious union under
the rule of Gustavus III, of agriculture, which was particularly praised
("senza te virtude / fra noi non vive"), of work, of mining, and of commerce.

> Tu felice Sveco
> l'arti e il commercio colla prima madre
> agricoltura abbracci. . . .[61]

Ceres was associated with the science for which Sweden was famous in
the world: botany,

> amica di Linneo, che il crin le adorna
> d'americani fior culti in Upsala.[62]

One voice now sounded throughout the north.

> Gustavo Wasa e libertà cantava.[63]

In the verses of Michelessi the compromise between republican tradition and reforming monarchy thus took on a particularly elegant and

---

[58] *La gazzetta di Milano*, no. 31, 29 July 1772 (Stockholm, 28 June). One might note
that the first foreign member of the order was Marquis de Mirabeau. Bain, *Gustavus III*,
vol. 1, p. 91 n. 1.

[59] *Notizie del mondo*, no. 67, 22 August 1772, p. 550 (Stockholm, 24 July).

[60] Ibid., no. 70, 1 September 1772, p. 578 (Stockholm, 4 August).

[61] "Without you virtue / does not live among us" "You happy Swede / embrace the arts
and commerce with the first mother / agriculture. . . ." "Per l'ordine reale di Wasa," in
Michelessi, *Operette*, p. lxi.

[62] "Friend of Linnaeus, who adorns her hair / with American flowers grown in Upsala." Ibid., p. lii.

[63] "It sang Gustavus Vasa and liberty." Ibid., p. liv.

composed form, balanced between Swedish history and classical tradition, between "virtue" and "beneficence."

The poem, the most significant one from the pen of Michelessi during his stay in Sweden, was published immediately in Stockholm.[64] But there were obstacles. He had wanted to add to his canto a Greek epigraph from Xenophon's *Memorabilia*. "Imagine," he finally had to confess, "in the capital of a kingdom not being able to find a printer with enough Greek characters to print at the head of a poem, so that they will have to put it in Italian, or wait until some old characters come from Upsala, which would be next year, given the promptness of this active folk."[65]

These details irritated him but did not distract him from his goals. Although he had a great desire to resume his pilgrimage and take his trip to Russia before the end of the summer, he felt he could not oppose the desires of Gustavus III. The king, as the months passed, seemed more and more disquieted. His initiatives seemed questionable to Michelessi. He consoled himself by thinking that "age will temper this youthful fire. Who knows how many mad things we would do ourselves if we became king at the age of twenty-six years."[66] At times he hid himself behind an impenetrable veil. "He has ordered me to remain here until the first of August, and would thus be 'very displeased if I left even one day earlier.'"[67] What was he trying to say? Michelessi was not the only one at court to ask this. The inauguration of the Order of Vasa was fixed for an earlier date, 17 July. Unable to resolve the mystery, there was nothing for Michelessi to do but resume his work as a publicist. On 20 July he sent to Bonomo Algarotti material that was to be printed in Venice. The speeches of the king, he said in the preface, "were just like those in ancient Rome. Gustavus speaks from the throne of liberty, as enemies of the king spoke in the Roman senate, a clear sign that not royalty, but violation of the laws leads to slavery, just as it is not the famous words 'free people,' but constant authority of the laws that proves the liberty of a nation. Men are always deceived by appearances. Often weak governments fear the doctor rather than the pain and reject the hand that can cure them."[68] In August he consigned all this material to the king. "He says he wants to look at it (although he will not be able to read it) and then send it off." As for the Latin version, it would not

---

[64] *Per l'ordine reale di Wasa instituito da S.M. Gustavo III re di Svezia, il giorno della sua incoronazione per l'avvaloramento dell'agricoltura, del commercio, delle mine e delle arti. Canto* (Stockholm: H. Fought, 1772). A copy is in Treviso, 1261.

[65] Treviso, 1260, mazzo 6, Stockholm, 11 August 1772.

[66] Ibid., Stockholm, 22 July 1772.

[67] Ibid., Stockholm, 23 June 1772.

[68] "Al conte Bonomo Algarotti, Michelessi." Dedication of the *Carteggio*, p. 5, Stockholm, 20 July 1772.

be possible to publish it in Stockholm because the speech of Gustavus III
was included; "for printing it in Swedish the printer is still in prison."[69]

But then events hastened onward. Michelessi received with disbelief
the first news of military movements in southern Sweden. Evidently
Gustavus III had decided to cut the Gordian knot. Even in Italy, from
the first advisories, it was understood that this was not a simple act of
force or a simple change of gears in government policy. Echoes of the
"extraordinary ferment" in the country showed that it was a "total subversion of the constitution of the Swedish kingdom."[70] Apparently it was
not a plot, but rather an insurrection, apparently spontaneous. The
preparation, it was said, came seemingly from the initiative of a single
individual, the "treasurer or rather public official of this city" (Stockholm), Gestrin, author of a book entitled *The Reign of Darkness*, who had
been arrested but was still quite influential.[71] The spark to action came
from the captain commanding the garrison of Christianstadt, who proclaimed in a manifesto that the orders composing the Diet had "not
taken care of the interests of the republic and the kingdom of Sweden."
"Instead of bringing prompt remedies to the misery that oppressed the
people, they have thought only of their own interests." The only remedy
"for so many ills" was "to put the sovereign power, of which he is so
worthy," at the feet of the king. Peasants and citizens of that locality had
"joined the troops of the captain." The movement rapidly assumed
large proportions. "The confederates have taken as their motto the following words: 'For God, the State, and the Fatherland.' "[72] As one can
see, the atmosphere was almost Polish. In fact, the insurgents were
called confederates. But their program was precisely the opposite of
that of their Polish namesakes: "The nation absolutely desires a sovereign king."[73] The success of the initiative in Christianstadt seemed modest at first. In the capital there was no "change in public tranquillity."
Measures the Senate took to ensure that "the spirit of revolution which
has appeared in that place does not spread to others" seemed successful
at first. "There will be no alteration," it was said, "at all in the constitu-

---

[69] Treviso, 1260, Stockholm, 11 August 1772.

[70] *Notizie del mondo*, no. 74, 15 September 1772, p. 610 (Hamburg, 25 August). This
gazette, in the final index for the year, collected the news of these events under the title
"Storia della rivoluzione di Svezia o sia mutazione del governo."

[71] Ibid., no. 71, 5 September 1772, p. 585 (Stockholm, 6 August). Again in no. 75, 19
September 1772, p. 619 (Hamburg, 28 August), it was said: "One cannot disprove that
the book of the fiscal agent Gestrin was not the cause of the uprising."

[72] Ibid., no. 74, 15 September 1772, pp. 608ff. (Helsingör, 24 August).

[73] Ibid., p. 609. On the same page of the gazette there are many notices of survivors
among the Polish confederates who sought refuge in Bavaria.

tion of this kingdom."[74] The king's brother, Prince Charles, made a move that seemed to place him against the rebels. It was a trick arranged by Gustavus III. His manifesto revealed a political position of deep uncertainty, which in reality was in support of the intentions of the king. "I exhort all inhabitants of the country not to abandon themselves to the old yoke, the old discord and differences, but instead to cooperate with me in restoring calm. Until the son of Hades who has brought us to this state of anxiety and misery is apprehended, a sword of destruction hangs over the heads of all, as much on citizens in their houses as on peasants in their fields, the mendicant in his hovel, and the babe in its cradle."[75]

The anguish reached its height on 19 August. The international situation forced the king to conclude matters: in Denmark the enemies of Struensee were now in power. On 5 August the partition of Poland was signed. The king could rightly fear that there might be a solution in Sweden similar to the one that had struck the kingdom of Stanislaus Augustus. The English government, which was repeatedly informed of the plans of Gustavus III, warned the Diet on 16 August.[76] The king could save himself only by acting immediately.[77] Thus, "on the morning of the nineteenth there was a total revolution in our government," reported a full narration of the events published in the *Notizie del mondo* on 22 September. "The Caps, that is, the republican party, finally had to succumb." Gustavus III had called up the guards, explaining to the officers, about two hundred, that "the government groaned under aristocratic tyranny" and that it was necessary to return "to the ancient and legitimate liberty Sweden had enjoyed under kings Gustavus I and Gustavus Adolphus." He assured them that "he would not do the least damage to the liberty of the country." To the request "if they wanted to help him in breaking this yoke, two captains responded 'no' and their swords were demanded immediately on their arrest; a third, it is said, fainted." The others accepted. When the two battalions of guards were united, "the king mounted on horseback and asked whether they were content with the powers that the great enjoyed in his kingdom; they said 'no' (as one can easily guess) . . . and amid cries of 'long live the king' they also pledged allegiance." The senators, who "were gathered in the Hall of the Council in the same palace," were unable to resist and were blocked

74 Ibid., no. 75, 19 September 1772, p. 616 (Stockholm, 18 August).

75 Ibid., p. 619 (Hamburg, 28 August). The manifesto was dated 15 August 1772.

76 See Roberts, "Great Britain and the Swedish Revolution of 1772–1773," in id., *Essays in Swedish History*, pp. 286ff., and on these developments in general see his essay "19 August 1772: An Ambivalent Revolution," in *L'Età dei Lumi*, vol. 1, pp. 563ff.

77 For a detailed narrative based on documents unknown to contemporaries, see Bain, *Gustavus III*, vol. 1, pp. 105ff.; Nordmann, *Grandeur et liberté de la Suède*, pp. 131ff.

by the guards. The king assured himself personally of the loyalty of the
artillery, to which he said he intended to reestablish "ancient Swedish
liberty as it was in 1680," renouncing "from this moment on odious unlimited royal power" and "absolute sovereignty" and declaring himself
to be "the first citizen of a truly free people." Then came the turn of the
ministers of foreign powers, to whom he explained that his person, and
the security of the state, had been menaced, and he assured them of his
pacific intentions. Many notables were arrested, all "with contacts in the
republican party": officials, judges, governors, burgomasters, and ecclesiastics. Meanwhile, an increasing number of persons heeded the orders of the king and followed his example, decking themselves with his
symbol—a handkerchief tied to an arm. In the evening, in the Arsenal,
he was welcomed with "a general 'long live the king' " by sailors and
common people. "All was quiet in the night; the king did the rounds
with a patrol in some of the streets, and his most trusted officers did the
same in other places."[78] The following day the assembly of the four orders received an address from him and heard of a preliminary plan for
a new constitution. An edict mentioned a plot to "introduce aristocratic
power over our faithful subjects in this kingdom," which fortunately
had been foiled by the king. Gustavus III explained to the assembly of
orders that he had been able to conclude his long struggle with the two
parties, which with their discord and vendettas were at the root of all
the evils of the country. It was their fault if "liberty, the most precious
of all rights of humanity," had degenerated into an "intolerable aristocratic despotism." The best citizens and officials, and the most zealous
magistrates, had been "sacrificed." "It seems that even the Supreme
Being had demonstrated his wrath at the unjust conduct of those in
power. The land had closed up its breast; famine, misery, and hunger
had devastated the country." The only means of escape was "a stable
and regulated government, as had been established in the ancient laws
of Sweden." To his "dear subjects" he promised "true liberty," the security that would be procured by "the laws for all your goods," "freedom
in all your trade, an impartial administration of justice, maintenance of
good order in the cities and in the open country . . . , and finally preservation of a pure piety stripped of fanaticism and superstition."[79]

[78] *Notizie del mondo*, no. 76, 22 September 1772, pp. 624ff. (Stockholm, 21 August):
"Exact account of what happened in Stockholm from 19 August 1772 to and including
the twenty-first."

[79] Ibid., no. 77, 26 September 1772, pp. 632ff. (Stockholm, 25 August). See no. 78, 29
September 1772, p. 640 (Stockholm, 28 August), where we see Gustavus III before the
assembly of orders "seated on the throne." "After having struck twice on the table with
the silver scepter that the kings of Sweden have carried from antiquity to impose silence,
His Majesty addressed the states thus."

As one sees, Gustavus III distorted the political language of his time. Liberty, despotism, and aristocracy became in his hand instruments of a policy that tended to substitute civil liberty, duly guaranteed by the monarchy, for the traditions of political liberty of the Swedish "republic." His program was monarchical, but he was still obliged to take into account the concrete reality of local tradition, of the constituted bodies before which he presented himself, and of the force and diversity of the movement he had provoked. He knew very well that the policy of recent years had menaced the nobility. He did not deny the bonds that connected him with the aristocratic world. He even defended it, as his later policy showed more clearly. He was anything but a demagogue. He attacked the nobility because he wanted them active around him, not in the opposition. What scandalized him most in their behavior was their demonstrated incapacity of collaborating with an absolutism that was respectful, and even the promoter, of civil liberty. As he keenly observed in the Sweden of his day, in the "clash of democracy with dying aristocracy," the mistake of the nobility was to prefer to "submit itself to democracy rather than to be protected by the monarchy, which extended its arms." The situation was similar in France, he observed. But at least there the state was solid, whereas Sweden advanced with great steps toward "anarchy." And in order to see what the outcome might be it was enough to look at nearby Poland. "The sacred names of religion and liberty have reduced the Poles to the state in which they now find themselves." These were his judgments two months earlier in his own "revolution" when he concluded: "I do not have the phlegm of the king of Poland." "Perhaps the parallel between the situation of my country and that of Poland makes my feelings more vivid and my interests more obvious."[80]

Michelessi, in Stockholm, followed the developments of August with passion. Surprised by events, and skeptical at first about the possible results, he informed Bonomo Algarotti of the rapid triumph of the king, always insisting on the fact that it was a bloodless revolution, without those disorders that "often accompany happenings of this nature."[81] As for Gustavus III, fear for his safety and admiration for his courage alternated in Michelessi's mind in those decisive days. "I went out immediately and found him with the artillery. . . . I found him on horse-

---

[80] Geffroy, *Gustave III*, vol. 1, pp. 264ff., letter to Madame de Boufflers dated 14 June 1772.

[81] Treviso, 1260, Stockholm, 25 August 1772. Bonomo Algarotti responded from Venice on 16 September, happy with the good news. "We will thus see Gustavus on the throne of Sweden in full sovereignty and Sweden governed by a wise and moderate king." (Treviso, 1263, Venice, 16 September 1772. This, like the rest of the source, was a draft of a letter.)

back all disheveled and perspiring," he wrote on 21 August. " 'My friend,' he said, 'can I trust the people? I was forced into this act, without which I would have been arrested tonight. . . .' I told him to stop wherever there were people gathered together, and instead of making them swear their allegiance, to speak and cry out, as he had just done." Michelessi was preoccupied particularly with European public opinion. What would "the gazettes of London and other free countries" say? There Gustavus III risked being taken for a "perjurer." "Saying one does not want to be a sovereign is well and good, but everything he does, and the cannons he surrounded the room with where the estates *freely* took their new oath and abjured the aristocracy, does not announce liberty." The greatest peril was now in the return to power of some senators and nobles, such as Scheffer and Bielke. "God knows what devilry will be done by these persons, odious to the whole nation." The only hope was in the courage and personal capacities of the king. "What is true is that Gustavus Vasa and Gustavus Adolphus could not have behaved better or with more courage." The political result appeared to him clearer and more precise than it was in reality. "Today Gustavus III is king, like those of Naples or Sardinia."[82] Everything seemed to depend on him, even the liberty of Sweden, a land that had not known how to defend itself. "With ignominy" seemed to him covered "this vile nation, which can thank God that Gustavus is a fine man. Without this it would let itself be enchained without the least difficulty."[83]

The important thing was to inform everyone, and particularly the Pope, who should not "ignore or wait to hear from the gazettes such an interesting event as a king who four days ago had the powers of the doge of Venice and today is an absolute sovereign, although he has solemnly renounced sovereignty, that is, despotism." "I will write to the nuncio in Vienna," he added, "about things in general, saying that I have already written to Rome." "I think it would please the Duke of Savoy, who has no minister here, to send him this news."[84] He assured everyone that the situation in the capital was quiet. "There is good news from all the provinces."[85] The only discordant notes came from the official religious ceremonies. At the *Te deum* "a f—— Lutheran preached for two hours comparing the king to Israel, Mars, Jesus Christ, the Holy Spirit, and then the organ, the hymns, and the communion where they ate and drank. In short, one had to stand up for four hours, because there were no benches or chairs around the king, who was annoyed at

---

[82] Ibid., Stockholm, 21 August 1772.
[83] Ibid., Stockholm, 10 September 1772.
[84] Ibid., Stockholm, 22 August 1772.
[85] Ibid., Stockholm, 25 August 1772.

all these pretty comparisons." Michelessi was even more irritated because in these days he was working ceaselessly to translate into Latin the king's declarations and speeches. "For thirty-eight hours I have written without taking off my clothes or sleeping for a minute. The king thinks one can do these translations easily. I would like you to see what a thing it is to translate from Swedish."

A heavy cloud obscured the political horizon: what would be the reaction of the two countries committed to the defense of Swedish liberty—Russia and Denmark? Still, the latter, alone, was not to be feared, and it seemed "impossible that the czarina, after having concluded one war for Poland, should want to take on another for Sweden."[86] He thought that the comparison with the kingdom of Stanislaus Augustus was inappropriate. Unlike Poland, there did not exist in Sweden "a single subject in revolt or opposition: thus the court of St. Petersburg has no dissenters, no confederates, to aid it, because there is no man who begs its assistance."[87]

How could one leave Sweden in the midst of all these adventures and problems? "Thus I passed the winter in Stockholm." He intended to visit Lapland "in the company of Gustavus, if war does not call him elsewhere, which I hope will not happen."[88] Meanwhile, despite some infirmity, he continued to be very busy. He took up again the work he had begun in the preceding months, collected as many documents as he could, and wrote his conclusions on the revolution. The work was soon published with the title *Lettre à M. Visconti archevêque d'Ephèse et nonce apostolique auprès de SS. MM. II. RR. et AA. sur la révolution arrivée en Suède le 19 août 1772*, with the place of Stockholm, "chez H. Fougt, imprimeur du roi." An appendix of documents offered readers the speeches of the king, the panegyric for Adolphus Federick, the final orders and decrees on the closing of the Diet, letters of the king to his brother, Charles, and so on. The *Lettre* was dated 3 November 1772.[89] The Italian text was included in the collection that appeared in Venice at the beginning of the following year.

The tone of the *Lettre* was set by a motto from Claudian: "*Nunquam libertas gratior extat quam sub rege pio*" (liberty is never more welcome than under a pious king). Republics generally arose out of revolts directed against kings when they became tyrants, but "the Swedes have never adopted a purely republican government, not even when, oppressed by

---

[86] Ibid., Stockholm, 28 August 1772.
[87] Ibid., Stockholm, 10 September 1772.
[88] Ibid., Stockholm, 10 November 1772.
[89] A copy is in Milan in the B. Braidense with the call number MM.I.2. It comes from the library of Albert Haller.

tyrants, they broke their yoke. This state is too large and its population is too sparse to be suited to that form of government, beyond what is dictated by the customs of the nation." Before 1720 Sweden had known "a more or less moderate monarchy." "The absolute sovereignty of Charles XI was even useful to the nation." Charles XII "was not a tyrant either, but good, affable, and honest. His obstinate wars were the result of education: the great, to make him leave his kingdom so as to govern it in the time of his absence, inspired him with a taste for military heroism." After his death the government of the country was changed. "A republican government . . . with a monarchical appearance" emerged. The Romans too had had their "sacrificial kings." This appearance was made necessary by the monarchical inclination, which Swedes had never abandoned.[90]

"Republican liberty" had soon shown that it was deleterious to the nation. "Sweden was without an army, without money, without industry, without either trade or population. All its glory seemed to expire with Charles XII. Two parties divided the nation and formed within it; one could say, two peoples."[91] Intentions and ideas were for the best, but the results were the worst possible. "Reading the constitution of 1720, it breathes order, independence, and liberty." But this meant only that "metaphysical systems imposed on the best form of government, when put into practice, do not always succeed." Even the Swedish example, like that of ancient Rome, showed that it was not enough to look at models of perfect republics or monarchies. In reality "a government is good or bad according to the qualities of those who govern."[92] In Sweden the two parties never succeeded in establishing a balance, which is what had happened in Italy in the past. "There was a perfect resemblance to parties that had arisen in the past in Florence: they were supported by two great powers, and the heads of both stood only for their own authority and particular interest." To be sure, in Tuscany there had been a resort to arms, but in Sweden "there were only continual diets, disputes, differences, and legal wranglings." But in one case as in the other, the only way out was through exhaustion of the parties. In Florence, "the sovereignty of the house of Medici put an end to these disturbances." What had happened in Sweden had been seen by Domenico Michelessi with his own eyes. "Can it not be said that from time to time men and circumstances repeat themselves?"[93] Even Gustavus III, as soon

[90] "Lettera a monsignor Visconti . . . sopra la rivoluzione di Svezia li 19 Agosto 1772," in *Carteggio*, pp. 229ff.

[91] Ibid., p. 231.

[92] Ibid., p. 232.

[93] Ibid., pp. 234–35.

as he had reached the throne, had done everything possible to reconcile all factions. But this was in vain, because they found their support outside of Sweden. "Thus in Florence to end the struggle of the Guelf and Ghibelline parties it would have been necessary to extinguish the influence of the powers that fomented them." "Reconciliation" proved to be impossible.[94] Gustavus III's aim to overcome all these difficulties was revealed to the eyes of Michelessi the day the king made his speech to the Diet. "I knew the king only as an amiable and well-educated prince; but in his speech I recognized the character of a sincere and courageous soul. He had no fear in telling the assembled states sensible truths."[95] Civil discord increased every day. "In France and in Italy blood would have been shed."[96] The nobility did not seem able to get a grip on that power which the king hurried to seize. The other orders did not succeed in finding a common formula. Meanwhile economic difficulties grew. "Did one party establish some useful measure? The other did everything possible to oppose it. . . . Were the measures bad? There was weak opposition. . . . Both sides were in a deadlock; everything was written about; all was discredited."[97] "In republics, as in monarchies, the general will can be only one; in Sweden there were two contradictory ones."[98] Alternately, "the nation became enslaved by one party and this had a limited number of heads."[99] The people did not know what the deputies did. "Are not representatives who can conclude everything definitively, without being obligated to give account, perhaps the rulers of those whom they represent? Do they perhaps not have more power than the nation that confers it on them?"[100] After having described in detail the stormy events that immediately preceded the end of the drama, Michelessi concluded by writing as follows: "There is no party without fanaticism. Sweden was no exception: it operated on all minds, as much as can occur in this naturally peaceful nation; it influenced every estate, every condition, and the people themselves."[101] The laws seemed to tie the hands of the king completely, who was impotent to protect even the civil liberty of Swedes, property, and justice. It was time for a "great change."[102] "To Gustavus III was finally given the task of putting an end to the discord and turbulence that lacerated his country. . . . Everything,

[94] Ibid., p. 236.
[95] Ibid., p. 237.
[96] Ibid., p. 238.
[97] Ibid., p. 240.
[98] Ibid., pp. 24ff.
[99] Ibid., p. 242.
[100] Ibid.
[101] Ibid., p. 251.
[102] Ibid., p. 256.

even his name, favored it."[103] Michelessi had no reason to color the events of August of 1772 with spontaneity. He described the coup d'état as the result of the will and courage of Gustavus III. He had participated in it too much not to celebrate it as a victory of a careful political plan.

One cannot admire enough the constancy, intrepidity, and presence of mind of that young prince. At the beginning of the revolution I went to the artillery. The king had honored me with too many acts of beneficence for me not to be fearful for his safety. He told me to enter; he was on horseback and deigned to address me to inform me with admirable precision of what had happened, the steps already taken and what remained to do; in the midst of the greatest peril he was as calm as he had been in the assembly. On the eve of this great day there had been a concert and dinner at the court—there were at least eighty persons—but the king seemed to be the most brilliant of all. I have seen a letter written during the concert on the plan for the following day, in which it was impossible to express better the sentiments of his fine spirit, nor to write better amid the greatest calm.[104]

Nor did Michelessi have less admiration for the political aspects of the king's actions. "Seated on the throne he made a speech that was a masterpiece of eloquence; he depicted with masculine vigor the excesses, disorders, and unhappiness into which disunity had plunged the state."[105] After a detailed description of the means by which Gustavus III succeeded in acquiring control of all the levers of power, Michelessi passed immediately, almost in conclusion, to tell how the king had abolished torture and how he had known how to end the session of the diet with dignity and vigor. In this way ended "the most happy revolution that history can tell."[106]

Echoes of this work were everywhere. A German translation appeared.[107] In Italy the *Lettre* helped to fix the developing image of events in Sweden, and of Gustavus III. An abridged version (without the personal testimony of Michelessi) appeared in the *Notizie del mondo* under the significant title "Account of the Swedish Revolution of 19 August 1772, as published by the court, which contains a description of the kingdom before the same, and of the causes that produced it. In this

[103] Ibid., p. 260. After many classical citations, a reference to Machiavelli's *Discorsi* was also included (see p. 256 n.).

[104] Ibid., pp. 263–64.

[105] Ibid., p. 267.

[106] Ibid., p. 281.

[107] *Des Herrn Abt Michelessi Schreiben an den Herrn Visconti . . . über die den 19. August 1772 in Schweden vorgegangene Staatsveränderung, nebst der nemen Regierungsform und andern dahin gehörige Reden und Schriften* (Greisswald: A. F. Röse, 1773). (As one sees, this version appeared in Swedish Pomerania.)

are the corrections of many errors not corrected in other accounts that were diffused in the kingdom and spread falsely abroad."[108]

From Vienna Michelessi received a letter from Abate Giuseppe Antonio Taruffi, the secretary of the nuncio Visconti to whom, as one remembers, the *Lettre* was addressed.[109] He thanked him for the "picture . . . of the most astonishing revolution that has ever been." "Without misrepresenting the candor of history, the force of genius makes itself felt at every turn: the fire of your young hero electrifies, so to speak, and penetrates your story." The work undoubtedly owed much "to the grandeur of events," "but one sees also that without the probe of Montesquieu it would not have been possible to indicate its course, nor without a pinch of Xenophon to trace its detail. Nothing could better demonstrate that history is a form of philosophy, but also, that to write it in an agreeable way, requires a philosophy like your own, full of sentiment and embellished with a taste for the arts, a philosophy resulting from a long study of the human heart, and a reflective reading of the ancient classics, which will always be our masters in matters of elegance." The nuncio Visconti was very grateful. "You can be sure that it will be a great pleasure to make so interesting a work known to those who can appreciate it, that is, to the select group of readers whose taste is informed by Horace."[110]

The Comte de Vergennes, the famous French ambassador in Stockholm, who was later minister of foreign affairs for Louis XVI, greatly appreciated Michelessi's *Lettre*. "The politician can perceive refined enlightened views; the philosopher a deep perception of chains of cause and effect; the man of erudition compensation for his labors in a felicitous application of examples from antiquity to modern times."[111]

Rome remained deaf as usual. "Those priests, until the day of judgment (or rather until a prince like Gustavus is born in Italy and drives them out of Rome), will be proud and full of themselves." What had happened in Sweden distanced him even more "from those Monsigneur b——s as they have always been, are, and will be."[112]

In Venice his friends went to a great deal of trouble to defend the image of Sweden that Michelessi had described. First they collected his prose and poetry, which were published by Pasquali at the beginning of 1773. The preface was written by Gaspare Gozzi. "The gazettes from

[108] *Notizie del mondo*, no. 19, 6 March 1773, pp. 146ff., and in the following numbers.
[109] On the ideas of Taruffi, see *Riformatori*, vol. 7, pp. 43–46ff.
[110] Treviso, 1261, "Vienna in Austria this 3 February 1773."
[111] L. Bonneville de Marsigny, *Le comte de Vergennes. Son ambassade en Suède, 1771–1774* (Paris: Plon, 1898), p. 248 n.
[112] Treviso, 1260, Stockholm, 6 November 1772. On 17 November he was still railing against "those priests, always proud when they should not be."

time to time have given news of you with praise and astonishment." He praised him for having learned Swedish, and at the same time for having made known there "good Italian letters and various works written in our language pleasing to his majesty the king, who these days is the admiration of Europe." Michelessi seemed to have entered the world of the north to such an extent that he felt he should conclude his presentation by saying: "Remember that you were born and educated in Italy."[113] Then the collection of materials about Gustavus III, which had been in preparation for some time, was completed. In Venice Bonomo Algarotti saw it through the press. Michelessi continued his translation.[114] He even found the time to translate into Italian "the funeral eulogy of Count Tessin done by Senator Höpken." "Tell me how many people in Venice you think would be capable of writing a similar discourse."[115]

Thus full of activity, and when he was making grand plans to travel and do further work—always with the hope in his heart of obtaining finally some benefit in France in the end to ensure his own independence, thanks perhaps to the intervention of Gustavus III—Michelessi became ill. He was cut down within a week, dying in Stockholm at the age thirty-seven, on 1 April 1773. The Italian and foreign gazettes talked of his demise.[116] The letters of condolence, carefully collected by Bonomo Algarotti, reflect a sense of surprise and sorrow for such an

---

[113] *Operette in prosa e in verso*, pp. iiiff. "Al signor abate Michelessi Gasparo Gozzi." Michelessi thanked him at the beginning of February "for trifles of mine printed by Pasquali." (Treviso, 1260, mazzo 7, Stockholm, 3 February 1773.)

[114] Treviso, 1260, Stockholm, 16 March 1773 (discussion of the title to give to the *Carteggio*), and Stockholm, 22 March (thanks for the "kind compliments you have paid me on the letter about the revolution" and injunctions to be sure French words printed by Pasquali would be correctly printed, because in the *Operette* there were quite a few errors, "whereas in Sweden Fougt, born in Lapland, printed French with the same correctness as [printers do] in Paris").

[115] Treviso, 1260, Stockholm, 17 November 1772. Michelessi's version was published posthumously: *Elogio al conte Tessin, senatore di Svezia ec. ec., recitato nell'Accademia reale delle scienze di Stockholm li XXV marzo 1771 da uno de' suoi membri il conte Giannandrea di Hoepken, senatore di Svezia, presidente del consiglio della Cancelleria, cancelliere dell'Università di Upsal* ..., translated from Swedish into Italian by Abate Domenico Michelessi (Venice: Giambattista Pasquali, 1774). Even though detached from the immediate struggle, this *Elogio* often alluded to the echoes in Sweden of events in Poland and considered the inevitable effects of open political discussion: "Liberty of judgment leads naturally to liberty to criticize, and liberty to criticize to a disposition toward an eventual revolution, a revolution always welcomed by the people who are so constituted that they cannot tolerate government or do without it."

[116] *Notizie del mondo*, no. 36, 4 May 1773, p. 284 (Stockholm, 2 April), and *Hamburgische Neue Zeitung*, no. 59, 13 April 1773 (a copy of the latter gazette is in Treviso, 1261); *Gazette de Nice*, no. 37, 10 May 1773, p. 146 (Stockholm, 9 April).

unexpected end. In this sad packet of letters appeared Vergennes (who had already written that "his genius" was "lively, happy, fertile, and brilliant" and that he had contributed much "to extend the celebrity of the king of Sweden in Italy"),[117] Bernis (who a little earlier had been surprised by the fact that an "Italian could write so well in French"),[118] Tanucci, and Kaspar Voght, from Hamburg ("the great Gustavus dropped tears on the news of his death. What a panegyric!").[119] The king of Sweden wanted to imitate the gesture Frederick II had made for Algarotti and promoted a monument dedicated to Michelessi.

> Optimo eruditissimo
> natione italo,
> Sveciae peramanter devincto,

one reads in one of the projects for an inscription, and

> natione italo
> adoptione sveco,

and even

> animo sveco,

as others proposed.[120]

Echoes of the interpretation that Michelessi had given to the Swedish revolution persisted for a long time in Europe. Let us open for instance the *Geschichte Gustaf's III* published by Ernest Ludwig Posselt in Karlsruhe in 1792. On the first page is an image that still symbolizes the thought of Michelessi: the king, invoking the Most High, succeeds in retaking the helm of Sweden, a ship terribly damaged by a tempest and that appears on the point of disappearing into the ocean. Underneath is an inscription: *Svecia servata* (Sweden saved). In the text, the author hardly begins his narrative of the revolution before basing it on what the Italian Abate had written, citing him continually.[121]

For Michelessi, as for all other observers when the revolution was over, attention naturally turned to the internal problems of the Swedish

---

[117] Bonneville de Marsigny, *Le comte de Vergennes. Son ambassade en Suède*, p. 248 n.

[118] Treviso, 1261, Rome, 20 February 1773.

[119] Ibid., Hamburg, 8 May 1773.

[120] "Most learned / Italian / bound to Sweden with love." "Italian / of Swedish adoption." "Swedish soul." Ibid., biographical information.

[121] Ernst Ludwig Posselt, *Geschichte Gustaf's III. Koenig der Schweden und Gothen* (Karlsruhe: Schmieder, 1792), pp. 60, 96, 110, 157, 176. Even the *Storia del regno e della vita di Gustavo III re di Svezia* (Venice: A. Zatta, 1792), which was published at the same time, was taken to a large extent from Michelessi. See vol. 2, pp. 53ff., 91ff.

kingdom: to the juridical, constitutional, and economic changes it underwent after the developments of August 1772. Gustavus III himself took the lead. Rapidly, almost repentantly, he turned to the problems of civil society. He had made use of the ideas of liberty, national history, the fear of disorder, and despotism to gain the throne. Now his task became to carry out reforms. His first moves undoubtedly showed ability. Before the end of August, when the churches were still sounding with "solemn thanks for the happy event," Gustavus III struck at a particularly odious aspect of the judicial system of the age of liberty and abolished torture. The reform was more than humanitarian; it was politically opportune. Torture had been practiced in Sweden in the age of the Diet's dominance, and it was widely employed in the political struggles of the years that preceded the revolution.[1] The king paid homage to *philosophie*. "He said," Michelessi had hastened to announce, "that it was the book *Dei delitti e delle pene* of the illustrious Beccaria that taught him this humanitarian trait."[2]

Thus, by order of the king (and not the initiative of the Diet) "the famous Chamber of the Rose" was suppressed on 27 August 1772. At the same time, as the *Notizie del mondo* reported, tribunals were ordered "to no longer make use of the cord or other instruments of torture to force criminals to confess, because torture generally serves only to confuse innocence with crime." "His Majesty ordered that torture chambers and other places of horror be closed forever, as miserable relics of disorders introduced in the administration of justice by the ignorance and barbarism of past centuries." Even in this edict, as in all the policies of Gustavus III, reflections of the past were mixed with the most modern ideas. The king affirmed that "the law of Sweden prohibited the use of the cord for inducing anyone to confess a crime." "And in fact," he explained, "there is nothing more contrary to humanity or more denigrating to the dignity of a generous people than the horrors of torture used against the accused and the harsh and violent treatment they are forced to undergo before their condemnation. For these reasons His Majesty wants these chambers of torment, which serve no purpose other than furthering tyranny and all most odious passions, suppressed in Sweden, so that there remain of them neither trace nor memory."[3]

Almost simultaneously, on 21 August, the new constitution was set down, a document also typical of the compromise on which the power

---

[1] Bain, *Gustavus III*, vol. 1, p. 162.

[2] Treviso, 1260, mazzo 1, Stockholm, 1 September 1772. A version of Beccaria's work appeared in Stockholm in 1770 and the translator, Johann Henrik Hochschield, dedicated it to the municipal council of the city. See Beccaria, *Dei delitti e delle pene*, p. 628.

[3] *Notizie del mondo*, no. 81, 6 October 1772, p. 657 (Stockholm, 4 September).

of Gustavus III was henceforth based.⁴ The basic aim was to ensure "that the ancient kingdom of Swedes and Goths remains always a free and an independent state." But the power of the senate was strongly checked and that of the Diet limited. The cabinet of the king was placed at the center of administration. The change was so great that it became necessary to dismiss the professor of public law from the University of Upsala.⁵ This was virtual absolutism but still was mitigated by past forms and traditions and by the search for a new relationship among the will to reform, efficiency of the state, and the need for liberty.

A growing interest for concrete problems that required a resolution soon prevailed, after the change of August 1772, not only in the political desires of the king, but also in broader public opinion. In his speech to the Diet of 9 September he said, "this happy revolution, effected by the Most High, has closed the wounds with which the body politic has been covered for more than a hundred years all at once and has united a people divided into factions into a free society, powerful, independent, and zealous for the true good of the country."⁶ But reality took on the task of showing that such miracles do not happen. The king could pride himself on the fact that no drop of blood had been shed in his coup, and he soon freed some of those who were imprisoned on that occasion.⁷ But the opposition did not remain silent, and there was news of the arrest of authors "of various books opposed to the present circumstances," who had gathered together in "nocturnal conventicles," had written "against the present form of government," and were denounced by the "printer to whom they had appealed."⁸ The king continued nonetheless his policy of generosity; even those who refused to swear fidelity to the new constitution were kept as functionaries. "The disunity of citizens," he said, "was close to causing the ruin of the country; I want to be king only to reunite its members."⁹

---

⁴ It is reproduced in its entirety in the *Notizie del mondo*, no. 79, 3 October 1772, pp. 648ff. (Stockholm, 1 September), and in the following numbers. Michelessi got hold of a Latin version of the original Swedish for the Pope, Treviso, 1260, mazzo 6, Drottningholm, 2 October 1772.

⁵ Ibid., no. 79, 3 October 1772, p. 649 (Stockholm, 1 September), and see no. 99, 12 December 1772, p. 809 (Stockholm, 10 November): "Because the recent revolution and the new form of government have brought a complete change in the system of public law in this realm, the king with his edict of 7 October past has suppressed the chair in this science at the University of Upsala, and Mr. Nils Rissel, who was the lector, was forced into retirement."

⁶ *Notizie del mondo*, no. 83, 17 October 1772, p. 680 (Stockholm, 15 September).

⁷ See, for example, ibid., no. 94, 24 November 1772, p. 767 (Stockholm, 23 October), news of the liberation of the "secretary of the order of peasants." There was also the rumor that his imprisonment "had driven him to madness."

⁸ Ibid., p. 768.

⁹ Ibid., no. 103, 26 December 1772, p. 840 (Stockholm, 24 November).

It seemed immediately necessary to attempt to alleviate the still grave economic situation in which the country found itself. A loan bank was instituted with the name General Bank of Assistance. Measures that the Diet had discussed at length in previous years were adopted, such as "the total prohibition of distillation of aquavit from grain," and some feast days were "abolished or postponed to the following Sundays."[10] There was an effort to organize assistance for the poor. A communication from Stockholm dated 9 December reads, "a society of well-to-do citizens who have taken the motto *Pro patria* was formed here. The aim of these patriots is to accumulate large funds to buy grain, destined to assist the different provinces of this kingdom, many of which are in great difficulty, despite the precaution of His Majesty, to the extent that he is able in the present circumstances to secure abundance everywhere."[11] A few months later a decree was read in churches creating houses "of employment for those who want to work." "Hundreds of women and children appeared in order to spin wool, hemp, and linen."[12] Even more difficult, and at first without result, was the effort to restore life to commerce, which was affected, among others, at the beginning of 1773, by the great failures of Dutch banks. "Commerce is in a kind of lethargy from which it will have difficulty recovering . . . the exchange continues on an uneven course," one read in the Florentine gazette of 6 March.[13] Thus it was necessary to reform the administration of the finances. Great plans were made in the spring of 1773. These were supposed to mark the moment of "recovery for all of Sweden, where the finances are in disorder. Thus one awaits with great impatience and curiosity the result of these regulations."[14] The current dispositions, and above all those of 8 March 1770, were "explained" and "interpreted," "in an attempt to encourage industry and the populace."[15] At the same time a new census

[10] Ibid., no. 99, 12 December 1772, pp. 809ff. (Stockholm, 10 November). See ibid., no. 47, 12 June 1773, p. 370 (Stockholm, 11 May): "The law prohibiting distillation is harshly enforced, and confiscations arising from it are very frequent." Still on 11 September there was the menace of "very severe penalties for violators." Existing stills were to serve only "to distill pears, apples, and other kinds of fruit," not "grain or feed." Ibid., no. 101, 19 December 1772, p. 825 (Stockholm, 18 November).

[11] Ibid., no. 3, 9 January 1773, p. 18 (Stockholm, 9 December 1772). See *Gazzetta di Parma*, no. 1, 3 January 1773 (Stockholm, 9 December).

[12] *Notizie del mondo*, no. 40, 18 May 1773, p. 316 (Stockholm, 21 April).

[13] Ibid., no. 19, 6 March 1773, p. 146 (Stockholm, 2 February). At the end of the year news came that Sweden was seeking a loan in Genova for "a million florins for the account of the Crown." Ibid., no. 100, 14 December 1773, p. 810 (Stockholm, 12 November). The loan was not granted. See Felloni, *Gli investimenti finanziari genovesi in Europa tra il Seicento e la restaurazione*.

[14] *Notizie del mondo*, no. 34, 27 April 1773, p. 266 (Stockholm, 29 March).

[15] Ibid., no. 39, 15 May 1773, p. 308 (Stockholm, 16 April).

of ecclesiastical property, and new taxation of it, was instituted.[16] The struggle to help beggars increased. "His Majesty has decided to take under his protection the poor and needy of his realm and hopes that true patriots will not stint themselves in order to diminish the number of these unfortunates." For this end he called on "women of the city and countryside," comparing them "to goddesses of Mount Ida, saying that their prize would be to receive the praise of the sovereign, and that this prize was much more precious than the beauty Paris gave to those goddesses." "Great results are expected from this flowering of rhetoric."[17] Fortunately the harvest of 1773 was satisfactory. Already in May, in anticipation of a good supply, the price of grain fell by 20 percent.[18] In June one saw "the beginning of a reappearance of plenty."[19] The inhabitants of the provinces gave signs of "extricating themselves from the penury they have suffered thus far."[20] But in July a blight of grain made prospects less rosy.[21] It became necessary to think of substitutes and to organize relief efforts.[22] At the same time there was recourse to one of the most discussed remedies of the preceding years, the prohibitions against luxury, squandering, and expensive living. But now traditional notions of sumptuary laws took a new form, typical of the "patriotic" spirit that animated the government. The *Pro patria* society, whose 1772 foundation we have seen, received from an anonymous donor a sum to serve as a prize for the best answer to the following question: "Whether in order to put an end to the folly of fashions, which change every day, and also to the contraband of forbidden goods, it might be useful to introduce a national costume in Sweden, appropriate to the climate, and different from that of other nations."[23] This competition was extraordinarily successful. At the beginning of 1774 the number of answers had reached fifty-four, "many from Germany, the Low Countries, and Switzerland."[24] There were plenty of discussions on the problem.[25] A

---

[16] Ibid., no. 40, 18 May 1773, p. 316 (Stockholm, 21 April).

[17] Ibid., no. 42, 25 May 1773, p. 333 (Stockholm, 27 April).

[18] Ibid., no. 51, 26 June 1773, p. 402 (Stockholm, 25 May).

[19] Ibid., no. 55, 10 July 1773, p. 434 (Stockholm, 11 June).

[20] Ibid., no. 59, 24 July 1773, p. 468 (Stockholm, 23 June).

[21] Ibid., no. 65, 14 August 1773, p. 514 (Stockholm, 17 July).

[22] Ibid., no. 56, 13 July 1773, p. 443 (Stockholm, 17 June) (potatoes); and no. 76, 21 September 1773, p. 619 (Stockholm, 17 August) ("The spirit of benevolence appears more and more in this reign"). No. 26, dated 29 March 1774, p. 203 (Stockholm, 25 February), announced the creation, "to prevent the consequences of a bad harvest," "of a commission," or "a kind of agricultural senate, composed of a certain number of governors of provinces and citizens distinguished for their zeal and knowledge for working toward the advancement or progress of agriculture."

[23] Ibid., no. 95, 27 November 1773, p. 771 (Stockholm, 26 October).

[24] Ibid., no. 19, 5 March 1774, p. 146 (Stockholm, 2 February).

[25] Ibid., no. 47, 11 June 1774, p. 371 (Stockholm, 20 May).

national costume was in fact adopted but was worn only for certain official ceremonies, without ever becoming popular. This, too, was a symbol of the "revolution" of 1772.[26]

At an economic level, the revolution did not initiate a radically new policy and was limited, although more energetically, to mobilizing existing forces and creating around the sovereign a series of political and social initiatives. But in a kind of first balance, in the spring of 1775, it was necessary to admit that the wounds declared healed in the summer of 1772 were still "bleeding" three years later. To be sure, one could place the weight of responsibility for the obstacles that were encountered on the past. Those "responsible for the party contrary to the public good," which, as it was necessary to admit, were far from having disappeared, could also be thought of as "results of anarchy," relics of the past; but the results were not consoling. The rhythm of change in Sweden was slow, much slower than the proclamations suggested. "This is a work that will require at least a generation."[27]

On the social level there were plenty of obstacles. The peasant world was disquieted in the kingdom of Sweden as well. And although in Sweden the existence of an "order" of peasants contained discontent and protest within constitutional channels, in the periphery of the realm of Gustavus III it took the form of a more open protest. "The peasants of Finland, who seek to extricate themselves from the authority of their lords, have sent His Majesty a deputation to beg him to declare them free, but they were told to think first of obeying, and if they then had reason to complain they would be shown every justice."[28] Even in Södermanland there broke out in June 1773 "a kind of revolution, those peasants having refused to pay feudal dues to the landlords." The courts proceeded "rigorously against delinquents." But "this rigor, instead of being a remedy, has increased the problem, and it is thought," the correspondent of the Florentine gazette added, "that the government will be obliged to prevent disorders that may result from the out-

[26] There is a description in the *Storia politica, filosofica e naturale del regno di Svezia* (Venice: Zatta, 1802), vol. 2, p. 45. *Réflexions sur l'utilité et les avantages d'un costume national,* by Gustavus III, is interesting. In his eyes the economic justifications for such a reform were clear. "When luxury establishes itself in a poor nation, it soon becomes a scourge." It was not new laws that were necessary, but a change of public opinion, following the example of Peter the Great, although in the opposite sense. This ruler had "reason to seek, so to speak, to pervert the nation." For Sweden, instead, it was indispensable to create a "national spirit." The Hungarians, Catherine II herself, and the Poles were providing an example of what should be followed, or even foreseen. "Let us hasten to forestall other countries." *Collection des écrits politiques, littéraires et dramatiques de Gustave III* (Stockholm: Charles Delén, 1803), vol. 1, pp. 210ff.

[27] *Notizie del mondo,* no. 24, 25 March 1775, p. 186 (Stockholm, 18 February).

[28] Ibid., no. 33, 24 April 1773, p. 258 (Stockholm, 26 March).

break of sedition."[29] At the end of the year the news from Finland was anything but reassuring. "The disturbances have not abated; some peasants there have again revolted against their lords; they do not want to pay impositions except to the king and recognize him as lord and master." Troops had been sent, "which have returned a part of the insurgents to their duty; the others have retreated to the Russian frontier, where they negotiate with the court through the king's minister in St. Petersburg. Some leaders of the rebellion have been captured and have received the punishment they deserved; others obtained their pardon by agreeing to fulfill their duty."[30] This was the winter of the revolt of Pugačev. The peasant movement I have just described on the margins between the Russian and Swedish worlds appears to have been guided by a vision that was similar to that of the rebel Cossacks. Even there, revolt against the nobility was filtered through an idolization of royal power, which was, in fact, directed against them. The Russian peasants attempted to circumvent this problem by creating a czar of their own, made in their own image and likeness. In Finland the peasants were soon forced to accept the severe reforming will of Gustavus III. As in Denmark at this time as well, there was discontent among mariners and workers. "There was, this past month," reflected the *Notizie del mondo* in a communication of 18 March 1774, "in Norrköping a bitter tumult among mariners and workers of that place, but the citizenry was able to prevent the sad consequences that might have occurred if the remedy had not been prompt."[31]

Despite the many difficulties, efforts, and counterefforts, the economic policy of the "revolution" of Gustavus III turned, as soon as the provisions and commercial situation began to improve, toward a greater liberalization. There were many discussions, numerous original works, and quite a few translations.[32] The influence of the physiocrats should not be exaggerated, even if they succeeded in converting Carl Fredrik Scheffer and in making their voices heard in the matter of education reform. The example of French liberal writers before physiocracy—Cantillon, Herbert, and Plumard de Dangeul—and of English writers—James Stuart and David Hume—and then, beginning in the second part of the seventies, of Adam Smith remained fundamental.[33]

Beginning in the summer of 1774, the *Notizie del mondo* informed

---

[29] Ibid., no. 55, 10 July 1773, p. 434 (Stockholm, 11 June).

[30] Ibid., no. 103, 25 December 1773, p. 835 (Stockholm, 23 November).

[31] Ibid., no. 32, 19 April 1774, p. 250 (Stockholm, 18 March).

[32] See the interesting statistics on the development of this economic discussion in Eli F. Heckscher, *Sveriges ekonomiska historia från Gustav Vasa* (Stockholm: Albert Bonniers förlag, 1949), pt. 2, vol. 2, pp. 817, 819.

[33] Ibid., pp. 837ff., especially pp. 870ff.

readers of the new direction Swedish policy was taking. "Since an abundant harvest is anticipated, the king, to avoid the falling in price of grain and to maintain credit abroad, has established free export. Such freedom has not been permitted in Sweden in more than a hundred years. He is to address the prohibition on distilling aquavit and the encouragement of agriculture."[34] Distillation was permitted again soon after, with the restriction that it would cease when the price of grain rose above a determined level.[35]

The Florentine *Gazzetta universale* focused on the new liberal reform policy of Gustavus III in June 1774. It knew well the obstacles that the king had to confront. "It is easier to conquer a kingdom than to uproot a national vice or to rid oneself of popular abuses and prejudices. The first undertaking is obtained by force, the second requires patience, constancy, and the influence of reason and the arts." Gustavus III had been able to utilize "both high and popular wisdom" to overcome resistance. He showed that he was able to use all means to spread his principles. Thus he transformed an experiment using different kinds of plows into one of "those country festivals similar to the ones in antiquity" and that are practiced "particularly in Asia." He presided over another such festival "to honor it with greater solemnity and joy." "In this way he hopes to procure the regulation of custom and taste of the nation through practice and experience, correcting defects and spreading necessary education through the realm." Particularly effective was the method he adopted to raise "the spirits of the nobility," which had finally ceased "to consume its revenues in idleness, neither knowing nor thinking where they came from." They were finally "taking up the tasks of administration," thus increasing "riches for themselves and for the whole state."[36] In 1775 Gustavus seconded Turgot's policy in France and showed his solidarity with him and with Louis XVI in the difficulties they encountered in instituting a more liberal policy. The letter he sent to the French minister is particularly significant. "An admirer in principle and by inclination of all those who devote themselves with zeal to the well-being of people and happiness of their country, I have heard with as much satisfaction as interest of your undertakings, and I have been all the more indignant to hear of the seditions and disorders that have arisen to disturb your work." He congratulated Turgot on his victory, and on being supported "by a king enlightened enough to know the price of your genius, and firm enough to support you against the assaults directed against you." What happened in France, he added, was

---

[34] *Notizie del mondo*, no. 72, 6 September 1774, p. 572 (Stockholm, 5 August).

[35] Ibid., no. 85, 22 October 1774, p. 676 (Stockholm, 20 September).

[36] *Gazzetta universale*, no. 50, 21 June 1774, p. 400, "Agricoltura."

always of great interest to him. "A singular resemblance between the circumstances in which I find myself and your position could not, I assure you, but increase that interest." The solidarity among reformers in distress inspired Gustavus III to send grain to France to alleviate the difficult situation there. Louis XVI, himself, responded, thanking him and explaining the situation: "The bad harvest and bad humor of some persons, whose acts were not concerted, led the wicked to pillage some markets. The peasants, misled by them and by a false rumor circulated of a fall in the price of bread, had the insolence to pillage markets in Versailles and Paris, which forced me to call up troops, who restored order without difficulty."[37]

Beyond these economic questions, political problems returned to the center of Gustavus III's preoccupations, as they did for Turgot and Louis XVI. In Sweden, as in France and everywhere else in Europe, the central question, when one looked at Scandinavia, remained that of liberty, that is, of the possibility of making reforms accepted and of increasing freedom. The different interpretations of the work of Gustavus III depended chiefly on the different answers given to this question. In France there were basically two positions: one stemming from the physiocratic movement, and the other from the followers of Rousseau and Mably. Le Mercier de la Rivière was the most important spokesman of the first. He had not been among those who crowded around the young hereditary prince of Sweden when he was in Paris, before the death of his father. He always tried to emphasize his own independence. But when he happened to travel to Stockholm his soul was won over, and he was delighted to be invited to lay down the groundwork for a project of reform in public instruction. He knew he had to deal with "a prince with a lively and penetrating spirit . . . already raised by education and the force of genius above the most common prejudices."[1] "Oh happy nation! Your leader does not limit his ambition to secure, through good laws, the happiness of the present generation; he also aims to secure, through instruction, that of future generations."[2] He became a great admirer of the "new Swedish constitution, because it gives the political body a movement and life it had almost entirely lost."[3] For centuries the Swedes had sought liberty, without ever finding it, "a lib-

---

[37] *Oeuvres de Turgot*, ed. Gustave Schelle (Paris: Alcan, 1922), vol. 4, pp. 471ff.

[1] Pierre-Paul-François Le Mercier de la Rivière, *De l'instruction publique ou considérations morales et politiques sur la nécessité, la nature et la source de cette instruction, ouvrage demandé par le roi de Suède* (Stockholm and Paris: Didot, 1775), "Avant-propos," pp. 1ff.

[2] Ibid., p. 3.

[3] Ibid., p. 4.

erty so dear that they had hardly found it when they lost it again." Gustavus III finally opened the way to "true liberty," to the only possible and appropriate one, "equidistant from oppression and anarchy."[4] His "astonishing revolution" had dissipated a "vain phantom," substituting for it "a regular constitution, made to ensure each of its members all the freedom they could reasonably enjoy."[5] He explained to the king's tutor, Count Scheffer, that this revolution was an integral part of a profound transformation taking place all over Europe: "Reason perfects itself, prejudices disappear, the rights of humanity begin to be known; we must believe that they will be respected."[6] Le Mercier de la Rivière expected to fill these high aspirations with a precise political and social content. "Happiness" and "moral good," he explained, could exist only in a society where all are left "fully free to contract exchanges as they please, fully free to employ all their faculties and all their talents in a manner that pleases them most and that seem best to them personally."[7] Property is the cornerstone of all free societies. "Remove the right of property and there are no other rights; remove the right of property and there are no laws: government and governed, all fall necessarily into an arbitrary abyss, a frightful chaos where pretensions continually clash."[8] Only property can guarantee equality. The system of public instruction of a country should above all "convince men that public order based on property rights makes them all equal among themselves, as much as possible." This was equality of rights, naturally; an equality "in fact" was inconceivable. Nor could one blame property for permitting the existence of great, disproportionate riches. The opposite was true: inequality was born from "outrages done to property rights."[9] Sweden under Gustavus III should thus aim for a more perfect economic freedom. Caught up in his enthusiasm for free trade, Le Mercier de la Rivière ultimately envisioned a society where relationships among people would depend "on things" and not "on persons" and thus would be capable of self-regulation through laws and unchanging relationships.[10] Liberty would be ensured when "each citizen is in a situation to understand that he depends only on his own will."[11] Still, to ensure such liberty a constitution and institutions were necessary. Hereditary monarchy counted among these. It alone had the "happy inability of

[4] Ibid., p. 5.
[5] Ibid., pp. 6ff.
[6] Ibid., "Lettre à monsieur le comte de Scheffer," p. 12.
[7] Ibid., "Objects principaux de l'instruction publique," p. 51.
[8] Ibid., p. 58.
[9] Ibid., pp. 62ff.
[10] Ibid., "Institutions sociales dont l'instruction publique a besoin," p. 90.
[11] Ibid., p. 92.

changing fundamental laws."¹² Another essential guarantee was freedom of the press, "a freedom always dangerous to error, always favorable to the truth."¹³ "Opposition and discussion" were indispensable.
The only limit was the obligation of authors to sign their works. "Why
hide oneself? Why not profess loudly what one holds to be reasonable
and true?" "Under a tyrannical government, prudence requires that defenders of reason and truth preserve their anonymity; they would have
everything to lose in making themselves known. But under a well-con-
stituted government, among men truly free, this conduct ceases to be
necessary and can only pass for folly and stupidity."¹⁴ This was a curious
conclusion for a book, written in 1774, that came out anonymously in
France the following year. As oppressive as the government of Louis xv
was thought to be in his last years, it was difficult to think the same of
that of his successor, which was soon dominated by the figure of Turgot.
Clearly Le Mercier de la Rivière considered the monarchy of Gustavus
iii to be not only a free government caught up in economic and social
reform, but also founded, in his view, on a solid constitutional base.

A different consideration of the problem of liberty stood at the center of the discussions that developed between Paris and Stockholm in
some other groups and currents often critical and hostile to the physiocrats. Among the followers of Rousseau and Mably, among Parisian admirers of Gustavus iii between the last years of Louis xv and the end of
the old regime—from Madame de Boufflers to Madame de Staël—there
gushed out from the example of Swedish experience a current of political reflections on nobility and monarchy, privileges and liberty, constitutions and law, that flowed in the end into the great river of nascent
European liberalism.

Even here, at the origins of the debate, stood Jean Jacques Rous-
seau.¹⁵ He had no confidence at all in the possibility of Sweden's conserving its liberty. At the beginning of 1772, even before the revolution
of Gustavus iii, he was convinced that hereditary monarchy and the
power of the senate would soon subject Sweden to the yoke "carried by
all nations" and from which, now that Corsica had fallen, only the Poles
were exempt.¹⁶ Mably, who was persuaded of the excellence and solidity
of the Swedish constitution, and was its strenuous defender, even when
it was undone by Gustavus iii, contradicted him. One could say that in

---

¹² Ibid., p. 103.
¹³ Ibid., p. 120.
¹⁴ Ibid., pp. 121ff.
¹⁵ Launay, "J. J. Rousseau et Gustave iii de Suède," pp. 496ff.
¹⁶ Rousseau, *Considérations sur le gouvernement de Pologne*, in *Oeuvres complètes*, vol. 3,
pp. 746, 992.

this preliberal discussion, Mably had the more doctrinaire position. He had explained to the Duke of Parma, through his brother Condillac, that Sweden was "civilized without having the defects of a civilized nation," and that it had ended up with a government that "was a masterpiece of modern legislation."[17] Its origin was not feudal tradition, but rather the "jealous love for liberty found in all Germanic peoples."[18] The Swedes, in fact, had chosen liberty after the death of Charles XII, creating a constitution that Mably thought clearly superior to that of the English.[19] The whole legislative power was entrusted to the diet. The relationship between the hereditary monarchy and the Senate was optimal. There were dangers, and the Swedish constitution needed retouches. But he thought the bases on which the liberty of that nation were erected were solid and rational.

Between the sixties and the seventies Mably took up these themes in one of his principal works, De la législation: Ou principes des loix, which appeared in 1776.[20] Even he could not close his eyes to the economic and social crisis of the country. Should one change direction and follow the English example, engaging in commerce, growing rich, and expanding beyond Europe? A Swede and an Englishman debated the problem at length in Mably's pages. At the center the following agonizing questions always remained: How to ensure and guarantee political liberty? How to avoid falling into despotism? The legislators of 1720 had been guided by these principles. "All interests not connected with liberty were neglected."[21] One should follow their example. Equality, frugality, and renunciation of any spirit of greed furnished the indispensable base. All temptation to favor aristocracy should be carefully avoided. The greatest attention was paid to the "populace." "One pays too little attention to the interests of that multitude which one calls the populace. . . . Instead of debasing them more each day, they should be taught to know their dignity. The more one humiliates them, the more the vanity of the rich and great will become intensified and oppressive: that is what cre-

[17] Gabriel Bonnot de Mably, "Lo studio della storia," in id., Scritti politici, ed. Aldo Maffey, vol. 1 (Turin: Utet, 1961), pp. 417, 426.

[18] Even recently the major historian of Sweden, Michael Roberts, has maintained that "Sweden was never a feudal country." Times Literary Supplement, 9 December 1977, p. 1434. And the same historian has emphasized the importance of medieval tradition as the root of Danish social life.

[19] Mably, "Lo studio della storia," pp. 417, 420.

[20] A. Maffey holds that it was written around 1760 and published later as such. But it is enough to read what Mably wrote about Pasquale Paoli, saying that he had taken refuge in London, to persuade oneself that these pages were at least revised later.

[21] Gabriel Bonnot de Mably, De la législation ou principes des loix (Amsterdam, 1776), vol. 1, p. 184.

ates slave wars, the revolts of peasants, and the uprisings of workers, which often endanger republics. When the legislator speaks of the multitudes, why does he always take on the tone of a menacing despot? . . . It is barbarous to punish the people for the stupidity to which they have been condemned."[22] Mably thus developed a whole program of changes in the relationship between the state and its poorest classes. "Because the lowest citizens have low and painful duties to carry out, raise their status and pay better those who work. Try to draw them out of the misery in which they languish. Mendicity dishonors and weakens government. All the alms of the rich cannot repair this evil."[23] If this plan of reform were adopted energetically it would be possible to transcend internal divisions that imperiled the state, such as those of "Hats and Caps, Whigs and Tories."[24] And this would permit one to confront one of the greatest problems of Swedish political life, that of class, and of the distinctions in orders and ranks. Here as well a spirit of reform should guide the governors. "I would like to preserve all privileges and prerogatives that confer only honor, but share with other orders all rights that confer authority. I do not think there will be great inconvenience or inequality of rank if it is all reduced to formalities of politeness and regard among individuals."[25] The peril of degenerating into an aristocracy was always present. It was precisely the privileges of nobles that had led in the seventeenth century to a loss of liberty. "If the other orders had been strong enough to resist the nobility, they would never have regarded the establishment of arbitrary monarchy as the only possible resource against the vexations of an unjust aristocracy."[26] If freedom was wanted, it was necessary to have guarantees for all, which would be equal to or stronger than those which absolutism seemed to promise. In Sweden it was necessary for ecclesiastics, bourgeois, and peasants, wiser than the plebs of ancient Rome, to convince themselves that their land belonged to them as much as to the nobility. "Without equality there is no true liberty."[27]

Thus one understands how Mably could think that the revolution of Gustavus III was an affront. He not only feared the frustration of those needs for liberty that were at the center of his program, but also had to recognize sadly that the king had been able to maneuver better than his adversaries among the orders and parties. Sweden, Mably said, "is a

[22] Ibid., pp. 237–38.
[23] Ibid., p. 238.
[24] Ibid., p. 242.
[25] Ibid., pp. 246–47.
[26] Ibid., p. 248. Mably naturally remembered the Danish example in this context.
[27] Ibid., p. 249.

great proof that nothing is impossible for an able legislator."[28] And he also had to confess that a pupil of his enemies the physiocrats—the supporters of legal despotism—had succeeded in undoing the work of a half-century of the age of liberty.

Instead, another one of his adversaries, Voltaire, abandoned himself to a hymn, a rather artificial one, to the young king, swallowing that compromise between monarchy and liberty that Gustavus III sought to have accepted outside and within the confines of his realm.

> Jeune et digne héritier du grand nom de Gustave
> souverain d'un peuple libre et roi d'un peuple brave
>
> . . . .
>
> Gustave a triomphé sitôt qu'il a paru.
>
> . . . .
>
> Un état divisé fut toujours malheureux,
> de sa liberté vante le prestige,
> dans son illusion sa misère l'afflige.[29]

Doubts, or better, the most pressing questions, came from the group of nobles in Paris that followed the actions of Gustavus III with increasing interest, and in the end frequently asked themselves what limits should be set to the absolute power the king of Sweden seemed to want to establish in his country. They were above all noblewomen, like Madame d'Egmont and de Boufflers, who were close to the court and at the same time sensitive to the opinions of the philosophes. They asked themselves more and more insistently what meaning the distant events of Sweden might have from this point of view. They had known Gustavus III during his stay in Paris and had admired him, seeing in him the brilliant example of a reforming sovereign, the precise opposite of the old king Louis XV, who proved more and more incapable of sustaining enthusiasm or hope, even when, as happened in these years, he abolished the Parlements in his attempt to substitute a more modern judicial system. Admiration turned to love in the soul of Jeanne-Sophie-Elisabeth-Louise-Armande-Septimanie de Wignerod du Plessis de Richelieu, daughter of the Maréchal De Richelieu and wife of Casimiro Pignatelli, Comte de Egmont, Grandee of Spain and *Lieutenant Général* of the French army. With knightly ardor Gustavus, even in Sweden, continued to consider her the lady of his dreams and carried her colors in tour-

---

[28] Ibid.

[29] "Young and worthy heir of the great name of Gustavus / sovereign of a free people, and king of a brave one / . . . / Gustavus triumphed as soon as he appeared. / . . . / A divided state was always unhappy, / vaunting the prestige of its liberty, / in its illusion its misery tormented it." Voltaire, *Oeuvres complètes*, vol. 10, p. 447, "Epître au roi de Suède Gustave III."

naments he organized.[30] Aristocratic superiority and disgust for the heavy and vulgar corruption of the court of Louis xv were mixed in the Comtesse d'Egmont with a broad and refined culture.[31] Warm sympathy also tied Gustavus III to Marie-Charlotte de Boufflers, the friend and protector of Jean Jacques, correspondent of Hume, and favorite of the Prince de Conti, a woman of great sensitivity whom destiny placed at the crossroads between the ways of philosophes and *parlementaires*, between the hopes of Rousseau and the constitutional aims of the French sovereign courts.[32] Nor should one forget that the fine days when Gustavus III met these gentlewomen were those when France, a little after the fall of Choiseul, was finding a way to finally break through the clouds of Louis xv's absolutist policy. Gustavus III had reached Paris on 4 February 1771. On 13 April Maupeou carried out his coup d'état against the Parlements. If, at a diplomatic level, the king of Sweden was more than inclined to accept the assistance of Versailles for his projected coup d'état, he still did not close his eyes or his heart to the smiles and precepts of legality, enlightenment, and freedom. It was too simple to believe, these ladies said, that the Parlements were limited to a judicial function. "This, to be sure, was their origin," but the monarchy had made them a substitute in a sense for the Estates-General. "The people thus became accustomed to considering them as an institution intended for them." Now the French monarchy intended to suppress them, to reaffirm its own absolutism. It forgot that, precisely because of "these phantoms of liberty," many could still convince themselves that they were free. By leveling the Parlements Louis xv had in reality persuaded his subjects that they were subject to an arbitrary power. Many turned to the past, however, to the history of France, in the hope of finding a

---

[30] Bain, *Gustavus III*, vol. 1, p. 221.

[31] Bonneville de Marsigny, *Le comte de Vergennes. Son ambassade en Suède*, pp. 110ff. See Marie-Célestine Amélie de Ségur D'Armaillé, *La comtesse d'Egmont fille du maréchal de Richelieu, 1740–1773. D'après ses lettres inédites à Gustave III* (Paris: Perrin, 1890). The letter she wrote to Gustavus III on 1 September 1771 was typical of her political position: "For myself, Sire, I reduce the whole question to this: that the Chancellor (Maupeou) might prove that the Parlement has no rights and that we have no law. But if the Parlement is nothing, we have need of an Estates-General. And if there are no laws in France, what rights can the king claim? Then nothing would remain besides natural law and custom. Now, the first of these would never create a despot, and the second would never suffer one in France" (pp. 228ff.).

[32] Paul-Emile Schazmann, *La comtesse de Boufflers* (Lausanne: Spes, 1933). This book contains many errors and lapses of judgment, but it is nonetheless useful. For fundamental documentation see the *Lettres de Gustave III à la comtesse de Boufflers et de la comtesse au roi*, published with an introduction and notes by M. Aurélien Vivie (Bordeaux: G. Gounouilhou, 1900).

guarantee of their liberty.[33] These considerations were addressed to Gustavus III and were at the beginning of a long and interesting debate. The Parisian noblewomen insisted on the necessity of historical guarantees for freedom in France, as in Sweden, and exhorted the young sovereign in every way to avoid absolutism. To be sure, they said, the struggle against corruption and the need to guarantee the independence of the country required deep changes. "An increase in your power is doubtless the first step toward those happy changes; but do not permit them to open the way to arbitrary power and take every means to make it impossible for your successors to establish it. May your reign become an age of restoration of a free and independent government, but never a source of absolute power!"

A monarchy limited by the laws seems to me the most happy of governments. Aristocratic republics soon retreat from justice and liberty; and democratic republics are not appropriate for large states. . . . Thus I think you will contribute to the happiness of Swedes by extending your authority; but, I repeat, if you do not place limits that will be impossible for your successors to cross, and make your people independent of the imbecility of a king, the fantasies of a mistress, and the ambitions of a minister, your success will become the first principle of abuse, and you will have to answer for it to posterity.[34]

King Gustavus, once his revolution was ended, explained to them that his new constitution had consecrated "the authority of the king without reducing the domination of the people, as did our ancient laws under Gustavus I and Gustavus Adolphus."[35] Nor did he hide from his admirers that this appeared to him to be basically "republican."[36] An action similar and parallel to that of Madame d'Egmont was carried out by Madame de Boufflers, the author of a memorial ad deterendum, *Effets du despotisme s'il s'établit en Suède.* And immediately after the revolution she repeated in a letter of 23 November 1772 that "absolute power is a mortal disease which, in secretly destroying moral qualities, ends up by

---

[33] Geffroy, *Gustave III*, vol. 1, pp. 235ff. Madame de Boufflers insisted continually on the basic defects of the French monarchy. "Among the ills that afflict us, that of changing the administration every time that one changes the administrator is not the least; the new ministers of whatever party, as soon as they are in place, think of nothing other than destroying the work of their predecessors, most of them to make a show of themselves, some of them believing that they are doing good; thus is born those problems that take from us all the advantages of a long reign . . . , and the immaturity of legislation." (*Lettres de Gustave III à la comtesse de Boufflers*, pp. 69ff.) Only legal tradition ensured by the Parlements was able to save the country from such instability.

[34] Ibid., pp. 241ff. The letter of the Comtesse D'Egmont is dated 1 September 1771. See Bonneville de Marsigny, *Le compte de Vergennes*, p. 156.

[35] Geffroy, *Gustave III*, p. 244.

[36] Bonneville de Marsigny, *Le comte de Vergennes*, p. 157.

destroying states."[37] When Madame de Staël, the wife of the Swedish ambassador in France, became a correspondent of Gustavus III, she took up again, with another style and energy, a long tradition of contrasts between the experience of Sweden and that of France.

In the years immediately following the revolution, the most difficult problem continued to be freedom of the press. At the beginning of 1774 one read the following in the *Notizie del mondo*: "Since freedom of the press is sometimes abused, the court of justice of this city [Stockholm] has begun discussing with the king whether this freedom should be permitted or not. The majority of the members are inclined, at least it is said, to impose limitations, because they believe that such liberty is entirely useless and consequently merits to be abolished. Meanwhile it is rumored that this delicate affair depends entirely on the will of His Majesty."[38] It seemed at first that the law of 1766 would be completely abolished and that a "court of censorship" would be set up. Freedom of the press was not at all "pleasing to the government and particularly to the court." But this intention rapidly aroused "great controversy."[39] It was said that "the larger part of the Senate" was "inclined to this suppression." "The public" feared that it would occur. But the king knew which side he should take. He made known that he was of a sentiment totally

---

[37] Geffroy, *Gustave III*, p. 267. On 19 November 1771 the countess wrote to the king: "Humanely speaking I understand the ambition of kings and even that of their ministers, who for a short time can share its fruits, but at the same time I understand the repugnance subjects have in submitting. But what I do not understand is the conduct of some persons who make themselves into apostles for absolute power, since it appears to be the most opposed to their natural interests." After the "revolution" of 18 September 1772 she wrote insisting that "a too arbitrary authority" would damage his reputation and glory. On 23 October she added that she did not like the idea that power "in the hands of an accomplished prince" was "the best government."

A maxim that one finds in different writers of antiquity, which the experience of all centuries confirms, and even a modern writer, on the fine arts, says and demonstrates is that when liberty leaves a country, the source of sublime thought and true glory is silenced.

In an undated fragment, also of 1772, the countess depicted to Gustavus III the destiny that awaited him if he took the road to absolutism.

The king will lose the most precious part of his happiness; he will be like the king of Prussia, who has no one to talk with; those who surround him will say yes or no depending only on the opinion he wants of them, in whatever circumstances. Deprived of the pleasure of conversation, there is even more reason that he will be deprived of that of sweetness and amity: truth will have difficulty reaching him (he will have to send for it from Paris). The hereditary prince, whatever pains one takes, will be less well educated.

In December 1772 she said to him that with the new constitution "the government seems to be either already entirely absolutist or in the process of becoming so." Her detailed examination of the new fundamental laws of the realm are interesting. *Lettres de Gustave III à la Comtesse de Boufflers*, pp. 42, 60, 65, 69, 71.

[38] *Notizie del mondo*, no. 10, 1 February 1774, p. 74 (Stockholm, 28 December 1773).

[39] Ibid., no. 30, 13 April 1774, p. 236 (Stockholm, 9 March).

contrary to the judges and senators and favored conserving "this precious privilege, which is a defense of the people against whatever injustice can be done to them."[40] In reality, he accepted, and even proclaimed, the principle of freedom of the press while imposing some limitations on it. The new regulation "differs little from the one made in 1766, so that the essentials of this liberty remain as before."[41] On 26 April 1774, in a great speech before the Senate, Gustavus III attacked abuses rather than the dispositions the Diet had adopted eight years earlier. "The estates perhaps never passed a law over which the nation has expressed greater satisfaction." It was born at a time "of uncertainty, in which interests and force often placed themselves close to the feet of justice." Why had it not preserved "a form of government based on liberty, security, and property"? This was "no longer a time when arbitrary power, left in the hands of the people, made everything uncertain and shifting. These times were no more. The law must be maintained with that rigor required by public tranquillity." The lessons of history were also favorable to its maintenance. "If it had been possible to enlighten the sovereign about his true advantages through the press in past centuries . . . perhaps Charles XI would not have taken the steps that made supreme power at the expense of general security odious. . . . If freedom of the press had been able to enlighten Charles XII as to his true glory, this generous prince would have preferred the satisfaction of governing a happy people to reigning over a vast unpopulated empire." And the lessons of history were as valid beyond the seas as in Sweden. "Freedom of the press did not exist in England when Charles I left his head on the block, or when James II fled and abandoned the kingdom to his ambitious cousin. The people did not obtain this right in a legal manner until the end of the reign of William III, or at the beginning of the reign of the House of Hanover, a house that has occupied the throne of England with greater glory and security than any other before it. If Wilkes has caused a stir, it should be attributed to the attention the government has unwisely given to his writings, rather than to their being published, for otherwise he would soon have been hated, like many others." One should never forget that "through freedom of the press the king comes to know the truth, which is often hidden from him with such care, and unfortunately with such success."[42]

This was a fine lesson in truth, like so many of Gustavus III's actions, and of reform policy in an age that was gradually becoming open to revolution. But, once again, the king of Sweden made use of his vision

---

[40] Ibid., no. 43, 28 May 1774, p. 338 (Stockholm, 26 April).
[41] Ibid., no. 44, 31 May 1774, p. 347 (Stockholm, 29 April).
[42] Ibid., no. 56, 12 July 1774, pp. 442ff. (Stockholm, 1 June).

for the end of preserving and increasing his own power. Absolutist aims were plenty in his nonetheless eloquent defense of the law of 1766. In the following years obstacles multiplied from the civil and religious authorities, in matters of freedom of the press. The result—as the Swedish scholar most preoccupied with this question tells us—was that "criticisms of the king and the government were brilliant in their absence, whereas praises flowed in torrents. Even the monopoly on production of alcohol, which clearly provoked lively discontent, drew nothing but praise in the press and in pamphlets." When finally, in 1778, J. G. Halldin dared to protest against the monopoly on alcohol, he was condemned to death "after a strange trial" and then was "immediately pardoned by the king, who even gave him a pension." "On this occasion, as on many others, the regime of Gustavus demonstrated a lack of restraint in law and justice." Often intervention was indirect. Corruption was rife. But on the other hand it is true that the effort to limit the import of foreign books remained ineffective. In 1780 censorship was officially reestablished.[43]

From a constitutonal point of view, in 1778 the delicate equilibrium that had resulted from the revolution was already twisted in a more monarchical direction. The Diet convoked in that year was particularly obsequious. Meanwhile, the aristocracy, guided by Alexis von Fersen, attempted to raise its head and restore life to parliamentary opposition. The king struck the nobility at its most sensitive point, in the notion of equality itself, which had kept the privileged classes united. A hierarchy of counts, barons, senatorial families, and rural gentlemen, with a separate vote for each of these categories, undermined still more the possibility of united action by the nobility. Against Fersen the king supported with great energy the economic and financial policy of the minister Liliencrantz. Religious tolerance was revived and enlarged. There was not even one opposing vote during the whole session of the Diet.[44]

In 1776 a writer attempted to evaluate the revolution of 1772. It was Ange Goudar again, who, in these years, one remembers, was continually involved with European events and their echoes in Italy. There was no doubt in his mind: the work of Gustavus III was not an isolated and insignificant incident, but a link in a long chain. "No event is isolated. Each revolution is preceded by another that gave birth to it."[1] The

---

[43] Stig Boberg, *Gustaf III och tryckfriheten, 1774–1787* (Gustavus III and the freedom of the press, 1774–1787) (Stockholm: Natur och Kultur, 1961), with a summary in French, pp. 343ff.

[44] Bain, *Gustavus III*, vol. 1, p. 182.

[1] Ange Goudar, *Discours oratoire contenant l'éloge de Gustave III roi de Suède* (Cologne,

problem of liberty gave universal significance to what had happened in
Stockholm. "There is an old idol on earth. . . . This idol is the name of
liberty, which one hears pronounced by all nations."² The Swedes had
believed in her, after having abandoned the policy of Charles xii, and a
new effort was made in the epoch of Adolphus Frederick, whose son,
Gustavus, had sought in philosophy, in Locke, Malebranche, and Montesquieu a new basis for his own action. "Happily for Gustavus his generation is one of the most enlightened." The obstacles he had to overcome were enormous. The uncertainty of French policy, and especially
the menacing power of Russia, seemed to bar every path. "A sky of brass
there has produced men of iron, a blind superstition that puts military
qualities on the same level as the precepts of religion. A heavy despotism
. . . the heroism of servitude" characterized Russia. How could one resist? Fruitlessly Gustavus had sought support in England, "proud of the
power of credit, which she owes only to the negligence of the industrious nations whose arts she has usurped."³ Nor, as was clear, would it
be possible to lean on Italy, which was "deprived of that force that gave
her the empire of the world." Venice was mistaken in its policy. "Genova, with its great riches, has no influence in Europe." Naples was
poor. "Tuscany, which might draw great advantages from its situation,
. . . is too small to become a great power."⁴ In this uncertain and weakened Europe Sweden should have acted on its own. But there "all spirit
of patriotism" was extinguished. The Senate had "become a despot."⁵
The king was a "prisoner in the midst of his capital." He had been
chained "at the foot of the throne where he reigns."⁶ Gustavus had long
sought the means of avoiding "a revolution."⁷ His situation was similar
to the one Charles i of England had to confront more than a century
earlier. But the results were quite different. He succeeded in changing
the spirit of the people. Without shedding a drop of blood he had made
it so that "all of Sweden, which a minute before had been favorable to a
republic, became immediately royalist."⁸ He had put liberty on his own
side. "Caesar only reformed the republic to make it feel his yoke; his

1776), p. 11. See the bibliography of F. L. Mars, "Addenda iii," *Casanova gleanings* 14
(1971): 31, and id., "Du nouveau sur Goudar," ibid. 19, new ser., no. 3 (1976): 48, where
it is said that the *Discours* was printed in Florence at the ducal printing press.

  ² Ibid., p. 18.
  ³ Ibid., p. 53.
  ⁴ Ibid., pp. 54ff.
  ⁵ Ibid., p. 58.
  ⁶ Ibid., p. 59.
  ⁷ Ibid., p. 60.
  ⁸ Ibid., p. 70.

glory was a tyranny; that of Gustavus is a triumph for liberty."[9] The new constitution he adopted was "the most perfect piece of legislation Sweden could receive at present."[10] Thus he had succeeded in establishing a model of universal validity. "Kings of the earth, monarchs who reign over the first nations of the world, when you make your reforms, follow the example of Gustavus." In short, he had succeeded in defending himself from the suspicion of tyranny, in reassuring the "intermediary powers," and in presenting himself as "a patriot king."[11]

Two years later, in 1778, Charles Francis Sheridan, who had been secretary of the British embassy during the revolution of Gustavus III, gave his own interpretation. He stated that another free country, Sweden, after so many others, seemed definitely to have taken the route of absolutism. Great Britain seemed more and more isolated in Europe. Its republican traditions seemed to be fading into a kind of ideological and political isolation. Sheridan took up again the considerations that Molesworth had made about Denmark one hundred years earlier, but he lacked the energy this Deist had been able to summon up in his polemics against continental despotism. Sheridan tried to understand the reasons for the revolution and to assess its results. It was a dignified and melancholy vision, resigned to taking flight from the "present almost general subversion of public liberty throughout Europe." The pressure to "conduct men into a state of political slavery seemed irresistible."[12] Everywhere he found evidence of the existence of forces intent on destroying liberty. "Italy once fitted with populous and independent cities, the seat of commerce, of riches and of liberty, is, in general, governed by the hand of despotism. In the few states that retain the name of republics, the bulk of the people, in general, suffers a severer degree of oppression than those exposed to who acknowledges but one master." If the Swiss had succeeded in conserving their liberty, they owed it "to the mountains, to poverty, and to courage." Spain, Portugal, and France had witnessed only "ineffectual struggles for liberty." To convince oneself it was enough to "consider the little ceremony with which the French monarchs, at this day, treat their parliaments." These had become rather "the instruments of the power of the sovereign than the guardians of the rights of the people."[13] Nor could more consoling spectacles be found in Austria and Prussia. The recent destiny of Danzig,

---

[9] Ibid., p. 75.

[10] Ibid., p. 76.

[11] Ibid., p. 77.

[12] Charles Francis Sheridan, *A history of the late revolution in Sweden, containing an account of the transactions of the three last diets in that country* (London: Edward and Charles Dilly, 1778), p. 1.

[13] Ibid., pp. 7ff.

overcome by disputes caused by the partition of Poland, could also give
a lesson to "free cities." Even in Holland the power of the stadholder
created a growing menace. The United Provinces were attentive only to
their mercantile interests and counted on contrasts among their neighbors to ensure their own survival. "The Dutch appear no longer to possess that martial and independent spirit which distinguished their ancestors." Poland, "the nobles of which, at least, were the freest in the
world," was now in the hands of absolute monarchy. "The dreadful despotism of Russia is well known."[14] In short, "arbitrary power seems, like
a plague, to have spread over almost the whole face of Europe, from
the coasts of the Mediterranean to the shores of the frozen ocean."[15]
Only the sea that divides it from the continent had defended England
from the general contagion. The Swedish revolution had been particularly unexpected and rapid, "which in one day had converted a government supposed to be the freest in Europe into an absolute monarchy."[16]
Even there the roots were now pulled out, which the "feudal system"
had planted throughout Europe, giving birth both to free governments
and to the monarchical reaction which the oppression of lords had not
failed to arouse. Guided by Montesquieu, and now by Robertson, Sheridan thus framed developments in Sweden within the whole history of
Europe in preceding centuries.[17] In their reaction to despotism, at the
beginning of the eighteenth century, the Swedes had undoubtedly exaggerated. The authority of the king had been too limited in their constitution of 1720. But they still had succeeded in creating a government
that was effectively free, taking care to found it on a division of power
between the monarchy "and a few haughty barons" while the rest of the
country trembled, as also happened elsewhere under "abject dependence." The "supreme power" of Sweden had then been "placed where
it ought to be, in the State general of the Kingdom." "Into these all
ranks of men were admitted and the meanest peasant, through his representative, as well as the proudest noble, bore a part in the legislature
of the country."[18] Why then had such a solid construction come to ruin?
In reality the people had not been ready to accept the constitution. Circumstances were against it, and time was lacking. "Liberty is not a plant
of sudden growth; time only can give it vigour. It will not take roots but
in a soil congenial to it; and, to be rendered flourishing or lasting, it
must be cultivated with care and defended with unremitting attention

[14] Ibid., p. 9.
[15] Ibid., p. 10.
[16] Ibid., p. 3.
[17] Ibid., pp. 12ff.
[18] Ibid., p. 41.

from the dangers which perpetually surround it."[19] Only experience could teach humanity how to cultivate it. The Swedish nobles were too poor and insufficiently independent. The distinctions among classes were too great. Bourgeois and clergy had attempted to concentrate on the interests of their own groups rather than on the general interests of the country. Corruption and foreign influence on one hand and the ability of Gustavus III on the other had done the rest. The constitution of 1720 had found no defenders in the upper or lower classes. There was truly a place in Sweden for a patriot king, as Bolingbroke had foreseen: "the most popular man in his country, a patriot king at the head of a united people."[20]

[19] Ibid., p. 139.
[20] Ibid., p. 318.

X

Constitutional Conflicts in the
Republic of Geneva

IN GENEVA THE PASSAGE FROM THE SIXTIES TO THE SEVENTIES ALSO
marked a decisive turn. From the conflicts between patricians and bourgeois that disturbed the eighteenth-century history of the republic,
which reached their height between 1763 and 1768, there was a development in the following three years from a two- to a three-part struggle.
Not only were patricians and bourgeois involved, but also *natifs*, the
group that, although born in Geneva, did not enjoy political rights. This
was also a problem in other European cities of this time—limiting ourselves to the Swiss world—in Berne and Zurich. But in Geneva the
struggle and debate were particularly intense, and the importance of
the natifs was particularly great. Also, the political and geographical position of the republic, between Switzerland, France, and Savoy, gave an
international dimension to the conflict, which might otherwise have
seemed quite local and provincial. Economic developments created new
bases of tension and new motives for resistance among the contenders.
It is enough to think of the highly specialized clock industry that was
tied to the world market and always subject to the possibility of the emigration of its workers. One does not need to add that the other important industry of Geneva, printing, was precisely suited to add ferment
to what already existed. In fact, as we will see, a large campaign of
printed pamphlets, sheets, and books accompanied all phases of the
struggle. Also, the intervention of men like d'Alembert, Rousseau, and
Voltaire transformed Geneva into a laboratory and sounding board for
important ideas of the Enlightenment.

Since 1757, when the article "Genève" was published in volume 7 of
the *Encyclopédie*, signed by d'Alembert but written in collaboration with
Voltaire, the religious, political, and moral nexus of the republic imposed itself on the attention of all. The city of Calvin had already taken

great steps, in the eyes of the philosophes: from the pyre of Servetus it had passed on to a diffused Socinianism. Now the work of civilization had to continue through the emergence of greater freedom in society and public opinion, which was to become more candid and tolerant. Introducing a theater would be an excellent way of obtaining this end. "A small republic would have the glory of informing Europe on this point, more important perhaps than one might think."[1] In vain people objected that Geneva was too small a place to become exemplary. "In the eyes of the philosopher," d'Alembert responded, "a republic of bees is not less interesting than the history of a great empire; is it not in small states that one finds the model of perfect public administration?"[2] This was true, Rousseau responded, on the condition that one did not ruin and corrupt the social fabric that already existed in Geneva. His celebrated *Lettre à M. d'Alembert* was not only a polemic against theaters, but also a defense and an illustration of Genevan social life, and above all of the typical form it assumed in *cercles*, "clubs," those mobile groups of friends, neighbors, hunters, shooters, and drinkers, men capable of cultivating and maintaining the "old simplicity" that alone could provide "a good constitution and good customs."[3] Addison, in his *Spectator*, had been wrong, Jean Jacques concluded, to criticize "coteries" in England, leaving the field to "cafes and low places." Geneva remained more faithful to the usages of the past. The names of these groups changed (from "*sociétés*" to "*cercles*"), but the substance remained the same.[4] "These honest and innocent institutions contain all that might contribute to form among men friends, citizens, soldiers, and consequently all that serves a free people."[5] The fear that Parisians, or Encyclopedists, or Voltaire, might corrupt Geneva became joined in the mind of Rousseau with the apprehension that his image of it, his own country, which he carried with him and which maintained itself tenaciously in his mind, might dissolve. All this induced him to think of Geneva as more static and conservative than it really was. It only needed the few years around 1762 to put him and Europe as a whole in confrontation with a Geneva caught up in the winds of a profound renewal. Rousseau released the tempest with his *Emile* and *Contrat social*. On 19 June 1762 the Petit Conseil condemned the two works to be burned. Rousseau himself, if he had re-

---

[1] *Encyclopédie* (Paris: Briasson, David, Le Breton, Durand, 1757), vol. 7, p. 577.

[2] Ibid., p. 578.

[3] Jean Jacques Rousseau, "Lettre à M. d'Alembert," in id., *Du Contrat social et autres oeuvres politiques*, ed. Jean Ehrard (Paris: Garnier, 1975), p. 214.

[4] Ibid., p. 202.

[5] Ibid., p. 208.

turned to Geneva, would have been arrested.[6] This was a measure desired by the patricians, and above all by the Tronchin, behind whom it
was not difficult to perceive the France of Voltaire. Against their action
was ranked the bourgeoisie, at the head of which was Jacques-François
De Luc, "an incarnation of the civic and religious virtues of old Geneva."[7] Voltaire called him "the Paoli of Geneva," a name that might
surprise us now, but contemporaries accepted it easily in the anxious
climate of the sixties.[8] The movement supporting Rousseau grew rapidly and did not stop even when the rejected Jean Jacques made his
gesture of publicly renouncing his Genevan citizenship—a gesture that
coincided within himself with a still greater idealization of Geneva and
a still more energetic defense of the deep and permanent elements of
its society and tradition.

The *Lettres écrites de la montagne* that De Luc asked him to write was
among the most effective works to issue from his pen. The events and
problems of Europe in these years were always present to him. He saw
Poland and its weakness at the opposite pole from Geneva.[9] The Wilkes
affair, in London, seemed to him both similar to and different from
what the Genevan magistrates had unleashed against him.[10] Everywhere
there seemed to arise the menace of "a besotted and stupid people, first
heated by unbearable vexations, and then covertly manipulated by cunning plots."[11] Precisely the opposite occurred in Geneva, where opposition and resistance to the patricians came from the best and most active
part of the population, from "the order midway between the rich and
poor, between heads of state and the plebs." "This order is composed of
men of more or less equal fortunes, standing, and education. They are
not so elevated as to have pretensions, nor so low as to have nothing to
lose. Their great and common interest is that the laws be observed, magistrates respected, the constitution sustained, and the state at peace."[12]
The Genevan constitution was "good and healthy."[13] It required defending against those who sought to twist it to their own advantage.

This was the limit, the intentional limit, of Rousseau's vision. He

[6] See Jean-Daniel Candaux's introduction to "Lettres écrites de la montagne," in Jean
Jacques Rousseau, *Oeuvres complètes*, ed. Bernard Gagnebin and Marcel Raymond (Paris:
Gallimard, 1961), vol. 3, p. clxii.

[7] Ibid., p. cliiii.

[8] Voltaire, *La guerre civile de Genève ou les amours de Robert Covelle. Poète héroïque.* New
edition (Besançon: Nicolas Grandvel, 1769), p. 39 n. f.

[9] Rousseau, "Lettres écrites de la montagne," p. 816.

[10] Ibid., p. 876.

[11] Ibid., p. 889.

[12] Ibid.

[13] Ibid., p. 894.

looked to the bourgeoisie alone. However, were these truly in a position to resist the external pressures that were then increasing? And up to what point was the bourgeoisie able to embody principles of liberty and equality, as Rousseau hoped? Between 1765 and 1768, inspired even by ideas of Jean Jacques, it made its greatest effort to wrest power from the patricians. But these, beginning in 1765, requested the mediation of France, Zurich, and Berne. And at the same time, behind the shoulders of the bourgeoisie, the new force of the natifs appeared, who sought recognition of their own rights more and more insistently. Little by little they became organized, turned to the mediating powers, and unexpectedly received vigorous and intelligent support from Voltaire, who was increasingly convinced that only through an introduction, not just of new ideas, but also of new social forces, could Geneva be reformed. He was not much interested in the republican constitution. Instead he was guided by an intricate series of reasonings extending from a desire to be useful to Choiseul to a Faustian need to make people prosperous and happy. Whatever the forces that stirred him to action, he contributed significantly to making the natifs a proving ground for Genevan egalitarianism, which Rousseau wanted to contain within republican tradition and which Voltaire attempted candidly to promote and utilize more broadly. The philosopher of Ferney did much to pull the natifs out of their small world of resentment and revenge and assist them to raise themselves to the level of a wider political vision. He guaranteed them their own legitimacy before patricians and bourgeois, as well as the reasonableness of their aspirations. He used them to strike at two adversaries at the same time: Rousseau and the Calvinists. He restored to himself and to philosophie the function of mediation, which the neighboring powers had found so difficult to carry out satisfactorily, without offending the republic's susceptibility or desire for independence.[14]

Georges Auzière, one of the most important leaders of the natifs, explained to him with great clarity, beginning in 1766, what the root of the problem was. There was not any difference, from a social point of view, between bourgeois and natifs, because both were "equal by birth and lived under the same laws." What divided them were the pretensions of the bourgeois, who were flattered by the panegyrics Rousseau had heaped upon them and by the title of "souverain" with which he distinguished them. "They thought of themselves as Polish nobles" and treated the natifs "like serfs." This was a typical contrast of the sunset of

[14] Jane Ceitac, *Voltaire et l'affaire des natifs* (Geneva: Droz, 1956); Nicola Matteucci, *Jacques Mallet du Pan* (Naples: Istituto italiano per gli studi storici, 1957); R. R. Palmer, *The Age of the Democratic Revolution*, vol. 1: *The Challenge*; Peter Gay, *Voltaire's Politics. The Poet as a Realist* (Princeton, N.J.: Princeton University Press, 1959).

the old regime when, as de Tocqueville noted for France, a general desire for equality corresponded with a more and more formal division of society into small, isolated, and enclosed entities. The more unjustifiable privileges became, the more they pricked social sensitivity. A deep sense of revolt was born from this, even in Geneva. Were the bourgeoisie not aware, a spokesman of the natifs asked, that "we could become Brutus in an instant, if they want to play Caesar"?[15]

Resentment grew stronger as the economic situation deteriorated. There were continual laments, in all the documentation of this polemic of the late sixties, about the stagnation of commerce and the artisan industry. Among the bourgeois the defense of corporate interests became harsher, and the effort to exclude rivals from any control of public affairs grew more rigid. In the general crisis the great famine of the winter of 1769–1770 struck a decisive blow. The specter of hunger—so widespread in Europe these years—did not spare Geneva. The system of provisioning of the republic, so admired by Galiani, was placed in serious difficulties by the general rise in the price of grain, and above all by the prohibitions on export imposed by the senate of Savoy. The Council of Geneva had to appeal to the sympathy of Minister Bogino and the benevolence of the old king, Carlo Emanuele III. This produced favorable results: in Turin it was well known that hunger would make the internal conflicts of the republic more serious. The patricians would have greater difficulty containing the pressure of bourgeois and natifs. To maintain political stability—which was desirable also in the eyes of the king of Sardinia for reasons of foreign policy, that is, to resist the increasing French influence—it was indispensable to provide needed supplies promptly. The conservative agreement between Geneva and Turin did not fail to be interpreted by malcontents as an attempt "to keep the people dependent on the Council," that is, on the patricians.[16]

Political discontent increased at the end of the sixties. The natifs no longer limited themselves to compiling declarations of protest (which were nonetheless still numerous), but put into motion a true mass movement. An assembly in Carouge, which met to listen to the councils of Voltaire, attracted more than one thousand persons (one should remember that the whole republic of Geneva numbered about 22,000). No one wanted to abandon legal means yet, but a general sense of the political weight that natifs were beginning to have began to spread. Still,

---

[15] Ceitac, *Voltaire et l'affaire des natifs*, p. 36.

[16] See Charles du Bois-Melly, "Relations de la Cour de Sardaigne et de la République de Genève depuis le traité de Turin (1754) jusqu'à la fin de l'année 1773," in *Miscellanea di storia patria*, vol. 28, 2d ser., p. 63. In his *Dialogues sur le commerce des bleds*, above all in book 2, Galiani discusses Geneva. See Galiani, *Opere*, pp. 376ff.

their political immaturity, the complex game of Voltaire—who wanted less than ever to break with the patricians, or the bourgeois, or even less with the France of Choiseul—as well as the external pressures of the mediating powers, led at first to a compromise, called the Edict of Conciliation, which was debated at length in the winter of 1767–1768 and was finally approved on 11 March 1768. To the constitutional concessions the patricians granted to the bourgeois were added others of a social and corporative nature favoring natifs. The patricians began the policy they continued in the seventies of extending "a paternal hand" to the natifs as a way of limiting the political pretensions of the bourgeoisie.[17] The same Georges Auxière, writing in 1767 to Tronchin, the *procureur général* who had requested and obtained the condemnation of the *Contrat social* and *Emile*, requested at least some concession: facilitating obtaining citizenship, "entry into all arts and trades" and "membership in all the guilds to trade freely," and admitting natifs "to positions as officers in bourgeois companies."[18] This was a program of slow social progress within the traditional forms of the republic, intended to persuade the patricians, and not to force their hand. But the tone of demands quickly became more insistent. Not only did demands for "equality among natifs and citizens begin," but the structure of the republic itself became a subject of debate. In contemporary eyes there seemed to be a balance, with the bourgeoisie on one side and the patricians on the other. The mediating powers maintained the balance. But "the natifs, through an inexplicable fatality, have now become as distant from questions agitating the republic as inhabitants of the shores of the Orinoco and must suppress the most natural sentiments if they listen to the voice of duty the constitution prescribes to them." Such silent submission was impossible. If the constitution was to be preserved it would be necessary to change its content by giving natifs the rights they demanded. "The health of the state" depended on this "change."[19]

The conciliation of 1768 tended nonetheless to maintain the existing balance. The wounds of the natifs remained open. A political novel by Jean-Pierre Bérenger, one of their leaders, entitled *Le natif ou Lettre de Théodore et d'Annette*, was an ingenious and faithful picture that tried to be a kind of *Anti-Nouvelle Héloïse*. It told the story of a marriage contracted between a natif and the daughter of a bourgeois. "The anecdotes and incidents were taken from the personal experiences of Georges Auzière" but contained general conclusions on the injustices of

---

[17] Ceitac, *Voltaire et l'affaire des natifs*, p. 121. The expression is from "Quelques considérations des natifs au procureur général Tronchin."

[18] Ibid., p. 117.

[19] Ibid., p. 120.

the existing order.[20] The discussion of the historical roots of the Genevan constitution—which continued uninterrupted in those years—ended with an appeal, a general claim of natural rights, and "maxims of reason, humanity, and the public good."[21]

The original solitary figures who carried on the battle after the conciliation of 1768 have been called "obscure heroes."[22] But more effective than their sporadic protest was the reinvigoration and transformation of the cercles in which Rousseau had seen the connective tissue of the bourgeoisie of Geneva, and which now, after 1768, were given by the most active among the natifs the aspect and function of embryonic political clubs. They generally met in an inn or a tavern. Only a few people made up the nucleus, from about twenty to only a few, depending on circumstances.[23] But their ability to unite and mobilize the populace was growing. Nor were these composed only of men, as Rousseau had imagined. Women had an important part, and they contributed to the unusually open discussions in these meetings. Their names are significant: a true roster of persons who counted in history, not only in Geneva, but in France and Europe in general in the following decades, from Mallet du Pan to Clavière, from Grenus to Cornuaud, not to mention individuals affiliated with Italy, the grandfather of our Vieusseux. Banquets, choruses, songs, and heated discussions characterized the meetings, scandalizing some and filling others with enthusiasm.[24]

When on 15 July 1769 the government, incited by the bourgeois, introduced new vexing limitations on the commercial activity of the natifs, they responded with a true and proper banquet campaign. At the beginning of the new year Isaac Cornuaud, a man of undoubted political capacity, placed himself at their head. He was not at all convinced that the natifs, in their quest for citizenship, had legal rights. He viewed with skepticism their effort to seek support for their cause from the Parlement of Grenoble. But he opposed the bourgeoisie, whom he had initially supported, and did not intend to further suffer the injustices he thought they were perpetrating. The arrest of a *natif* who had sung a song in a café "to answer a bourgeois" put the natifs in a state of agitation.[25] The trial of the prisoner was anticipated with disquiet and impatience. Some spoke of the death penalty. A crowd surrounded the

[20] Ibid., pp. 131ff.

[21] Ibid., p. 133.

[22] Ibid., p. 143ff.

[23] Ibid., p. 153.

[24] The principal evidence is in *Mémoires de Isaac Cornuaud sur Genève et la révolution, de 1770 à 1795*, ed. Emilie Cherbuliez (Geneva: A. Jullien, 1912).

[25] Ibid., pp. 97ff. The precedents and the facts of 1770 are set forth clearly in Albert Choisy, "La prise d'armes de 1770 contre les natifs," in *Etrennes genevoises* (Geneva: Editions Atar, 1925), pp. 47ff.

courthouse. Mallet du Pan summed up for the defense. The sentence was relatively light: six months of house arrest. A riot broke out when the prisoner appeared, and a cortege formed to bring home the hero of the day. Seditious songs, insults, jokes, and tricks against citizens were plentiful. The next day the bourgeois reacted. The condemned man was arrested again (he had evaded the sentence of house arrest). More influential bourgeois asked the Council to act against the growing menace of the natifs. "Very properly and through a unanimous vote of the council . . . it was decided . . . to call out the whole city and the garrison, and in effect, to sound the alarm."[26]

The *Notizie del mondo* explained these events clearly to its readers in the issue of 10 March. "Our city," a correspondent wrote from Geneva on 23 February, "found itself in the past days in the midst of grave disturbances caused by these nationals [their translation of *natifs*]."[27] Even *La Gazzetta di Milano* of 21 March announced that "the spirit of independence has caused a grave disturbance in this city in the past days."[28] The Florentine gazette referred to the origins of the disturbances.

For a long time the nationals have demanded certain privileges of the Council, which they enjoyed in previous times, but which had been annuled in large part through subsequent mediation. The Council has informed them that there was no way to recover them. After this reply injurious writings began to be distributed, which were immediately burned. The said nationals were not intimidated by this; rather they became more audacious, going to the magistrates and arrogantly demanding reestablishment of their old privileges. The magistrates, desiring to repress such audacity, arrested many, who were judged with much clemency. The third time they pronounced sentence against one of the said nationals named Persequerre [actually he was called Guillaume Resseguerre], who was condemned to house arrest for six months, there was a large tumult of people at the city hall, who accompanied the criminal to the prison, where he went to pay the usual fine. There four of the strongest . . . took him on their shoulders and carried him triumphantly through the city, with sprigs of laurel in their hair, and they cried victory to the crowd. When the Council was informed of this, it sent four officials the following day to rearrest the man and put him back in prison.

The reaction of the natifs was not long in coming. "The protest grew even greater, with a parade of infuriated people to the city hall, almost all armed privately with pistols. After repeated appeals from the citizenry to the Magnificent Council about the heatedness of spirits and imminent peril to the republic, a general alarm was sounded, and the whole garrison and citizenry was called to arms."[29]

[26] Choisy, "La prise d'armes," p. 67.

[27] *Notizie del mondo*, no. 20, 10 March 1770, p. 157 (Geneva, 23 February).

[28] *La Gazzetta di Milano*, no. 16, 21 March 1770 (Geneva, 23 February).

[29] *Notizie del mondo*, no. 20, 10 March 1770, p. 157 (Geneva, 23 February).

This was an informed and substantially precise account, even if clearly favorable to the "citizenry" and the government. In Venice the *Mercurio storico e politico* presented things in a similar light. After having narrated the attempted sedition "of nationals and inhabitants," it concluded: "If we had waited a half-hour we would have been lost, but Providence. . . ."[30] However, none of the Italian periodicals that I have seen reported the grave incidents that accompanied the subsequent violent reaction of bourgeois and patricians. Before the bell of St. Peter's had struck, "three natifs were sacrificed to the furor of citizens." "A young courageous natif, Chalet, an engraver and a grenadier, already wounded, took his sword in his hand and was killed where he stood by the notary Richard. An inoffensive old man, father Olivier, aged seventy-three years, a simple spectator who had come out in his dressing gown, was assassinated by Sergeant Frarin, who according to Cornuaud had a grudge against him. A third, little-esteemed natif, Chevalier, saw the blood of his friends flowing; he armed himself, descended, tried to fire and failed; in his haste he had put the bullet behind the powder; he was seized, disarmed, and soon, stabbed from behind, he died, struck by his cousin, a citizen." "The night was passed in arms, terror, and suspicion. The wind and rain raged. . . . In improvised places of detention, where wood for heat was requisitioned from the hospital, the natif prisoners became the butts of the reproaches, threats, and insults of their guards."[31] These facts struck Voltaire deeply. In France and Geneva the discussion of the constitutional and social problems of the republic became more and more complex.[32] The *Notizie del mondo* limited itself to reporting the arrests, and then in detail the repressive measures the rulers of the republic took through an edict of 22 February and a whole series of condemnations and expulsions. It had been a vain hope that the edict of 1768 would succeed in creating an equilibrium. The magistrates had been obliged to state "with extreme sorrow" that the "stubborn criminal ambition" of the natifs had not disappeared. "Presuming not to know the condition the laws impose on them, they claim that natives of the city are equal in number to those whom our edicts call 'citizens,' an imaginary and absurd proposition that would totally undo our constitution." "To attempt this perfidious act," they have "formed an association among themselves, have acted by all possible means to increase their party, . . . and have formed assemblies, or clubs, to discuss their political interests," frequently distributing their views in print. Finally they attempted to impede the normal course of justice. Thus the

---

[30] *Mercurio storico e politico*, vol. 628, March 1770, p. 45, Geneva.

[31] Choisy, *La prise d'armes*, p. 69.

[32] Ceitac, *Voltaire et l'affaire des natifs*, pp. 155ff.

Council acted well to "call citizens, bourgeois, and natives to arms." The majority of the natives had even remained faithful to the government. The republic reconfirmed the edicts of 1738 and 1768, stating that "anyone who maintains in speech or writing that natifs enjoy rights other than those enumerated . . . or either within the city or without make any plot, gang, threat, or act tending to change the status of natifs will be punished for disturbing public peace and tranquillity, as the case demands, even with the death sentence."[33] The "cercles" listed by name in the edict were "disbanded". "Those who have frequented them are forbidden to found any others for the discussion of affairs of state." A new oath was required of suspects: "To be faithful to the state, obedient to magistrates, and submissive to the present constitution of the republic, and particularly to the present edict." Those who refused would be expelled from Geneva. Meanwhile, expelled were also those who were considered particularly guilty:[34] "George Auzière, maker of box hinges (whom we already know), Jean Pierre Béranger[35] (whom we have seen in action), Jean Pierre Mottu, called 'The Jonquil,' maker of boxes,[36] Eduard Luya, clockmaker,[37] Philippe Pouzait, clockmaker, Davide François Pouzait, rug maker,[38] Pierre Rival, clockmaker,[39] and Guillaume Henri Valentin, clockmaker."[40]

[33] *Notizie del mondo*, no. 22, 17 March 1770, pp. 173ff. (Geneva, 3 March).

[34] Ibid., no. 23, 20 March 1770, pp. 180ff. (Geneva, 20 February). See the list in Choisy, *La prise d'armes*, p. 71.

[35] As we read in *Mémoires de Isaac Cornuaud*, p. 119, Béranger was "the principal writer among the protesting natifs." In 1772 he had published the *Histoire de Genève*. Cornuaud openly criticized this work, as well as the political conduct of its author. "Born proud, and naturally prejudiced against the great and the rich, he hid his defects for a long time under a veil of moderation, but his *Histoire de Genève* made his principles and political conduct clear; it was generally a cloth of trivialities." The *Gazzetta di Parma*, no. 9, 2 March 1773 (Geneva, 10 February), spoke of Béranger's *Histoire de Genève* and wrote that its "distribution had been prohibited under harsh punishment."

[36] On this "singular and original" man, see *Mémoires de Isaac Cornuaud*, p. 119: "He sacrificed to the cause of the natifs his time, his small fortune, his health, and his tranquillity. . . . he was a very honest man, with a candid and generous soul."

[37] Ibid., p. 118: "He had a spirit of substance and thoughtfulness, but was naturally serious, in bad health, and taciturn. . . . He had a large family; already poorly off before his exile, sorrow shortened his days."

[38] Ibid., pp. 120ff. The second of these two brothers distinguished himself in the tumult of 1770. His exile in Versoix was difficult. "He worked in the neighboring countryside both in Switzerland and France, and even in the territory of the republic. . . . He was one of the natifs who was best informed of the pretensions of the party: he knew the matter thoroughly and had made original observations."

[39] Ibid., p. 121. The brother of a well-known actor, he was a good orator. "It was he who addressed the old man of Ferney in the name of his fellows, on feast days."

[40] Ibid., p. 122. Cornuaud was most hostile to him: "Liar, false, violent, a hypocrite, and full of vanity and pettiness, he never had any principles."

The edict of 22 February 1770 even made some concessions, not on a political or even a social level, but on a corporate one. "In order to give natifs who have shown they are faithful and obedient a demonstration of benevolence, in the future natifs will no longer pay taxes to the Hospital when they marry, they will no longer pay market fees, along with citizens and bourgeois they will be admitted in the military exercises for prizes in marksmanship, their admission to the *jurands* was preserved as stated in the edict of 1768, and it was established that beginning with the year 1774 a *maître jurand* would always be chosen among the corps of natifs for all trades where there was more than one *maître jurand*."[41]

These were niggardly and archaic concessions, insufficient to satisfy a movement that had animated a significant group of artisans, that had shown itself capable, as we have seen, of reflecting on its own destiny, of listening critically to the voices of Rousseau and Voltaire, and of seeking autonomously some way to reform the republic of Geneva.

[41] *Notizie del mondo*, no. 23, 20 March 1770, pp. 180ff. (Geneva, 20 February).

XI

The French Reform Crisis

EVENTS IN FRANCE BETWEEN 24 DECEMBER 1770 AND 12 MAY 1776, that is, between the dismissal of Choiseul and the fall of Turgot, were decisive for the fate of the old regime. The throne changed hands: Louis XVI replaced Louis XV in 1774. The ministers were replaced. The Parlements were at first defeated and then returned triumphant. A foreign policy still dominated by the consequences of the Seven Years' War gave way to French intervention in the War of American Independence. The moral and intellectual climate changed significantly. In these years the last great attempt to reform France by maintaining, or even restoring, traditional institutions occurred, an attempt that was also inspired by the new economic and political ideas of the Enlightenment.

I will not take up again here, even in summary, the narrative and interpretation of these decisive years, which Furio Diaz has done very well in his work entitled *Filosofia e politica nel Settecento francese*.[1] Chapter 6 is entitled "The Power Struggle between Crown and Parlements" and contains a detailed examination of the affair of the Parlement of Bretagne and the Maupeou reform, as seen through the doubts and problems these facts aroused in the minds of Voltaire, the philosophes, and their adversaries. Chapter 8 is entitled the "Effort and Failure of Turgot." The subtitle, "The Philosophes Will Not Reign," tells us of the dramatic importance of the events. Beginning with these pages, here are recent books on the years 1770–1776 in France that help us follow the discussion Furio Diaz opened.

A book by Lucien Laugier is not particularly stimulating: *Un ministère réformateur sous Louis XV. Le triumvirat (1770–1774)* (Paris: La pensée universelle, 1975). The monarchical orthodoxy, the calculated admiration for the policy of the period of Louis XV, and the consistently apologetic stance toward men like Maupeou, Terray, d'Aiguillon astonish

---

[1] Diaz, *Filosofia e politica nel Settecento francese.*

the reader, who is obliged to ask how such an antiquated historical-political vision could survive in modern France. But an attentive reading suggests why there should be such a residue of ideas here from the Action Française and its historian Gaxotte (who wrote the introduction to this book). Nationalism and admiration for administrative and bureaucratic technique periodically seduce a few French historians with the monarchical ideals of the old regime. Otherwise Lucien Laugier's work is useful precisely because of its bureaucratic pedantry and detail, which succeed in tracing a striking picture of the internal conflicts in the French government in the last years of Louis xv.

The book by Edgar Faure, *La disgrâce de Turgot: 12 Mai 1776*, has a different tone and value. It appeared in the collection *Trente journées qui ont fait la France*, published by Gallimard (Paris, 1961). The parliamentary tradition of French republicanism in the nineteenth and twentieth centuries, and a radical spirit, emerges here triumphantly. Edgar Faure brings to this work all the vivacity and intelligence he showed in the political crises of his own time. People are valued for their merit in debate, in intrigue, in the daily struggle for power. All ideological reverence or regret is forgotten. Modern liberty is like the air, without which all debate, all life, and all affirmation are unthinkable. Is this perspective too modern for a historical understanding of a man like Turgot? In fact, Edgar Faure does not resist much the temptation to utilize present reality to explain the reality of the eighteenth century. He lacks historical distance. For instance, his view that the Parlements were forced into demagogy by the false position they found themselves in in their struggle with the monarchy is illuminating but risks not taking a more important factor sufficiently into account: the broad and deep diffusion of the new ideas, aims, and convictions of the Enlightenment around the year 1770. If the *Parlementaires* were demagogic, this resulted not from political logic alone, but also from the general need for moral and intellectual change that obliged even French magistrates to search out for new directions. Nevertheless, Edgar Faure's book, precisely because it is openly the work of a contemporary political figure ready to relive the crises of the past (he has recently published, in the same collection, another large volume on 17 July 1720: *La banqueroute de Law*), rediscovers for us a sense of the drama, as well as the importance of Turgot's experience. It is filled with numerous detailed observations on the strategy of reform, on the lost opportunities, and also on the true efforts of the *philosophe* and *économiste* who arrived in power between 1774 and 1776. In order to include the developments of these years more precisely in the history of economic and political discussion of the French Enlightenment one should turn to the excellent book by Douglas Dakin, *Turgot and the Ancien Régime in France* (London: Methuen, 1939), to the two posthumous volumes by Georges Weulersse, *La physiocratie à la fin du règne de Louis XV (1770–1774)* and *La physiocratie sous les ministères de Turgot et de Necker (1774–1781)* (both published in Paris, by the Presses Universitaires de France, in 1959 and 1950), and to the still fundamental work by Herbert Lüthy, *La banque protestante en France de la Révocation de l'Edit de Nantes à la Révolution* (Mouton: La Haye, 1959–61). Among more recent publications, of particular importance is the volume by Keith Michael Baker, *Condorcet: From Natural Philosophy to Social Mathematics* (University of Chicago Press, 1975), which reexamines the problem of the intervention of Condorcet in the reform attempt by Turgot. A useful collection of Turgot's *Ecrits économiques* was edited by Bernard Cazes in the collections *Perspectives de l'économique* by the Parisian editor Calmann-Levy in 1970. Roberto Finzi has published a similar collection of texts, entitled *Le ricchezze, il progresso e la storia universale* (Turin: Piccola Biblioteca Einaudi, 1978), where interest is concentrated, aside from the more strictly economic thought of Turgot, on his philosophical ideas and his vision of the evolution of human society, thus restoring him to philosophie, from which political history had attempted to separate him. This anthology thus takes up the way opened half a century ago by Gustave Schelle in his still fundamental edition of the *Oeuvres de Turgot et documents le concernant* (Paris: Alcan, 1913–33), in five volumes.

There were many echoes, even in Italy, of the great turning point of the French old regime at the beginning of the seventies, between Choiseul and Turgot.

It is enough to open the *Notizie del mondo* at the end of 1770 and follow the numerous communications published there on the conflicts between the French monarchy and the Parlements, and on the ever more weighty intervention of the ministers of Louis XV to break the resistance of the law courts, to realize that, even among Italians, there was an awareness of the larger significance contained in these disputes. The fall of Choiseul (24 December 1770), the action of the Abbé Terray and of the ministers d'Aiguillon and Maupeou were not understood merely as a repetition of an old quarrel about competence, or a judicial contest to the nth degree. Even in Italy it was clear that more important values were at play: the idea itself of law and a constitution, a certain tradition of liberty, a growing repugnance for the arbitrary methods of government, and also a kind of desperation at the sight of France in the hands of a corrupt court, that was incompetent, and at the same time both oppressive and despotic.

Even those philosophes, like Voltaire, who insisted on trying to utilize monarchical power—and the influence they thought they could exercise over its ministers—for continuing the battle against privilege and the backwardness and cruelty of the judicial caste, were struck by a

growing sense of aversion and uncertainty when confronted with the
lack of intelligence and decision the French government demonstrated
in its daily operations. Those among the Encyclopedists, such as Diderot, Helvétius, or Deleyre, who for some time had declared their autonomy and independence when confronted with official policy, there
was a growing discouragement, almost a despair for that reform program to which they had devoted their existence. Diderot said to Catherine II that, despite the just criticism leveled at the French judicial system, to tear down the legality and traditions of the Parlements was to
bring into the open the despotic character of the French monarchy.
"There was a veil between the head of the despot and our eyes on which
the multitude admired a great image of liberty. Soothsayers had long
looked through little holes in the fabric and knew well what it concealed;
the veil was torn away and tyranny showed its face openly. When a people is not free, the opinion it has of its liberty is still precious." When the
illusion of liberty was removed, France felt enslaved. "Do not expect any
more great things either in war, or the sciences, or in letters and the
arts." A profound sense of abasement pervaded the country.[2] Diderot
asked himself how one could escape from the insufferable sense of
oppression, or get off one's back the sensation of being corrupt and decadent. Before his eyes appeared the image of Medea, who "returned
her father to youth by cutting him into pieces and having him boiled."[3]
Over Helvétius, descended the blackest pessimism as he persuaded himself more and more that there was no way out for France, humiliated as
it was in the present, and expecting nothing in the future besides invasion and conquest. "My fatherland is now under the yoke of despotism;
thus it will produce no more famous writers. . . . This fallen nation is
the scorn of Europe. No salutary crisis will restore its liberty; it will die
of consumption. Conquest is the only remedy for its misfortunes, and
chance and circumstance will decide the effectiveness of this remedy."[4]
As for Alexandre Deleyre, he wrote at that time in his testament:
"France, where I was born, has fallen into corruption under the yoke of
despotism. The nation is too blind and too base to seek or be able to
escape."[5]

[2] Denis Diderot, *Mémoires pour Catherine II*, ed. Paul Vernière (Paris: Garnier, 1966), p.
20.

[3] Denis Diderot, "Réfutation suivie de l'ouvrage d'Helvétius intitulé L'homme," in id.,
Oeuvres complètes, ed. J. Assézat (Paris: Garnier, 1875), vol. 2, p. 276.

[4] Dedication of Claude-Adrien Helvétius, *De l'homme, de ses facultés intellectuelles et de
son éducation. Ouvrage posthume* (London: Société typographique, 1773).

[5] See Franco Venturi, "Un encyclopédiste: Alexandre Deleyre," in id., *Europe des lumières. Recherches sur le 18e siècle* (Paris and The Hague: Mouton, 1971), p. 76. On the
whole moral crisis of these years see also the rich work by Durand Echeverria, *The Mau-*

The philosophes discovered with surprise the horror of being in a path seemingly without exit. They did not hide their pessimism even when writing to friends in Italy. Thus, for example, Baron d'Holbach, in a letter to Father Frisi on 1 December 1771, speaking of the recently published *Meditazioni* by Pietro Verri, confessed that it would be difficult to publish a French translation. "For some time now here the press has been so controlled that it has been almost impossible to utter the slightest truths; we are reduced to savoring those that come to us from foreign countries."[6] Even Italy, although traditionally notorious for its oppressive censorship, could seem a refuge of liberty in the eyes of Baron d'Holbach when compared with the oppression that had settled on France in the last years of Louis xv.

To be sure, we do not sense in Italian gazettes and writings quite the same degree of participation in the French drama at the beginning of the seventies. Accents similar to those of Diderot or Helvetus do not appear in the Florentine *Notizie del mondo*. But read, for instance, the sheet dated 3 November 1770. The documents themselves were eloquent on the crisis of the Parlements. At issue was a "remonstrance of the *Cour des aides*" on the trial pending against the Duc d'Aiguillon: "Consternation is universal in your realm," proclaimed the judges addressing themselves to the sovereign. "The spirit of lawlessness joins forces with the spirit of despotism against the courts." "It is known in all your kingdom that nowadays the Parlement of Brittany represents the opinion of an entire province. The nobility has the same opinion as the magistrates, and the same sentiments have been adopted by the merchant, the peasant, and the artisan." Those who would accept substitutes for magistrates legally in possession of their charges were called "vile spirits." "The person of the judicial magistrate must be inviolable." The king had embarked on a route filled with grave perils. "We will not discuss the terrible prospect of a reversal of law which will be necessary to preserve royal authority, an ill-fated expedient for so many monarchies, but that nonetheless seems likely to be adopted by your council." Nor did the Parlement of Brittany hide from the sovereign that the struggle had become "known to all of Europe."[7] This was to say something not that different from what Diderot had explained to Catherine ii. The parallel protest of the Parlement of Bordeaux was published on 13 Au-

---

peou Revolution. A study in the History of Libertarianism, France, 1770–1774 (Baton Rouge: Louisiana State University Press, 1985).

6 "Une lettre du baron d'Holbach," published by F. Venturi in *Studies on Voltaire and the Eighteenth Century*, fasc. 2 (1956), p. 286.

7 *Notizie del mondo*, no. 88, 3 November 1770, p. 716 (Paris, 15 October).

gust 1770.[8] As for the Parisian tribunal, it denounced "the project to change the form of government and substitute for the steady force of law the irregular blows of arbitrary power."[9]

After the surprising fall of Choiseul, the atmosphere became more tense.[10] *Lits de Justice*, acts of authority, and arrests multiplied and were always reported in detail in the Florentine journals. La Harpe, the well-known writer of tragedies, was imprisoned in the Bicêtre. "The famous Rousseau has left this capital without anyone's knowing where he has gone."[11] With the 9 March 1771 issue the *Notizie del mondo* began to publish the "vote of the Parlement of Rouen," reporting, on 19 March, that "the court was suspended through suppression of a law that for more than eight hundred years had ensured inviolability to a free nation, sovereigns who loved it, and free and quiet subjects to the sovereign." Instead of "erecting despotism into law," the monarch would do better to think of "convoking the Estates General," which would be able to "tell him the abuses committed in his name." "Resistance" against arbitrary rule was a duty when "the rights of different orders of citizens" were under attack.[12] In April 1771 a declaration by the nobility affirmed that "the constitution of the government and the rights of the people" had been abused in the king's attempt to substitute for them "a despotism without bounds, without limits, and consequently without rights." The nobility recalled its own "right of assembly." It did not forget that "the nation, in its assemblies, had charged the Parlements with defending its rights." It was time, in other words, to resist the efforts of those who sought to suppress the Parlements and to substitute "despotism" for liberty.[13]

Declarations and counterdeclarations, protests and counterclaims, multiplied in the spring of 1771. Minute details were provided on the establishment and structure of the new court system, the "new Parlement." A cold and hostile atmosphere surrounded it.[14] The royal pronouncements were translated in full, but they were unable to counter effectively the hopes and passions the old Parlements had succeeded in

[8] Ibid., no. 84, 20 October 1770, pp. 683ff. (Paris, 1 October), and then in a long series of sucessive issues.

[9] Ibid., no. 86, 27 October 1770, p. 699 (Paris, 8 October).

[10] Ibid., no. 3, 8 January 1771, p. 18 (Paris, 25 December) ("This affair has raised astonishment in people").

[11] Ibid., no. 15, 19 February 1771, p. 114 (Paris, 5 February). The same communication is in *La Gazzetta di Milano*, no. 9, 27 February 1771 (Paris, 7 February).

[12] *Notizie del mondo*, no. 23, 19 March 1771, pp. 176ff., "Fine del voto del parlamento di Roano."

[13] Ibid., no. 28, 6 April 1771, p. 216 (Paris, 18 March).

[14] Ibid., no. 37, 7 May 1771, pp. 287ff. (Paris, 23 April).

raising. The protest of the princes of the blood was considered "one of the most interesting memorials of the present history of this kingdom." Even they had not hesitated to appeal to "law," "rights," and "liberty."[15] Beside the manifesto of the high nobility stood the protest of the "judges of the Châtelet," and there also came news of the exile inflicted on recalcitrant magistrates.[16] Books maintaining the illegality of the new judges were "shredded and burned by the hand of the executioner for being seditious and denigratory to the authority of the king."[17] The new court did its best to appear tolerant in religious matters and supportive of peace between church and state.[18] "After the creation of the new Parlement there has been no further trouble with the church, and no one has refused the sacraments, which leads one to believe that the disturbances of the past were the work of riotous spirits making use of the division between Parlements and church to foment discord."[19] The frequent internal conflicts of the new judicial body were followed with great interest.[20] Rumors of changes continued, creating a climate of uncertainty and disquiet.[21] The government attempted to stifle the debate. "The ferment created by the changes that have taken place in the courts, which are not yet entirely accomplished," one reads in April 1772, "continues to elicit clandestine, but really public, libelles." The example of a book was cited, "with the title *Inauguration de Pharamond, ou Exposition des loix fondamentales de la monarchie françoise, avec les preuves de leur exécution, perpétuées sous les trois races de nos roix*. The contents of this work, down to the medallion in the frontispiece, show the spirit of discontent." In two other works "the actions taken in the past year are bitterly criticized with continual ironies." On the official side rejoinders appeared in other libelles. But the most usual response was to condemn works of protest "to be shredded and burned publicly by the executioner."[22] On the other hand, the most insidious means were taken to

---

[15] Ibid., no. 43, 28 May 1771, pp. 335ff. (Paris, 14 May. It continues in the following issues, until no. 47, 11 June 1771, p. 368.)

[16] Ibid., no. 50, 22 June 1771, pp. 391ff. (Paris, 4 June).

[17] Ibid., no. 51, 25 June 1771, p. 399 (Paris, 11 June).

[18] Ibid., no. 57, 16 July 1771, pp. 447ff. (Paris, 2 July).

[19] Ibid., no. 104, 28 December 1771, p. 802 (Paris, 9 December).

[20] See, for example, ibid., no. 61, 30 July 1771, p. 479 (Paris, 16 July).

[21] See, for example, ibid., no. 67, 20 August 1771, p. 527 (Paris, 6 August), for information about the well-known attorney general Dupaty and the rumors circulating about the suppression of the "Parlement of Besançon." See also William Doyle, "Dupaty (1746–1788): A Career in the Late Enlightenment," *Studies on Voltaire and the Eighteenth Century*, no. 230 (1985): 1ff.

[22] Ibid., no. 29, 11 April 1772, pp. 225ff. (Paris, 23 March). This was the *Inauguration de Pharamond, ou Exposition desoix fondamentales de la monarchie françoise, avec les preuves de leur exécution, perpétuées sous les trois races de nos roix* (n.p., 1772), probably the work of Mar-

distribute the literature of opposition. There was a detailed account in the Florentine gazette of an episode of a blind man who lived beside "the Church of the Holy Spirit" ("every church has its blind man") and who was sent to distribute a new "prayer to St. Brigid," which in reality was "a libelle against the Lord Chancellor."[23] From Bordeaux and Aix-en-Provence echoes of protests and resistance continued to arrive. The act with which the Parlement of the latter city was dismissed moved "to repentance even those who brought the orders of the king," those, that is, who were charged with the removal of the traditional magistrates.[24]

At the end of 1772 echoes of the dispute began little by little to be lost in silence. The life of France was too varied for its attention to be fixed forever on political and judicial problems. Instead, in the last years of Louis xv attention, even in Italy, was directed more and more toward administrative and economic problems. And with the death of the king a new epoch began.

The *Nuove di diverse corti e paesi* of 30 May 1774 announced the death of Louis xv. "At three o'clock in the afternoon [of 10 May], with perfect resignation to divine will and religious sentiment worthy of the eldest son of the Church, he surrendered his soul to its creator."[1] It was the end of a long reign (he had been consecrated in Reims in 1722). Even through the aulic mournful style of official prose there came an awareness that a period of French history had closed with his death and that a new epoch was beginning. Certainly "many glorious victories" would be remembered (forgetting the not few hard defeats); certainly "the acquisition of Lorraine" could add to the positive balance of his account (there was no mention of Corsica), as well as the construction of "many sumptuous edifices devoted to religion, many public monuments, great roads opened throughout the realm to ease commerce." But even Italian readers were aware of how false the boast sounded of his having "given a luminous protection to the arts and sciences."[2] Still, a new France had been born during the long reign of Louis xv, and it had as its symbol that *Encyclopédie* which had survived thanks to the faithfulness and ability of Diderot and his collaborators, despite the

tin Morizot. It contained a reproduction of a medal representing a king, with scepter and sword, raised on a shield by two warriors, with the inscription *Unus omnium votis* (One by the vote of all). This was a symbol of the ancient election of kings.

[23] Ibid., no. 89, 5 November 1771, p. 682 (Paris, 21 October).

[24] Ibid., no. 94, 23 November 1771, p. 721 (Paris, 5 November).

[1] *Nuove di diverse corti e paesi*, no. 22, 30 May 1774, p. 173 (Paris, 12 May).

[2] Ibid.

thousand difficulties and contradictions in the public, religious, and intellectual life of the age of Louis xv.

But it was chiefly the last years of the old king that made his death seem a liberation and colored the future of his grandson, Louis xvi, with rosy colors of sweet hope. The flight of Du Barry and the collapse of all those who had made their fortunes through the king's last favorite (events minutely recorded in the gazette of Lugano), gave the change of reign the significance of a purging and purification. There came rapidly, with the first news from Paris, word of the intention of the new court to change the tone of government and satisfy in some way the desire for novelty, honesty, and cleanliness that steadily manifested itself more strongly in France. Whereas Louis xv was famous for his laziness and indifference, the new sovereign "rises from bed early and works for seven or eight hours a day." Neither the life of the court nor foreign affairs attracted his interest in particular; instead he was interested in "the high price of bread, [which he] wants to curb in the whole kingdom, and have the price of foodstuffs reduced so that even the lowest classes of his subjects can pay for them." "The affability and love of the people of this august sovereign could not be greater. . . . It is not with pomp and great expense that he has proposed to make the magnificence of his throne shine gloriously; rather he intends to found its splendor on a noble simplicity of manners, on order, decency, and the exact observance of respective duties, a virtue he holds in high esteem and requires as much in the great as in the people."[3] The contrast with the defunct king was clear. Explicit, if vague, was the promise—stated by Louis xvi in the edict registered by the Parlement on 30 May—to take "those paths that can make our people happy." He did not forget, it was hastily added, that this happiness "depended chiefly on a wise administration of finance."[4] The primacy of economics was thus recognized from the first official act of the new reign.

But the political problems remained open. D'Aiguillon was replaced by Vergennes in the ministry of foreign affairs.[5] Choiseul returned to favor through the queen and in a way proposed his own candidacy for the political leadership of France.[6] The procedures of the police and censorship, which had become more repressive in the last years of Louis xv, were lightened. "It is reported from France," one read in the *Notizie*

---

[3] Ibid., no. 23, 6 June 1774, p. 182 (Paris, 23 May).

[4] Ibid., no. 25, 20 June 1774, p. 195 (Paris, 6 June). The preamble of the edict with which Louis xvi opened his reign is also reproduced in the *Notizie del mondo*, no. 50, 21 June 1774, p. 394 (Paris, 6 June).

[5] *Nuove di diverse corti e paesi*, no. 26, 27 June 1774, p. 205 (Paris, 13 June), where it was noted, naturally, that Vergennes was the French ambassador in Stockholm.

[6] Ibid., no. 28, 11 July 1774, p. 221 (Paris, 1 July).

del mondo, "that the king has sent away all those functionaries of the post intended to open letters, saying that a caution permissible in wartime is improper in time of peace."[7] This was one of the first steps in a long series of changes in the "police" of Paris and France. With the anticipation of a more benevolent censorship, Voltaire published, "with the name of the author," "an elegy of Louis xv that was equidistant from adulation and satire."[8] Thus he also contributed to that reassessment of the policy of the past, and the start of a new era, that took many forms, at the court, among ministers, in the administration, and among writers and publicists.[9]

In the summer the problem of the Parlements returned to the center of attention. The new magistrates were nervous and "in much agitation as to the part to play with regard to the rumor of their approaching annihilation." In vain Chancellor Maupeou tried to reassure his judges, telling them in the name of the king "to remain quiet and not be disturbed about public discussion." But pressure increased from the men who had been dismissed and exiled in the last years of Louis xv. At the time of his funeral, the princes of the blood declared they would not attend if "the present Parlement were invited."[10] In Paris, the common rumor was that the king would soon relent. "It is said that all members of the old Parlements, and even the Seigneur de la Chalotais, that is, all those who had been exiled during the previous reign, would be recalled." Nor did this involve only the judicial world. The figure of another famous exile now appeared on the horizon: "Mr. Voltaire . . . might perhaps return to Paris."[11] This was a significant sign. Animated by the rising wave of rejection of arbitrary procedure, despotism, and the corruption of the preceding reign, Voltaire and the Parlements reemerged together, although they were great enemies, as is known.

Nevertheless, conservative resistance was not lacking. There were several efforts to explain to the young king the great risks the monarchy ran in restoring the Parlements to their ancient functions and traditional privileges. "Be assured," one read in the *Nuove di diverse corti e paesi,* "that a high-ranking minister has addressed the king as follows: 'Your Majesty, do not be deceived by the false prejudices of those rising spirits who pursue their own interests in general disorder. Do not de-

---

[7] *Notizie del mondo,* no. 53, 2 July 1774, p. 422 (Parma, 28 June).

[8] *Nuove di diverse corti e paesi,* no. 26, 27 June 1774, p. 205 (Paris, 13 June).

[9] We could add even among artists. It is symbolic that precisely at the decisive moment of the crisis of the summer of 1773, "Chevalier Gluck presented to the King, to the Queen, and to their Royal Highnesses an opera of his composition entitled *Orfeo,*" ibid., no. 31, 1 August 1774, p. 245 (Paris, 22 July). Thus a new sensibility found expression.

[10] *Nuove di diverse corti e paesi,* no. 30, 25 July 1774, p. 240 (Paris, 15 July).

[11] *Notizie del mondo,* no. 57, 16 July 1774, p. 450 (Paris, 4 July).

stroy, Sire, a work undertaken for twenty years that was the object of deep reflection of your august grandfather.' "[12] But it was too late to go against the current. "The partisans of the old Parlement . . . double their efforts to prevail."[13]

When the news of these Parisian disputes arrived in Italy, the knot was already cut. The events of 24 August were "striking." As the Abbé Véri wrote in his diary, "The expected revolution took place this morning." The Spanish ambassador, the famous Count of Aranda, remembering the saint of the day, said: "Behold a St. Bartholomew of ministers," and added, "it is not a massacre of innocents."[14] And the day 24 August 1774 has remained as "the St. Bartholomew of ministers"; it saw the posthumous collapse of the policy of Louis xv. Maupeou had to abandon "his glorious post as grand chancellor," making it easy to foresee that the old Parlement would soon be restored. "The Abbé Terray," controller general of the finances, was dismissed with the order to "present his accounts and consign his papers to Mr. Turgot, who has been named by His Majesty to replace him in this charge." Thus the economic management of the country changed hands. Sartine, a man of great culture and a friend of Diderot, became "secretary of state for the department of marine affairs" (which through the control of ports gave him a large influence over French commerce). Lenoir was nominated "lieutenant of the police of Paris," a key administration position in these years. "The transport of joy with which the news was received in Paris last Wednesday, toward five o'clock in the evening, was inexpressible. All citizens congratulated themselves most expressively and showered the king, the queen, the royal princes, and Mr. Maurepas" with blessings. The palace of justice was the center of demonstrations of joy, mixed with "several biting sarcasms" directed against the justices introduced by Louis xv and Maupeou. Then followed a series of measures taken against the former ruling clique, including the archbishop of Paris, who was exiled to Conflans. The creatures of the Abbé Terray were dismissed, and benevolent and propitiating measures were directed at the most representative members of the opposition. The "most respectable magistrate, M. de la Chalotais, after most difficult experiences," began to feel the "effects of royal bounty."[15] As the *Notizie del mondo* reported, this new benevolence for the Breton judge was to be regarded as "the

---

[12] *Nuove di diverse corti e paesi*, no. 31, 1 August 1774, p. 245 (Paris, 22 July).

[13] Ibid., no. 36, 5 September 1774, p. 284 (Paris, 24 August).

[14] See Edgar Faure, *La disgrâce de Turgot: 12 Mai 1776* (Paris: Gallimard, 1961), p. 33. This definition was reported in the *Notizie del mondo*, no. 75, 17 September 1774, p. 595 (Leiden, 2 September).

[15] *Nuove di diverse corti e paesi*, no. 37, 12 September 1773, p. 293 (Paris, 2 September).

highest point of this very fortunate revolution."[16] Finally France was governed by "a king who was a friend of truth and recognized merit" and by "ministers who enjoy the esteem of the public and confidence of the nation."

But in this idyllic "fortunate revolution" the first signs of a more obscure and violent movement appeared. "One of the disgraced ministers," one reads in the same gazette, "was in danger of losing his life [in crossing a river] to reach his home, since some riotous peasants wanted to cut the rope of his skiff, but the agility of the boatmen in getting him to the other side freed him."[17] These were small local scenes of disquiet that hardly disturbed the bright horizon of the ascent to the throne of Louis XVI and the rise to power of a new governing clique, headed by the philosopher and economist Turgot.

Outside France, and throughout the world, the scene seemed favorable for a new experiment. Precisely in these days the long Russo-Turkish war ended. The turbulence within Russia, Poland, and Sweden seemed to subside. The news from the English world, and from beyond the ocean, seemed to foreshadow an imminent conflict between the colonies and the mother country. But these were marginal preoccupations in a Europe that turned its gaze more and more toward France. There, under the best auspices and with the greatest hopes, seemed to begin an exceptional experiment in reform and renewal.[18] As the *Notizie del mondo* wrote in November, translating the rosy prose that arrived in waves from beyond the Alps, "our young monarch, as a true Telemachus, has taken good sense for his mentor; for his council experience, probity, and sagacity; economics is his treasury. He has for companions tenderness; for sons all his subjects; and for sovereign the truth. What will so many courtiers become? If possible . . . gentlemen."[19]

The atmosphere beyond the Alps was reflected clearly in the pages of Italian gazettes of the autumn of 1774. Anxious and full of hope, France followed the first steps of the new minister with anticipation. It was ready to let itself be carried away by enthusiasm but feared obstacles that could be glimpsed in the shadows: the intrigues of the adversaries of reform. It welcomed with joy the punishment of the men responsible

[16] *Notizie del mondo*, no. 75, 17 September 1774, p. 595 (Leiden, 2 September).

[17] *Nuove di diverse corti e paesi*, no. 38, 19 September 1774, p. 301 (Paris, 9 September).

[18] There is a very interesting 1774 survey of Europe in the *Tableau de l'Europe* by Alexandre Deleyre, which came out in that year and soon appeared in an Italian version: *Prospetto attuale dell'Europa* (attributed, as usual, to the Abbé Raynal) (London, 1778). See Venturi, "Alexandre Deleyre," pp. 77ff. There is also the letter with which Catherine II thanked Grimm, on 30 April 1774, for sending this work, in Sirio, vol. 13 (1874), p. 442.

[19] *Notizie del mondo*, no. 93, 19 November 1774, p. 737 (Paris, 31 October).

for previous policies. It was suspended uncertainly between protest and reform, between a will to free itself from the past and a desire to construct a new future. The figure of Turgot seemed imposing precisely because of his calmness, firmness, and lucidity at a moment when all seemed to seek out their own ways. When he was named minister of the merchant marine the *Nuove di diverse corti e paesi* said he was "much esteemed for his integrity and desire for hard work."[1] Appreciation and praise for him grew rapidly. But it was impossible not to see the weight of obstacles looming before him. Up to what point was it possible to reconcile the economic reform he wanted with the control and opposition of the Parlements, which had now returned to exercise their functions? Would the good will of the young king, the court, and ministers be sufficient to remedy the deficit in the finances and problems of provisioning and open the door to that profound transformation of the whole of French society which the philosophes had proclaimed necessary for years? For the present, in the enthusiasm of 1774, sentimentalism and optimism disguised the obstacles, coloring them with benevolent suspense. But the very multiplicity of the objects of reform—the system of justice, political rights, grain, artisan trades—divided attention in different directions, opening a horizon that was complex, changing, and veiled. This contrasted clearly with the hard, energetic, and precise aims of the American colonists, which, even in Italian journals, were reported along with news that came from the France of Turgot.

Turgot was not well known in Italy, and even in France he was better known within the political and intellectual elite than by nascent public opinion. Few of his writings had circulated: the articles of the *Encyclopédie* were on philosophy; his writings on history and economics had generally remained in manuscript form and were not widely diffused, and his most important political acts were closed in the archives of the intendency of Limoges and of Parisian ministries. Within the elite itself opinion about him was divided. Among the Encyclopedists it was well known that he had belonged to the right wing of the movement, so to speak, and that, along with d'Alembert, he had abandoned the great undertaking in 1759. For this reason Diderot, who much admired him, did not like him at all. Among the physiocrats he was considered an economist of exceptional ingenuity but not a member of the "sect." Thus, despite the great admiration that surrounded him among philosophes and économistes, the support he received during his reforming ministry of 1774–1775 was not great or energetic. The group around him included the young Condorcet and a series of writers of second or third rank, among whom the most typical was Boncerf. This situation

---

[1] *Nuove di diverse corti e paesi*, no. 33, 15 August 1774, p. 262 (Paris, 5 August).

was due to the position of Turgot himself, midway between philosophe and *grand commis*, between economist and statesman, writer and functionary. The situation was also due, in large part, to the detachment of many French philosophes from the task of reform, which had been supplanted, in the minds of many, by the need for a more integral transformation of society. This was already clear in 1766, during the debate on the work of Beccaria. Turgot and Malesherbes (who was now at the side of the new minister) were favorable to *Dei delitti e delle pene*. But Diderot countered the reform program of the Milanese with a will for a complete transformation, for a rebirth, which would fill the works of the last part of his life, from his collaboration in the *Histoire* of Raynal to his *Essai sur Sénèque*. In 1774, less than a decade later, the divergence was enlarged, made deeper and wider by the deluding and difficult political experience of the last years of Louis xv. Voltaire did not hide the fact that the party of the philosophes was profoundly divided. The ministry of Turgot was the last political effort of those who still believed in reform, and at the center of this effort were the immediate economic problems of the nation. But many of the philosophes had their eyes fixed on broader and more distant horizons.

On 13 September 1774 the great edict was promulgated, which reversed the protective policy of Terray and established free trade in grain. The Florentine journals hastened to publish the good news and circulate among Italians the text of the new law in full, which could only be "welcome to all readers sensible to the good of humanity," one read in the *Notizie del mondo*.[2] But in the last months of the year, the great quantity of details about the reestablishment of the Parlements, the extraordinary hopes of public happiness forecast for France, the commotion of well-thinking minds, and the tears shed in every corner of the realm began to be mixed with the first echoes of opposition and the growing difficulties that the new liberal law on the grain trade might encounter. The harvest had been poor. The search for bread became more pressing and widespread. Local administrative authorities, rather than applying the new regulations, multiplied their own interventions, reviving age-old practices and habits. Some of the Parlements revived

---

[2] *Notizie del mondo*, no. 83, 15 October 1774, p. 658 (Paris, 3 October). The follow-up to the decree was published in no. 85, 22 October 1774, p. 673 (Paris, 10 October), and in no. 86, 25 October 1774, p. 682 (Paris, 10 October). In the latter issue it was noted that the *Gazzetta di commercio, arti e finanze*, which came out in Paris, had begun to debate on the edict. The *Gazzetta universale*, which had been published in Florence for about a year, summarized it in no. 85, 15 October 1774, p. 658 (Paris, 3 October), and then published it in its entirety beginning with no. 97, 3 December 1774, pp. 775ff. In the *Nuove di diverse corti e paesi* it was necessary to wait for no. 3, 16 January 1775, p. 21 (Paris, 30 December 1774), to read the long preamble of the edict.

their opposition to the economic policy of the government. Others, it is true, supported Turgot, as the *Gazzetta universale* hastened to note.[3] At the court the campaign against the minister continued. "The new controller general Turgot, a subject of great merit and wisdom," one reads in the same gazette, "is exposed to the cruel wind of envy, and there is an attempt to make him lose the place the king conferred on him so willingly." "Various zealots" whispered that "this minister was not very attached to religion." Finally, one morning, turning to Maurepas, Louis XVI said: "They say that Turgot does not go to mass, what do you think?" The answer from the minister was quick: "The Abbé Terray went every morning."[4]

Discussion about the historical and economic bases of the new economic policy was resumed in Paris. For ten years, since the edict of 1764, a debate continued on the respective merits of Sully and Colbert, who were seen as symbols of the two contradictory positions the state might assume with regard to agriculture. A correspondent of the *Gazzetta universale* referred directly to this and did not forget to mention the intervention in the debate of the "Abbé G. of Naples" against the laws of 1763 and 1764. Galiani's *Dialogues*, to which this alluded, had been supported by the government of Terray and "circulated with interest and applause throughout the realm," whereas his adversary, Morellet, was refused permission to print his refutation, and the Abbé Baudeau found it impossible to express his opinion. Only the "obscurity" of another polemicist, the author of a work entitled *Récréations économiques*, had protected him from a similar "public proscription."[5] Finally, the moment for freedom of the press had come. "Now all the above-mentioned works, either printed or suppressed, are sold publicly and triumphantly in Paris."[6]

The *Gazzetta universale* opened the discussion on the general theme of Turgot's policy. One contributor, although favorable in general to free trade in grain, still clung to the idea of establishing a maximum price, which, when exceeded, would require intervention. "Otherwise

---

[3] *Gazzetta universale*, no. 2, 7 January 1775, p. 9 (Paris, 23 December 1774). "The freedom of trade in grain has contented particularly our southern provinces." The Parlement of Toulouse had offered its thanks to the ministry.

[4] *Gazzetta universale*, no. 4, 14 January 1775, p. 25 (Paris, 29 December 1774). The notice is also in the *Nuove di diverse corti e paesi*, no. 4, 23 January 1775, p. 28 (Paris, 9 January).

[5] This was the *Récréations économiques, ou Lettres de l'auteur des Représentations aux magistrats, à M. le chevalier Zanobi, principal interprète des Dialogues sur le commerce des blés* (Paris: Delalain and Lacombe, 1770), by the abbé Pierre-Joseph-Antoine Roubaud.

[6] *Gazzetta universale*, no. 4, 15 January 1775, p. 32, *Notizie di lettere, arti, agricoltura, ecc.* On Galiani and Turgot, see Galiani, *Opere*, p. lxxxix.

the avidity of many merchants . . . would soon make the price of products rise even during the most abundant season."[7] Soon after the Tuscan
gazette returned to a more orthodox liberalism (and it is possible that
this followed intervention by the grand ducal government). "Innumerable," we read in February, "have been the praises and thanks pouring
in to the king of France from the different Parlements of the realm,
from magistrates, communities, and individuals, because of his law on
free trade in grain, which is regarded by the wise as a foundation of
happiness and basis of perpetual prosperity for agriculture and commerce." Some objections were still raised. "Some weak and timid spirits"
thought it opportune to "apply remedies to liberty through a regulation
of prices, and other measures to prevent serious disadvantages." The
Gazzetta universale wanted to "expose their doubts, fears, and advice
openly." But it was best to state clearly that "the most excellent economists and politicians" were opposed to their measures. It was necessary
to hold fast to the principle of liberty. "When it is at its beginning, and
the system is not yet established, some might take advantage of the situation in which the state finds itself due to past regulation, but liberty
will change these circumstances, and when legislation removes other restrictions of the old system, which are incompatible with the full exercise
of free trade, all the feared inconveniences, monopolies, excessive and
unjust prices, and more important, peril of a lack of subsistence for the
people will disappear by themselves." The *Gazzetta universale* had published "the aforementioned article" in order to "have the opportunity to
refute it."[8]

Meanwhile the gazettes of the winter of 1774–1775 referred to other
numerous reforms that Turgot desired, projected, and discussed. He
intended "to remove many little impositions with which merchants are
taxed." The *Gazzetta universale* thought "an operation of this kind should
have been done before the edict on the freedom of trade in grain. . . .
If the peasant had known that he would have to make no more payments, he would gladly accept the risk of prices in different markets and
prefer this to other prospects." The "beneficial effects" of freedom
would be felt all the more. "Mr. Turgot is even seriously thinking of
putting begging to an end, wanting to give to those truly in need the
immense sums of charitable assistance collected throughout the king-

---

[7] *Gazzetta universale*, no. 11, 7 February 1775, pp. 86ff., "Politica."

[8] Ibid., no. 13, 14 February 1775, p. 103. "Politica." There was a similar polemic in
the *Notizie del mondo*, no. 15, 20 February 1776, p. 113 (Paris, 30 January), disputing the
work of Marc-Ferdinand Grouber de Groubentall de Linière, *La finance politique réduite au
principe et en pratique pour servir de système général en France* (Paris Grangé, 1775). "All is
unjust and moribund in regulations that were once regarded as laws of nature," it concluded.

dom."⁹ Military reform was considered, beginning with a provision that could not help touching the hearts of all. "For some time humanity has trembled to see unhappy deserters receive the death penalty; they are often pushed to desertion by fear of a severe punishment for some light involuntary act, and not for lack of zeal for their sovereign." Finally France would show the example of abolishing "that barbarous law." "The king has substituted for it a new one, forced labor on the public roads."¹⁰ At the same time, "in the same council," the *corvées* were "abolished, because the king has considered how harmful it is to subject the most useful and poorest of his people to work so prejudicial to agriculture." "He has also ordered that those condemned to the galleys work on the corvées along with deserters." "It was reserved for Louis XVI," concluded the gazette, "to cast his gaze over such important objects and prefer public work on land to the galleys, which are a mere illusory punishment of no benefit."¹¹

Turgot as minister thus found himself at the crossroads between the ideas of Beccaria and those of the physiocrats, coloring both with a humanitarianism typical of the first years of Louis XVI. In March a first step toward a general transformation of public administration was taken; Turgot deliberated about this for some time, making motions in this direction during his ministry but still not being able to lay the basic foundations for reform. Turgot, one read in the *Gazzetta universale*, "is to propose in the council a new plan for public administration advantageous both to the sovereign and the people."¹² The minister still seemed to have wind in his sails in the winter of 1774–1775. On the occasion of his first effort to moderate the avidity of the Tax Farms, the *Nuove di diverse corti e paesi* wrote that the policy of the "enlightened minister" was energetic and that "he would continue to have the approval of his monarch as long as his aims were to assist the people."¹³

But the attack was soon joined, and in a violent and insidious manner, surprising Turgot at the culminating moment of his career. It did

---

⁹ *Gazzetta universale*, no. 6, 21 January 1774, p. 41 (Paris, 3 January).

¹⁰ *Notizie del mondo*, no. 12, 11 February 1775, p. 91 (Paris, 24 January). This measure was also referred to in the *Gazzetta universale*, no. 12, 11 February 1775, p. 89 (Paris, 24 January).

¹¹ *Notizie del mondo*, no. 12, 11 February 1775, p. 91 (Paris, 24 January). See *Gazzetta universale*, no. 12, 11 February 1775, p. 89 (Paris, 24 January). See also in the *Gazzetta universale*, no. 93, 21 November 1775, p. 737 (Paris, 7 November), the news of many "needy in the charge of the state" sent to "public works." "The land will have its galleys as well as the sea, as is wisely practiced in some states of Italy."

¹² *Gazzetta universale*, no. 24, 25 March 1775, p. 186 (Paris, 7 March).

¹³ *Nuove di diverse corti e paesi*, no. 14, 3 April 1775, p. 109 (Paris, 20 March).

not come from the court, but from needy crowds in places where bread had become scarcest and most expensive in the spring of 1775. Between March and April began the tumult later called the "guerre des farines." The uprising in Dijon and the disturbances around Paris initiated by "peasants who had come to buy foodstuffs" were first announced in the *Gazetta universale* and the *Notizie del mondo* on 20 and 23 May. Their cause seemed obvious: "the great increase in the price of bread."[1] In Pontoise people had begun "to sack three barges loaded with grain" destined for Paris. In Saint-Germain there was "at the time of the market another tumult." The bakers were sacked. In Versailles the same happened. "The bread of the city was carried off without any payment." "Some peasants, who prided themselves on having been in the revolution of St. Germain and Versailles," returned to the dock and asked for flour. It was emphasized that this was purely a rural movement. "No artisans or workmen were involved in the incident." The king continued to support Turgot. "The whole guard of Paris, watch and ward, made their rounds day and night."[2] The *Notizie del mondo* reported as follows on 6 June: "An example has been made of some of the guiltiest, at Versailles as at Paris, in the Place de Grève. Two reaching the scaffold in that place thought of making their fate more interesting by crying out: 'I die for bread! Help, friends, help!' But their cries were lost in the wind." Besides these punitive measures the government strongly supported the proposition that there was "no scarcity, no high price of grain, that had caused these incidents"; instead, there had been a plot by "persons with discontented criminal minds who tried to rouse the lowest plebs against a sovereign adored in all of France," who "from the moment of his ascent to the throne has given only proofs of goodness and paternal benevolence."[3] Even the *Gazzetta universale* asserted in decisive tones that "the sedition had its sole origin in a cabal and the ill-will of different people." "The rioters wore signs on their clothes to recognize one another. . . . they printed false decrees of the council, spread seditious manifestos, and dared to advertise their actions, saying that they wanted to assault Paris and Versailles."[4]

The plot theory was upheld officially and believed by many contemporaries, among whom were Voltaire and Galiani. It was taken up again,

---

[1] *Gazzetta universale*, no. 40, 20 May 1775, p. 314 (Paris, 4 May), and no. 41, 23 May 1775, p. 321 (Paris, 8 May). See *Notizie del mondo*, no. 40, 20 May 1775, p. 313 (Paris, 2 May) ("mutiny in Dijon"). There is a detailed description of the "guerre des farines" (27 April–10 May) furnished by George Rudè in the *Annales historiques de la Révolution française*, April–June 1956, pp. 139ff., and by Faure in *Le disgrâce de Turgot*, pp. 249ff.

[2] *Gazzetta universale*, no. 41, 23 May 1775, p. 321 (Paris, 8 May).

[3] *Notizie del mondo*, no. 45, 6 June 1775, p. 354 (Paris, 22 May).

[4] *Gazzetta universale*, no. 43, 30 May 1775, p. 338 (Paris, 16 May).

if with much circumspection, by the majority of historians but has not stood up to recent, more careful analysis. The "guerre des farines" remained, as E. Faure has maintained, a link connecting the hunger riots of earlier times with the movement of crowds at the start of the French Revolution. The energetic and rapid action of Turgot limited the immediate political results. But his entire program of reform, benevolent and humanitarian, rational and calm though it was, could not help but receive a hard blow. It became more difficult for him, even in matters of the grain trade, to follow the route of liberalization, even if, as the *Notizie del mondo* emphasized from the beginning, the chief aim of the government was to contain the resistance "without restricting the liberty of trade," using "the most moderate means, most adapted to the general good to return grain to a more moderate price," and distributing "thanks and premiums to those who brought in foreign grain."[5]

In Tuscany Turgot's experience aroused both interest and a barely concealed sense of superiority and pride. Freeing the grain trade—Tuscans were convinced—had been effected earlier in the grand duchy, more completely, and at less cost than in France.[6] In the summer of 1775 Salustio Bandini's *Discorso economico* was published in Florence. It was a good occasion to speak of the local roots of a liberal policy that had borne such good fruits in the last decade. The initiative for publishing Bandini's work, which had remained so long in manuscript, said the *Notizie del mondo*, was to give "praise to the philosophic prince on the throne [of Tuscany], who demonstrates the happiness of the times in which we live."[7] "That active creative spirit called the 'spirit of enterprise,'" which Bandini had shown in his writings and his "familiar discourse," should continue to inspire the work of transformation and reform in Tuscany.[8] An ample summary of Bandini's *Discorso economico* was provided to the readers of the Florentine journal, with the note that "with low prices not only is agriculture depressed and discouraged, but decadence has spread to industry, where at first a low price might seem useful, and the philosopher finds that periods of low prices are the true cause of scarcity."[9] After having summarized the entire thought of Bandini it concluded: "It is remarkable that in 1737 a priest could have seen so far in political economy, to things not yet shown in the immortal writings of many famous men beyond the Alps, and even by our own sec-

---

[5] *Notizie del mondo*, no. 40, 20 May 1775, p. 313 (Paris, 2 May).

[6] Franco Venturi, "Quattro anni di carestia in Toscana," *R. stor. ital.*, fasc. 4 (December 1976): 649ff.

[7] *Notizie del mondo*, no. 59, 25 July 1775, p. 470 (Florence, 24 July).

[8] Ibid., no. 60, 29 July 1775, p. 478 (Florence, 29 July).

[9] Ibid., no. 62, 5 August 1775, p. 493. "Segue l'Estratto del Discorso economico del Bandini."

retary Francesco Pagnini." And even more important, "We have had the rare pleasure of having seen the useful projects of our author realized in the wise legislation of Peter Leopold, our duke, and then imitated by the greatest monarchs of Europe."[10] Bandini and the grand duke had, in short, opened a road that France was trying to follow through all the difficulties that readers discovered in other columns of the same gazette.

The discussion of what was happening in the Paris of Turgot continued to be followed in Florence with particular attention. In August the *Notizie del mondo* reported a eulogy Voltaire had written in a letter to "Ephémérides," where he showed that he was convinced "that agriculture is the foundation of everything" and attributed to the reforming minister "a greatness of vision equal to and a philosophy more solid than that of Sully or Colbert."[11] The political debate became more and more heated. In the united chambers of the Parlement, the *avocat* Séguier condemned two books entitled *Catéchisme du citoyen* and *L'Ami des loix,* saying that they tended to "raise the nation against the sovereign." He was struck by the republican spirit of these works. "Let us leave to history," he concluded, the "fanaticism" of "ancient republics buried under the ruins of Greece and Italy."[12] The assembly of the clergy denounced the *Histoire* of Raynal, and it was said that the author had to flee Paris "to seek exile."[13] The name of Linguet was often mentioned, along with his projects and misfortunes.[14]

The ferment contrasted with the profound loyalty to the monarchy and enthusiasm for the young king, of which the Florentine gazettes furnished frequent testimonials with the consecration of Louis xvi in

[10] Ibid., no. 65, 15 August 1775, p. 518. "Fine dell'Estratto." On Salustio Bandini, see *Riformatori*, vol. 3, pp. 881ff. On F. Pagnini, see Franco Venturi, "Scienza e riforma nella Toscana del Settecento: Targioni Tozzetti, Lapi, Montelatici, Fontana e Pagnini," *R. stor. ital.*, fasc. 1 (March 1977): 98ff.

[11] Ibid., no. 67, 22 August 1775, p. 530 (Paris, 8 August).

[12] *Gazzetta universale*, no. 59, 25 July 1775, p. 465 (Paris, 11 July). This was the *Catéchisme du citoyen, ou Eléments du droit public français par demandes et par réponses* (Geneva [actually Bordeaux], 1775), a work by the *avocat* Guillaume-Joseph Saige; and the *Ami des loix* ([n.p., n.d.] but Paris, 1775), attributed to the *avocat* Jacques-Claude Martin de Mariveaux. On both see the thorough treatment, also rich in bibliography, by Keith Michael Baker, "French Political Thought at the Accession of Louis xvi," *Journal of Modern History* 50 (June 1978): 279ff., and by the same author: "The Language of Liberty in Eighteenth-Century Bordeaux: Early Writings of Guillaume-Joseph Saige," in *L'Età dei Lumi*, vol. 1, pp. 331ff.

[13] *Gazzetta universale*, no. 77, 26 September 1775, p. 612 (Paris, 12 September). This gazette, returning to the argument of no. 102, 23 December 1775, p. 810 (Paris, 12 December), wrote that this work "would be one of the best of our century if it were not filled with reflections that are too pointed."

[14] See, for example, *Notizie del mondo*, no. 15, 20 February 1776, p. 113 (Paris, 30 January).

Reims and appearances of the sovereign in the midst of his people. The sparks of the *guerre des farines* were hardly spent when a large number of Parisians crowded "to see the royal mantle that His Majesty will wear on the day of his consecration: the crown, the scepter, the carriage, and finally the horses, which are of the greatest magnificence."[15] After the ceremony, which was minutely described in a separate work appearing as a supplement to the *Gazzetta universale*, the writer Marmontel spoke in a long letter, published in full, of the emotion that had swept everyone present.[16] But doubts and rumors of a possible change of ministers persisted.[17] To all appearances the situation improved, thanks above all to the abundance of the harvests. "Our countryside now assures us of most abundant harvests, and meanwhile the government has taken measures to ensure that proprietors will not be molested by evildoers, since it wants the harvest carried from the fields to the granaries with all security."[18]

With the coming of the summer the series of reforms and projects that had characterized the first phase of Turgot's administration resumed. Malesherbes released "two hundred persons imprisoned with *lettres de cachet*." "One is assured that the same minister has requested all intendants in the provinces to send immediately an exact count of those who are in prison, banned, or exiled because of such letters."[19] An "act of justice and beneficence that merits the applause of all nations" was accomplished by giving "considerable gratifications and pensions" to La Chalotais, father and son, "well known for the long misfortunes they have suffered."[20] In October came word that Turgot had presented to the king "a plan by which it is intended to abolish all the tax farms." This plan was not easy to implement, commented the *Gazzetta universale*, given that "the greatest lords have interests in the finances."[21]

---

[15] *Gazzetta universale*, no. 47, 13 June 1775, p. 369 (Paris, 30 May).

[16] Ibid., no. 56, 15 July 1775, p. 441 (Paris, 27 June).

[17] Ibid., no. 58, 22 July 1775, p. 457 (Paris, 11 July).

[18] Ibid., no. 62, 5 August 1775, p. 490 (Paris, 18 July).

[19] Ibid., no. 68, 26 August 1775, p. 537 (Paris, 15 August). Malesherbes seemed "destined to break the chains of all the unfortunates. . . . Under his administration was reborn that noble liberty, a positive sign of good government, and wherever sovereigns distribute bounty they need not fear that subjects will shun their administration," one read in no. 89, 7 November 1775, p. 705 (Paris, 24 October).

[20] Ibid., no. 74, 16 September 1775, p. 585 (Paris, 29 August). The *Nuove di diverse corti e paesi*, no. 39, 25 September 1775, p. 310 (Paris, 12 September), described Malesherbes at the castle of Vincennes, "where he found some prisoners whose crimes were entirely unknown, and others who from their long imprisonment had lost the use of their reason." "He soon released the first and one hopes that this virtuous minister with his zealous inquiries will discover the horrors committed by those in charge, some with persons condemned for a simple indiscretion or an imprudence."

[21] *Gazzetta universale*, no. 82, 14 October 1775, p. 650 (Paris, 3 October).

With the beginning of the new year, 1776, a new theme emerged in
the center of the whole complex of the French reform movement: the
abolition of the guilds. The *Gazzetta universale* referred in detail to the
posthumous work of Bigot de Sainte-Croix, *Essai sur la liberté du commerce et de l'industrie*, published by Baudeau in Paris in 1775, which defended the necessity of liberating artisans from all corporative restraints.[22] "This work much resembles a short history called *Chinki*,"
published from the pen of the Abbé Coyer. "Tuscany was the first place
in Italy to receive the said work *Chinki*. Under its current enlightened
government the state has destroyed and continues to destroy all obstacles to the advantages derived from freedom of trade and industry."[23]
The *Notizie del mondo* also spoke of this *Cochin Chinese History That can
Benefit Other Countries*, which "eight years ago was sold clandestinely in
this capital [Paris] and is attributed to the Abbé Coyer," and "now enjoys
much popularity and is sold publicly." Lively and effective was this history of a "well-appointed laborer" who became "miserable" because of
restrictions, taxes, and obstacles that hinder his path.[24] But the reforms
planned by Turgot in this area encountered more and more tenacious
resistance. The Parlement held that "liberty conceded to anyone and
everyone to follow what occupation pleases them most, since conceded
to persons for the most part corrupt, will open the door to an infinity of
abuses and disorders and carry to ruin a quantity of families, the best
commercial houses, and the best-appointed artisans." These arguments,
it was understood, did not persuade the Florentine gazette, which hastened to invite the Parlementaires to "reflect that the inconvenience that
might result would be small in comparison with the advantages of such
a well-designed measure."[25] But it could not conceal that in Paris "the
public is divided into two parties by these innovations." Linguet had expressed an opinion contrary to the ideas of Bigot de Sainte-Croix.[26] The
government saw itself obliged to censor "several memoirs against the
suppression of the so-called *jurandes*, or guilds of arts and trades."[27] "Enlightened people applauded the edict that suppressed all trade guilds
and other privileges." In Paris alone "as many as 118" had been

[22] Ibid., no. 6, 20 January 1776, p. 47, "Notizie Letterarie," Paris.
[23] Ibid., no. 7, 23 January 1776, p. 55. "Notizie letterarie," Paris. See the announcement of this Tuscan version published in Florence by Allegrini and Pagani in the *Notizie
letterarie*, no. 2, 10 March 1770, col. 17. The echo, in this conservative period, was negative: "Its merit derives not from the translator's choice, but from the purity of the Tuscan
language."
[24] *Notizie del mondo*, no. 31, 16 April 1776, p. 231 (Paris, 1 April).
[25] *Gazzetta universale*, no. 19, 5 March 1776, p. 145 (Paris, 13 February).
[26] Ibid., no. 21, 12 March 1776, p. 161 (Paris, 27 February).
[27] Ibid., no. 24, 23 March 1776, p. 185 (Paris, 6 March).

counted. "Everything was a corporation, even the flower sellers. The tailors, carpetmakers, innkeepers, bakers, were all distinct bodies." Even in this case Florence applauded what was happening in Paris. "This liberty cannot help but be very advantageous to the public."[28] But the narrative of actions and reactions it aroused demonstrated that Turgot's task was becoming more and more difficult.

Another theme, not less controversial, also emerged. "On 23 [February] a work entitled *Les inconvéniens des droits féodaux* was denounced to the Parlement, and the following day it was condemned to be burned for containing assertions dangerous to property rights and existing law."[29] The Parlement, with this condemnation, succeeded in placing an impassable limit on Turgot's reform activity. He had been able to touch the corvées, the guilds, and economic restrictions. But feudal rights were inviolable. The state could not enter the privileged world of nobles and lords. The Florentine gazette was quite amazed by this presupposition. The book by Pierre-François Boncerf, *Les inconvéniens des droits féodaux*, appeared to contain, according to the *Notizie del mondo*, only "explanations and declarations of propositions already published by other writers, and it is not just recently that the feudal system has been called a relic of ancient barbarity." It was still necessary to "uproot the old abuses and give agriculture and commerce that activity which liberty alone can procure."[30] The greater part of readers, the *Gazzetta universale* noted, "have recognized in this work the praiseworthy object of combatting feudal barbarism and drying up streams of litigants by simplifying trials." Did it not intend "to strike at the constitution of the French monarchy and rouse vassals against their lords, or against the sovereign himself, by making all feudal and seigneurial rights seem usurpations, vexations, or odious and ridiculous violence, suggesting supposed means for their abolition"?[31] Evidently, in defending feudal rights, what was wanted, really, was to attack Turgot. The *avocat* Séguier saw parading

---

[28] Ibid., no. 34, 27 April 1776, p. 267 (Paris, 9 April). The *Nuove di diverse corti e paesi*, no. 15, 8 April 1776, p. 116 (Paris, 25 March), after having noted that "all the preambles" of the laws of Turgot were "very interesting," furnished a translation of the decree that "abolished matriculation in the guilds." An excellent background for the problem of the guilds in France is by Steven Kaplan, "Réflexions sur la police du monde du travail, 1700–1815," *Révue Historique*, no. 529 (January–March, 1979): 17ff.

[29] *Notizie del mondo*, no. 23, 19 March 1776, p. 177 (Paris, 26 February).

[30] Ibid. The tone of Boncerf's work, published in Paris by Valade in 1776, was firm and insistent, but not violent. The numerous mishaps that came from *cens*, *banalités*, and feudal rights of all kinds were denounced with great precision. In a second edition, by the same publisher, there was an appendix, on pp. 65ff., entitled "Arrêt de la Cour du Parlement qui condamne une brochure intitulée: Les inconvéniens des droits féodaux" and dated 23 February 1776.

[31] *Gazzetta universale*, no. 24, 23 March 1776, p. 185 (Paris, 6 March).

behind the work of Boncerf "a secret party, a hidden agent, that by means of an attack from within seeks to destroy the foundations of the state, like those volcanoes which after having announced themselves with underground noises and successive earthquakes suddenly erupt." Was the aim, perhaps, to incite the peasants against their lords? "It was true that this project was displayed only in a veiled manner, and that it was only insinuated that inhabitants of the countryside had no other choice than to appeal to their lords to demand suppression and redemption of seigneurial dues, which could not be denied them if all vassals were united and agreed on the same offer. But it was uncertain whether such multitudes collected in the different castles of each lord, after having requested suppression and offered indemnity, might become more heated by the maxims spread about and require what might not be freely given." And why should the French state support such an operation? In reality writers like Boncerf were demanding nothing less than the "destruction of the property of all lords, because feudal rights, work services, *banalités, cens,* and others of this kind are an integral part of property."[32]

Against such an open and clear reaction the agreement of the Florentine narrator was with the French minister and the pamphleteer Boncerf. The latter had cited the example of England, where, in the sixteenth century "lands dependent on the church and on monks" had been freed, and he did not miss emphasizing how "the need for liberty, for things or persons, expresses itself in all times and places." He even cited the edict of 20 January 1772, through which "the king of Sardinia had freed all serfs in the duchy of Savoy," and he did not fail to mention that "Russia seeks to free its slaves and make them proprietors."[33] For the Tuscan journalist examples and precedents even closer to home were introduced, from the regulation of entails in the epoch of Richecourt to the daily reforms of Peter Leopold. Distant and strange, instead, must have seemed the preoccupations that emerged in the words of Séguier: the peril of a more radical subversion and the fear and suspicion of a revolutionary outcome of reform. In Paris one feared living on top of a volcano, but not in Florence.

This was all the more true because in France that philosophie which Séguier had attacked with particular violence was strongly present and alive, and certainly not by chance. "With what fatalism do writers today

---

[32] *Notizie del mondo,* no. 24, 23 March 1776, pp. 186ff. (Paris, 4 March).

[33] Boncerf, *Les inconvéniens des droits féodaux* (London and Paris: Valade, 1776), p. 62. On p. 55 n., Boncerf, on the evidence of the traveler Pierre-Jean Grosley, noted that "in Italy, where feudal rights have little content, the countryside is more densely populated in comparison with the cities."

make such a study of destroying and overturning everything?" And he continued to say that "if the systematic spirit guiding the pen of that writer [Boncerf] should unfortunately take control of the multitudes, the constitution of the monarchy would soon be seen to totter." He saw before his eyes already a horrible spectacle in the future: "Vassals will not be slow to rise against their lords, and the people against their sovereign. The most cruel anarchy will necessarily result from an independence that has become all the more terrible because nothing will be able to prevent or stop its effects."[34] Precisely at that time a book called *Théologie portative* had come into his hands, which contained the orthodox polemics against the followers of d'Holbach.[35] This provided a not recent, but always good, occasion to fulminate against "false philosophy," which seeks nothing less than "to destroy under the pretext of instructing," and against "that occult and active group which appears to be employed only in preparing itself, under cover of darkness, so as to bring forth suddenly a revolution in belief, government, and customs."[36]

Not a revolution, but a reform movement was taking place in Tuscany, the *Notizie del mondo* emphasized still further. It was a reform movement that followed a different rhythm, more harmonious and gradual, than the experiment taking place in Paris. In Florence the obstacles that Turgot encountered seemed already to have been overcome. "The more good a sovereign does, the more good it is easy for him to do. As he advances in his illustrious career, his stride becomes daily more rapid. 'O happy times,' said Tacitus about the reign of Trajan, 'when one obeys only the laws, when one can think freely and can say freely what one thinks. . . .' " "This is exactly what Tuscany seeks and admires. Ever new benefits, new freedoms, new liberties, new encouragements for commerce, industry, and agriculture, new rights given to property."[37] There followed the edict of 11 March 1776, which abolished "various restrictions and aggravations prejudicial to industry or limiting property rights" in Pistoia. Whereas in France, one reads in ¬ later issue of the same journal, the Parlements did not even permit discussion of the problems of feudal rights; "recently the grand duchy of Tuscany, with an edict dated 11 December 1775, has suppressed the privileges over mills for grain and olives, because through this right proprietors, sure that work was not lacking, have neglected milling and raised prices. Our prince has also ordered that mills belonging to the

[34] Ibid., pp. 67, 70.

[35] *Théologie portative ou Dictionnaire abrégé de la religion chrétienne*, by M. l'Abbé Bernier, licencié en théologie (London, 1768).

[36] *Notizie del mondo*, no. 25, 26 March 1776, p. 184 (Paris, 7 March).

[37] Ibid., pp. 187ff. (Florence, 25 March).

ducal government not be more privileged than others." But Peter Leopold was not the only one to undertake a gradual dismemberment of
feudal rights. "The king of Sardinia, as well, with an edict of December
1771, had ordered the liberation of lands subject to feudal obligations,
and tributes proceeding from fiefs, because such rights are a burden not
only for debtors, but often for proprietors as well, either because of disputes about exacting particular rights, or because of the difficulty and
expense of renewing them, which is an unending source of litigation
and abuse.[38]

This was a cautious satisfaction with what had been accomplished,
which did not make one close one's eyes to the obstacles that reformers
were destined to encounter in their path. There remained much to do
in changing the mentality of an entire population. Hard and obstinate
were the prejudices urban citizens nurtured toward "inhabitants of the
countryside," who were thought of as a "kind of slaves who should satisfy one's needs without having the right even to one's compassion."[39]
To change social relations so deeply rooted as these was anything but
easy. The French case provided an example. "The operation of Mr.
Turgot cannot help but make some discontented because each time a
minister of finance has the courage to reform abuses and introduce
economies in state expenditures, from the profusion of which so many
grow fat, there is always someone who will measure public utility against
private interest and disclaim novelties as if they were injustices."[40]

Less than a month later "the celebrated Mr. Turgot" was dismissed
from office. "This unexpected blow has made a most vivid impression
on the public. It is generally held that the arts and commerce, the cultivator and the artisan, have lost a protector and father in this illustrious
subject who shares with the great Sully the glory of having been a god-
father, at the foot of the throne, of humanity's cause against despotism
and oppression."[41] About the same news the *Gazzetta universale* commented: "It is said that the author upheld with too much vigor the maxims of a book entitled *Les inconvéniens des droits féodaux*, which has given
rise in the great to a jealous preservation of their rights."[42] The greatest
reform experiment of the century had been cut short.

---

[38] Ibid., no. 34, 27 April 1776, pp. 257ff. (Paris, 8 April).

[39] Ibid., no. 31, 16 April 1776, p. 232 (Orléans, 10 March).

[40] Ibid., no. 35, 30 April 1776, p. 264 (Paris, 15 April).

[41] Ibid., no. 44, 1 June 1776, p. 336 (Paris, 14 May). Even the *Nuove di diverse corti e
paesi*, no. 22, 27 May 1776, p. 171 (Paris, 13 May), wrote, "The common word is that the
arts, commerce, peasants, and the poor have lost in Mr. Turgot a protector and father,
which they will have difficulty finding in another subject."

[42] *Gazzetta universale*, no. 43, 28 May 1776, p. 337 (Paris, 14 May).

XII

⟨ornament⟩

Constitution,
Liberty, and Revolution in the
Britannic World

THE BRITANNIC WORLD IN THE SECOND HALF OF THE EIGHTEENTH century, even before it was divided between the United Kingdom and the United States of America, was a constellation, a conglomeration, rather than a truly unified political body, as France, Spain, and Russia might be thought to have been at that time, despite their internal differences. It is enough to remember that England, Scotland, Ireland, and the different colonies jealously preserved traditions and autonomous forms of self-government. It was not a question of administrative divisions, as for example in the Hapsburg empire. A degree of political liberty, which contemporaries often called "republican," made the internal ties of the Britannic world quite original and different from those of other European countries. So varied was this political constellation that even recently historians have asked themselves whether it is truly possible to contain such a complex world within the scope of a single glance.[1] The answer to this question must be, I hold, in the affirmative, but on the condition of bearing in mind that the problem of the organization of liberty itself was one of the bonds keeping together lands that were so distant and diverse.

Almost a half-century has now passed since the publication of the books of Namier and Butterfield which marked a decisive change in modern historical research on the Britannic world in the eighteenth century. Lewis Namier's work, *The Structure of Politics at the Accession of George III*, was published in 1929, followed a year later by his *England in*

---

[1] See the brilliant article by John G. A. Pocock in polemic with A.J.P. Taylor, "British History: A Plea for a New Subject," *Journal of Modern History* 47, no. 4 (December 1975): 601ff.

the Age of the American Revolution.[2] In 1931 Herbert Butterfield wrote his reflections on historiography entitled *The Whig Interpretation of History.*[3] Although quite different in their approach, these books marked the end of a political, oratorical, and constitutional vision of the age of the Georges and inaugurated a new direction of research on the social, political, and intellectual structures of eighteenth-century England. They attempted to come closer to historical reality by criticizing ideologies inherited from the past, especially the idea of a Whig-Tory polarization in eighteenth-century England. Namier rose above the masks of political justifications to the real interests of individuals and groups. The governing class was stripped of its traditional cloak and shown in its daily struggle for place, protection, influence, and local and national prestige. The sources on which its history was based changed. From speeches and declarations one passed to private letters and whispered confidences, from the history of institutions to that of pressure groups. Moved by a curious and sometimes contradictory love-hate relationship with the governing class he knew so well, Namier showed us the great solidarity, the tenacity, the ever renewed energy of a conservative oligarchy, which was capable of extraordinary adaptations and mutations. It was certainly not by chance that at the center of the picture was George III, a figure who remains enigmatic despite the elementary nature of his political reactions; mysterious even though seemingly obvious. Thanks to Namier and his followers we know the English ruling class better than any other patriciate or bureaucracy in the Europe of the late eighteenth century, better even, in my opinion, than what has emerged from the valuable studies in France of the Breton nobility or the Parisian Parlementaries. This advantage is due to Namier's extraordinary curiosity about each single individual and about each little group of the gentry, and especially to his exceptional capacity for reconstructing the most hidden mechanisms of life in a free country like England. The House of Commons was a unique phenomenon in Europe in the eighteenth century. Unique and exceptional still seems the effort of this English historian to penetrate into its recesses and to illuminate its shadows.

After Butterfield and Namier, the intimate history of the British ruling class in the eighteenth century became the preferred field of some of the most fruitful of English historiography. It is enough to think of the fine essay by Richard Pares, *King George III and the Politicians* (Ox-

---

[2] See Franco Venturi, "Sir Lewis Namier," in id., *Historiens du XXe siècle* (Geneva: Droz, 1966), pp. 92ff.

[3] See Sir Denis Brogan, "Sir Herbert Butterfield as a Historian: An Appreciation," in *The Diversity of History: Essays in Honour of Sir Herbert Butterfield*, ed. John H. Elliott and H. G. Koenigsberger (London: Routledge and Kegan, 1970), pp. 1ff.

ford: Clarendon Press, 1953), or of the fundamental work by J. H. Plumb, *Sir Robert Walpole*, 2 vols. (London: Cresset, 1956–60). The figures of Chatham, North, Shelburne, Burke, and so on, were reexamined. Research on Parliament was enlarged. Thanks above all to Lucy S. Sutherland this work extended to the world of great commercial companies, to the City, and to the mercantile classes. The collection of essays in honor of Namier, which Richard Pares and A.J.P. Taylor (*Essays Presented to Sir Lewis Namier*) published in 1961, can be considered a point of arrival of a whole movement of research and renewal begun a quarter of a century earlier.

Then, in the fifties and sixties, signs of weariness began to appear. The project of writing detailed biographies of all members of the House of Commons (the Namierite utopia) was dropped. It seemed tiresome and perhaps useless to rummage endlessly in the innumerable deposits of documents left by a conservative class that was aware of the value of its own memories and curious about any sign of individualism and even eccentricity in its ancestors. Once the animating breath of Namier's great personality stopped, the English governing class of the eighteenth century went back to an appearance of an immense, scattered, and abandoned boneyard. But from the historiographical desert a means of escape was found by a route still open to the historians of the British world, the way where social and intellectual history meet.

At first there was a transition from studying the governing class to studying the new forces and organizations that began to appear on the political scene in the eighteenth century. There was not much interest in reexamining the social structure of England (the historians of the incipient Industrial Revolution were, often vigorously, seeing to that), but rather in observing closely, more closely than ever before, how the debate—which up to that point generally had been confined to the chambers of Parliament, the Cabinet, the court, and country houses and salons—spread to less well-to-do inhabitants of the cities, to tradesmen, artisans, and farmers. The first to respond to this interest was George Rudé, in *Wilkes and Liberty: A Social Study of 1763 to 1774* (Oxford: Clarendon Press, 1962). He chose precisely the moment when the whole organization of the British oligarchy was challenged, for the first time in the eighteenth century, when the first efforts of reform appeared, and when in a large part of the population a spirit began to germinate which is difficult to describe without using the general but effective term *radical*. Rudé's work tried to be both a political history and an investigation of social history. He followed events as they came but stopped to ask himself at every turn the identity of the people moving in the front of the scene and in the background. One could say that this was an effort to apply a Namierite method, no longer to an elite, but to a crowd, a

mass of electors, protestors, and so on. The historiographical effort
risked being unsuccessful, because the documents concerning the electors of Wilkes were unfortunately much less typical and significant than
those concerning Chatham, Shelburne, and Burke. Wilkes himself, a
point of contact between Parliament and the crowd, was not easy to understand or reveal, and he remains, even in the accurate pages of Rudé,
a figure of small historical stature.

Walter James Shelton took a further step toward better understanding the popular world in his book *English Hunger and Industrial Disorders:
A Study of Social Conflict during the First Decade of George III's Reign* (London: Macmillan, 1973). This was an investigation of the food riots that
followed the famine of 1766 and a detailed description of the distress of
workers in London and other English centers in the last years of the
decade. This is one of the closest studies thus far made of one of the
numerous parallel popular movements that have appeared in different
parts of Europe during this period.

The decisive historiographical step was taken when this deepening
of social history joined an effort to reconstruct in all its different aspects
the moral and intellectual life of the years after the accession to the
throne of George III (1760), which saw a worsening of conflicts within
the governing class and the formation of opposition, resistance, and
even rebellion outside of and against it. The passage from the sixties to
the seventies in the Britannic world began to appear in all its complexity, as a crisis of the governing class, and as a period of emergence of
new political forms and energies.

With regard to the British Isles, the most recent and important work
on this subject is that of John Brewer, *Party Ideology and Popular Politics
at the Accession of George III* (Cambridge: Cambridge University Press,
1976). The part of this work that has succeeded least, in my opinion, is
the first, which is concerned with the ideology of parties, that is, the
ideas and feelings of the governing class. At this level the analysis of
Namier and his followers remains more effective than the description,
however valuable, by John Brewer, of the constitutional mechanisms of
Great Britain in the years of undercurrents and combinations that followed the Seven Years' War. The most original part of the work is "An
Alternative Structure of Politics," the examination of those forces and
political and social institutions which began to appear at the center of
the scene in these years: the press, propaganda, and new personalities.
There is an admirable chapter entitled "The Press in the 1760s," which
succeeds in giving a concrete idea of the great development of gazettes,
reviews, and periodicals of all types in Wilkes's London, as well as in
many provincial cities. Counting only periodicals liable to the stamp tax,
that is, the most stable and important gazettes, there was an annual

printing of 7,300,000 copies in 1750. In 1760 this had already reached 9,400,000. In 1775 it had risen to 12,600,000 (the equivalent of 34,700 copies a day). In 1760 London had four daily newspapers and five or six serials published three times a week. The number of periodicals of all kinds was eighty-nine. In 1770 the number of journals published three times a week had risen to three, and the number published sporadically (including Wilkes's *North Britain*) had multiplied rapidly. There was also a notable development of gazettes in the provinces, thirty-five in 1761, and eighty in 1780. Circulation of individual issues was, depending on circumstances, 1,500 to 5,000 copies (note the detailed figures furnished by Brewer for the *Public Advertiser* on page 144). The number of pamphlets also multiplied, with 500 to 5,000 copies in each printing. The network of cafes, inns, and taverns where periodicals could be obtained became more complex and varied, and around them vivid discussions developed. In 1737 there were 551 cafes in London, 207 inns, and 447 taverns, some of which were transformed into true and proper political clubs. Circulating libraries also grew in number, in the capital and in the provinces. This was the background against which the Wilkes movement arose, with its specific propaganda and organization, and with its truly new "ritual" detached from and opposed to the traditional one. Thus emerged during the sixties and at the beginning of the seventies "Two Political Nations," as Brewer entitles the concluding part of his work.

The "new nation" that was arising was divided from its origins internally into two currents, one directed toward reform of the English political system, and the other toward separation of the American colonies from the British Empire. Their political and ideological roots were the same, their passions and hopes were similar, and their language was often identical. But in the sixties a divergence began which widened rapidly in the years before 1776: reform or independence? No statesman was able to dominate this dilemma: no one succeeded in holding together internal reformers and American patriots. Neither Chatham in the governing elite nor Wilkes in the "new nation" was up to it. The undercurrent we have found present in different forms throughout Europe in these years, that fermented in the conflict between Russia and Poland, that was not absent in Denmark and Sweden, and that emerged in a more extreme form in the France of Turgot, Raynal, and Diderot, assumed in the Britannic world the form of an unavoidable political conflict, leading on one side to a birth of radicalism and the parliamentary reform movement, and on the other side to the birth of a true and proper "new nation," the free America of the United States.

American historians have demonstrated recently, with great mastery, how profoundly rooted in English tradition were the ideas that

carried the American colonists to rebel against George III, as if this were
a civil war, not only in the sense of the community of origin of the combatants—which is evident—but in the truer sense of a common passion
for forms of liberty, which the revolutions of the seventeenth century
had planted deeply in the souls of Englishmen on both sides of the
ocean. A true flowering of historiography has rediscovered the roots of
this "republican" tradition. Caroline Robbins—English by origin and
American by adoption—was the pioneer. J.G.A. Pocock, who also
passed from the British world to the United States, traced the sixteenth-
and seventeenth-century origins of ideas that returned to action in the
years preceding the struggle for American independence. Bernard Bailyn has reconstructed in great detail the culture, traditions, and ideas of
the "new nation" that was forming in the American colonies during the
eighteenth century, assimilating, adapting, and transforming the legacy
inherited from "republicans," from Deists, and from English dissidents.
This minute and patient work was synthesized lucidly in the essay "The
Origins of American Politics," which appeared in 1967. In a larger
work, *The Ordeal of Thomas Hutchinson* (Cambridge, Mass.: Harvard University Press, 1974), the problem of the "two nations" in England—the
ruling elite and new currents—was taken up again by the American historian through the biography of a man who was considered by his compatriots in Boston as the principal responsible for the insupportable economic and political oppression that George III and his Parliament
attempted, according to them, to impose on the free American colonists.
For Thomas Hutchinson was American himself—of five generations—
and he was closely connected with the mercantile and political life of the
colonies. Not nationality, but ideas, not interests, but a conception of
liberty, made this man the designated victim of the New England revolutionaries. The dividing line between Old and New England was not
geographic; it passed through London as much as it did through Boston. The biography Bernard Bailyn has given us of this not exceptional,
and therefore characteristic, man helps us to understand how and why,
in a seemingly homogeneous world, there developed those deep fissures
that led rapidly to civil war, to the division of the English empire, and
to the birth of the United States. There is in these pages, however, an
element of regret, of nostalgia, almost as if the contests and struggles in
Boston in the sixties and seventies carried within them signs of a still
present historical injustice. Other books have also appeared recently to
restate the problem of the relationship between the English desire for
reform and the American Revolution. First there is a general picture,
written with great care, competence, and the evident intention of furnishing a synthesis of what has been written in the last decades on this
argument, by Ian R. Christie and Benjamin W. Labaree, *Empire or Inde-*

pendence, 1760–1776: A British-American Dialogue on the Coming of the American Revolution (Oxford: Phaidon, 1976). In 1982 a synthesis of this broad historical debate by Ian R. Christie appeared, with the title *Wars and Revolutions: Britain 1760–1815*, published by Edward Arnold in his *New History of England*. There is also the more problematical book by Colin Bonwick, *English Radicals and the American Revolution* (Chapel Hill: University of North Carolina Press, 1977).

A common characteristic in many of these works is the absence of an international perspective, a vision that goes beyond the British Isles and the American colonies. It is not that the authors demonstrate that they do not know the diplomatic and military events of these years, which are naturally always present before their eyes. It is not that developments of the Enlightenment are not taken into account, or that there is not a discussion of the extent to which these joined or opposed the "republican" traditions of the British world. What is often lacking is a specific reference to events in Russia and Poland, Corsica and Greece, Denmark and Sweden, and an effort to see how these were connected with the aspirations and ideas of English radicals and American colonials. In this regard, one who showed the way was Bernard Bailyn. In a few pages of vivid synthesis, taken from American gazettes, he showed how the drama overtaking Polish peasants sacked by the troops of Catherine II was seen along the Atlantic coast, how even there were echoes of the fear of despotism that Maupeou raised in France, of the concern Italian "bandits" caused, and regrets that Rome and Greece, once centers of virtue, knowledge, and greatness, were now reduced, one to a hospice for "a flock of fat monks and a few hungry lay inhabitants," the other to "a few base gibbering slaves, kept in ignorance and chains by the Turkish monarchy."[4] Thus the fear of a general decline of all peoples into despotism, which was so diffused everywhere between the sixties and the seventies, had a substantial part in moving the American colonists to resistance and then to revolt. The sense of an overhanging menace, of a corruption penetrating everything, almost as if it were a feared disease, carried many in the Britannic world toward reform, and in the colonies toward independence.[5] In other words, the world that saw the

[4] Bernard Bailyn, *The Origins of American Politics*. I have used the Vintage Books edition (New York, 1970), pp. 149ff.

[5] A particularly vivid expression of the sense of urgency that seized American patriots in the years before the revolution is in a letter William Bradford wrote to James Madison on 1 August 1774.

To use Shakespeare's expression, 'The times seem to be out of joint': our being attacked on the one hand by the Indians, and on the other, our liberties invaded by a corrupt, ambitious, and determined ministry, is bringing things to foretell some great event. In Europe the states entertain a general suspicion on each other. They seem to be looking forward to some great revolution, and stand as if it was

rise of Wilkes and Jefferson was closely connected with the one we have thus far studied. As an indication of this, once again, we will observe things through the curious and attentive eyes of Italians.

I certainly do not intend to redo here, after more than half a century, the work of Arturo Graf, *L'anglomania e l'influsso inglese in Italia nel secolo XVIII*, which was published in Turin in 1911, following with him and multiplying ad libitum Britain's multiple echoes of customs, ideas, and attitudes in Italy. And I do not intend either—which could be more interesting—to reexamine in its entirety the importance that the economic and social experience of England in the eighteenth century had in stimulating and forming Italian reform movements, from Genovesi to Vasco, from Pietro Verri to Filangieri. Wherever economic problems were discussed in Italy at that time, wherever a new relationship began between the individual and society, the British world was present and active. The problem I intend to examine is more limited chronologically, but also more intense and concrete; and I will try to use the most varied sources, to see how much Italians were aware and how they interpreted developments between the sixties and the seventies in London and Boston, New York and Philadelphia.

Vincenzio Martinelli and Alessandro Verri, two Italians typical of two different generations, regions, and mentalities, encountered each other in London in the winter of 1766–1767. The first was a Tuscan, a man of sixty-four years, an expert on different lands, including southern Italy, a historian, publicist, and language master who had emigrated to London. In the eyes of Alessandro Verri, a twenty-five-year-old still animated by the heat, polemics, and enthusiasm of *Il Caffè*, Martinelli could not help but seem a typical, traditional Italian intellectual. "He is a good old man, very much alive; he praises himself much and wants to be admired. I, pardoning this defect as an incorrigible fault of age, and in human sympathy with his passions, captured his great friendship. I told him that Beccaria admired him: that pleased him. Otherwise he is like other Italian literary men: most careful of the harmony of his style;

with their hands on their swords. . . . The obstinate and bloody contention of the Turks and Russians, the overthrow of liberty in Sweden and Corsica, the death of Lewis, and the accession of the young ambitious monarch to the Throne of France lead us to imagine there is something at hand that shall greatly augment the history of the world.

His millenarian vision, an anticipation of the "conclusion of the drama," was born from this view. *The Papers of James Madison* (Chicago: University of Chicago Press, 1962), vol. 1: 1751–1779, pp. 117ff. There is a perceptive analysis of how the idea of republican virtue was transformed into American national feeling in three central figures of these years in Edmund S. Morgan, *The Meaning of Independence: John Adams, George Washington, and Thomas Jefferson* (Charlottesville: Virginia University Press, 1976).

a poor logician; with some wit, which he uses to criticize merit; little enthusiasm; a pedant; a talker devoured by vanity, envy, and sarcasm; a virtuoso of impertinence. Despite this dowry of vices, which I think always accompanies our erudites, he has heart and fire."[1] This contrast of generations expressed the profound break the Enlightenment of the sixties produced in Italy. But still, Martinelli, in his thirty years of contact with the British world, showed he was anything but insensitive and narrow-minded: his works merit attentive reading.[2]

He had arrived in London at the end of 1748 and rapidly introduced himself to the world of diplomacy and the oligarchy that succeeded Walpole, establishing relations with the Chesterfields, Grenvilles, Pulteneys, Townshends, and so on. This was a solid and compact world, with its own habits and ideas, very different from the Italian one, and strong in its apparent immobility. He soon persuaded himself that comparisons between Britannic reality and other lands in Europe were illusory. Members of the French Parlements had nothing in common with members of the English Parliament, as Montesquieu had said in his *Esprit des loix*, "the first are chosen and removable at the pleasure of the sovereign, whereas the second only recognize the authority of the people who have confided in them."[3] Neither the principles from which Montesquieu departed nor his theories about climate seemed sufficient to him. The distinction Montesquieu made between monarchy and despotism seemed to have little solidity. In reality, in "certain monarchies, like the English and Swedish, where government is a mixture of the three states, monarchical, aristocratic, and democratic, the prince can exercise prerogatives assigned to him only by the fundamental constitution of government." There were then other monarchies, "such as Naples, Portugal, Saxony," where the powers of the sovereign are equally limited by traditional privileges. "But in general, when we speak of monarchy in Europe, we mean a prince . . . the absolute lord of the lives and goods of his subjects." It was useless to harbor illusions. "The true power of monarchies

---

[1] *Carteggio di Pietro e di Alessandro Verri dal 1766 al 1797*, vol. 1, pt. 1, pp. 234ff., London, 27 January 1767. See also in the same volume pp. 363ff., Florence, 15 May 1767, where Martinelli is cited with other Italian literary figures "with a very bad humor. . . . There is a painter of some kind and a virtuoso with this person's character." See the excellent edition edited by Gianmarco Gaspari of the *Viaggio a Parigi e Londra (1766–1767)*. *Carteggio di Pietro e Alessandro Verri* (Milan: Adelphi, 1980), pp. 618ff.

[2] Benedetto Croce, "Un letterato italiano in Inghilterra: Vincenzio Martinelli," in id., *La letteratura italiana del Settecento* (Bari: Laterza, 1949), pp. 256ff.; E. H. Thorne, "Vincenzio Martinelli in England, 1748–1774," *Italian Studies* (1956): 92ff.

[3] Vincenzio Martinelli, *Lettere famigliari e critiche* (London: John Nourse, bookseller in the Strand, 1758), p. 64, "Al Sign. Giacomo Greenville sopra il libro intitolato *Esprit des loix*," London, n.d.

not mixed or limited is despotic, most despotic."[4] Martinelli viewed the old republics with sympathy and admiration, and especially Venice.[5] Reopening his polemic with Montesquieu, he declared he was against venality of offices, which seemed to him "a kind of feudalism," and against feudal jurisdictions, with which Richelieu had had to struggle so much in France. "Nor would the kingdom of England ever have been able to reach such felicity as I have seen if Henry VII had not cut off the head of that horrible monster."[6] Always attuned to French culture, he found it too attached to these absolutistic privileges. Martinelli even found them in Voltaire. He criticized chiefly the *Siècle de Louis XIV*.[7] He did not think that the ideas on which Jean Jacques Rousseau based his *Discourses* were realistic, but he did not hide his sympathy for such independent thought, or his admiration for "Monsieur Rousseau, certainly one of the most perceptive geniuses of our century."[8] His conclusions were explicit: civil liberty was limited everywhere but reached its greatest possible range in those governments "where democracy is fully developed and justices are obliged to observe precisely the letter of the law."[9] Certainly, liberty was often "imaginary," depending entirely on the "liberty people believe they enjoy."[10] But the fruits it bore in the form of customs, ideas, and way of life in a land like England, where there was freedom of the press, and where men in prison did not lose their passion for "our liberties," were extraordinary. "A man working with horses and wagons, his head often exposed to sun or ice, badly dressed, and worse fed" could believe he was "the freest man on earth" for having had a boxing match with "a properly dressed person."[11]

In 1752 Martinelli tried to contrast his nascent vision of England with the difficulties of Europe of his day. His *Istoria critica della vita civile* was dedicated to Charles Townshend, "Member of the House of Commons and one of the Lords of Trade and Plantations of Great Britain," one of the most eccentric, intelligent, and unstable members of the English aristocracy. He was then at the beginning of his brief and stormy

[4] Ibid., pp. 70ff. "Al medesimo, sopra le divisioni che l'autore dello Spirito delle Leggi fa de' differenti governi," London, n.d.

[5] Ibid., pp. 74ff., "Al medesimo, sopra gli Inquisitori di stato della repubblica di Venezia," London, n.d.

[6] Ibid., p. 96, "Al medesimo, sulla vendita delle cariche pubbliche e sulle private giurisdizioni feudali," London, n.d.

[7] Ibid., pp. 106ff., "A mylord Pulteney a Richemond sopra il secolo di Luigi XIV," London, n.d.

[8] Ibid., p. 269, "Al sign. Carlo Townsend, sopra il libro della origine e fondamenti della disuguaglianza tra gli uomini, pubblicato da Mr. Rousseau," London, n.d.

[9] Ibid., p. 337, "Al sign. Roberto Hudgkinsons, sopra la libertà," London, n.d.

[10] Ibid., p. 340.

[11] Ibid., p. 342.

political career as a member of the Board of Trade and Plantations and
became famous fifteen years later, in 1767, on the eve of his death, for
the financial legislation directed at the colonies which traditionally carries his name and which fanned the flames, then inextinguishable, of
the American revolt.[12] Besides Townshend, who financed the publication of his book, there was a "list of subscribers," which shows us the
ambience in which Martinelli moved and the political class to which he
offered his experience as a man who had known closely the miseries of
lands without liberty (he depicted, for example, a picture of Naples with
its low-life "*lazzari*" and "*banchèri*"); he kept vivid in his mind his love for
the free traditions of Tuscany and Venice.[13] If, in this as in his other
works, he often spoke of literature and of teaching the Tuscan tongue,
this stemmed not only from a kind of professional duty (which is what
the English chiefly wanted), but also to a large extent from his awareness
of a still vivid liberty in Italian poets and writers. And this did not come
only from the past: Ludovico Antonio Muratori, Antonio Cocchi, and
Marco Foscarini were his natural points of reference among contemporaries. The pages, for instance, that he dedicated in his *Istoria* to discussing the work of Muratori, *Dei difetti della giurisprudenza*, provided an
opportunity to develop a polemic against entails, primogeniture, and
the privileges of the nobility in general. He knew well, from direct experience, the arrogance of feudal lords in southern Italy. If the situation
was better in Tuscany, the reason was past liberties in that part of Italy.
It was precisely because it had been governed "for many centuries" by
democratic republics, where "equality involved even those of inferior
circumstances," that its rulers "govern their subjects with moderation."[14]
He did not forget the limitation of feudal jurisdictions, not only in England and France, but also by Vittorio Amadeo II in the kingdom of
Sardinia.[15]

Nevertheless, despite the accuracy of many of his observations, Martinelli did not have sufficient energy to escape the prison of what he
himself called "our Italian decadence."[16] He looked carefully at the
models that appeared before him in Great Britain. He showed, for example, how good it might be to imitate the Irish academies, which of-

---

[12] Vincenzio Martinelli, *Istoria critica della vita civile* (London: George Woodfall at
Charing-Cross, 1752), p. 3. See one of the last and most insightful biographies by Sir
L. Namier, *Charles Townshend: His Character and Career. The Leslie Stephen Lecture* (Cam-
bridge: Cambridge University Press, 1959).

[13] Martinelli, *Istoria critica*, p. 39. See p. 138: "In Naples, where I have long lived. . . ."
In fact he lived there for eight years, as a functionary of Carlo di Borbone.

[14] Ibid., p. 199.

[15] Ibid., p. 200.

[16] Ibid., p. 163.

fered prizes to those who developed industries (and he was one of the first examples of an Italian writer to mention this function which would soon be taken on everywhere in Europe, and even in Italy, by economics academies).[17] A true center of energy was lacking in his desire for reform. The section "Of Liberty," with which he ended his book, was vague.[18] England remained for him an admired model but difficult to imitate. It was enough to think of education, so full of defects in Italy, and so energetic in Great Britain: "An Englishman begins, one could say in his swaddling clothes, as the Romans did, to hear talk of government. The details of government, as they unfold, are discussed before him continually. Books, when the time comes, are given him to read on these matters. Nourished in this way, the head of an Englishman of seventeen or eighteen years is filled with ideas, and his mouth with words, of fatherland, liberty, common good, arts, commerce, and sciences."[19] The result of such an education of the governing class is clear: whereas "in other communities in Europe" the public good was desired "by some prince," or "by a few private citizens," in England there was a "constant will" of the state to "do good for its people."[20]

Clearly, this was praise and exaltation of the English ruling class, of that Whig oligarchy with which Martinelli had become more and more involved. This political world seemed nearly immobile, but it was profoundly changing between the fifties and sixties, when England was engaged in the Seven Years' War and George III succeeded George II. The evidence of "republican" tradition became more and more visible, a tradition that had never disappeared, and regained vigor when stimulated by the external and internal problems Great Britain found itself obliged to confront. In 1761 Martinelli was in contact with the most important survivor of this tradition: Thomas Hollis. Hollis contributed to journals, wrote books and pamphlets, printed them, had them bound with splendid bindings, in which were stamped symbols of liberty, and distributed them on both sides of the ocean—even in Italy, which was, in fact, always present to him as a symbol of ancient liberty and current oppression.[21] He kept a detailed diary of his varied activities as a propagandist, which is now preserved at the Houghton Library at Harvard University. Italians in London often appear in it, such as Baretti and the artists Bartolozzi and Cipriani (who were also friends of Martinelli), and Italian erudites with whom Hollis was in contact are frequently mentioned, as

[17] Ibid., p. 237.
[18] Ibid., pp. 295ff.
[19] Ibid., p. 154.
[20] Ibid., p. 155.
[21] Robbins, *The Eighteenth-Century Commonwealthmen*, pp. 384ff.

well as Gabriele Prince of Torremuzza, Vito d'Amico, Benedetto di Catania, Algarotti, Celesia, Piranesi, and Abate Venuti.[22] And here in his diary is also Martinelli, on 25 May 1761: "Signor Martinelli breackfasted [*sic*] with me. Much ingenious conversation with him. Promised to assist him generally, if occasion should present."[23] A few days later he was advised to continue to write and publish collections of letters, "which, if its subjects are well chosen, may be exceedingly useful both in this country and in Italy."[24] Then Hollis was entirely taken up by the activity of sending out books (to Venuti, for example, he sent the life of Milton written by Toland, and to the English consuls in Genova and Livorno "some *bagatelli*," as he called them, that is, Deist and republican works). But busy as he was in spreading his ideas from America to Transylvania, he did not forget Martinelli. When he returned from a visit to Italy in 1765, he had a long conversation with him and gave him "some curious satyrical papers, manuscripts sent to me lately by Don Clemente from Naples."[25] He became more and more involved in the campaign to support the Corsican revolt, favored the rebels of Madrid in 1766 (with the motto *Pro republica semper*), collected portraits of Rousseau, one of which was by Vallaperta, "a Milanese painter" not further identified, without forgetting the events of his private life, as for example, on 24 April 1766 he wrote: "Played on my flute at night."[26] In 1770 he intended to have published two letters he had requested of Martinelli on the problems: "What gave rise to *cicisbeism*?" and "Why do nations usually lose their liberties as they become polished?" This occasioned another long conversation with Martinelli: "He stayed with me till ten, an ingenious, vain old man!"[27]

In Italy, meanwhile, the editions of Martinelli's *Istoria critica* multiplied: a second appeared at Bologna, edited by Antonio Giandolini, and a third at Naples in 1764, dedicated to the Duke of York. In a long preface the author returned to his preferred themes, above all to the problem of fiefs, which he said he took up "always having had and preserving due respect for so many worthy feudal nobles who not only have not abused this prerogative, but make use of every means to make the people subject to them happy."[28]

---

[22] See Francis Blackburne, *Memoires of Thomas Hollis* (London: n.p., 1782), vol. 1, pp. 59ff.

[23] Cambridge., Mass., Harvard University, Houghton Library, English MS., 1191, Thomas Hollis, *Diary*, vol. 2, F. 8.

[24] Ibid., p. 9.

[25] Ibid., vol. 3, n.p.

[26] Ibid., vol. 4, n.p.

[27] Ibid., vol. 6, 8 January 1770, n.p.

[28] Vincenzio Martinelli, *Istoria critica della vita civile . . . terza edizione emendata ed accres-*

But if Martinelli continued to discuss themes that were dear to him, he became involved in the sixties in a much more arduous task, that of writing a history of England. It was an act of homage to that English oligarchy he so admired (and he did not fail to write at length, for instance, of the Walpole family), but it was above all an effort to make known to Italians that England which was growing in power and wealth and acquiring an "influence so much greater than it ever had before in all parts of the globe."[29] The voyage he made to Italy in 1764 persuaded him of the need for this task. It struck him that things he had told his compatriots "as much of the finances as of the customs of these realms . . . arrived in my account as such wonders as if they came, not from England a short distance away, but from California or the distant shores of the Tartar sea." Such ignorance risked having practical consequences: "In the last wars one saw its all-too-evident effects."[30]

Looking through Martinelli's three thick volumes, it is not hard to conclude, despite his good will, that he did not succeed in interesting Italians in developments in Great Britain with a chronicle that attempted to be impartial; instead, it was cold. Inspired by Rapin de Toyras, it lacked the political passion of the Huguenot historian, and it ended in the reign of Queen Anne, at just the point where it might have begun to satisfy Italian curiosity about the contemporary Britannic world. Still, its political orientation was clear. In a conversation with the exiled Paoli and the writers Goldsmith and Johnson, the first of these observed, "Martinelli is a Whig." None of those present denied this fact. Johnson advised Martinelli not to venture, in writing his history, into the contemporary era. "A foreigner who attaches himself to a political party in this country is in the worst state that can be imagined."[31]

At the end of 1774, one year after the publication of the third and last volume of his *Istoria d'Inghilterra*, Martinelli abandoned London and returned to Tuscany.[32] But echoes of what was happening in the Britannic world reached him there as well. He again began to illustrate "the constitutional history" of England in its fundamental aspects, and he

ciuta dall'autore all'altezza reale del Serenissimo Odoardo duca di York (Naples: Giovanni Gravier, 1764), "Prefazione dell'autore," p. x.

[29] *Istoria d'Inghilterra scritta da Vincenzio Martinelli al Sig. Luca Corsi, dedicata all'Ill.mo Signor Tommaso Walpole, divisa in tre tomi* (London: Pietro Molini, libraio nel Mercato del fieno, 1770), vol. 1, p. 1. Alessandro Verri was a guest of Molini, Martinelli's editor, during his stay in London.

[30] Ibid.

[31] Cited by Thorne, "Vincenzio Martinelli in England," p. 103. The conversation took place on 15 April 1773.

[32] See the annotations of Giuseppe Palli Bencivenni reported in Salvatore Rota, "L'illuminismo a Genova: Lettere di P. P. Celesia a F. Galiani," *Miscellanea storica ligure*, year 5 (1973), no. 1, vol. 2, pp. 81ff.

succeeded in giving these age-old developments a nonconventional out-look, "putting into relief hesitations and deviations" and "discrediting the idea of liberty . . . inherited from the Saxons."[33] Martinelli resumed his polemic against feudalism. "The vivid image of this form of government still remains in Poland and in those parts of Germany from which the ancestors of the Saxons passed into Britanny. The Franks and Normans introduced this kind of government into France, as did the Huns, the Goths, and the Lombards into Italy, and the Vandals into Spain and Portugal." It had required a long and difficult process for the inhabitants of the British Isles to liberate themselves from this system of government. "To give the English that true personal liberty, which the Anglo-Saxons took from them, and create that happy government, which this nation has finally come to enjoy, has required a purge of thirteen centuries." How many traces have remained in the words and customs of Europe of these early "hurtful customs"! "In Italy feudalism infests liberty to such a degree that the word *baron* is an odious one, and even today one says in insult: you are a baron, he is a baron." Everywhere is used a salutation "with the vile preface *servitor vostro*." Whenever he heard this, he could do "no less than murmur in his heart: you still have a Gothic air."[34]

Coming then to narrate the origin and development of the English colonies, he did not hide elements of abuse and violence that accompanied the development of the India Company, but he confined himself largely to describing admiringly the solid foundations of places like Pennsylvania, where "security of property" and "the liberty of persons" were the "bases of government" and where "tolerance" was ensured. True, to the 150,000 white inhabitants of Pennsylvania it was necessary to add about "30,000 black slaves," but the conscience of the inhabitants had begun to counteract this inequality and injustice. "Not long ago," he related, "one of the Quakers . . . in one of their meetings rose and said: 'How long will we continue to have two consciences, two measures, two scales, one favorable to ourselves, the other disfavorable to our fellows? With what face dare we lament that Parliament wants to impose a yoke on us, depriving us of the rights of citizens, we who for a century have remorselessly held in chains so many of our equals, our brothers. . . . And we are Christians and Englishmen?' "[35]

Other colonies Martinelli described displayed similar contrasts (even

[33] Croce, "Un letterato italiano in Inghilterra," pp. 272ff.

[34] *Istoria del governo d'Inghilterra e delle sue colonie in India e nell'America settentrionale, scritta da Vincenzio Martinelli, a sua eccellenza il sig. principe D. Lorenzo Corsini* (Florence: Gaetano Cambiagi, 1776), pp. 34, 36, 40. See *Notizie del mondo*, no. 63, 6 August 1776, p. 383 (Florence, 5 August).

[35] Ibid., pp. 89ff.

the witches of Salem made an appearance). But one problem dominated the others, the revolt against the mother country. "The outcome of the differences between England and her colonies is in the mind of God." But how could one forget that, since antiquity, at a certain point sooner or later, there was always a separation from the mother country? A recent example further confirmed the rule. The conflict in the Britannic world seemed similar to that of the "Genoese against the Corsicans." Even these had defended "their liberty." "Thus, when the wisdom of government does not take expedients to remove the causes of discontent, it can be confidently foretold that there will be shameful losses and tearful victories even for descendants in the third and fourth degree of the present generation."[36] Martinelli's hopes were directed to Lord Chatham, who once before had saved England from a difficult situation and might now again show his exceptional political skill. He was in fact "another Cromwell in his unearthing of the most hidden secrets of princes . . . scrupulous in keeping his word . . . most wise in the pursuit of merit."[37] The great figure of Pitt dominated the picture Martinelli took with him to Tuscany in the seventies when the American storm broke out on the horizon.[38]

Thus, Martinelli's was a long and fruitful discovery of the Britannic world. It continually brought forth elaborate comparisons between his native land and the adopted one, where he lived for thirty years. By contrast, a more youthful and enthusiastic discovery was made by Alessandro Verri, his interlocutor in the winter of 1766–1767, who was less well prepared to understand England (a land whose language he did not know). He was less learned and cultivated, but he felt immediately at home on the streets of London, as if this were precisely the place that he had dreamed of with his brother and friends in the years of *Il Caffè*. Unexpectedly, he was there. Within eight days of his arrival he wrote to his brother Pietro. "I find London the best of all cities in which to live. What a fine thing it would be to bring here all the fellowship of *Il Caffè*. I assure you that we would all be in the best possible state, with perfect freedom and tranquillity."[39] Finally it was no longer a matter, as it was for the French philosophes, of a hoped-for, desired, and requested freedom. In England liberty was a custom, a part of daily life, not a hope

[36] Ibid., p. 126.

[37] Ibid., p. 160ff.

[38] A second edition of the *Istoria del governo d'Inghilterra* appeared in Pescia in 1777. Nothing was added to the Florentine edition, but it was dedicated to "Jacopo Finocchietti, nobile pisano e livornese," and was the first product of the Società tipografica, established shortly before in Pescia.

[39] *Carteggio di Pietro e di Alessandro Verri*, vol. 1, pt. 1, p. 123 (London, 15 December 1766).

but a reality. "In Paris there is always talk of the police; in London no one ever talks of them and all goes well."[40] There was even the freedom of boxing matches. This was not a land made for distinguished refined lords, but a kingdom of common people. "The people are free and sovereign; they feel their freedom and show their feelings with a roughness and license appropriate to themselves. They seek everywhere new expressions of independence."[41] Inconvenient, but inspiring enthusiasm. As for ideas, everyone is mentor to himself. "Do you want to believe nothing? You're the boss. Do you want to believe little? You're the boss. . . . Do you want to organize a sect? You're the boss. Do you want to call the king a b——? Go right ahead. My serving man says it a hundred times a day. . . . Tolerance of opinion, much discussed in philosophy, is a truth here known by all porters and a maxim of the government. Every Englishman says: 'My sovereign is the law,' and to know if an action is allowed asks: 'Is there a law that prevents it?' . . . Here these two great basic maxims are known by all."[42]

With these eyes Alessandro observed men and women, the theaters and academies, the roads and monuments, avoiding the circles of diplomacy in which he had contacts, ignoring the circles of politics and government, and concentrating instead on observing, with cool objectivity, even the most abnormal aspects of a society that was so different from the one in which he had grown up. He looked at this reality with the eyes of a Hogarth, and sometimes with the spirit of a Sterne.[43] He even forgot the Milanese discussions on penal law, at the time when the English version of *Dei delitti e delle pene* was published, and adopted a detached tone when describing to his brother a brutal hanging.[44] He was not concerned with strictly constitutional issues, and little with political economy. He was concerned with science in order to meet Franklin and other learned men rather than for a specific interest. When finally, at the Royal Society, he was exposed to the propaganda of Thomas Hollis, who had distributed a *Crucifixion*, with the inscription "Behold the fate of a reformer," he found it "very beautiful," but even here, he noted, the "English are surprised at nothing. Nothing astonishes them."[45]

[40] Ibid., p. 126.

[41] Ibid., p. 128. See ibid., p. 248 (London, 29 January 1767), for the relevant discussion with Pietro.

[42] Ibid., pp. 146–47 (London, 21 December 1766).

[43] On Hogarth, see ibid., p. 155 (Milan, 20 January 1767); p. 173 (Milan, 24 January 1767); and p. 264 (London, 10 February 1767). On Sterne, p. 183 (London, 6 January 1767); and p. 284 (Paris, 1 March 1767).

[44] Ibid., p. 211 (on the work of Beccaria), and pp. 213ff. (London, 15 January 1767) (on the hanging).

[45] Ibid., p. 201 (London, 12 January 1767). A reproduction of the engraving is in Venturi, *Settecento riformatore*, vol. 1, fig. 68, facing p. 393.

Certainly Alessandro Verri was a genuine admirer of British liberty, but he did not want to be seduced by the problems it opened before his eyes, attempting instead, as he wrote to his brother with a revealing phrase, to "take refuge in liberty," in personal and private freedom.[46] And he would do just this, soon, when he had left England and was in Rome again. He seemed barely aware of the tensions besetting the structure of British politics in these years. He had known Wilkes in Paris, in November 1766: "A man of great spirit, of much learning, infinitely likable."[47] He thought that the disputes he had impassioned in his own country were abating and that he would be able to return to London. This was a good solution as long as one tried to forget the facts. In fact, the internal conflicts of Great Britain were rapidly intensifying. Pietro Verri was well informed of them in Milan, although not by his brother. What his friend Henry Lloyd told him at the beginning of 1768 was quite dramatic and important.[48] A year and a half later, in September 1769, Pietro was convinced that "a civil war seems inevitable in England. The corruption is in Parliament itself; the constitution is undermined by it, there is no remedy other than to return to a state of nature and reset the machine."[49] In other words, one was on the brink of a revolution.

For many Italians the English crisis of the late sixties was perceived mainly through the debate about the Corsican rebellion, the French intervention there, and the exile of Pasquale Paoli.[1] Other aspects of Italian participation in British problems of the late sixties could certainly be drawn from the impressions and judgments of a man like Baretti, who returned to London in 1766 and was soon involved in polemics regarding relations with Italy.[2] Nor should we forget the curious reaction of Ferdinando Galiani, who was in London for three weeks in November–December 1767. As he wrote to Tanucci, he found the nation "rather

[46] *Carteggio di Pietro e di Alessandro Verri*, vol. 1, pt. 1, p. 181 (Milan, 27 January).

[47] Ibid., p. 113 (Paris, 26 November 1766).

[48] See Franco Venturi, *Le vite incrociate di Henry Lloyd e Pietro Verri: Corso 1976–1977* (Turin: Tirrenia-Stampatori, 1977), pp. 39ff., and id., "Le avventure di generale Henry Lloyd," *R. Stor. ital.*, nos. 2–3 (June 1979): 369ff.

[49] *Carteggio di Pietro e di Alessandro Verri*, vol. 3, p. 73 (Milan, 23 September 1769).

[1] See Venturi, "Il dibattito francese e britannico sulla rivoluzione di Corsica," pp. 643ff., and Id., "Il dibattito in Italia sulla rivoluzione di Corsica," pp. 40ff.

[2] See the article by Mario Fubini, "Giuseppe Baretti," in *DBI*, vol. 6, pp. 329ff. For the surroundings in which Baretti moved, see Noel Blakiston, "Dr. Johnson and Italy," in fasc. 4 of the *Italian Institution of Culture in London: Art and Ideas in Eighteenth Century Italy* (Rome: Ed. di storia e letteratura, 1960), pp. 64ff.

similar to Italy and quite distant from France."[3] And when the minister responded to him with great surprise, the abbé insisted, indicating that he did not mean to speak of "all of Italy, but only the parts with living or extinct republics: Tuscany and Lombardy." Even the seriousness of the English was "the same in the two places, that is, in London, and in Venice or Genova."[4] But, he added, the English could never hope to reach the level of Italians in the past, "when they were a single nation, as they would be again if one monarchy returned."[5] Great Britain struck him for its economic fragility, for lacking many products, and for its artful politics. It was the "offspring of great industry, infinite trouble, and great parsimony," but it had finally fallen victim to natural human relaxation and weariness.[6] Now it was in a real crisis, he reasoned paradoxically.

Nor should we forget the *Vita* of Alfieri where he speaks of his voyage to England in 1768. It is interesting to compare it with what we have read in Alessandro Verri's letters.

Just as Paris displeased me from its first appearance, England pleased me, and London most of all. The roads, the inns, the horses, the women, the general well-being, the life and activity of that island, the cleanliness and comfort of even the smallest houses, the lack of beggars, the constant movement of money and industry, distributed equally between the provinces and the capital; all these true and unique gifts of that fortunate and free country astonished me before, and in two other voyages besides the one I have just made, and I have never changed my opinion, there being too much difference between England and the remainder of Europe in the diffusion of public happiness resulting from better government. Thus, although I did not then study the constitution deeply, the mother of such prosperity, I know enough of it from observing and appreciating its divine effects.[7]

An English witness of primary importance might have reciprocated this growing interest of Italian writers for the life and problems of England, the same Wilkes who visited Italy in the first months of 1765, passing through Milan and remaining at length in Naples. But his visit was an unfortunate one. Besides his amorous adventures and misfortunes, Wilkes was not able to detach his thought from his own turbulent political life, from the attack on George III in number 45 of his journal, the *North Briton*, from the persecutions to which he had been subjected, and from the people of London who had saved him from the hands of his

---

[3] Galiani, *Opere*, p. 947, London, 8 December 1767.
[4] Ibid., p. 947 n., Paris, 8 February 1768.
[5] Ibid., p. 947, London, 8 December 1767.
[6] Ibid., p. 948.
[7] Alfieri, *Vita*, p. 83.

enemies, a salvation that sent him into exile. The Italian gazettes were filled with the facts, as John Murray, the English consul in Venice, reported with displeasure when he attempted to make known the official, sweetened version of these unfortunate occurrences.[8] Wilkes did little or nothing to persuade Italians of the justice of his cause, as he had succeeded in doing in Paris among the central group of philosophes, where he appealed particularly to Holbach. In Italy his contacts with the world of culture and politics remained cold and measured. In Lombardy Prince Trivulzio received him "in the noblest manner, and in the evening carried me to the countess Simonetta, who is the first lady of Milan." He visited the Duke of Modena and Firmian, "the first minister," with whom he remained in discussion for four hours. He seemed to begin to accustom himself to the country and to understand Italian so as to read "tolerably well their best authors."[9] But his encounter with Naples, where he arrived on 26 February 1765, made him more disdainful and discontented. "I was never more disappointed than in the inhabitants of Italy. I expected to see a very clever and polite people. On the contrary, you cannot imagine anything more ignorant, more ill-bred or more coarse than they are." He even wrote, in exile from England, in a pornographic poem, that the conversation of Italians "is shocking to a modest ear." The roads in Italy were terrible. Glass was missing in the windows and was replaced with sheets of paper. "For three days I could get nothing to eat but red herrings, eggs, and bread."[10] He tried to contact his compatriots, English gentlemen living in Turin, Florence, Rome, and naturally Naples. He asked that portraits of British republicanism heroes be sent to him, "Hampden, Sidney etc., given me by Mr Hollis, and those of lord Temple and Mr Pitt."[11] He was writing a history of England and collecting the poetry, also libertine, of his friend Charles Churchill. In short, he did everything possible to "breath the spirit of liberty even in this land of slaves." His grand hope was to return to England and fight for liberty. "I am ready, whenever the standard of liberty is set up, to fight under it."[12]

Three years later, in March 1768, Wilkes was in London again, first as a candidate for the city, and then for the House of Commons, seeking election for the Middlesex borough of London. He won unexpectedly.

---

[8] PRO SP 99/69, F. 138, n.d., from the end of 1764.

[9] *The Correspondence of the late John Wilkes with his friends* . . . printed . . . by John Almon in five volumes (London: Richard Phillips, 1805), vol. 2, p. 124, Parma, 16 January 1765. On the countess Teresa di Simonetta, see *Carteggio di Pietro e di Alessandro Verri*, vol. 1, pt. 1, p. 159 n.

[10] *The correspondence of the late John Wilkes*, vol. 2, p. 168, Naples, 21 May 1765.

[11] Ibid., p. 195, Naples, 25 March 1765.

[12] Ibid., p. 201, Naples, 28 May 1765.

The courts, although with uncertainty and hesitation, reopened the accusation against him of having published attacks on the king and various morally offensive tracts. He was condemned to twenty-two months in prison. Thus, the governing class challenged the "riotous spirit" that had grown rapidly in England in those years, "almost to the point of revolution."[13] Blue cockades numbered forty-five (of the *North Briton*) and the cry "Wilkes and Liberty" accompanied a series of disturbances, attacks on ministers, and illuminations of joy for the triumph of the people unleashed. The prison incarcerating Wilkes became a center of permanent agitation. "Never since the Revolution, not even in the years 1715 and 1745, were we in such a critical and an alarming situation as the present one," wrote the London correspondent of the *Nouvelles extraordinaires de divers endroits*, the so-called gazette of Leiden, on 3 June 1768.[14] The situation became worse and still more tense when on 2 February 1769, after much hesitation, the government denied Wilkes his seat in Parliament. On 16 February 1769 he was unanimously reconfirmed by his electors. The day after, the House confirmed his expulsion. Other reelections and denials followed. The Commons received into the House a rival of Wilkes who had received fewer votes. In the City Wilkes was again elected alderman. More and more violent incidents accompanied each of these episodes. Wilkes remained in prison, but he had succeeded in inspiring a great movement in London and the provinces. Questions involving the election of deputies and rule by the majority were brought openly into discussion, just when parallel questions were straining more seriously the relationship between the English mother country and the American colonies. The character and power of Parliament itself were in doubt.

Italian gazettes and journals followed the development of these debates with growing interest, translating the principal documents and describing the incidents, demonstrations, encounters, and protests. The *Gazzetta estera*, which began publishing in Florence in April 1767, although preoccupied with the gloomy news from Russia, Poland, Sweden, and beyond the seas, could not avoid considering the problem of the nature and situation of the British government. It took the occasion of a book published in London to inquire whether the aristocratic English system would sooner or later not fall into a kind of absolute mon-

---

[13] William Edward Lecky, *A History of England in the Eighteenth Century* (London: Longmans, 1921), vol. 3, p. 319.

[14] *Nouvelles extraordinaires de divers endroits*, no. 47, 10 June 1768 (London, 3 June).

archy.[1] After discussing the question for three issues, it concluded the following: "The people, tired of the oppression of the great, feeling that they have lost their liberty, and being more willing to submit to an indulgent patron than to two or three hundred petty tyrants, will address themselves to the sovereign and demand, as a special grace, the establishment of an absolute monarchy."[2] The following months news confirmed the "deplorable" "situation in which England found itself." "The liberty of Great Britain is in flux. . . . True patriotism, the basis of the constitution, has disappeared."[3] Some had dared to defend absolute government.[4] And this was happening just when in America, especially in Boston, the effort to defend liberty was growing more energetic. In the mother country people were unemployed and discontented. The winter was hard in Gloucester. "Provisions here continue to be very dear. Thousands of persons die of hunger for lack of employment in textile employment. It is difficult to observe without emotion the many poor creatures begging for bread in the open countryside. Their faces, their appearance, all announce the most terrible misery. What is worse is not knowing what remedy to take, although it is all too clear that if circumstances do not change the country will be lost."[5] In Newcastle the contrast between rich and poor increased. "We have the sorrow of seeing our farmers swimming in luxury, their daughters showing off the most costly and ridiculous fashions. . . . All our hope is concentrated on the current Parliament. . . . Our poor mechanics live mostly on potatoes, which have kept thousands from starving, and these potatoes cost twice what they did in 1764."[6] In Scotland, "the poor die of misery and hunger." It is hoped that taxes will be reduced. "There is talk of taking action against luxury through the establishment of sumptuary laws," something that "was contrary to liberty." "The immense debts," the decline of trade with America, all combined to increase the "misery of the people."[7] Whereas the colonists began to show that they were ready for sacrifice and hardship, the English government remained uncertain and incapable of finding a solution.

[1] *Gazzetta estera*, no. 26, 29 September 1767, p. 107 (London, 4 September), "Ragionamento sul governo britannico."

[2] Ibid., no. 28, 13 October 1767, p. 115 (London, 15–18 September), "Continuazione del Ragionamento sul governo britannico."

[3] Ibid., no. 36, 8 December 1767, p. 147 (The Hague, 20 November).

[4] Ibid., no. 37, 15 December 1767, p. 152 (The Hague, 27 November), "Segue il Discorso sopra la libertà britannica."

[5] Ibid., no. 42, 19 January 1768, p. 172 (Gloucester, 9 December 1767), "Estratto di una lettera scritta da Petbury."

[6] Ibid., p. 173 (Newcastle, 8 December).

[7] Ibid., no. 44, 2 February 1768, p. 181 (London, 29 December 1767, and London, 1 January 1768).

Against this background the appearance of Wilkes was an exceptional and emotional event, a hope among many preoccupations and delusions. In March 1768 it was reported from London that "the crowd of people was incredible, all were hastening to go to see Mr. Wilkes and attest with repeated acclamations their satisfaction to see him elected. He pronounced to the citizenry a speech worthy of his talents." All around, in the provinces, disturbances continued. "In Lancaster and in Preston" there were wounded. These "disorders show up the liberty of old England very badly."[8] The epicenter of the movement was the capital. "The city of London and Westminster, as well as all the County of Middlesex, have been in violent agitation for three days because of the election of their representatives to Parliament. The people have generally shown much extravagance in expressing their zeal and attachment for Mr. Wilkes." Public subscriptions were launched to pay his debts. London was crossed with processions in his honor. A large number of people wore blue cockades "on which were written Wilkes and Liberty: no. 45." It was difficult to pass through "the principal streets" without hearing these words. "The people have broken all the windows in the house of the Lord Mayor and committed many other excesses." "There is no example in memory" of a similar "affair," the gazette concluded. The speech with which Wilkes thanked his electors was reported in full, as a typical document of the "glorious cause of liberty."[9] A week later one read: "The election of Mr. Wilkes continues to divide opinion. . . . His antagonists prepare to hotly dispute the legitimacy of his nomination in the next session of Parliament," while the popular support he elicited in London grew.[10] The *Gazzetta estera* stopped publication in May and was replaced in August by the *Gazzetta di Firenze*. From its first issue it provided an ample picture of the situation in England. The breaking point was approaching. "The signs of discontent are too visible here, as much as in America, to be dissimulated. Here the mass of people is reduced to poverty to an extent unknown until the present. The public debt is enormous and the luxury that has grown proportionally only serves to increase the deceptive appearance of prosperity and to poison the rich, while the poor are reduced to despair. Our colonies are still rich, it is true—frugality and industry still reign there—but animated as they are by a spirit of independence and discontent with the mother country, what assistance can we hope for? A new war or some other provocation could soon remove them entirely from our dominion." Thus a policy of peace was needed, even if this meant abandoning

[8] Ibid., no. 1, 5 April 1768, p. 1 (London, 18 March).
[9] Ibid., no. 4, 26 April 1768, p. 15 (London, 29 March and 1 April).
[10] Ibid., no. 5, 3 May 1768, p. 19 (London, 8 April).

Corsica to its destiny. Any other initiative "would be less an act of generosity than a foolish romantic folly." But should one thus abandon all struggle for liberty? The defender of a policy of peace believed he had to assure his listeners that he too was an admirer "of the brave and disinterested Paoli." One of his critics—whose argument was carried in the columns of the *Gazzetta di Firenze*—insisted on the strategic and political necessity of an English intervention. The "oppressed" Corsicans should be "assisted."[11] The "merchants" of the capital were also moving in this direction.[12] But problems and doubts were ever growing. The imprisonment of Wilkes, the subscription for Paoli, and "the petition of the inhabitants of Boston"[13] were themes that continued to intersect during the remainder of the summer. In October the journal changed its name to *Notizie del mondo*. It followed closely the final defense of the Corsicans, but there was an equal amount of news about the conflict in Great Britain, where the motto "Wilkes and Liberty" continued to resound.[14] "The nation," a correspondent from London reported, "seems generally unhappy" with the lack of assistance for Paoli.[15] In the capital and provinces "the scarcity caused by the illicit manipulation by persons intent on enriching themselves in a few days on public misery" remained "excessive."[16] Differences with the American colonies were becoming more serious. Nor were things quieter in the following year, 1769. "England is in a state of violent agitation," the *Mercurio storico e politico* in Venice reported, summarizing the events of that year.[17] "A single man . . . , the celebrated Mr. John Wilkes," had become the "idol of a large part of the nation."[18] The *Foglio ordinario* of Naples spoke in February of the "embarrassment of the ministry . . . especially in a situation where daily affairs require serious and constant attention" (alluding evidently to Corsica, the Russo-Turkish war, and America).[19] In April it described in detail the actions of the "most zealous" partisans of Wilkes and the "disquiet of the people," as the propaganda of the *North Briton* and "other publications that adopt the same ideas" increased.[20] There were not many issues of the gazette of Lugano in which one did not hear echoes of hammer blows of the name Wilkes, who "declaims vigorously against

[11] *Gazzetta di Firenze*, no. 1, 23 August 1768, pp. 2ff. (London, 5 August).
[12] Ibid., no. 2, 27 August 1768, p. 10 (London, 5 August).
[13] Ibid., no. 3, 30 August 1768, p. 18 (London, 9 August).
[14] *Notizie del mondo*, no. 21, 1 November 1768, p. 163 (London, 14 October).
[15] Ibid., no. 34, 17 December 1768, p. 257 (London, 27 November).
[16] Ibid., no. 35, 20 December 1768, p. 274 (London, 2 December).
[17] *Mercurio storico e politico*, vol. 676, January 1770, p. 3, "Compendio dei principali avvenimenti dell'anno 1769."
[18] Ibid.
[19] *Foglio ordinario*, no. 8, 21 February 1769 (London, 13 January).
[20] Ibid., no. 16, 18 April 1769 (London, 12 March).

the conduct of the ministry and the procedure of Parliament in this regard and invites his compatriots to hold firm for the maintenance of
their liberty and privileges, which they want to destroy." These voices,
as the gazette recognized, were "apt to embitter souls and nourish the
discontent unfortunately already prevalent in these realms."[21] As the
Florentine *Notizie del mondo* reported a little later, "Mr. John Wilkes continues to keep the whole city in agitation. . . . On the sixth and seventh
of this month [January] he gave presents to all the prisoners of Kings
Bench, the Fleet, and other prisons of this capital. Recently he invited
to dinner in his prison the members of the Common Council of the
Farrigdon-Without district, where he was elected alderman. Six of the
sixteen guests attended the dinner, the other ten made excuses. The
dinner was magnificent, composed of different meats his friends sent to
him."[22]

The columns of this gazette thus were transformed into a pictur-
esque course in British constitutional law, leading Italian readers
through a meander full of surprises and unexpected situations. The
terms themselves were not easy to translate. For example, the "freehold-
ers," electors of Wilkes at Middlesex, were barely recognizable in the
Italian version as "*feudatari*" (fief-holders).[23] But this opacity did not
prevent one's guessing the extraordinary complexity and liberty of a
land where municipal councils held banquets in prison, where freedom
of the press was defended so tenaciously, where the people of London
controlled the streets, and where money for political subscriptions was
not lacking. The weakness and uncertainty of the government were
clear, incapable as it was of a firm policy, and deprived of effective support in the population at large. The effort to rally more moderate elements in the provinces and capital failed in the spring of 1769. The
County of Essex sent a delegation to the court as a testimony "of the
most profound respect and inviolable fidelity toward His Majesty." "But
this county has thus far found no others to imitate it." Among London
merchants "few subscribed."[24] The universities of Cambridge and Oxford intervened without effect. There was a fruitless attempt to rally a
cortège of three hundred merchant carriages in the City. "The low people gave them manifest signs of resentment, whistling, murmuring, and

---

[21] *Supplimento* to the *Nuove di diverse corti e paesi*, no. 2, 9 January 1759 (London, 20
December 1768).

[22] *Notizie del mondo*, no. 9, 31 January 1769, p. 67 (London, 12 January).

[23] See, for example, ibid., no. 3, 10 January 1769, p. 19 (London, 20 December 1768).
Already no. 5, 16 January 1770, p. 34 (London, 25 December 1769), spoke of "landhold-
ers of the County of Middlesex."

[24] *Supplimento* to the *Nuove di diverse corti e paesi*, no. 13, 27 March 1769 (London, 10
March). See *Notizie del mondo*, no. 27, 4 April 1769, p. 209 (London, 14 March).

throwing mud at them." At Temple Bar they encountered a barricade. The horses were unhitched. "Finally, many merchants, finding it dangerous to proceed, returned to their houses." The people organized a kind of macabre masquerade as a reminder of past incidents and above all of the tumult of 10 May 1765. They went about crying: "Long live the King, Wilkes, and Liberty." A corps of cavalry intervened, and sixteen people were arrested. Few indeed were the merchants who succeeded in reaching the Court of St. James. "For having risked their lives they were admitted to an audience."[25]

After news of this kind Italian readers naturally wanted to know the political principles on which such an extraordinarily broad liberty was based. The documents concerning Wilkes could in part satisfy such curiosity. But his language was certainly not that of a philosopher. These were appeals, not explanations or clarifications. But the events themselves seemed to speak for him: "It is about whether the people have an inherent right in the constitution to be represented in Parliament by a man who is freely elected. . . . This is a right as old as our constitution and one of the fundamental principles of the form of our government, according to which the third part of legislative power is reserved for the people. This right began with the first weak ray of liberty in our island and will survive to its last convulsive breath. . . . This right of the people conforms no less to reason than to positive law. . . . On this public foundation I will always stand firm, nor will any peril disturb my duty."[26] His declaration after his fourth reelection was equally energetic: "As long as the British constitution keeps its vigor and ancient form, you will never have in the House of Commons anyone other than representatives you voluntarily select."[27]

The *Notizie del mondo* finally attempted to provide a more general interpretation of the British constitution. "Since we have received a recent excellent essay on the constitution, liberty, rights, and privileges of the English, it has been thought useful for the public to include it in this journal," one read on 17 October 1769.[28] Two issues were devoted to the effort of explaining the principles of the "great Locke" and of Great Britain. "This nation prides itself on having a government close to perfection, where true maxims of political, or rather civil, society are always seen to flourish with great progress and vigor." In the British Isles

---

[25] *Notizie del mondo*, no. 30, 15 April 1769, p. 232 (London, 24 March). See *Supplimento* to the *Nuove di diverse corti e paesi*, no. 16, 17 April 1769 (London, 24 March).

[26] *Nuove di diverse corti e paesi*, no. 17, 24 April 1769 (London, 7 April).

[27] Ibid., no. 20, 15 May 1769 (London, 28 April). See *Notizie del mondo*, no. 39, 16 May 1769, pp. 305ff. (London, 28 April).

[28] *Notizie del mondo*, no. 83, 17 October 1769, p. 678 (London, 26 September).

power was not embodied, as happened elsewhere, "in a prince or a few lords," nor was it "arbitrary or despotic."[29] There a person was free. After many attempts and experiments over the centuries, there had finally arrived the "memorable revolution when the prince and princess of Orange ascended the throne." From that time even arbitrary acts, such "as [the ones that] occurred in 1763 with Mr. Wilkes," could and should have been corrected and repaired. "Keeping civil rights alive, particularly the act of *habeas corpus*, is always of greatest importance in the opinion of the English." Any "sign of despotism" or "horrible apprehension of tyranny" would only "stir the people to an uprising."[30] Here this "Essay" was interrupted, and one seeks in vain in the following issues of the Florentine gazette for the fulfillment of the promise "To be continued." But even in such a mutilated state the few pages synthesize the lessons that came to Italy in that period from the England of Wilkes.

It was not an easy lesson: the agitation for liberty was joined by others for higher wages.[31] The repression became violent at times.[32] Amid the demonstrations, banquets, tumults, and executions was born a new political movement, with its symbols, clubs, and permanent organizations, for the defense of the rights of citizens.[33] A new kind of

[29] Ibid., p. 679.

[30] Ibid., no. 84, 21 October 1769, p. 686 (London, 29 September), "Segue la scrittura d'Inghilterra."

[31] Ibid., no. 86, 28 October 1769, p. 702 (London, 6 October): "The weavers have resumed their disturbances and have made a pact among themselves promising to no longer serve their principals except for so much money for each batch of silk or other." The "company" of the workers keeps watch to seek out those who "for necessity or for avarice work for less than the established price . . . to beat them up and even kill them." "The militia does not want to do violence against its fellow citizens, and the number of justices of the peace, constables, and night guards is insufficient to contain so many people."

[32] Ibid., no. 103, 26 December 1769, p. 838 (London, 8 December), describes how "two weavers were hanged." "These unfortunates protested their innocence to their last breath and gave the sheriffs a sworn declaration to that effect. The crowd of people who had come to witness it was enormous and nearly prevented the execution; when it was barely ended, they took the gallows furiously and went to plant it in front of the house of the master weaver who had insisted that the sentence be carried out as a warning to others. The plebs attempted to knock down the door of his house and a detachment of guards on horseback was needed to quiet the tumult."

[33] See, for example, ibid., no. 93, 21 November 1769, p. 758 (London, 31 October): "great fireworks in St. George's fields in honor of the birthday of Sig. Wilkes"; the "society of the protectors of the rights of the people" gave him, besides 300 pounds, "a great silver cup capable of containing four bottles, appraised to be worth 100 pounds sterling. On it were engraved his figure with a liberty cap and on the other side the famous Magna Carta." In no. 54, of 8 July 1769, p. 434 (London, 16 June), the *Notizie del mondo* had already spoken of the creation of the society of "defenders of the rights and privileges of the nation." "These actually form quite a respectable body." "They have written circulars

politics emerged in England, and even at a distance, in Italy, it was possible to sense the excitement and disquiet.

The increasingly frequent information arriving from beyond the ocean at the end of the sixties was inserted, naturally, into this framework. This was a further element in the general crisis of the Britannic world rather than an indication of a nascent American consciousness, which developed slowly over an extended period, under the influence of commercial, financial, juridical, and constitutional conflicts. The radical movement seemed at first stronger and more influential in London than in Boston, New York, or Philadelphia. Also, at the beginning of the seventies the conviction of the possibility of an accord, a reconciliation between the colonies and the mother country, was strong and deep. Only with the silting up and slowing down of the Wilkes movement in England did the conflict beyond the sea bob up into the foreground. Even from the Italian observation post, what was seen for a long time were the problems and tensions of the British world: American reality emerged very slowly. One has to look in the gazettes—the chief font of information—naturally with the dateline London, for reflections of what was happening beyond the seas. And it was—quite rightly— through English eyes that American reality was interpreted in Italy, at least until 1775. To see the colonies separated from the mother country before the effective break is to write the story of a divorce without having told of the long period of cohabitation, and risks deducing wrongly that Italians knew little or were not very interested in the origins of the American Revolution. It was only that they saw and interpreted events within a European and British framework.[34]

to invite the counties to interest themselves in the common cause, and contributions come from all parts of the realm and beyond, as far as America." A few days later, the same journal announced the preparation of a festival on the occasion of the anniversary of the "famous Shakespeare, tragic and comic poet who flourished in the sixteenth century," and hastened to add that even the Magna Carta would soon be solemnly remembered as the "foundation of English liberty." "All the sons of liberty will be invited to commemorate the glorious day in which such a great privilege was granted." *Notizie del mondo*, no. 57, 18 July 1769, p. 458 (London, 30 June).

[34] See Vittorio Gabrieli, "The Impact of American Political Ideas in Eighteenth Century Italy," in *Contagious Conflict*, ed. A.N.J. den Hollander (Leiden: Brill, 1973); Piero del Negro, *Il mito americano nella Venezia del Settecento*, seconda edizione (Padova: Liviana Editore, 1986); Giorgio Spini, Anna Maria Martellone, Raimondo Luraghi, Tiziano Bonazzi, and Roberto Ruffilli, *Italia e America dalla metà del Settecento all'imperialismo* (Padova: Marsilio, 1976) (where the failure to rely on gazettes distorts the vision of relations between Italy and America before 1775). These studies contain a recent bibliography. The connection between the nascent United States of America and the different European states has become a privileged terrain of research in these recent years, on the occasion of the bicentennial of the Declaration of Independence. It is enough to think, to cite only two examples, that there appeared in Belgrade in 1976 a work by D. Živojinović on the relations

In Italy, as well as elsewhere, the Seven Years' War revived strong interest in America. Two large informative works were published in Italy in 1763 at the conclusive moment of the conflict: the *Gazzettiere americano* in Livorno and the *Storia degli stabilimenti europei in America* in Venice.[1] Both tended to satisfy a diffused curiosity about the land, plants, animals, and people of the New World rather than to arouse a discussion of the political life of that continent. Even the illustrations attempted to show exotic and strange aspects of life beyond the ocean. The Venetian work began with an engraving of "an Indian couple of North America." It was taken from a painting executed by the "most ingenious and excellent painter" Benjamin West when he was traveling through Livorno. The engraving was made by Francesco Bartolozzi, who was about to move to England.[2] The book was large, detailed, and thought provoking. The author was William Burke. His more famous cousin Edmund reviewed it. Altogether it was a publisher's undertaking regarding a land about which discussion was lively and candid. Following a history of European colonization, from south to north, there was a survey of the fundamental problems of the "English establishments"— religious sects, witchcraft, economics, slavery, the legal system, which differed from colony to colony; one problem after another was examined in detail. Confronted with such an unexpected world the Italian translator had a symptomatic reaction, struck as he was by the fact that Italy was now one of the few European lands, almost the only one, that did not participate directly in the life of the American continent. How could one not be surprised that "in the wide spaces of this new world, discovered by an Italian, among all the nations of Europe (except the

between America and the republic of Ragusa, and that the Soviet scholar N. N. Bolchovitinov in the same year published in Moscow a book on Russia and the War of Independence. On Poland, see Zofia Libiszowska, *Opinia Polska wobec rewolucji amerikańskiej w XVIII wieku* (Polish opinion and the American Revolution of the eighteenth century) (Łodz: Żaklad narodowij im. Ossolińskich, 1962). The most complete and best-documented work is by Horst Dippel, *Germany and American Revolution*, translated from German and published by the Institute for the Early American History and Culture of Williamsburg, Virginia (Chapel Hill: University of North Carolina Press, 1977).

[1] See Eric W. Cochrane, "Il *Gazzettiere americano* di Livorno e l'America nella letteratura del Settecento," *Quaderni di cultura e di storia sociale*, new ser., 3, no. 1 (January 1954): 43ff.

[2] *Storia degli stabilimenti europei in America, divisa in sei parti, nella quale oltre una breve notizia della scoperta e conquiste fatte in quella parte del mondo, de' costumi e maniere de' popoli originari, si dà un'esatta descrizione delle colonie colà stabilite, dell'estensione, clima, prodotti e commercio loro, indole e disposizione degli abitanti: Si accennano gl'interessi de' potentati d'Europa in riguardo a si fatti stabilimenti e le mire politiche e di commercio degli uni rispetto agli altri*, tradotta in italiano dalla seconda edizione inglese (Venice: Giambattista Novello, 1763), vol. 2: *Il traduttore a chi legge*, vol. 1, p. iii.

Greeks, who for the empire and barbarism they languish under could
be called Asiatic), only the Italians did not have some establishment, and
no Italian had ever attempted to found one"? His vision of the American world suggested the idea of emigration. The "generous prudence
of the English" would not deny the necessary land, "especially for raising silkworms." Nor did British colonies lack places "where permission
for the free and public exercise of the Catholic religion still remains."
Who could doubt the need to find a place to which so many poor people
could go? "And oh! how many there are (and who does not know our
Italy?) who, reduced to a low state and lacking employment, or in difficulties for some other reason, become useless and dangerous to themselves, a burden to the state, and troublesome to their neighbors. They
live far from their native land, wandering from one province of Europe
to another without finding anyone who will utilize their ability and honest industry." Among the "English people" they would find a "good, glorious, and free country."[3] Nor would their adaptation be difficult, even
if they possessed habits or temperaments quite different from the
American colonists. The book he was in the course of translating assured him of this. In chapter 8 of part 6 he assured that "a variety of
characters" was indispensable for the formation of a new country. Even
"those who love risk and uncertainty" among "persons of low or modest
condition," who would be "at best dangerous members of a regulated
and well-ordered community," could be of great utility in the "West Indies." There, as well, would find "asylum" the unfortunate, the unhappy, debtors, the poor, the "despised of their homeland, who, should
they want to after a time, might return, wealthy and with good reputa-
tions."[4] With such people, "excepting a few," were populated the "establishments" of America. "And in the New World, from the ardor of hot
visionary men, from the imprudence of youth, from the corruption of
usual custom, and even from the misery and criminality of abandoned
lost people," as the English authors concluded, "we have derived the
great store of our wealth, force, and strength."[5] In this way, colonization
only followed a natural process. "Humors appear in animate bodies,
which can be harmful; but drained opportunely they provide good material for the production of new bodies. Providence is a great teacher,
which often reaches its ends by ways and means that seem contradictory,
since earthquakes, whirlwinds, storms, and floods are as necessary for
the well-being of the universe as calm and serenity. Life and beauty
come from death and corruption, and the best medicine is often made

[3] Ibid., vol. 2, pp. iiiff.
[4] Ibid., pp. 124ff.
[5] Ibid., p. 127.

with the most lethal poisons. This, to whoever examines it well, is the order of nature, and perhaps one could think, without arrogance, that this is an example for governments."[6]

The storms, even in the North American colonies, would arrive soon enough. Already in the chapter that followed the one I have cited Burke explained clearly the origin of the conflict that broke out at the end of the sixties: war had posed more and more acutely the problem of the colonies' participating in the cost of defending and administering these lands beyond the sea. Should one impose new taxes on the colonies? Would this not lead to the ruin of their commerce, already menaced by French competition? Would not the expense of maintaining governors, and local administration in general, be too great? Thus, a lightening of burdens, rather than new taxes, was necessary to permit the colonies to persevere and "be more useful to their ancient fatherland."[7]

Little more than a year after the end of the war (and after the publication of Burke's book in Venice) similar considerations of the need to change the financial relationship between the colonies and the mother country developed into a fundamental economic and legal conflict. In 1764 the British government began to examine measures that led to a grave crisis two years later.[8] Giovanni Molinari, the editor of the *Gazzetta estera* in Florence, came to preliminary conclusions when he added a preface to the first volume of his journal that had appeared between April 1767 and March 1768.[9] Two great events had distinguished that period in America: the "quiet and peaceful expulsion of the Society of Jesus from Paraguay" and the "reasoned and constant resolution of the English colonies to resist their own destruction by banning all foreign merchandise and introducing on their own soil the manufacture of necessities and luxuries alike."[10] A correspondent from North America had already given readers of the *Gazzetta estera* on 1 September 1767 a vivid idea of the atmosphere this resistance created, the organization resulting from it, and the principles guiding it. "Letters from Boston in New England," one read, "tell us that on the fourteenth of the past month [August 1767] a number of prosperous citizens gathered under what they call their Liberty Tree to celebrate the day. After the usual

---

[6] Ibid., p. 128.

[7] Ibid., p. 136.

[8] Edmund S. Morgan and Helen M. Morgan, *The Stamp Act Crisis: Prologue to Revolution* (New York and London: Collier-Macmillan, 1962).

[9] On him, as in general on the Tuscan gazettes, see the excellent work by Maria Augusta Timpanaro Morelli, "Persone e momenti del giornalismo politico a Firenze dal 1766 al 1799 in alcuni documenti dell'Archivio di Stato di Firenze," *Rass. arch. stato* 31, no. 2 (May–August 1971): 413ff.

[10] *Gazzetta estera*, vol. 1 (April 1787–March 1768), "Prefazione."

toasts required of all faithful subjects, they drank to the following: (1) that the House of Representatives in America defend with vigor what it has wisely resolved, (2) that they maintain a stable union and fidelity among sons of liberty in America, (3) that each man who in case of danger does not defend the cause of his country be the object of the general scorn of the sons of virtue and liberty, (4) that the day that sees America bend to slavery be the last of its existence."[11] At the beginning of 1768 an "extract from the gazette of Boston in New England was published, at the beginning of which could be read in italic letters *Save your coins and you will save your country*." It told of an assembly held on 28 October 1767, with "Mr. James Otis assuming the function of moderator." There had been a reading "of a petition to the inhabitants" signed "*Philopatriae*," which recommended "economy and industry." The conclusions were clear: "To bring us out of these unhappy and embarrassing circumstances it is absolutely necessary to advance industry, economy, and manufacture among us, and by these means to prevent the useless import of European goods, the excessive use of which threatens poverty and ruin for our country."[12] The Americans had even succeeded in "introducing great savings" in funerals.[13] This policy had immediate results in England, where everyone lamented the reduction in maritime traffic. At the beginning of 1768 the government was presented with a difficult alternative: if it showed firmness, it risked "perhaps anticipating a development that is feared and does not seem very distant," that is, a break with the colonies. To maintain silence meant "nurturing that contempt the Americans show for us."[14] But what right, basically, did the English government have to impose taxes on the American colonies? The *Gaz-*

---

[11] *Gazzetta estera*, no. 32, 10 November 1767, p. 131 (New York, 1 September).

[12] Ibid., no. 41, 12 January 1768 (Boston, 2 November 1767), p. 169. On the "Boston gazette" see Arthur M. Schlesinger, *Prelude to Independence: The Newspaper War on Britain, 1764–1776* (New York: Vintage Books, 1957), particularly ch. 5: "Boston: Foundry of Propaganda." On James Otis in those years, "the most formidable enemy of royal government in America," called the "American Hampden," see John C. Miller, *Sam Adams: Pioneer in Propaganda* (Stanford, Calif.: Stanford University Press, 1966), pp. 8ff. The figure of Hampden was often reevoked in those years. On another occasion, when the valorous commander Montgomery fell in the assault on Quebec, the general congress in Philadelphia compared him to Hampden, and the *Notizie del mondo*, no. 28, 6 April 1776, p. 210 (London, 15 March), explained that Hampden was "one of the most constant patriots to oppose the arbitrary power that cost the life of the unfortunate Charles I." It narrated the principal episodes of the life of Hampden and his death "in an action against the Royalists in 1643." "Mr. Hume, although otherwise not very favorable to the fanaticism of liberty, praised him highly."

[13] *Gazzetta estera*, no. 48, 1 March 1768, p. 197 (Boston in New England, 16 December 1767).

[14] Ibid., no. 44, 2 February 1768, p. 181 (London, 1 January).

zetta estera referred generally to a speech of Lord Camden, in which he maintained with much energy that this was in reality an "illegitimate act, absolutely contrary to the fundamental laws of our constitution, a constitution founded on eternal and immutable laws of nature, a constitution whose foundation and center are liberty, and which reverberates liberty throughout. . . ." Taxation and representation "were united inseparably." "God united them, and no British parliament can separate them. Anyone who would attempt it would kill us." Even attempting to pose the question historically in an effort to find the distant roots of such an absolute truth was a great error. A recent historian (Hume) had done harm in "trying to fix the time of the establishment of the House of Commons." This "had begun with the constitution and grew with it." Together with that "practiced politician" and "great man" John Locke it is always best to base oneself only on the fundamental and undeniable basic rights of Englishmen. "The ancestors of the Americans did not leave their native country and expose themselves to perils and calamities to see themselves reduced to a state of slavery; they have not renounced their rights."[15]

These arguments were resumed beginning with the first issue of the *Gazzetta di Firenze*, in the summer of 1768. In London there was an attempt to demonstrate "a vigorous resistance to the pretensions" of the American colonists, "but tempered with moderation, following the counsel of Lord Chatham, who was consulted in this emergency." In Boston, for the moment, only "the 64th and 65th regiments of infantry, which will be supported by a few warships under orders of Lord Colville, would be sent."[16] From Boston continued to come news of protests, crystallized in declarations of principle. "The inhabitants . . . , legally united," asked "that the British constitution be considered the foundation of their security and honor. Through this constitution it is established that no man shall be governed by foreign laws or taxed only by himself or his legally and freely elected representative if he has not first given his consent." Instead, "in open violation of these fundamental rights of Britons, laws have been imposed on us, and taxes, to which we not only have not consented, but against which we have made the most serious representations." To this the reply had been to send an "armed

[15] Ibid., no. 45, 9 February 1768 (Leiden, 22 January). On Charles Pratt, Baron (and then Earl) Camden, friend of William Pitt, defender of John Wilkes, tenacious opponent of the coercive measures taken against the American colonists, and, as Horace Walpole wrote, "a uniform Whig," see Alan Valentine, *The British Establishment, 1760–1784: An Eighteenth-Century Biographical Dictionary* (Norman: University of Oklahoma Press, 1970), vol. 2, pp. 719ff. For the speech cited here see Lawrence Henry Gipson, *The Coming of the Revolution, 1763–1775* (London: Hamish Hamilton, 1954), pp. 112ff.

[16] *Gazzetta di Firenze*, no. 1, 23 August 1768, p. 2 (London, 5 August).

troop that takes, forces, and imprisons our fellow citizens."[17] "Among the people threats appropriate only to the mouths of barbarians have been spread." Impeding the commerce of the colonies was the equivalent of reducing them "to scarcity and desolation." The colonists saw themselves constrained by a tragic choice. "To fight our mother country is, in our opinion, a most riotous and terrible thing, but to give in abjectly without resistance . . . is so humiliating and vile. . . ." They had no choice other than being obliged "to do too much" or having to expose themselves "to the shame and regret of having done too little." Other colonies began to confront this dilemma. "The inhabitants of New York have set up a subscription for the levy of a national regiment."[18] The English government seemed heedless of the consequences that American resistance might have for the entire British world. One should treat the colonists beyond the sea as one would if "subjects of the three reigns of England, Scotland, and Ireland proclaimed their independence."[19] Meanwhile the rebellion grew: from Philadelphia came the report "dated 21 July . . . that there is a general ferment in the continental colonies." In South Carolina the state of mind was similar: "The people generally aspire to cut the shackles of their enchained liberty and are ready to oppose with every force everything that might cast a shadow of oppression."[20] In the autumn the *Notizie del mondo* became the *Gazzetta di Firenze*, but its tone did not change: "disturbances" in London, uprisings and tumults in America.[21] From the capital news of a visit by the king of Denmark was mixed with news of demonstrations and the cry "Wilkes and Liberty."[22] In New York, "the merchants . . . had resolved to follow the example of those in Boston not to receive from Great Britain any kind of merchandise, directly or indirectly."[23] If all the American colonists acted in this way the loss to Great Britain would be worth more than three million pounds sterling.[24]

After the trickle of encounters an unexpected quiet followed in 1769, even a hope of a coming reconciliation. In the House of Commons the discussion of "American affairs" and the "election of a Member of Parliament for the County of Middlesex" developed as parallel

[17] Ibid., no. 2, 27 August 1768, pp. 10ff. (London, 5 August).

[18] Ibid., no. 3, 30 August 1768, pp. 18ff. (London, 9 August).

[19] Ibid., no. 5, 6 September 1768, p. 34 (London, 19 August).

[20] Ibid., no. 12, 1 October 1768, pp. 98ff. (London, 16 September).

[21] *Notizie del mondo*, no. 18, 22 October 1768 (London, 30 September), and no. 19, 25 October 1768, p. 145 (London, 4 October).

[22] Ibid., no. 21, 1 November 1768, p. 163 (London, 14 October).

[23] Ibid., no. 23, 8 November 1768, p. 178 (London, 18 October).

[24] Ibid., no. 30, 3 December 1768, p. 235 (London, 11 November).

themes.[25] From London came word that the colonies would be treated with every possible leniency. "No doubt there will soon be a happy outcome."[26] But in the colonies the reality was different. "From Boston we hear that soldiers quartered in the city and seamen on warships in the port are in conflict and separated by mutual hatred."[27] Then, just as the conflict between Wilkes and Parliament was growing again, more reassuring news arrived. "Yesterday letters arrived from New York, which took thirty-two days to get here; they report that there is calm in Boston."[28] On both sides of the Atlantic the fundamental political problem remained of defining the powers of Parliament. "It is said," we read in a June communication, "that there is on the agenda a project to change the form of government in our American colonies, according to which those provinces would no longer be subject to the British Parliament but depend only on the Crown, like the realm of Ireland. They would have a parliament, with rights to make laws and impose taxes subject to the approval of the court. They would have their own viceroy, who would be accountable to the Crown alone. There is reason to believe that, with the approval of this project, the Americans would be content."[29] The return of Chatham to the government restored hope. Some said that "the coming year will be called the year of patriotism."[30] There was much talk "of reducing the duration of Parliament" from seven to three years.[31] Even regarding America there was a need for "an act of special clemency," of "royal authority," and "of Parliament." This was important "because commerce suffers greatly from the disputes between the capital and the colonies."[32] Not long after, even Chatham was deprived of these hopes.[33] At the end of August "the agents of the American colonies" insisted to the secretaries of state that "their affairs have become

[25] Ibid., no. 1, 3 January 1769, pp. 3ff. (London, 16 December 1768).

[26] Ibid., no. 5, 17 January 1769, p. 34 (London, 30 December).

[27] Ibid., no. 27, 4 April 1769, p. 212 (Philadelphia, 5 January). In the same days the *Nuove di diverse corti e paesi*, no. 15, 10 April 1769 (London, 23 March), spoke of the expense "caused by the sending of troops to Boston to oblige the inhabitants of New England to obey the acts of Parliament, whose object was to establish a fixed revenue in North America."

[28] *Notizie del mondo*, no. 45, 6 June 1769, p. 358 (London, 16 May). See *Nuove di diverse corti e paesi*, no. 23, 5 June 1769 (London, 16 May).

[29] *Notizie del mondo*, no. 45, 6 June 1769, p. 358 (London, 16 May). See *Nuove di diverse corti e paesi*, no. 23, 5 June 1769 (Lonon, 16 May).

[30] *Notizie del mondo*, no. 58, 22 July 1769, p. 471 (London, 27 June).

[31] Ibid., no. 60, 29 July 1769, p. 486 (London, 7 July).

[32] Ibid., no. 61, 1 August 1769, p. 494 (London, 11 July).

[33] Ibid., no. 62, 5 August 1769, p. 502 (London, 14 July) (his violent speech "against seditious spirits who . . . have attempted to divide us. . . ." "Under the veil of patriotism I see no one other than malcontents who are against their fatherland").

more and more difficult to accommodate."[34] "Trade between England
and North America is reduced. . . . only one ship has been loaded for
New York and Philadelphia and three for Carolina."[35] A "Supplement"
of the *Nuove di diverse corti e paesi* reported from London that the court
had received from North America "news that cannot be considered with
indifference. The common people of Boston have insulted officials of
the customshouse in the streets and treated them so badly that they were
obliged to find refuge in the headquarters of the garrison."[36] All this
occurred just when London was affected by high prices, workers
showed resistance, and navies of the port were agitating. Still, the year
1769 ended on another note of optimism: "The affairs of North America have taken a good turn, and it is commonly believed that Parliament
will repeal the acts that have caused so much restlessness in the colonies."[37] This, in fact, occurred, as is known, after much more shuffling.
The Townshend duties, except for the one on tea, were repealed.[38]

---

[34] Ibid., no. 74, 16 September 1769, p. 602 (London, 25 August).

[35] Ibid., no. 79, 3 October 1769, p. 645 (London, 15 September). A description of the
difficult trade situation is also in the *Gazzetta di Milano*, no. 4, 24 January 1770 (London,
2 January).

[36] *Supplimento* to the *Nuove di diverse corti e paesi*, no. 49, 4 December 1769 (London, 10
November).

[37] *Notizie del mondo*, no. 101, 19 December 1769, p. 822 (London, 28 November).

[38] The readers of the *Notizie del mondo* could follow closely the long development of
these measures: ibid., no. 15, 20 February 1770, p. 114 (London, 2 February) (American
orders to merchants in Bristol, "if Parliament will revoke the acts that impose taxes on the
Americans"); no. 17, 27 February 1770, p. 131 (London, 9 February) (London merchants
ask the Commons to "revoke the act of taxation so lamented by the Americans"); no. 22,
17 March 1770, p. 170 (London, 23 February): "On the fifth of the coming month the
petition of the Americans will be examined, and it is believed that the parliamentary acts
will be revoked that have caused so much dissension in those provinces"; no. 25, 27 March
1770, p. 194 (London, 6 March) (first reading of the revocation of the impositions; in vain
the opposition proposes that even tea be exempted); no. 35, 1 May 1770, p. 274 (London,
13 April) ("the king has signed the decree for the revocation of several duties exacted
from the colonists, but they are not content because all have not been removed"). The
readers of the *Gazzetta di Milano* were also broadly informed, although with fewer details
than readers of the *Notizie del mondo*: no. 8, 21 February 1770 (London, 2 February)
("those against the ministry move seas and mountains to support the idol of England and
martyr of liberty [Wilkes]." Lord North replaces the Duke of Grafton. "This revolution
will be very favorable to the party of the opposition, to the Americans, and to Wilkes");
no. 13, 28 March 1770 (London, 2 March) ("the pretensions of the Americans keep the
ministry troubled, which otherwise seems willing to second their petitions"); no. 14, 4
April 1770 (London, 9 March) ("it was decided to revoke all taxes imposed on those colonies, except the one on tea. The opposition party openly upholds the aims of the Americans; thus one foresees new turmoil and new misfortunes. . . . The disorder in the assemblies and tribunals of the whole kingdom is connected with an abyss of corruption and
disgrace. England's present situation is very close to what was described in other times by

But even in the *Notizie del mondo* it was clear that these differences were helping to spread beyond the ocean ideas and convictions that touched a deeper chord than that of mercantile interests and even constitutional debates. "The American-English inhabitants of the northern part of that hemisphere have prohibited entry of all English books to their parts, except the history of Mrs. Macauley, which is written in a very free style, and they call it the foundation of liberty."[39] Republicanism, which initially had been only one element in American political culture, was becoming its center. Even on an economic level it was not possible to hide the fact that relations between England and America were changing: "We have heard," it was said in January, "that much merchandise has been sent to our American colonies from France and Holland."[40] Thus there was progress toward greater and greater autonomy in economic affairs: "Such circumstances have given them an opportunity to demand permission to trade in all parts of the world; they have desired this for a long time, but up to now they have not dared demand it."[41]

Meanwhile, through a thousand conflicts, hesitations, and discussions, on 5 March 1770 the Boston Massacre occurred, leaving a deep gap between England and the colonies. The news arrived in London soon after the liberation of Wilkes from prison, who was carried triumphantly by his partisans. In all his words and deeds there was "always the same spirit of liberty that so shines out in his writings."[1] The columns of the *Gazzetta di Firenze* were full of "sentiments of liberty and patriotism" that he expressed even on this occasion. In the same issue the *Notizie del mondo* announced that the House of Commons was examining "the unfortunate news received a little earlier from New England, where there was a great tumult until the evening of the third of last March, because of three young civilians and three soldiers. The consequences of the encounter have been so great that two regiments there had to withdraw into Fort William. Consternation has spread through the whole place, and now there is talk of sending four regiments with

Dio Cassius: the government languishes, the laws are not adapted to the times and not enforced, and society maintains itself more out of habit than authority").

[39] *Notizie del mondo*, no. 97, 5 December 1769, p. 790 (London, 17 November).

[40] Ibid., no. 11, 6 February 1770, p. 82 (London, 19 January).

[41] Ibid., no. 24, 24 March 1770, p. 186 (London, 2 March).

[1] Ibid., no. 37, 8 May 1770, p. 291 (London, 20 April). See no. 38, 12 May 1770, p. 299 (London, 20 April) ("letter of April 18 to the electors of Middlesex," in which there was talk of "a most corrupt and despotic ministry, which every day has the vileness to give desperate blows to the vital parts of the constitution").

four warships."[2] "The court has sent instructions to General Gage, who commands our troops in America, to quiet the aforementioned disorders in Boston."[3] In the Commons the seesaw between those who wanted moderation and "temperament" and those who demanded severe punishment was revived, adding that tolerance "would only serve to incite more audacious attempts to gain independence."[4] The debate was prolonged. "The slaughter in Boston" seemed for a moment to have parted the veil and made colonial independence seem attainable.[5] Certainly agitation was gaining more autonomy on both sides of the ocean. In the Commons "Mr. Burke, the celebrated orator and author of *Thoughts on the Present Discontents*, attempted to indicate possible solutions. Alexander Wedderburn asserted: "We conquered America in the reign of Charles II, and in the reign of George III we have lost it, since it can no longer be considered part of the British empire." "Lord Selburne spoke with much vivacity and spirit. . . . Lord Chatham proposed again to prorogue the current Parliament, but this did not go to the vote."[6]

Wilkes, although he made a great effort, was no longer at the center of the political discussion. He sought and found support in the City, but greater problems were pressing.[7] Even as a publicist, another writer with the pseudonymous name Junius became the sentry and was continually cited, even in Italian journals.[8] In America the colonists raised an inalterable principle: only "provincial assemblies" would be able to impose taxes.[9] Thus they sent back the tea that had arrived from England.[10] "The general assembly of the Province of Massachusetts Bay," convoked on 7 June in Boston, openly disobeyed Governor Hutchin-

[2] Ibid., no. 39, 15 May 1770, p. 307 (London, 27 April).

[3] Ibid., no. 40, 19 May 1770, p. 314 (London, 27 April).

[4] Ibid., no. 41, 22 May 1770, p. 331 (London, 4 May).

[5] Ibid., no. 44, 2 June 1770, p. 363 (London, 11 May).

[6] Ibid., no. 45, 5 June 1770, p. 372 (London, 15 May). *Thoughts on the cause of the present discontents* was published in London by J. Dodsley in 1770. On A. Wedderburn, see Valentine, *The British Establishment*, vol. 2, pp. 914ff.

[7] Ibid., no. 77, 25 September 1770, p. 630 (London, 7 September): "The nation's enthusiasm for him is much diminished."

[8] See, for example, *La gazzetta di Milano*, no. 11, 10 January 1770 (London, 10 December 1769): "The noted satirical writer who with the name Junius has attacked the ministry with a license that would be energetically suppressed in any other land. . . ."

[9] *Notizie del mondo*, no. 54, 7 July 1770, p. 442 (London, 15 June).

[10] Ibid., no. 55, 10 July 1770, p. 450 (London, 19 July); no. 58, 21 July 1770, p. 474 (London, 29 June); no. 61, 31 July 1770, p. 499 (London, 13 July) ("it is calculated that through these differences our nation loses one thousand guineas a day, besides the rights that should belong to the government"). See *La gazzetta di Milano*, no. 17, 25 April 1770, "the women of Boston have formed an association in which they have bound themselves to make no future use of tea" until it is free of all taxes.

son.[11] It was now a question of force. It was said that "the restive colonies" would be "forced to obedience by arms."[12] Ships and troops would subdue "those who do not want to submit to the laws of the British Parliament."[13]

Then, almost without one's being aware of it, the tension diminished. Today historians still discuss the reasons for the truce established tacitly between the end of 1770 and the end of 1773 (the Boston Tea Party took place on 16 December 1773).[14] These were years of economic recovery and commercial prosperity: in the ports of the Atlantic people preferred to pay the existing taxes and submit to the limits the English Parliament continued to impose rather than to see a profitable trade ended again. Still, there were incidents, often caused by the inefficiency and corruption of those sent from London to enforce the economic policy of the mother country. The narrative of these incidents brought to light an essential fact: the central points of the problem had arisen at the beginning of the seventies. The colonies had by no means renounced their self-administration and their defense of what in the past had been their privileges, which now were taking on in their eyes more and more the form and value of rights.

It seems certain that the first work printed on the European continent intended to provide a general picture of American grievances was the *Précis de l'état actuel des colonies angloises dans l'Amérique Septentrionale.* To it was added, in an appendix, the declaration Franklin made before the House of Commons in 1767. It was in fact printed, one reads on the cover, by the bookseller Reycends, in Milan, in 1771.[15] The author was Domenic von Blackford, a friend of Caminer and of Pelli, whom we have encountered earlier; he was also the translator of the *Essai sur la littérature russe*, which appeared in Livorno, also in 1771, at the time of the Orlov expedition to the Mediterranean. This is a small and significant symbol of the curiosity that united the entire European world, from Russia to the American colonies. As one sees, an able journalist of German origin such as D. von Blackford could have published in Milan,

---

[11] *Notizie del mondo*, no. 65, 14 August 1770, p. 531 (London, 27 July). See no. 82, 13 October 1770, p. 668 (London, 21 September).

[12] Ibid., no. 73, 11 September 1770, p. 597 (London, 24 August).

[13] Ibid., no. 74, 15 September 1770, p. 605 (London, 23 August).

[14] For this period as well, see the small, but intelligent and perceptive book by Edmund S. Morgan, *The Birth of the Republic* (Chicago: University of Chicago Press, 1956), pp. 51ff.

[15] Piero del Negro has studied and described it in "Saggio di una bibliografia delle opere relative agli Stati Uniti apparse in Italia nel Settecento," in Spini et al., *Italia e America*, pp. 151ff., where nonetheless the identity of the author is not given.

in French, the first tally sheet of American aspirations and, in French, in Livorno, the first history of Russian literature.[16]

A symbol—of a quite different importance—of this cosmopolitan vision, which continued to expand on the other side of the Atlantic Ocean as well, was Benjamin Franklin. Even in Italy there were numerous testimonials to the admiration that surrounded him.[17] Let us add another little testimony to the many that have been collected. In the *Gazzetta di Milano* of September 1772 a correspondent from Paris provided news that was distorted by a printing error but nevertheless revealing: "The Royal Academy of Sciences has elected as a new foreign associate in place of the late Baron Vanswietten, Mr. Tranklin [*sic*] of Philadelphia."[18] The celebrated doctor of Maria Theresa, the censor of the Austrian empire, was replaced by a scientist from Philadelphia. A generation had passed. The world had changed and grown. The *Gazzetta universale*, at the beginning of 1774, wrote that "the name of Mr. Franklin is equally celebrated in this and the other hemisphere. He is one of the greatest geniuses of our century."[19]

But the American ferment was not destined to dissolve into radiant cosmopolitan visions. At the beginning of 1773 the gazette of Mantova received "bad news from London." The American "people" were taking "measures to protect themselves from the despotic acts of the governors and other civil and military officials kept there by our court."[20] The *Notizie del mondo* reported incidents in Rhode Island.[21] The same journal did not fail to note another significant phenomenon of those years: the growing Scottish and Irish emigration to America.[22] As for the colonies, it seemed almost normal that "all the provincial assemblies" had established "a regular correspondence" among themselves in order to communicate "the deliberations of the British Parliament with regard to the colonies and to consult on the measures to take."[23] The new reality ma-

---

[16] Venturi, "Qui est le traducteur de l'Essai sur la littérature russe?" pp. 217ff.

[17] See Antonio Pace, *Benjamin Franklin and Italy* (Philadelphia: American Philosophical Society, 1958); del Negro, *Il mito americano*; Carlo Mangio, "Illuministi italiani e rivoluzione americana," in Spini et al., *Italia e America*, p. 46 and the index.

[18] *Gazzetta di Milano*, no. 38, 16 September 1772 (Paris, 27 August).

[19] *Gazzetta universale*, no. 6, 18 January 1774, p. 46, *Notizie letterarie* (review of Franklin's *Oeuvres*, translated by Jacques Barbeu du Bourg).

[20] *Mantova*, no. 8, 19 February 1773 (London, 29 January).

[21] *Notizie del mondo*, no. 21, 13 March 1773, p. 161 (London, 19 February).

[22] Ibid., no. 38, 11 May 1773, p. 300 (London, 20 April); no. 61, 31 July 1773, p. 482 (London, 9 July) ("the emigration of Scots and Irish for North America has been so frequent and in such numbers for some time that the government is justifiably perturbed. Such emigration is the cause of the decline of cloth manufacture and of the resolution of many to raise considerably the price of their goods").

[23] *Notizie del mondo*, no. 62, 3 August 1773, p. 490 (London, 13 June).

tured rapidly. Projects for a new "plan of legislation for the colonies were begun." New York would become "the capital of that continent . . . and every colony would maintain representatives in the general assembly in the same way as in the British Parliament." "America becomes more and more populous and provides itself with the means to have no need of Great Britain." In vain Hutchinson explained, when confronted with similar hopes, that it was necessary to have "moderation in what is called Anglican liberty."[24] Soon he was obliged to give up and to request "to return to England."[25]

The "spirit of opposition" was growing in the colonies. New "confederations" kept being formed among them, intended to "try different officials of the Crown who . . . had usurped in those parts an authority incompatible" with traditional Britannic liberty.[26] At the beginning of 1774 the news from New York could not help but "concern the government of the India Company for the total refusal of those inhabitants to accept tea. . . . On 5 November in different places a gallows on a cart was carried about, which had an effigy whose chest had a painted teapot with the words 'tea, three shillings a pound of tax' and other signs and inscriptions, all expressing the disdain of the people for such impositions." Ten days later one read the following: "The price of stock of the India Company has fallen noticeably."[27]

The first news that reached Italy (with the usual gap of about two months) of the Boston Tea Party, of the destruction, that is, on 16 December 1773, of a cargo of tea that had arrived in Boston Harbor, seemed at first just another riot. "The people, in less than four hours, threw into the sea all the tea, consisting of 342 cases, without damaging the ship or other merchandise. It is thought that the same will take place in Philadelphia and New York."[1] But minds were prepared, in the win-

[24] Ibid., no. 67, 21 August 1773, p. 530 (London, 30 July).

[25] Ibid., no. 73, 11 September 1773, p. 594 (London, 20 August). See ibid., no. 59, 23 July 1774, p. 466 (London, 1 July) (arrival in England). The *Gazzetta universale* paid attention to his politics and his misfortunes in no. 53, 2 July 1774, p. 417 (London, 10 June). On these developments, see Bailyn, *The Ordeal of Thomas Hutchinson*, pp. 221ff.

[26] *Gazzetta universale*, no. 5, 15 January 1774, pp. 33ff. (London, 24 December 1773).

[27] Ibid., no. 11, 5 February 1774, p. 81 (London, 14 January), and no. 14, 15 February 1774, p. 106 (London, 25 January).

[1] *Notizie del mondo*, no. 13, 12 February 1774, p. 97 (London, 21 January). In no. 15, 19 February 1774, p. 114 (London, 28 January), one read the following in the same gazette: "The day before yesterday a ship of our nation arrived in the Thames with 600 cases of tea aboard destined for Philadelphia, but this was sent back since unloading them there is forbidden." In no. 21, 12 March 1774, p. 161 (London, 18 February), one read: "The inhabitants of Charles-town have followed the example of those of New York: on 31

ter of 1773–1774, to receive this news as the announcement of a revolution. The international framework in which these distant events were inserted underscored their tragedy: the first news of the Pugačev revolt appeared side by side with the news from Massachusetts. One was used to news of the refusal to pay taxes imposed by the English Parliament, which the American colonists had practiced in different forms for many years. What was new was the political will emerging behind these acts of resistance. It was becoming clearer in London how difficult it would be "to repress the disobedience of the Americans." "The business is becoming very serious. If we are to believe the news from those parts, the colonies of New England, New York, Pennsylvania, Carolina, and Rhode Island are ready to raise 100,000 men to oppose our troops."[2] Soon after the *Notizie del mondo* referred to talk in London of "sending troops and warships to the colonies to put down their audacity and make them return to their duty." "But it is necessary to consider seriously the state things are in before using force against the Americans. In fact, the latest news is that all the colonies have taken up arms to protect their privilege of being taxed only by their own assemblies. The inhabitants of Boston and Philadelphia encourage each other to break relations with the British government." The governors were on the defensive. "They have deployed the few troops they have in order to prevent disorders and popular uprisings, placed artillery before their houses, and brought armed ships in the ports so as to at least halt the discontent in those parts."[3] In February there was word of 240,000 men the colonists could use against "any attempt our troops might make if the government should resolve to reduce the colonists to obedience through force."[4] In reporting these figures the *Notizie del mondo* wrote that this force could have become even greater if it proved true that "the Americans have resolved to give out free land to any soldiers sent there from England, Scotland, or Ireland."[5]

What should have been done? This question was much discussed in England during the spring and summer of 1774. The debates and official resolutions were widely reported in the Florentine journals, in the *Gazzetta universale*, as well as in the *Notizie del mondo*. George III thundered against the "insufferable cabals and stratagems thus far put into

December they voluntarily carried all their tea into the marketplace and burned it in sight of everyone."

[2] *Gazzetta universale*, no. 14, 15 February 1774, p. 106 (London, 25 January). The same news in the *Nuove di diverse corti e paesi*, no. 7, 14 February 1774, p. 54 (London, 28 January).

[3] *Notizie del mondo*, no. 17, 26 February 1774, p. 130 (London, 4 February).

[4] *Gazzetta universale*, no. 19, 5 March 1774, p. 145 (London, 11 February).

[5] *Notizie del mondo*, no. 19, 5 March 1774, p. 145 (London, 11 February).

operation by the North Americans."[6] The suspicion began to grow that
"in such a combustion of things a power jealous of our greatness could
easily profit from these disturbances to place itself in possession of several fine provinces in North America."[7] The proposal to punish the port
of Boston by prohibiting any shipping evoked opposition, or, as the *Notizie del mondo* reported, "much disagreement."[8] That would have caused
"the ruin, or rather total destruction of that place." It would be better
to be content with a fine. There was the grave risk that these punitive
measures would encourage the colonists to assist one another.[9] Americans living in London "made every effort to have suspended the decree
depriving Boston of its commerce."[10] Boston, meanwhile, responded
with a kind of legal schism "obliging all the judges of the province, except Mr. Oliver, who is of their party, to sign a solemn act concluding
that the laws of Great Britain have no legal force in that part of America."[11] American firmness met continual hesitation and uncertainty in
London. The words were haughty and violent, but the deeds slow and
halting. Even launching the fleet that was to punish the rebels was delayed, to "know the effect the strong resolution taken against them will
have on the colonists."[12] The debate in London became more heated.[13]
"In the time some take here to maintain the dependency of the colonies,
others hold that the Americans are ill-treated and protest in a sensible
manner that the conduct of the ministry toward them can be considered
so many attempts made against their liberty and patience, and that they
are right to act in consequence." If the differences grow worse "the results may prove dangerous to both sides."[14] Resistance became stronger
in the House of Commons. "Several Members of Parliament observe
that there is an intention in the colonies to introduce a form of military
government and thus raise strong opposition. . . . Lord Chatham, called

---

[6] Ibid., no. 26, 29 March 1774, p. 202 (London, 8 March).

[7] *Gazzetta universale*, 29 March 1774, p. 202 (London, 8 March). This sheet, like the
Notizie del mondo, echoed in the following months the possiblity of a French and Spanish
intervention.

[8] *Notizie del mondo*, no. 28, 5 April 1774, p. 218 (London, 15 March).

[9] *Gazzetta universale*, no. 30, 12 April 1774, p. 234 (London, 28 March).

[10] Ibid., no. 32, 19 April 1774, p. 249 (London, 29 March). In no. 41, 21 May 1774,
p. 321 (29 April), the same sheet reported that "the act against the city of Boston" had
been adopted by 95 votes to 32.

[11] *Notizie del mondo*, no. 29, 9 April 1774, p. 226 (London, 18 March).

[12] *Gazzetta universale*, no. 33, 23 April 1774, p. 257 (London, 1 April).

[13] See, for example, *Notizie del mondo*, no. 41, 21 May 1774, p. 322 (London, 29 April).

[14] *Notizie del mondo*, no. 30, 12 April 1774, p. 235 (London, 22 March). The *Nuove di
diverse corti e paesi*, no. 19, 9 May 1774, p. 149 (London, 22 April), wrote: "The measure is
currently at its climax and a drop more would give the final push to the fury of the Americans."

in public gazettes the comet of his country, . . . loudly condemned the conduct of the Americans but declared that the measures the ministry took were rigid, oppressive, and tyrannical."[15] The growing emigration to the New World was viewed with anxiety. A series of articles made even Italian readers aware that England was suffering continually the loss of artisans and workmen leaving their homeland to seek a better life. The propaganda intended to slow their steps was ineffective. In vain it was reported that "the larger part of those who go to settle in Pennsylvania are sold as slaves and treated as brutes."[16] In fact, the emigration was assuming significance and political weight.[17] "One cannot call a project to form an independent empire in the New World chimerical if one reflects on the great number of persons passing from this realm and from Ireland to establish themselves in our American colonies." There were reportedly 20,000 in Pennsylvania, "and similar proportions in all the other colonies." Developments in recent months show a similar trend. "This proves," the *Gazzetta universale* concluded, "that the colonists are heading toward independence and are ready to repel force with force."[18]

"The Americans risk everything in order to preserve their liberty."[19] Not only that, but in Boston the number of incidents directed against "royal officials and those inhabitants who adhere to the British government" grew, and still more important, the colonies began to establish the basis for a "general convention."[20] "The colony of Pennsylvania, one of the largest, moved by the fate of the inhabitants of Boston, whose commerce is threatened with destruction, has advised them in a letter to be firm, prudent, and moderate in all they do in order to preserve the common liberty."[21] The authoritarian acts of the English government only justified the colonists' resistance. "The proclamation of General Gage . . . has had an unfortunate effect."[22] "It is generally thought that this severity will have bad consequences, despite the fact that the party of

---

[15] *Gazzetta universale*, no. 48, 14 June 1774, p. 378 (London, 27 May).

[16] Ibid., no. 29, 9 April 1774, p. 226 (London, 18 March).

[17] See ibid., no. 65, 13 August 1774, p. 514 (London, 22 July), where there was talk that 43,720 Irish had emigrated since 25 July 1769. Numerous also were "the English, Scots, Germans, and inhabitants of the Isle of Man." The *Notizie del mondo*, no. 88, 1 November 1774, p. 698 (London, 11 October), said there had formed "in Spitalfields a society called Migrants. Each member paid six shillings a week for the cost of the passage to America. None would embark until the necessary sum had been collected to transport the whole society. The contributions of those who die remain for the benefit of the survivors."

[18] *Gazzetta universale*, no. 52, 28 June 1774, p. 411 (London, 7 June).

[19] Ibid., no. 53, 2 July 1774, p. 417 (London, 10 June).

[20] Ibid., no. 55, 9 July 1774, p. 434 (London, 17 June).

[21] Ibid., no. 64, 9 August 1774, p. 506 (London, 19 July).

[22] Ibid., no. 74, 13 September 1774, p. 586 (London, 23 August).

the ministry prides itself on perfect submission."[23] "New York, Pennsylvania, Maryland, and Virginia" declared their solidarity with Boston.[24] The government of Boston, transferred to Salem, widened its influence.[25] All were impatient "to know what the deliberations of the provincial assembly were," which had also transferred to Salem.[26] They read the answer in the *Nuove di diverse corti e paesi*: "The colonies are unanimously resolved not to submit to taxes of Parliament if these are not established by their provincial assemblies." On these bases, in Salem "resolution becomes stronger daily.... People go in crowds to the churches to sign their agreement on the communion tables, where is written *pro aris, pro focis*" (for altars and hearths).[27] In Philadelphia, while still denying the idea of independence, the provincial assembly continued to establish its own administration and to support the resistance of Boston.[28] In all parts now, noted the *Gazzetta universale*, they are preparing for the "general congress to be held in Philadelphia to protest what the ministry of Great Britain has ordered."[29] The "deputies from the colonies" had already set out.[30]

There were plenty of people, even in the mother country, who continued to sympathize with the colonists, to seek a policy of understanding and indulgence, and even to admire the decision and courage of the Americans. But the situation was quite different from what it had been at the end of the sixties, in everything concerning the relationship between internal English politics and the American rebellion. In the autumn of 1774 all the gazettes, even the Italian ones, were full of Wilkes's electoral speeches and of his triumph in Middlesex as a candidate for

[23] *Notizie del mondo*, no. 55, 9 July 1774, p. 434 (London, 17 June).

[24] Ibid., no. 56, 12 July 1774, p. 442 (London, 21 June).

[25] Ibid., no. 58, 19 July 1774, p. 457 (London, 28 June). See Ibid., no. 77, 24 September 1774, p. 611 (London, 2 September).

[26] Ibid., no. 62, 2 August 1774, p. 490 (London, 12 July).

[27] *Nuove di diverse corti e paesi*, no. 37, 12 September 1774, p. 295 (London, 26 August). See *Gazzetta universale*, no. 74, 13 September 1774, p. 586 (London, 23 August). In this report the expression "sign the agreement" is given as "join the league."

[28] *Nuove di diverse corti e paesi*, no. 40, 3 October 1774, p. 319 (London, 16 September). See no. 45, 7 November 1774, p. 359 (London, 21 October), and no. 47, 21 November 1774, p. 374 (London, 1 November). (The general congress in Philadelphia has approved the "conduct of Bostonians to not want to submit to the new law of Parliament. Thus it ordered a general contribution in all North America to indemnify the damage to their commerce and for their subsistence, for as long as circumstances require this." They were asked to abstain from any "disorder," "but at the same time to show that firmness which can make their enemies understand that for a cause so important to the liberty of the country they should behave in such a manner as to merit the approval of all wise men in any free land.")

[29] *Gazzetta universale*, no. 78, 27 September 1774, p. 617 (London, 9 September).

[30] *Notizie del mondo*, no. 78, 27 September 1774, p. 618 (London, 6 September).

the prestigious office of Lord Mayor of London. He went from victory to victory. The governing class had finally accepted him as a recipient of its favors. But he was still the champion of the antiministerial party, and he did not hide his sympathies for the colonists across the ocean. He always presented himself as the "intrepid defender of the English constitution" and never tired of talking about this theme.[31] But it was precisely this which separated him from the Americans. They did not accept the authority of Parliament. Wilkes affirmed it (even while holding that this authority should be exercised in a different manner). The defense of the constitution, and of liberty, was for him the first (and, in some sense, the only) end of his actions. In Boston and Philadelphia there was a scrambling search in a new direction. Wilkes's direction led to the preservation of English constitutional liberty and to radical reform. As the *Gazzetta universale* wrote, Wilkes had become the "*gonfaloniere*" (the Tuscan translation of the title Lord Mayor) of London and had thus entered the old political structure, which he expected to utilize and change, and certainly not cut down or destroy.[32] The position of the colonies led instead, with rapid steps, to civil war and independence. While the tensions became greater in New England, Wilkes fought a rear-guard action in defense of English republicanism. When it was a question of deciding in the London Council whether to celebrate the

[31] See, for example, the electoral platform of Wilkes and Glynn in *Notizie del mondo*, no. 85, 22 October 1774, p. 675 (London, 30 September), and Wilkes's two-hour speech after his election as Lord Mayor, in *Nuove di diverse corti e paesi*, no. 44, 1 November 1774, p. 351 (London, 14 October), where, after having described the celebration for Wilkes, Boston was spoken of: "Everyone predicts that we are about to see a civil war break out in America if the new Parliament does not resolve to take the means to calm agitated spirits." See also *Notizie del mondo*, no. 89, 5 November 1774, pp. 707ff. (London, 14 October).

[32] See, for example, *Gazzetta universale*, no. 34, 29 April 1775, p. 265 (London, 7 April): "It was resolved in a general assembly convoked by the Lord Mayor Wilkes and the council of this city to present to the king a humble petition as a request and to demand of His Majesty, in the most respectful terms, to hear the lament of their fellow citizens in America caused by the recent acts of Parliament, since the petitioners must also experience similar damages, as a mercantile nation. . . ." They then requested that "the ministers who had proposed such measures be dismissed from his councils." "It was established that Lord Chatham and Mr. Burke should be thanked for the plans made by them for a reconciliation between the British government and the colonies." In the end it was concluded "that the resolutions regarding the election in Middlesex be erased from the registers, where the election of Mr. Wilkes was disallowed for representation of that county." When these words were printed in the gazette, no one in Florence would have known that the civil war in New England had in fact begun ten days earlier, on 29 April 1775. The *Gazzetta universale*, no. 84, 21 October 1775, p. 666 (London, 29 September), concluded that "the Americans could not have worse advocates than the Middlesex councilors. . . . All is animosity in their meetings. They are filled with the injuries they say Mr. Wilkes has done to them in the recent election, and they sacrifice to their passions and to a spirit of revenge."

"anniversary of the martyrdom of King Charles I," Wilkes opposed the matter "and applied the words of Milton to that king, *ipso Nerone neronior* (more Neronian than Nero himself), but finally with a plurality of 112 votes to 83 it was resolved to observe the holiday."[33] His action in favor of the Americans took the form of a solemn remonstrance presented to George III, full of eloquent words, but unable to influence the situation.[34]

As in all of Europe during these years, in the British world those who had a sense of institutions, of rights, of the constitution, and of liberty, in contrast with the absolutist state, often lacked a sense of the necessity to reform and the need even to utilize the state mechanism to change society and the economy. This was the case in Sweden in the "time of liberty," in France of the Parlements, and in Poland of the confederations. From this point of view the divorce between the English Parliament and the American colonists was only a confirmation of the general ineptitude shown, in the late eighteenth century, by archaic oligarchic and "republican" structures to change and reform themselves and society at large. The great novelty, the great difference, between British and American experience on one hand consisted of the fact that, in the end, England preserved and maintained a parliamentary and constitutional tradition; on the other hand—no less important—beyond the ocean the need for reform was for the first time embodied not in a sovereign, a state, or even a group of philosophers, party, or sect, but in a people, capable of preserving the indelible imprint of British liberty, but abandoning, if only partially and with difficulty, the privileges this had assumed in the mother country. For the first time there was an organic union of the desire for a constitution—which was alive in the English governing class as much as it was in the plebs of London who applauded Wilkes, in the tradition of "true Whigs," in the ideas of Locke, "commonwealthmen," and "classical republicans"—with the desire for equality and the new ideals of the European Enlightenment that had also slowly but deeply penetrated beyond the ocean. It was not by chance that the most famous figure among the colonists was Benjamin Franklin, or that the drafter of the Declaration of Independence was Jefferson, the most enlightened American. It was precisely this tempestuous fusion of the constitutional and the reform elements, of tradition and Enlightenment innovation, that made the American Revolution the only victor among the many movements that emerged and erupted

[33] *Notizie del mondo*, no. 15, 21 February 1775, p. 113 (London, 1 February).

[34] Ibid., no. 35, 2 May 1775, pp. 273ff. (London, 11 April) (where the text of the remonstrance is printed in full).

from Russia to Poland, from Sweden to France, in the first general crisis
of the old regime.

The autumn and the winter of 1774–1775 again were a period of
waiting—the last—before the definitive split between the colonies and
the mother country. The atmosphere was particularly confused and uncertain. Under a continual menace of repression the organs of self-government in the colonies became consolidated. But in the English government the hope of taking in hand again men and things which tended
more and more to operate autonomously was not dead. "The affairs in
Boston and the whole continent," we read at the beginning of November in the *Notizie del mondo*, "are in a state of extreme confusion. All civil
officials have refused to take part in the execution of parliamentary acts
concerning the colonies and have signed a declaration in that regard.
The administration of justice is almost suspended. Discontents spread
the fires of discord everywhere. Americans in general, and those in Massachusetts in particular, have in effect raised the standard of rebellion.
The inhabitants of Boston on one side and the royal troops on the other
are constantly on the watch. It seems that each party only awaits the
moment to decide their differences with arms."[1] General Gage, in Boston, brought out his cannon. But the inhabitants stood firm, comforted
by promises of assistance and defense "from nearby cities" in case of
attack. In London, despite the growing tension, works openly favorable
to Americans continued to appear. Even the imminent outbreak of civil
war did not suspend freedom of the press. "A small book has appeared,"
one reads in the *Notizie del mondo* on 12 November, "entitled *American
independence the interest and glory of Great Britain*. This work tended to
demonstrate that in matters of taxation, as well as in commerce, manufacture, and government, the colonies had the right to be totally independent from British legislation."[2] How was it possible to tolerate that
much audacity in opposing the policy of government? the *Gazzetta uni-*

---

[1] *Notizie del mondo*, no. 89, 5 November 1774, p. 707 (London, 14 October). See also
no. 94, 22 November, pp. 748ff. (London, 1 November).

[2] Ibid., no. 91, 12 November 1774, p. 722 (London, 21 October). This was the work
by the famous radical polemicist John Cartwright, *American independence the interest and
glory of Great Britain; or, Arguments to prove that not only in taxation, but in trade, manufactures
and government the colonies are entitled to an entire independency of the British legislature and that
it can only be by a formal declaration of these rights and forming thereupon a friendly league with
them that the true and lasting welfare of both countries can be promoted. In a series of letters to the
legislature. To which are added copious notes, containing reflexions on the Boston and Quebec acts
and a full justification of the people of Boston for destroying the British-taxed tea, submitted to the
judgment not of those who have none but borrowed party-opinions, but the candid and honest* (London: Printed for the author by H. S. Woodfall, 1774).

versale asked at the beginning of the following year. In February a pamphlet entitled *The Present Crisis with Respect to America Considered* came out, as well as number 3 of the periodical the *Crisis*. "We do not know what to think when we see two works that are so little likely to calm spirits appear together." "The first, which was published by Thomas Becker, is no more than the second part of a book that was published a short time ago; the other is a weekly sheet opposing the government, but its editor cannot but please the ministry by demonstrating the need for censorship of the press, which was introduced during the reign of Charles II and abolished by the same prince as contrary to the rights of free citizens and the constitution."[3] Nor were works quite different from those just indicated lacking in London, like the one "written against the colonists" entitled *The interest of the merchants and manufacturers of Great Britain*, which the *Notizie del mondo* summarized at length in March 1775. The colonists appeared to be ungrateful in the eyes of the merchants of the mother country. Their arguments finally brought this out explicitly: "Up to now we have made our fortune by making use of your capital and good will. Now we expect to enjoy it as we like and increase it as much as possible; do not involve yourselves more than necessary in our affairs." The "merchants and manufacturers" could not help interpreting the revolt in the colonies as a "potential ruin of their commerce and loss of their funds."[4]

The pamphlet by Samuel Johnson, *Taxation no tyranny; an answer to the revolutions and address of the American Congress*, proceeded in the same direction, but with a different energy. It was amply reviewed in *Notizie del mondo*. This recognized how deep were the roots of the idea that any taxation required the consent of those to whom it was applied. "The

[3] *Gazzetta universale*, no. 23, 21 March 1775, p. 178 (London, 28 February). *The Crisis* of William Moore came out in 91 issues between 1775 and 1776; it was openly favorable to American independence. This journal was called "a false libel, infamous and seditious, likely to alienate the affection of subjects from their sovereign and government and to disturb the peace of the realm." The two Houses condemned it to be "burned by the public executioner." On *The present crisis with respect to America considered* (London: T. Becket, 1775), "a peer in the party of opposition" noted that "pernicious maxims of this kind had cost two of our kings dearly," *Notizie del mondo*, no. 23, 21 March 1775, p. 179 (London, 27 February). See also ibid., no. 32, 22 April 1775, pp. 250ff. (London, 31 March).

[4] *Notizie del mondo*, no. 19, 7 March 1775, pp. 150ff. (London, 14 February). This was the work of William Knox, *The interest of the merchants and manufacturers of Great Britain* (London: T. Cadell, 1774), and numerous other editions. A work by the same author, *The present state of the nation*, which appeared in 1768 in various editions, was translated into Italian by Michele Torcia with the title *Stato presente della nazione inglese soprattuto concernente il suo commercio e le sue finanze, diretto al re ed alle due Camere del Parlamento* (Naples: V. Flauto, 1775).

people will not refuse to pay taxes required for the common good. . . . Do they not have the right to examine and judge their necessity?" But one should not confuse the right to control taxation with legislative power. "There is a distinction between legislative right and the right to grant subsidies." "Now the Americans, not having any deputies in this House, are not represented in it." But they could not for this reason consider themselves exempt from taxation. Even in this they had the duty to respect the British constitution. "The sovereign who receives his authority from his subjects does not obtain it except on certain conditions; there has been a contract between them and the prince which cannot be altered; now this contract exists in England, and it is perhaps the only land where there is a similar one." In other lands it had been cancelled or hidden. It was precisely because of this constitutional character that England was right in taxing the colonists, whereas these were guilty of "rebellion."[5]

Confronted with the brilliant light of the British political climate and economy, Florentine journalists paid more and more attention to what was said and done on both sides of the Atlantic and continually sought out new sources of information. In April 1775 the *Notizie del mondo* published a long review of the Reverend Andrew Burnaby's *Travels through the middle settlements in North America in the years 1759 and 1760*. Rev. Burnaby was well known in Tuscany; he had lived for some time in Livorno and had been in close contact with Pasquale Paoli. He expressed the anxiety of having to choose between England and America, to both of which he felt closely bound, and he felt they should never be separated from one another. With the hope of a coming reconciliation he provided detailed information about the current economic and political situation in the colonies.[6] The *Notizie del mondo* looked with hope to Franklin until the end. If he had delayed his departure for Philadelphia, they wrote in November, it was because by staying where he was he might still be useful as an intermediary. "At the time he was to depart, a Lord requested that he come to his house, and after a long conference persuaded him of the need to delay his voyage until after the opening of Parliament, where he promised to do all he could to reduce things to a happy reconciliation."[7] Vain hopes. The reality (expressed by the *Gaz-*

---

[5] *Notizie del mondo*, no. 48, 17 June 1775, pp. 378ff. (London, 26 May).

[6] Ibid., no. 29, 11 April 1775, p. 226 (London, 21 March); no. 31, 18 April 1775, pp. 244ff. (London, 28 March); and no. 33, 25 April 1775, pp. 260ff. (London, 4 April). No. 47, 13 June 1775, pp. 370ff. (London, 23 May), published the "Descrizione della provincia di Massachuset's-Bay, estratta dai Viaggi recentemente pubblicati dal sig. Burnaby." ("The character of the inhabitants of this province is very polished in comparison with what it was, but puritanism and a certain spirit of persecution are not entirely extinct," p. 372.)

[7] Ibid., no. 98, 6 December 1774, p. 778 (London, 15 November). The same notice was in the *Gazzetta universale*, no. 98, 6 December 1774, p. 777 (London, 15 November).

zetta universale at the beginning of the year) was that Massachusetts had already become "an independent government."[8] A few days later it added: "The general congress in Philadelphia has published its first resolutions," approving what had been done in Massachusetts and recommending that "all the colonies follow its example."[9] In vain General Gage sought to restore understanding with the Bostonians, explaining that "Great Britain could not conceive of the idea of destroying or reducing to slavery any people of the world." And in vain, at the same time, in London, the "antiministerial party" attempted to stay the hand of the "party of the court."[10] In America, the military problem took precedence over any other, on both sides. General Gage was everyone's adversary, "because of which he remains armed day and night for fear of being surprised."[11] He made every effort to disband the militia that the provincial assembly sitting in Cambridge had established in October 1774.[12] In all, throughout the colonies, similar militias "amount to 60,000 men."[13] The "provincial congress of Massachusetts, in its meetings of 5, 9 and 10 December, had approved without reservation all that had been concluded and resolved by the general congress in Philadelphia . . . and recommended that its inhabitants persist in their resolution 'to triumph or die in defense of the country.' "[14] Local incidents multiplied. "Some letters from Boston that arrived by way of Edinburgh report that the people of Salem set fire to the house of a person they hated; that the flames spread to the customshouse and consumed it en-

---

[8] *Gazzetta universale*, no. 1, 3 January 1775, p. 3 (London, 13 December 1774).

[9] Ibid., no. 2, 7 January 1775, p. 11 (London, 16 December 1774). The complete text of the "famous resolution of the congress of Philadelphia" is in the *Notizie del mondo*, no. 5, 17 January 1775, pp. 34ff. (London, 27 December 1774); no. 7, 24 January 1775, pp. 51ff. (London, 3 January); no. 8, 28 January 1775, pp. 58ff. (London, 6 January); and 31 January 1775, pp. 66ff. (London, 10 January).

[10] *Notizie del mondo*, no. 3, 10 January 1775, pp. 18ff. (London, 20 December 1774). On internal differences in the English governing class, see ibid., no. 6, 21 January 1775, p. 43 (London, 30 December). On the efforts of Lord Chatham, supported by Shelburne, Camden, the Duke of Richmond, and the Marquis of Rockingham, to reach a "happy accommodation," see no. 13, (14 February) (with ample information on the parliamentary debate), and no. 18, 4 March 1775, pp. 137ff. (London, 10 February) (discussion in the House of Peers). On the intervention of Lord North on 20 February 1775 in "a harangue with mixed expressions of candor and firmness, of threats and promises, of war and peace," arousing the responses of Colonel Barré and of Edmund Burke, who interpreted it as "an effort to divide the colonies," see no. 21, 14 March 1775, p. 162 (London, 21 February). "Finally the plan of the ministry is formed and it will be unalterably executed," the government declared at the end of March, no. 32, 22 April 1775, p. 250 (London, 31 March).

[11] *Gazzetta universale*, no. 6, 21 January 1775, p. 45 (London, 30 January).

[12] Ibid., no. 8, 28 January 1775, p. 58 (London, 6 January).

[13] Ibid., no. 10, 4 February 1775, p. 74 (London, 13 January).

[14] *Notizie del mondo*, no. 10, 4 February 1775, p. 77 (London, 13 January).

tirely, along with twenty other houses, and many lost their lives; that two
regiments of General Gage's troops had deserted to join those inhabitants; and that everything, in short, is in disorder there." The situation
was not better in the "Island of Rhodes," that is, Rhode Island.[15] "This
is a fire that smolders sullenly under the ashes and could break out with
more violence."[16] "One can see clearly," the *Gazzetta universale* wrote,
"that in the colonies there are persons who want to take things in hand
and shed blood."[17] If New England remained the center of agitation,
the state of mind of the other colonies was not more peaceful. "Virginia
now has at arms 15,000 infantrymen, 1,000 cavalry, and 5,000 freed
Negroes. It was reported in a letter written from Baltimore, Maryland,
in December that the provincial assembly had occupied the arsenal, with
15,000 weapons and a great quantity of powder, and that it had been
resolved that every male inhabitant of that province from fifteen to fifty
years must be armed and in the army."[18] "A letter from Annapolis, capital of the province of Maryland," we read some days later, "written on
31 December, confirms that the people of the whole colony are divided
into companies under trial officers, who drill them daily in the use of
weapons, and that the spirit of liberty is so widespread that almost all
individuals are firmly resolved to sacrifice all they hold most dear to
patriotism, even commerce."[19] From Philadelphia one learned that
"every province is inclined to take up arms to oppose the execution of
parliamentary acts, that there has been high mortality among the royal
troops, and that the tenth regiment mutinied and consequently was disarmed at night for refusing to execute three soldiers of this body condemned to death for desertion."[20] General Gage remained in Boston, in
"supreme command of the army of the Crown." "The colonies on their
part have instituted a day of general fasting to summon divine assistance
and to pray to God to bless the weapons they have been obliged to take
up to preserve their rights."[21]

Then suddenly, in June 1775, the first news of the April encounters
in Lexington and Concord between "royal troops and the colonial mili-

[15] Ibid., no. 13, 15 February 1775, p. 98 (London, 24 January).

[16] Ibid., no. 16, 25 February 1775, p. 123 (London, 3 February).

[17] *Gazzetta universale*, no. 31, 18 April 1775, p. 241 (London, 28 March).

[18] *Notizie del mondo*, no. 20, 11 March 1775, p. 154 (London, 17 February). On the
situation in Virginia see *Gazzetta universale*, no. 46, 10 June 1775, p. 362 (London, 19 May),
"Lettera della Virginia che passa per esser scritta da un forestiero stabilito in quella provincia." The continuation and end are in no. 49, 10 June 1775, p. 387.

[19] *Notizie del mondo*, no. 21, 14 March 1775, p. 162 (London, 21 February).

[20] Ibid., no. 33, 25 April 1775, p. 260 (London, 4 April).

[21] Ibid., no. 35, 2 May 1775, p. 273 (London, 11 April).

tia" arrived. Four packed columns of the Florentine gazette described these first battles and the further mobilization of the population. "All the colleges of New England, from which the students have voluntarily withdrawn, now serve as quarters for the provincial troops."[1] When echoes of these events reached Virginia, "General Washington left immediately to join the provincial troops near Boston." In New York the people rose at the news of the encounter in Concord and attacked "the city hall, took arms deposited there for the king's troops, and thence went to the port to take all the munitions." According to news from Virginia there was fear of "a general rebellion by Negroes throughout the continent because, since the suspension of commerce with Great Britain, they no longer receive greatly needed commodities from Europe."[2]

Between 19 April 1775, the date of the first encounter, and 4 July of the following year, when the Declaration of Independence was published in Philadelphia, news of battles, and of dead and wounded, accumulated in the Italian gazettes. But above the sounds of battle rose the voices of those who wanted to explain the reason and method of their struggle. A letter from Boston indignantly rejected the accusation that prisoners were mistreated. "We fight," they said, "through a longing to maintain our liberties and not through enmity for the British, whom we have learned to love and respect. In reality we do not blame our persecution on the English people, but only on certain persons who are both our and their enemies."[3] Of "our common liberty" the Bostonians spoke, turning their attention to the inhabitants of Canada.[4] In August the *Gazzetta universale* mentioned the ideas and writings of "Mr. Dickinson, one of the members of the assembly of Philadelphia, who is famous for his patriotic writings, among which in particular is his *Letters from a farmer in Pennsylvania*."[5]

In one way or another the logic of war made its iron hand felt as much in England as in America. The social results of the conflict were hard. In London "workers of the admiralty," one reads in August, "refuse to work without an increase in salary." They say they will even "be obliged to leave the dry docks forever if their pay is not increased and

[1] Ibid., no. 50, 24 June 1775, p. 394ff. (London, 2 June), and *Gazzetta universale*, no. 50, 24 June 1775, pp. 394ff. (London, 3 June).

[2] *Gazzetta universale*, no. 51, 27 June 1775, p. 402 (London, 2 June).

[3] *Notizie del mondo*, no. 55, 11 July 1775, p. 435 (London, 23 June).

[4] Ibid., no. 67, 22 August 1775, pp. 530ff. (London, 1 August), "Agli abitanti oppressi del Canada."

[5] *Gazzetta universale*, no. 61, 1 August 1775, p. 482 (London, 11 July). Apparently the author of this report understood the word *farmer*, as "tenant," not as "cultivator." This was the famous *Letters from a farmer in Pennsylvania to the inhabitants of the British colonies* by John Dickinson, which appeared in numerous editions in 1768.

they are not given at least two shillings six pence a day."[6] In Boston, it was said, General Gage promised a "reward of 500 pounds sterling to anyone who would place in his hands Adams and Handek" (Samuel Adams and John Hancock), while he promised "an amnesty and general pardon to any other rebels who will lay down their arms." "Up to now the Americans have made no disposition about this, but in the present state of affairs it would not be surprising for them to respond with a law of retaliation to the martial law of Mr. Gage, which could be a proper declaration of war made with a great manifesto to justify themselves to all nations."[7]

In September more interest was aroused by the "declaration that the general congress of the confederated colonies of North America has published on 6 July." "We thought it was too interesting not to communicate it to our readers," wrote the *Notizie del mondo*. It started with the affirmation that "government was instituted to promote the welfare of humankind and ought to be administered for the attainment of that end"; it recited the long history of the relations between England and the American colonies; it rejected brusquely the "despotism" of Parliament and reasserted solidarity with Boston, which had been unjustly attacked. "The legislature of Great Britain, however, stimulated by an inordinate passion for a power, not only unjustifiable, but which they know to be peculiarly reprobated by the very constitution of that kingdom, and desperate of success in any mode of contest, where regard should be had to truth, law, or right, have at length, deserting those, attempted to effect their cruel and impolitic purpose of enslaving those colonies by violence." The representatives of the colonies declared they were all concordantly resolved to die as free men rather than live as slaves. In conclusion, they said to England, "We have not raised armies with ambitious designs of separating from Great Britain and establishing independent states. We fight not for glory or for conquest. We exhibit to mankind the remarkable spectacle of a people attacked by unprovoked enemies, without any imputation or even suspicion of offence. They boast of their privileges and civilization, and yet proffer no milder conditions than *servitude* or *death*."[8] The contrast with the prose with

---

[6] *Notizie del mondo*, no. 62, 5 August 1775, p. 491 (London, 17 July). The *Gazzetta universale*, no. 78, 30 September 1775, p. 618 (London, 8 September), gave detailed information about a "great uprising among the sailors in the port of Liverpool," caused by the fact that "they wanted to give them twenty shillings instead of the thirty agreed on to go into the slave trade of Negroes on the coasts of Guinea." "The uprising did not end until the arrival of a large detachment of troops, which restored calm in this city, after the arrest of fifty of the most seditious."

[7] *Notizie del mondo*, no. 64, 12 August 1775, p. 508 (London, 21 July).

[8] Ibid., no. 72, 9 September 1775, pp. 569ff. (London, 18 August); no. 73, 12 Septem-

which George III declared the Americans "traitors and rebels" was impressive: "Misled by dangerous and ill-designing men . . . ," he declared, they overturn "the public peace" and attempt to destroy "lawful commerce . . . to the oppression of our loyal subjects . . . by arraying themselves in hostile manner to withstand the execution of the law."[9]

The reasoned moderation that dominated the documents arriving from America was highly appreciated by correspondents in our gazettes.[10] But they did not conceal that this moderation derived in part from internal contrasts in the Congress at Philadelphia.[11] In February 1776 the *Gazzetta universale* announced the following: "The Americans of the Congress formed in Philadelphia under the name of the United Colonies of North America have signed a confederation, or perpetual union, made up of twelve articles. . . . This observes the same spirit of order that is in nearly all their pronouncements. Each colony will preserve its own laws, usages, rights, privileges, and so on. The general congress will meet in each colony by turn. It will have authority to make war and peace, conclude alliances, decide differences that may arise among the colonies themselves, form new ones, and so on." The confederation was to last until the resolution of all problems. "When this happens the colonies will return to their union with Great Britain, but if matters are not concluded as they wish, this plan will become a permanent confederation."[12] A new military order was created, the Order of Liberty, with its device "*Congressus populusque americanus* (the Congress and people of America), and a star from which hangs a liberty cap attached to a chain."[13] A new flag had already been displayed in the summer "in the presence of the whole American army drawn up near Cambridge," after "an animated and touching speech by the chaplain of the Putnam regiment" and "a fervent prayer." On one side was written *Appeal to Heaven*, and on the other *Qui transtulit sustinet* (Who came upholds).[14]

Together with the growing pressure caused by military necessity and

ber 1775, pp. 578ff. (London, 25 August); no. 74, 16 September 1775, pp. 586ff. (London, 25 August). The conclusion of this declaration is reproduced in another version, in the *Nuove di diverse corti e paesi*, no. 36, 4 September 1775, p. 287 (London, 18 August). See also *Gazzetta universale*, no. 71, 5 September 1775, p. 561 (London, 18 August).

[9] *Nuove di diverse corti e paesi*, no. 37, 11 September 1775, p. 293 (London, 25 August).

[10] *Notizie del mondo*, no. 23, 19 March 1776, p. 178 (London, 27 February).

[11] Ibid., no. 35, 30 April 1776, p. 264 (London, 8 April). ("The congress of Philadelphia is much divided on the proposition of making the colonies into a free and independent state.")

[12] *Gazzetta universale*, no. 13, 13 February 1776, p. 98 (London, 19 January). The text is in the *Notizie del mondo*, no. 13, 13 February 1776, pp. 98ff. (London, 19 January, and in the following numbers).

[13] *Gazzetta universale*, no. 20, 9 March 1776, p. 155 (London, 16 February).

[14] *Notizie del mondo*, no. 81, 10 October 1775, p. 642 (London, 19 September).

the creation of new structures and new political symbols, the discussion of political forms and ideas, which continued vividly and deeply in 1775 and 1776, was of great—or rather decisive—importance. This was one of the most extraordinarily fertile periods in the history of the eighteenth century (and not only of that century): the age of Adam Smith and Gibbon, of Tom Paine and Richard Price, not counting the innumerable books and other writings that attempted to draw up a balance of reform and revolution in preceding years and throw open the doors to the future.[15]

There were strong echoes of this debate everywhere in Europe. The *Notizie del mondo* devoted two columns to a new edition of a book that had already appeared in 1774 and was republished in the autumn of 1775: Granville Sharp's *A declaration of the people's natural right to a share in the legislature, which is the fundamental principle of the British constitution of state.* How had the lacerations between Great Britain and its colonies come about? "Blood has already been spilled, the colonists have great advantages, they are on their own ground, they know the land; . . . this civil war will inevitably cost the English dearly, and the outcome will not be favorable; it is enough to calculate the population of Great Britain and that of English America, and the distance that separates the two regions, to understand that it will be difficult for the first to subject the second and make them submit by force." It was necessary to return to the roots of the evil, to the violation done by the English to the "fundamental principle" of their constitution, that is, that "no community, no colony, can be subjected legally to acts of a parliament if it is not a participant in these acts itself, that is, through its representatives." If geographical distance made impossible the application of these "rights of the people," one should form "an assembly . . . independent of the Parliament of Great Britain," as had happened, for instance, in Ireland. In America, instead, the powers of the governors was increased and there was an effort to impose the laws of the English Parliament. The consequences then unleashed had perhaps demonstrated that "the result of desiring too much is to be left with nothing."[16] At the same time there were many writers in London who insisted on the notion that application of the British constitution alone would ensure liberty, certainly not the enthusiasm of rebels beyond the seas. "Who was wrong? The king for having preserved the constitution, the ministry for having maintained our laws and our best interests, or the Americans, who through

---

[15] See the excellent delineation of this *annus mirabilis* in Bernard Bailyn, "Seventeen Seventy-Six. The Year of Challenge: A World Transformed," *Journal of Law and Economics* 19 (October 1976): 437ff.

[16] *Notizie del mondo*, no. 86, 28 October 1775, pp. 682ff. (London, 6 October).

strange enthusiasm have wanted to destroy our happy system of government and sacrifice our lives, our liberty, our interests, and all that we hold most dear through anarchy and usurpation?"[17] The civil war posed new and difficult moral problems. "Lord North," one read in November, "in order to avoid the charges made against the ministry of arming subjects against each other, proposed to authorize military officers to renounce their places whenever they were called to service of which they disapproved."[18] This naturally led to the employment of "foreign troops," which in fact began to occur. Edmund Burke referred in a long speech to the Commons, also in November, "to the source of the unhappy break between England and the colonies" and proposed a "project of accommodation" based on the abolition of all English taxation and the restriction of the "jurisdiction of Parliament over the colonies to the regulation of commerce alone."[19] On the twenty-seventh of the same month Wilkes compared the position of the American Congress with that of the English Parliament. The first did not groan, like the second, "under the unsupportable weight of 140 millions of debt, the interest of which absorbs all revenue. Neither does it have to provide annual pensions to many persons in office, who are hungry and useless; indulgence weakens neither their bodies nor their spirits. They present themselves as so many youths untroubled by a multitude of private debts. We, on the contrary, resemble poor fathers: aged, weak, indigent, and degenerate, due to our extravagances." It was not true, he added, that "freedom of the press is entirely lost in America." "Freedom of the press is the foundation of our liberty, and it is lost only in Boston, where General Gage commands the troops of the ministry. The press is still free in Water-Town, which is seven miles from Boston, and in Philadelphia, Newport, Williamsburg, and the remainder of North America." Even the odious proclamation of General Gage against "Samuel Adams and John Hancock, two worthy persons, and I dare to say two true patriots . . . has been reprinted in all the public sheets of America."[20] On 15 December "members of the opposition and particularly the Dukes of Manchester and Richmond maintained firmly, arousing a great debate, that the 'present conduct of the Americans is less an open rebellion than a legitimate resistance to preserve the natural rights of humanity.' "[21] Before the end of the year a small work entitled *A proposition for the present peace and future government of the British colonies in North America* appeared

---

[17] Ibid., no. 89, 7 November 1775, p. 706 (London, 17 October).
[18] Ibid., no. 95, 28 November 1775, pp. 744ff. (London, 7 November).
[19] Ibid., no. 101, 19 December 1775, p. 792 (London, 28 November).
[20] Ibid., no. 103, 26 December 1775, pp. 808ff. (London, 5 December).
[21] Ibid., no. 3, 9 January 1776, p. 18 (London, 19 December 1775).

in London.[22] It called to mind the "trite but true proverb that the short-est follies are the best" and proposed to "end divisions" by convoking in America an assembly composed of a small number of members selected, some from the government, and the others among "representatives of the bodies of each province." "The deputies selected by the councils of each province will represent the rights of the Crown, and the others those of the people." Thus, the rights of the constitution of Great Brit-ain would be extended to America, "uniting, as they are in Europe, the two powers that are divided and that do not combine, or at least should not combine, if not for the good."[23]

More profound and effective was the intervention of Richard Price, reported the *Notizie del mondo* in April 1776. The "famous little book by Doctor Price, containing observations on the nature of civil liberty, the principles of government, and the equity and policy of the war against the Americans," had reached its fifth edition.[24] "This work is generally to the taste of the nation, but the ministry finds in it some ideas capable of dissolving the obedience of the people toward their legislators and governors, as well as some unjust assertions founded on mistaken cal-culations regarding the state of national finance, which have already been refuted in part. However that is, one cannot say that this work does not leave in the human heart a germ of patriotism, which no other work of its kind is capable of conceiving or developing there."[25] The nucleus of Price's work, as a recent historian has written, consisted not of a radical critique of the mode of election of the English Parliament, but of the negation of its sovereignty. Only the people were sovereign. If one had to choose, he concluded, between anarchy and despotism, there is no doubt one would prefer the first. "There is *no* situation," he wrote, "*none whatever*, in which one state may rightfully impose authority over another. The only acceptable association of peoples or states are *voluntary* assemblages in which no element rules the other by its own determination."[26] It was symptomatic of the atmosphere of uncertainty that reigned in London in the spring of 1776 that the work of Price, the

[22] *A proposition for the present peace and future government of the British colonies in North America* (London: W. Davis, 1775).

[23] *Notizie del mondo*, no. 5, 16 January 1776, p. 35 (London, 26 December 1775).

[24] Ibid., no. 29, 9 April 1776, p. 217 (London, 19 March). *Observations on the nature of civil liberty, the principles of governement and the justice and policy of the war with America* was published in London in February. At the end of the year thirteen editions had appeared in England and twelve others in Dublin, Philadelphia, New York, Boston, Charleston, Edinburgh, Leiden, and Paris.

[25] The same information and the same considerations, slightly paraphrased, were in the *Gazzetta universale*, no. 29, 9 April 1776, p. 227 (London, 19 March).

[26] Bailyn, "Seventeen Seventy-Six. The year of challenge," p. 440.

Notizie del mondo noted, was presented to and accepted by the London City Council. "Mr. Saxby pronounced in past days in the Assembly of the Common Council great praise of the well-known book by Doctor Price, and made two propositions: that the Court of the Common Council thank the author for his just, impartial, and intelligent reflections on the nature of civil liberty, the current state of decadence of the nation, the inhuman and unjust war being made against the American colonies; and, second, his equitable plan to preserve the realm from the ruin that threatens it." On Price, for his "courage in so critical a time," was conferred "the citizenship of this capital," and he was also given "a gold snuffbox valued at fifty pounds sterling."[27]

Before April ended, another fundamental book of the times came to the attention of the Italian public: Tom Paine's *Common Sense*. The *Notizie del mondo* mistakenly attributed it to "Mr. Adams" but rightly underlined its importance. "It rejects absolutely any idea of reconciliation and incites the colonies to independence." Europe was in his eyes not only distant, but repellant. "Divided into too many realms," it produced only wars, whose consequences fall on the American colonies, ruining their trade. Why should one continue to be tied to it? "Our products will find a market in all the ports of Europe, and our imports will be paid for from wherever they come." Even from a political point of view "a government of our own is our natural right." It was time to form "a government of our own."[28] The conclusion, printed in its entirety on 21 May, insisted on the fact that French and Spanish assistance would come only if the Americans were decisively favorable to independence. Only in that way would it be possible to ensure "the health of the colonies."[29]

"The captain of a ship that had arrived in Bristol from Philadelphia," one read in a communication from London at the end of May, intimated that the Congress itself was now taking this direction. "The aforementioned book, entitled *Common Sense*, has made a strong impression on the majority." Even those of a different opinion continued to bear arms in anticipation of concessions that England would make. In London *Common Sense* was reprinted "and it is read with even more interest because of the refutation Doctor Price made of the same."[30] The deepening of the discussion, together with the grave military news arriving from America—which was reflected in Italian gazettes as well as in those

[27] *Notizie del mondo*, no. 31, 16 April 1776, p. 234 (London, n.d.).

[28] Ibid., no. 35, 30 April 1776, pp. 264ff. (London, 8 April).

[29] Ibid., no. 41, 21 May 1776, pp. 313ff. (London, 30 April). See also *Gazzetta universale*, no. 41, 21 May 1776, p. 323 (London, 3 May).

[30] *Notizie del mondo*, no. 50, 22 June 1776, p. 385 (London, 31 May). See *Gazzetta universale*, no. 50, 22 June 1776, p. 394 (London, 31 May).

of Europe as a whole—pushed the English government in the spring of 1776 toward an attempt to control public opinion, which was becoming more inflamed in the British world as elsewhere. Lord North proposed to the Commons a further tax on journals. "Many people consider them sheets that do more ill than good, whereas others consider them from quite a different point of view." Certainly one had seen "these sheets insult persons imprudently every day and present in a false light" the measures of the government. There had been grave effects of "calumnies and falsities spread and repeated in the course of a year in 12,230,000 sheets," reaching the hands of readers who are induced to read them "from a vain and foolish curiosity."[31]

This was a peevish note, which only made, in the minds of curious readers, the large, confident, and firm tones of the voices that came from America seem to rise in even greater contrast. The decision was now made. "Little by little the form of government adopted by the United Colonies has taken on an aspect that makes one believe that all hope of reconciliation is past."[32] The general congress, on 15 May, considered "the establishment of any government under the council and authority of Great Britain opposed to reason and conscience" and deliberated whether from now on "all legislative power" should be exercised "under the authority of the people of these colonies for the preservation of internal peace, virtue, and good order, as well as for the defense of ourselves, and of our liberty and property, against the invasion of our enemies." Each colony should adopt "that government which the representatives of the people judge most conducive to the prosperity and security of their constituents in particular, and America in general."[33] The delegates from Boston uttered words that were "not less decisive." "We have seen the humble representations of these colonies to the king of Great Britain repulsed repeatedly with contempt. . . . Against our prayers has been turned the sword, liberty has no other choice than chains. . . . The hopes we founded on effective support of the British people have long vanished." It was time for the Congress to persuade itself of the "necessity of making a public declaration of independence."[34]

The declaration came, on 4 July 1776. On 2 September the *Notizie del mondo* and the *Gazzetta universale* offered readers this decisive document as a scoop. "Now that the sword is drawn for the defense of all

[31] *Gazzetta universale*, no. 40, 18 May 1776, p. 314 (London, 26 April).
[32] Ibid., no. 55, 9 July 1776, p. 436 (London, 21 June).
[33] *Notizie del mondo*, no. 61, 30 July 1776, p. 461 (London, 9 July).
[34] Ibid., p. 462.

that is most dear to them, the Americans will not return it to its sheath until they receive ample satisfaction for the cruel acts of oppression they have been made to suffer." Reflecting on the difficult tests of the past, they concluded: "We, therefore, the representatives of the United states of America in General Congress assembled, appealing to the supreme judge of the world for the rectitude of our intentions, do, in the name and by the authority of the good people of these colonies, solemnly publish and declare that these United Colonies are and of right ought to be free and independent states; that they are absolved from all allegiance to the British Crown."[1] "A clamorous moment for this confederation," the *Gazzetta universale* stated on 14 September as it published the text of the declaration in full. The *Notizie del mondo* did the same, alerting readers that this was a document of unusual energy. "In the present circumstances and in the state of animosity in which the colonists find themselves, it is not surprising or offensive that there are very strong expressions in it."[2] High sounding indeed, translated into Tuscan, was the celebrated text by Jefferson, the crystallization of a historical epoch: "We hold these truths to be self-evident: that all men are created equal; that they are endowed by their creator with certain inalienable rights; that among these are life, liberty, and the pursuit of happiness: that to secure these rights, governments are instituted among men, deriving their just powers from the consent of the governed; that whenever any form of government becomes destructive of these ends, it is the right of the people to alter or to abolish it, and to institute new government, laying its foundation on such principles, and organizing its powers in such form, as to them shall seem most likely to effect their safety and happiness."[3]

[1] Ibid., no. 71, 3 September 1776, p. 543 (London, 13 August), and *Gazzetta universale*, no. 71, 3 September 1776, p. 562 (London, 16 August).

[2] Ibid., no. 74, 14 September 1776, p. 567 (London, 23 August).

[3] Ibid. The full text, with some variants, is in the *Gazzetta universale*, no. 74, 14 September 1776, pp. 586ff. (London, 23 August).

Index

(Names of publishers are included only before 1800. Numbers in italics refer to the illustrations following p. 232)